The New Testament
English Version for the Deaf

The New Testament
English Version for the Deaf

TRANSLATED FROM THE GREEK TEXT

BAKER BOOK HOUSE
Grand Rapids, Michigan

PREFACE

It is urgent that all people have the Bible in a language they understand. Present English versions of the Scriptures—designed for hearing persons—do not meet the special needs of most deaf people, because the deaf have not had the advantage of speech in developing their knowledge and usage of the English language.

This is a translation of the Bible designed especially for deaf people. It is not a revision of existing English versions. Rather, it is a serious translation, based directly on the original Greek of the New Testament. As such, it is not a paraphrase. Ideas not found in the Greek text are not introduced, and nothing expressed in the Greek text is omitted.

Although the full meaning of the Greek text is expressed in the translation, the sense of the original has been restructured into the closest natural equivalents in English for the deaf community. (For example, pronouns such as "he," "she," and "they" are usually replaced by names, as is the practice in sign language.) The result is an English translation that communicates effectively to the deaf.

Although the use of English was a practical necessity for this version of the Scriptures, great care was taken to speak primarily to the deaf and not to the hearing. The translators and their advisors have tried to be sensitive to an important fact which most hearing persons do not understand—that a deaf person is not simply a hearing person who cannot hear. The translators have learned to appreciate the unique thought patterns of the deaf person's mind and to respect the intricate structure of his independent language.

The result of this effort might appear to be a simple English version of the New Testament, but it is much more than that. It is a carefully constructed translation, designed to communicate to those who are deaf. Although the language used will not be familiar to those accustomed to standard English versions, it does convey to the deaf the meaning that was originally intended.

It is the purpose of this translation to provide the deaf with their own Bible for personal reading and study and to aid the vital ministry of those who teach the deaf, giving them relief from the need to "translate" existing English versions as they teach.

Brief explanations or synonyms of certain words in the text are placed in parentheses and italicized. Words or phrases that need fuller explanation are followed by an asterisk (*) and explained in footnotes at the bottom of the page. In addition, Scripture quotations are identified and variant readings are frequently given in footnotes. Italicized words are sometimes supplied in the text to make the meaning clear.

CONTENTS

Matthew	1		1 Timothy	532
Mark	91		2 Timothy	542
Luke	145		Titus	549
John	237		Philemon	554
Acts	301		Hebrews	556
Romans	387		James	585
1 Corinthians	424		1 Peter	594
2 Corinthians	457		2 Peter	604
Galatians	478		1 John	610
Ephesians	491		2 John	619
Philippians	503		3 John	621
Colossians	512		Jude	623
1 Thessalonians	520		Revelation	626
2 Thessalonians	527			

Matthew

The Family History of Jesus

1 This is the family history of Jesus Christ. He came from the family of David. David came from the family of Abraham.
² Abraham was the father of Isaac,
Isaac was the father of Jacob,
Jacob was the father of Judah and his brothers,
³ Judah was the father of Perez and Zerah.
   (Their mother was Tamar.)
Perez was the father of Hezron,
Hezron was the father of Ram,
⁴ Ram was the father of Amminadab,
Amminadab was the father of Nahshon,
Nahshon was the father of Salmon,
⁵ Salmon was the father of Boaz.
   (Boaz' mother was Rahab.)
Boaz was the father of Obed.
   (Obed's mother was Ruth.)
Obed was the father of Jesse,
⁶ Jesse was the father of King David.

David was the father of Solomon.
   (Solomon's mother had been Uriah's wife.)
⁷ Solomon was the father of Rehoboam,
Rehoboam was the father of Abijah,
Abijah was the father of Asa,
⁸ Asa was the father of Jehoshaphat,
Jehoshaphat was the father of Joram,
Joram was the father of Uzziah,
⁹ Uzziah was the father of Jotham,
Jotham was the father of Ahaz,

Ahaz was the father of Hezekiah,
[10]Hezekiah was the father of Manasseh,
Manasseh was the father of Amon,
Amon was the father of Josiah,
[11]Josiah was the father of Jechoniah and his brothers.
(This was during the time that the *Jewish* people were taken to Babylon *to be slaves*.)

[12]After they were taken to Babylon:
Jechoniah was the father of Shealtiel,
Shealtiel was the father of Zerubbabel,
[13]Zerubbabel was the father of Abiud,
Abiud was the father of Eliakim,
Eliakim was the father of Azor,
[14]Azor was the father of Zadok,
Zadok was the father of Achim,
Achim was the father of Eliud,
[15]Eliud was the father of Eleazar,
Eleazar was the father of Matthan,
Matthan was the father of Jacob,
[16]and Jacob was the father of Joseph. Joseph was the husband of Mary. And Jesus was born from Mary. He is called the Christ.*

[17]So there were fourteen generations from Abraham to David. And there were fourteen generations from David until the time when the people were taken to Babylon. And there were fourteen generations from the time when the people were taken to Babylon until Christ was born.

The Birth of Jesus Christ

[18]The mother of Jesus Christ was Mary. And this is how the birth of Jesus happened. Mary was engaged to marry Joseph. But before they married, Mary learned that she was pregnant with a child. Mary was pregnant by *the power of* the Holy Spirit. [19]Mary's husband, Joseph, was a good man. He did not want to embarrass Mary before the people. So he planned to divorce her secretly.

Christ   The "anointed one" (the Messiah) or chosen one of God.

²⁰But after Joseph thought about this, an angel of the Lord came to Joseph in a dream. The angel said, "Joseph, son of David, don't be afraid to accept Mary to be your wife. The baby that is in her is from the Holy Spirit.* ²¹She will give birth to a son. You will name the son Jesus.* Give him that name because he will save his people from their sins."

²²All this happened to make clear the full meaning of the things the Lord said through the prophet*: ²³"The virgin* will be pregnant and will give birth to a son. They will name him Immanuel."* (Immanuel means, "God with us.")

²⁴When Joseph woke up, he did the thing that the angel from the Lord told him to do. Joseph married Mary. ²⁵But Joseph had no sexual union with Mary until she gave birth to the son. And Joseph named the son Jesus.

Wise Men Come to Visit Jesus

2 Jesus was born in the town of Bethlehem in Judea. He was born during the time when Herod* was king. After Jesus was born, some wise men from the east came to Jerusalem. ²The wise men asked people, "Where is the new baby that is the king of the Jews? We saw the star that shows he was born. We saw the star rise in the sky in the east. We came to worship him."

³King Herod heard about this new king of the Jews. Herod was troubled about this. And all the people in Jerusalem were worried too. ⁴Herod called a meeting of all the leading priests and teachers of the law. Herod asked them where the Christ* was to be born. ⁵They answered, "In the town of Bethlehem in Judea. The prophet* wrote about this *in the Scriptures**:

⁶ 'Bethlehem, in the land of Judah,
    you are important among the rulers of Judah.

Holy Spirit   Also called the Spirit of God, the Spirit of Christ, and the Comforter. He is joined
    with God and Christ. He does the work of God among people in the world.
Jesus   The name Jesus means "salvation."
prophet   Person who spoke for God. He often told things that would happen in the future.
virgin   A pure girl who is not married.
"The virgin...Immanuel"   Quotation from Isaiah 7:14.
Herod   Herod I (Herod the Great), ruler (king) of Judea 40-4 B.C.
Christ   The "anointed one" (the Messiah) or chosen one of God.
Scriptures   Holy Writings—the Old Testament.

3

> Yes, a ruler will come from you,
>   and that ruler will lead Israel, my people.' "   *Micah 5:2*

⁷Then Herod* had a secret meeting with the wise men from the east. Herod learned from the wise men the exact time they first saw the star. ⁸Then Herod sent the wise men to Bethlehem. Herod said to the wise men, "Go and look carefully to find the new baby. When you find the baby, come tell me. Then I can go worship him too."

⁹The wise men heard the king and then left. They saw the same star they had seen in the east. The wise men followed the star. The star went before them until it stopped above the place where the baby was. ¹⁰The wise men were very happy to see the star. They were filled with joy. ¹¹The wise men came to the house where the baby was. They saw the baby with his mother, Mary. The wise men bowed down and worshiped the baby. Then the wise men opened the gifts they brought for the baby. They gave the baby treasures of gold, frankincense,* and myrrh.* ¹²But God warned the wise men in a dream. God warned them not to go back to Herod. So the wise men went home to their own country a different way.

Jesus' Parents Take Him to Egypt

¹³After the wise men left, an angel of the Lord came to Joseph in a dream. The angel said, "Get up! Take the baby and his mother and escape to Egypt. Herod will start looking for the baby. Herod wants to kill him. So stay in Egypt until I tell you *it is safe*."

¹⁴So Joseph got up, and left for Egypt with the baby and the baby's mother. They left during the night. ¹⁵Joseph stayed in Egypt until Herod died. This happened to make clear the full meaning of what the Lord said through the prophet.* The Lord said, "I called my son to come out of Egypt."*

Herod   Herod I (Herod the Great), ruler (king) of Judea 40-4 B.C.
frankincense, myrrh   Very expensive and sweet-smelling perfumes.
prophet   Person who spoke for God. He often told things that would happen in the future.
"I called...Egypt"   Quotation from Hosea 11:1.

Herod Kills the Baby Boys in Bethlehem

[16]Herod saw that the wise men had fooled him. Herod was very, very angry. So Herod gave an order to kill all the boys in Bethlehem and in all the area around Bethlehem. Herod had learned from the wise men the time *the baby was born*. It was now two years from that time. So Herod said to kill all the boys who were two years old and younger. [17]So the thing God said through the prophet* Jeremiah happened:

[18]"A sound was heard in Ramah.
  It was bitter crying and much sadness.
Rachel cries for her children;
  and she cannot be comforted,
    because her children are dead."   *Jeremiah 31:15*

Joseph and Mary Return from Egypt with Jesus

[19]After Herod died, an angel of the Lord came to Joseph in a dream. This happened while Joseph was in Egypt. [20]The angel said, "Get up! Take the baby and his mother and go to Israel. The people who were trying to kill the baby are now dead."

[21]So Joseph took the baby and the baby's mother and went to Israel. [22]But Joseph heard that Archelaus was now king in Judea. Archelaus became king when his father Herod died. So Joseph was afraid to go there. Joseph was warned in a dream. So Joseph left there and went to the area of Galilee. [23]Joseph went to a town called Nazareth and lived there. And so the thing happened that God said through the prophets*: "*The Christ* will be called a Nazarene.*"

The Work of John the Baptizer

3 At that time, John the Baptizer* came and began preaching. He preached in the desert area of Judea. [2]John said, "Change your hearts and lives, because the kingdom of heaven is

---

prophets   People who spoke for God. Their writings are part of the Old Testament.
Nazarene   A person from the city of Nazareth.
Baptizer   John is called the Baptizer because he had the work of baptizing people.

5

coming soon.'' ³John the Baptizer is the one that Isaiah the prophet* was talking about. Isaiah said:

"There is a person shouting in the desert*:
'Prepare the way for the Lord;
make his paths straight.' ''

Isaiah 40:3

⁴John's clothes were made from camel's hair. John had a leather belt around his waist. For food, John ate locusts* and wild honey. ⁵People went to hear John preach. The people came from Jerusalem and all Judea and all the area around the Jordan river. ⁶People told the sins they had done, and John baptized* them in the Jordan river.

⁷Many of the Pharisees* and Sadducees* came to the place where John was baptizing people. When John saw them he said to them: "You are all snakes! Who warned you to run away from God's anger that is coming? ⁸You must do the things that show that you have really changed your hearts and lives. ⁹And don't think that you can boast and say to yourselves, 'Abraham is our father.' I tell you that God could make children for Abraham from these rocks here. ¹⁰The ax is now ready to cut down the trees.* Every tree that does not make good fruit will be cut down and thrown into the fire.

¹¹"I baptize you with water to show that you changed your hearts and lives. But there is a person coming later who is greater than I am. I am not good enough to carry his shoes for him. He will baptize you with the Holy Spirit* and with fire. ¹²He will come ready to clean the grain.* He will separate the good grain from the straw. He will put the good part of the grain into his barn. And he will burn the part that is not good. He will burn it with a fire that cannot be stopped."

---

prophet A person who spoke for God. He often told things that would happen in the future.
desert The area is called a desert because no people lived there.
locusts Insects like grasshoppers. The law of Moses said locusts could be eaten (Lev. 11:21-22).
baptized A Greek word meaning to immerse, dip, or bury a person or thing briefly under water.
Pharisees Pharisees were a Jewish religious group that followed all the Old Testament and other Jewish laws and customs very carefully.
Sadducees A leading Jewish religious group. They followed only the first five books of the Old Testament. They believed that people don't have another life after death.
trees The people who don't accept Jesus. They are like "trees" that will be cut down.
Holy Spirit Also called the Spirit of God, the Spirit of Christ, and the Comforter. He is joined with God and Christ. He does the work of God among people in the world.
clean the grain The grain means people. John uses this idea to show how Jesus will separate the good people from the bad people.

6

Jesus Is Baptized by John

¹³At that time Jesus came from Galilee to the Jordan river. Jesus came to John and wanted John to baptize* him. ¹⁴But John tried to say that he was not good enough to baptize Jesus. John said, "Why do you come to me to be baptized? I should be baptized by you!"

¹⁵Jesus answered, "Let it be this way for now. We should do all things that are right." So John agreed to baptize Jesus.

¹⁶Jesus was baptized* and he came up out of the water. The sky opened and he saw God's Spirit coming down on him like a dove. ¹⁷And a voice spoke from heaven. The voice said, "This (*Jesus*) is my Son and I love him. I am very pleased with him."

The Temptation of Jesus

4 Then the Spirit* led Jesus into the desert.* Jesus was taken there to be tempted by the devil. ²Jesus ate nothing for 40 days and nights. After this, he was very hungry. ³The devil came to Jesus to tempt him. The devil said, "If you are the Son of God, tell these rocks to become bread."

⁴Jesus answered, "It is written *in the Scriptures*,*

'A person does not live only by eating food.
True life comes from the words
that God says.' "   *Deuteronomy 8:3*

⁵Then the devil led Jesus to the holy city (*Jerusalem*). The devil put Jesus on a very high place on the temple.* ⁶The devil said, "If you are the Son of God, jump off. Why? Because it is written *in the Scriptures*,

'God will command his angels for you,
and their hands will catch you,
so that you will not hit your foot
on a rock.' "   *Psalm 91:11-12*

---

baptize   A Greek word meaning to immerse, dip, or bury a person or thing briefly under water.
Spirit   The Holy Spirit. Also called the Spirit of God, the Spirit of Christ, and the Comforter. He is joined with God and Christ. He does the work of God among people in the world.
desert   The area is called a desert because no people lived there.
Scriptures   Holy Writings—the Old Testament.
temple   The special building in Jerusalem where God commanded the Jews to worship.

⁷Jesus answered him, "It also says *in the Scriptures*,

'You must not tempt the Lord your God.' " *Deuteronomy 6:16*

⁸Then the devil led Jesus to the top of a very high mountain. The devil showed Jesus all the kingdoms of the world, and all the great things that are in those kingdoms. ⁹The devil said, "If you will bow down and worship me, I will give you all these things."

¹⁰Jesus said to the devil, "Go away from me, Satan! It is written *in the Scriptures*,*

'You must worship the Lord your God.
Serve only him!' " *Deuteronomy 6:13*

¹¹So the devil left Jesus. And then some angels came to Jesus and helped him.

Jesus Begins His Work in Galilee

¹²Jesus heard that John was put in prison. So Jesus went back to Galilee. ¹³Jesus did not stay in Nazareth. He went and lived in Capernaum, a town near the lake (*Lake Galilee*). Capernaum is in the area near Zebulun and Naphtali. ¹⁴Jesus did this to make happen what the prophet* Isaiah said:

¹⁵"The land of Zebulun and the land of Naphtali,
    the way to the sea, past the Jordan River,
Galilee, the land of non-Jewish people—
¹⁶those people live in darkness (*sin*),
    but they have seen a great light;
    the light has come for those people who live
        in the land that is dark like a grave." *Isaiah 9:1-2*

Jesus Chooses Some Followers

¹⁷From that time Jesus began to preach. This is what he said: "Change your hearts and lives, because the kingdom of heaven is coming soon."

¹⁸Jesus was walking by Lake Galilee. He saw two brothers, Simon (called Peter) and Simon's brother Andrew. The two brothers were fishermen and they were fishing in the lake with a

Scriptures Holy Writings—the Old Testament.
prophet Person who spoke for God. He often told things that would happen in the future.

net. [19]Jesus said, "Come follow me. I will make you a different kind of fishermen. You will work to gather people, *not fish*." [20]Simon and Andrew left their nets and followed Jesus.

[21]Jesus continued walking by Lake Galilee. He saw two other brothers, James and John, the sons of Zebedee. The two brothers were in a boat with their father, Zebedee. They were preparing their nets to catch fish. Jesus told the brothers to come with him. [22]So the brothers left the boat and their father, and they followed Jesus.

Jesus Teaches and Heals People

[23]Jesus went everywhere in the country of Galilee. Jesus taught in the synagogues* and preached the good news about the kingdom of heaven. And Jesus healed all the people's diseases and sicknesses. [24]The news about Jesus spread all over Syria. And people brought all the sick people to Jesus. These sick people were suffering from different kinds of diseases and pain. Some people were suffering with very bad pain, some people had demons* inside them, some people were epileptics,* and some people were paralyzed (*crippled*). Jesus healed all these people. [25]Many, many people followed Jesus. These people were from Galilee, the Ten Towns,* Jerusalem, Judea, and the area across the Jordan River.

Jesus Teaches the People

5 Jesus saw the many people that were there. So Jesus went up on a hill and sat down. His followers came to him. [2]Jesus taught the people. He said:

> [3] "Those people who *know they* have
>   great spiritual needs are blessed.
>   The kingdom of heaven belongs to those people.
> [4] Those people who are sad now are blessed.
>   God will comfort those people.

synagogues   Synagogues were buildings where Jews gathered to read and study the Scriptures.
demons   Demons are evil spirits from the devil.
epileptics   People with a bad disease that causes them sometimes to lose control of their bodies, and maybe faint, shake strongly, or not be able to move.
Ten Towns   Greek, "Decapolis," an area east of Lake Galilee. It once had ten main towns.

⁵ Those people who are humble are blessed.
    Everything will belong to them.
⁶ Those people who want to be right with God
      more than anything else are blessed.
    God will fill them with goodness.
⁷ Those people who give mercy to other people are blessed.
    Mercy will be given to them.
⁸ Those people who are pure in their thinking are blessed.
    Those people will be with God.
⁹ Those people who work to make peace are blessed.
    God will call those people his sons.
¹⁰Those people who are treated badly
      for doing good things are blessed.
    The kingdom of heaven belongs to those people.

¹¹"People will say bad things against you and hurt you. They will lie and say all kinds of evil things against you because you follow me. But when people do those things to you, you are blessed. ¹²Be happy and glad. You have a great reward waiting for you in heaven. People did those same bad things to the prophets* who lived before you."

You Are like Salt and You Are like Light

¹³"You are the salt of the earth. But if the salt loses its taste, then it cannot be made salty again. Salt is good for nothing if it loses its salty taste. It must be thrown out and people walk on it.

¹⁴"You are the light that gives light to the world. A city that is built on a hill cannot be hidden. ¹⁵And people don't hide a light under a bowl. No. People put the light on a lamp table. Then the light shines for all the people in the house. ¹⁶In the same way you should be a light for other people. Live so that people will see the good things you do. Live so that people will praise your Father in heaven."

Jesus and the Writings of the Old Testament

¹⁷"Don't think that I have come to destroy the law *of Moses* or the *teaching of the* prophets.* I have not come to destroy their

prophets People who spoke for God. Their writings are part of the Old Testament.

teachings. I came to give full meaning to their teachings. ¹⁸I tell you the truth. Nothing will disappear from the law until heaven and earth are gone. The law will not lose even the smallest letter or the smallest part of a letter before the end of all things. ¹⁹A person should obey every commandment, even a commandment that does not seem important. If a person refuses to obey any commandment and teaches other people not to obey that commandment, then that person will be the least important in the kingdom of heaven. But the person who obeys the law and teaches other people to obey the law will be great in the kingdom of heaven. ²⁰I tell you that you must be better people than the teachers of the law and the Pharisees.* If you are not better people, then you will not enter the kingdom of heaven."

Jesus Teaches About Anger

²¹"You have heard that it was said to our people long ago, 'Don't kill any person.* And any person who kills will be judged.' ²²But I tell you, don't be angry with another person. Every person is your brother. If you are angry with other people, you will be judged. And if you say bad things to another person, you will be judged by the Jewish council. And if you call another person a fool, then you will be in danger of the fire of hell.

²³"So when you offer your gift to God, think about other people. If you are offering your gift before the altar,* and you remember that your brother has something against you, ²⁴then leave your gift there at the altar. Go and make peace with that person. Then come and offer your gift.

²⁵"If your enemy is taking you to court, then become friends with him quickly. You should do that before you go to court. If you don't become his friend, then he might give you to the judge. And the judge might give you to a guard to put you in jail. ²⁶And I tell you that you will not leave that jail until you have paid everything you owe."

Pharisees   Pharisees were a Jewish religious group that followed all the Old Testament and other Jewish laws and customs very carefully.
'Don't kill...person'   Quotation from Exodus 20:13, Deuteronomy 5:17.
altar   An altar is a place where sacrifices or gifts are offered to God.

Jesus Teaches About Sexual Sin

²⁷"You have heard that it was said, 'Don't do the sin of adultery.'* ²⁸But I tell you that if a person looks at a woman and wants to sin sexually with her, then that person has already done that sin with the woman in his mind. ²⁹If your right eye makes you sin, then take it out and throw it away. It is better to lose one part of your body than to have your whole body thrown into hell. ³⁰If your right hand makes you sin, then cut it off and throw it away. It is better to lose one part of your body than for your whole body to go into hell."

Jesus Teaches About Divorce

³¹"It was also said, 'Any person who divorces his wife must give her a written notice of divorce.'* ³²But I tell you that any person who divorces his wife is causing his wife to be guilty of adultery.* The only reason for a person to divorce his wife is if his wife had sexual relations with another man. And any person who marries that divorced woman is guilty of adultery."

Jesus Teaches About Making Promises

³³"You have heard that it was said to our people long ago, 'When you make a vow (*promise*), don't break that promise. Keep the vows (*promises*) that you make to the Lord.'* ³⁴But I tell you, never make a vow.* Don't make a vow using the name of heaven, because heaven is God's throne. ³⁵Don't make a vow using the name of the earth, because the earth belongs to God. Don't make a vow using the name of Jerusalem, because that is the city of the great King (*God*). ³⁶And don't even say that your own head is proof that you will keep your vow.* You cannot make one hair on your head become white or black. ³⁷Say only 'yes' if you mean yes, and say only 'no' if you mean no. If you must say more than 'yes' or 'no,' it is from the Evil One (*the devil*)."

'Don't...adultery'   Quotation from Exodus 20:14, Deuteronomy 5:18.
'Any person...divorce'   Quotation from Deuteronomy 24:1.
adultery   Breaking a marriage promise by doing sexual sin.
'When...Lord'   Quotation from Leviticus 19:12, Numbers 30:2, Deuteronomy 23:21.
vow   A very strong promise that a person makes, often using the name of something important.

Jesus Teaches About Fighting Back

³⁸"You have heard that it was said, 'An eye for an eye, and a tooth for a tooth.'* ³⁹But I tell you, don't stand against an evil person. If someone hits you on the right cheek, then turn and let him hit the other cheek too. ⁴⁰If a person wants to sue you in court and take your coat, then let him have your overcoat too. ⁴¹If a soldier forces you to walk with him one mile, then go with him two miles. ⁴²If a person asks you for something, then give to him. Don't refuse to give to a person who wants to borrow from you."

Love All People

⁴³"You have heard that it was said, 'Love your friends* and hate your enemies.' ⁴⁴But I tell you, love your enemies. Pray for those people who do bad things to you. ⁴⁵If you do this, then you will be true sons of your Father in heaven. Your Father lets the sun rise for the good people and for the bad people. Your Father sends rain to people that do good and to people that do wrong. ⁴⁶If you love only the people who love you, then you will get no reward. Even the tax collectors* do that. ⁴⁷And if you are nice only to your friends, then you are no better than other people. Even the people without God are nice to their friends. ⁴⁸So you must be perfect, the same as your Father in heaven is perfect."

Jesus Teaches About Giving to Other People

6 "Be careful! When you do good things, don't do those things in front of people. Don't do those things for people to see you. If you do that, then you will have no reward from your Father in heaven.

²"When you give to poor people, don't announce that you are giving. Don't do like the hypocrites* do. They blow trumpets before they give so that people will see them. They do that in the synagogues* and on the streets. They want other people to give

'An eye...tooth' Quotation from Exodus 21:24, Leviticus 24:20, Deuteronomy 19:21.
'Love your friends' Quotation from Leviticus 19:18.
tax collectors Jews hired by the Romans to collect taxes. They often cheated their people.
hypocrites People who act like they are good but are not.
synagogues Synagogues were buildings where Jews gathered to read and study the Scriptures.

honor to them. I tell you the truth. Those hypocrites already have their full reward. ³So when you give to poor people, give very secretly. Don't let any person know what you are doing. ⁴Your giving should be done in secret. Your Father can see the things that are done in secret. And he will reward you.''

Jesus Teaches About Prayer

⁵''When you pray, don't be like the hypocrites.* The hypocrites love to stand in the synagogues* and on the street corners and pray loudly. They want people to see them pray. I tell you the truth. They already have their full reward. ⁶When you pray, you should go into your room and close the door. Then pray to your Father that cannot be seen. Your Father can see the things that are done in secret. And he will reward you.

⁷''And when you pray, don't be like those people who don't know God. They continue saying things that mean nothing. Don't pray like that. They think that God will hear them because of the many things they say. ⁸Don't be like those people. Your Father knows the things you need before you ask him. ⁹So when you pray, you should pray like this:

'Our Father in heaven,
we pray that your name will always be kept holy.
¹⁰We pray that your kingdom will come,
and that the things you want will be done,
here on earth and also in heaven.
¹¹Give us the food we need for each day.
¹²Forgive the sins we have done,
the same as we have forgiven the people
that did wrong to us.
¹³Don't cause us to be tempted (*tested*);
but save us from the Evil One (*the devil*).'

¹⁴Yes, if you forgive other people for the things they do wrong, then your Father in heaven will also forgive you for the things you do wrong. ¹⁵But if you don't forgive the wrong things people do to you, then your Father in heaven will not forgive the wrong things you do.''

---

hypocrites People who act like they are good but are not.
synagogues Synagogues were buildings where Jews gathered to read and study the Scriptures.

Jesus Teaches About Fasting

[16]"When you fast,* don't make yourselves look sad. Don't be like the hypocrites.* The hypocrites do that. They make their faces look strange so that they can show people that they are fasting. I tell you the truth, those hypocrites already have their full reward. [17]So when you fast, make yourself look nice. Wash your face. [18]Then people will not know that you are fasting. But your Father that you cannot see will see you. Your Father sees the things that are done in secret. And he will reward you."

God Is More Important Than Money

[19]"Don't save treasures for yourselves here on earth. Moths and rust will destroy treasures here on earth. And thieves can break into your house and steal the things you have. [20]So save your treasure in heaven. The treasures in heaven cannot be destroyed by moths or rust. And thieves cannot break in and steal that treasure. [21]Your heart will be where your treasure is.

[22]"The eye is a light for the body. If your eyes are good, then your whole body will be full of light. [23]But if your eyes are evil, then your whole body will be full of darkness (*sin*). And if the only light you have is really darkness, then you have the worst darkness.

[24]"No person can serve two masters at the same time. He will hate one master and love the other master. Or he will follow one master and refuse to follow the other master. So you cannot serve God and money at the same time."

Don't Worry

[25]"So I tell you, don't worry about the food you need to live. And don't worry about the clothes you need for your body. Life is more important than food. And the body is more important than clothes. [26]Look at the birds in the air. They don't plant or harvest or save food in barns. But your heavenly Father feeds those birds. And you know that you are worth much more than

---

fast   To fast is to live without food for a special time of prayer and worship to God.
hypocrites   People who act like they are good but are not.

those birds. [27]You cannot add any time to your life by worrying about it.

[28]"And why do you worry about clothes? Look at the flowers in the field. See how they grow. They don't work or make clothes for themselves. [29]But I tell you that even Solomon, the great and rich king, was not dressed as beautifully as one of these flowers. [30]God clothes the grass in the field like that. That grass is living today, but tomorrow it is thrown into the fire to be burned. So you know that God will clothe you much more. Don't have so little faith! [31]Don't worry and say, 'What will we eat?' or 'What will we drink?' or 'What will we wear?' [32]All the people who don't know God try to get these things. Don't worry, because your Father in heaven knows that you need these things. [33]The thing you should want most is God's kingdom and being right with him. Then all these other things you need will be given to you. [34]So don't worry about tomorrow. Each day has enough trouble of its own. Tomorrow will have its own worries.''

Jesus Teaches About Judging Other People

7 "Don't judge other people, and God will not judge you. [2]You will be judged in the same way that you judge other people. And the forgiveness you give to other people will be given to you.

[3]"Why do you notice the small piece of dust that is in your brother's eye, but you don't notice the big piece of wood that is in your own eye? [4]Why do you say to your brother, 'Let me take that little piece of dust out of your eye'? Look at yourself first! You still have that big piece of wood in your own eye! [5]You are a hypocrite*! First, take the wood out of your own eye. Then you will see clearly to take the dust out of your brother's eye.

[6]"Don't give holy things to dogs. Don't throw your pearls to pigs. *Dogs and pigs don't care about those things.* They will only walk on those things and then turn and hurt you.''

Continue to Ask God for the Things You Need

[7]"Continue to ask, and God will give to you. Continue to search, and you will find. Continue to knock, and the door will

hypocrite A person who acts like he is good but is not.

open for you. ⁸Yes, if a person continues asking, that person will receive. If a person continues looking, that person will find. And if a person continues knocking, the door will open for that person.

⁹"Do any of you have a son? If your son asked for bread, would you give him a rock? No! ¹⁰Or if your son asked for a fish, would you give him a snake? No! ¹¹*You are not like God*—you are evil. But you know how to give good things to your children. So surely your heavenly Father will give good things to those people who ask him."

The Most Important Rule

¹²"Do to other people the same things you want them to do to you. This is the meaning of the law *of Moses* and the *teaching* of the prophets.*"

The Way to Heaven and the Way to Hell

¹³"Enter through the narrow gate *that opens the way to heaven*. The road that leads to hell is a very easy road. And the gate to hell is very wide. Many people enter that gate. ¹⁴But the gate that opens the way to real life is very small. And the road to real life is very difficult (*hard*). Only a few people find that road."

The Things People Do Show the Kind of People They Are

¹⁵"Be careful of false prophets.* They come to you and look *gentle* like sheep. But they are really dangerous *like* wolves. ¹⁶You will know these people because of the things they do. Good things don't come from bad people, the same as grapes don't come from thorn bushes. And figs don't come from thorny weeds. ¹⁷In the same way, every good tree gives good fruit. And bad trees give bad fruit. ¹⁸A good tree cannot give bad fruit. And a bad tree cannot give good fruit. ¹⁹Every tree that does not give good fruit is cut down and thrown into the fire. ²⁰You will know these false people by the fruit they give (*things they do*).

prophets   People who spoke for God. Their writings are part of the Old Testament.
false prophets   People who say they speak for God but do not really speak God's truth.

²¹"Not every person who says that I am his Lord will enter the kingdom of heaven. The only people who will enter the kingdom of heaven are those people who do the things that my Father in heaven wants. ²²On the last day many people will say to me, 'You are our Lord! We spoke for you. And for you we forced out demons* and did many miracles.*' ²³Then I will tell those people clearly, 'Go away from me, you people that do wrong. I never knew you.' "

A Wise Person and a Foolish Person

²⁴"Every person who hears these things I say and obeys these things is like a wise man. The wise man built his house on rock. ²⁵It rained hard, and the water rose. The winds blew and hit that house. But the house did not fall, because the house was built on rock. ²⁶But the person who hears the things I teach and does not obey those things is like a foolish man. The foolish man built his house on sand. ²⁷It rained hard, the water rose, and the winds blew and hit that house. And the house fell with a loud noise."

²⁸When Jesus finished saying these things, the people were amazed at his teaching. ²⁹Jesus did not teach like their teachers of the law. Jesus taught like a person who had authority (*power*).

Jesus Heals a Sick Man

8 Jesus came down from the hill. Many, many people followed him. ²Then a man sick with leprosy* came to Jesus. The man bowed down before Jesus and said, "Lord, you have the power to heal me if you want."

³Jesus touched the man. Jesus said, "I will heal you. Be healed!" And immediately the man was healed from his leprosy.* ⁴Then Jesus said to him, "Don't tell any person about what happened. But go and show yourself to the priest.* And offer the gift that Moses commanded *for people who are made well*. This will show people that you are healed."

---

demons   Demons are evil spirits from the devil.
miracles   Miracles are powerful works or great things done by the power of God.
leprosy   A very bad skin disease.
show...priest   The law of Moses said a priest must say when a Jew with leprosy was well.

Jesus Heals a Soldier's Servant

⁵Jesus went to the city of Capernaum. When he entered the city, a Roman army officer* came to Jesus and begged for help. ⁶The officer said, "Lord, my servant is at home. He is very sick in bed. He can't move his body and has much pain."

⁷Jesus said to the officer, "I will go and heal him."

⁸The officer answered, "Lord, I am not good enough for you to come into my house. All you need to do is command that my servant be healed, and he will be healed. ⁹I myself am a man under the authority (*power*) of other men. And I have soldiers under my authority. I tell one soldier, 'Go,' and he goes. And I tell another soldier, 'Come,' and he comes. I say to my servant, 'Do this,' and my servant obeys me. *I know that you also have power like this.*"

¹⁰When Jesus heard this, he was amazed. Jesus said to those people who were with him, "I tell you the truth. This man has more faith than any person I have found, even in Israel. ¹¹Many people will come from the east and from the west. Those people will sit and eat with Abraham, Isaac, and Jacob* in the kingdom of heaven. ¹²And those people (*the Jews*) who should have the kingdom will be thrown out. They will be thrown outside into the darkness. In that place people will cry and grind their teeth *with pain.*"

¹³Then Jesus said to the officer,* "Go home. Your servant will be healed the way you believed he would." And at that same time his servant was healed.

Jesus Heals Many People

¹⁴Jesus went to Peter's house. There Jesus saw that Peter's mother-in-law was in bed with a high fever. ¹⁵Jesus touched her hand and the fever left her. Then she stood up and began to serve Jesus.

¹⁶That evening people brought to Jesus many people who had demons* inside them. Jesus spoke and the demons left the

---

officer A centurion, a Roman army officer who had authority over 100 soldiers.
Abraham, Isaac, and Jacob Three of the most important Jewish leaders of the past.
demons Demons are evil spirits from the devil.

people. Jesus healed all the people that were sick. [17]Jesus did these things to make happen what Isaiah the prophet* said. Isaiah said,

> "He took our diseases
> and carried away our sicknesses."

Isaiah 53:4

People Want to Follow Jesus

[18]Jesus saw that all the people were around him. So Jesus told his followers to go to the other side of the lake. [19]Then a teacher of the law came to Jesus and said, "Teacher, I will follow you any place you go."

[20]Jesus said to him, "The foxes have holes to live in. The wild birds have nests to live in. But the Son of Man* has no place where he can rest his head."

[21]Another man, one of Jesus' followers, said to Jesus, "Lord, let me go and bury my father first. *Then I will follow you.*"

[22]But Jesus said to him, "Follow me, and let the people that are dead bury their own dead."

Jesus Stops a Storm

[23]Jesus got into a boat and his followers went with him. [24]After the boat left the shore, a very bad storm began on the lake. The waves covered the boat. But Jesus was sleeping. [25]The followers went to Jesus and woke him. They said, "Lord, save us! We will drown!"

[26]Jesus answered, "Why are you afraid? You don't have enough faith." Then Jesus stood up and gave a command to the wind and the sea. The wind stopped and the sea became very calm.

[27]The men were amazed. They said, "What kind of man is this? Even the wind and the sea obey him!"

Jesus Heals Two Men Troubled with Demons

[28]Jesus arrived at the other side of the lake in the country of the

---

prophet Person who spoke for God. He often told things that would happen in the future.
Son of Man Jesus. Jesus was God's Son, but this name showed that Jesus was a man, too. In Daniel 7:13-14, this is the name for the Messiah (Christ).

Gadarene* people. There, two men came to Jesus. They had demons* inside them. These men lived in the burial caves. They were very dangerous. So people could not use the road by those caves. ²⁹The two men came to Jesus and shouted, "What do you want with us, Son of God? Did you come here to punish us before the right time?"

³⁰Near that place there was a large herd of pigs feeding. ³¹The demons begged Jesus, "If you make us leave these men, please send us into that herd of pigs."

³²Jesus said to them, "Go!" So the demons left those men and went into the pigs. Then the whole herd of pigs ran down the hill and into the lake. All the pigs drowned in the water. ³³The men who were caring for the pigs ran away. They went into town and told the people what happened. They told about all that happened with the pigs and with the men who had demons. ³⁴Then the whole town went out to see Jesus. When all the people saw Jesus, they begged him to leave their area.

Jesus Heals a Crippled Man

9 Jesus got into a boat and went back across the lake to his own town. ²Some people brought to Jesus a man who was paralyzed (*crippled*). The man was lying on his bed. Jesus saw that these people had much faith. So Jesus said to the paralyzed man, "Be happy, young man. Your sins are forgiven."

³Some of the teachers of the law heard this. They said to themselves, "This man (*Jesus*) speaks like he is God—that is blasphemy*!"

⁴Jesus knew they were thinking this. So Jesus said, "Why are you thinking evil thoughts? ⁵Which is easier: to tell this paralyzed man, 'Your sins are forgiven,' or to tell him, 'Stand up and walk'? ⁶But I will prove to you that the Son of Man* has power on earth to forgive sins." Then Jesus said to the paralyzed man, "Stand up. Take your bed and go home." ⁷And the man stood up and went home. ⁸The people saw this and they were amazed. The people praised God for giving power like this to men.

Gadarene From Gadara, an area southeast of Lake Galilee.
demons Demons are evil spirits from the devil.
blasphemy Saying things against God.
Son of Man Jesus. Jesus was God's Son, but this name showed that Jesus was a man, too. In Daniel 7:13-14, this is the name for the Messiah (Christ).

21

Jesus Chooses Matthew

⁹When Jesus was leaving, he saw a man named Matthew. Matthew was sitting in the tax office. Jesus said to him, "Follow me." Then Matthew stood up and followed Jesus.

¹⁰Jesus ate dinner at Matthew's house. Many tax collectors* and other bad people came and ate with Jesus and his followers. ¹¹The Pharisees* saw that Jesus was eating with these people. The Pharisees asked Jesus' followers, "Why does your teacher eat with tax collectors and other bad people?"

¹²Jesus heard the Pharisees say this. So Jesus said to the Pharisees, "Healthy people don't need a doctor. It is the sick people that need a doctor. ¹³I will tell you something. Go and learn what it means: 'I don't want animal sacrifices. I want kindness *among people*.'* I did not come to invite good people. I came to invite people who *know they are* sinners."

Jesus Is Not Like Other Religious Jews

¹⁴Then the followers of John* came to Jesus. They said to Jesus, "We and the Pharisees* fast* often. But your followers don't fast. Why?"

¹⁵Jesus answered, "*When there is a wedding*, the friends of the bridegroom* are not sad while he is with them. But the time will come when the bridegroom will leave them. The friends are sad when the bridegroom leaves. Then they will fast.*

¹⁶"When a person sews a patch over a hole on an old coat, that person never uses a piece of cloth that is not yet shrunk. If he does, the patch will *shrink and* pull away from the coat. Then the hole will be worse. ¹⁷Also, people never pour new wine into old wine bags.* Why? Because the old bags will break. The wine will spill and the wine bags will be ruined. But people always pour new wine into new wine bags. Then the wine and the wine bags will continue to be good."

tax collectors   Jews hired by the Romans to collect taxes. They often cheated their people.
Pharisees   Pharisees were a Jewish religious group that followed all the Old Testament and other Jewish laws and customs very carefully.
'I don't...people'   Quotation from Hosea 6:6.
John   John the Baptizer, who preached to people about Christ's coming (Matthew 3, Luke 3).
fast   To fast is to live without food for a special time of prayer and worship to God.
bridegroom   A man ready to be married.
wine bags   Bags made from the skin of an animal and used for holding wine.

Jesus Gives Life to a Dead Girl
and Heals a Sick Woman

¹⁸While Jesus was saying these things, a ruler of the synagogue* came to him. The ruler bowed down before Jesus and said, "My daughter has just died. But come and touch her with your hand and she will live again."

¹⁹So Jesus stood up and went with the ruler. Jesus' followers went too.

²⁰There was a woman who had been bleeding for twelve years. The woman came behind Jesus and touched the bottom of his coat. ²¹The woman was thinking, "If I can touch his coat, then I will be healed."

²²Jesus turned and saw the woman. Jesus said, "Be happy, dear woman. You are made well because you believed." Then the woman was healed.

²³Jesus continued going with the ruler, and went into the ruler's house. Jesus saw people there who make music for funerals. And he saw many people there crying *because the girl died.* ²⁴Jesus said, "Go away. The girl is not dead. She is only asleep." But the people laughed at Jesus. ²⁵After the people were put out of the house, Jesus went into the girl's room. Jesus held the girl's hand and the girl stood up. ²⁶The news about this spread all around the area.

Jesus Heals More People

²⁷When Jesus was leaving there, two blind men followed him. The blind men said loudly, "Show kindness to us, Son of David*!"

²⁸Jesus went inside, and the blind men went with him. Jesus asked the men, "Do you believe that I am able to make you see again?" The blind men answered, "Yes, Lord, we believe."

²⁹Then Jesus touched their eyes and said, "You believe that I can make you see again, so this will happen." ³⁰Then the men were able to see again. Jesus warned them very strongly. Jesus

---

synagogue   A synagogue was a building where Jews gathered to read and study the Scriptures.
Son of David   Name for the Christ, who was from the family of David, king of Israel.

said, "Don't tell any person about this." ³¹But the blind men left and spread the news about Jesus all around that area.

³²When the two men were leaving, some people brought another man to Jesus. This man could not talk because he had a demon* inside him. ³³Jesus forced the demon to leave the man. Then the man who couldn't talk was able to speak. The people were amazed and said, "We have never seen anything like this in Israel."

³⁴But the Pharisees* said, "The leader of demons (*the devil*) is the one that gives him (*Jesus*) power to force demons out."

Jesus Feels Sorry for the People

³⁵Jesus traveled through all the towns and villages. Jesus taught in their synagogues* and told people the Good News about the kingdom. And Jesus healed all kinds of diseases and sicknesses. ³⁶Jesus saw the many people and felt sorry for them. Jesus felt sorry for the people because the people were worried and helpless. The people were like sheep without a shepherd to lead them. ³⁷Jesus said to his followers, "There are many, many people to harvest (*save*). But there are only a few workers to help harvest them. ³⁸God owns the harvest (*people*). Pray to him that he will send more workers to help gather his harvest."

Jesus Sends His Apostles to Tell About God's Kingdom

10 Jesus called his twelve followers together. Jesus gave them power over evil spirits. Jesus gave them power to heal every kind of disease and sickness. ²These are the names of the twelve apostles*: Simon (also called Peter) and his brother Andrew; James, son of Zebedee, and his brother John; ³Philip and Bartholomew; Thomas and Matthew, the tax collector; James, son of Alphaeus, and Thaddaeus; ⁴Simon the Zealot* and Judas Iscariot. Judas is the one who turned against Jesus.

demon   Demons are evil spirits from the devil.
Pharisees   Pharisees were a Jewish religious group that followed all the Old Testament and other Jewish laws and customs very carefully.
synagogues   Synagogues were buildings where Jews gathered to read and study the Scriptures.
apostles   The men Jesus taught and chose to be his special helpers.
Zealot   The Zealots or "Enthusiasts" were a Jewish political group.

⁵Jesus gave these twelve apostles* some orders. Then he sent them *to tell people about the kingdom*. Jesus said, "Don't go to the non-Jewish people. And don't go into any town where the Samaritans* live. ⁶But go to the people of Israel (*the Jews*). They are like sheep that are lost. ⁷When you go, preach this: 'The kingdom of heaven is coming soon.' ⁸Heal sick people. Give dead people life again. Heal those people who have leprosy.* Force demons* to leave people. I give you these powers freely. So help other people freely. ⁹Don't carry any money with you—gold or silver or copper. ¹⁰Don't carry a bag. Take for your trip only the clothes and shoes you are wearing. Don't take a walking stick. A worker should be given the things he needs.

¹¹"When you enter a city or town, find some good person there and stay in his house until you leave. ¹²When you enter that house say, 'Peace be with you.' ¹³If the people in that home welcome you, then they are worthy of your peace. Let your peace stay there. But if the people don't welcome you, then they are not worthy of your peace. Take back the peace you wished for them. ¹⁴And if a home or town refuses to welcome you or listen to you, then leave that place. Shake their dust off your feet.* ¹⁵I tell you the truth. On the judgment day it will be worse for that town than for the towns of Sodom and Gomorrah.*"

Jesus Warns His Apostles About Troubles

¹⁶"Listen! I am sending you, and you will be like sheep among wolves. So be smart like snakes. But also be like doves and do nothing wrong. ¹⁷Be careful of people. They will arrest you and take you to be judged. They will whip you in their synagogues.* ¹⁸You will be taken to stand before governors and kings. People will do this to you because of me. You will tell about me to those kings and governors and to the non-Jewish people. ¹⁹When you

---

apostles   The men Jesus taught and chose to be his special helpers.
Samaritans   Samaritans were people from Samaria. These people were part Jew, but the Jews did not accept them as true Jews. Samaritans and Jews hated each other.
leprosy   A very bad skin disease.
demons   Demons are evil spirits from the devil.
shake...feet   A warning. It showed that they were finished talking to these people.
Sodom and Gomorrah   Cities that God destroyed to punish the evil people who lived there.
synagogues   Synagogues were buildings where Jews gathered to read and study the Scriptures.

are arrested, don't worry about what to say or how you should say it. At that time you will be given the things to say. ²⁰It will not really be you speaking. The Spirit of your Father will be speaking through you.

²¹"Brothers will turn against their own brothers and give them to be killed. Fathers will turn against their own children and give them to be killed. Children will fight against their own parents and find ways for their parents to be killed. ²²All people will hate you because you follow me. But the person who continues strong until the end will be saved. ²³When you are treated badly in one city, go to another city. I tell you the truth. You will not finish going through all the cities of Israel before the Son of Man* comes again.

²⁴"A servant is not better than his teacher. A servant is not better than his master. ²⁵A student should be satisfied to become like his teacher. A slave should be satisfied to become like his master. If the head of the family is called Beelzebul (*the devil*), then the other members of the family will be called worse names!"

Fear God, Not People

²⁶"So don't be afraid of those people. Everything that is hidden will be shown. Everything that is secret will be made known. ²⁷I tell you these things in the dark (*secretly*). But I want you to tell these things in the light. I speak these things quietly and only to you. But you should tell these things freely to all people. ²⁸Don't be afraid of people. They can only kill the body. They cannot kill the soul. The only one you should fear is the One (*God*) who can destroy the body and the soul. He can send the body and the soul to hell. ²⁹When birds are sold, two small birds cost only a penny. But not even one of those little birds can die without your Father allowing it. ³⁰God even knows how many hairs are on your head. ³¹So don't be afraid. You are worth much more than many birds."

Son of Man Jesus. Jesus was God's Son, but this name showed that Jesus was a man, too. In Daniel 7:13-14, this is the name for the Messiah (Christ).

Telling People About Your Faith in Jesus

³²"When a person stands before other people and says he believes in me, then I will say that person belongs to me. I will say this before my Father in heaven. ³³But when a person stands before people and says he does not believe in me, then I will say that person does not belong to me. I will say this before my Father in heaven.

³⁴"Don't think that I have come to bring peace to the earth. I did not come to bring peace. I came to bring a sword. ³⁵I have come to make this happen:

> 'A son will be against his father,
> a daughter will be against her mother,
> a daughter-in-law will be against her mother-in-law.
> ³⁶ A man's enemies will be members
> of his own family.'

Micah 7:6

³⁷"Any person who loves his father or mother more than he loves me is not good enough to follow me. Any person who loves his son or daughter more than he loves me is not good enough to follow me. ³⁸If a person will not accept the cross (*suffering*) that will be given to him when he follows me, then that person is not good enough for me. ³⁹Any person who loves his life *more than he loves me* will lose true life. Any person who gives up his life for me will find true life. ⁴⁰The person who accepts you also accepts me. And the person who accepts me also accepts the One (*God*) who sent me. ⁴¹Any person who meets a prophet* and accepts him will get the reward of a prophet. And any person who accepts a good man because that man is good will get the reward of a good man. ⁴²If any person helps one of these little ones because they are my followers, then that person will truly get his reward. That person will get his reward even if he only gave my follower a cup of cold water."

Jesus and John the Baptizer

11 Jesus finished telling these things to his twelve followers. Then Jesus left there and went to the towns in Galilee to teach and preach.

prophet Person who spoke for God. He often told things that would happen in the future.

²John the Baptizer* was in prison. He heard about the things Christ was doing. So John sent some of his followers to Jesus. ³John's followers asked Jesus, "Are you the man that *John said* was coming, or should we wait for another man?"

⁴Jesus answered, "Go back to John and tell him about the things that you hear and see: ⁵Blind people are able to see again; crippled people are able to walk again; people who have leprosy* are healed; deaf people can hear again; dead people are raised from death; and the Good News is told to the poor people. ⁶The person who can accept* me is blessed (*happy*)."

⁷While John's followers were leaving, Jesus began talking to the people about John. Jesus said, "What did you people go out to the desert to see? A weed* blown by the wind? No! ⁸Really, what did you go out to see? A man dressed in fine clothes? No! Those people who wear fine clothes live in kings' palaces. ⁹So what did you go out to see? A prophet*? Yes, and I tell you, John is more than a prophet. ¹⁰This Scripture* was written about John:

'Listen! I send my helper ahead of you.

He will prepare the way for you.' *Malachi 3:1*

¹¹I tell you the truth: John the Baptizer* is greater than any man who has ever lived. But even the least important person in the kingdom of heaven is greater than John. ¹²Since the time John the Baptizer came until now, the kingdom of heaven has been going forward strongly.* People using force have been trying to get the kingdom. ¹³All the prophets* and the law *of Moses* spoke until the time John came. They told about the things that would happen. ¹⁴And if you will believe the things the law and the prophets said, then you will believe that John is Elijah. The law and the prophets said he would come. ¹⁵You people who hear me, listen!

¹⁶"What can I say about the people that live today? What are they like? The people today are like children sitting in the market

---

Baptizer   John is called the Baptizer because he had the work of baptizing people.
leprosy   A very bad skin disease.
can accept   Literally, "is not offended by."
weed   Literally, "reed." It means that John is not weak like a reed blown by the wind.
prophet   Person who spoke for God. He often told things that would happen in the future.
Scripture   A part of the Holy Writings—the Old Testament.
has...strongly   This could also be translated, "has suffered violence."

place. One group of children calls to the other group,

> [17]'We played music for you, but you did not dance;
>   we sang a sad song, but you were not sad.'

[18]*Why do I say people are like that?* Because John* came and he did not eat like other people or drink wine. And people say, 'He has a demon* inside him.' [19]The Son of Man* came eating like other people and drinking wine, and people say, 'Look at him! He eats too much and drinks too much wine. He is a friend of tax collectors* and other bad people.' But wisdom is shown to be right by the things it does.''

Jesus Warns People Who Don't Believe

[20]Then Jesus criticized the cities where he did most of his miracles.* Jesus criticized those cities because the people there did not change their lives and stop sinning. [21]Jesus said, ''It will be bad for you Chorazin (*a city*)! It will be bad for you Bethsaida (*a city*)! I did many miracles in you. If those same miracles had happened in Tyre and Sidon,* then those people in Tyre and Sidon would have changed their lives a long time ago. Those people would have worn sackcloth* and put ashes on themselves to show that they were sorry for their sins. [22]But I tell you, on the day of judgment it will be worse for you than for Tyre and Sidon. [23]And you, Capernaum, will you be saved? No! You will be thrown down to hell! I did many miracles in you. If those same miracles had happened in Sodom, Sodom would *have stopped sinning and would* still be a city today. [24]But I tell you it will be worse for you in the day of judgment than for Sodom.''

Jesus Offers Rest to People Who Accept Him

[25]Then Jesus said, ''I thank you, Father, Lord of heaven and earth. I praise you because you have hidden these things from the

John   John the Baptizer, who preached to people about Christ's coming (Matthew 3, Luke 3).
demon   Demons are evil spirits from the devil.
Son of Man   Jesus. Jesus was God's Son, but this name showed that Jesus was a man, too. In Daniel 7:13-14, this is the name for the Messiah (Christ).
tax collectors   Jews hired by the Romans to collect taxes. They often cheated their people.
miracles   Miracles are powerful works or great things done by the power of God.
Tyre and Sidon   Towns where very bad people lived.
sackcloth   A rough cloth of animal hair. People sometimes wore it to show sadness.

wise and smart people. But you have shown these things to people who are like little children. ²⁶Yes, Father, you did this because this is what you really wanted to do.

²⁷"My Father has given me all things. No person knows the Son—only the Father knows the Son. And no person knows the Father—only the Son knows the Father. And the only people who will know about the Father are those people the Son chooses to tell.

²⁸"Come to me all you people who are tired and have heavy burdens. I will give you rest. ²⁹Accept my work and learn from me. I am gentle and humble in spirit. And you will find rest for your souls. ³⁰Yes, the work that I ask you to accept is easy. The burden I give you to carry is not heavy."

Some Jews Criticize Jesus and His Followers

12 About that same time, Jesus was walking through the fields of grain on a Sabbath day.* Jesus' followers were with him, and they were hungry. So the followers began to pick the grain and eat it. ²The Pharisees* saw this. They said to Jesus, "Look! Your followers are doing something that is against the *Jewish* law to do on the Sabbath day.*"

³Jesus answered, "You have read what David did when he and the people with him were hungry. ⁴David went into God's house. David and the people with him ate the bread that was offered to God. It was against the law for David or the people with him to eat that bread. Only the priests were allowed to eat it. ⁵And you have read in the law *of Moses* that on every Sabbath day* the priests in the temple break the law about the Sabbath day. But the priests are not wrong for doing that. ⁶I tell you that there is something here that is greater than the temple.* ⁷The Scripture* says, 'I don't want animal sacrifices; I want kindness *among people*.'* You don't really know what those words mean. If you

Sabbath day   Seventh day of the Jewish week. It was a special religious day for the Jews.
Pharisees   Pharisees were a Jewish religious group that followed all the Old Testament and other Jewish laws and customs very carefully.
temple   The special building in Jerusalem where God commanded the Jews to worship.
Scripture   A part of the Holy Writings—the Old Testament.
'I don't...people'   Quotation from Hosea 6:6.

understood those words, then you would not judge those people who have done nothing wrong.

⁸"The Son of Man* is Lord (*ruler*) over the Sabbath day." *

Jesus Heals a Man's Crippled Hand

⁹Jesus left that place and went into their synagogue.* ¹⁰In the synagogue, there was a man with a crippled hand. Some Jews there were looking for a reason to accuse Jesus of doing wrong. So they asked Jesus, "Is it right to heal on the Sabbath day?"*

¹¹Jesus answered, "If any of you has a sheep, and the sheep falls into a ditch on the Sabbath day, then you will take the sheep and help it out of the ditch. ¹²Surely a man is more important than a sheep. So the law *of Moses* allows people to do good things on the Sabbath day."

¹³Then Jesus said to the man with the crippled hand, "Let me see your hand." The man put his hand out for Jesus, and the hand became well again, the same as the other hand. ¹⁴But the Pharisees* left and made plans to kill Jesus.

Jesus Does the Things God Chose Him to Do

¹⁵Jesus knew what the Pharisees* were doing. So Jesus left that place. Many people followed Jesus, and he healed all the sick people. ¹⁶But Jesus warned the people not to tell other people who he was. ¹⁷Jesus did these things to make happen what Isaiah the prophet* said. Isaiah said,

¹⁸"Here is my servant; I (*God*) have chosen him.
    I love him and I am pleased with him;
  I will put my Spirit on him,
    And he will tell about the way
      I will judge the non-Jewish people fairly.

Son of Man   Jesus. Jesus was God's Son, but this name showed that Jesus was a man, too. In Daniel 7:13-14, this is the name for the Messiah (Christ).
Sabbath day   Seventh day of the Jewish week. It was a special religious day for the Jews.
synagogue   Synagogues were places where Jews gathered to read and study the Scriptures.
Is it right...Sabbath day   It was against Jewish law to work on the Sabbath day.
Pharisees   Pharisees were a Jewish religious group that followed all the Old Testament and other Jewish laws and customs very carefully.
prophet   Person who spoke for God. He often told things that would happen in the future.

¹⁹He will not argue or shout;
    People will not hear his voice in the streets.
²⁰He will not break the reed that is already bent;
    He will not stop the light
        that has almost stopped burning.
  He will continue until he makes fair judgment
      win the victory.
²¹   All people will hope in him.''

Isaiah 42:1-4

Jesus' Power Is from God

²²Then some people brought a man to Jesus. This man was blind and could not talk because he had a demon* inside him. Jesus healed the man and the man could talk and see. ²³All the people were amazed. The people said, "Maybe this man (*Jesus*) is the Son of David* *that God promised to send to us*!''

²⁴The Pharisees* heard the people saying this. The Pharisees said, "Jesus uses the power of Beelzebul (*the devil*), to force demons out of people. Beelzebul is the ruler of demons.''

²⁵Jesus knew the things that the Pharisees* were thinking. So Jesus said to them, "Every kingdom that is fighting against itself will be destroyed. And every city that is divided cannot continue. And every family that is divided cannot succeed. ²⁶So if Satan (*the devil*) forces out his own demons,* then Satan is divided. And his kingdom will not be able to continue. ²⁷You say that I use the power of Satan when I force out demons. If that is true, then what power do your people use when they force out demons? So your own people prove that you are wrong. ²⁸But I use the power of God's Spirit to force out demons. This shows that the kingdom of God has come to you.

²⁹"If a person wants to enter a strong man's house and steal his things, first the person must tie the strong man. Then the person can steal the things from the strong man's house.

³⁰"If a person is not with me, then he is against me. The person who does not work with me is working against me. ³¹So I tell you,

demon   Demons are evil spirits from the devil.
Son of David   Name for the Christ, who was from the family of David, king of Israel.
Pharisees   Pharisees were a Jewish religious group that followed all the Old Testament and other Jewish laws and customs very carefully.
If...demons   Literally, "If Satan forces out Satan.''

people can be forgiven of every sin they do. And people can be forgiven for every bad thing they say. But if a person speaks against (*refuses to accept*) the *Holy* Spirit,* then that person will not be forgiven. ³²Any person who says things against the Son of Man* can be forgiven. But any person who says things against the Holy Spirit will not be forgiven. They will not be forgiven now or in the future.''

The Things You Do Show What You Are

³³''If you want good fruit, you must make the tree good. If your tree is not good then it will have bad fruit. A tree is known by the kind of fruit it gives. ³⁴You snakes! You are evil people! How can you say anything good? The mouth speaks the things that are in the heart. ³⁵A good person has good things saved in his heart. And so he speaks the good things that come from his heart. But an evil person has evil saved in his heart. So he speaks the evil things that come from his heart. ³⁶And I tell you that people will have to explain about every careless thing they have said. This will happen on the day of judgment. ³⁷The words you have said will be used to judge you. Some of your words will make you right, but some of your words will make you guilty.''

The Jewish Leaders Ask Jesus to Do a Miracle

³⁸Then some of the Pharisees* and teachers of the law answered Jesus. They said, ''Teacher, we want to see you do a miracle* as a sign (*proof*).''

³⁹Jesus answered, ''Evil and sinful people are the ones who want to see a miracle for a sign (*proof*). But no miracle will be given as a sign to those people. The only sign will be the miracle that happened to the prophet* Jonah. ⁴⁰Jonah was in the stomach of the big fish for three days and three nights. In the same way,

---

Holy Spirit   Also called the Spirit of God, the Spirit of Christ, and the Comforter. He is joined with God and Christ. He does the work of God among people in the world.

Son of Man   Jesus. Jesus was God's Son, but this name showed that Jesus was a man, too. In Daniel 7:13-14, this is the name for the Messiah (Christ).

Pharisees   Pharisees were a Jewish religious group that followed all the Old Testament and other Jewish laws and customs very carefully.

miracle   Miracles are powerful works or great things done by the power of God.

prophet   Person who spoke for God. He often told things that would happen in the future.

the Son of Man* will be in the grave three days and three nights. ⁴¹And on the Judgment Day the men from Nineveh* will stand up with you people that live today, and they will show that you are wrong (*guilty*). Why? Because when Jonah preached to those people, they changed their lives. And I tell you that I am greater than Jonah! ⁴²On the judgment day, the Queen of the South* will stand up with you people that live today and she will show that you are wrong (*guilty*). Why? Because that queen traveled from far, far away to listen to Solomon's wise teaching. And I tell you that I am greater than Solomon!''

People Today Are Full of Evil

⁴³"When an evil spirit *of the devil* comes out of a person, that spirit travels through dry places looking for a place to rest. But that spirit finds no place to rest. ⁴⁴So the spirit says, 'I will go back to the home (*person*) I left.' When the spirit comes back to that person, the spirit finds that home (*person*) still empty. That home is swept clean and made neat. ⁴⁵Then the evil spirit goes out and brings seven other spirits more evil than itself. Then all the spirits go into that person and live there. And that person has even more trouble than he had before. It is the same way with the evil people that live today.''

Jesus' Followers Are His True Family

⁴⁶While Jesus was talking to the people his mother and brothers stood outside. They wanted to talk to Jesus. ⁴⁷A person told Jesus, "Your mother and brothers are waiting for you outside. They want to talk to you.''

⁴⁸Jesus answered, "Who is my mother? Who are my brothers?'' ⁴⁹Then Jesus pointed to his followers and said, "See! These people are my mother and my brothers. ⁵⁰My true brother and sister and mother are those people who do the things that my Father in heaven wants.''

Son of Man   Jesus. Jesus was God's Son, but this name showed that Jesus was a man, too. In Daniel 7:13-14, this is the name for the Messiah (Christ).
Nineveh   The city where Jonah preached to warn the people. Read Jonah 3.
Queen of the South   The Queen of Sheba. She traveled 1000 miles to learn God's wisdom from Solomon. Read 1 Kings 10:1-13.

Jesus Uses a Story About a Farmer Planting Seed

13 That same day Jesus went out of the house and sat by the lake (*Lake Galilee*). ²Many, many people gathered around Jesus. So Jesus got into a boat and sat in the boat. All the people stayed on the shore. ³Then Jesus used stories to teach the people many things. Jesus said: "A farmer went out to plant his seed. ⁴While the farmer was planting, some seed fell by the road. The birds came and ate all that seed. ⁵Some seed fell on rocky ground. The ground there did not have enough dirt. The seed grew very fast there, because the ground was not deep. ⁶But when the sun rose, it burned the plants. The plants died because they did not have deep roots. ⁷Some other seed fell among thorny weeds. The weeds grew and stopped the good plants from growing. ⁸Some other seed fell on good ground. In the good ground, the seed grew and made grain. Some plants had 100 grains, other plants had 60 grains, and some had 30 grains. ⁹You people who hear me, listen!"

Why Jesus Used Stories to Teach

¹⁰The followers came to Jesus and asked, "Why do you use these stories to teach the people?"

¹¹Jesus answered, "Only you can know the secret truths about the kingdom of heaven. Those other people cannot know these secret truths. ¹²The person who has *faith* will be given more. And that person will have all he needs. But the person who refuses *to believe* will lose even the little *faith* he has. Everything will be taken from him. ¹³This is why I use these stories to teach the people: The people see, but they don't see. The people hear, but they don't really understand. ¹⁴So these people show that the things Isaiah said about them are true:

'You people will listen and you will hear,
but you will not understand.
You people will look and you will see,
but you will not understand what you see.
¹⁵Yes, the hearts (*minds*) of these people (*the Jews*)
are now hard.
These people have ears, but they don't listen.

35

> And these people refuse to see *the truth*.
> This has happened so that these people will not
> see with their eyes,
> hear with their ears,
> understand with their minds.
> This has happened so that they will not
> turn to me to heal them.'
> *Isaiah 6:9-10*

¹⁶But you are blessed. You understand the things you see with your eyes. And you understand the things you hear with your ears. ¹⁷I tell you the truth. Many prophets* and good people wanted to see the things that you now see. But they did not see these things. And many prophets and good people wanted to hear the things that you now hear. But they did not hear these things."

Jesus Explains the Story About the Planting of the Seeds

¹⁸"So listen to the meaning of that story about the farmer. ¹⁹What is the seed that fell by the path? That seed is like the person who hears the teaching about the kingdom but does not understand it. The Evil One (*the devil*) comes and takes away the things that were planted in that person's heart. ²⁰And what is the seed that fell on rocky ground? That seed is like the person who hears the teaching and quickly accepts that teaching with joy. ²¹But that person does not let that teaching go deep into his life. He keeps that teaching only a short time. When trouble or persecution* comes because of the teaching he accepted, then he quickly quits. ²²And what is the seed that fell among the thorny weeds? That seed is like the person who hears the teaching but lets worries about this life and love for money stop that teaching from growing. So that teaching does not make fruit* in that person's life. ²³But what is the seed that fell on the good ground? That seed is like the person who hears the teaching and understands it. That person grows and makes fruit, sometimes 100 times more, sometimes 60 times more, and sometimes 30 times more."

---

prophets People who spoke for God. Their writings are part of the Old Testament.
persecution Being hurt by other people or suffering bad things from them.
make fruit To make fruit is to have in your life the good things God wants.

Jesus Uses a Story About Wheat and Weeds

²⁴Then Jesus told them another story. Jesus said, "The kingdom of heaven is like a man who planted good seed in his field. ²⁵That night, all the people were asleep. The man's enemy came and planted weeds among the wheat. Then the enemy went away. ²⁶Later, the wheat grew and heads of grain grew on the wheat plants. But at the same time the weeds also grew. ²⁷Then the man's servants came to him and said, 'You planted good seed in your field. Where did the weeds come from?'

²⁸"The man answered, 'An enemy planted weeds.'

"The servants asked, 'Do you want us to go pull the weeds?'

²⁹"The man answered, 'No, because when you pull up the weeds, you might also pull up the wheat. ³⁰Let the weeds and the wheat grow together until the harvest time. At the harvest time I will tell the workers this: 'First gather the weeds and tie them together to be burned. Then gather the wheat and bring it to my barn.' "

Jesus Uses More Stories to Teach the People

³¹Then Jesus told the people another story: "The kingdom of heaven is like a mustard seed. A person plants that seed in his field. ³²That seed is one of the smallest of all seeds. But when the seed grows, it is one of the largest garden plants. It becomes a tree, big enough for the wild birds to come and make nests in its branches."

³³Then Jesus told the people another story: "The kingdom of heaven is like yeast that a woman mixes into a big bowl of flour to make bread. The yeast makes all the dough (*bread*) rise."

³⁴Jesus used stories to tell all these things to the people. Jesus always used stories to teach the people. ³⁵This is the same as what the prophet* said:

> "I will speak using stories;
> I will tell things that have been secrets
> since the world was made." *Psalm 78:2*

---

prophet Person who spoke for God. He often told things that would happen in the future.

Jesus Explains the Story About the Wheat and the Weeds

³⁶Then Jesus left the people and went into the house. His followers came to him and said, "Explain to us the meaning of the story about the weeds in the field."

³⁷Jesus answered, "The person who planted the good seed in the field is the Son of Man.* ³⁸The field is the world. And the good seed are all of God's children in the kingdom. The weeds are those people who belong to the Evil One (*the devil*). ³⁹And the enemy who planted the bad seed is the devil. The harvest time is the end of the world.* And the workers who gather are God's angels.

⁴⁰"The weeds are pulled up and burned in the fire. It will be the same at the end of this world.* ⁴¹The Son of Man* will send his angels, and his angels will find the people who cause sin and all people who do evil. The angels will take those people out of his kingdom. ⁴²The angels will throw those people into the place of fire. In that place the people will be crying and grinding their teeth *with pain*. ⁴³Then the good people will shine like the sun. They will be in the kingdom of their Father. You people who hear me, listen!"

Stories About a Treasure and About a Pearl

⁴⁴"The kingdom of heaven is like a treasure hidden in a field. One day a man found the treasure, and then hid the treasure in the field again. The man was very happy to find the treasure. The man went and sold everything that he owned to buy that field.

⁴⁵"Also, the kingdom of heaven is like a salesman looking for fine pearls. ⁴⁶One day the salesman found a very great pearl. The salesman went and sold everything he had to buy that pearl."

A Story About a Fishing Net

⁴⁷"Also, the kingdom of heaven is like a net that was put into the lake. The net caught many different kinds of fish. ⁴⁸The net became full, so the fishermen pulled the net to the shore. The

Son of Man   Jesus. Jesus was God's Son, but this name showed that Jesus was a man, too. In Daniel 7:13-14, this is the name for the Messiah (Christ).
world   Literally, "this age," or "this time."

fishermen sat down and put all the good fish in baskets. Then they threw away the bad fish. ⁴⁹It will be the same at the end of this world.* The angels will come and separate the evil people from the good people. ⁵⁰The angels will throw the evil people into the place of fire. In that place the people will cry and grind their teeth *with pain*."

⁵¹Jesus asked his followers, "Do you understand all these things?"

The followers answered, "Yes, we understand."

⁵²Then Jesus said to the followers, "So every teacher of the law who has been taught about the kingdom of heaven is like the owner of a house. That person has new things and old things saved in that house. And that person brings out those new things and old things."

Jesus Goes to His Home Town

⁵³When Jesus finished teaching with these stories, he left there. ⁵⁴Jesus went to the town where he grew up. Jesus taught the people in the synagogue,* and the people were amazed. The people said, "Where did this man get this wisdom and this power to do miracles*? ⁵⁵This is only the son of the carpenter. And his mother is Mary. His brothers are James, Joseph, Simon and Judas. ⁵⁶And all his sisters are here with us. So where does this man get this wisdom and the power to do these things?" ⁵⁷And the people refused to accept Jesus.

But Jesus said to the people, "Other people give honor to a prophet.* But people in that prophet's own town or own home don't give honor to him."

⁵⁸The people there did not believe in Jesus. So Jesus did not do many miracles there.

---

world   Literally, "this age," or "this time."
synagogue   Synagogues were places where Jews gathered to read and study the Scriptures.
miracles   Miracles are powerful works or great things done by the power of God.
prophet   Person who spoke for God.

Herod Hears About Jesus

14 At that time Herod,* the ruler *of Galilee*, heard the things people said about Jesus. ²So Herod said to his servants, "Jesus is really John the Baptizer.* He is risen from death. That is why he is able to do these miracles.*"

How John the Baptizer Was Killed

³Before this time, Herod* had arrested John and put John into prison. Herod arrested John because of Herodias. Herodias was the wife of Philip, Herod's brother. ⁴Herod arrested John because John told Herod: "It is not right for you to have Herodias." ⁵Herod wanted to kill John, but he was afraid of the people. The people believed that John was a prophet.*

⁶On Herod's birthday, the daughter of Herodias danced for Herod and his group. Herod was very pleased with her. ⁷So Herod promised that he would give her anything she wanted. ⁸Herodias told her daughter what to ask for. So she said to Herod, "Give me the head of John the Baptizer here on this plate." ⁹King Herod was very sad. But he had promised to give the daughter anything she wanted. And the people eating with Herod had heard his promise. So Herod ordered that the thing she asked be done. ¹⁰He sent men to cut off John's head in the prison. ¹¹And the men brought John's head on a plate and gave it to the girl. Then the girl took the head to her mother, Herodias. ¹²John's followers came and got his body and buried it. Then they went and told Jesus what happened.

Jesus Feeds More Than 5,000 People

¹³When Jesus heard what happened to John, Jesus left in a boat. Jesus went alone to a place where there were no people. But the people heard that Jesus left. So the people left their towns and followed Jesus. They went by land to the same place Jesus went. ¹⁴When Jesus arrived there, he saw many, many people there.

Herod Herod Antipas, the son of Herod the Great.
Baptizer John is called the Baptizer because he had the work of baptizing people.
miracles Miracles are powerful works or great things done by the power of God.
prophet Person who spoke for God. He often told things that would happen in the future.

Jesus felt sorry for them and he healed the people that were sick.

¹⁵Late that afternoon, the followers came to Jesus and said, "No people live in this place. And it is already late. Send the people away so they can go to the towns and buy food for themselves."

¹⁶Jesus answered, "The people don't need to go away. You give them some food to eat."

¹⁷The followers answered, "But we have only five loaves of bread and two fish."

¹⁸Jesus said, "Bring the bread and the fish to me." ¹⁹Then Jesus told the people to sit down on the grass. Jesus took the five loaves of bread and the two fish. Jesus looked into the sky and thanked God for the food. Then Jesus divided the loaves of bread. Jesus gave the bread to the followers and the followers gave the bread to the people. ²⁰All the people ate and were filled. After the people finished eating, the followers filled twelve baskets with the pieces of food that were not eaten. ²¹There were about 5,000 men there who ate. There were also women and children.

Jesus Walks on the Lake

²²Then Jesus made the followers get into the boat. Jesus told them to go to the other side of the lake (*Lake Galilee*). Jesus said that he would come later. Jesus stayed there to tell the people they could go home. ²³After Jesus said good-bye to the people, he went up into the hills. Jesus went there alone to pray. It was late, and Jesus was there alone. ²⁴At this time, the boat was already far away on the lake. The boat was having trouble because of the waves. The wind was blowing against it.

²⁵Between three and six o'clock in the morning, Jesus' followers were still in the boat. Jesus came to them. He was walking on the water. ²⁶The followers saw Jesus walking on the water and they were very afraid. They said, "It's a ghost!" The followers shouted with fear.

²⁷But Jesus quickly spoke to them. Jesus said, "Don't worry! It's me! Don't be afraid."

²⁸Peter said, "Lord, if that is really you, then tell me to come to you on the water."

²⁹Jesus said, "Come, Peter."

Then Peter left the boat and walked on the water to Jesus. ³⁰But while Peter was walking on the water, he saw the wind and the waves. Peter became afraid and began sinking down into the water. Peter shouted, "Lord, save me!"

³¹Then Jesus caught Peter with his hand. Jesus said, "Your faith is small. Why did you doubt?"

³²After Peter and Jesus were in the boat, the wind became calm. ³³Then those followers in the boat worshiped Jesus and said, "Truly you are the Son of God."

³⁴After they crossed the lake, they came to the shore at Gennesaret. ³⁵The people in that place saw Jesus. They knew who he was. So they told the other people all around there that Jesus had come. The people brought all their sick people to Jesus. ³⁶The people begged Jesus to let them only touch his coat to be healed. And all the sick people who touched Jesus' coat were healed.

God's Law Is More Important than Rules That People Make

15 Then some Pharisees* and teachers of the law came to Jesus. They came from Jerusalem and asked Jesus, ²"Why do your followers not obey the rules given to us by our great people who lived before us? Your followers don't wash their hands before they eat!"

³Jesus answered, "And why do you refuse to obey God's command so that you can follow those rules you have? ⁴God said, 'Respect *and obey* your father and mother.'* And God also said, 'Any person who says bad things to his father or mother must be killed.'* ⁵But you teach that a person can say to his father or mother, 'I have something I could use to help you. But I will not use it to help you. I will give it to God.' ⁶You teach that person to not honor his father. So you teach that it is not important to do what God said. You think that it is more important to follow those rules you have. ⁷You are hypocrites*! Isaiah was right when

---

Pharisees   Pharisees were a Jewish religious group that followed all the Old Testament and other Jewish laws and customs very carefully.
'Respect...mother'   Quotation from Exodus 20:12, Deuteronomy 5:16.
'Any person...killed'   Quotation from Exodus 21:17.
hypocrites   People who act like they are good but are not.

he spoke about you. Isaiah said:

⁸ 'These people say they honor me,
but they don't really make me an important part
of their lives.
⁹ Their worship of me is worthless.
The things they teach are only rules
that people have made.' "   *Isaiah 29:13*

¹⁰Jesus called the people to him. Jesus said, "Listen and understand what I am saying. ¹¹It is not the things a person puts in his mouth that make him wrong. It is the things a person says with his mouth that make him wrong."

¹²Then the followers came to Jesus and asked, "Do you know that the Pharisees* are angry because of what you said?"

¹³Jesus answered, "Every plant that my Father in heaven has not planted himself will be pulled up by the roots. ¹⁴Stay away from the Pharisees. They lead the people, but they are like blind men leading other blind men. And if a blind man leads another blind man, then both men will fall into a hole."

¹⁵Peter said, "Explain to us what you meant when you told *about what makes a person wrong.*"

¹⁶Jesus said, "You still have trouble understanding? ¹⁷Surely you know that all the food that enters a man's mouth goes into the stomach. Then that food goes out of the body. ¹⁸But the bad things a person says with his mouth come from the way a person thinks. And these are the things that make a person wrong. ¹⁹All these bad things begin in a person's mind: evil thoughts, murder, adultery,* sexual sins, stealing, lying, saying bad things against other people. ²⁰These things make a person wrong. But not washing his hands before he eats does not make a person wrong."

Jesus Helps a Non-Jewish Woman

²¹Jesus left that place and went to the area of Tyre and Sidon. ²²A Canaanite woman from that area came to Jesus. The woman shouted, "Lord, Son of David,* please help me! My daughter has

---

Pharisees Pharisees were a Jewish religious group that followed all the Old Testament and other Jewish laws and customs very carefully.
adultery Breaking a marriage promise by doing sexual sin.
Son of David Name for the Christ, who was from the family of David, king of Israel.

a demon* inside her and she is suffering very much.''

²³But Jesus did not answer the woman. So the followers came to Jesus and begged him, ''Tell the woman to go away. She is following us and shouting.''

²⁴Jesus answered, ''God sent me only to the lost people* of Israel (*the Jews*).''

²⁵Then the woman came to Jesus again. She bowed before Jesus and said, ''Lord, help me!''

²⁶Jesus answered, ''It is not right to take the children's bread and give it to the dogs.''

²⁷The woman said, ''Yes, Lord, but even the dogs eat the pieces of food that fall from their master's table.''

²⁸Then Jesus answered, ''Woman, you have great faith! I will do the thing you wanted me to do.'' And at that time the woman's daughter was healed.

Jesus Heals Many People

²⁹Then Jesus left that place and went to the shore of Lake Galilee. Jesus went up on a hill and sat down.

³⁰Many, many people came to Jesus. These people brought many other sick people and put the sick people before Jesus. There were people who could not walk, blind people, crippled people, deaf people, and many others. Jesus healed all these people. ³¹People were amazed when they saw that people who could not speak were able to speak again. Crippled people were made strong again. People who could not walk were able to walk again. The blind were able to see again. All the people thanked the God of Israel (*the Jews*) for this.

Jesus Feeds More than 4,000 People

³²Jesus called his followers to him and said, ''I feel sorry for these people. They have been with me three days, and now they have nothing to eat. I don't want to send them away hungry. They might faint while going home.''

---

demon Demons are evil spirits from the devil.
people Literally, ''sheep.''

³³The followers asked Jesus, "Where can we get enough bread to feed all these people? We are far away from any town."

³⁴Jesus asked, "How many loaves of bread do you have?"

The followers answered, "We have seven loaves of bread, and a few small fish."

³⁵Jesus told the people to sit on the ground. ³⁶Jesus took the seven loaves of bread and the fish. Then Jesus gave thanks to God for the food. Jesus divided the food and gave it to the followers. The followers gave the food to the people. ³⁷All the people ate and were full. After this, the followers filled seven baskets with the pieces of food that were not eaten. ³⁸There were about 4,000 men there who ate. The women and children ate too. ³⁹After they ate, Jesus told the people they could go home. Jesus got into the boat and went to the area of Magadan.

The Jewish Leaders Want Jesus to Do Something Wrong

16 The Pharisees* and Sadducees* came to Jesus. They wanted to try to make Jesus do something wrong. So they asked Jesus to show them a miracle* to prove that he was from God.

²Jesus answered, "When you people see the sunset, you know what the weather will be. If the sky is red, then you say we will have good weather. ³And in the morning you watch the sunrise. If the sky is dark and red, then you say that it will be a rainy day. These things are signs of the weather. You see these signs in the sky and you know what they mean. In the same way, you see the things that are happening now. These things are also signs. But you don't know the meaning of these signs. ⁴Evil and sinful people are the kind of people that want a miracle* for a sign (*proof*). But those people will have no sign—only the sign of. Jonah.*" Then Jesus left that place and went away.

Pharisees Pharisees were a Jewish religious group that followed all the Old Testament and other Jewish laws and customs very carefully.

Sadducees A leading Jewish religious group. They followed only the first five books of the Old Testament. They believed that people don't have another life after death.

miracle Miracles are powerful works or great things done by the power of God.

sign of Jonah Jonah's three days in the big fish are like Jesus' three days in the grave.

MATTHEW 16

Jesus Warns Against the Jewish Leaders

⁵Jesus and his followers went across the lake. But the followers forgot to bring bread. ⁶Jesus said to the followers, "Be careful! Guard against the yeast (*bad influence*) of the Pharisees* and the Sadducees.*"

⁷The followers discussed the meaning of this. They said, "Did Jesus say this because we forgot to bring bread?"

⁸Jesus knew that the followers were talking about this. So Jesus asked them, "Why are you talking about not having bread? Your faith is small. ⁹You still don't understand? Remember the five loaves of bread that fed the 5,000 people? And remember that you filled many baskets *with bread after the people finished eating*? ¹⁰And remember the seven loaves of bread that fed the 4,000 people? Remember that you filled many baskets *with bread after the people finished eating*? ¹¹So I was not talking to you about bread. Why don't you understand that? I am telling you to be careful and guard against the yeast (*bad influence*) of the Pharisees* and the Sadducees.*" ¹²Then the followers understood what Jesus meant. Jesus was not telling them to guard against the yeast used in bread. Jesus was telling them to guard against the teaching of the Pharisees and the Sadducees.

Peter Says That Jesus Is the Christ

¹³Jesus went to the area of Caesarea Philippi. Jesus said to his followers, "I am the Son of Man.* Who do the people say I am?"

¹⁴The followers answered, "Some people say you are John, the Baptizer.* Other people say you are Elijah.* And some people say that you are Jeremiah* or one of the prophets.*"

¹⁵Then Jesus said to his followers, "And who do you say I am?"

Pharisees Pharisees were a Jewish religious group that followed all the Old Testament and other Jewish laws and customs very carefully.

Sadducees A leading Jewish religious group. They followed only the first five books of the Old Testament. They believed that people don't have another life after death.

Son of Man Jesus. Jesus was God's Son, but this name showed that Jesus was a man, too. In Daniel 7:13-14, this is the name for the Messiah (Christ).

Baptizer John is called the Baptizer because he had the work of baptizing people.

Elijah A man who spoke for God about 800 years before Christ.

Jeremiah Man who spoke for God hundreds of years before Christ.

prophets People who spoke for God. Their writings are part of the Old Testament.

46

¹⁶Simon Peter answered, "You are the Christ,* the Son of the living God."

¹⁷Jesus answered, "You are blessed, Simon son of Jonah. No person taught you that. My Father in heaven showed you who I am. ¹⁸So I tell you, you are Peter.* And I will build my church on this rock. The power of hell* will not be able to defeat my church. ¹⁹I will give you the keys of the kingdom of heaven. The things you don't allow on earth will be the things that God does not allow. The things you make free on earth will be the things that God has made free." ²⁰Then Jesus warned his followers not to tell any person that he was the Christ.*

Jesus Tells His Followers That He Must Die

²¹From that time Jesus began telling his followers that he must go to Jerusalem. Jesus explained that the older Jewish leaders, the leading priests, and the teachers of the law would make him suffer many things. And Jesus told his followers that he must be killed. Then, on the third day, he would be raised from death.

²²Peter spoke to Jesus alone. Peter began to criticize Jesus. Peter said, "God save you from those things, Lord! Those things will never happen to you!"

²³Then Jesus said to Peter, "Go away from me, Satan*! You are not helping me! You don't care about the things of God. You only care about things that people think are important."

²⁴Then Jesus said to his followers, "If any person wants to follow me, he must say 'No' to the things he wants. That person must accept the cross (*suffering*) that is given to him, and he must follow me. ²⁵The person who wants to save his life will lose it. And every person who gives his life for me will save it. ²⁶It is worth nothing for a person to have the whole world, if he loses his soul. A person could never pay enough to buy back his soul. ²⁷The Son of Man* will come again with his Father's glory, and with his angels. At that time, the Son of Man will reward each

Christ   The "anointed one" (the Messiah) or chosen one of God.
Peter   The Greek name "Peter," like the Aramaic name "Cephas," means "rock."
power of hell   Literally, the "gates of Hades."
Satan   Name for the devil meaning "the enemy."
Son of Man   Jesus. Jesus was God's Son, but this name showed that Jesus was a man, too. In Daniel 7:13-14, this is the name for the Messiah (Christ).

47

person for the things he has done. ²⁸I tell you the truth. There are some people standing here who will see the Son of Man coming with his kingdom before they die."

Three Followers See Jesus Talking with Moses and Elijah

17 Six days later, Jesus took Peter, James, and John the brother of James and went up on a high mountain. They were all alone there. ²While these followers watched him, Jesus was changed. His face became bright like the sun. And his clothes became white as light. ³Then two men were there, talking with Jesus. The men were Moses and Elijah.*

⁴Peter said to Jesus, "Lord, it is good that we are here. If you want, I will put three tents here—one for you, one for Moses, and one for Elijah."

⁵While Peter was talking, a bright cloud came over them. A voice came from the cloud. The voice said, "This (*Jesus*) is my Son and I love him. I am very pleased with him. Obey him!"

⁶The followers with Jesus heard this voice. They were very afraid, so they fell to the ground. ⁷But Jesus came to the followers and touched them. Jesus said, "Stand up. Don't be afraid." ⁸The followers looked up, and they saw that Jesus was now alone.

⁹Jesus and the followers were walking down the mountain. Jesus commanded the followers, "Don't tell any person about the things you saw on the mountain. Wait until the Son of Man* has been raised from death. Then you can tell people about what you saw."

¹⁰The followers asked Jesus, "Why do the teachers of the law say that Elijah* must come first *before the Christ* comes*?"

¹¹Jesus answered, "They are right to say that Elijah is coming. And it is true that Elijah will make all things the way they should be. ¹²But I tell you, Elijah has already come. People did not know who he was. People did to him all the *bad* things they wanted to

---

Moses and Elijah   Two of the most important Jewish leaders in the past.
Son of Man   Jesus. Jesus was God's Son, but this name showed that Jesus was a man, too. In Daniel 7:13-14, this is the name for the Messiah (Christ).
Elijah   A man who spoke for God about 800 years before Christ.
Christ   The "anointed one" (the Messiah) or chosen one of God.

48

do. It is the same with the Son of Man.* Those same people will make the Son of Man suffer." ¹³Then the followers understood that Jesus meant John the Baptizer was really Elijah.

Jesus Heals a Sick Boy

¹⁴Jesus and the followers went back to the people. A man went to Jesus and bowed before him. ¹⁵The man said, "Lord, be kind to my son. He has epilepsy* and is suffering very much. My son often falls into the fire or into the water. ¹⁶I brought my son to your followers, but they could not heal him."

¹⁷Jesus answered, "You people have no faith. Your lives are all wrong. How long must I stay with you? How long must I continue to be patient with you? Bring the boy here." ¹⁸Jesus gave a strong command to the demon* inside the boy. Then the demon came out of the boy, and the boy was healed.

¹⁹Then the followers came to Jesus alone. They said, "We tried to force the demon out of the boy, but we could not. Why were we not able to make the demon go out?"

²⁰Jesus answered, "You were not able to make the demon go out, because your faith is too small. I tell you the truth. If your faith is as big as a mustard seed,* then you can say to this mountain, 'Move from here to there.' And the mountain will move. All things will be possible for you." ²¹*

Jesus Talks About His Death

²²Later, the followers met together in Galilee. Jesus said to the followers, "The Son of Man* will be given into the control of some men. ²³Those men will kill the Son of Man. But on the third day the Son of Man will be raised from death." The followers were very sad to hear that the Son of Man would die.

Son of Man   Jesus. Jesus was God's Son, but this name showed that Jesus was a man, too. In Daniel 7:13-14, this is the name for the Messiah (Christ).
epilepsy   A bad disease that causes a person sometimes to lose control of his body, and maybe faint, shake strongly, or not be able to move.
demon   Demons are evil spirits from the devil.
mustard seed   This seed is very, very small, but the plant grows taller than a man.
Verse 21   Some copies add: "That kind of spirit comes out only if you use prayer and fasting."

Jesus Teaches About Paying Taxes

²⁴Jesus and his followers went to Capernaum. In Capernaum, some men came to Peter. They were the men who collected the two-drachma tax.* They asked, "Does your teacher pay the two-drachma tax?"

²⁵Peter answered, "Yes, Jesus pays the tax."

Peter went into the house where Jesus was. Before Peter could speak, Jesus said to him, "The kings on the earth get different kinds of taxes from people. But who are the people who pay the taxes? Are these people the king's children? Or is it other people who pay the taxes? What do you think?"

²⁶Peter answered, "The other people pay the taxes."

Jesus said to Peter, "Then the children of the king don't have to pay taxes. ²⁷But we don't want to make these tax collectors* angry. So *pay the tax in this way*: Go to the lake and fish. After you catch the first fish, open the fish's mouth. Inside its mouth you will find a four-drachma coin. Take that coin and give it to the tax collectors. That will pay the tax for you and me."

Jesus Tells His Followers Who Is the Greatest

18 At that time the followers came to Jesus and asked, "Who is the greatest in the kingdom of heaven?"
²Jesus called a little child to come to him. Jesus stood the child before the followers. ³Then Jesus said, "I tell you the truth. You must change and become like little children *in your hearts*. If you don't do this, you will never enter the kingdom of heaven. ⁴The greatest (*most important*) person in the kingdom of heaven is the person who makes himself humble like this child.

⁵"If a person accepts a little child like this in my name, then that person accepts me. ⁶If one of these little children believes in me, and another person causes that child to sin, then it will be very bad for that person. It would be better for that person to have a large rock tied around his neck and be drowned in the deep sea. ⁷I feel sorry for the people in the world because of the things that make people sin. Those things must happen. But it will be

---

two-drachma tax   A tax that every Jew had to pay once each year for the temple.
tax collectors   Jews hired by the Romans to collect taxes. They often cheated their people.

very bad for the person that causes those things to happen. ⁸If your hand or your foot makes you sin, cut it off and throw it away. It is better for you to lose part of your body but have life forever. That is much better than to have two hands and two feet but be thrown into the fire (*hell*) that burns forever. ⁹If your eye makes you sin, take it out and throw it away. It is better for you to have only one eye but have life forever. That is much better than to have two eyes but be thrown into the fire of hell."

Jesus Uses a Story About a Lost Sheep

¹⁰"Be careful. Don't think these little children are worth nothing. I tell you that these little children have angels in heaven. And those angels are always with my Father in heaven. ¹¹*

¹²"If a man has 100 sheep, but one of the sheep becomes lost, then the man will leave the other 99 sheep on the hill. He will go to look for the lost sheep. Right? ¹³And if the man finds the lost sheep, the man is happier about that one sheep than about the 99 sheep that were never lost. I tell you the truth. ¹⁴In the same way, your Father in heaven does not want any of these little children to be lost."

When a Person Does Something Wrong Against You

¹⁵"If your brother *or sister* does something wrong to you, go and tell that person what he did wrong. Do this alone with that person. If that person listens to you, then you have helped that person to be your brother again. ¹⁶But if that person refuses to listen, then go to him again and bring one or two people with you. Then there will be two or three other people who will be able to tell all that happened. ¹⁷If that person refuses to listen to them, then tell the church (*group of believers*). If that person refuses to listen to the church, then treat him like he is a person who does not believe in God. Treat him like he is a tax collector.*

¹⁸"I tell you the truth. The things you don't allow on earth will be the things that God does not allow. The things you allow on earth will be the things that God allows.

Verse 11 Some Greek copies add verse 11: "The Son of Man came to save lost people."
tax collector A Jew hired by the Romans to collect taxes. Tax collectors often cheated people.

[19]"Also, I tell you that if two of you on earth agree about something, then you can pray for it. And the thing you ask for will be done for you by my Father in heaven. [20]This is true, because if two or three people are together believing in me, I am there with them."

Story About a Servant Who Would Not Forgive

[21]Then Peter came to Jesus and asked, "Lord, when my brother continues to do something wrong to me, how many times must I forgive him? Should I forgive him as many as seven times?"

[22]Jesus answered, "I tell you, you must forgive him more than seven times. You must continue to forgive him even if he does wrong to you seventy-seven times."

[23]"So the kingdom of heaven is like a king who decided to collect the money that his servants owed him. [24]The king began to collect his money. One servant owed the king several million dollars worth of gold and silver. [25]The servant was not able to pay the money to his master, the king. So the master ordered that everything the servant owned should be sold, even the servant's wife and children. The money would be used to pay the king what the servant owed.

[26]"But the servant fell on his knees and begged, 'Be patient with me. I will pay you everything I owe.' [27]The master felt sorry for his servant. So the master told the servant he did not have to pay. The master let the servant go free.

[28]"Later, that same servant found another servant who owed him a few dollars worth of silver. The servant grabbed the other servant around the neck and said, 'Pay me the money you owe me!'

[29]"The other servant fell on his knees and begged him, 'Be patient with me. I will pay you everything I owe.'

[30]"But the first servant refused to be patient. The servant told the judge that the other servant owed him money, and the other servant was thrown into prison. The servant had to stay in prison until he could pay everything he owed. [31]All the other servants saw what happened. They were very sorry. So they went and told their master everything that happened.

³²"Then the master called his servant in and said, 'You evil servant. You owed me much money, but you begged me to forgive your debt. So I told you you did not have to pay anything. ³³So you should have given the same mercy to that other man who is a servant with you. You should have given him the same mercy that I gave you.' ³⁴The master was very angry, so he put the servant in prison to be punished. And the servant had to stay in prison until he could pay everything he owed.

³⁵"This king did the same as my heavenly Father will do to you. You must truly forgive your brother *or sister*, or my heavenly Father will not forgive you.''

Jesus Teaches About Divorce

19 After Jesus said all these things, he left Galilee. Jesus went into the area of Judea on the other side of the Jordan river. ²Many people followed Jesus. Jesus healed the sick people there.

³Some Pharisees* came to Jesus. They tried to make Jesus say something wrong. They asked Jesus, "Is it right for a man to divorce his wife for any reason he chooses?''

⁴Jesus answered, "Surely you have read this *in the Scriptures**: When God made the world, 'he made people male and female.'* ⁵And God said, 'So a man will leave his father and mother and be joined to his wife. The two people will become one body.'* ⁶So the two people are not two, but one. God joined those two people together. So no person should separate them.''

⁷The Pharisees* asked, "So why did Moses give a command allowing a man to divorce his wife by writing a certificate of divorce?''

⁸Jesus answered, "Moses allowed you to divorce your wives because you refused to accept God's teaching. But divorce was not allowed in the beginning. ⁹I tell you that any person who divorces his wife and marries another woman is guilty of the sin of adultery.* The only reason for a person to divorce and marry

Pharisees   Pharisees were a Jewish religious group that followed all the Old Testament and other Jewish laws and customs very carefully.

Scriptures   Holy Writings—the Old Testament.

'he made...female'   Quotation from Genesis 1:27 or 5:2.

'So...body'   Quotation from Genesis 2:24.

adultery   Breaking a marriage promise by doing sexual sin.

53

again is if his first wife had sexual relations with another man."

¹⁰The followers said to Jesus, "If that is the only reason a man can divorce his wife, then it is better not to marry."

¹¹Jesus answered, "Not every person can accept this truth *about marriage*. But God has made some people able to accept it. ¹²There are different reasons why some men cannot marry.* Some men were born without the ability to make children. Other men were made that way later in life by other people. And other men have given up marriage because of the kingdom of heaven. But the person who can *marry* should accept this teaching *about marriage*.*"

Jesus Welcomes Children

¹³Then the people brought their little children to Jesus so that Jesus could put his hands on* them and pray for them. When the followers saw this, they told the people to stop bringing their children to Jesus. ¹⁴But Jesus said, "Let the little children come to me. Don't stop them, because the kingdom of heaven belongs to people who are like these children." ¹⁵After Jesus put his hands on the children he left there.

A Rich Young Man Asks Jesus an Important Question

¹⁶A man came to Jesus and asked, "Teacher, what good thing must I do to have life forever?"

¹⁷Jesus answered, "Why do you ask me about what is good? Only God is good. But if you want to have life forever, obey the commandments."

¹⁸The man asked, "Which commandments?"

Jesus answered, " 'You must not kill people, you must not do the sin of adultery,* you must not steal, you must not lie, ¹⁹you must respect *and obey* your father and mother, and you must love other people like you love yourself.'* "

²⁰The young man said, "I have obeyed all these things. What else do I need?"

some men cannot marry   Literally, "some men are eunuchs."
But...marriage   This may also mean, "The person who can accept this teaching about not marrying should accept it."
put his hands on them   Showing that Jesus gave special blessings to these children.
adultery   Breaking a marriage promise by doing sexual sin.
'Love...yourself'   Quotation from Leviticus 19:18.

²¹Jesus answered, "If you want to be perfect, then go and sell all the things you own. Give the money to the poor people. If you do this, you will have a rich treasure in heaven. Then come and follow me!"

²²But when the man heard this, he was very sad. The man was very rich *and wanted to keep his money*. So he left Jesus.

²³Then Jesus said to his followers, "I tell you the truth. It will be very hard for a rich person to enter the kingdom of heaven. ²⁴Yes, I tell you that it is easier for a camel to go through the eye of a needle than for a rich person to enter the kingdom of God."

²⁵When the followers heard this they were very surprised. They asked, "Then who can be saved?"

²⁶Jesus looked at his followers and said, "This is something that people cannot do themselves. But God can do all things."

²⁷Peter said to Jesus, "We left everything we had and followed you. So what will we have?"

²⁸Jesus said to the followers, "I tell you the truth. When the new world is made, the Son of Man* will sit on his great throne. And all of you who followed me will also sit on thrones. You will sit on twelve thrones and you will judge the twelve family groups of Israel. ²⁹And every person who has left houses, brothers, sisters, father, mother, children, or farms to follow me will get much more than he left. And that person will have life forever. ³⁰Many people who have the highest place in life now will have the lowest place in the future. And many people who have the lowest place now will have the highest place in the future."

Jesus Uses a Story About Workers on a Farm

20 "The kingdom of heaven is like a man who owned some land. The man grew grapes on his land. One morning, the man went out very early to hire some other people to work in his field. ²The man agreed to pay the workers one silver coin* for working that day. Then the man sent the people into the field to work.

Son of Man   Jesus. Jesus was God's Son, but this name showed that Jesus was a man, too. In Daniel 7:13-14, this is the name for the Messiah (Christ).
silver coin   A Roman denarius. One coin was the average pay for one day's work.

³"At about nine o'clock the man went to the market place and saw some other people standing there. These people were doing nothing. ⁴So the man said to them, 'If you go and work in my field, I will pay you what your work is worth.' ⁵So the people went to work in the field.

"The man went out again about twelve o'clock and again at three o'clock. Both times the man hired some other people to work in his field. ⁶At about five o'clock the man went to the market place again. He saw some other people standing there. The man asked them, 'Why did you stand here all day doing nothing?'

⁷"The people answered, 'No person gave us a job.'

"The man said to them, 'Then you can go and work in my field.'

⁸"At the end of the day, the owner of the field said to the boss of all the workers, 'Call the workers and pay all of them. Start by paying the last people I hired. Then pay all of them, ending with the workers I hired first.'

⁹"The workers who were hired at five o'clock came to get their pay. Each worker got one silver coin. ¹⁰Then those workers who were hired first came to get their pay. Those workers thought they would be paid more than the other workers. But each one of those workers also received one silver coin. ¹¹When they got their silver coin, these workers complained to the man who owned the land. ¹²The workers said, 'Those people were hired last and worked only one hour. But you paid them the same as us. And we worked hard all day in the hot sun.'

¹³"But the man who owned the field said to one of those workers, 'Friend, I am being fair with you. You agreed to work for one silver coin. Right? ¹⁴So take your pay and go. I want to give the man who was hired last the same pay that I gave you. ¹⁵I can do what I want with my own money. Are you jealous because I am good *to those people*?'

¹⁶"So the people who have the last place now will have the first place in the future. And the people who have the first place now will have the last place in the future.''

Jesus Talks About His Own Death

¹⁷Jesus was going to Jerusalem. His twelve followers were with him. While they were walking, Jesus gathered the followers together and spoke to them privately. Jesus said to them, ¹⁸"We are going to Jerusalem. The Son of Man* will be given to the leading priests and the teachers of the law. The priests and teachers of the law will say that the Son of Man must die. ¹⁹They will give the Son of Man to the non-Jewish people. Those people will laugh at him and beat him with whips, and then kill him on a cross. But on the third day after his death, he will be raised to life again."

A Mother Asks Jesus to Do Something Special for Her Sons

²⁰Then the wife of Zebedee came to Jesus. Her sons were with her. The mother bowed before Jesus and asked him to do something for her.

²¹Jesus said, "What do you want?"

She said, "Promise that one of my sons will sit at your right side in your kingdom. And promise that the other son will sit at your left side in your kingdom."

²²So Jesus said, "You don't understand what you are asking. Can you accept the kind of suffering* that I must have?"

The sons answered, "Yes, we can!"

²³Jesus said to them, "Truly you will suffer the same things that I will suffer. But I cannot choose the person that will sit at my right side or my left side. My Father has decided who will have those places. He has prepared those places for those people. Those places belong to them."

²⁴The other ten followers heard this. They became angry with the two brothers. ²⁵Jesus called all the followers together. Jesus said, "You know that the rulers of the non-Jewish people love to show their power over the people. And their important leaders love to use all their authority over the people. ²⁶But it should not

---

Son of Man   Jesus. Jesus was God's Son, but this name showed that Jesus was a man, too. In Daniel 7:13-14, this is the name for the Messiah (Christ).

accept...suffering   Literally, "drink the cup." Jesus used the idea of drinking from a cup to mean accepting the terrible things that would happen to him.

be that way with you. If one of you wants to become great, then he must serve you like a servant. ²⁷If one of you wants to become first, then he must serve you like a slave. ²⁸It is the same with the Son of Man.* The Son of Man did not come for other people to serve him. The Son of Man came to serve other people. The Son of Man came to give his life to save many people.''

Jesus Heals Two Blind Men

²⁹When Jesus and his followers were leaving Jericho, many, many people followed Jesus. ³⁰There were two blind men sitting by the road. The blind men heard that Jesus was coming by. So the blind men shouted, ''Lord, Son of David,* please help us!''

³¹All the people criticized the blind men. They told the blind men not to speak. But the blind men shouted more and more, ''Lord, Son of David, please help us!''

³²Jesus stopped and said to the blind men, ''What do you want me to do for you?''

³³The blind men answered, ''Lord, we want to be able to see.''

³⁴Jesus felt sorry for the blind men. Jesus touched their eyes and they were able to see. Then the blind men followed Jesus.

Jesus Enters Jerusalem like a King

21 Jesus and his followers were coming closer to Jerusalem. But first they stopped at Bethphage at the hill called the Mount of Olives.* There Jesus sent two of his followers into the town. ²Jesus said to the followers, ''Go to the town you can see there. When you enter it you will find a donkey tied there. With the donkey you will find a young donkey. Untie the two donkeys and bring them to me. ³If any person asks you why you are taking the donkeys, tell that person, 'The Master needs these donkeys. He will send them back soon.' ''

Son of Man   Jesus. Jesus was God's Son, but this name showed that Jesus was a man, too. In Daniel 7:13-14, this is the name for the Messiah (Christ).
Son of David   Name for the Christ, who was from the family of David, king of Israel.
Mount of Olives   A hill covered with olive trees near the city of Jerusalem.

⁴This happened to make clear the full meaning of what the prophet* said:

> ⁵ "Tell the city of Zion,
> 'Now your king is coming to you.
> He is humble and he is riding on a donkey.
> He is riding on a young donkey,
> born from a work animal.' "   *Zechariah 9:9*

⁶The followers went and did what Jesus told them to do. ⁷The followers brought the mother donkey and the young donkey to Jesus. They put their coats on the donkeys, and Jesus sat on the coats. ⁸*Jesus rode along the road to Jerusalem*. Many people spread their coats on the road for Jesus. Other people cut branches from the trees and spread the branches on the road. ⁹Some of the people were walking ahead of Jesus. Other people were walking behind Jesus. Those people shouted,

> "Praise to the Son of David*!
> God bless the One who comes
> in the name of the Lord!
> Praise to God in heaven!"   *Psalm 118:26*

¹⁰Then Jesus went into Jerusalem. All the people in the city were confused. They asked, "Who is this man?"

¹¹The many people following Jesus answered, "This man is Jesus. He is the prophet* from the town of Nazareth in Galilee."

Jesus Goes to the Temple

¹²Jesus went into the temple.* He threw out all the people who were selling and buying things there. Jesus turned over the tables that belonged to the men who were exchanging different kinds of money. And Jesus turned over the benches of those men who were selling doves. ¹³Jesus said to all the people there, "It is written *in the Scriptures*, 'My house will be called a house for

---

prophet   Person who spoke for God. He often told things that would happen in the future.
Son of David   Name for the Christ, who was from the family of David, king of Israel.
temple   The special building in Jerusalem where God commanded the Jews to worship.

prayer.'* But you are changing God's house into 'a hiding place for thieves.'* "

¹⁴Some blind people and some crippled people came to Jesus in the temple.* Jesus healed these people. ¹⁵The leading priests and the teachers of the law saw what Jesus did. They saw that Jesus was doing great things and saw the children praising Jesus in the temple. The children were saying, "Praise to the Son of David.*" All these things made the priests and the teachers of the law angry.

¹⁶The leading priests and the teachers of the law asked Jesus, "Do you hear the things these children are saying?" Jesus answered, "Yes. Have you read the Scripture* that says, 'You (*God*) have taught children and babies to give praise'*?"

¹⁷Then Jesus left that place and went out of the city to Bethany. Jesus stayed there that night.

Jesus Shows His Followers the Power of Faith

¹⁸Early the next morning, Jesus was going back to the city. Jesus was very hungry. ¹⁹Jesus saw a fig tree beside the road. Jesus went to the fig tree *to get a fig to eat*. But there were no figs on the tree. There were only leaves. So Jesus said to the tree, "You will never again have fruit!" And then the tree dried up and died.

²⁰The followers saw this. They were very surprised. They asked, "How did the fig tree dry up and die so quickly?"

²¹Jesus answered, "I tell you the truth. If you have faith and no doubts, you will be able to do the same as I did to this tree. And you will be able to do more. You will be able to say to this mountain, 'Go, mountain, fall into the sea.' And if you have faith, then it will happen. ²²If you believe, then you will get anything you ask for in prayer."

'My house...prayer' Quotation from Isaiah 56:7.
'a hiding place for thieves' Quotation from Jeremiah 7:11.
temple The special building in Jerusalem where God commanded the Jews to worship.
Son of David Name for the Christ, who was from the family of David, king of Israel.
Scripture A part of the Holy Writings—the Old Testament.
'You...praise' Quotation from the Septuagint (Greek) version of Psalm 8:3.

The Jewish Leaders Doubt Jesus' Authority

²³Jesus went to the temple. While Jesus was teaching there, the leading priests and the older leaders of the people came to Jesus. They said to Jesus, "Tell us! What authority (*power*) do you have to do these things? Who gave you this authority?"

²⁴Jesus answered, "I will ask you a question too. If you answer me, then I will tell you what authority I have to do these things. ²⁵Tell me: When John baptized* people, did that come from God or from man?"

The priests and the Jewish leaders talked about Jesus' question. They said to each other, "If we answer, 'John's baptism was from God,' then Jesus will say, 'Then why didn't you believe John?' ²⁶But if we say, 'It was from man,' then *all the people will be angry with us*. We are afraid of the people because they all believe that John was a prophet.*"

²⁷So they answered Jesus, "We don't know *where John's authority came from*."

Then Jesus said, "Then I won't tell you what authority I have to do these things!"

Jesus Uses a Story to Teach the Jewish Leaders

²⁸"Tell me what you think about this: There was a man who had two sons. The man went to the first son and said, 'Son, go and work today in my field of grapes.'

²⁹"The son answered, 'I will not go.' But later the boy decided he should go, and the boy went.

³⁰"Then the father went to the other son and said, 'Son, go and work today in my field of grapes.' The son answered, 'Yes, sir, I will go and work.' But the boy did not go.

³¹"Which of the two sons obeyed his father?"

The Jewish priests and leaders answered, "The first son."

Jesus said to them, "I tell you the truth. *You think* the tax collectors* and the prostitutes* *are bad people. But they* will

---

baptized   A Greek word meaning to immerse, dip, or bury a person or thing briefly under water.
prophet   Person who spoke for God. He often told things that would happen in the future.
tax collectors   Jews hired by the Romans to collect taxes. They often cheated their people.
prostitutes   Women who are paid by men who use them for sexual purposes.

enter the kingdom of God before you enter. [32]John came showing you the right way to live. And you did not believe John. But the tax collectors and prostitutes believed John. And you saw that the tax collectors and prostitutes believed him. But you still refused to change and believe him.''

God Sends His Son

[33]''Listen to this story: There was a man who owned a field. He planted the field with grapes. The man put a wall around the field and dug a hole for a wine press.* Then the man built a tower. The man leased the land to some farmers. Then the man left for a trip. [34]Later, it was time for the grapes to be picked. So the man sent his servants to the farmers to get his share of the grapes.

[35]''But the farmers grabbed the servants and beat one. They killed another one, and then killed a third servant with rocks. [36]So the man sent some other servants to the farmers. The man sent more servants than he sent the first time. But the farmers did the same thing to the servants that they did the first time. [37]So the man decided to send his son to the farmers. The man said, 'The farmers will respect my son.'

[38]''But when the farmers saw the son, they said to each other, 'This is the owner's son. This field will be his. If we kill him, then his field will be ours!' [39]So the farmers took the son, threw him out of the field, and killed him.

[40]''So what will the owner of the field do to these farmers when he comes?''

[41]The Jewish priests and leaders said, ''He will surely kill those evil men. Then he will lease the field to some other farmers. He will lease it to farmers that will give him his share of the crop at harvest time.''

[42]Jesus said to them, ''Surely you have read this in the Scriptures*:

'The stone that the builders did not want
     became the cornerstone* (*most important stone*).

---

wine press   Place dug in rock used to mash grapes and collect the juice for making wine.
Scriptures   Holy Writings—the Old Testament.
cornerstone   The first and most important rock of a building.

> The Lord did this,
> and it is wonderful to us.'   *Psalm 118:22-23*

⁴³"So I tell you that the kingdom of God will be taken away from you. God's kingdom will be given to people who do the things God wants in his kingdom. ⁴⁴The person who falls on this stone will be broken. And if the stone falls on a person, then it will crush that person."

⁴⁵The leading priests and the Pharisees* heard these stories that Jesus told. They knew that Jesus was talking about them. ⁴⁶They wanted to find a way to arrest Jesus. But they were afraid of the people, because the people believed that Jesus was a prophet.*

Story About a King Inviting People to a Wedding Dinner

22 Jesus used stories to say some other things to the people. Jesus said, ²"The kingdom of heaven is like a king that prepared a wedding feast for his son. ³The king invited some people to the feast. When the feast was ready, the king sent his servants to tell those people to come. But the people refused to come to the king's feast.

⁴"Then the king sent some more servants. The king said to the servants, 'I have already invited those people. So tell them that my feast is ready. I have killed my best bulls and calves to be eaten. Everything is ready. Come to the wedding feast.'

⁵"*The servants went and told the people to come.* But the people refused to listen to the servants. Those people went to do other things. One person went to work in his field, and another person went to his business. ⁶Some of the other people grabbed the servants, beat them, and killed them. ⁷The king was very angry. The king sent his army to kill those people who killed his servants. And the army burned their city.

⁸"After that, the king said to his servants, 'The wedding feast is ready. I invited those people, but they were not good enough to come to my feast. ⁹So go to the street corners and invite all the people you see. Tell them to come to my feast.' ¹⁰So the servants

---

Pharisees Pharisees were a Jewish religious group that followed all the Old Testament and other Jewish laws and customs very carefully.
prophet Person who spoke for God. He often told things that would happen in the future.

went into the streets. The servants gathered all the people they could find. The servants brought good people and bad people to the place where the wedding feast was ready. And that place was filled with people.

¹¹"Then the king came in to see all the people. The king saw a man there who was not dressed in the right clothes for a wedding. ¹²The king said, 'Friend, how were you allowed in here? You are not wearing the right clothes for a wedding.' But the man said nothing. ¹³So the king told some servants, 'Tie this man's hands and feet. Throw the man out into the darkness. In that place, people will cry and grind their teeth *with pain.*'

¹⁴"Yes, many people are invited. But only a few are chosen."

Some Jewish Leaders Try to Trick Jesus

¹⁵Then the Pharisees* left the place where Jesus was teaching. They made plans to catch Jesus saying something wrong. ¹⁶The Pharisees sent some men to Jesus *to trick him.* They sent some of their own followers and some men from the group called Herodians.* These men said, "Teacher, we know that you are an honest man. We know that you teach the truth about God's way. You are not afraid of what other people think about you. All men are the same to you. ¹⁷So tell us what you think. Is it right to pay taxes to Caesar*? Yes or no?"

¹⁸But Jesus knew that these men were trying to trick him. So Jesus said, "You hypocrites*! Why are you trying to catch me saying something wrong? ¹⁹Show me a coin used for paying tax." The men showed Jesus a silver coin.* ²⁰Then Jesus asked, "Whose picture is on the coin? And whose name is written on the coin?"

²¹The men answered, "It is Caesar's picture and Caesar's name."

Then Jesus said to them, "Give to Caesar the things that are Caesar's. And give to God the things that are God's."

Pharisees   Pharisees were a Jewish religious group that followed all the Old Testament and other Jewish laws and customs very carefully.
Herodians   A political group that followed Herod and his family.
Caesar   The name or title given to the emperor (ruler) of Rome.
hypocrites   People who act like they are good but are not.
silver coin   A Roman denarius. One coin was the average pay for one day's work.

²²Those men heard what Jesus said, and they were amazed. They left Jesus and went away.

Some Sadducees Try to Trick Jesus

²³That same day some Sadducees* came to Jesus. (Sadducees believe that no person will rise from death.) The Sadducees asked Jesus a question. ²⁴They said, "Teacher, Moses told us that if a married man dies and he had no children, then his brother must marry the woman. Then they will have children for the dead brother. ²⁵There were seven brothers among us. The first one married but died. He had no children. So his brother married the woman. ²⁶Then the second brother also died. The same thing happened to the third brother and all the other brothers. ²⁷The woman was the last to die. ²⁸But all seven men had married her. So when people rise from death, whose wife will she be?"

²⁹Jesus answered, "You don't understand because you don't know what the Scriptures* say. And you don't know about the power of God. ³⁰At the time when people rise from death, there will be no marriage. People will not be married to each other. All people will be like the angels in heaven. ³¹Surely you have read what God said to you about the rising from death? ³²God said, 'I am the God of Abraham, the God of Isaac, and the God of Jacob.'* *This means that* God is the God of living people, not dead people."

³³All the people heard this. The people were amazed at Jesus' teaching.

Which Commandment Is the Most Important?

³⁴The Pharisees* learned that Jesus told the Sadducees* things they could not argue with. So the Pharisees met together. ³⁵One Pharisee was an expert in the law *of Moses*. That Pharisee asked Jesus a question to test him. ³⁶The Pharisee said, "Teacher,

---

Sadducees   A leading Jewish religious group. They followed only the first five books of the Old Testament. They believed that people don't have another life after death.
Scriptures   Holy Writings—the Old Testament.
Abraham...Isaac...Jacob   Three of the most important leaders of in the Old Testament.
'I am...Jacob'   Quotation from Exodus 3:6.
Pharisees   Pharisees were a Jewish religious group that followed all the Old Testament and other Jewish laws and customs very carefully.

which commandment in the law is the most important?"

³⁷Jesus answered, " 'Love the Lord your God. You must love him with all your heart, all your soul, and all your mind.'* ³⁸This is the first and most important commandment. ³⁹And the second commandment is like the first: 'Love other people the same as you love yourself.'* ⁴⁰All of the law and the writings of the prophets* take their meaning from these two commandments."

Jesus Asks the Pharisees a Question About the Christ

⁴¹So while the Pharisees* were together, Jesus asked them a question. ⁴²Jesus said, "What do you think about the Christ*? Whose son is he?"

The Pharisees answered, "The Christ is the Son of David.*"

⁴³Then Jesus said to the Pharisees, "Then why did David call him 'Lord'? David was speaking by the power of the *Holy Spirit.* David said,

⁴⁴"The Lord (*God*) said to my Lord (*Christ*):
    Sit by me at my right side.

I will put your enemies under your control.*'   *Psalm 110:1*

⁴⁵David calls the Christ 'Lord.' So how can he be David's son?" ⁴⁶None of the Pharisees could answer Jesus' question. And after that day no person was brave enough to ask Jesus any more questions *to trick him*.

Jesus Criticizes the Jewish Religious Leaders

23 Then Jesus spoke to the people and to his followers. Jesus said, ²"The teachers of the law and the Pharisees* have the authority (*power*) to tell you what the law of Moses says. ³So you should obey the things they say. You should do all the things

---

'Love...mind'   Quotation from Deuteronomy 6:5.
'Love...yourself'   Quotation from Leviticus 19:18.
prophets   People who spoke for God. Their writings are part of the Old Testament.
Pharisees   Pharisees were a Jewish religious group that followed all the Old Testament and other Jewish laws and customs very carefully.
Christ   The "anointed one" (the Messiah) or chosen one of God.
Son of David   Name for the Christ, who was from the family of David, king of Israel.
Holy Spirit   Also called the Spirit of God, the Spirit of Christ, and the Comforter. He is joined with God and Christ. He does the work of God among people in the world.
control   Literally, "feet." Being under a person's feet means being under his control.

they tell you to do. But their lives are not good examples for you to follow. They tell you to do things, but they don't do those things themselves. ⁴They make strict rules that are hard for people to obey. They try to force other people to obey all those rules. But they themselves will not try to follow any of those rules.

⁵"The only reason they do good things is for other people to see them. They wear special boxes* full of Scriptures.* They make these boxes bigger and bigger. And they make their special prayer clothes very long *so that people will see them*. ⁶Those Pharisees* and teachers of the law love to get the most important seats at the feasts. And they love to get the most important seats in the synagogues.* ⁷They love for people to show respect to them in the market places. And they love to have people call them 'Teacher.'

⁸"But you must not be called 'Teacher.' You are all brothers and sisters together. You have only one Teacher. ⁹And don't call any person on earth 'Father.' You have one Father. He is in heaven. ¹⁰And you should not be called 'Master.' You have only one Master, the Christ.* ¹¹The person who serves you like a servant is the greatest person among you. ¹²Every person who makes himself better than other people will be made humble. Every person who makes himself humble will be made great.

¹³"It will be bad for you teachers of the law and Pharisees.* You are hypocrites*! You close the way for people to enter the kingdom of heaven. You yourselves don't enter. And you stop the people who are trying to enter. ¹⁴*

¹⁵"It will be bad for you teachers of the law and Pharisees.* You are hypocrites*! You travel across the seas and across different countries to find one person who will follow your ways.

---

special boxes Small leather boxes containing four important Scriptures. Some Jews tied these to the forehead and left arm, probably to show they were very religious.
Scriptures Holy Writings—the Old Testament.
Pharisees Pharisees were a Jewish religious group that followed the Old Testament and other Jewish laws and customs very carefully.
synagogues Synagogues were buildings where Jews gathered to read and study the Scriptures.
Christ The "anointed one" (the Messiah) or chosen one of God.
hypocrites People who act like they are good but are not.
Verse 14 Some Greek copies add verse 14: "It will be bad for you, teachers of the law and Pharisees. You are hypocrites. You take away widows' houses, and you make long prayers so that people can see you. So you will have a worse punishment."

When you find that person, you make him worse than you are. And you are so bad that you belong in hell!

[16] "It will be bad for you teachers of the law and Pharisees.* You guide the people, but you are blind. You say, 'If any person uses the name of the temple* to make a promise, that means nothing. But if any person uses the gold that is in the temple to make a promise then he must keep that promise.' [17] You are blind fools! Which is greater: the gold, or the temple? The temple makes that gold holy. *So the temple is greater.* [18] And you say, 'If any person uses the altar* to make a promise, that means nothing. But if any person uses the gift on the altar to make a promise, then he must keep his promise.' [19] You are blind. You see (*understand*) nothing! Which is greater: the gift, or the altar? The altar makes the gift holy. *So the altar is greater.* [20] The person who uses the altar to make a promise is really using the altar and also everything on the altar. [21] And the person who uses the temple* to make a promise is really using the temple and also everything in the temple. [22] The person who uses heaven to make a promise is also using God's throne and the One who sits on that throne.

[23] "It will be bad for you teachers of the law and Pharisees.* You are hypocrites*! You give God one-tenth of everything you own—even your mint, dill, and cummin.* But you don't obey the really important teachings of the law—being fair, showing mercy, and being honest. These are the things you should do. And you should also continue to do those other things. [24] You guide the people, but you are blind! Think about a person picking a little fly out of his drink and then swallowing a camel! You are like that*!

[25] "It will be bad for you teachers of the law and Pharisees.* You are hypocrites*! You wash clean the outside of your cups and dishes. But inside they are full of things that you got by

---

Pharisees Pharisees were a Jewish religious group that followed all the Old Testament and other Jewish laws and customs very carefully.

temple The special building in Jerusalem where God commanded the Jews to worship.

altar An altar is a place where sacrifices or gifts are offered to God.

hypocrites People who act like they are good but are not.

mint, dill, and cummin Small plants grown in gardens and used for spices. Only very religious people would be careful enough to give a tenth of these plants.

You...that! Meaning, "You worry about the smallest mistakes but do the biggest sins."

cheating other people and pleasing yourselves. ²⁶Pharisees, you are blind! First make the inside of the cup clean and good. Then the outside of the cup can be truly clean.

²⁷"It will be bad for you teachers of the law and Pharisees.* You are hypocrites*! You are like tombs* that are painted white. The outside of those tombs looks fine. But inside, the tombs are full of the bones of dead people. And all kinds of unclean things are inside there. ²⁸It is the same with you. People look at you and think that you are good. But on the inside you are full of hypocrisy* and evil.

²⁹"It will be bad for you teachers of the law and Pharisees.* You are hypocrites*! You build tombs for the prophets.* And you show honor to the graves of people who lived good lives. ³⁰And you say, 'If we had lived during the time of our fathers (*ancestors*), we would not have helped them kill these prophets.' ³¹You give proof that you are children (*descendants*) of those people who killed the prophets. ³²And you will finish the sin that your fathers started!

³³"You are snakes! You are from a family of poisonous snakes! You will not escape God. You will all be judged guilty and go to hell! ³⁴So I tell you this: I send to you prophets* and wise men and teachers. You will kill some of these people. You will hang some of them on crosses. You will beat some of these people in your synagogues.* You will chase them from town to town. ³⁵So you will be guilty for all the good people who have been killed on earth. You will be guilty for the killing of that good man Abel.* And you will be guilty for the killing of Zechariah,* son of Berachiah. He was killed between the temple* and the altar.* You will be guilty for the killing of all the good people who lived between the time of Abel and the time of Zechariah. ³⁶I

Pharisees Pharisees were a Jewish religious group that followed all the Old Testament and other Jewish laws and customs very carefully.
hypocrites People who act like they are good but are not.
tombs Small buildings made to show respect for important persons who had died.
hypocrisy Acting like you are good when you are not.
prophets People who spoke for God. Their writings are part of the Old Testament.
synagogues Synagogues were buildings where Jews gathered to read and study the Scriptures.
Abel...Zechariah In the Hebrew Old Testament, the first and last men to be murdered.
temple The special building in Jerusalem where God commanded the Jews to worship.
altar An altar is a place where sacrifices or gifts are offered to God.

tell you the truth. All of these things will happen while you people are still living."

Jesus Feels Sorry for the People of Jerusalem

³⁷"O Jerusalem, Jerusalem! You kill the prophets.* You kill with rocks those men that God sent to you. Many, many times I wanted to help your people. I wanted to gather your people together, like a hen gathers her chicks under her wings. But you did not let me. ³⁸Now your home will be left completely empty. ³⁹I tell you, you will not see me again until that time when you will say, 'Blessed is the one who comes in the name of the Lord (God).'"

Jesus Talks About the Future Destruction of the Temple

24 Jesus left the temple* and was walking away. But his followers came to him to show him the temple's buildings. ²Jesus asked the followers, "See all these buildings? I tell you the truth. *All these buildings will be destroyed*. Every stone will be thrown down to the ground. Not one stone will be left on another."

³Later, Jesus was sitting at a place on the Mount of Olives.* The followers came to be alone with Jesus. They said, "You told us that the temple would be destroyed. Tell us when this will happen. And what will happen to show us that it is time for you to come again and time for the world* to end?"

⁴Jesus answered: "Be careful! Don't let any person fool you. ⁵Many people will come and use my name. They will say, 'I am the Christ.*' And they will fool many people. ⁶You will hear about wars and stories about wars that are being fought. But don't be afraid. These things must happen before the end comes. ⁷Nations will fight against other nations. Kingdoms will fight against other kingdoms. There will be times when there is no food for people to eat. And there will be earthquakes in different

---

prophets   People who spoke for God. Their writings are part of the Old Testament.
temple   The special building in Jerusalem where God commanded the Jews to worship.
Mount of Olives   A hill covered with olive trees near the city of Jerusalem.
world   Literally, "this age," or "this time."
Christ   The "anointed one" (the Messiah) or chosen one of God.

places. [8]These things are like the first pains when something new is born.

[9]"Then people will treat you badly. People will give you *to the rulers* to be persecuted (*hurt*) and killed. All people will hate you. All these things will happen to you because you believe in me. [10]At that time, many believers will lose their faith. They will turn against each other and hate each other. [11]Many false prophets* will come. They will cause many people to believe wrong things. [12]There will be more and more evil in the world. So most believers will stop showing love. [13]But the person who continues strong to the end will be saved. [14]The Good News about *God's* kingdom will be preached in the whole world. It will be told to every nation. Then the end will come.

[15]"Daniel the prophet* spoke about 'a terrible thing that causes destruction.'* You will see this terrible thing standing in the holy place (*the temple*)." (You should understand what this means.) [16]"At that time, the people in Judea should run away to the mountains. [17]People should run away without wasting the time to stop for anything. If a person is on the roof of his house, he must not go down to get things out of his house. [18]If a person is in the field, he must not go back to get his coat. [19]At that time, it will be bad for women who are pregnant or have small babies! [20]Pray that it will not be winter or a Sabbath day* when these things happen and you have to run away. [21]Why? Because at that time there will be much trouble. There will be more trouble than has ever happened since the beginning of the world. And nothing as bad as that will ever happen again. [22]God has decided to make that terrible time short. If that time was not made short, then no person would continue living. But God will make that time short to help the people he has chosen. [23]At that time, some person might say to you, 'Look, there is the Christ*!' Or another person might say, 'There he is!' But don't believe them. [24]False Christs and false prophets* will come and do great things and miracles.*

false prophets   People who say they speak for God but do not really speak God's truth.
prophet   Person who spoke for God. He often told things that would happen in the future.
'a terrible thing that causes destruction'   Mentioned in Daniel 9:27, 12:11 (cf. Daniel 11:31).
Sabbath day   Seventh day of the Jewish week. It was a special religious day for the Jews.
Christ   The "anointed one" (the Messiah) or chosen one of God.
miracles   False miracles—powerful acts done by the power of Satan.

They will do these things to the people God has chosen. They will do these things to try to fool his people, if that is possible. ²⁵Now I have warned you about this before it happens.

²⁶"Some person might tell you, 'The Christ* is there in the desert!' But don't go into the desert to look for the Christ. Another person might say, 'There is the Christ in that room!' But don't believe that. ²⁷When the Son of Man* comes, he will be seen by all people. It will be like lightning flashing in the sky that can be seen everywhere. ²⁸*My coming will be clear, the same as* any time you see vultures* gathering, you know there is a dead body.

²⁹"Soon after the trouble of those days, this will happen:

'The sun will become dark,
    and the moon will not give light.
The stars will fall from the sky,
    and everything in the sky will be changed.'   *Isaiah 13:10; 34:4*

³⁰"At that time, there will be something in the sky that shows the Son of Man* coming. All the people of the world will cry. All the people will see the Son of Man coming on the clouds in the sky. The Son of Man will come with power and great glory. ³¹The Son of Man will use a loud trumpet to send his angels all around the earth. The angels will gather his chosen people from every part of the earth.

³²"The fig tree teaches us a lesson: When the fig tree's branches become green and soft, and new leaves begin to grow, then you know that summer is near. ³³It is the same with these things that I told you would happen. When you see all these things happening, you will know that the time* is near, ready to come. ³⁴I tell you the truth. All these things will happen while the people of this time* are still living! ³⁵The whole world, earth and sky, will be destroyed, but the words I have said will never be destroyed!"

Christ   The "annointed one" (the Messiah) or chosen One of God.
Son of Man   Jesus. Jesus was God's Son, but this name showed that Jesus was a man, too. In Daniel 7:13-14, this is the name for the Messiah (Christ).
vultures   Birds that eat dead animals.
time   The time that Jesus has been talking about when something very important will happen. In Luke Jesus says that it is the time for God's kingdom to come (Luke 21:31).
the people of this time   This can also mean "the people of this nation."

Only God Knows When the Time Will Be

³⁶"No person knows when that day or time will be. The Son and the angels in heaven don't know when that day or time will be. Only the Father knows. ³⁷When the Son of Man* comes, it will be the same as the thing that happened during Noah's time. ³⁸In those days before the flood, people were eating and drinking. People were marrying and giving their children to be married. The people were still doing those things until the day Noah entered the boat. ³⁹Those people knew nothing about what was happening. But then the flood came and all those people were destroyed. It will be the same when the Son of Man comes. ⁴⁰Two men will be working together in the field. One man will be taken and the other will be left. ⁴¹Two women will be grinding grain with a mill.* One woman will be taken and the other woman will be left.

⁴²"So always be ready. You don't know the day your Lord will come. ⁴³Remember this: If the owner of the house knew what time the thief was coming, then the owner would be ready for him. The owner would watch and not let the thief enter his house. ⁴⁴So you also must be ready. The Son of Man* will come at a time when you don't expect him.

⁴⁵"Who is the wise and trusted servant? The master trusts one servant to give the other servants their food at the right time. Who is the servant that the master trusts to do that work? ⁴⁶When the master comes and finds that servant doing the work he gave him, that servant will be very happy. ⁴⁷I tell you the truth. The master will choose that servant to take care of everything the master owns. ⁴⁸But what will happen if that servant is evil and thinks that his master will not come back soon? ⁴⁹Then that servant will begin to beat the other servants. That servant will eat the food and get drunk with other people like him. ⁵⁰Then the master of that servant will come when that servant is not ready. It will be a time when that servant is not expecting the master. ⁵¹Then the master will punish that servant. The master will send

---

Son of Man Jesus. Jesus was God's Son, but this name showed that Jesus was a man, too. In Daniel 7:13-14, this is the name for the Messiah (Christ).
mill Two large, round, flat rocks used for grinding grain to make flour.

him away to be with the hypocrites.* And in that place people will cry and grind their teeth *with pain*."

Story About Ten Girls Waiting for the Bridegroom

25 "At that time the kingdom of heaven will be like ten girls that went to wait for the bridegroom.* They brought their lamps with them. ²Five of the girls were foolish. And five of the girls were wise. ³The five foolish girls brought their lamps, but they did not bring more oil for the lamps to burn. ⁴The wise girls brought their lamps and more oil in jars. ⁵The bridegroom was very late. All the girls became tired and began sleeping.

⁶"At midnight someone announced, 'The bridegroom is coming! Come and meet him!'

⁷"Then all the girls woke up. The girls made their lamps ready. ⁸But the foolish girls said to the wise girls, 'Give us some of your oil. The oil in our lamps is all gone.'

⁹"The wise girls answered, 'No! The oil we have might not be enough for all of us. But go to the people that sell oil and buy some for yourselves.'

¹⁰"So the five foolish girls went to buy oil. While they were gone, the bridegroom came. The girls who were ready went in with the bridegroom to the wedding feast. Then the door was closed and locked.

¹¹"Later the other girls came. The girls said, 'Sir, sir, open the door to let us in.'

¹²"But the bridegroom answered, 'I tell you the truth. I don't know you.'

¹³"So always be ready. You don't know the day or the time *when the Son of Man* will come*."

Story About Three Servants Using Their Master's Money

¹⁴"*The kingdom of heaven is* like a man leaving home to travel to another place for a visit. Before the man left, he talked with his servants. The man told his servants to take care of the things he

---

hypocrites   People who act like they are good but are not.
bridegroom   A man ready to be married.
Son of Man   Jesus. Jesus was God's Son, but this name showed that Jesus was a man, too. In Daniel 7:13-14, this is the name for the Messiah (Christ).

owned while he was gone. ¹⁵The man decided how much each servant would be able to care for. The man gave one servant five bags of money. The man gave another servant two bags of money. And the man gave a third servant one bag of money. Then that man left. ¹⁶The servant who got five bags of money went quickly to invest the money. Those five bags of money earned five more. ¹⁷It was the same with the servant who had two bags of money. That servant invested the money and earned two more. ¹⁸But the servant who got one bag of money went away and dug a hole in the ground. Then the servant hid his master's money in that hole.

¹⁹"After a long time the master came home. The master asked the servants what they did with his money. ²⁰The servant who got five bags of money brought five more bags of money to the master. The servant said, 'Master, you trusted me to care for five bags of money. So I used your five bags of money to earn five more.'

²¹"The master answered, 'You did right. You are a good servant that can be trusted. You did right with that small amount of money. So I will let you care for much greater things. Come and share my happiness with me.'

²²"Then the servant who got two bags of money came to the master. The servant said, 'Master, you gave me two bags of money to care for. So I used your two bags of money to earn two more.'

²³"The master answered, 'You did right. You are a good servant that can be trusted. You did right with a small amount of money. So I will let you care for much greater things. Come and share my happiness with me.'

²⁴"Then the man who got one bag of money came to the master. The man said, 'Master, I knew that you were a very hard man. You harvest things you did not plant. You gather crops where you did not put any seed. ²⁵So I was afraid. I went and hid your money in the ground. Here is the one bag of money you gave me.'

²⁶"The master answered, 'You are a bad and lazy servant! You say you knew that I harvest things I did not plant, and that I gather crops where I did not put any seed. ²⁷So you should have

put my money in the bank. Then, when I came home, I would get my money back. And I would also get the interest that my money earned.'

²⁸"*So the master told his other servants*, 'Take the one bag of money from that servant and give it to the servant that has ten bags of money. ²⁹Every person who uses what he has will get more. That person will have much more than he needs. But the person who does not use what he has will have everything taken away from him.' ³⁰Then the master said, 'Throw that useless servant outside, into the darkness! In that place people will cry and grind their teeth *with pain*.' "

The Son of Man Will Judge All People

³¹"The Son of Man* will come again. He will come with great glory. All his angels will come with him. He will be king and sit on his great throne. ³²All the people of the world will be gathered before the Son of Man. Then the Son of Man will separate all people into two groups. This is like a shepherd separates the sheep from the goats. ³³The Son of Man will put the sheep (*good people*) on his right and the goats (*bad people*) on his left.

³⁴"Then the king will say to those good people on his right, 'Come. My Father has given you great blessings. Come and get the kingdom God promised you. That kingdom has been prepared for you since the world was made. ³⁵You can have this kingdom, because I was hungry and you gave me food to eat. I was thirsty, and you gave me something to drink. I was alone and away from home, and you invited me into your home. ³⁶I was without clothes, and you gave me clothes. I was sick, and you cared for me. I was in prison and you came to visit me.'

³⁷"Then the good people will answer, 'Lord, when did we see you hungry and give you food? When did we see you thirsty and give you something to drink? ³⁸When did we see you alone and away from home and invite you into our home? When did we see you without clothes and give you clothes? ³⁹When did we see you sick or in prison and care for you?'

Son of Man   Jesus. Jesus was God's Son, but this name showed that Jesus was a man, too. In Daniel 7:13-14, this is the name for the Messiah (Christ).

⁴⁰"Then the king will answer, 'I tell you the truth. Anything you did for any of my people* here, you also did for me.'

⁴¹"Then the king will say to those bad people on his left, 'Go away from me. God has said that you will be punished. Go into the fire that burns forever. That fire was prepared for the devil and his helpers. ⁴²You must go away, because I was hungry and you gave me nothing to eat. I was thirsty and you gave me nothing to drink. ⁴³I was alone and away from home and you did not invite me into your home. I was without clothes and you gave me no clothes. I was sick and in prison and you did not care for me.'

⁴⁴"Then those people will answer, 'Lord, when did we see you hungry or thirsty? When did we see you alone and away from home? Or when did we see you without clothes or sick or in prison? When did we see these things and not help you?'

⁴⁵"Then the king will answer, 'I tell you the truth. Anything you refused to do for any of my people* here, you refused to do for me.'

⁴⁶"Then those bad people will go away. They will have punishment forever. But the good people will go and have life forever."

The Jewish Leaders Plan to Kill Jesus

26 After Jesus finished saying all these things, he said to his followers, ²"You know that the day after tomorrow is the day for the Passover Feast.* On that day, the Son of Man* will be given to his enemies to be killed on a cross."

³Then the leading priests and the older Jewish leaders had a meeting at the palace where the high priest* lived. The high priest's name was Caiaphas. ⁴In the meeting, they tried to find a way to arrest Jesus. They planned to lie so that they could arrest Jesus and kill him. ⁵The men in the meeting said, "We cannot

---

any of my people   Literally, "one of the least of these brothers of mine."
Passover Feast   Important holy day for Jews. They ate a special meal on this day every year to remember that God freed them from slavery in Egypt in the time of Moses.
Son of Man   Jesus. Jesus was God's Son, but this name showed that Jesus was a man, too. In Daniel 7:13-14, this is the name for the Messiah (Christ).
high priest   The most important Jewish priest and leader.

arrest Jesus during the feast. We don't want the people to become angry and cause a riot.''

A Woman Does Something Special for Jesus

⁶Jesus was in Bethany. He was at the house of Simon the leper.* ⁷While Jesus was there, a woman came to him. She had an alabaster* jar filled with very expensive perfume. The woman poured this perfume on Jesus' head while Jesus was eating.

⁸The followers saw the woman do this and became upset at the woman. The followers asked, ''Why waste that perfume? ⁹That perfume could be sold for much money and the money could be given to poor people.''

¹⁰But Jesus knew what happened. Jesus said, ''Why are you troubling this woman? She did a very good thing for me. ¹¹You will always have poor people with you. But you will not always have me. ¹²This woman poured perfume on my body. She did this to prepare me for burial after I die. ¹³I tell you the truth. The Good News* will be told to people in all the world. And in every place where the Good News is told, the story of what this woman did will also be told. The thing she has done will be told and people will remember her.''

Judas Becomes an Enemy of Jesus

¹⁴Then one of the twelve followers went to talk to the leading priests. This was the follower named Judas Iscariot. ¹⁵Judas said, ''I will give you Jesus. What will you pay me for doing this?'' The priests gave Judas 30 silver coins. ¹⁶After that time Judas waited for the best time to give Jesus to the priests.

Jesus Eats the Passover Meal with His Followers

¹⁷On the first day of the Feast of Unleavened Bread,* the followers came to Jesus. The followers said, ''We will prepare

---

leper   A person who has leprosy, a very bad skin disease.
alabaster   A beautiful kind of stone that can be carved to make things.
Good News   The news that God has made a way through Christ for people to have their sins
   forgiven and live with God. When people accept this truth, God accepts them.
Feast of Unleavened Bread   Same as Passover Feast, the most important holy day for Jews. On
   this day they ate a special meal with bread that was made without yeast.

everything for you to eat the Passover Feast.* Where do you want us to have the feast?''

18 Jesus answered, "Go into the city. Go to a man I know. Tell him that the teacher says, 'The chosen time is near. I will have the Passover Feast with my followers at your house.' '' 19The followers obeyed the thing that Jesus told them to do and they prepared the Passover Feast.

20In the evening Jesus was sitting at the table with the twelve followers. 21They were all eating. Then Jesus said, "I tell you the truth. One of you twelve here will soon be against me.''

22The followers were very sad to hear this. Each follower said to Jesus, "Surely I will not be against you, Lord!''

23Jesus answered, "The man who has dipped his hand into the same bowl with me is the person who will be against me. 24The Son of Man* will go *and die*. The Scriptures* say this will happen. But it will be very bad for the person who gives the Son of Man to his enemies to be killed. It would be better for that person if he were never born.''

25Then Judas said to Jesus, "Teacher, surely I will not be against you!'' (Judas is the one who would give Jesus to his enemies.)

Jesus answered, "Yes, it is you.''

The Lord's Supper

26While they were eating, Jesus took some bread. Jesus thanked God for the bread and divided it. He gave the bread to his followers. Jesus said, "Take this bread and eat it. This bread is my body.''

27Then Jesus took a cup of wine. Jesus thanked God for it and gave it to the followers. Jesus said, "Every one of you drink this. 28This wine is my blood. My blood (*death*) begins the new agreement *from God to his people*. This blood is given for many people to forgive their sins. 29I tell you this: I will not drink this wine again until that day when we are together in my Father's

---

Passover Feast   Important holy day for Jews. They ate a special meal on this day every year to remember that God freed them from slavery in Egypt in the time of Moses.

Son of Man   Jesus. Jesus was God's Son, but this name showed that Jesus was a man, too. In Daniel 7:13-14, this is the name for the Messiah (Christ).

Scriptures   Holy Writings—the Old Testament.

kingdom and the wine is new. Then I will drink it again with you.''

³⁰All the followers sang a song. Then they went out to the Mount of Olives.*

Jesus Tells His Followers They Will All Leave Him

³¹Jesus told the followers, ''Tonight you will lose your faith because of me. It is written *in the Scriptures**:

'I will kill the shepherd,
and the sheep will run away.'   *Zechariah 13:7*

³²But *after I die*, I will rise from death. Then I will go into Galilee. I will be there before you go there.''

³³Peter answered, ''All the other followers may lose their faith because of you. But I will never lose my faith.''

³⁴Jesus answered, ''I tell you the truth. Tonight you will say you don't know me. You will say this three times before the rooster crows.''

³⁵But Peter answered, ''I will never say that I don't know you. I will even die with you.'' And all the other followers said the same thing.

Jesus Prays Alone

³⁶Then Jesus went with his followers to a place called Gethsemane. Jesus said to his followers, ''Sit here while I go there and pray.'' ³⁷Jesus told Peter and the two sons of Zebedee to come with him. Then Jesus began to be very sad and troubled. ³⁸Jesus said to Peter and the two sons of Zebedee, ''My soul is full of sorrow. My heart is breaking with sadness. Stay awake here with me and wait.''

³⁹Then Jesus walked a little farther away from them. Jesus fell on the ground and prayed, ''My Father, if it is possible, don't give me this cup* of suffering. But *what you want is more important*. Do what you want, not what I want.'' ⁴⁰Then Jesus

Mount of Olives   A hill covered with olive trees near the city of Jerusalem.
Scriptures   Holy Writings—the Old Testament.
cup   Jesus is talking about the bad things that will happen to him. Accepting these things
will be very hard, like drinking a cup full of something that tastes very bad.

went back to his followers. Jesus found his followers sleeping. Jesus said to Peter, "You men could not stay awake with me for one hour? ⁴¹Stay awake and pray that you will not be tempted. Your spirit wants to do what is right. But your body is weak."

⁴²Then Jesus went away a second time and prayed, "My Father, if it is not possible for this painful thing to be taken from me, and if I must do it, then I pray that what you want will be done."

⁴³Then Jesus went back to the followers. Again Jesus found them sleeping. Their eyes were very tired. ⁴⁴So Jesus left them and went away one more time and prayed. This third time he prayed, he said the same thing.

⁴⁵Then Jesus went back to the followers and said, "You are still sleeping and resting? The time has come for the Son of Man* to be given to sinful people. ⁴⁶Stand up! We must go. Here comes the man who is giving me *to my enemies.*"

Jesus Is Arrested

⁴⁷While Jesus was still speaking, Judas came there. Judas was one of the twelve followers. Judas had many people with him. These people were sent from the leading priests and the older leaders of the people. These people with Judas had swords and clubs. ⁴⁸Judas planned to do something to show the people which man was Jesus. Judas said, "The man I kiss is Jesus. Arrest him." ⁴⁹So Judas went to Jesus and said, "Hello, teacher!" Then Judas kissed Jesus.

⁵⁰Jesus answered, "Friend, do the thing you came to do."

Then the men came and grabbed Jesus and arrested him. ⁵¹When that happened, one of the followers with Jesus grabbed his sword and pulled it out. This follower hit the servant of the high priest with the sword and cut off his ear.

⁵²Jesus said to the man, "Put your sword back in its place. People who use swords will be killed with swords. ⁵³Surely you know I could ask my Father and he would give me more than

---

Son of Man Jesus. Jesus was God's Son, but this name showed that Jesus was a man, too. In Daniel 7:13-14, this is the name for the Messiah (Christ).

twelve armies of angels. ⁵⁴But this thing must happen this way so that it will be like the Scriptures* said."

⁵⁵Then Jesus said to all the people, "You came to get me with swords and clubs like I am a criminal. Every day I sat in the temple teaching. You did not arrest me there. ⁵⁶But all these things have happened so that it will be like the prophets* wrote." Then all of Jesus' followers left him and ran away.

Jesus Before the Jewish Leaders

⁵⁷Those men who arrested Jesus led him to the house of Caiaphas, the high priest.* The teachers of the law and the older Jewish leaders were gathered there. ⁵⁸Peter followed Jesus, but he did not come near Jesus. Peter followed Jesus to the yard of the high priest's house. Peter went into the yard and sat with the guards. Peter wanted to see what would happen to Jesus.

⁵⁹The high priest* and the Jewish council tried to find something that Jesus had done wrong so that they could kill him. All the things said against Jesus were false. ⁶⁰Many people came and told false things about Jesus. But the council could find no real reason to kill Jesus. Then two people came and said, ⁶¹"This man (*Jesus*) said, 'I can destroy the temple of God and build it again in three days.' "

⁶²Then the high priest* stood and said to Jesus, "These people have said things against you. Do you have something to say about these charges against you? Are these people telling the truth?" ⁶³But Jesus said nothing.

Again the high priest* said to Jesus, "You are now under oath. I command you by the power of the living God to tell us the truth. Tell us, are you the Christ,* the Son of God?"

⁶⁴Jesus answered, "Yes, I am. But I tell you, in the future you will see the Son of Man* sitting at the right side of God. And you will see the Son of Man coming on the clouds of heaven."

Scriptures   Holy Writings—the Old Testament.
prophets   People who spoke for God. Their writings are part of the Old Testament.
high priest   The most important Jewish priest and leader.
Christ   The "anointed one" (the Messiah) or chosen one of God.
Son of Man   Jesus. Jesus was God's Son, but this name showed that Jesus was a man, too. In Daniel 7:13-14, this is the name for the Messiah (Christ).

⁶⁵When the high priest* heard this, he was very angry. He tore his clothes and said, "This man has said things that are against God! We don't need any more witnesses. You all heard him say these things against God. ⁶⁶What do you think?"

The Jews answered, "He is guilty, and he must die."

⁶⁷Then the people there spit in Jesus' face. And they hit him with their fists. Other people slapped Jesus. ⁶⁸They said, "Show us that you are a prophet,* Christ! Tell us who hit you!"

Peter Is Afraid to Say He Knows Jesus

⁶⁹At that time, Peter was sitting in the yard. A servant girl came to Peter. The girl said, "You were with Jesus, that man from Galilee."

⁷⁰But Peter said that he was never with Jesus. He said this to all the people there. Peter said, "I don't know what you are talking about."

⁷¹Then Peter left the yard. At the gate, another girl saw him. The girl said to the people there, "This man was with Jesus of Nazareth."

⁷²Again, Peter said that he was never with Jesus. Peter said, "I promise to God that I don't know this man, Jesus!"

⁷³A short time later, some people standing there went to Peter and said, "We know you are one of those men who followed Jesus. We know this because of the way you talk."

⁷⁴Then Peter began to curse. He said strongly, "I promise to God that I don't know this man, Jesus!" After Peter said this, a rooster crowed. ⁷⁵Then Peter remembered what Jesus had told him: "Before the rooster crows, you will say three times that you don't know me." Then Peter left that place and cried bitterly.

Jesus Is Taken to Governor Pilate

27 Early the next morning, all the leading priests and older leaders of the people decided to kill Jesus. ²They tied Jesus with chains. Then they led him to Pilate the governor. They gave Jesus to Pilate.

---

high priest The most important Jewish priest and leader.
prophet Person who spoke for God. He often told things that would happen in the future.

Judas Kills Himself

³Judas saw that they had decided to kill Jesus. Judas was the one who gave Jesus to his enemies. When Judas saw what happened, he was very sorry for what he did. So he gave the 30 silver coins back to the priests and the leaders. ⁴Judas said, "I sinned. I gave you an innocent man to be killed."

The Jewish leaders answered, "We don't care! That's a problem for you, not us."

⁵So Judas threw the money into the temple. Then Judas left that place and hanged himself.

⁶The leading priests picked up the silver coins in the temple. They said, "Our law does not allow us to keep this money with the temple money, because this money has paid for a man's death." ⁷So they decided to use the money to buy a field called Potter's Field. This field would be a place to bury people who died while visiting *in Jerusalem*. ⁸That is why that field is still called the Field of Blood. ⁹So the thing happened that Jeremiah the prophet* said:

> "They took 30 silver coins. That was how much the Jewish people decided to pay for his (*Jesus'*) life. ¹⁰They used those 30 silver coins to buy the potter's field, like the Lord commanded."*

Governor Pilate Questions Jesus

¹¹Jesus stood before Pilate the governor. Pilate asked him questions. He said, "Are you the king of the Jews?"

Jesus answered, "Yes, I am."

¹²When the leading priests and the older Jewish leaders accused Jesus, he refused to answer.

¹³So Pilate said to Jesus, "You hear these people accusing you of all these things. Why don't you answer?"

¹⁴But Jesus said nothing to answer Pilate. Pilate was very surprised at this.

---

prophet Person who spoke for God. He often told things that would happen in the future.
"They...commanded" See Zechariah 11:12-13 and Jeremiah 32:6-9.

Pilate Tries but Fails to Free Jesus

¹⁵Every year at the Passover* time the governor would free one person from the prison. This was always a person that the people wanted to be made free. ¹⁶At that time there was a man in prison who was known to be very bad. His name was Barabbas. ¹⁷All the people gathered at Pilate's house. Pilate asked the people, "I will free one man for you. Which man do you want me to free: Barabbas, or Jesus who is called the Christ*?" ¹⁸Pilate knew that the people gave Jesus to him because the people were jealous.

¹⁹Pilate said these things while he was sitting in the place for judging. While he was sitting there, his wife sent this message to him. The message said, "Don't do anything with that man (*Jesus*). He is not guilty. And today I had a dream about him and it troubled me very much."

²⁰But the leading priests and older Jewish leaders told the people to ask for Barabbas to be made free and for Jesus to be killed.

²¹Pilate said, "I have Barabbas and Jesus. Which do you want me to make free for you?"

The people answered, "Barabbas!"

²²Pilate asked, "So what should I do with Jesus, the one called the Christ?"

All the people answered, "Kill him on a cross!"

²³Pilate asked, "Why do you want me to kill him? What wrong has he done?"

But all the people shouted louder, "Kill him on a cross!"

²⁴Pilate saw that he could do nothing to make the people change. And he saw that the people were becoming upset. So Pilate took some water and washed his hands* so that all the people could see. Then Pilate said, "I am not guilty of this man's death. You are the ones who are doing it!"

²⁵All the people answered, "We will be responsible for his death. We accept for ourselves and for our children any punishment for his death."

Passover Important holy day for Jews. They ate a special meal on this day every year to remember that God freed them from slavery in Egypt in the time of Moses.
Christ The "anointed one" (the Messiah) or chosen one of God.
washed his hands Jewish religious custom that the Pharisees thought was very important.

²⁶Then Pilate freed Barabbas. Pilate told some soldiers to beat Jesus with whips. Then Pilate gave Jesus to the soldiers to be killed on a cross.

Pilate's Soldiers Tease Jesus

²⁷Then Pilate's soldiers brought Jesus into the governor's palace. All the soldiers gathered around Jesus. ²⁸The soldiers took off Jesus' clothes and put a red robe on him. ²⁹Then the soldiers used thorny branches to make a crown. They put this crown of thorns on Jesus' head. Then they put a stick in Jesus' right hand. After the soldiers did all these things, they bowed before him and teased him. They said, "Hello, king of the Jews!" ³⁰The soldiers spit on Jesus. Then they took his stick and hit him on the head many times. ³¹After they finished teasing Jesus, the soldiers took off the robe and put his own clothes on him again. Then they led Jesus away to be killed on a cross.

Jesus Is Killed on a Cross

³²The soldiers were going out of the city with Jesus. The soldiers forced another man there to carry the cross for Jesus. This man's name was Simon from Cyrene. ³³They came to the place called Golgotha. (Golgotha means The Place of the Skull.) ³⁴At Golgotha, the soldiers gave Jesus wine to drink. This wine was mixed with gall.* Jesus tasted the wine but refused to drink it. ³⁵The soldiers nailed Jesus to a cross. Then the soldiers gambled with dice to decide who would get Jesus' clothes. ³⁶The soldiers sat there and continued watching Jesus. ³⁷The soldiers put a sign above Jesus' head with the charge against him written on it. The sign said: "THIS IS JESUS, THE KING OF THE JEWS." ³⁸Two robbers were nailed to crosses beside Jesus. One robber was put beside Jesus on the right and the other was put on the left. ³⁹People walked by and said bad things to Jesus. People shook their heads ⁴⁰and said, "You said you could destroy the temple and build it again in three days. So save yourself! Come down from that cross, if you are really the Son of God!"

---

gall   Probably a drink of wine mixed with drugs to help a person feel less pain.

⁴¹The leading priests, the teachers of the law, and the older Jewish leaders were also there. These men teased Jesus the same as the other people. ⁴²They said, "He saved other people. But he can't save himself! People say he is the king of Israel. If he is the king, then he should save himself by coming down from the cross. Then we will believe in him. ⁴³He trusted God. So let God save him now, if God really wants him. He himself said, 'I am the Son of God.' " ⁴⁴And in the same way, the robbers who were being killed on crosses beside Jesus also said bad things to him.

Jesus Dies

⁴⁵At noon the whole country became dark. This darkness continued for three hours. ⁴⁶At about three o'clock Jesus cried with a loud voice, "Eli, Eli, lema sabachthani?" This means, "My God, my God, why have you left me alone?"

⁴⁷Some of the people standing there heard this. The people said, "He is calling Elijah."

⁴⁸Quickly one of the people ran and got a sponge. That person filled the sponge with vinegar and tied the sponge to a stick. Then he used the stick to give the sponge to Jesus to drink from it. ⁴⁹But the other people said, "Don't bother him (*Jesus*). We want to see if Elijah will come to save him."

⁵⁰Again Jesus cried with a loud voice. Then he died.*

⁵¹When Jesus died, the curtain in the temple* was torn into two pieces. The tear started at the top and tore all the way to the bottom. Also, the earth shook and rocks were broken. ⁵²All the graves opened, and many of God's people in the graves were raised from death. ⁵³Those people came out of the graves. After Jesus was raised from death, those people went into the holy city (*Jerusalem*), and many people saw them.

⁵⁴The army officer and the soldiers guarding Jesus saw this earthquake and everything that happened. They were very afraid and said, "He really was the Son of God!"

⁵⁵Many women were standing away from the cross, watching. These were the women that followed Jesus from Galilee to care

---

died Literally, "he let his spirit leave."
curtain in the temple A curtain divided the "most holy place" from the other part of the temple, the special building in Jerusalem where God commanded the Jews to worship him.

for him. ⁵⁶Mary Magdalene, Mary the mother of James and Joseph, and the mother of James and John* were there.

Jesus Is Buried

⁵⁷That evening a rich man named Joseph came to Jerusalem. Joseph was a follower of Jesus from the town of Arimathea. ⁵⁸Joseph went to Pilate and asked to have Jesus' body. Pilate gave orders for the soldiers to give Jesus' body to Joseph. ⁵⁹Then Joseph took the body and wrapped it in a new linen cloth. ⁶⁰Joseph put Jesus' body in a new tomb (*grave*) that Joseph had dug in a wall of rock. Then he closed the tomb by rolling a very large stone to cover the entrance. After he did these things, Joseph went away. ⁶¹Mary Magdalene and the other woman named Mary were sitting near the tomb.

The Tomb of Jesus Is Guarded

⁶²That day was the day called Preparation day.* The next day, the leading priests and the Pharisees* went to Pilate. ⁶³They said, "Sir, we remember that while that liar was still alive he said, 'After three days I will rise from death.' ⁶⁴So give the order for the tomb to be guarded well until after three days. His followers might come and try to steal the body. Then they could tell the people that he has risen from death. Then that lie will be even worse than when Jesus lived."

⁶⁵Pilate said, "Take some soldiers and go guard the tomb the best way you know." ⁶⁶So they all went to the tomb and made it safe from thieves. They did this by sealing the stone in the entrance and then putting soldiers there to guard it.

The Followers Learn That Jesus Has Risen from Death

28 The day after the Sabbath day* was the first day of the week. At dawn on the first day, Mary Magdalene and the

---

James and John   Literally, "the sons of Zebedee."
Preparation day   Friday, the day before the Sabbath day.
Pharisees   Pharisees were a Jewish religious group that followed all the Old Testament and other Jewish laws and customs very carefully.
Sabbath day   Seventh day of the Jewish week. It was a special religious day for the Jews.

other woman named Mary went to look at the tomb.*

²At that time there was a very strong earthquake. An angel of the Lord came from the sky. The angel went to the tomb and rolled the stone away from the entrance. Then the angel sat on the stone. ³The angel was shining very bright like lightning. His clothes were white like snow. ⁴The soldiers guarding the tomb were very afraid of the angel. They shook with fear and became like dead men.

⁵The angel said to the women, "Don't be afraid. I know that you are looking for Jesus, the one who was killed on the cross. ⁶But Jesus is not here. He is risen from death like he said he would. Come and see the place where his body was. ⁷And go quickly and tell his followers. Tell them: 'Jesus has risen from death. He is going into Galilee. He will be there before you. You will see him there.' " Then the angel said, "I have told you everything."

⁸So the women left the tomb quickly. They were afraid, but they were also very happy. They ran to tell his followers what happened. ⁹While the women were running to tell the followers, Jesus was standing there before them. Jesus said, "Hello!" The women went to Jesus. They held him at his feet and worshiped him. ¹⁰Then Jesus said to the women, "Don't be afraid. Go and tell my brothers (*followers*) to go to Galilee. They will see me there."

The Soldiers Tell the Jewish Leaders What Happened

¹¹The women went to tell the followers. At the same time, some of the soldiers that were guarding the tomb* went into the city. They went to tell the leading priests everything that happened. ¹²Then the priests met with the older Jewish leaders and made a plan. They paid the soldiers much money *to tell a lie*. ¹³They said to the soldiers, "Tell the people that Jesus' followers came during the night and stole the body while you were sleeping. ¹⁴If the governor hears about this, we will satisfy him and save you from trouble." ¹⁵So the soldiers kept the money and obeyed the priests. And that story is still spread among the Jews even today.

---

tomb   A grave dug in a wall of rock.

Jesus Talks to His Followers

[16]The eleven followers went to Galilee. They went to the mountain where Jesus told them to go. [17]On the mountain the followers saw Jesus. They worshiped him. But some of the followers did not believe that it was really Jesus. [18]So Jesus came to them and said, "All power in heaven and on earth is given to me. [19]So go and make followers of all people in the world. Make people my followers by baptizing them in the name of the Father and the Son and the Holy Spirit.* [20]Teach those people to obey everything that I have told you. You can be sure that I will be with you always. I will continue with you until the end of the world."

Holy Spirit   Also called the Spirit of God, the Spirit of Christ, and the Comforter. He is joined with God and Christ. He does the work of God among people in the world.

Mark

John the Baptizer Prepares for the Coming of Jesus

1 The Good News* about Jesus Christ, the Son of God,* begins ²with what the prophet* Isaiah wrote about:

"I (*God*) will send my helper* ahead of you.
My helper will prepare the way for you.   *Malachi 3:1*
³ There is a person shouting in the desert:
'Prepare the way for the Lord.
Make his paths straight.' "   *Isaiah 40:3*

⁴So John the Baptizer* came. John told people to change their hearts and lives and be baptized* so that their sins could be forgiven. John was baptizing people in the desert area. ⁵All the people from Judea and Jerusalem went out to John. These people told about the sins they had done, and then were baptized by John in the Jordan river. ⁶John wore clothes made from camel's hair. John had a leather belt around his waist. He ate locusts* and wild honey. ⁷This is what John preached to the people: "There is a person coming later who is greater than I am. I am not good enough to kneel down and untie his shoes. ⁸I baptize you with water. But that person who is coming will baptize you with the Holy Spirit.*"

Good News   The news that God has made a way through Christ for people to have their sins forgiven and live with God. When people accept this truth, God accepts them.
the Son of God   Some Greek copies omit these words.
prophet   Person who spoke for God. He often told things that would happen in the future.
helper   Literally, "messenger," a person who is sent with news to tell other people.
Baptizer   John is called the Baptizer because he had the work of baptizing people.
baptized   A Greek word meaning to be immersed, dipped, or buried in water.
locusts   Insects like grasshoppers. The law said locusts could be eaten (Leviticus 11:21-22).
Holy Spirit   Also called the Spirit of God, the Spirit of Christ, and the Comforter. He is joined with God and Christ. He does the work of God among people in the world.

Jesus Is Baptized and Goes Away to Be Tempted

⁹At that time Jesus came from the town of Nazareth in Galilee to the place where John was. John baptized Jesus in the Jordan river. ¹⁰While Jesus was coming up out of the water, he saw the sky open. The Holy Spirit* came down to Jesus like a dove. ¹¹A voice came from heaven and said: "You are my son. I love you, and I am very pleased with you."

¹²Then the Spirit sent Jesus into the desert alone. ¹³Jesus was in the desert 40 days. He was there with the wild animals. While Jesus was in the desert, he was tempted by Satan (*the devil*). Then angels came and helped Jesus.

Jesus Chooses Some Followers

¹⁴After this, John was put into prison. Jesus went into Galilee and preached the Good News* from God. ¹⁵Jesus said, "The right time is now here. The kingdom of God is near. Change your hearts and lives and believe the Good News!"

¹⁶Jesus was walking by Lake Galilee. Jesus saw Simon* and Simon's brother, Andrew. These two men were fishermen, and they were throwing a net into the lake to catch fish. ¹⁷Jesus said to them, "Come and follow me. I will make you a different kind of fishermen. You will work to gather people, not fish." ¹⁸So Simon and Andrew left their nets and followed Jesus.

¹⁹Jesus continued walking by Lake Galilee. He saw two more brothers, James and John, the sons of Zebedee. They were in their boat, preparing their nets to catch fish. ²⁰Their father Zebedee and the men who worked for him were in the boat with the brothers. When Jesus saw the brothers he told them to come. They left their father and followed Jesus.

Holy Spirit   Also called the Spirit of God, the Spirit of Christ, and the Comforter. He is joined with God and Christ. He does the work of God among people in the world.
Good News   The news that God was sending Christ to make a way for people to have their sins forgiven and live with God.
Simon   Simon is later called Peter.

Jesus Heals a Man Who Had an Evil Spirit

²¹Jesus and his followers went to Capernaum. On the Sabbath day* Jesus went into the synagogue* and taught the people. ²²The people there were amazed at Jesus' teaching. Jesus did not teach like their teachers of the law. Jesus taught like a person who had authority (*power*). ²³While Jesus was in the synagogue, a man was there who had an evil spirit *from the devil* inside him. The man shouted, ²⁴"Jesus of Nazareth! What do you want with us? Did you come to destroy us? I know who you are—God's Holy One!"

²⁵Jesus said strongly, "Be quiet! Come out of the man!" ²⁶The evil spirit made the man shake. Then the spirit made a loud noise and came out of the man.

²⁷The people were amazed. They asked each other, "What is happening here? This man is teaching something new. And he teaches with authority (*power*)! He even gives commands to evil spirits, and the spirits obey him." ²⁸So the news about Jesus spread quickly everywhere in the area of Galilee.

Jesus Heals Many People

²⁹Jesus and the followers left the synagogue. They all went with James and John to the home of Simon* and Andrew. ³⁰Simon's mother-in-law was very sick. She was in bed and had fever. The people there told Jesus about her. ³¹So Jesus went to her bed. Jesus held her hand and helped her stand up. The fever left her, and she was healed. Then she began serving them.

³²That night, after the sun went down, the people brought many sick people to Jesus. They also brought people who had demons* inside them. ³³All the people in the town gathered at the door of that house. ³⁴Jesus healed many people that had different kinds of sicknesses. Jesus also forced many demons to leave people. But Jesus would not allow the demons to speak, because the demons knew who he was.*

Sabbath day Seventh day of the Jewish week. It was a special religious day for the Jews.
synagogue Synagogues were places where Jews gathered to read and study the Scriptures.
Simon Simon is later called Peter.
demons Demons are evil spirits from the devil.
who he was The demons knew that Jesus was the Christ, the Son of God.

Jesus Prepares to Tell People the Good News

³⁵The next morning, Jesus woke up very early. Jesus left the house while it was still dark. He went to a place to be alone and pray. ³⁶Later, Simon* and his friends went to look for Jesus. ³⁷They found Jesus and said, "All the people are looking for you!"

³⁸Jesus answered, "We should go to another place. We can go to other towns around here. Then I can preach in those places also. That is why I came." ³⁹So Jesus traveled everywhere in Galilee. He preached in the synagogues* and forced demons* to leave people.

Jesus Heals a Sick Man

⁴⁰A man that had leprosy* came to Jesus. The man bowed on his knees and begged Jesus, "I know that you can heal me if you want."

⁴¹Jesus felt sorry for the man. So Jesus touched the man and said, "I want to heal you. You are healed!" ⁴²Then the sickness left the man, and he was healed.

⁴³Jesus told the man to go. But Jesus warned him strongly. Jesus said, ⁴⁴"Don't tell any person about what I did for you. But go and show yourself to the priest. And offer a gift to God because you have been healed. Offer the gift that Moses commanded.* This will show the people that you are healed." ⁴⁵The man left there and told all the people he saw that Jesus had healed him. So the news about Jesus spread. And that is why Jesus could not enter a town if people saw him. Jesus stayed in places where people did not live. But people came from all the towns to the places where Jesus was.

Jesus Heals a Crippled Man

2 A few days later, Jesus came back to Capernaum. The news spread that Jesus was back home. ²Many, many people

Simon   Simon is later called Peter.
synagogues   Synagogues were buildings where Jews gathered to read and study the Scriptures.
demons   Demons are evil spirits from the devil.
leprosy   A very bad skin disease.
Moses commanded   Read about this in Leviticus 14:1-32.

gathered to hear Jesus preach. The house was full. There was no place to stand, not even outside by the door. Jesus was teaching these people. ³Some people brought a paralyzed (*crippled*) man to Jesus. Four men were carrying the paralyzed man. ⁴But they could not bring the man to Jesus because the house was full of people. So the men went to the roof above Jesus and made a hole in the roof. Then they lowered the bed with the paralyzed man on it. ⁵Jesus saw that these men had much faith. So Jesus said to the paralyzed man, "Young man, your sins are forgiven."

⁶Some of the teachers of the law were sitting there. They saw what Jesus did, and they said to themselves, ⁷"Why does this man say things like that? He is saying things that are against God. Only God can forgive sins."

⁸Jesus knew that these teachers of the law were thinking those things about him. So Jesus said to them, "Why are you thinking these things? ⁹Which is easier: to tell this crippled man, 'Your sins are forgiven,' or to tell him, 'Stand up. Take your bed and walk'? ¹⁰But I will prove to you that the Son of Man has power on earth to forgive sins." So Jesus said to the paralyzed man, ¹¹"I tell you, stand up. Take your bed and go home." ¹²The paralyzed man stood up. He took his bed and walked out of the room. All the people could see him. The people were amazed and praised (*thanked*) God. They said, "This is the most amazing thing we have ever seen!"

¹³Jesus went to the lake again. Many people followed him there. So Jesus taught them. ¹⁴Jesus was walking beside the lake, and he saw a tax collector* named Levi, the son of Alphaeus. Levi was sitting in the tax office. Jesus said to him, "Follow me." Then Levi stood up and followed Jesus.

¹⁵Later that day, Jesus ate at Levi's house. There were many tax collectors* and other bad people eating there with Jesus and his followers. There were many of these people that followed Jesus. ¹⁶The teachers of the law (they were Pharisees*) saw Jesus eating with these tax collectors and other bad people. They asked

tax collector   A Jew hired by the Romans to collect taxes. Tax collectors often cheated people.
Pharisees   Pharisees were a Jewish religious group that followed all the Old Testament and other Jewish laws and customs very carefully.

Jesus' followers, "Why does he (*Jesus*) eat with tax collectors and sinners?"

¹⁷Jesus heard this, and he said to them, "Healthy people don't need a doctor. It is the sick people that need a doctor. I did not come to ask good people *to change*. I came to ask bad people *to change their lives*."

Jesus Is Not Like Other Religious Leaders

¹⁸The followers of John* and the Pharisees* were fasting.* Some people came to Jesus and said, "John's followers fast,* and the followers of the Pharisees fast. But your followers don't fast. Why?"

¹⁹Jesus answered, "*When there is a wedding,* the friends of the bridegroom* are not sad while he is with them. They cannot fast (*be sad*) while the bridegroom is still there. ²⁰But the time will come when the bridegroom will leave them. The friends are sad when the bridegroom leaves. Then they will fast.

²¹"When a person sews a patch over a hole on an old coat, that person never uses a piece of cloth that is not yet shrunk. If he does, the patch will *shrink and* pull away from the coat. Then the hole will be worse. ²²Also, people never pour new wine into old wine bags.* Why? Because the new wine will break the bags, and the wine will be ruined with the wine bags. People always put new wine into new wine bags."

Some Jews Criticize Jesus and His Followers

²³On the Sabbath day,* Jesus was walking through some grain fields. Jesus' followers were walking with him. The followers picked some grain *to eat*. ²⁴The Pharisees* saw this and said to Jesus, "Why are your followers doing that? It is against the *Jewish* law to do that on the Sabbath day."

²⁵Jesus answered, "You have read what David did when he and the people with him were hungry and needed food. ²⁶It was

John   John the Baptizer who preached to the Jews about Christ's coming (Mark 1:4-8).
Pharisees   Pharisees were a Jewish religious group that followed all the Old Testament and other Jewish laws and customs very carefully.
fasting, fast   To fast is to live without food for a special time of prayer and worship to God.
bridegroom   A man ready to be married.
wine bags   Bags made from the skin of an animal and used for holding wine.
Sabbath day   Seventh day of the Jewish week. It was a special religious day for the Jews.

during the time of Abiathar the high priest. David went into God's house and ate the bread that was offered to God. And the law *of Moses* says only priests can eat that bread. David also gave some of the bread to those people with him.''

²⁷Then Jesus said to the Pharisees,* "The Sabbath day* was made to help people. People were not made to be ruled by the Sabbath day. ²⁸So the Son of Man* is Lord (*master*) of every day, even the Sabbath.''

Jesus Heals a Man Who Has a Crippled Hand

3 Another time Jesus went into the synagogue.* In the synagogue, there was a man with a crippled hand. ²Some Jews there wanted to see Jesus do something wrong so that they could accuse him. So those people watched him closely. They wanted to see if Jesus would heal the man on a Sabbath day.* ³Jesus said to the man with the crippled hand, "Stand up here so that all the people can see you.''

⁴Then Jesus asked the people, "Which thing is right to do on the Sabbath day: to do good, or to do evil? Is it right to save a life or to destroy one?'' The people said nothing to answer Jesus.

⁵Jesus was angry and he looked at the people. But he felt very sad because they were stubborn. Jesus said to the man, "Let me see your hand.'' The man put his hand out for Jesus. His hand was healed. ⁶Then the Pharisees* left and made plans with the Herodians* about a way to kill Jesus.

Many People Follow Jesus

⁷Jesus went away with his followers to the lake. Many people from Galilee followed him. ⁸Many, many people also came from Judea, from Jerusalem, from Idumea, from the area across the Jordan river, and from the area around Tyre and Sidon. These people came because they heard about all the things Jesus was doing. ⁹Jesus saw the many people. So he told his followers to get

Pharisees   Pharisees were a Jewish religious group that followed all the Old Testament and other Jewish laws and customs very carefully.
Sabbath day   Seventh day of the Jewish week. It was a special religious day for the Jews.
Son of Man   Jesus. Jesus was God's Son, but this name showed that Jesus was a man, too. In Daniel 7:13-14, this is the name for the Messiah (Christ).
synagogue   Synagogues were places where Jews gathered to read and study the Scriptures.
Herodians   A political group that followed Herod and his family.

a small boat and make it ready for him. *Jesus wanted to get into the boat* so that the many, many people would not push against him. ¹⁰Jesus had healed many people. So all the sick people were pushing toward him to touch him. ¹¹Some people had evil spirits *from the devil* inside them. When the evil spirits saw Jesus, they bowed before him and shouted, "You are the Son of God!" ¹²But Jesus commanded the spirits strongly not to tell people who he was.

Jesus Chooses His Twelve Apostles

¹³Then Jesus went up on a hill. Jesus told some men to come to him. These were the men Jesus wanted. These men went to Jesus. ¹⁴Jesus chose twelve men and called them apostles.* Jesus wanted these twelve men to be with him, and he wanted to send them to other places to preach. ¹⁵And Jesus wanted these men to have the power to force demons* out of people. ¹⁶These are the names of the twelve men Jesus chose: Simon (Jesus gave him the name Peter); ¹⁷James and John, the sons of Zebedee (Jesus gave them the name Boanerges. This name means "Sons of Thunder"); ¹⁸Andrew, Philip, Bartholomew, Matthew, Thomas, James the son of Alphaeus, Thaddaeus, Simon the Zealot,* ¹⁹and Judas Iscariot. Judas is the one who gave Jesus to his enemies.

Some Jewish Leaders Say Jesus Has a Devil in Him

²⁰Then Jesus went home. But again many people gathered there. There were so many people that Jesus and his followers could not eat. ²¹Jesus' family heard about all these things. They went to get him because people said that Jesus was crazy.

²²And the teachers of the law from Jerusalem said, "Beelzebul (*the devil*) is living inside him (*Jesus*)! He uses power from the ruler of demons* to force demons out of people."

²³So Jesus called the people together and used stories to teach the people. Jesus said, "Satan will not force his own demons* out of people. ²⁴A kingdom that fights against itself cannot continue. ²⁵And a family that is divided cannot succeed. ²⁶And if Satan is against himself and fights against his own people, then he cannot

apostles   The men Jesus taught and chose to be his special helpers.
demons   Demons are evil spirits from the devil.
Zealot   There was a Jewish political group known as the Zealots or "Enthusiasts."

continue. That would be the end of Satan. ²⁷If a person wants to enter a strong man's house and steal his things, first the person must tie the strong man. Then the person can steal the things from the strong man's house. ²⁸I tell you the truth. All sins that people do can be forgiven. And all the bad things people say against God can be forgiven. ²⁹But any person who says bad things against (*refuses to accept*) the Holy Spirit* will never be forgiven. He is guilty of a sin that continues forever.''

³⁰Jesus said this because the teachers of the law said that Jesus had an evil spirit (*devil*) inside him.

Jesus' Followers Are His True Family

³¹Then Jesus' mother and brothers came there. They stood outside and sent a person in to tell Jesus to come out. ³²Many people were sitting around Jesus. They said to Jesus, ''Your mother and brothers are waiting for you outside.''

³³Jesus asked, ''Who is my mother? Who are my brothers?'' ³⁴Then Jesus looked at those people sitting around him. He said, ''These people are my mother and my brothers! ³⁵My true brother and sister and mother are those people who do the things God wants.''

Jesus Uses a Story About a Farmer Planting Seed

4 Another time Jesus began teaching by the lake. Many, many people gathered around Jesus. So Jesus got into a boat and went out on the lake. All the people stayed on the shore next to the water. ²Jesus taught the people from the boat. Jesus used many stories to teach them. He said, ³''Listen! A farmer went out to plant his seed. ⁴While the farmer was planting, some seed fell by the road. The birds came and ate all that seed. ⁵Some seed fell on rocky ground. The ground there did not have enough dirt. The seed grew very fast there because the ground was not deep. ⁶But the sun rose and the plants were burned. The plants died because they did not have deep roots. ⁷Some other seed fell among thorny weeds. The weeds grew and stopped the good plants from

Holy Spirit Also called the Spirit of God, the Spirit of Christ, and the Comforter. He is joined with God and Christ. He does the work of God among people in the world.

growing. So those plants did not make grain. ⁸Some other seed fell on good ground. In the good ground, the seed began to grow. It grew and made grain. Some plants had 30 grains, other plants had 60 grains, and some had 100 grains.''

⁹Then Jesus said, ''You people who hear me, listen!''

Jesus Tells Why He Used Stories

¹⁰Later, Jesus was away from the people. The twelve apostles* and Jesus' other followers asked him about the stories.

¹¹Jesus said, ''Only you can know the secret truth about the kingdom of God. But to those other people, I tell everything by using stories. ¹²I do this so that:

'They will look and look, but never really see;
    they will listen and listen, but never understand.
If they saw and understood,
    they might change and be forgiven.' ''   Isaiah 6:9-10

Jesus Explains the Story About the Farmer Planting Seed

¹³Then Jesus said to the followers, ''Do you understand this story? If you don't, then how will you understand any story? ¹⁴The farmer is like a person who plants God's teaching in people. ¹⁵Sometimes the teaching falls on the path. This is like some people. Those people hear the teaching of God. But Satan (*the devil*) comes and takes away the teaching that was planted in them. ¹⁶Other people are like the seed planted on rocky ground. They hear the teaching and quickly accept it with joy. ¹⁷But those people don't allow the teaching to go deep into their lives. They keep that teaching only a short time. When trouble or persecution* comes because of the teaching they accepted, they quickly quit. ¹⁸Other people are like the seed planted among the thorny weeds. These people hear the teaching. ¹⁹But then these things come into their lives: the worries of this life, the love of money, and wanting all kinds of other things. These things stop the teaching from growing. So that teaching does not make fruit*

apostles   The men Jesus taught and chose to be his special helpers.
persecution   Being hurt by other people or suffering bad things from them.
make fruit   To make fruit is to have in your life the good things God wants.

in the lives of those people. ²⁰Other people are like the seed planted on the good ground. They hear the teaching and accept it. Then they grow and make fruit—sometimes 30 times more, sometimes 60 times more, and sometimes 100 times more."

You Must Use What You Have

²¹Then Jesus said to them, "Do you take a lamp and hide it under a bowl or under a bed? No! You put the lamp on a lamp table. ²²Everything that is hidden will be made clear. Every secret thing will be made known. ²³You people who hear me, listen!

²⁴"Think carefully about the things you hear. The way you give is the way God will give to you. But God will give you more than you give. ²⁵The person who *uses what he* has will be given more. The person who does not *use what he* has will have everything taken away from him."

Jesus Uses a Story About Seed

²⁶Then Jesus said, "The kingdom of God is like a man who plants seed in the ground. ²⁷The seed begins to grow. It grows night and day. It is not important if the man is sleeping or awake; the seed still grows. The man does not know how the seed grows. ²⁸Without any help, the ground grows grain. First the plant grows, then the head, and then all the grain in the head. ²⁹When the grain is ready, the man cuts it. This is the harvest time."

Jesus Uses a Story About the Mustard Seed

³⁰Then Jesus said, "What can I use to show you what the kingdom of God is like? What story can I use to explain it? ³¹The kingdom of God is like a mustard seed. The mustard seed is the smallest seed that you plant in the ground. ³²But when you plant this seed, it grows and becomes the largest of all the plants in your garden. It has branches that are very big. The wild birds can come and make nests there and be protected from the sun."

³³Jesus used many stories like these to teach them. He taught them all that they could understand. ³⁴Jesus always used stories to teach the people. But when Jesus and his followers were alone together, Jesus explained everything to them.

Jesus Stops a Storm

³⁵That day, at evening, Jesus said to his followers, "Come with me across the lake." ³⁶Jesus and the followers left the people there. They went in the same boat that Jesus was already sitting in. There were also other boats with them. ³⁷A very bad wind came on the lake. The waves were coming over the sides and into the boat. The boat was almost full of water. ³⁸Jesus was inside the boat, sleeping with his head on a pillow. The followers went to him and woke him. They said, "Teacher, do you care about us? We will drown!"

³⁹Jesus stood up and commanded the wind and the waves to stop. Jesus said, "Quiet! Be still!" Then the wind stopped and the sea became calm.

⁴⁰Jesus said to his followers, "Why are you afraid? You still have no faith?"

⁴¹The followers were very afraid and asked each other, "What kind of man is this? Even the wind and the sea obey him!"

Jesus Frees a Man from Evil Spirits

5 Jesus and his followers went across the lake to the area where the Gerasene people lived. ²When Jesus got out of the boat, a man came to him from the caves where dead people are buried. This man had an evil spirit *from the devil* living inside him. ³This man lived in the burial caves. No person could tie him. Even chains could not keep this man tied. ⁴Many times, people had used chains to tie the man's hands and feet. But the man broke the chains on his hands and feet. No person was strong enough to control him. ⁵Day and night the man walked around the burial caves and on the hills. The man would scream and cut himself with rocks.

⁶While Jesus was far away, the man saw him. The man ran to Jesus and bowed down before Jesus. ⁷⁻⁸Jesus said to the man, "You evil spirit, come out of that man." So the man shouted with a loud voice, "What do you want with me, Jesus, Son of the Most High God? I beg you to promise to God that you will not punish me!"

⁹Then Jesus asked the man, "What is your name?"

The man answered, "My name is Legion,* because there are many spirits inside me." ¹⁰The spirits inside the man begged Jesus again and again not to send them out of that area.

¹¹A large herd of pigs was eating on a hill near there. ¹²The evil spirits begged Jesus, "Send us to the pigs. Let us go into them." ¹³So Jesus allowed them to do this. The evil spirits left the man and went into the pigs. Then the herd of pigs ran down the hill and into the lake. All the pigs were drowned. There were about 2,000 pigs in that herd.

¹⁴The men who had the work of caring for the pigs ran away. The men ran to the town and to the farms. They told all the people what happened. The people went out to see what happened. ¹⁵The people came to Jesus. They saw the man who had the many evil spirits. The man was sitting and was wearing clothes. His mind was right again. The people were afraid. ¹⁶Some people were there and saw what Jesus did. These people told the other people what happened to the man that had the demons* living in him. And they also told about the pigs. ¹⁷Then the people began to beg Jesus to leave their area.

¹⁸Jesus was preparing to leave in the boat. The man who was freed from the demons begged to go with Jesus.

¹⁹But Jesus did not allow the man to go. Jesus said, "Go home to your family and friends. Tell them about all the things the Lord did for you. Tell them that the Lord was good to you." ²⁰So the man left and told the people in the Ten Towns* about the great things Jesus did for him. All the people were amazed.

Jesus Gives Life to a Dead Girl and Heals a Sick Woman

²¹Jesus went in the boat back across to the other side of the lake. There, many people gathered around him by the lake. ²²A ruler from the synagogue* came to that place. His name was Jairus. Jairus saw Jesus and bowed down before him. ²³The ruler begged and begged Jesus. He said, "My little daughter is dying.

Legion   Means very many. A legion was about 5,000 men in the Roman army.
demons   Demons are evil spirits from the devil.
Ten Towns   Greek, "Decapolis," an area east of Lake Galilee. It once had ten main towns.
synagogue   Synagogues were places where Jews gathered to read and study the Scriptures.

Please come and put your hands on her. Then she will be healed and will live.''

²⁴So Jesus went with the ruler. Many people followed Jesus. They were pushing very close around him.

²⁵While Jesus was going with the ruler, a woman was following him. This woman had been bleeding for the past twelve years. ²⁶The woman suffered very much. Many doctors tried to help her. All the money she had was spent. But she was not improving. Her sickness was becoming worse. ²⁷The woman heard about Jesus. So she followed Jesus with the people and touched his coat. ²⁸The woman thought, ''If I can touch his clothes, that will be enough to heal me.'' ²⁹When the woman touched his coat, her bleeding stopped. The woman felt that her body was healed from the suffering. ³⁰And Jesus felt power go out from him. So he stopped and turned around. Then he asked, ''Who touched my clothes?''

³¹The followers said to Jesus, ''There are many people pushing against you. But you ask, 'Who touched me?' ''

³²But Jesus continued looking for the person who touched him. ³³The woman knew that she was healed. So she came and bowed at Jesus' feet. The woman was shaking with fear. She told Jesus the whole story. ³⁴Jesus said to the woman, ''Dear woman, you are made well because you believed. Go in peace. You will have no more suffering.''

³⁵Jesus was still there speaking. Some men came from the house of Jairus, the synagogue* ruler. The men said, ''Your daughter is dead. There is now no need to bother the teacher (*Jesus*).''

³⁶But Jesus did not care what the men said. Jesus said to the synagogue ruler, ''Don't be afraid; only believe.''

³⁷Jesus let only Peter, James, and John the brother of James go with him to Jairus' house. ³⁸Jesus and these followers went to the house of Jairus, the synagogue* ruler. Jesus saw many people there crying loudly. There was much confusion. ³⁹Jesus entered the house and said to the people, ''Why are you people crying and making so much noise? This child is not dead. She is only

---

synagogue   Synagogues were places where Jews gathered to read and study the Scriptures.

sleeping." ⁴⁰But all the people laughed at Jesus. Jesus told the people to leave the house. Then Jesus went into the room where the child was. He brought the child's father and mother and his three followers into the room with him. ⁴¹Then Jesus held the girl's hand and said to her, "Talitha, koum!" (This means, "Little girl, I tell you to stand up!") ⁴²The girl stood up and began walking. (The girl was twelve years old.) The father and mother and the followers were amazed. ⁴³Jesus gave the father and mother very strict orders not to tell people about this. Then Jesus told them to give the girl some food to eat.

Jesus Goes to His Home Town

6 Jesus left there and went back to his home town. His followers went with him. ²On the Sabbath day* Jesus taught in the synagogue.* Many people heard him teach and were amazed. These people said, "Where did this man get this teaching? How did he get this wisdom? Who gave it to him? And where did he get the power to do these miracles*? ³He is only the carpenter. And his mother is Mary. He is the brother of James, Joses, Judas, and Simon. And his sisters are here with us." The people did not accept Jesus.

⁴Jesus said to the people, "Other people give honor to a prophet.* But in his own town with his own people and in his own home, a prophet does not get honor." ⁵Jesus was not able to do many miracles* in that town. The only miracles he did were to heal some sick people by putting his hands on them. ⁶Jesus was very surprised because those people did not have faith.

Then Jesus went to other villages in that area and taught. ⁷Jesus called the twelve followers together. Jesus sent them out in groups of two. Jesus gave them power over evil spirits. ⁸This is what Jesus told his followers: "Take nothing for your trip. Take only a stick for walking. Take no bread, no bag, and no money in your pockets. ⁹Wear shoes, and take only the clothes you are wearing. ¹⁰When you enter a house, stay in that house until you

Sabbath day   Seventh day of the Jewish week. It was a special religious day for the Jews.
synagogue   Synagogues were places where Jews gathered to read and study the Scriptures.
miracles   Miracles are powerful works or great things done by the power of God.
prophet   Person who spoke for God. He often told things that would happen in the future.

leave that town. ¹¹If any town refuses to listen to you or refuses to accept you, then leave that town. Shake their dust off your feet.* This will be a warning to them."

¹²The followers left there and went to other places. They preached to the people and told them to change their hearts and lives. ¹³The followers forced many demons* out of people. And the followers put olive oil on* sick people and healed them.

Herod Thinks Jesus Is John the Baptizer

¹⁴King Herod heard about Jesus, because Jesus was now famous. Some people said, *"He (Jesus) is* John the Baptizer. He is risen from death. That is why he (*Jesus*) can do these miracles."

¹⁵Other people said, "He is Elijah."

Other people said, "Jesus is a prophet.* He is like the prophets that lived long ago."

¹⁶Herod heard these things about Jesus. He said, "I killed John by cutting off his head. Now John has been raised from death!"

¹⁷Herod himself had given orders for his soldiers to arrest John. So John was put into prison. Herod did this to please his wife, Herodias. Herodias was the wife of Philip, Herod's brother. But then Herod married Herodias. ¹⁸John told Herod that it was not right for him to be married to his brother's wife. ¹⁹So Herodias hated John. She wanted to kill him. But Herodias was not able to persuade Herod to kill John. ²⁰Herod was afraid to kill John. Herod knew that all the people thought John was a good and holy man. So Herod protected John. Herod enjoyed listening to John preach. But John's preaching always bothered Herod.

²¹Then the right time came for Herodias to cause John's death. It happened on Herod's birthday. Herod gave a dinner party for the most important government leaders, the commanders of his army, and the most important people in Galilee. ²²The daughter of Herodias came to the party and danced. When she danced,

---

Shake...feet A warning. It showed that they were finished talking to these people.
demons Demons are evil spirits from the devil.
put...oil on Oil was used like a medicine, so that is probably how the followers used it.
prophet Person who spoke for God. He often told things that would happen in the future.

Herod and the people eating with him were very pleased.

So King Herod said to the girl, "I will give you anything you want." ²³Herod promised her, "Anything you ask for I will give it to you. I will even give you half of my kingdom."

²⁴The girl went to her mother and asked, "What should I ask King Herod to give me?" Her mother answered, "Ask for the head of John the Baptizer."

²⁵Quickly the girl went back in to the king. The girl said to the king, "Please give me the head of John the Baptizer. Bring it to me now on a plate."

²⁶King Herod was very sad. But he had promised to give the girl anything she wanted. And the people eating there with Herod heard his promise. So Herod did not want to refuse the thing she asked for. ²⁷So the king sent a soldier to cut off John's head and bring it. So the soldier went and cut off John's head in the prison. ²⁸Then the soldier brought John's head back on a plate. He gave the head to the girl. Then the girl gave the head to her mother. ²⁹John's followers heard about what happened. So they came and got John's body. They put it in a tomb (*grave*).

Jesus Feeds More Than 5,000 People

³⁰The apostles* *that Jesus sent to preach* came back to Jesus. They gathered around Jesus and told him about all the things they did and taught. ³¹Jesus and his followers were in a very busy place. There were many, many people. Jesus and his followers did not even have time to eat. Jesus said to his followers, "Come with me. We will go to a quiet place to be alone. There we will get some rest."

³²So Jesus and his followers went away alone. They went in a boat to a place where there were no people. ³³But many people saw them leave. The people knew it was Jesus. So people from all the towns ran to the place where Jesus was going. The people were there before Jesus arrived. ³⁴When Jesus arrived there, he saw many people waiting. Jesus felt sorry for them, because they were like sheep without a shepherd *to care for them*. So Jesus taught the people many things.

apostles The men Jesus taught and chose to be his special helpers.

[35]At this time, it was late in the day. So Jesus' followers came to him. They said, "No people live in this place. And it is already very late. [36]So send the people away. They need to go to the farms and towns around here to buy some food to eat."

[37]But Jesus answered, "You give them some food to eat."

The followers said to Jesus, "We can't buy enough bread to feed all these people! We would all have to work a month to earn enough money to buy that much bread!"

[38]Jesus asked the followers, "How many loaves of bread do you have now? Go and see."

The followers counted their loaves of bread. They came to Jesus and said, "We have five loaves of bread and two fish."

[39]Then Jesus said to the followers, "Tell all the people to sit in groups on the green grass." [40]So all the people sat in groups. There were about 50 or 100 people in each group. [41]Jesus took the five loaves and two fish. He looked up to the sky and thanked God for the bread. Then Jesus divided the bread and gave it to his followers. Jesus told his followers to give the bread to the people. Then Jesus divided the two fish and gave the fish to the people. [42]All the people ate and were full. [43]After the people finished eating, the followers filled twelve baskets with the pieces of bread and fish that were not eaten. [44]There were about 5,000 men there who ate.

Jesus Walks on the Water

[45]Then Jesus told the followers to get into the boat. Jesus told them to go to the other side of the lake to Bethsaida. Jesus said that he would come later. Jesus stayed there to tell the people they could go home. [46]After Jesus said good-bye to the people, he went into the hills to pray.

[47]That night, the boat was still in the middle of the lake. Jesus was alone on the land. [48]Jesus saw the boat far away on the lake. He saw the followers working hard to row the boat. The wind was blowing against them. Sometime between three and six o'clock in the morning, Jesus went to the boat. Jesus was walking on the water. Jesus continued walking until he was almost past the boat. [49]But the followers saw Jesus walking on the water. They thought he was a ghost. The followers shouted with fear. [50]All the

followers saw Jesus and were very afraid. But Jesus spoke to the followers and said, "Don't worry! It's me! Don't be afraid." ⁵¹Then Jesus got into the boat with the followers. And the wind became calm. The followers were amazed. ⁵²They had seen Jesus make more bread from five loaves. But they did not understand what it meant. They were not able to understand it.

⁵³The followers of Jesus crossed the lake. They came to shore at Gennesaret. They tied the boat there. ⁵⁴When they were out of the boat, the people saw Jesus. They knew who he was. ⁵⁵The people ran *to tell other people* everywhere in that area *that Jesus was there*. The people brought sick people on beds to every place Jesus went. ⁵⁶Jesus went into towns and cities and farms around that area. And every place Jesus went, the people brought sick people to the market places. They begged Jesus to let them touch any part of his coat. And all the people who touched him were healed.

God's Law Is More Important than Rules that People Make

7 Some Pharisees* and some teachers of the law came from Jerusalem. They gathered around Jesus. ²The Pharisees and teachers of the law saw that some of Jesus' followers ate food with hands that were not clean. ("Not clean" means that they did not wash their hands *in the way the Pharisees said people must*.) ³The Pharisees and all the Jews never eat before washing their hands in this special way. They do this to follow the teaching given to them by their people who lived before them. ⁴And when the Jews buy something in the market, they never eat it until they wash it in a special way. They also follow other rules from their people who lived before them. They follow rules like the washing of cups, pitchers, and pots.

⁵The Pharisees* and the teachers of the law said to Jesus, "Your followers don't follow the rules given to us by our great people who lived before us. Your followers eat their food with hands that are not clean. Why do they do this?"

Pharisees Pharisees were a Jewish religious group that followed all the Old Testament and other Jewish laws and customs very carefully.

⁶Jesus answered, "You are all hypocrites.* Isaiah was right when he spoke about you. Isaiah wrote,

'These people say they honor me,
but they don't really make me an important
part of their lives.
⁷ Their worship of me is worthless.
The things they teach are only rules
that people have made.'   *Isaiah 29:13*

⁸You have stopped following the commands of God. Now you follow the teachings of men."

⁹Then Jesus said to them: "You think you are smart! You ignore the commands of God so that you can follow your own teachings! ¹⁰Moses said, 'Respect *and obey* your father and mother.'* Then Moses also said, 'Any person who says bad things to his father or mother should be killed.'* ¹¹But you teach that a person can say to his father or mother, 'I have something I could use to help you. But I will not use it to help you. I will give it to God.' ¹²You are telling that person that he does not have to do anything for his father or mother. ¹³So you are teaching that it is not important to do what God said. You think that it is more important to follow those rules you teach people. And you do many things like that."

¹⁴Jesus called the people to him again. He said, "Every person should listen to me and understand what I am saying. ¹⁵There is nothing a person puts into his body that makes him wrong. A person is made wrong by the things that come from him." ¹⁶*

¹⁷Then Jesus left the people and went into the house. The followers asked Jesus about this story. ¹⁸Jesus said, "You still have trouble understanding? Surely you know that nothing that enters a man from the outside can make him wrong. ¹⁹Food does not go into a person's mind. Food goes into his stomach. Then that food goes out of his body." (When Jesus said this, he meant that there is no food that is wrong for people to eat.)

²⁰And Jesus said, "The things that come from a man are the things that make him wrong. ²¹All these bad things begin inside a

hypocrites People who act like they are good but are not.
'Honor...mother' Quotation from Exodus 20:12, Deuteronomy 5:16.
'Any person...killed' Quotation from Exodus 21:17.
Verse 16 Some Greek copies add verse 16: "You people who hear me, listen!"

person, in his mind: bad thoughts, sexual sins, stealing, murder, ²²adultery,* selfishness, doing bad things to people, lying, doing sinful things, jealousy, saying bad things about people, boasting, and foolishness. ²³All these evil things come from inside a person. These things make a person wrong.''

Jesus Helps a Non-Jewish Woman

²⁴Jesus left that place and went to the area around Tyre. Jesus went into a house there. But Jesus did not want the people in that area to know he was there. But Jesus could not stay hidden. ²⁵A woman heard that Jesus was there. Her little daughter had an evil spirit *from the devil* inside her. So the woman came to Jesus and bowed down near his feet. ²⁶The woman was not a Jew. She was Greek, born in Phoenicia, an area in Syria. The woman begged Jesus to force the demon* out of her daughter.

²⁷Jesus told the woman: ''It is not right to take the children's bread and give it to the dogs. First let the children eat all they want.''

²⁸The woman answered, ''That is true, Lord. But the dogs under the table can eat the pieces of food that the children don't eat.''

²⁹Then Jesus told the woman, ''That is a very good answer. You may go. The demon* has left your daughter.''

³⁰The woman went home and found her daughter lying on the bed. The demon was gone.

Jesus Heals a Deaf Man

³¹Then Jesus left the area around Tyre and went through Sidon. Jesus went to Lake Galilee. Jesus went through the area of the Ten Towns.* ³²While he was there, some people brought a man to him. This man was deaf and could not talk. The people begged Jesus to put his hand on the man *to heal him*.

³³Jesus led the man away from the people to be alone with him. Jesus put his fingers in the man's ears. Then Jesus spit and touched the man's tongue. ³⁴Jesus looked up to the sky and made

adultery Breaking a marriage promise by doing sexual sin.
demon Demons are evil spirits from the devil.
Ten Towns Greek, ''Decapolis,'' an area east of Lake Galilee. It once had ten main towns.

a breathing sound. Jesus said to the man, "Ephphatha!" (This means, "Open!") ³⁵When Jesus did this, the man was able to hear. The man was able to use his tongue and spoke clearly.

³⁶Jesus commanded the people not to tell any person about what happened. Jesus always commanded people not to tell other people about him. But this only caused the people to tell about him more and more. ³⁷The people were really amazed. The people said, "Jesus does everything in a good way. Jesus makes deaf people able to hear. And people who can't talk—Jesus makes them able to talk."

Jesus Feeds More Than 4,000 People

8 Another time, there were many people *with Jesus*. The people had nothing to eat. So Jesus called his followers to him. Jesus said, ²"I feel sorry for these people. They have been with me for three days. And now they have nothing to eat. ³I should not send them home hungry. If they leave without eating, they will faint while going home. Some of these people live a long way from here."

⁴Jesus' followers answered, "But we are far away from any towns. Where can we get enough bread to feed all these people?"

⁵Jesus answered, "How many loaves of bread do you have?"

The followers answered, "We have seven loaves of bread."

⁶Jesus told the people to sit on the ground. Then Jesus took the seven loaves and gave thanks to God. Jesus divided the bread and gave the pieces to his followers. Jesus told the followers to give the bread to the people. The followers obeyed him. ⁷The followers also had a few small fish. Jesus gave thanks for the fish and told the followers to give the fish to the people. ⁸All the people ate and were full. Then the followers filled seven baskets with the pieces of food that were not eaten. ⁹There were about 4,000 men who ate. After they ate, Jesus told them to go home. ¹⁰Then Jesus went in a boat with his followers to the area of Dalmanutha.

Study Guide
Mark 7:24-37

1. Jesus went to Tyre and Sidon to ( ) receive attention, (✓) to avoid attention.

2. What did the Syrophoenician woman want Jesus to do? *get the devil out of her daughter*

3. Did "the children" (v. 27) refer to Jews or Gentiles? *Jews*

4. Because of the woman's persistence, ( ) Jesus refused her request, (✓) her daughter was healed.

5. The man brought to Jesus had (✓) hearing, ( ) ambulatory, ( ) speech, ( ) sight problems.

6. What actions did Jesus do in connection with the man's healing? *put his fingers in the man's ears then spit & touched the man's tongue*

7. The man was healed (✓) immediately, ( ) gradually.

8. Jesus wanted the people to tell everyone about the healing. True *False*

9. The people were (✓) astonished, ( ) unimpressed by Jesus' healings.

The Pharisees Want Jesus to Do Something Wrong

¹¹The Pharisees* came to Jesus and asked him questions. They wanted to try to make Jesus do something wrong. So they asked Jesus to do a miracle* to show that he was from God. ¹²Jesus made a sad sound like he was troubled. He said, "Why do you people ask to see a miracle as proof? I tell you the truth. No proof like that will be given to you." ¹³Then Jesus left the Pharisees. Jesus went in the boat to the other side of the lake.

Jesus Warns Against the Jewish Leaders

¹⁴The followers had only one loaf of bread with them in the boat. They forgot to bring more bread. ¹⁵Jesus warned them, "Be careful! Guard against the yeast* of the Pharisees* and the yeast of Herod."

¹⁶The followers discussed the meaning of this. They said, "He said this because we have no bread."

¹⁷Jesus knew that the followers were talking about this. So Jesus asked them, "Why are you talking about having no bread? You still don't see or understand? Are you not able to understand? ¹⁸Do you have eyes that can't see? Do you have ears that can't hear? Remember what I did before, when we did not have enough bread? ¹⁹I divided five loaves of bread for 5,000 people. Remember how many baskets you filled with pieces of food that were not eaten?"

The followers answered, "We filled twelve baskets."

²⁰"And remember that I divided seven loaves of bread for 4,000 people. Remember how many baskets you filled with pieces of food that were not eaten?"

The followers answered, "We filled seven baskets."

²¹Then Jesus said to them, *"You remember these things I did, but you still don't understand?"*

Pharisees   Pharisees were a Jewish religious group that followed all the Old Testament and other Jewish laws and customs very carefully.

miracle   Miracles are powerful works or great things done by the power of God.

yeast   Used here as a symbol of bad influence.

Jesus Heals a Blind Man in Bethsaida

²²Jesus and his followers came to Bethsaida. Some people brought a blind man to Jesus. They begged Jesus to touch the man. ²³So Jesus held the blind man's hand and led him out of the village. Then Jesus spit on the man's eyes. Jesus put his hands on the blind man and asked him, "Can you see now?"

²⁴The blind man looked up and said, "Yes, I see people. They look like trees walking around."

²⁵Again Jesus put his hands on the blind man's eyes. Then the man opened his eyes wide. His eyes were healed, and he was able to see everything clearly. ²⁶Jesus told him to go home. Jesus said, "Don't go into the town."

Peter Says that Jesus Is the Christ

²⁷Jesus and his followers went to the towns in the area of Caesarea Philippi. While they were traveling, Jesus asked the followers, "Who do people say I am?"

²⁸The followers answered, "Some people say you are John the Baptizer.* Other people say you are Elijah.* And other people say that you are one of the prophets.*"

²⁹Then Jesus asked, "Who do you say I am?"

Peter answered, "You are the Christ.*"

³⁰Jesus told the followers, "Don't tell any person who I am."

³¹Then Jesus began to teach his followers that the Son of Man* must suffer many things. Jesus taught that the Son of Man would not be accepted by the older Jewish leaders, the leading priests, and the teachers of the law. Jesus taught that the Son of Man must be killed and then rise from death after three days. ³²Jesus told them everything that would happen. He did not keep anything secret. Peter spoke to Jesus alone. Peter told Jesus *not to say those things*. ³³But Jesus turned and looked at his followers. Then he criticized Peter. Jesus said to Peter, "Go away

---

Baptizer John is called the Baptizer because he had the work of baptizing people.
Elijah A man who spoke for God about 800 years before Christ.
prophets People who spoke for God. Their writings are part of the Old Testament.
Christ The "anointed one" (the Messiah) or chosen one of God.
Son of Man Jesus. Jesus was God's Son, but this name showed that Jesus was a man, too. In Daniel 7:13-14, this is the name for the Messiah (Christ).

Study Guide
Mark 8:27—9:1

1. The setting was in the towns of _Caesarea_ _Philippi_.

2. Who did the people think Jesus was?
   John the Baptist, Elijah, one of prophets

3. Which of the disciples responded to Jesus' question? _Peter_

4. Jesus taught them about (choose one):
   (✓) His suffering, ( ) His glorification,
   ( ) His ministry.

5. How did Peter respond to this teaching?
   he rebuked Jesus

6. How did Jesus respond to Peter's reaction?
   opposed God's plan

7. What three things did Jesus demand of His followers? _denying self   cross bearing   will following_

8. Jesus said, "Whosoever _will_ _save_ his life shall _lose_ it, but whosoever _shall_ _lose_ his life for my sake . . . shall _save_ it."

2

from me, Satan*! You don't care about the things of God. You care only about things that people think are important.''

³⁴Then Jesus called the people to him. His followers were also there. Then Jesus said, "If any person wants to follow me, he must say 'No' to the things he wants. That person must accept the cross (*suffering*) that is given to him, and he must follow me. ³⁵The person who wants to save his life will lose it. And every person who gives his life for me and for the Good News* will save his life forever. ³⁶It is worth nothing for a person to have the whole world, if he loses his soul *in hell*. ³⁷A person could never pay enough to buy back his soul. ³⁸The people that live now are living in a sinful and evil time. If any person is ashamed of me and my teaching, then I* will be ashamed of that person. I will be ashamed of that person at the time I come with the glory of my Father and the holy angels.''

9 Then Jesus said to the people, "I tell you the truth. Some of you people standing here will see the kingdom of God come before you die. The kingdom of God will come with power.''

Three Followers See Jesus Talking with Moses and Elijah

²Six days later Jesus took Peter, James, and John and went up on a high mountain. They were all alone there. While these followers watched him, Jesus was changed. ³Jesus' clothes became shining white. The clothes were whiter than any person could make them. ⁴Then two men were there, talking with Jesus. The men were Moses and Elijah.* ⁵Peter said to Jesus, "Teacher, it is good that we are here. We will put three tents here—one for you, one for Moses, and one for Elijah.'' ⁶Peter did not know what to say, because he and the other two followers were very afraid.

Satan Name for the devil meaning "the enemy."
Good News The news that God has made a way through Christ for people to have their sins forgiven and live with God. When people accept this truth, God accepts them.
I Literally, "the Son of Man."
Moses and Elijah Two of the most important Jewish leaders in the past.

⁷Then a cloud came and covered them. A voice came from the cloud. The voice said, "This (*Jesus*) is my Son, and I love him. Obey him!"

⁸Then Peter, James, and John looked, but they saw only Jesus there alone with them.

⁹Jesus and the followers were walking back down the mountain. Jesus commanded the followers, "Don't tell any person about the things you saw on the mountain. Wait until after the Son of Man* rises from death. Then you can tell people what you saw."

¹⁰So the followers obeyed Jesus and said nothing about what they saw. But they discussed what Jesus meant about rising from death. ¹¹The followers asked Jesus, "Why do the teachers of the law say that Elijah must come first?"

¹²Jesus answered, "They are right to say that Elijah must come first. Elijah makes all things the way they should be. But why does the Scripture* say that the Son of Man* will suffer much and that people will think he is worth nothing? ¹³I tell you that Elijah has already come. And people did to him all the *bad* things they wanted to do. The Scriptures said this would happen to him."

Jesus Heals a Sick Boy

¹⁴Then Jesus, Peter, James, and John went to the other followers. They saw many people around them. The teachers of the law were arguing with the followers. ¹⁵When the people saw Jesus, they were very surprised. They ran to him to welcome him.

¹⁶Jesus asked, "What are you arguing with the teachers of the law about?"

¹⁷A man answered, "Teacher, I brought my son to you. My son has a spirit *from the devil* inside him. This spirit stops my son from talking. ¹⁸The spirit attacks my son and throws him on the ground. My son foams from his mouth, grinds his teeth, and becomes very stiff. I asked your followers to force the evil spirit out, but they could not."

Son of Man Jesus. Jesus was God's Son, but this name showed that Jesus was a man, too. In Daniel 7:13-14, this is the name for the Messiah (Christ).
Scripture A part of the Holy Writings—the Old Testament.

¹⁹Jesus answered, "You people don't believe! How long must I stay with you? How long must I continue to be patient with you? Bring the boy to me!"

²⁰So the followers brought the boy to Jesus. When the *evil* spirit saw Jesus, the spirit attacked the boy. The boy fell down and rolled on the ground. The boy was foaming from his mouth.

²¹Jesus asked the boy's father, "How long has this been happening to the boy?"

The father answered, "Since he was very young. ²²The spirit often throws him into a fire or into water to kill him. If you can do anything for him, please feel sorry for us and help us."

²³Jesus said to the father, "You said, 'Help him if you can.' All things are possible for the person who believes."

²⁴The father became very excited. He said, "I do believe. Help me to believe more!"

²⁵Jesus saw that all the people were running there to see what was happening. So Jesus spoke to the evil spirit. Jesus said, "You evil spirit that makes this boy deaf and stops him from talking—I command you to come out of this boy and never enter him again!"

²⁶The *evil* spirit screamed. The spirit caused the boy to fall on the ground again, and then the spirit came out. The boy looked like he was dead. Many people said, "He is dead!" ²⁷But Jesus held the boy's hand and helped the boy stand.

²⁸Jesus went into the house. His followers were alone with him there. They said, "We could not force that evil spirit out. Why?"

²⁹Jesus answered, "That kind of spirit can be forced out only by using prayer."

Jesus Talks About His Death

³⁰Then Jesus and his followers left that place. They went through Galilee. Jesus did not want the people to know where they were. ³¹Jesus wanted to teach his followers alone. Jesus said to them, "The Son of Man* will be given to people who will kill him. After three days, he will rise from death." ³²But the

---

Son of Man   Jesus. Jesus was God's Son, but this name showed that Jesus was a man, too. In Daniel 7:13-14, this is the name for the Messiah (Christ).

followers did not understand what Jesus meant. And they were afraid to ask him what he meant.

Jesus Tells His Followers Who Is the Greatest

³³Jesus and his followers went to Capernaum. They went into a house. Then Jesus said to his followers, "I heard you arguing on the road today. What were you arguing about?" ³⁴But the followers did not answer, because their argument on the road was about which one of them was the greatest.

³⁵Jesus sat down and called the twelve apostles* to him. Jesus said, "If any person wants to be the most important, then he must make all other people more important than himself. That person must serve all other people."

³⁶Then Jesus took a small child. Jesus stood the child before the followers. Jesus held the child in his arms and said, ³⁷"If a person accepts children like these in my name, then that person also accepts me. And if a person accepts me, then that person is also accepting the One (*God*) who sent me."

Any Person Not Against Us Is for Us

³⁸Then John said, "Teacher, we saw a man using your name to force demons* out of a person. He is not one of us. So we told him to stop, because he does not belong to our group."

³⁹Jesus said, "Don't stop him. Any person who uses my name to do powerful things will not say bad things about me. ⁴⁰The person who is not against us is with us. ⁴¹I tell you the truth. If a person helps you by giving you a drink of water because you belong to the Christ,* then that person will truly get his reward.

⁴²"If one of these little children believes in me, and another person causes that child to sin, then it will be very bad for that person. It would be better for that person to have a large rock tied around his neck and be drowned in the sea. ⁴³If your hand makes you sin, cut it off. It is better for you to lose part of your body but have life forever. That is much better than to have two hands

---

apostles   The men Jesus taught and chose to be his special helpers.
demons   Demons are evil spirits from the devil.
Christ   The "anointed one" (the Messiah) or chosen one of God.

and go to hell. In that place the fire never stops. ⁴⁴* ⁴⁵If your foot makes you sin, cut it off. It is better for you to lose part of your body but have life forever. That is much better than to have two feet and be thrown into hell. ⁴⁶* ⁴⁷If your eye makes you sin, take it out. It is better for you to have only one eye but have life forever. That is much better than to have two eyes and be thrown into hell. ⁴⁸The worms that eat the people in hell never die. In hell the fire is never stopped. ⁴⁹Every person will be punished* with fire.

⁵⁰"Salt is good. But if the salt loses its salty taste, then you cannot make it salty again. So, be full of goodness. And have peace with each other."

Jesus Teaches About Divorce

10 Then Jesus left that place. He went into the area of Judea and across the Jordan river. Again, many people came to him. And Jesus taught the people like he always did.

²Some Pharisees* came to Jesus. They tried to make Jesus say something wrong. They asked Jesus, "Is it right for a man to divorce his wife?"

³Jesus answered, "What did Moses command you to do?"

⁴The Pharisees said, "Moses allowed a man to divorce his wife by writing a certificate of divorce."

⁵Jesus answered, "Moses wrote that commandment for you because you refused to accept God's teaching. ⁶But when God made the world, 'God made people male and female.'* ⁷'That is why a man will leave his father and mother and be joined to his wife. ⁸And the two people will become one body.'* So the two people are not two, but one. ⁹God has joined those two people together. So no person should separate them."

¹⁰Later, the followers and Jesus were in the house. The followers asked Jesus again about the question of divorce. ¹¹Jesus answered, "Any person who divorces his wife and marries another woman is guilty of sin against his wife. He is guilty of the

Verse 44   Some Greek copies of Mark add verse 44, which is the same as verse 48.
Verse 46   Some Greek copies of Mark add verse 46, which is the same as verse 48.
punished   Literally, "salted."
Pharisees   Pharisees were a Jewish religious group that followed all the Old Testament and other Jewish laws and customs very carefully.
'God made...female'   Quotation from Genesis 1:27.
'That is...body'   Quotation from Genesis 2:24.

sin of adultery.* ¹²And the woman who divorces her husband and marries another man is also guilty of adultery.''

Jesus Accepts Children

¹³People brought their small children to Jesus, so that Jesus could touch them. But the followers told the people to stop bringing their children to Jesus. ¹⁴Jesus saw what happened. He did not like his followers telling the children not to come. Jesus said to them, "Let the little children come to me. Don't stop them, because the kingdom of God belongs to people who are like these little children. ¹⁵I tell you the truth. You must accept the kingdom of God like a little child accepts things, or you will never enter it.'' ¹⁶Then Jesus held the children in his arms. Jesus put his hands on them and blessed them.

A Rich Young Man Asks Jesus a Question

¹⁷Jesus started to leave, but a man ran to him and bowed on his knees before Jesus. The man asked, "Good teacher, what must I do to get the life that never ends?''

¹⁸Jesus answered, "Why do you call me good? No person is good. Only God is good. ¹⁹*But I will answer your question.* You know the commandments: 'You must not kill, you must not do the sin of adultery,* you must not steal, you must not lie, you must not cheat, and you must respect *and obey* your father and mother.'* ''

²⁰The man said, "Teacher, I have obeyed all these commandments since I was a boy.''

²¹Jesus looked at the man. Jesus felt love for him. Jesus said, "There is still one more thing you need to do. Go and sell everything you have. Give the money to the poor people. You will have a reward in heaven. Then come and follow me.''

²²The man was very sorry to hear Jesus say this, and he left. The man was sad because he was very rich *and wanted to keep his money.*

---

adultery Breaking a marriage promise by doing sexual sin.
'You...mother' Quotation from Exodus 20:12-16, Deuteronomy 5:16-20.

²³Then Jesus looked at his followers and said to them, "It will be very hard for a rich person to enter the kingdom of God!"

²⁴The followers were amazed at what Jesus said. But Jesus said again, "My children, it is very hard to enter the kingdom of God! ²⁵And it will be very hard for rich people to enter the kingdom of God! It would be easier for a camel to go through the eye of a needle!"

²⁶The followers were more amazed and said to each other, "Then who can be saved?"

²⁷Jesus looked at the followers and said, "This is something that people cannot do themselves. It must come from God. God can do all things."

²⁸Peter said to Jesus, "We left everything to follow you!"

²⁹Jesus said, "I tell you the truth. Every person who has left his home, brothers, sisters, mother, father, children, or farm for me and for the Good News* ³⁰will get a hundred times more than he left. Here in this world that person will get more homes, brothers, sisters, mothers, children, and farms. And with those things, that person will have persecutions.* But he will also have a reward in the world that is coming. That reward is life forever. ³¹Many people who have the highest place now will have the lowest place in the future. And the people who have the lowest place now will have the highest place in the future."

Jesus Talks Again About His Death

³²Jesus and the people with him were going to Jerusalem. Jesus was leading the people. Jesus' followers were amazed. But those people who followed behind them were afraid. Jesus gathered the twelve apostles* again and talked with them alone. Jesus told them what would happen in Jerusalem. ³³Jesus said, "We are going to Jerusalem. The Son of Man* will be given to the leading priests and teachers of the law. The priests and the teachers of the law will say that the Son of Man must die. They will give the Son of Man to the non-Jewish people. ³⁴Those people will laugh at

Good News   The news that God has made a way through Christ for people to have their sins forgiven and live with God. When people accept this truth, God accepts them.

persecutions   Being hurt by other people or suffering bad things from them.

apostles   The men Jesus taught and chose to be his special helpers.

Son of Man   Jesus. Jesus was God's Son, but this name showed that Jesus was a man, too. In Daniel 7:13-14, this is the name for the Messiah (Christ).

him and spit on him. They will beat him with whips and kill him. But on the third day after his death, he will rise to life again.''

James and John Ask Jesus to Do a Special Thing for Them

³⁵Then James and John, sons of Zebedee, came to Jesus. They said, "Teacher, we want to ask you to do something for us."

³⁶Jesus asked, "What do you want me to do for you?"

³⁷The sons answered, "You will have glory *in your kingdom*. Let one of us sit at your right, and let one of us sit at your left."

³⁸Jesus said, "You don't understand what you are asking. Can you accept the kind of suffering that I must have.* And can you be baptized with the same kind of baptism* that I must have?"

³⁹The sons answered, "Yes, we can!"

Jesus said to the sons, "You will suffer the same things that I will suffer. And you will be baptized with the same baptism that I must have. ⁴⁰But I cannot choose the person that will sit at my right or my left. There are some people who will have those places. Those places are prepared for them."

⁴¹The other ten followers heard this. They became angry with James and John. ⁴²Jesus called all the followers together. Jesus said, "The non-Jewish people have men they call rulers. You know that those rulers love to show their power over the people. And their important leaders love to use all their authority over the people. ⁴³But it should not be that way with you. If one of you wants to become great, then he must serve you like a servant. ⁴⁴If one of you wants to become the most important, then he must serve all of you like a slave. ⁴⁵In the same way, the Son of Man* did not come for other people to serve him. But the Son of Man came to serve other people. The Son of Man came to give his life to save many people."

Jesus Heals a Blind Man

⁴⁶Then they came to the town of Jericho. Jesus was leaving that town with his followers and many other people. A blind man

accept...have   Literally, "drink the cup." Jesus used the idea of drinking from a cup to mean accepting the terrible things that would happen to him.
baptized...baptism   Has a special meaning here—being "baptized" or "buried" in troubles.
Son of Man   Jesus. Jesus was God's Son, but this name showed that Jesus was a man, too. In Daniel 7:13-14, this is the name for the Messiah (Christ).

named Bartimaeus (son of Timaeus) was sitting by the road. This man was always begging for money. ⁴⁷The blind man heard that Jesus from Nazareth was walking by. The blind man shouted, "Jesus, Son of David,* please help me!"

⁴⁸Many people criticized the blind man. They told him not to speak. But the blind man shouted more and more, "Son of David, please help me!"

⁴⁹Jesus stopped and said, "Tell the man to come here."

So they called the blind man. They said, "Be happy! Stand up! Jesus is calling you." ⁵⁰The blind man stood quickly. He left his coat there and went to Jesus.

⁵¹Jesus asked the man, "What do you want me to do for you?"

The blind man answered, "Teacher, I want to see again."

⁵²Jesus said, "Go. You are healed because you believed." Then the man was able to see again. He followed Jesus on the road.

Jesus Enters Jerusalem like a King

11 Jesus and his followers were coming closer to Jerusalem. They came to the towns of Bethphage and Bethany at the Mount of Olives.* There Jesus sent two of his followers to do something. ²Jesus said to the followers, "Go to the town you can see there. When you enter it, you will find a young donkey tied there. No person has ever ridden this donkey. Untie the donkey and bring it here to me. ³If any person asks you why you are taking the donkey, tell that person, 'The Master needs this donkey. He will send it back soon.'"

⁴The followers went into the town. They found a young donkey tied in the street near the door of a house. The followers untied the donkey. ⁵Some people were standing there and saw this. The people asked, "What are you doing? Why are you untying that donkey?" ⁶The followers answered the way Jesus told them to answer. The people let the followers take the donkey. ⁷The followers brought the donkey to Jesus. The followers put their coats on the donkey, and Jesus sat on it. ⁸Many people spread their coats on the road for Jesus. Other people cut branches in the fields and spread the branches on the road. ⁹Some of the people

Son of David   Name for the Christ, who was from the family of David, king of Israel.
Mount of Olives   A hill covered with olive trees near the city of Jerusalem.

were walking ahead of Jesus. Other people were walking behind him. All the people shouted,

"Praise God!
God bless the one who comes
in the name of the Lord!   *Psalm 118:26*

[10]God bless the kingdom of our father David!
That kingdom is coming!
Praise to God!"

[11]Jesus went into Jerusalem and went to the temple.* Jesus looked at everything in the temple. But it was already late. So Jesus went to Bethany with the twelve apostles.*

[12]The next day, Jesus was leaving Bethany. He was hungry. [13]Jesus saw a fig tree with leaves. So Jesus went to the tree to see if it had any figs growing on it. But Jesus found no figs on the tree. There were only leaves. It was not the right time for figs to grow. [14]So Jesus said to the tree, "People will never eat fruit from you again." Jesus' followers heard him say this.

Jesus Goes to the Temple

[15]Jesus went to Jerusalem. He went into the temple.* Jesus began to throw out the people who were selling and buying things there. Jesus turned over the tables that belonged to the people who were exchanging different kinds of money. And Jesus turned over the benches of those people who were selling doves. [16]Jesus refused to allow any person to carry things through the temple. [17]Then Jesus taught the people. He said, "It is written in the Scriptures,* 'My house will be called a house for prayer for all people.'* But you are changing God's house into a 'hiding place for thieves.'*"

[18]The leading priests and the teachers of the law heard these things. They began trying to find a way to kill Jesus. They were afraid of Jesus because all the people were amazed at his teaching. [19]That night, Jesus and his followers left the city.

---

temple   The special building in Jerusalem where God commanded the Jews to worship him.
apostles   The men Jesus taught and chose to be his special helpers.
Scriptures   Holy Writings—the Old Testament.
'My house...people'   Quotation from Isaiah 56:7.
'hiding place for thieves'   Quotation from Jeremiah 7:11.

Jesus Shows His Followers the Power of Faith

²⁰The next morning, Jesus was walking with his followers. They saw the fig tree *that Jesus spoke to the day before*. The fig tree was dry and dead, even the roots. ²¹Peter remembered the tree and said to Jesus, "Teacher, look! Yesterday, you told that fig tree to die. Now it is dry and dead!"

²²Jesus answered, "Have faith in God. ²³I tell you the truth. You can say to this mountain, 'Go, mountain, fall into the sea.' And if you have no doubts in your mind and believe that the thing you say will happen, then God will do it for you. ²⁴So I tell you to ask for things in prayer. And if you believe that you have received those things, then they will be yours. ²⁵When you are praying, and you remember that you are angry with another person about something, then forgive that person. If you do this, then your Father in heaven will also forgive your sins." ²⁶*

The Jewish Leaders Doubt Jesus' Authority

²⁷Jesus and his followers went again to Jerusalem. Jesus was walking in the temple.* The leading priests, the teachers of the law, and the older Jewish leaders came to Jesus. ²⁸They said to Jesus, "Tell us! What authority (*power*) do you have to do these things? Who gave you this authority?"

²⁹Jesus answered, "I will ask you a question. You answer my question. Then I will tell you whose authority I use to do these things. ³⁰Tell me: When John baptized* people, did that come from God or from man? Answer me!"

³¹These Jewish leaders talked about Jesus' question. They said to each other, "If we answer, 'John's baptism was from God,' then Jesus will say, 'Then why didn't you believe John?' ³²But if we say, 'John's baptism was from man,' *then the people will be angry with us*." (These leaders were afraid of the people. All the people believed that John was a prophet.*)

Verse 26 Some early Greek copies add verse 26: "But if you don't forgive other people, then your Father in heaven will not forgive your sins."

temple The special building in Jerusalem where God commanded the Jews to worship him.

baptized A Greek word meaning to immerse, dip, or bury a person or thing briefly under water.

prophet Person who spoke for God. He often told things that would happen in the future.

125

³³So the leaders answered Jesus, "We don't know the answer."

Jesus said, "Then I will not tell you what authority I use to do these things."

God Sends His Son

12 Jesus used stories to teach the people. Jesus said, "A man planted a field with grapes. The man put a wall around the field and dug a hole for a wine press.* Then the man built a tower. The man leased the field to some farmers. Then the man left for a trip. ²Later, it was time for the grapes to be picked. So the man sent a servant to the farmers to get his share of the grapes. ³But the farmers grabbed the servant and beat him. They sent the servant away with nothing. ⁴Then the man sent another servant to the farmers. The farmers hit this servant on the head. They showed no respect for him. ⁵So the man sent another servant. The farmers killed this servant. The man sent many other servants to the farmers. The farmers beat some of the servants, and killed the others.

⁶"The man had one person left to send to the farmers. This person was the man's son. The man loved his son. But the man decided to send the son to the farmers. The son was the last person he could send. The man said, 'The farmers will respect my son.'

⁷"But the farmers said to each other, 'This is the owner's son. This field will be his. If we kill him, then his field will be ours.' ⁸So the farmers took the son, killed him, and threw him out of the field.

⁹"So what will the man who owns the field do? He will go to the field and kill those farmers. Then he will give the field to other farmers. ¹⁰Surely you have read this Scripture*:

'The stone that the builders did not want
    became the cornerstone* (*most important stone*).
¹¹The Lord did this,
    and it is wonderful to us.' "

Psalm 118:22-23

---

wine press   Place dug in rock used to mash grapes and collect the juice for making wine.
Scripture   A part of the Holy Writings—the Old Testament.
cornerstone   The first and most important rock of a building.

¹²These Jewish leaders heard this story that Jesus told. They knew that this story was about them. So they wanted to find a way to arrest Jesus. But they were afraid of the people. So the Jewish leaders left Jesus and went away.

The Jewish Leaders Try to Trick Jesus

¹³Later, the Jewish leaders sent some Pharisees* and some men from the group called Herodians* to Jesus. They wanted to catch Jesus saying something wrong. ¹⁴The Pharisees and Herodians went to Jesus and said, "Teacher, we know that you are an honest man. You are not afraid of what other people think about you. All men are the same to you. And you teach the truth about God's way. Tell us: Is it right to pay taxes to Caesar*? Yes or no? Should we pay taxes, or should we not pay taxes?"
¹⁵But Jesus knew that these men were really trying to trick him. Jesus said, "Why are you trying to catch me saying something wrong? Bring me a silver coin. Let me see it." ¹⁶They gave Jesus a coin and Jesus asked, "Whose picture is on the coin? And whose name is written on it?" They answered, "It is Caesar's picture and Caesar's name."
¹⁷Then Jesus said to them, "Give to Caesar the things that are Caesar's. And give to God the things that are God's." The men were amazed at what Jesus said.

Some Sadducees Try to Trick Jesus

¹⁸Then some Sadducees* came to Jesus. (Sadducees believe that no person will rise from death.) The Sadducees asked Jesus a question. ¹⁹They said, "Teacher, Moses wrote that if a married man dies and he had no children, then his brother must marry the woman. Then they will have children for the dead brother. ²⁰There were seven brothers. The first brother married but died. He had no children. ²¹So the second brother married the woman.

Pharisees Pharisees were a Jewish religious group that followed all the Old Testament and other Jewish laws and customs very carefully.
Herodians A political group that followed Herod and his family.
Caesar The name or title given to the emperor (ruler) of Rome.
Sadducees A leading Jewish religious group. They followed only the first five books of the Old Testament. They believed that people don't have another life after death.

But he also died and had no children. The same thing happened with the third brother. ²²All seven brothers married the woman and died. None of the brothers had any children with the woman. The woman was last to die. ²³But all seven brothers had married her. So at the time when people rise from death, whose wife will the woman be?"

²⁴Jesus answered, "Why did you make this mistake? Is it because you don't know what the Scriptures* say? Or because you don't know about the power of God? ²⁵When people rise from death, there will be no marriage. People will not be married to each other. All people will be like angels in heaven. ²⁶Surely you have read what God said about people rising from death. In the book where Moses wrote about the *burning* bush, it says that God told Moses this: 'I am the God of Abraham, the God of Isaac, and the God of Jacob.*'* ²⁷*This means that* God is the God of living people, not dead people. You Sadducees* are wrong!"

Which Commandment Is Most Important?

²⁸One of the teachers of the law came to Jesus. He heard Jesus arguing with the Sadducees* and the Pharisees.* He saw that Jesus gave good answers to their questions. So he asked Jesus, "Which of the commandments is most important?"

²⁹Jesus answered, "The most important commandment is this: 'People of Israel, listen! The Lord our God is the only Lord. ³⁰Love the Lord your God. You must love him with all your heart, all your soul, all your mind, and all your strength.'* ³¹The second most important commandment is this: 'Love other people the same as you love yourself.'* These two commandments are the most important commandments."

³²The man answered, "That was a good answer, Teacher. You were right when you said these things. God is the only Lord, and

---

Scriptures Holy Writings—the Old Testament.
Abraham...Isaac...Jacob Three of the most important leaders in the Old Testament.
'I am...Jacob' Quotation from Exodus 3:6.
Sadducees A leading Jewish religious group. They followed only the first five books of the Old Testament. They believed that people don't have another life after death.
Pharisees Pharisees were a Jewish religious group that followed all the Old Testament and other Jewish laws and customs very carefully.
'People...strength' Quotation from Deuteronomy 6:4-5.
'Love...yourself' Quotation from Leviticus 19:18.

there is no other God. [33]And a person must love God with all his heart, all his mind, and all his strength. And a person must love other people the same as he loves himself. These commandments are more important than all the animals and sacrifices we offer to God.''

[34]Jesus saw that the man answered him wisely. So Jesus said to the man, "You are close to the kingdom of God." And after that time, no person was brave enough to ask Jesus any more questions.

[35]Jesus was teaching in the temple.* Jesus asked, "Why do the teachers of the law say that the Christ* is the son of King David? [36]With the help of the Holy Spirit* David himself says:

> 'The Lord (*God*) said to my Lord (*Christ*):
> Sit by me at my right side.
> I will put your enemies under your control.*'   *Psalm 110:1*

[37]David himself calls the Christ 'Lord.' So how can the Christ be David's son?'' Many people listened to Jesus and were very pleased.

[38]Jesus continued teaching. Jesus said, "Be careful of the teachers of the law. They like to walk around wearing clothes that look important. And they love for people to show respect to them in the market places. [39]They love to get the most important seats in the synagogues.* And they love to get the most important seats at the feasts. [40]They are mean to widows* and steal their homes. Then they try to make themselves look good by saying long prayers. God will punish these people very much.''

A Widow Shows the Meaning of True Giving

[41]Jesus sat near the temple money box* where people put their gifts. He watched the people put money in the box. Many rich

---

temple   The special building in Jerusalem where God commanded the Jews to worship him.
Christ   The "anointed one" (the Messiah) or chosen one of God.
Holy Spirit   Also called the Spirit of God, the Spirit of Christ, and the Comforter. He is joined with God and Christ. He does the work of God among people in the world.
control   Literally, "feet." Being under a person's feet means being under his control.
synagogues   Synagogues were buildings where Jews gathered to read and study the Scriptures.
widows   A widow is a woman whose husband has died.
money box   Special box in the Jewish place for worship where people put their gifts to God.

people gave much money. ⁴²Then a poor widow* came and gave two very small copper coins. These coins were not even worth a penny.

⁴³Jesus called his followers to him. Jesus said, "I tell you the truth. This poor widow gave only two small coins. But she really gave more than all those rich people. ⁴⁴The rich people have plenty; they gave only what they did not need. This woman is very poor. But she gave all she had. And she needed that money to help her live."

Jesus Tells About the Future Destruction of the Temple

13 Jesus was leaving the temple.* One of his followers said to him, "Look, Teacher! This temple has very beautiful buildings with very big stones."

²Jesus said, "You see all these great buildings? All these buildings will be destroyed. Every stone will be thrown down to the ground. Not one stone will be left on another."

³Later, Jesus was sitting at a place on the Mount of Olives.* He was alone with Peter, James, John, and Andrew. They could all see the temple. Those followers asked Jesus, ⁴"Tell us, Jesus, when will all these things happen? And what will show us that it is time for these things to happen?"

⁵Jesus said to the followers: "Be careful! Don't let any person fool you. ⁶Many people will come and use my name. They will say, 'I am the One.' And they will fool many people. ⁷You will hear about wars and stories about wars that are being fought. But don't be afraid. These things must happen before the end comes. ⁸Nations will fight against other nations. Kingdoms will fight against other kingdoms. There will be times when there is no food for people to eat. And there will be earthquakes in different places. These things are like the first pains when something new is born.

⁹"You must be careful. People will arrest you and take you to be judged. They will beat you in their synagogues.* You will be

---

widow   A widow is a woman whose husband has died.
temple   The special building in Jerusalem where God commanded the Jews to worship him.
Mount of Olives   A hill covered with olive trees near the city of Jerusalem.
synagogues   Synagogues were buildings where Jews gathered to read and study the Scriptures.

forced to stand before kings and governors. You will tell them about me. This will happen to you because you follow me. [10]Before these things happen, the Good News* must be told to all people. [11]You will be arrested and judged. But don't worry about what you should say. Say the things God gives you to say at that time. It will not really be you speaking. It will be the Holy Spirit* speaking.

[12]"Brothers will turn against their own brothers and give them to be killed. Fathers will turn against their own children and give them to be killed. Children will fight against their own parents and find ways for their parents to be killed. [13]All people will hate you because you follow me. But the person who continues strong until the end will be saved.

[14]"You will see 'a terrible thing that causes destruction.'* You will see this thing standing in the place where it should not be." (You should understand what this means.) "At that time, the people in Judea should run away to the mountains. [15]People should run away without wasting time to stop for anything. If a person is on the roof of his house, he must not go down to take things out of his house. [16]If a person is in the field, he must not go back to get his coat. [17]At that time, it will be bad for women who are pregnant or have small babies. [18]Pray that these things will not happen in winter. [19]Why? Because those days will be full of much trouble. There will be more trouble than has ever happened since the beginning, when God made the world. And nothing as bad as that will ever happen again. [20]God has decided to make that terrible time short. If that time was not made short, then no person could continue living. But God will make that time short to help his special people that he has chosen. [21]At that time, some person might say to you, 'Look, there is the Christ*!' Or another person might say, 'There he is!' But don't believe them. [22]False Christs and false prophets will come and do great things and miracles. They will do these things to the people God has chosen. They will do these things to try to fool his people, if that is

Good News   The news that God has made a way through Christ for people to have their sins forgiven and live with God. When people accept this truth, God accepts them.

Holy Spirit   Also called the Spirit of God, the Spirit of Christ, and the Comforter. He is joined with God and Christ. He does the work of God among people in the world.

'a terrible thing that causes destruction'   Mentioned in Daniel 9:27, 12:11 (cf. Daniel 11:31).

Christ   The "anointed one" (the Messiah) or chosen one of God.

possible. ²³So be careful. Now I have warned you about all this before it happens.

²⁴"During the days after this trouble happens,

'The sun will become dark,
and the moon will not give light.
²⁵The stars will fall from the sky,
and everything in the sky will be changed.'   *Isaiah 13:10; 34:4*

²⁶"Then people will see the Son of Man* coming in the clouds with power and great glory. ²⁷The Son of Man will send his angels all around the earth. The angels will gather his chosen people from every part of the earth.

²⁸"The fig tree teaches us a lesson: When the fig tree's branches become green and soft, and new leaves begin to grow, then you know that summer is near. ²⁹It is the same with these things that I told you would happen. When you see all these things happening, then you will know that the time* is near, ready to come. ³⁰I tell you the truth. All these things will happen while the people of this time are still living. ³¹The whole world, earth and sky, will be destroyed. But the words I have said will never be destroyed.

³²"No person knows when that day or time will be. The Son and the angels in heaven don't know when that day or time will be. Only the Father knows. ³³Be careful! Always be ready! You don't know when that time will be. ³⁴This is like a man who goes on a trip and leaves his house. The man lets his servants take care of the house. He gives each servant a special job to do. One servant has the work of guarding the door. The man tells this servant to always be ready. This is the same as I am now telling you. ³⁵So you must always be ready. You don't know when the owner of the house will come back. He might come in the afternoon, or at midnight, or in the early morning, or when the sun rises. ³⁶The owner might come back quickly. If you are always ready, then he will not find you sleeping. ³⁷I tell you this, and I say this to every person: 'Be ready!' "

Son of Man   Jesus. Jesus was God's Son, but this name showed that Jesus was a man, too. In Daniel 7:13-14, this is the name for the Messiah (Christ).

time   The time that Jesus has been talking about when something very important will happen. In Luke, Jesus says that it is the time for God's kingdom to come (Luke 21:31).

The Jewish Leaders Plan to Kill Jesus

14 It was now only two days before the Passover Feast* and the Feast of Unleavened Bread.* The leading priests and teachers of the law were trying to find a way to use some lie to arrest Jesus. Then they could kill him. ²They said, "But we cannot arrest Jesus during the feast. We don't want the people to become angry and cause a riot."

A Woman Does Something Special for Jesus

³Jesus was in Bethany. He was eating in the house of Simon the leper.* While Jesus was there a woman came to him. The woman had an alabaster* jar filled with very expensive perfume. This perfume was made of pure nard.* The woman opened the jar and poured the perfume on Jesus' head.

⁴Some of the followers there saw this. They became upset and complained to each other. The followers asked, "Why waste that perfume? ⁵That perfume was worth a full year's work. It could be sold and the money could be given to poor people." The followers criticized the woman strongly.

⁶Jesus said, "Don't bother the woman. Why are you troubling her? She did a very good thing for me. ⁷You will always have poor people with you. You can help them any time you want. But you will not always have me. ⁸This woman did the only thing she could do for me. She poured perfume on my body. She did this before I die to prepare me for burial. ⁹I tell you the truth. The Good News* will be told to people in all the world. And in every place where the Good News is told, the story of what this woman did will also be told. The thing she has done will be told and people will remember her."

Passover Feast Important holy day for Jews. Jews ate a special meal on this day every year to remember that God freed them from slavery in Egypt in the time of Moses.
Feast of Unleavened Bread Same as Passover Feast. On this day they ate a special meal with bread that was made without yeast.
leper A person who has leprosy, a very bad skin disease.
alabaster A beautiful kind of stone that can be carved to make things.
nard A very expensive oil from the root of the nard plant. It was used like a perfume.
Good News The news that God has made a way through Christ for people to have their sins forgiven and live with God. When people accept this truth, God accepts them.

[10]Then one of the twelve apostles* went to talk to the leading priests. This was the follower named Judas Iscariot. Judas wanted to give Jesus to them. [11]The leading priests were very happy about this. They promised to pay Judas for doing this. So Judas waited for the best time to give Jesus to them.

[12]It was now the first day of the Feast of Unleavened Bread.* This was a time when the Jews always sacrificed* (killed) the Passover lambs.* Jesus' followers came to him. They said, "We will go and prepare everything for you to eat the Passover Feast.* Where do you want us to have the feast?"

[13]Jesus sent two of his followers into the city. Jesus said to them, "Go into the city. You will see a man carrying a jar of water. The man will come to you. Follow that man. [14]That man will walk into a house. Tell the person who owns the house, 'The Teacher asks that you show us the room where he and his followers can eat the Passover Feast.*' [15]The owner will show you a large room upstairs. This room is ready for you. Prepare the food for us there."

[16]So the followers left and went into the city. Everything happened the way Jesus said. So the followers prepared the Passover Feast.*

[17]In the evening, Jesus went to that house with the twelve apostles.* [18]While they were all eating, Jesus said, "I tell you the truth. One of you twelve will be against me—one of you eating with me now."

[19]The followers were very sad to hear this. Each follower said to Jesus, "Surely I will not be against you!"

[20]Jesus answered, "The man who is against me is one of you twelve. He is the one who dips his bread into the same bowl with me. [21]The Son of Man* will go and die. The Scriptures* say this will happen. But it will be very bad for the person who gives the

---

apostles   The men Jesus taught and chose to be his special helpers.

Feast of Unleavened Bread   Same as Passover Feast, the most important holy day for Jews. On this day they ate a special meal with bread that was made without yeast.

sacrificed   To sacrifice is to offer something or kill something as a gift to God.

Passover lambs   Part of the celebration of the Passover Feast was the sacrifice of lambs.

Passover Feast   Important holy day for Jews. They ate a special meal on this day every year to remember that God freed them from slavery in Egypt in the time of Moses.

Son of Man   Jesus. Jesus was God's Son, but this name showed that Jesus was a man, too. In Daniel 7:13-14, this is the name for the Messiah (Christ).

Scriptures   Holy Writings—the Old Testament.

134

Son of Man* to his enemies to be killed. It would be better for that person if he were never born.''

The Lord's Supper

²²While they were eating, Jesus took some bread. Jesus thanked God for the bread and divided it. He gave the bread to his followers. Jesus said, "Take this bread. This bread is my body.''

²³Then Jesus took a cup of wine. He thanked God for it and gave it to the followers. All the followers drank from the cup.

²⁴Then Jesus said, "This wine is my blood. My blood (*death*) begins the new agreement *from God to his people*. This blood is given for many people. ²⁵I tell you the truth. I will not drink this wine again until that day when I drink it in the kingdom of God and the wine is new.''

²⁶All the followers sang a song. Then they went out to the Mount of Olives.*

Jesus Tells His Followers that They Will All Leave Him

²⁷Then Jesus told the followers, "You will all lose your faith. It is written *in the Scriptures**:

'I will kill the shepherd,
  and the sheep will run away.'   Zechariah 13:7

²⁸But *after I die*, I will rise from death. Then I will go into Galilee. I will be there before you go there.''

²⁹Peter answered, "All the other followers may lose their faith. But I will never lose my faith.''

³⁰Jesus answered, "I tell you the truth. Tonight you will say you don't know me. You will say this three times before the rooster crows twice.''

³¹But Peter answered strongly, "I will never say that I don't know you. I will even die with you.'' And all the other followers said the same thing.

Son of Man   Jesus. Jesus was God's Son, but this name showed that Jesus was a man, too. In Daniel 7:13-14, this is the name for the Messiah (Christ).
Mount of Olives   A hill covered with olive trees near the city of Jerusalem.
Scriptures   Holy Writings—the Old Testament.

Jesus Prays Alone

³²Jesus and his followers went to a place named Gethsemane. Jesus said to his followers, "Sit here while I pray." ³³Jesus told Peter, James, and John to come with him. Then Jesus began to be very troubled and full of sorrow. ³⁴Jesus said to Peter, James, and John, "My soul is full of sorrow. My heart is breaking with sadness. Wait here and stay awake."

³⁵Jesus walked a little more away from them. Then Jesus fell on the ground and prayed. Jesus prayed that, if it was possible, he would not have this time of suffering. ³⁶Jesus prayed, "Abba,* Father! You can do all things. Let me not have this cup* *of suffering*. But do what you want, not what I want."

³⁷Then Jesus went back to his followers. Jesus found his followers sleeping. Jesus said to Peter, "Simon, why are you sleeping? You could not stay awake with me for one hour? ³⁸Stay awake and pray that you will not be tempted. Your spirit wants to do what is right. But your body is weak."

³⁹Again Jesus went away and prayed the same thing. ⁴⁰Then Jesus went back to the followers. Again Jesus found them sleeping. Their eyes were very tired. The followers did not know what they should say to Jesus.

⁴¹After Jesus prayed a third time, he went back to his followers. Jesus said to them, "You are still sleeping and resting? That's enough! The time has come for the Son of Man* to be given to sinful people. ⁴²Stand up! We must go. Here comes the man who is giving me to my enemies."

Jesus Is Arrested

⁴³While Jesus was still speaking, Judas came there. Judas was one of the twelve apostles.* Judas had many people with him. These people were sent from the leading priests, the teachers of the law, and the older Jewish leaders. These people with Judas had swords and clubs.

Abba Name that a child called his father. It was used like the English word "daddy."
cup Jesus is talking about the bad things that will happen to him. Accepting these things will be very hard, like drinking a cup full of something that tastes very bad.
Son of Man Jesus. Jesus was God's Son, but this name showed that Jesus was a man, too. In Daniel 7:13-14, this is the name for the Messiah (Christ).
apostles The men Jesus taught and chose to be his special helpers.

⁴⁴Judas planned to do something to show the people which man was Jesus. Judas said, "The man I kiss is Jesus. Arrest him and guard him while you lead him away." ⁴⁵So Judas went to Jesus and said, "Teacher!" Then Judas kissed Jesus. ⁴⁶Then the men grabbed Jesus and arrested him. ⁴⁷One of the followers standing near Jesus grabbed his sword and pulled it out. This follower hit the servant of the high priest* with the sword and cut off his ear.

⁴⁸Then Jesus said, "You came to get me with swords and clubs like I am a criminal. ⁴⁹Every day I was with you teaching in the temple.* You did not arrest me there. But all these things have happened so that it will be like the Scriptures* said." ⁵⁰Then all of Jesus' followers left him and ran away.

⁵¹There was a young man there who was a follower of Jesus. He was wearing only a linen cloth. The people also grabbed this man. ⁵²The cloth he was wearing came off, and he ran away wearing nothing.

Jesus Before the Jewish Leaders

⁵³The people who arrested Jesus led him to the house of the high priest.* All the leading priests, the older Jewish leaders, and the teachers of the law were gathered there. ⁵⁴Peter followed Jesus, but he did not come near Jesus. Peter followed Jesus to the yard of the high priest's house. Peter went into the yard. Peter was sitting there with the guards. He was warming himself by their fire.

⁵⁵The leading priests and all the Jewish council tried to find something that Jesus had done wrong so they could kill him. But the council could find no proof that would allow them to kill Jesus. ⁵⁶Many people came and told false things against Jesus. But the people all said different things—none of them agreed.

⁵⁷Then some people stood and said something false against Jesus. They said, ⁵⁸"We heard this man (*Jesus*) say, 'I will destroy this temple* that men made. And three days later, I will build another temple—a temple not made by men.' " ⁵⁹But also the things these people said did not agree.

high priest   The most important Jewish priest and leader.
temple   The special building in Jerusalem where God commanded the Jews to worship him.
Scriptures   Holy Writings—the Old Testament.

⁶⁰Then the high priest* stood before all the people and said to Jesus, "These people said things against you. Do you have something to say about these charges against you? Are these people telling the truth?" ⁶¹But Jesus said nothing. He did not answer.

The high priest* asked Jesus another question: "Are you the Christ,* the Son of the blessed *God*?"

⁶²Jesus answered, "Yes, I am the Son of God. And in the future you will see the Son of Man* sitting at the right side of the Great One (*God*). And you will see the Son of Man coming on the clouds of heaven."

⁶³When the high priest* heard this, he was very angry. He tore his clothes and said, "We don't need any more witnesses! ⁶⁴You all heard him say these things against God. What do you think?"

All the people said that Jesus was wrong. They said he was guilty and must be killed. ⁶⁵Some of the people there spit at Jesus. They covered Jesus' eyes and hit him with their fists. They said, "Show us that you are a prophet*!" Then the guards led Jesus away and beat him.

Peter Is Afraid to Say He Knows Jesus

⁶⁶At that time, Peter was still in the yard. A servant girl of the high priest* came to Peter. ⁶⁷The girl saw Peter warming himself at the fire. She looked closely at Peter.

Then the girl said, "You were with Jesus, that man from Nazareth."

⁶⁸But Peter said that he was never with Jesus. He said, "I don't know or understand what you are talking about." Then Peter left and went to the entrance of the yard.

⁶⁹The servant girl saw Peter there. Again the girl said to the people who were standing there, "This man is one of those people *that followed Jesus.*" ⁷⁰Again Peter said that it was not true.

---

high priest   The most important Jewish priest and leader.
Christ   The "anointed one" (the Messiah) or chosen one of God.
Son of Man   Jesus. Jesus was God's Son, but this name showed that Jesus was a man, too. In Daniel 7:13-14, this is the name for the Messiah (Christ).
prophet   Person who spoke for God. He often told things that would happen in the future.

A short time later, some people were standing near Peter. The people said, "We know you are one of those people *that followed Jesus*. You are from Galilee, *the same as Jesus*."

⁷¹Then Peter began to curse. He said strongly, "I promise to God that I don't know this man you are talking about."

⁷²After Peter said this, the rooster crowed the second time. Then Peter remembered what Jesus told him: "Before the rooster crows twice, you will say three times that you don't know me." Then Peter was very sad and began to cry.

Governor Pilate Questions Jesus

15 Very early in the morning, the leading priests, the older Jewish leaders, the teachers of the law, and all the Jewish council decided what to do with Jesus. They tied Jesus and led him to Pilate, *the governor*. They gave Jesus to Pilate.

²Pilate asked Jesus, "Are you the king of the Jews?" Jesus answered, "Yes, that is right."

³The leading priests accused Jesus of many things. ⁴So Pilate asked Jesus another question. Pilate said, "You can see that these people are accusing you of many things. Why don't you answer?"

⁵But Jesus still did not answer. Pilate was very surprised at this.

Pilate Tries but Fails to Free Jesus

⁶Every year at the Passover* time the governor would free one person from the prison. He would free any person the people wanted him to free. ⁷At that time, there was a man named Barabbas in prison. He was in prison with the rebels. These rebels were guilty of murder during a riot. ⁸The people came to Pilate and asked him to free a prisoner like he always did.

⁹Pilate asked the people, "Do you want me to free the king of the Jews?" ¹⁰Pilate knew that the leading priests had given Jesus to him because they were jealous of Jesus. ¹¹But the leading priests persuaded the people to ask Pilate to free Barabbas, not Jesus.

Passover Important holy day for Jews. They ate a special meal on this day every year to remember that God freed them from slavery in Egypt in the time of Moses.

¹²Pilate asked the people again, "So what should I do with this man you call the king of the Jews?"

¹³The people shouted, "Kill him on a cross!"

¹⁴Pilate asked, "Why? What wrong has he done?"

But the people shouted louder and louder, "Kill him on a cross!"

¹⁵Pilate wanted to please the people. So Pilate freed Barabbas for them. Then he told the soldiers to beat Jesus with whips. Then Pilate gave Jesus to the soldiers to be killed on a cross.

¹⁶Pilate's soldiers brought Jesus into the governor's palace (called the Praetorium). They called all the other soldiers together. ¹⁷The soldiers put a purple robe on Jesus. Then they used thorny branches to make a crown. They put this crown of thorns on Jesus' head. ¹⁸Then they called to Jesus. They said, "Hello, king of the Jews!" ¹⁹The soldiers hit Jesus on the head many times with a stick. They also spit on Jesus. Then *they teased Jesus by* bowing on their knees and worshiping him. ²⁰After they finished teasing Jesus, the soldiers took off the purple robe and put his own clothes on him again. Then they led Jesus out of the palace to be killed on a cross.

Jesus Is Killed on a Cross

²¹There was a man from Cyrene walking into the city. The man was Simon, the father of Alexander and Rufus. Simon was walking into the city from the fields. The soldiers forced Simon to carry the cross for Jesus. ²²They led Jesus to the place called Golgotha. (Golgotha means "The Place of the Skull.") ²³At Golgotha, the soldiers tried to give Jesus wine to drink. This wine was mixed with myrrh.* But Jesus refused to drink it. ²⁴The soldiers nailed Jesus to a cross. Then the soldiers divided Jesus' clothes among themselves. They gambled with dice to decide which clothes each soldier would get.

²⁵It was nine o'clock in the morning when they nailed Jesus to the cross. ²⁶There was a sign with the charge against Jesus written on it. The sign said: "THE KING OF THE JEWS." ²⁷They also put two robbers on crosses beside Jesus. They put one robber beside

---

myrrh   Myrrh was mixed with wine and this was used as a drug to help a person feel less pain.

Jesus on the right, and they put the other robber beside Jesus on the left. ²⁸* ²⁹People walked by and said bad things to Jesus. People shook their heads and said, "You said you could destroy the temple* and build it again in three days. ³⁰So save yourself! Come down from that cross!"

³¹The leading priests and the teachers of the law were also there. These men teased Jesus the same as the other people did They said to themselves, "He saved other people. But he can't save himself. ³²If he is really the Christ,* the king of Israel, then he should *save himself by* coming down from the cross now. We will see this, and then we will believe in him." The robbers who were being killed on the crosses beside Jesus also said bad things to him.

Jesus Dies

³³At noon the whole country became dark. This darkness continued until three o'clock. ³⁴At three o'clock Jesus cried with a loud voice, "Eloi, Eloi, lama sabachthani." This means, "My God, my God, why have you left me alone?"

³⁵Some of the people standing there heard this. The people said, "Listen! He is calling Elijah."

³⁶One man there ran and got a sponge. The man filled the sponge with vinegar and tied the sponge to a stick. Then he used the stick to give the sponge to Jesus to drink from it. The man said, "We should wait now and see if Elijah will come to take him down from the cross."

³⁷Then Jesus cried with a loud voice and died.

³⁸When Jesus died, the curtain in the temple* was torn into two pieces. The tear started at the top and tore all the way to the bottom. ³⁹The army officer that was standing there before the cross saw what happened when Jesus died. The officer said, "This man really was the Son of God!"

⁴⁰Some women were standing away from the cross, watching. Some of these women were Mary from the town of Magdala,

Verse 28   Some Greek copies add verse 28: "And the Scripture happened that says, 'They put him with the criminals.' "
curtain in the temple   A curtain divided the "most holy place" from the other part of the temple, the special building in Jerusalem where God commanded the Jews to worship him.
Christ   The "anointed one" (the Messiah) or chosen one of God.

Salome, and Mary the mother of James and Joses. (James was her youngest son.) ⁴¹These were the women that followed Jesus in Galilee and cared for him. Many other women were also there. These women had come with Jesus to Jerusalem.

Jesus Is Buried

⁴²This day was called Preparation day.* (That means the day before the Sabbath day.*) It was becoming dark. ⁴³A man named Joseph from Arimathea was brave enough to go to Pilate and ask for Jesus' body. Joseph was an important member of the Jewish council. He was one of the people who wanted the kingdom of God to come. ⁴⁴Pilate was surprised to hear that Jesus was already dead. Pilate called the army officer who guarded Jesus. Pilate asked the officer if Jesus was already dead. ⁴⁵The officer told Pilate that Jesus was dead. So Pilate told Joseph he could have the body. ⁴⁶Joseph bought some linen cloth. Joseph took the body *from the cross* and wrapped the body in the linen. Then Joseph put the body in a tomb (*grave*) that was dug in a wall of rock. Then Joseph closed the tomb by rolling a very large stone to cover the entrance. ⁴⁷Mary from Magdala and Mary the mother of Joses saw the place where Jesus was put.

The Followers Learn that Jesus Has Risen from Death

16 The next day after the Sabbath day,* Mary from Magdala, Salome, and Mary the mother of James bought some sweet-smelling spices. They wanted to put the spices on Jesus' body. ²Very early on that day, the first day of the week, the women were going to the tomb. It was very early after sunrise. ³The women said to each other, "There is a large rock covering the entrance of the tomb. Who will move the rock for us?"

⁴Then the women looked and saw that the stone was moved. The stone was very large, but it was moved away from the entrance. ⁵The women walked into the tomb. They saw a young

---

Preparation day Friday, the day before the Jewish Sabbath day.
Sabbath day Seventh day of the Jewish week. It was a special religious day for the Jews.

man there wearing a white robe. The man was sitting on the right side of the tomb. The women were afraid.

⁶But the man said, "Don't be afraid. You are looking for Jesus from Nazareth, the one who was killed on a cross. He has risen from death! He is not here. Look, here is the place they put him when he was dead. ⁷Now go and tell his followers. And *be sure to* tell Peter. Tell them, 'Jesus is going into Galilee. He will be there before you. You will see him there like he told you before.' "

⁸The women were very afraid and confused. They left the tomb and ran away. The women did not tell about what happened, because they were afraid.*

Some Followers See Jesus

⁹Jesus rose from death early on the first day of the week. Jesus showed himself first to Mary from Magdala. One time in the past, Jesus had forced seven demons* to leave Mary. ¹⁰After Mary saw Jesus, she went and told his followers. His followers were very sad and were crying. ¹¹But Mary told them that Jesus was alive. Mary said that she had seen Jesus. But the followers did not believe her.

¹²Later, Jesus showed himself to two followers while they were walking in the country. But Jesus did not look the same as before he was killed. ¹³These followers went back to the other followers and told them what happened. Again, the followers did not believe them.

Jesus Talks to the Apostles

¹⁴Later Jesus showed himself to the eleven followers while they were eating. Jesus criticized the followers because they had little faith. They were stubborn and refused to believe the people who said that Jesus had risen from death.

¹⁵Jesus said to the followers, "Go everywhere in the world. Tell the Good News* to every person. ¹⁶Any person who believes and is baptized* will be saved. But the person who does not believe

Verse 8 Some early Greek copies end the book with verse 8.
demons Demons are evil spirits from the devil.
Good News The news that God has made a way through Christ for people to have their sins forgiven and live with God. When people accept this truth, God accepts them.
baptized A Greek word meaning to immerse, dip, or bury a person or thing briefly under water.

will be judged guilty. [17]And the people who believe will be able to do these things as proof: They will use my name to force demons* out of people. They will speak in languages they never learned. [18]Those people will hold snakes without being hurt. And those people will drink poison without being hurt. Those people will touch sick people and the sick people will be healed.''

[19]After the Lord Jesus said these things to the followers, he was carried up into heaven. There, Jesus sat at the right side of God. [20]The followers went everywhere in the world and told the Good News* to people. And the Lord helped them. The Lord proved that the Good News they told people was true. He proved this by giving the followers power to do miracles.*

demons   Demons are evil spirits from the devil.
Good News   The news that God has made a way through Christ for people to have their sins forgiven and live with God. When people accept this truth, God accepts them.
miracles   Miracles are powerful works or great things done by the power of God.

Luke

1 Dear Theophilus,
Many people have tried to give a history of the things that happened among us. ²Some people saw those things from the beginning, and they did the work of spreading the teaching about Jesus. Those people have given that teaching to us. ³I studied everything carefully from the beginning, your Excellency.* Then I thought I should write it for you. So I put it in order in a book. ⁴I write these things so that you can know that what you have been taught is true.

Zechariah and Elizabeth

⁵During the time when Herod* ruled Judea, there was a priest named Zechariah. Zechariah belonged to Abijah's group.* Zechariah's wife came from the family of Aaron. Her name was Elizabeth. ⁶Zechariah and Elizabeth were truly good people before God. They did everything that was right and everything the Lord (*God*) commanded. They were without fault. ⁷But Zechariah and Elizabeth had no children; Elizabeth could not have a baby. And both of them were very old.

⁸Zechariah was serving as a priest before God for his group. ⁹The other priests chose him to offer the incense.* So Zechariah went into the temple* of the Lord (*God*) to offer the incense. ¹⁰There were many, many people outside. They were praying at the time the incense was offered. ¹¹Then, on the right side of the incense table, an angel of the Lord (*God*) came and stood before

---

Excellency   This word was used to show respect to an important person like a king or ruler.
Herod   Herod I (Herod the Great), ruler (king) of Judea 40-4 B C
Abijah's group   The Jewish priests were divided into 24 groups. See 1 Chronicles 24.
incense   Special dried tree sap used for a sacrifice. It was burned to make a sweet-smelling smoke.
temple   The special building in Jerusalem where God commanded the Jews to worship him.

Zechariah. [12]When he saw the angel, Zechariah was confused and very afraid. [13]But the angel said to him, "Zechariah, don't be afraid. Your prayer has been heard by God. Your wife, Elizabeth, will give birth to a baby boy. You will name him John. [14]You will be very, very happy. Many people will be happy because of his birth. [15]John will be a great man for the Lord *God*. He will never drink wine or liquor. Even at the time when John is being born, he will be filled with the Holy Spirit.* [16]John will help many Jews return to the Lord their God. [17]John himself will go first before the Lord. John will be powerful like Elijah.* He will have the same spirit Elijah had. He will make peace between fathers and their children. Many people are not obeying God. John will bring those people back to the right way that people should think. He will make people ready for the *coming of* the Lord."

[18]Zechariah said to the angel, "How can I know that what you say is true? I am an old man, and my wife is also old."

[19]The angel answered him, "I am Gabriel. I stand before God. God sent me to talk to you and to tell you this good news. [20]Now, listen! You will not be able to talk until the day when these things happen. You will lose your speech. Why? Because you did not believe what I told you. But these things will really happen."

[21]Outside, the people were still waiting for Zechariah. They were surprised that he was staying so long in the temple.* [22]Then Zechariah came outside, but he could not speak to them. So the people knew that Zechariah had seen a vision* inside the temple. Zechariah could not speak. He could only make signs to the people. [23]When Zechariah's time of service was finished, he went home.

[24]Later, Zechariah's wife, Elizabeth, became pregnant. So she did not go out of her house for five months. Elizabeth said, [25]"Look what the Lord (*God*) has done for me! My people were ashamed* of me, but now the Lord has taken away that shame."

Holy Spirit Also called the Spirit of God, the Spirit of Christ, and the Comforter. He is joined with God and Christ. He does the work of God among people in the world.
Elijah A man who spoke for God about 800 years before Christ.
temple The special building in Jerusalem where God commanded the Jews to worship him.
vision A vision is something like a dream that God used to speak to people.
ashamed The Jews thought it was a shame for women not to have children.

The Virgin Mary

²⁶⁻²⁷During Elizabeth's sixth month of pregnancy, God sent the angel Gabriel to a virgin* girl who lived in Nazareth, a town in Galilee. The girl was engaged to marry a man named Joseph from the family of David. Her name was Mary. ²⁸The angel came to her and said, "Greetings! The Lord (*God*) is with you. He wants to bless you."

²⁹But Mary was very confused about what the angel said. Mary wondered, "What does this mean?"

³⁰The angel said to her, "Don't be afraid, Mary, because God has blessed you. ³¹Listen! You will become pregnant. You will give birth to a baby boy. And you will name him Jesus. ³²He will be great (*important*). People will call him the Son of the Most High (*God*). The Lord God will give him the authority of King David, his ancestor. ³³Jesus will rule over the people of Jacob forever. Jesus' kingdom will never end."

³⁴Mary said to the angel, "How will this happen? I am not married!"

³⁵The angel said to Mary, "The Holy Spirit* will come to you and the power of the Most High (*God*) will cover you. The baby will be holy. He will be called the Son of God. ³⁶Now listen! You know that Elizabeth, your relative, is very old. But she is also pregnant with a son. The woman who could not have a baby has been pregnant for six months! ³⁷God can do anything!"

³⁸Mary said, "I am the servant girl of the Lord (*God*). Let this thing happen to me!" Then the angel went away.

Mary Visits Zechariah and Elizabeth

³⁹Mary got up and went quickly to a town in the hill country of Judea. ⁴⁰She went into Zechariah's house and greeted Elizabeth. ⁴¹When Elizabeth heard Mary's greeting, the unborn baby inside Elizabeth jumped. Then Elizabeth was filled with the Holy Spirit.* ⁴²Elizabeth said with a loud voice, "God has blessed you (*Mary*) more than any other woman. And God has blessed the baby which you will give birth to. ⁴³You are the mother of my

virgin   A pure girl who is not married.
Holy Spirit   Also called the Spirit of God, the Spirit of Christ, and the Comforter. He is joined
    with God and Christ. He does the work of God among people in the world.

Lord, and you have come to me! Why has something so good happened to me? ⁴⁴When I heard your voice, the baby inside me jumped with joy. ⁴⁵You are blessed because you believed what the Lord (*God*) said to you. You believed this would happen.''

Mary Praises God

⁴⁶Then Mary said,

⁴⁷''My soul praises the Lord (*God*);
  my heart is happy because God is my Savior.
⁴⁸I am not important.
  But God has accepted me,
    his servant girl.
  From now on, all people will say that I am blessed,
⁴⁹ because the Powerful One (*God*)
    has done great things for me.
  His name is very holy.
⁵⁰ God will always give mercy
    to those people who worship him.
⁵¹God's arm is strong.
  He scatters those people who are
    proud and boastful.
⁵²God brings down rulers from their thrones,
  and he raises up the humble people.
⁵³God fills hungry people with good things,
  but he sends rich, selfish people
    away with nothing.
⁵⁴God has helped his people who serve him.
  He gave them his mercy.
⁵⁵God has done what he promised to our ancestors,
  to Abraham and to his children forever.''

⁵⁶Mary stayed with Elizabeth for about three months. Then Mary went home.

The Birth of John

⁵⁷When it was time for Elizabeth to give birth, she had a boy. ⁵⁸Her neighbors and relatives heard that the Lord (*God*) was very good to her. They were happy for her.

⁵⁹When the baby was eight days old, they came to circumcise* him. They wanted to name him Zechariah because this was his father's name. ⁶⁰But his mother said, "No! He will be named John."

⁶¹The people said to Elizabeth, "But no one in your family is named John!" ⁶²Then they made signs to his father, "What would you like to name him?"

⁶³Zechariah asked for something to write on. Then Zechariah wrote, "His name is John." All the people were surprised. ⁶⁴Then Zechariah could talk again. He began to praise God. ⁶⁵And all their neighbors became afraid. In all the hill country of Judea people continued talking about all these things. ⁶⁶All the people who heard about these things wondered about them. They thought, "What will this child (*John*) become when he grows up?" The people could see that the Lord (*God*) was with this child.

Zechariah Praises God

⁶⁷Then Zechariah, John's father, was filled with the Holy Spirit.* He told the people what would happen:

⁶⁸"Let us thank the Lord God of Israel (*the Jews*).
　　God has come to help his people
　　　and has given them freedom.
⁶⁹God has given us a powerful Savior
　　　from the family of God's servant, David.
⁷⁰God said that he would do this.
　　He said it through his holy prophets*
　　　who lived long ago.
⁷¹God will save us from our enemies
　　　and from the power of all those who hate us.
⁷²God said he would give mercy to our fathers.
　　And he remembered his holy promise.
⁷³God promised Abraham, our father (*ancestor*),
　　　that he would free us from the

circumcise　To cut off the foreskin. This was done to every Jewish baby boy. It was a physical mark of the agreement that God made with Abraham (Genesis 17:9-14).
Holy Spirit　Also called the Spirit of God, the Spirit of Christ, and the Comforter. He is joined with God and Christ. He does the work of God among people in the world.
prophets　People who spoke for God. Their writings are part of the Old Testament.

[74]   power of our enemies,
      so that we could serve him without fear.
[75]We will be righteous and good before God
      as long as we live.
[76]"Now you, little boy, will be called a prophet*
      of the Most High (*God*).
   You will go first before the Lord
      to make the people ready for the Lord's coming.
[77]You will make his people know
      that they will be saved.
   They will be saved by having
      their sins forgiven.
[78]With the loving mercy of our God,
      a new Day from heaven will shine upon us.
[79]God will help the people who live in darkness,
      in the fear of death.
   He will lead us in the way that goes toward peace."

[80]And so the little boy (*John*) was growing up and becoming stronger in spirit. John lived in a place away from other people, until the time when he came out *to preach* to Israel (*the Jews*).

The Birth of Jesus

2 At that time, Augustus Caesar* sent out an order to all people in the countries that were under Roman rule. The order said that all people must write their name in a book (*register*). [2]This was the first registration.* It happened while Quirinius was governor of Syria. [3]All people traveled to their own towns to be registered.

[4]So Joseph left Nazareth, a town in Galilee. He went to the town of Bethlehem in Judea. This town was known as the town of David. Joseph went there because he was from the family of David. [5]Joseph registered with Mary because she was engaged to marry him. (Mary was now pregnant.) [6]While Joseph and Mary were in Bethlehem, the time came for Mary to have the baby.

prophet   Person who spoke for God. He often told things that would happen in the future.
Caesar   The name or title given to the emperor (ruler) of Rome.
registration   Census. A counting of all the people and the things they own.

[7]She gave birth to her first son (*Jesus*). There were no rooms left in the hotel. So Mary wrapped the baby with cloths and laid the baby in a box where cattle are fed.

Some Shepherds Hear About Jesus

[8]That night, some shepherds were in the fields there watching their sheep. [9]An angel of the Lord (*God*) stood before the shepherds. The glory of the Lord was shining around them. The shepherds became very afraid. [10]The angel said to them, "Don't be afraid, because I am telling you some good news. It will make all the people very happy. [11]Today your Savior was born in David's town. He is Christ,* the Lord. [12]This is how you will know him: You will find a baby wrapped in cloths and lying in a feeding box."

[13]Then a very large group of angels from heaven joined the first angel. All the angels were praising God, saying:

[14]"Give glory to God in heaven,
and on earth let there be peace to
the people that please God."

[15]The angels left the shepherds and went back to heaven. The shepherds said to each other, "We will go to Bethlehem and see this thing that has happened. We will see this thing the Lord (*God*) told us about."

[16]So the shepherds went quickly and found Mary and Joseph. The baby was lying in the feeding box. [17]The shepherds saw the baby. Then they told what the angels said about this child. [18]Everyone was surprised when they heard what the shepherds told them. [19]Mary hid these things in her heart; she continued to think about them. [20]The shepherds went back to their sheep, praising God and thanking him for everything that they had seen and heard. It was just as the angel had told them.

[21]When the baby was eight days old, he was circumcised,* and he was named Jesus. This name was given by the angel before the baby began to grow inside Mary.

Christ   The "anointed one" (the Messiah) or chosen one of God.
circumcised   To have the foreskin cut off. This was done to every Jewish baby boy. It was a physical mark of the agreement that God made with Abraham (Genesis 17:9-14).

Jesus Is Presented in the Temple

²²The time came for Mary and Joseph to do the things the law of Moses taught about being made pure.* Joseph and Mary brought Jesus to Jerusalem so they could present him to the Lord (*God*). ²³It is written in the law of the Lord (*God*): "When the first boy in every family is born, he shall be called 'special for the Lord.' " ²⁴The law of the Lord also says that the people must give a sacrifice*: "You must sacrifice two young doves or two young pigeons."* So Joseph and Mary went to Jerusalem to do this.

Simeon Sees Jesus

²⁵A man named Simeon lived in Jerusalem. He was a good man and very religious. Simeon was waiting for the time when God would help Israel (*the Jews*). The Holy Spirit* was in him. ²⁶The Holy Spirit told Simeon that he would not die before he saw the Christ* from the Lord (*God*). ²⁷The Spirit led Simeon to the temple.* Mary and Joseph went to the temple to do what the Jewish law said they must do. They brought the baby Jesus to the temple. ²⁸Simeon held the baby in his arms and thanked God:

²⁹"Now, Lord (*God*), you can let me, your servant,
  die in peace like you said.
³⁰I have seen your Salvation* with my own eyes.
³¹ You prepared him (*Jesus*) before all people.
³²He (*Jesus*) is a light for all the people
  of the world to see.
He will bring honor to
  your people, Israel (*the Jews*)."

³³Jesus' father and mother were amazed at what Simeon said about him. ³⁴Then Simeon blessed them and said to Mary, "Many Jews will fall and many will rise because of this boy. He

pure   The law of Moses said that 40 days after a Jewish woman gave birth to a baby, she must be cleansed by a ceremony at the temple. Read Leviticus 12:2-8.
sacrifice   An offering or gift to God.
"You...pigeons"   Quotation from Leviticus 12:8.
Holy Spirit   Also called the Spirit of God, the Spirit of Christ, and the Comforter. He is joined with God and Christ. He does the work of God among people in the world.
Christ   The "anointed one" (the Messiah) or chosen one of God.
temple   The special building in Jerusalem where God commanded the Jews to worship him.
Salvation   Simeon was talking about Jesus. The name Jesus means "salvation."

will be a sign (*proof*) from God that some people will not accept. ³⁵The things that people think in secret will be made known. The things that will happen will make your heart very sad.''

Anna Sees Jesus

³⁶Anna, a prophetess,* was there at the temple.* She was from the family of Phanuel in the Asher tribe (*family group*). Anna was very old. She had been married for seven years. ³⁷Then her husband died and she lived alone. She was now 84 years old. Anna was always at the temple; she never left. She worshiped God by fasting* and praying day and night. ³⁸Anna was standing there at that same time, thanking God. She talked about Jesus to all people who were waiting for God to free Jerusalem.

Joseph and Mary Return Home

³⁹Joseph and Mary finished doing everything that the law of the Lord commanded. Then they went home to Nazareth, their own town in Galilee. ⁴⁰The little boy (*Jesus*) was growing. He became stronger and wiser. God's blessings were with him.

Jesus As a Boy

⁴¹Every year Jesus' parents went to Jerusalem for the Passover Feast.* ⁴²When Jesus was twelve years old, they went to the feast like they always did. ⁴³When the feast days were finished, they went home. But the boy Jesus stayed in Jerusalem. His parents did not know about it. ⁴⁴Joseph and Mary traveled for a whole day. They thought that Jesus was with them in the group. They began to look for him among their family and close friends. ⁴⁵But Joseph and Mary did not find Jesus in the group. So they went back to Jerusalem to look for him there. ⁴⁶After three days they found him. Jesus was sitting in the temple* with the religious teachers, listening and asking them questions. ⁴⁷Everyone heard him. They were amazed at his understanding and wise answers.

prophetess A woman who spoke for God.
temple The special building in Jerusalem where God commanded the Jews to worship him.
fasting To fast is to live without food for a special time of prayer and worship to God.
Passover Feast Important holy day for Jews. They ate a special meal on this day every year to remember that God freed them from slavery in Egypt in the time of Moses.

⁴⁸When Jesus' parents saw him, they were amazed. His mother said to him, "Son, why did you do this to us? Your father and I were very worried about you. We have been looking for you."

⁴⁹Jesus said to them, "Why did you have to look for me? You should have known that I must be where my Father's (*God's*) work is!" ⁵⁰But they did not understand the meaning of what he said to them.

⁵¹Jesus went with them to Nazareth. He obeyed everything his parents said. His mother was still thinking about all these things. ⁵²Jesus continued to learn more and more. He grew taller. People liked Jesus, and he pleased God.

The Preaching of John

3 It was the 15th year of the rule of Tiberius Caesar.* These men were under Caesar:

Pontius Pilate, the ruler of Judea;
Herod,* the ruler of Galilee;
Philip, Herod's brother, the ruler of Iturea and Trachonitis;
Lysanias, the ruler of Abilene.

²Annas and Caiaphas were the high priests.* At that time, a command from God came to John, the son of Zechariah. John was living in the desert. ³John went through the whole area around the Jordan river. He preached to the people. John told the people to change their hearts and lives and to be baptized* so that their sins would be forgiven. ⁴This is like the words written in the book of Isaiah the prophet*:

"There is a person shouting in the desert:
'Prepare the way for the Lord.
  Make his paths straight.
⁵ Every valley will be filled.
  And every mountain and hill will be made flat.
Roads with turns will be made straight.
  And rough roads will be made smooth.

Caesar   The name or title given to the emperor (ruler) of Rome.
Herod   Herod Antipas, son of Herod the Great, tetrarch (ruler) of Galilee and Perea.
high priests   The most important Jewish priests and leaders.
baptized   A Greek word meaning to immerse, dip, or bury a person or thing briefly under water.
prophet   Person who spoke for God. He often told things that would happen in the future.

⁶ Every person will know about
the salvation of God!' ''

Isaiah 40:3-5

⁷People came to be baptized* by John. John said to them,
"You are like poisonous snakes! Who warned you to run away
from God's anger that is coming? ⁸You must do the things that
will show that you have really changed your hearts. Don't *boast
and* say, 'Abraham is our father.' I tell you that God can make
children for Abraham from these rocks here. ⁹The ax is now
ready to cut down the trees.* Every tree that does not make good
fruit will be cut down and thrown into the fire."

¹⁰The people asked John, "What should we do?"

¹¹John answered, "If you have two coats, share with the person
who does not have one. If you have food, share that too."

¹²Even the tax collectors* came to John. They wanted to be
baptized.* They said to John, "Teacher, what should we do?"

¹³John said to them, "Don't take more taxes from people than
you have been ordered to take."

¹⁴The soldiers asked John, "What about us? What should we
do?"

John said to them, "Don't make people give you money. Don't
tell lies about anyone. Be happy with the pay you get."

¹⁵All the people were hoping *for the Christ* to come*, and they
wondered about John. They thought, "Maybe he is the Christ."

¹⁶John answered everyone, "I baptize* you in water, but there
is a person coming later who can do more than I can. I am not
good enough to untie his shoes* for him. He will baptize you with
the Holy Spirit* and with fire. ¹⁷He will come ready to clean the
grain.* He will separate the good grain from the straw. He will
put the good part of the grain into his barn. Then he will burn the
part that is not good. He will burn it with a fire that cannot be

---

baptized   A Greek word meaning to immerse, dip, or bury a person or thing briefly under water.
trees   The people who do not accept Jesus. They are like "trees" that will be cut down.
tax collectors   Jews hired by the Romans to collect taxes. They often cheated their people.
Christ   The "anointed one" (the Messiah) or chosen one of God.
baptize   A Greek word meaning to immerse, dip, or bury a person or thing briefly under water.
shoes   Literally, "sandals," open shoes tied to the bottom of the feet with leather strings.
Holy Spirit   Also called the Spirit of God, the Spirit of Christ, and the Comforter. He is joined
   with God and Christ. He does the work of God among people in the world.
clean the grain   The grain means people. John uses this idea to show how Jesus will separate the
   good people from the bad people.

stopped." [18]And John continued to preach the Good News,*
saying many other things to help the people.

How John's Work Later Ended

[19](John criticized Governor Herod.* John criticized Herod for
the bad thing he did with Herodias, the wife of Herod's brother.
John also criticized Herod for the many other bad things Herod
did. [20]So Herod did another bad thing: He put John in jail. This
was added to all the other bad things Herod did.)

Jesus Is Baptized by John

[21]*Before John was put into prison*, all the people were being
baptized* by him. Then Jesus came and was baptized too. While
Jesus was praying, the sky opened. [22]The Holy Spirit* came down
on him. The Spirit looked like a real dove. Then a voice came
from heaven and said, "You are my Son. I love you, and I am
very pleased with you!"

The Family History of Joseph

[23]When Jesus began to teach, he was about 30 years old. People
thought that Jesus was Joseph's son.

> Joseph was the son of Eli.
> [24]Eli was the son of Matthat.
> Matthat was the son of Levi.
> Levi was the son of Melchi.
> Melchi was the son of Jannai.
> Jannai was the son of Joseph.
> [25]Joseph was the son of Mattathias.
> Mattathias was the son of Amos.
> Amos was the son of Nahum.
> Nahum was the son of Esli.
> Esli was the son of Naggai.

Good News The news that God has made a way through Christ for people to have their sins
forgiven and live with God. When people accept this truth, God accepts them.
Herod Herod Antipas, son of Herod the Great, tetrarch (ruler) of Galilee and Perea.
baptized A Greek word meaning to immerse, dip, or bury a person or thing briefly under water.
Holy Spirit Also called the Spirit of God, the Spirit of Christ, and the Comforter. He is joined
with God and Christ. He does the work of God among people in the world.

[26]Naggai was the son of Maath.
Maath was the son of Mattathias.
Mattathias was the son of Semein.
Semein was the son of Josech.
Josech was the son of Joda.
[27]Joda was the son of Joanan.
Joanan was the son of Rhesa.
Rhesa was the son of Zerubbabel.
Zerubbabel was the son of Shealtiel.
Shealtiel was the son of Neri.
[28]Neri was the son of Melchi.
Melchi was the son of Addi.
Addi was the son of Cosam.
Cosam was the son of Elmadam.
Elmadam was the son of Er.
[29]Er was the son of Joshua.
Joshua was the son of Eliezer.
Eliezer was the son of Jorim.
Jorim was the son of Matthat.
Matthat was the son of Levi.
[30]Levi was the son of Simeon.
Simeon was the son of Judah.
Judah was the son of Joseph.
Joseph was the son of Jonam.
Jonam was the son of Eliakim.
[31]Eliakim was the son of Melea.
Melea was the son of Menna.
Menna was the son of Mattatha.
Mattatha was the son of Nathan.
Nathan was the son of David.
[32]David was the son of Jesse.
Jesse was the son of Obed.
Obed was the son of Boaz.
Boaz was the son of Salmon.
Salmon was the son of Nahshon.
[33]Nahshon was the son of Amminadab.
Amminadab was the son of Admin.
Admin was the son of Arni.

Arni was the son of Hezron.

Hezron was the son of Perez.

Perez was the son of Judah.

[34]Judah was the son of Jacob.

Jacob was the son of Isaac.

Isaac was the son of Abraham.

Abraham was the son of Terah.

Terah was the son of Nahor.

[35]Nahor was the son of Serug.

Serug was the son of Reu.

Reu was the son of Peleg.

Peleg was the son of Eber.

Eber was the son of Shelah.

[36]Shelah was the son of Cainan.

Cainan was the son of Arphaxad.

Arphaxad was the son of Shem.

Shem was the son of Noah.

Noah was the son of Lamech.

[37]Lamech was the son of Methuselah.

Methuselah was the son of Enoch.

Enoch was the son of Jared.

Jared was the son of Mahalaleel.

Mahalaleel was the son of Cainan.

[38]Cainan was the son of Enos.

Enos was the son of Seth.

Seth was the son of Adam.

Adam was the son of God.

Jesus Is Tempted by the Devil

4 Jesus returned from the Jordan river. He was full of the Holy Spirit.* The Spirit led Jesus into the desert. [2]There the devil tempted Jesus for 40 days. Jesus ate nothing during that time. When those days were finished, Jesus was very hungry.

[3]The devil said to Jesus, "If you are the Son of God, tell this rock to become bread."

Holy Spirit   Also called the Spirit of God, the Spirit of Christ, and the Comforter. He is joined with God and Christ. He does the work of God among people in the world.

⁴Jesus answered, "It is written *in the Scriptures**:

'A person does not live only
    by eating food.' " *Deuteronomy 8:3*

⁵Then the devil took Jesus and showed him all the kingdoms of the world in a moment of time. ⁶The devil said to Jesus, "I will give you all these kingdoms and all the power and glory that is in them. It has all been given to me. I can give it to any person I want. ⁷I will give it all to you, if you will only worship me."

⁸Jesus answered, "It is written *in the Scriptures**:

'You must worship the Lord your God.
    Serve only him!' " *Deuteronomy 6:13*

⁹Then the devil led Jesus to Jerusalem. The devil put Jesus on a very high place of the temple.* He said to Jesus, "If you are the Son of God, jump off! ¹⁰It is written *in the Scriptures*:

'God will command his angels
    to take care of you.' *Psalm 91:11*

¹¹It is also written:

'Their hands will catch you
    so that you will not hit your foot
    on a rock.' " *Psalm 91:12*

¹²Jesus answered, "But it also says *in the Scriptures*:

'You must not test (*doubt*)
    the Lord your God.' " *Deuteronomy 6:16*

¹³The devil finished tempting Jesus in every way and went away to wait until a better time.

Jesus Teaches the People

¹⁴Jesus went back to Galilee with the power of the Holy Spirit.* Stories about Jesus spread all over the area around Galilee. ¹⁵Jesus began to teach in the synagogues.* All the people praised him.

Scriptures Holy Writings—the Old Testament.
temple The special building in Jerusalem where God commanded the Jews to worship him.
Holy Spirit Also called the Spirit of God, the Spirit of Christ, and the Comforter. He is joined with God and Christ. He does the work of God among people in the world.
synagogues Synagogues were buildings where Jews gathered to read and study the Scriptures.

¹⁶Jesus traveled to Nazareth, the town where he grew up. On the Sabbath day* he went to the synagogue* like he always did. Jesus stood up to read. ¹⁷The book of Isaiah the prophet* was given to him. Jesus opened the book and found the place where this is written:

> ¹⁸"The Spirit of the Lord (*God*) is in me.
>> God chose me to tell the Good News
>>> to people who have nothing.
>> God sent me to tell people who are prisoners *to sin*
>>> that they are free,
>>> and to tell the blind that they can see again.
>> God sent me to free the weak people
>>> from their suffering,
> ¹⁹   and to announce the year for the Lord (*God*)
>> to show kindness to people."   *Isaiah 61:1-2*

²⁰Jesus closed the book. He gave the book back and sat down. Every person in the synagogue watched Jesus closely. ²¹Jesus began to speak to them. He said, "While you heard me reading these words just now, the words were coming true!"

²²All the people said good things about Jesus. They were amazed at the beautiful words that Jesus spoke. The people said, "*How can he speak like this*? He is only Joseph's son, isn't he?"

²³Jesus said to them, "I know that you will tell me the old saying: 'Doctor, heal yourself.' You want to say, 'We heard about some things that you did in Capernaum. Do those same things here in your own home town!' " ²⁴Then Jesus said, "I tell you the truth. A prophet* is not accepted in his own home town. ²⁵What I say is true. During the time of Elijah* it did not rain in Israel for three and a half years. There was no food anywhere in the whole country. There were many widows* in Israel during that time. ²⁶But Elijah was sent to none of those widows *in Israel*. Elijah was sent only to a widow in Zarephath, a town in Sidon.

Sabbath day   Seventh day of the Jewish week. It was a special religious day for the Jews.
synagogue   Synagogues were places where Jews gathered to read and study the Scriptures.
prophet   Person who spoke for God. He often told things that would happen in the future.
Elijah   A man who spoke for God about 800 years before Christ.
widows   A widow is a woman whose husband has died.

²⁷And there were many people with leprosy* living in Israel during the time of the prophet Elisha.* But none of those people were healed; the only one was Naaman. And Naaman was from the country of Syria, *not from Israel*."

²⁸All the people in the synagogue* heard these things. The people became very, very angry. ²⁹The people got up and forced Jesus to go out of town. Their town was built on a hill. They brought Jesus to the edge of the hill. The people wanted to throw him off. ³⁰But Jesus walked through the middle of them and went away.

Jesus Heals a Man Who Has an Evil Spirit

³¹Jesus went to Capernaum, a city in Galilee. On the Sabbath day* Jesus taught the people. ³²They were amazed at what Jesus taught; the things he said were powerful. ³³In the synagogue* there was a man who had an evil spirit from the devil inside him. The man shouted with a loud voice, ³⁴"Jesus of Nazareth! What do you want with us? Did you come here to destroy us? I know who you are—God's Holy One!" ³⁵But Jesus warned the evil spirit to stop. Jesus said, "Be quiet! Come out of the man!" The evil spirit threw the man down on the ground before all the people. Then the evil spirit left the man and did not hurt him.

³⁶The people were amazed. They said to each other, "What does this mean? With authority and power he (*Jesus*) commands evil spirits and they come out." ³⁷And so the news about Jesus spread to every place in the whole area.

Jesus Heals a Woman

³⁸Jesus left the synagogue.* He went to Simon's* house. Simon's mother-in-law was very sick. She had a high fever. They asked Jesus to do something to help her. ³⁹Jesus stood very close to her and commanded the sickness to leave her. The sickness left her. Then she got up and began serving them.

---

leprosy   A very bad skin disease.
Elisha   A man who spoke for God after the time of Elijah.
synagogue   Synagogues were places where Jews gathered to read and study the Scriptures.
Sabbath day   Seventh day of the Jewish week. It was a special religious day for the Jews.
Simon   Simon's other name was Peter. He later became one of Jesus' apostles.

Jesus Heals Many Other People

⁴⁰When the sun went down, the people brought their sick friends to Jesus. They had many different kinds of sickness. Jesus put his hands on each sick person and healed them. ⁴¹Demons* came out of many people. The demons shouted, "You are the Son of God." But Jesus gave a strong command for the demons not to speak. The demons knew Jesus was the Christ.*

Jesus Goes to Other Towns

⁴²The next day, Jesus went to a place to be alone. The people looked for Jesus. When the people found Jesus, they would not let him leave. ⁴³But Jesus said to them, "I must tell the Good News about God's kingdom to other towns, too. This is why I was sent."

⁴⁴Then Jesus preached in the synagogues* in Judea.

Peter, James, and John Follow Jesus

5 Jesus stood beside Lake Gennesaret (*Galilee*). Many people pushed to get all around him. They wanted to hear the teachings of God. ²Jesus saw two boats at the shore of the lake. The fishermen were washing their nets. ³Jesus got into the boat that belonged to Simon.* Jesus asked Simon to push off a little from the shore. Then Jesus sat down in the boat and continued to teach the people on the shore.

⁴Jesus finished speaking. He said to Simon, "Take the boat into the deep water. If all of you will put your nets into the water, you will catch some fish."

⁵Simon answered, "Master, we worked hard all night trying to catch fish, but we caught nothing. But you say I should put the nets into the water; so I will." ⁶The fishermen put their nets into the water. Their nets became so full of fish that the nets began to

---

demons   Demons are evil spirits from the devil.
Christ   The "anointed one" (the Messiah) or chosen one of God.
synagogues   Synagogues were places where Jews gathered to read and study the Scriptures.
Simon   Simon's other name was Peter. He later became one of Jesus' apostles.

break. [7]They called to some friends in another boat to come and help them. The friends came and both boats were filled so full of fish that they were almost sinking.

[8-9]The fishermen were all amazed at the many fish they caught. When Simon Peter saw this, he bowed down before Jesus and said, "Go away from me, Lord. I am a sinful man!" [10]James and John, the sons of Zebedee, were amazed too. (James and John worked together with Simon.)

Jesus said to Simon, "Don't be afraid. From now on you will work to gather people, *not fish*!"

[11]The men brought their boats to the shore. They left everything and followed Jesus.

Jesus Heals a Sick Man

[12]One time Jesus was in a town where a very sick man lived. This man was covered with leprosy.* When the man saw Jesus, he bowed before Jesus and begged him, "Lord, heal me. I know you can if you want to."

[13]Jesus said, "I want to heal you. Be healed!" Then Jesus touched the man. Immediately the leprosy* disappeared. [14]Then Jesus said, "Don't tell anyone about what happened. But go show yourself to the priest.* And offer a gift *to God* for your healing like Moses commanded. This will show people that you are healed."

[15]But the news about Jesus spread more and more. Many people came to hear Jesus and to be healed of their sicknesses. [16]Jesus often went away to other places to be alone so that he could pray.

Jesus Heals a Crippled Man

[17]One day Jesus was teaching the people. The Pharisees* and teachers of the law were sitting there too. They had come from

---

leprosy A very bad skin disease.
show...priest The law of Moses said a priest must say when a Jew with leprosy was well.
Pharisees Pharisees were a Jewish religious group that followed all the Old Testament and other Jewish laws and customs very carefully.

every town in Galilee and from Judea and Jerusalem. The Lord (*God*) was giving Jesus the power to heal people. [18]There was a man who was paralyzed (*crippled*). Some men carried him on a small bed. The men tried to bring him and put him down before Jesus. [19]But there were so many people that the men could not find a way to Jesus. So the men went up on the roof and lowered the crippled man down through a hole in the ceiling. They lowered the bed *into the room* so that the crippled man was lying before Jesus. [20]Jesus saw that these men believed. Jesus said to the sick man, "Friend, your sins are forgiven."

[21]The Jewish teachers of the law and the Pharisees* thought to themselves, "Who is this man (*Jesus*)? He is saying things that are against God! Only God can forgive sins."

[22]But Jesus knew what they were thinking. He said, [23]"Which is easier: to tell this crippled man, 'Your sins are forgiven,' or to tell him, 'Stand up and walk'? [24]But I will prove to you that the Son of Man* has power on earth to forgive sins." So Jesus said to the paralyzed man, "I tell you, stand up! Take your bed and go home!"

[25]Then the man stood up before the people there. He picked up his bed and walked home, praising God. [26]All the people were fully amazed. They began to praise God. The people were filled with much respect *for God's power*. They said, "Today we saw amazing things!"

Levi Follows Jesus

[27]After this, Jesus went out and saw a tax collector* sitting in the tax office. His name was Levi. Jesus said to him, "Follow me!" [28]Levi got up, left everything, and followed Jesus.

[29]Then Levi gave a big dinner for Jesus. The dinner was at Levi's house. At the table, there were many tax collectors* and some other people too. [30]But the Pharisees* and those men who

---

Pharisees   Pharisees were a Jewish religious group that followed all the Old Testament and other Jewish laws and customs very carefully.

Son of Man   Jesus. Jesus was God's Son, but this name showed that Jesus was a man, too. In Daniel 7:13-14, this is the name for the Messiah (Christ).

tax collector   A Jew hired by the Romans to collect taxes. Tax collectors often cheated people.

taught the law for the Pharisees* began to complain to the followers of Jesus, "Why do you eat and drink with tax collectors* and other bad people?"

³¹Jesus answered them, "Healthy people don't need a doctor. It is the sick people that need a doctor. ³²I have not come to ask good people to change. I have come to ask bad people to change their hearts and lives!"

Jesus Answers a Question About Fasting

³³They said to Jesus, "John's followers often fast* and pray, the same as the Pharisees.* But your followers eat and drink all the time."

³⁴Jesus said to them, "*When there is a wedding*, you cannot make the friends of the bridegroom* fast (*be sad*) while the bridegroom is still with them. ³⁵But the time will come when the groom will be taken away from them. Then his friends will fast."

³⁶Jesus told them this story: "No person takes cloth off a new coat to cover a hole on an old coat. Why? Because he ruins the new coat, and the cloth from the new coat will not be the same as the old cloth. ³⁷People never pour new wine into old wine bags. Why? Because the new wine will break the bags, and the wine will spill out and the wine bags will be ruined. ³⁸People always put new wine into new wine bags. ³⁹No person who drinks old wine wants new wine. Why? Because he says, 'The old wine is better.' "

Jesus Is Lord over the Sabbath Day

6 One time, on a Sabbath day,* Jesus was walking through some grain fields. His followers picked the grain, rubbed it in their hands, and ate it. ²Some Pharisees* said, "Why are you doing that? It is against the law *of Moses* to do that on the Sabbath day."

Pharisees   Pharisees were a Jewish religious group that followed all the Old Testament and other Jewish laws and customs very carefully.
tax collectors   Jews hired by the Romans to collect taxes. They often cheated their people.
fast   To fast is to live without food for a special time of prayer and worship to God.
bridegroom   A man ready to be married.
Sabbath day   Seventh day of the Jewish week. It was a special religious day for the Jews.

³Jesus answered, "You have read about what David did when he and the people with him were hungry. ⁴David went into God's house. David took the bread that was offered to God and ate it. And David gave some of the bread to the people with him. This was against the law *of Moses*. The law says that only the priests can eat that bread." ⁵Then Jesus said to the Pharisees,* "The Son of Man* is Lord (*Master*) over the Sabbath day."

Jesus Heals a Man on the Sabbath Day

⁶On another Sabbath day,* Jesus went into the synagogue.* Jesus taught the people. A man with a crippled right hand was there. ⁷The teachers of the law and the Pharisees* were waiting to see if Jesus would heal on the Sabbath day. They wanted to see Jesus do something wrong so that they could accuse him. ⁸But Jesus knew what they were thinking. He said to the man with the crippled hand, "Get up and stand before these people." The man got up and stood there. ⁹Then Jesus said to them, "I ask you, which thing is right to do on the Sabbath day: to do good, or to do evil? Is it right to save a life or to destroy one?" ¹⁰Jesus looked around at all of them. Jesus said to the man, "Let me see your hand." The man put his hand out. His hand was healed. ¹¹The Pharisees and the teachers of the law became very, very angry. They said to each other, "What can we do to Jesus?"

Jesus Chooses His Twelve Apostles

¹²At that time, Jesus went out to a mountain to pray. He stayed there all night praying to God. ¹³The next morning, Jesus called his followers. He chose twelve of them. Jesus named these twelve men "apostles."* They were: ¹⁴Simon (Jesus named him Peter) and Andrew, Peter's brother; James and John, Philip and Bartholomew; ¹⁵Matthew, Thomas, James (the son of Alphaeus),

---

Pharisees   Pharisees were a Jewish religious group that followed all the Old Testament and other Jewish laws and customs very carefully.
Son of Man   Jesus. Jesus was God's Son, but this name showed that Jesus was a man, too. In Daniel 7:13-14, this is the name for the Messiah (Christ).
Sabbath day   Seventh day of the Jewish week. It was a special religious day for the Jews.
synagogue   Synagogues were places where Jews gathered to read and study the Scriptures.
apostles   The men Jesus taught and chose to be his special helpers.

and Simon (called the Zealot*), ¹⁶Judas (the son of James) and Judas Iscariot. This Judas was the one who gave Jesus to his enemies.

Jesus Teaches the People and Heals Them

¹⁷Jesus and the apostles* came down from the mountain. Jesus stood on a flat place. A large group of his followers were there. Also, there were many people from all around Judea, Jerusalem, and the seacoast cities of Tyre and Sidon. ¹⁸They all came to hear Jesus teach and to be healed of their sicknesses. Jesus healed those people who were troubled by evil spirits *from the devil*. ¹⁹All the people were trying to touch Jesus, because power was coming out from him. Jesus healed them all!

²⁰Jesus looked at his followers and said,
"Poor people, you are blessed (*happy*),
because God's kingdom belongs to you.
²¹You people who are hungry now, you are blessed,
because you will be filled.
You people who are crying now, you are blessed,
because you will laugh *with joy*.
²²"You are blessed when people hate you and are mean to you. They will say that you are bad because you belong to the Son of Man.* When they say this, you are blessed. ²³At that time, be full of joy, because you have a great reward in heaven. Their fathers (*ancestors*) were mean to the prophets* in the same way that these people are mean to you.

²⁴"But it will be bad for you,
you rich people,
because you had your easy life.
²⁵It will be bad for you people
who are full now,
because you will be hungry.

Zealot   The Zealots or "Enthusiasts" were a Jewish political group.
apostles   The men Jesus taught and chose to be his special helpers.
Son of Man   Jesus. Jesus was God's Son, but this name showed that Jesus was a man, too. In Daniel 7:13-14, this is the name for the Messiah (Christ).
prophets   People who spoke for God. Their writings are part of the Old Testament.

> It will be bad for you people
> who are laughing now,
> because you will be sad and cry.

²⁶"It is bad when all people say good things about you. Their fathers (*ancestors*) always said good things about the false prophets.*"

Love Your Enemies

²⁷"I say to you people who are listening to me, love your enemies. Do good and be kind to those people who hate you. ²⁸Bless those people who say bad things to you. Pray for those people who are mean to you. ²⁹If a person hits you on the side of your face, let him hit the other side too. If a person takes away your coat, let him have your shirt too. ³⁰Give to every person who asks you. When a person takes something that is yours, don't ask for it back. ³¹Do for other people what you want them to do for you. ³²If you love only those people who love you, should you get some special praise for doing that? No! Even sinners love the people who love them! ³³If you do good only to those people who do good to you, should you get some special praise for doing that? No! Even sinners do that! ³⁴If you loan things to people, always hoping to get something back, should you get some special praise for that? No! Even sinners lend to other sinners so that they can get the same amount back! ³⁵So love your enemies. Do good to them, and lend to them without hoping to get anything back. If you do these things, you will have a great reward. You will be sons of the Most High (*God*). Yes, because God is good even to the people who are full of sin and not thankful. ³⁶Give love and mercy the same as your Father gives love and mercy."

Look at Yourselves

³⁷"Don't judge other people, and you will not be judged. Don't condemn (*find guilty*) other people, and you will not be condemned. Forgive other people *for the wrongs they do to you*, and you will be forgiven. ³⁸Give to other people, and you will receive. You will be given much. It will be poured into your

---

false prophets   People who say they speak for God but do not really speak God's truth.

hands—more than you can hold. You will be given so much that it will spill into your lap. The way you give to other people is the way God will give to you."

³⁹Jesus told them this story: "Can a blind man lead another blind man? No! Both of them will fall into a hole. ⁴⁰A student is not better than his teacher. But when the student has fully learned, then he will be like his teacher.

⁴¹"Why do you notice the small piece of dust that is in your brother's eye, but you don't see the big piece of wood that is in your own eye? ⁴²You say to your brother, 'Brother, let me take that little piece of dust out of your eye.' Why do you say this? You cannot see that big piece of wood in your own eye! You are a hypocrite*! First, take the piece of wood out of your own eye. Then you will see clearly to take the dust out of your brother's eye."

Two Kinds of Fruit

⁴³"A good tree does not give bad fruit. Also, a bad tree does not give good fruit. ⁴⁴Each tree is known by the fruit it gives. Do people gather figs from thorn bushes? No! Do people get grapes from bushes? No! ⁴⁵A good person has good things saved in his heart. And so he brings good things out of his heart. But an evil person has evil things saved in his heart. So he brings out bad things. A person speaks the things that are in his heart."

Two Kinds of People

⁴⁶"Why do you call me, 'Lord, Lord,' but you are not doing what I say? ⁴⁷Every person who comes to me and listens to my words and obeys ⁴⁸is like a man building a house. He digs deep and builds his house on strong rock. Then the floods come, and the water tries to wash the house away. But the flood cannot move the house, because the house was built well (*strong*). ⁴⁹But the person who hears my words and does not obey is like a man who does not build his house on strong rock. When the floods come, the house falls down easily. And that house is completely destroyed."

hypocrite   A person who acts like he is good but is not.

Jesus Heals a Servant

7 Jesus finished saying all these things to the people. Then Jesus went into Capernaum. ²In Capernaum there was a Roman army officer.* The officer had a servant who was very sick; he was near death. The officer loved the servant very much. ³When the officer heard about Jesus, he sent some older Jewish leaders to him. The officer wanted the men to ask Jesus to come and save the life of his servant. ⁴The men went to Jesus. They begged Jesus *to help the officer*. They said, "This officer is worthy to have your help. ⁵He loves our people and he built the synagogue* for us."

⁶So Jesus went with the men. Jesus was coming near the officer's house when the officer sent friends to say, "Lord, you don't need to come into my house. I am not good enough to be with you. ⁷That is why I did not come to you myself. You only need to give the order and my servant boy will be healed. ⁸*I understand your authority*. I am a man under the authority (*power*) of other men. And I have soldiers under my authority. I tell one soldier, 'Go,' and he goes. And I tell another soldier, 'Come,' and he comes. And I say to my servant, 'Do this,' and my servant obeys me."

⁹When Jesus heard this, he was amazed. Jesus turned to the people who were following him. Jesus said, "I tell you, this is the most faith I have seen anywhere—even in Israel!"

¹⁰The group that was sent to Jesus went back to the house. There they found that the servant was healed.

Jesus Brings a Man Back to Life

¹¹The next day Jesus went to a town called Nain. Jesus' followers and a large group of people were traveling with him. ¹²When Jesus came near the town gates, he saw a funeral. A mother, who was a widow,* had lost her only son. Many people from the town were there with the mother while her son was being carried out. ¹³When the Lord (*Jesus*) saw her, he felt very sorry

---

officer A centurion, a Roman army officer who had authority over 100 soldiers.
synagogue Synagogues were places where Jews gathered to read and study the Scriptures.
widow A widow is a woman whose husband has died.

for her in his heart. Jesus said to her, "Don't cry." ¹⁴Jesus walked to the coffin* and touched it. The men who were carrying the coffin stopped. Jesus said to the dead boy, "Young man, I tell you, get up!" ¹⁵Then the boy sat up and began to talk. Jesus gave him to his mother.

¹⁶All the people were amazed. They were praising God. They said, "A great prophet has come to us!" And they said, "God is taking care of his people."

¹⁷This news about Jesus spread into all Judea and into all the places around there.

John Asks a Question

¹⁸John's followers told John about all these things. John called for two of his followers. ¹⁹John sent them to the Lord (*Jesus*) to ask, "Are you the One who is coming, or should we wait for another person?"

²⁰So the men came to Jesus. They said, "John the Baptizer* sent us to you with this question: 'Are you the One who is coming, or should we wait for another person?' "

²¹At that time, Jesus healed many people of their sicknesses, diseases, and evil spirits *from the devil*. Jesus healed many blind people so that they could see again. ²²Then Jesus said to John's followers, "Go tell John the things that you saw and heard here. Blind people are healed and can see. Crippled people are healed and can walk. People with leprosy* are healed. Deaf people are healed and can hear. Dead people are given life. And the Good News *about God's kingdom* is given to the poor people. ²³The person who can accept* me is blessed!"

²⁴When John's followers left, Jesus began to tell the people about John: "What did you people go out into the desert to see? A weed* blown by the wind? ²⁵What did you go out to see? A man dressed in fine clothes? No. Those people who have fine, nice clothes live in kings' houses. ²⁶Really, what did you go out to

---

coffin A wooden box in which dead bodies are placed to be buried.
Baptizer John is called the Baptizer because he had the work of baptizing people.
leprosy A very bad skin disease.
can accept Literally, "is not offended by."
weed Literally, "reed." It means that John is not weak like a reed blown by the wind.

see? A prophet*? Yes, and I tell you, John is more than a prophet. ²⁷This was written about John:

'Listen! I send my helper*
    ahead of you.
He will prepare the way for you.'   *Malachi 3:1*

²⁸I tell you, John is greater than any man ever born. But even the least important person in the kingdom of God is greater than John.''

²⁹(When the people heard this, they all agreed that God's teaching was good. Even the tax collectors* agreed. These were the people who were already baptized* by John. ³⁰But the Pharisees* and teachers of the law refused to accept God's plan for themselves; they did not let John baptize them.)

³¹*Then Jesus said,* "What shall I say about the people of this time? What can I compare them to? What are they like? ³²The people of this time are like children sitting in the market place. One group of children calls to the other children and says,

'We played music for you, but you did not dance.
    We sang a sad song, but you did not cry.'

³³John the Baptizer* came and did not eat *like other people* or drink wine. And you say, 'He has a demon* inside him.' ³⁴The Son of Man* came eating *like other people* and drinking wine. And you say, 'Look at him! He eats too much and drinks too much wine! He is a friend of the tax collectors* and other bad people!' ³⁵But wisdom is shown to be right by the things it does.''

Simon the Pharisee

³⁶One of the Pharisees* asked Jesus to eat with him. Jesus went into the Pharisee's house and sat at the table. ³⁷At that time there

prophet   Person who spoke for God. He often told things that would happen in the future.
helper   Literally, ''messenger,'' a person who is sent with news to tell other people.
tax collectors   Jews hired by the Romans to collect taxes. They often cheated their people.
baptized   A Greek word meaning to immerse, dip, or bury a person or thing briefly under water.
Pharisees   Pharisees were a Jewish religious group that followed all the Old Testament and other Jewish laws and customs very carefully.
Baptizer   John is called the Baptizer because he had the work of baptizing people.
demon   Demons are evil spirits from the devil.
Son of Man   Jesus. Jesus was God's Son, but this name showed that Jesus was a man, too. In Daniel 7:13-14, this is the name for the Messiah (Christ).

was a sinful woman in the town. She knew that Jesus was eating at the Pharisee's* house. So the woman brought some perfume. ³⁸She stood at Jesus' feet, crying. Then she began to wash his feet with her tears. She dried Jesus' feet with her hair. She kissed his feet many times and rubbed them with perfume. ³⁹The Pharisee who asked Jesus to come to his house saw this. He thought to himself, "If Jesus were a prophet,* he would know that the woman who is touching him is a sinner!"

⁴⁰Jesus said to the Pharisee,* "Simon, I have something to say to you."

Simon said, "Teacher, you can speak. *I am listening.*"

⁴¹Jesus said, "There were two men. Both men owed money to the same banker. One man owed the banker 500 silver coins.* The other man owed the banker 50 silver coins. ⁴²The men had no money, so they could not pay their debt. But the banker told the men that they did not have to pay him. Which one of those two men will love the banker more?"

⁴³Simon, *the Pharisee*, answered, "I think it would be the one who owed him the most money."

Jesus said to Simon, "You are right." ⁴⁴Then Jesus turned to the woman and said to Simon, "Do you see this woman? When I came into your house, you gave me no water for my feet. But she washed my feet with her tears and dried my feet with her hair. ⁴⁵You did not kiss me, but she has been kissing my feet since I came in! ⁴⁶You did not rub my head with oil, but she rubbed my feet with perfume. ⁴⁷I tell you that her many sins are forgiven. This is clear, because she showed great love. But the person who feels only a little need to be forgiven will feel only a little love when he is forgiven."

⁴⁸Then Jesus said to her, "Your sins are forgiven."

⁴⁹The people sitting at the table began to think to themselves, "Who does this man (*Jesus*) think he is? How can he forgive sins?"

⁵⁰Jesus said to the woman, "Because you believed, you are saved *from your sins*. Go in peace."

Pharisee Pharisees were a Jewish religious group that followed all of the Old Testament and other Jewish laws and customs very carefully.
prophet Person who spoke for God. He often told things that would happen in the future.
silver coins One coin, a denarius, was the average pay for one day's work.

The Group with Jesus

8 The next day, Jesus traveled through some cities and small
towns. Jesus preached and told the Good News about God's
kingdom. The twelve apostles* were with him. ²There were also
some women with him. Jesus had healed these women of
sicknesses and evil spirits *from the devil*. One of the women was
named Mary. She was from a town called Magdala. Seven
demons had come out of her. ³Also with these women were:
Joanna, the wife of Chuza (Herod's* helper), Suzanna, and
many other women. These women used their own money to help
Jesus and his apostles.*

Jesus Uses a Story About a Farmer Planting Seed

⁴Many people came together. People came to Jesus from every
town. Jesus told the people this story:
⁵"A farmer went out to plant his seed. While the farmer was
planting, some seed fell beside the road. People walked on the
seed, and the birds ate all this seed. ⁶Some seed fell on rock. This
seed began to grow, but then died because the seed had no water.
⁷Some seed fell among thorny weeds. This seed grew, but later the
weeds stopped the good plants from growing. ⁸And some seed fell
on good ground. This seed grew and made 100 times more
grain."
Jesus finished the story. Then Jesus said, "You people who
hear me, listen!"
⁹Jesus' followers asked him, "What does this story mean?"
¹⁰Jesus said, "You have been chosen to know the secrets of the
kingdom of God. But I use stories to speak to other people. I do
this so that:

'They look, but don't see;
and they listen, but they
don't understand.'

Isaiah 6:9

¹¹"This is what the story means: The seed is God's teaching.
¹²What is the seed that fell beside the path? That is like the people

---

apostles   The men Jesus taught and chose to be his special helpers.
Herod   Herod Antipas, son of Herod the Great, tetrarch (ruler) of Galilee and Perea.

who hear God's teaching, but then the devil comes and takes the teaching away from their hearts. So those people cannot believe the teaching and be saved. [13]What is the seed that fell on rock? That is like the people who hear God's teaching and accept it gladly. But these people don't have deep roots. They believe for a while. But then trouble comes. They stop believing and turn away from God. [14]What is the seed that fell among the thorny weeds? That is like the people who hear God's teaching, but they let the worries, riches, and pleasures of this life stop them from growing. So they never make good fruit. [15]And what is the seed that fell on the good ground? That is like the people who hear God's teaching with a good, honest heart. They obey God's teaching and patiently make good fruit.''

Use the Truth You Have

[16]"No person lights a lamp and then covers it with a bowl or hides it under a bed. Instead, that person puts the lamp on a lamp table so that the people who come in will have enough light to see. [17]Everything that is hidden will become clear. Every secret thing will be made known. [18]So be careful how you listen. The person who has something will be given more. But to the person who has nothing, this will happen: Even what he thinks he has will be taken away from him.''

Jesus' Followers Are His True Family

[19]Jesus' mother and brothers came to visit him. There were so many people that Jesus' mother and brothers could not get close to him. [20]Someone said to Jesus, "Your mother and your brothers are standing outside. They want to see you.''

[21]Jesus answered them, "My mother and my brothers are those people who listen to God's teaching and obey it!''

The Followers See Jesus' Power

[22]One day Jesus and his followers got into a boat. Jesus said to them, "Come with me across the lake.'' And so they started across. [23]While they were sailing, Jesus slept. A big storm blew

down on the lake. The boat began to fill with water. They were in danger. ²⁴The followers went to Jesus and woke him. They said, "Master! Master! We will drown!"

Jesus got up. He gave a command to the wind and the waves. The wind stopped, and the lake became calm. ²⁵Jesus said to his followers, "Where is your faith?"

The followers were afraid and amazed. They said to each other, "What kind of man is this? He commands the wind and the water, and they obey him!"

A Man with Demons Inside Him

²⁶Jesus and his followers sailed across the lake from Galilee. They sailed to the area where the Gergesene people live. ²⁷When Jesus got out of the boat, a man from that town came to Jesus. This man had demons* inside him. For a long time he had worn no clothes. He lived in the caves where dead people are buried, not in a house. ²⁸⁻²⁹He had often been taken, put in jail, and tied with chains. But the man would always break the chains, and the demon inside him would force him to go out to the places where no people lived. Then Jesus commanded the evil spirit (*the demon*) to come out of this man. The man hurried to Jesus and shouted with a loud voice, "What do you want with me, Jesus, Son of the Most High God? Please, don't punish me!"

³⁰Jesus asked him, "What is your name?"

The man answered, "Legion."* (He said his name was "Legion" because many demons* had gone into him.) ³¹The demons begged Jesus not to send them into the eternal darkness.* ³²On that hill there was a big herd of pigs eating. The demons begged Jesus to allow them to go into the pigs. So Jesus allowed the demons to do this. ³³Then the demons came out of the man and went into the pigs. The herd of pigs ran down the hill and into the lake. All the pigs drowned.

³⁴The men who were caring for the pigs ran away. The men told the story in the fields and in the town. ³⁵People went out to see what happened. The people came to Jesus and found the man

demons Demons are evil spirits from the devil.
Legion Means very many. A legion was about 5,000 men in the Roman army.
eternal darkness Literally, "the abyss," something like a pit or hole that has no end.

sitting there at the feet of Jesus. The man had clothes on and his mind was right again; the demons* were gone. The people became afraid. ³⁶The men who saw these things happen told the other people all about how Jesus made the man well. ³⁷All the people asked Jesus to go away. The people were all very afraid. So Jesus got into the boat and went back to Galilee. ³⁸The man that Jesus healed begged to go with Jesus.

But Jesus sent the man away, saying, ³⁹"Go back home and tell people what God did for you."

So the man went all over town telling what Jesus had done for him.

Jesus Gives Life to a Dead Girl and Heals a Sick Woman

⁴⁰When Jesus went back to Galilee, the people welcomed him. Everyone was waiting for him. ⁴¹A man named Jairus came to Jesus. Jairus was a ruler of the synagogue.* Jairus bowed down at the feet of Jesus and begged him to come to his house. ⁴²Jairus had only one daughter. She was twelve years old, and she was dying.

While Jesus was going *to Jairus' house*, the people came all around him. ⁴³A woman was there who had been bleeding for twelve years. She had spent all her money on doctors, but no doctor was able to heal her. ⁴⁴The woman came behind Jesus and touched the bottom of his coat. At that moment, her bleeding stopped. ⁴⁵Then Jesus said, "Who touched me?"

All the people said they had not touched Jesus. Peter said, "Master, the people are all around you and are pushing against you."

⁴⁶But Jesus said, "Someone touched me! I felt power go out from me." ⁴⁷When the woman saw that she could not hide, she came forward, shaking. She bowed down before Jesus. While all the people listened, she told why she touched Jesus. Then she said that she was healed immediately when she touched him. ⁴⁸Jesus

---

demons Demons are evil spirits from the devil.
synagogue Synagogues were places where Jews gathered to read and study the Scriptures.

said to her, "My daughter, you are made well because you believed. Go in peace."

⁴⁹While Jesus was still speaking, a person came from the house of the synagogue* ruler (*Jairus*) and said, "Your daughter has died! Don't bother the teacher (*Jesus*) now."

⁵⁰Jesus heard this. He said to Jairus, "Don't be afraid! Just believe and your daughter will be well."

⁵¹Jesus went to the house. Jesus let only Peter, John, James, and the girl's father and mother go inside with him. Jesus did not let any other person go inside. ⁵²All the people were crying and feeling sad because the girl was dead. But Jesus said, "Don't cry. She is not dead; she is only sleeping."

⁵³The people laughed at Jesus, because they knew that the girl was dead. ⁵⁴But Jesus held her hand and called to her, "Little girl, stand up!" ⁵⁵Her spirit came back into her and she stood up immediately. Jesus said, "Give her something to eat." ⁵⁶The girl's parents were amazed. Jesus told them not to tell any person about what happened.

Jesus Sends the Twelve Apostles

9 Jesus called the twelve apostles* together. He gave the apostles power to heal sicknesses, and power over all demons.* ²Jesus sent the apostles to tell about God's kingdom and to heal the sick. ³He said to the apostles, "When you travel, don't take a walking stick. Also, don't carry a bag, food, or money. Take for your trip only the clothes you are wearing. ⁴When you go into a house, stay there until it is time to leave. ⁵If the people in the town will not welcome you, go outside the town and shake their dust off of your feet.* This will be a warning to them."

⁶So the apostles went out. They traveled through all the towns. They told the Good News* and healed people everywhere.

---

synagogue Synagogues were places where Jews gathered to read and study the Scriptures.
apostles The men Jesus taught and chose to be his special helpers.
demons Demons are evil spirits from the devil.
shake...feet A warning. It showed that they were finished talking to these people.
Good News The news that God has made a way through Christ for people to have their sins forgiven and live with God. When people accept this truth, God accepts them.

Herod Is Confused About Jesus

⁷Governor Herod* heard about all these things that were happening. He was confused because some people said, "John the Baptizer* is risen from death." ⁸Other people said, "Elijah* has come to us." And some other people said, "One of the prophets* from long ago has risen from death." ⁹Herod said, "I cut off John's head. So who is this man (*Jesus*) I hear these things about?" Herod continued trying to see Jesus.

Jesus Feeds More Than 5,000 People

¹⁰When the apostles* came back, they told Jesus the things they had done on their trip. Then Jesus took them away to a town called Bethsaida. There, Jesus and his apostles could be alone together. ¹¹But the people learned where Jesus went. They followed him. Jesus welcomed them and talked with them about God's kingdom. He healed the people that were sick.

¹²Late in the afternoon, the twelve apostles* came to Jesus and said, "No people live in this place. Send the people away. They need to find food and places to sleep in the farms and towns around here."

¹³But Jesus said to the apostles,* "You give them something to eat."

The apostles said, "We have only five loaves of bread and two fish. Do you want us to go buy some food for all these people?" ¹⁴(There were about 5,000 men there.)

Jesus said to his followers, "Tell the people to sit in groups of about 50 people."

¹⁵So the followers did this and all the people sat down. ¹⁶Then Jesus took the five loaves of bread and two fish. Jesus looked up into the sky and thanked God for the food. Then Jesus divided the food and gave it to the followers. Jesus told the followers to give the food to the people. ¹⁷All the people ate and were filled. And there was much food left. Twelve baskets were filled with the pieces of food that were not eaten.

Herod   Herod Antipas, son of Herod the Great, tetrarch (ruler) of Galilee and Perea.
Baptizer   John is called the Baptizer because he had the work of baptizing people.
Elijah   A man who spoke for God about 800 years before Christ.
prophets   People who spoke for God. Their writings are part of the Old Testament.
apostles   The men Jesus taught and chose to be his special helpers.

Jesus Is the Christ

¹⁸One time Jesus was praying alone. His followers came together there. Jesus asked them, "Who do the people say I am?"

¹⁹The followers answered, "Some people say you are John, the Baptizer.* Other people say you are Elijah.* And some people say you are one of the prophets* from long ago who has come back to life."

²⁰Then Jesus said to his followers, "And who do you say I am?"

Peter answered, "You are the Christ* from God."

²¹Jesus warned them not to tell this to anyone. Then Jesus said, ²²"The Son of Man* must suffer many things. He will be rejected by the older Jewish leaders, the leading priests, and teachers of the law. The Son of Man will be killed. But after three days he will be raised from death."

²³Jesus continued to say to all of them, "If any person wants to follow me, he must say 'No' to the things he wants. That person must accept the cross (*suffering*) that is given to him every day, and he must follow me. ²⁴The person who wants to save his life will lose it. And every person who gives his life for me will save it. ²⁵It is worth nothing for a person to have the whole world, if he himself is destroyed or lost. ²⁶If any person is ashamed of me and my teaching, then I* will be ashamed of that person. I will be ashamed of that person at the time I come with my glory and with the glory of the Father and the holy angels. ²⁷I tell you the truth. Some of you people standing here will see the kingdom of God before you die."

Moses, Elijah, and Jesus

²⁸About eight days after Jesus said these things, he took Peter, James, and John and went up on a mountain to pray. ²⁹While

---

Baptizer John is called the Baptizer because he had the work of baptizing people.
Elijah A man who spoke for God about 800 years before Christ.
prophets People who spoke for God. Their writings are part of the Old Testament.
Christ The "anointed one" (the Messiah) or chosen one of God.
Son of Man Jesus. Jesus was God's Son, but this name showed that Jesus was a man, too. In Daniel 7:13-14, this is the name for the Messiah (Christ).
I Literally, "the Son of Man" (Jesus).

Jesus was praying, his face began to change. His clothes became shining white. ³⁰Then two men were talking with Jesus. The men were Moses and Elijah.* ³¹Moses and Elijah were shining bright too. They were talking with Jesus about his death that would happen in Jerusalem. ³²Peter and the others were asleep. But they woke up and saw the glory of Jesus. They also saw the two men who were standing with Jesus. ³³When Moses and Elijah were leaving, Peter said, "Master, it is good that we are here. We will put three tents here—one for you, one for Moses, and one for Elijah." (Peter did not know what he was saying.)

³⁴While Peter was saying these things, a cloud came all around them. Peter, James, and John became afraid when the cloud covered them. ³⁵A voice came from the cloud. The voice said, "This is my Son. He is the One I have chosen. Obey him."

³⁶When the voice finished, only Jesus was there. Peter, James, and John said nothing. At that time they told no person about what they had seen.

Jesus Heals a Boy Who Has an Evil Spirit

³⁷The next day, Jesus, Peter, James, and John came down from the mountain. A large group of people met Jesus. ³⁸A man in the group shouted to Jesus, "Teacher, please come and look at my son. He is the only child I have. ³⁹An evil spirit *from the devil* comes into my son, and then he shouts. He loses control of himself and he foams from the mouth. The evil spirit continues to hurt him and almost never leaves him. ⁴⁰I begged your followers to make the evil spirit leave my son, but they could not do it."

⁴¹Jesus answered, "You people that live now have no faith. Your lives are all wrong. How long must I be with you and be patient with you?" Then Jesus said to the man, "Bring your son here."

⁴²While the boy was coming, the demon* threw the boy on the ground. The boy lost control of himself. But Jesus gave a strong command to the evil spirit. Then the boy was healed. And Jesus gave the boy back to his father. ⁴³All the people were amazed at the great power of God.

Moses and Elijah Two of the most important Jewish leaders in the past.
demon Demons are evil spirits from the devil.

LUKE 9

Jesus Talks About His Death

The people were still amazed about all the things Jesus did. Jesus said to his followers, 44"Remember these words: The Son of Man* will be given into the control of some men." 45But the followers did not understand what Jesus meant. The meaning was hidden from them so that they could not understand it. But the followers were afraid to ask Jesus about what he said.

The Most Important Person

46Jesus' followers began to have an argument about which one of them was the greatest (*most important*). 47Jesus knew what they were thinking. So Jesus took a little child and stood the child beside him. 48Then Jesus said to the followers, "If a person accepts a little child like this in my name, then that person accepts me. And when a person accepts me, that person accepts the One (*God*) who sent me. The person among you who is the most humble—that person is a great (*important*) person."

Any Person Not Against You Is for You

49John answered, "Master, we saw a person using your name to force demons* out of people. We told him to stop because he does not belong to our group."

50Jesus said to him, "Don't stop him, because if a person is not against you, then he is for you."

A Samaritan Town

51The time was coming near when Jesus would leave and go back to heaven. He traveled toward Jerusalem. 52Jesus sent some men ahead of him. The men went into a town in Samaria to make everything ready for Jesus. 53But the people there would not welcome Jesus because he was going toward Jerusalem. 54James and John, the followers of Jesus, saw this. They said, "Lord, do

Son of Man Jesus. Jesus was God's Son, but this name showed that Jesus was a man, too. In Daniel 7:13-14, this is the name for the Messiah (Christ).
demons Demons are evil spirits from the devil.

you want us to call fire down from heaven and destroy those people?" *

⁵⁵But Jesus turned and scolded them.* ⁵⁶Then Jesus and his followers went to another town.

Following Jesus

⁵⁷They were all traveling along the road. Someone said to Jesus, "I will follow you any place you go."

⁵⁸Jesus answered, "The foxes have holes to live in. The wild birds have nests to live in. But the Son of Man* has no place where he can rest his head." ⁵⁹Jesus said to another man, "Follow me!"

But the man said, "Lord, let me go and bury my father first."

⁶⁰But Jesus said to him, "Let the people that are dead bury their own dead! You must go and tell about the kingdom of God."

⁶¹Another man said, "I will follow you, Lord, but first let me go and say good-bye to my family."

⁶² Jesus said, "If any person begins to plow a field, but looks back, he is not prepared for the kingdom of God."

Jesus Sends the 72 Men

10 After this, the Lord (*Jesus*) chose 72* more men. Jesus sent the men out in groups of two. He sent them ahead of him into every town and place where he planned to go. ²Jesus said to them, "There are many, many people to harvest (*save*). But there are only a few workers to help harvest them. God owns the harvest (*people*). Pray to God that he will send more workers to help gather his harvest. ³You can go now. But listen! I am sending you, and you will be like sheep among wolves. ⁴Don't carry a purse, a bag, or shoes. Don't stop to talk with people on the road. ⁵Before you go into a house, say, 'Peace be with this home.' ⁶If a peaceful man lives there, your blessing of peace will stay with

---

Verse 54 Here, some Greek copies of Luke add: "...like Elijah did."
Verse 55 Here, some copies add: "And Jesus said, 'You don't know what kind of spirit you belong to. ⁵⁶The Son of Man did not come to destroy the souls of men but to save them.' "
Son of Man Jesus. Jesus was God's Son, but this name showed that Jesus was a man, too. In Daniel 7:13-14, this is the name for the Messiah (Christ).
72 Luke probably wrote 72, but many Greek copies of Luke say 70.

him. If the man is not peaceful, then your blessing of peace will come back to you. ⁷Stay in the peaceful house. Eat and drink what the people there give you. A worker should be given his pay. Don't leave that house to stay in another house. ⁸If you go into a town and the people welcome you, eat the food they give you. ⁹Heal the sick people that live there. Then tell them, 'The kingdom of God is soon coming to you!' ¹⁰But if you go into a town, and the people don't welcome you, then go out into the streets of that town and say, ¹¹'Even the dirt (*dust*) from your town that sticks to our feet we wipe off against you. But remember that the kingdom of God is coming soon.' ¹²I tell you, on the judgment day it will be worse for the people of that town than for the people of Sodom.*"

Jesus Warns People Who Don't Believe

¹³"It will be bad for you, Chorazin (*a city*)! It will be bad for you, Bethsaida (*a city*)! I did many miracles* in you. If those same miracles had happened in Tyre and Sidon,* then those people in Tyre and Sidon would have changed their lives and stopped sinning a long time ago. Those people would have worn sackcloth* and put ashes on themselves to show that they were sorry for their sins. ¹⁴But on the judgment day it will be worse for you than for Tyre and Sidon. ¹⁵And you, Capernaum (*a city*), will you be saved*? No! You will be thrown down to hell!

¹⁶"When a person listens to you, that person is really listening to me. But when a person refuses to accept you, that person is really refusing to accept me. And when a person refuses to accept me, he is refusing to accept the One (*God*) who sent me."

Satan Falls

¹⁷When the 72* men came back from their trip, they were very happy. They said, "Lord, even the demons* obeyed us when we

---

Sodom A town where very bad people lived. God punished them by destroying their city.
miracles Miracles are powerful works or great things done by the power of God.
Tyre and Sidon Towns where very bad people lived.
sackcloth A rough cloth of animal hair. People sometimes wore it to show sadness.
saved Literally, "lifted up to heaven."
72 Luke probably wrote 72, but many Greek copies of Luke say 70.
demons Demons are evil spirits from the devil.

used your name!'' [18]Jesus said to the men, "I saw Satan (*the devil*) falling like lightning from the sky. [19]Listen! I gave you power to walk on snakes and scorpions.* I gave you more power than the Enemy (*the devil*) has. Nothing will hurt you. [20]The spirits obey you. This is true. And be happy. Why? Not because you have this power, but be happy because your names are written in heaven.''

Jesus Prays to the Father

[21]Then the Holy Spirit* made Jesus feel very happy. Jesus said, "I thank you, Father, Lord of heaven and earth. I praise you because you have hidden these things from the wise and smart people. But you have shown these things to people who are like little children. Yes, Father, you did this because this is what you really wanted to do.

[22]"My Father has given me all things. No person knows who the Son is—only the Father knows. And only the Son knows who the Father is. The only people who will know about the Father are those people the Son chooses to tell.''

[23]Then Jesus turned to his followers. They were there alone with him. Jesus said, "You are blessed to see the things you now see! [24]I tell you, many prophets* and kings wanted to see the things that you now see. But they did not see these things. And many prophets and kings wanted to hear the things that you now hear. But they did not hear these things.''

Story About the Good Samaritan

[25]Then a teacher of the law stood up. He was trying to test Jesus. He said, "Teacher, what must I do to get life forever?''

[26]Jesus said to him, "What is written in the law? What do you read there?''

---

scorpions   A scorpion is an insect that stings with a bad poison.
Holy Spirit   Also called the Spirit of God, the Spirit of Christ, and the Comforter. He is joined with God and Christ. He does the work of God among people in the world.
prophets   People who spoke for God. Their writings are part of the Old Testament.

²⁷The man answered, "Love the Lord your God. You must love him with all your heart, all your soul, all your strength, and all your mind."* Also, "You must love other people the same as you love yourself."*

²⁸Jesus said to him, "Your answer is right. Do this and you will have life forever."

²⁹But the man wanted to show that the way he was living was right. So he said to Jesus, "But who are these other people I must love?"

³⁰To answer this question, Jesus said, "A man was going down the road from Jerusalem to Jericho. Some robbers surrounded him. They tore off his clothes and beat him. Then the robbers left the man lying there on the ground. He was almost dead. ³¹It happened that a Jewish priest was going down that road. When the priest saw the man, he did not stop to help him; he walked away. ³²Next, a Levite* came near. The Levite saw the hurt man, but he went around him. He would not stop to help him either; he just walked away. ³³Then a Samaritan* man traveled down that road. He came to the place where the hurt man was lying. The Samaritan saw the man. He felt very sorry for the hurt man. ³⁴The Samaritan went to him and poured olive oil and wine* on his wounds. Then he covered the man's wounds with cloth. The Samaritan had a donkey. He put the hurt man on his donkey. He took the hurt man to an inn.* At the inn, the Samaritan cared for him. ³⁵The next day, the Samaritan brought out two silver coins* and gave it to the man who worked at the inn. The Samaritan said, 'Take care of this hurt man. If you spend more money on him, I will pay it back to you when I come again.' "

³⁶Then Jesus said, "Which one of these three men (*the priest, the Levite, or the Samaritan*) do you think showed love to the man who was hurt by the robbers?"

"**You...mind**"   Quotation from Deuteronomy 6:5.
"**Love...yourself**"   Quotation from Leviticus 19:18.
Levite   Levites were men from the family group of Levi who helped the Jewish priests with their work in the temple. Read 1 Chronicles 23:24-32.
Samaritan   Samaritans were people from Samaria. These people were part Jew, but the Jews did not accept them as true Jews. Samaritans and Jews hated each other.
olive oil and wine   Oil and wine was used like medicine to soften and clean wounds.
inn   A place where travelers stay overnight, the same as a motel today.
silver coins   One coin, a denarius, was the average pay for one day's work.

[37]The teacher of the law answered, "The one who helped him."

Jesus said to him, "Then you go and do the same *for other people*!"

Mary and Martha

[38]While Jesus and his followers were traveling, Jesus went into a town. A woman named Martha let Jesus stay at her house. [39]Martha had a sister named Mary. Mary was sitting at Jesus' feet and listening to him teach. But her sister Martha was doing the housework. [40]Martha became angry because she had so much work to do. Martha went in and said, "Lord, don't you care that my sister has left me alone to do all the housework? Tell her to help me!"

[41]But the Lord answered her, "Martha, Martha, you are getting worried and upset about too many things. [42]Only one thing is important. Mary has made the right choice; and it will never be taken away from her."

Jesus Teaches About Prayer

11 One time Jesus was praying in a place. When Jesus finished praying, one of his followers said to him, "John taught his followers how to pray. Lord, please teach us how to pray too."

[2]Jesus said to them, "When you pray, pray like this:

'Father, we pray that your name will always be kept holy.
We pray that your kingdom will come.
[3] Give us the food we need for each day.
[4] Forgive us the sins we have done,
     because we forgive every person
          who has done wrong to us.
And don't cause us to be tempted (*tested*).' "

Continue to Ask

[5-6]Then Jesus said to them, "Suppose one of you went to your friend's house very late at night and said to him, 'A friend of mine has come into town to visit me. But I have nothing for him to eat. Please give me three loaves of bread.' [7]Your friend inside

the house answers, 'Go away! Don't bother me! The door is already locked. My children and I are in bed. I cannot get up and give you the bread now.' ⁸I tell you, maybe friendship is not enough to make him get up to give you the bread. But he will surely get up to give you what you need if you continue to ask. ⁹So I tell you, continue to ask, and God will give to you. Continue to search, and you will find. Continue to knock, and the door will open for you. ¹⁰Yes, if a person continues asking, that person will receive. If a person continues looking, that person will find. And if a person continues knocking, the door will open for that person. ¹¹Does any of you have a son? What would you do if your son asked you for a fish? Would any father give his son a snake? No! You would give him a fish. ¹²Or, if your son asks for an egg, would you give him a scorpion*? No! ¹³*You are like all other people*—you are evil. But you know how to give good gifts to your children. So surely your heavenly Father knows how to give the Holy Spirit* to those people who ask him.''

Jesus' Power Is from God

¹⁴One time Jesus was sending a demon* out of a man who could not talk. When the demon came out, the man was able to speak. The people were amazed. ¹⁵But some of the people said, ''Jesus uses the power of Beelzebul (*the devil*) to force demons* out of people. Beelzebul is the ruler of demons.''

¹⁶Other people wanted to test Jesus. They asked Jesus to show them a sign (*proof*) from heaven. ¹⁷But Jesus knew the things they were thinking. So Jesus said to the people, ''Every kingdom that is divided and fights against itself will be destroyed. And a family that fights against itself will break apart. ¹⁸So if Satan (*the devil*) is fighting against himself, then how will his kingdom continue? You say that I use the power of Beelzebul (*the devil*) to force out demons*. ¹⁹But if I use the power of Beelzebul to force out demons, then what power do your people use when they force out demons? So your own people prove that you are wrong. ²⁰But I

---

scorpion A scorpion is an insect that stings with a bad poison.
Holy Spirit Also called the Spirit of God, the Spirit of Christ, and the Comforter. He is joined with God and Christ. He does the work of God among people in the world.
demon(s) Demons are evil spirits from the devil.

use the power of God to force out demons. This shows that the kingdom of God has come to you!

²¹"When a strong man with many weapons guards his own house, then the things in his house are safe. ²²But suppose a stronger man comes and defeats him. The stronger man will take away the weapons that the first man trusted to keep his house safe. Then the stronger man will do what he wants with the other man's things.

²³"If a person is not with me, he is against me. The person who does not work with me is working against me."

The Empty Man

²⁴"When an evil spirit *from the devil* comes out of a person, that spirit travels through dry places, looking for a place to rest. But that spirit finds no place to rest. So the spirit says, 'I will go back to the home (*person*) I left.' ²⁵When the spirit comes back to that person, the spirit finds that home (*person*) swept clean and made neat. ²⁶Then the evil spirit goes out and brings seven other spirits more evil than itself. Then all the evil spirits go into that person and live there. And that person has even more trouble than he had before."

The People Who Are Truly Happy

²⁷When Jesus said these things, a woman with the people there began to speak. She said to Jesus, "Your mother is blessed (*happy*), because she gave birth to you and fed you."

²⁸But Jesus said, "The people who hear the teaching of God and obey it—they are the people who are truly happy!"

Give Us Proof!

²⁹The group of people grew larger and larger. Jesus said, "The people that live today are evil. They ask for a miracle* as a sign (*proof*) from God. But no miracle will be given as a sign to them. The only sign will be the sign of Jonah.* ³⁰Jonah was a sign for

---

miracle Miracles are powerful works or great things done by the power of God.
sign of Jonah Jonah's three days in the big fish are like Jesus' three days in the grave.

those people who lived in Nineveh. It is the same with the Son of Man.* The Son of Man will be a sign for the people of this time. ³¹On the judgment day the Queen of the South* will stand up with the men that live now and she will show that they are wrong (*guilty*). Why? Because that queen came from far, far away to listen to Solomon's wise teaching. And I tell you that I am greater than Solomon! ³²On the judgment day the men of Nineveh will stand up with the people that live now, and they will show that you are wrong (*guilty*). Why? Because when Jonah preached to those people, they changed their hearts and lives. And I tell you that I am greater than Jonah!''

Be a Light for the World

³³''No person takes a light and puts it under a bowl or hides it. Instead, a person puts the light on a lamp table so that the people who come in can see. ³⁴Your eye is a light for the body. If your eyes are good, then your whole body will be full of light. But if your eyes are evil, then your whole body will be full of darkness (*sin*). ³⁵So be careful! Don't let the light in you become dark. ³⁶If your whole body is bright, and none of it is dark, then you will shine bright like lightning.''

Jesus Criticizes the Pharisees

³⁷While Jesus spoke, a Pharisee* asked Jesus to eat with him. So Jesus came and sat at the table. ³⁸But the Pharisee was surprised when he saw that Jesus did not wash *his hands** first before the meal. ³⁹The Lord (*Jesus*) said to him, ''You Pharisees clean the outside of the cup and the dish. But inside you are full of things you got by cheating other people and being evil. ⁴⁰You are foolish! The same One (*God*) who made what is outside also made what is inside. ⁴¹So give the things in your cups and dishes to the people who need it. Then you will be fully clean. ⁴²But it will be bad for you Pharisees! You give God one-tenth of

Son of Man   Jesus. Jesus was God's Son, but this name showed that Jesus was a man, too. In Daniel 7:13-14, this is the name for the Messiah (Christ).

Queen of the South   The Queen of Sheba. She traveled 1000 miles to learn God's wisdom from Solomon. Read 1 Kings 10:1-13.

Pharisee   Pharisees were a Jewish religious group that followed all of the Old Testament and other Jewish laws and customs very carefully.

wash his hands   Jewish religious custom that the Pharisees thought was very important.

everything you own—even your mint, your rue, and every other little plant in your garden. But you forget to be fair to other people and to love God. These are the things you should do. And you should also continue to do those other things—*like giving* one-tenth. ⁴³It will be bad for you Pharisees,* because you love to get the most important seats in the synagogues.* And you love for people to show respect to you in the market places. ⁴⁴It will be bad for you, because you are like hidden graves. People walk on them without knowing it.''

Jesus Talks to the Jewish Teachers

⁴⁵One of the teachers of the law said to Jesus, "Teacher, when you say these things *about the Pharisees,* you are criticizing our group too."

⁴⁶Jesus answered, "It will be bad for you, you teachers of the law! You make strict rules that are very hard for people to obey.* You try to force other people to obey those rules. But you yourselves don't even try to follow any of those rules. ⁴⁷It will be bad for you, because you build tombs* for the prophets.* But these are the same prophets that your fathers (*ancestors*) killed! ⁴⁸And now you show all people that you agree with what your fathers did. They killed the prophets, and you build tombs for the prophets! ⁴⁹This is why the Wisdom of God said, 'I will send prophets and apostles* to them. Some of my prophets and apostles will be killed by evil men. Others will be treated badly.' ⁵⁰So you people that live now will be punished for the deaths of all the prophets who were killed since the beginning of the world. ⁵¹You will be punished for the killing of Abel.* And you will be punished for the killing of Zechariah.* Zechariah was killed between the altar* and the temple.* Yes, I tell you that you people who live now will be punished for them all.

Pharisees   Pharisees were a Jewish religious group that followed all the Old Testament and other Jewish laws and customs very carefully.
synagogues   Synagogues were buildings where Jews gathered to read and study the Scriptures.
You make...obey   Literally, "You put heavy burdens on people that are hard for them to carry."
tombs   Small buildings made to show respect for important persons who had died.
prophets   People who spoke for God. Their writings are part of the Old Testament.
apostles   The men Jesus taught and chose to be his special helpers.
Abel...Zechariah   In the Hebrew Old Testament, the first and last men to be murdered.
altar...temple   This altar was the place where sacrifices were offered to God outside the temple, the building in Jerusalem where God commanded the Jews to worship him.

⁵²"It will be bad for you, you teachers of the law. You have hidden the key to learning about God. You yourselves would not learn, and you stopped others from learning too."

⁵³When Jesus was leaving, the teachers of the law and the Pharisees* began to give him much trouble. They tried to make Jesus answer questions about many things. ⁵⁴They were trying to find a way to catch Jesus saying something wrong.

Don't Be Like the Pharisees

12 Many thousands of people came together. There were so many people that they were stepping on each other. Before Jesus spoke to the people, he said to his followers, "Be careful of the yeast (*bad influence*) of the Pharisees.* I mean that they are hypocrites.* ²Everything that is hidden will be shown. Everything that is secret will be made known. ³The things you say in the dark (*secretly*) will be told in the light (*openly*). The things you whisper in a secret room will be shouted from the top of the house."

Fear Only God

⁴Then Jesus said to the people, "I tell you, my friends, don't be afraid of people. People can kill the body, but after that they can do nothing more to hurt you. ⁵I will show you the One to fear. You should fear him (*God*) who has the power to kill you and also to throw you into hell. Yes, he is the One you should fear.

⁶"When birds are sold, five small birds cost only two pennies. But God does not forget any of them. ⁷Yes, God even knows how many hairs you have on your head. Don't be afraid. You are worth much more than many birds."

Don't Be Ashamed of Jesus

⁸"I tell you, if any person stands before other people and says that he believes in me, then I* will say that person belongs to me.

Pharisees Pharisees were a Jewish religious group that followed all the Old Testament and other Jewish laws and customs very carefully.

hypocrites People who act like they are good but are not.

I Literally, "the Son of Man" (Jesus).

I will say this before the angels of God. ⁹But if any person stands before people and says he does not believe in me, then I* will say that person does not belong to me. I will say this before the angels of God.

¹⁰"If a person says something against the Son of Man,* he can be forgiven. But a person who says bad things against (*refuses to accept*) the Holy Spirit* will not be forgiven.

¹¹"When men bring you into the synagogues* before the leaders and other important men, don't worry about how you will answer their questions. Don't worry about what you will say. ¹²At that time the Holy Spirit* will teach you what you must say."

Jesus Warns Against Selfishness

¹³One of the men in the crowd said to Jesus, "Teacher, *our father just died*. Tell my brother to share with me the things our father owned."

¹⁴But Jesus said to him, "Who said that I should be your judge or decide how to divide your father's things between you two?" ¹⁵Then Jesus said to them, "Be careful and guard against all kinds of selfishness. A person's life is not measured by the many things he owns."

¹⁶Then Jesus used this story: "There was a rich man who had some land. His land grew a very good crop of food. ¹⁷The rich man thought to himself, 'What will I do? I have no place to keep all my crops.' ¹⁸Then the rich man said, 'I know what I will do. I will tear down my barns and build bigger barns! I will put all my wheat and good things together in my new barns. ¹⁹Then I can say to myself, I have many good things stored. I have saved enough for many years. Rest, eat, drink, and enjoy life!' ²⁰But God said to that man, 'Foolish man! Tonight you will die. So what about the things you prepared for yourself? Who will get those things now?'

²¹"This is how it will be for the person who saves things only for himself. To God that person is not rich."

I Literally, "the Son of Man" (Jesus).
Son of Man Jesus. Jesus was God's Son, but this name showed that Jesus was a man, too. In Daniel 7:13-14, this is the name for the Messiah (Christ).
Holy Spirit Also called the Spirit of God, the Spirit of Christ, and the Comforter. He is joined with God and Christ. He does the work of God among people in the world.
synagogues Synagogues were buildings where Jews gathered to read and study the Scriptures.

LUKE 12

Putting God's Kingdom First

²²Jesus said to his followers, "So I tell you, don't worry about the food you need to live. Don't worry about the clothes you need for your body. ²³Life is more important than food. And the body is more important than clothes. ²⁴Look at the birds. They don't plant or harvest. Birds don't save food in houses or barns. But God takes care of them. And you are worth much more than birds. ²⁵None of you can add any time to your life by worrying about it. ²⁶If you cannot do the little things, then why worry about the big things? ²⁷Look at the wild flowers. See how they grow. They don't work or make clothes for themselves. But I tell you that even Solomon, the great and rich king, was not dressed as beautifully as one of these flowers. ²⁸God clothes the grass in the field like that. That grass is living today, but tomorrow it will be thrown into the fire to be burned. So you know that God will clothe you much more. Don't have so little faith! ²⁹So don't always think about what you will eat or what you will drink. Don't worry about it. ³⁰All the people in the world try to get those things. Your Father (*God*) knows that you need those things. ³¹The thing you should want is God's kingdom. Then all these other things you need will be given to you."

Don't Trust in Money

³²"Don't fear, little flock (*group*). Your Father (*God*) wants to give you the kingdom. ³³Sell the things you have and give that money to people who need it. The riches of this world don't continue. So get the kind of riches that continue. Get the treasure of heaven. That treasure continues forever. Thieves can't steal your treasure in heaven, and moths can't destroy it. ³⁴Your heart will be where your treasure is."

Always Be Ready

³⁵"Be ready! Be fully dressed and have your lights shining. ³⁶Be like servants who are waiting for their master to come home from a wedding party. The master comes and knocks. The servants open the door for the master. ³⁷Those servants will be blessed when their master comes home, because he sees that his servants

194

are ready and waiting for him. I tell you the truth. The master will dress himself for work and tell the servants to sit at the table. Then the master will serve them. ³⁸Those servants might have to wait until midnight or later for their master. But they will be happy when their master comes in and finds them still waiting. ³⁹Remember this: If the owner of the house knew what time a thief was coming, then the owner would not allow the thief to enter his house. ⁴⁰So you also must be ready! The Son of Man* will come at a time when you don't expect him!''

Who Is the Trusted Servant?

⁴¹Peter said, ''Lord, did you tell this story for us or for all people?''

⁴²The Lord said, ''Who is the wise and trusted servant? The master trusts one servant to give the other servants their food at the right time. Who is the servant that the master trusts to do that work? ⁴³When the master comes and finds that servant doing the work he gave him, that servant will be very happy. ⁴⁴I tell you the truth. The master will choose that servant to take care of everything the master owns. ⁴⁵But what will happen if that servant is evil and thinks that his master will not come back soon? That servant will begin to beat the other servants, men and women. He will eat and drink and get drunk. ⁴⁶Then the master of that servant will come when that servant is not ready. It will be a time when that servant is not expecting the master. Then the master will punish that servant. The master will send him away to be with the other people who don't obey.

⁴⁷''That servant knew what his master wanted him to do. But that servant did not make himself ready or try to do what his master wanted. So that servant will be punished very much! ⁴⁸But what about the servant who does not know what his master wants? The servant does things that deserve punishment. But he will get less punishment than the servant who knew what he should do. Any person who has been given much will be responsible for much. Much more will be expected from the person who has been given more.''

Son of Man Jesus. Jesus was God's Son, but this name showed that Jesus was a man, too. In Daniel 7:13-14, this is the name for the Messiah (Christ).

People Will Not Agree About Jesus

⁴⁹Jesus continued speaking, "I came to bring fire to the world. I wish it were already burning! ⁵⁰I must be baptized with a *different kind of* baptism.* I feel very troubled until it is finished. ⁵¹Do you think that I came to give peace to the world? No! I came to divide the world! ⁵²From now on, a family with five people will be divided, three against two, and two against three.

⁵³A father and son will be divided:
The son will be against his father.
The father will be against his son.
A mother and her daughter will be divided:
The daughter will be against her mother.
The mother will be against her daughter.
A mother-in-law and her daughter-in-law will be divided:
The daughter-in-law will be against her mother-in-law.
The mother-in-law will be against her daughter-in-law."

Understanding the Times

⁵⁴Then Jesus said to the people, "When you see clouds growing bigger in the west, you say, 'A rainstorm is coming.' And soon it begins to rain. ⁵⁵When you feel the wind begin to blow from the south, you say, 'It will be a hot day.' And you are right. ⁵⁶Hypocrites*! You can understand the weather. Why don't you understand what is happening now?"

Settle Your Problems

⁵⁷"Why can't you decide for yourselves what is right? ⁵⁸When a person is suing you, and you are going with him to court, try hard to settle it on the way. If you don't settle it, he may take you to the judge. The judge will throw you into jail. ⁵⁹You will not get out of there until they have taken everything you have."

---

baptized...baptism Has a special meaning here—being "baptized" or "buried" in troubles.
hypocrites People who act like they are good but are not.

Change Your Hearts

13 At that time some people were there with Jesus. These people told Jesus about what happened to some people from Galilee. Pilate* killed those people while they were worshiping. Pilate mixed their blood with the blood of the animals they were sacrificing* *to God.* ²Jesus answered, "Do you think this happened to those people because they were more sinful than all other people from Galilee? ³No, they were not! But if all of you don't change your hearts and lives, then you will be destroyed like those people were! ⁴What about those 18 people who died when the tower of Siloam fell on them? Do you think those people were more sinful than all the people who live in Jerusalem? ⁵They were not! But I tell you if you don't change your hearts and lives, then you will all be destroyed too!"

The Useless Tree

⁶Jesus told this story: "A man had a fig tree. He planted the tree in his garden. The man came looking for some fruit on the tree, but he found none. ⁷The man had a servant who took care of his garden. So the man said to his servant, 'I have been looking for fruit on this tree for three years, but I never find any. Cut it down! Why should it waste the ground?' ⁸But the servant answered, 'Master, let the tree have one more year to make fruit. Let me dig up the dirt around it and put on some plant food. ⁹Maybe the tree will make fruit next year. If the tree still doesn't make fruit, then you can cut it down.' "

Jesus Heals a Woman on the Sabbath Day

¹⁰Jesus taught in one of the synagogues* on the Sabbath day.* ¹¹In that synagogue there was a woman who had a spirit *from the devil* inside her. This spirit had made the woman crippled for 18 years. Her back was always bent; she could not stand up straight.

Pilate   Pontius Pilate was the Roman governor of Judea from 26 A.D. to 36 A.D.
sacrificing   To offer a gift or kill an animal as an offering to God.
synagogues   Synagogues were buildings where Jews gathered to read and study the Scriptures.
Sabbath day   Seventh day of the Jewish week. It was a special religious day for the Jews.

¹²When Jesus saw her, he called to her, "Woman, your sickness has gone away from you!" ¹³Jesus put his hands on her. Then she was able to stand up straight. She praised God.

¹⁴The synagogue* leader was angry because Jesus healed on the Sabbath day.* The leader said to the people, "There are six days for work. So come to be healed on one of those days. Don't come for healing on the Sabbath day."

¹⁵The Lord (*Jesus*) answered, "You people are hypocrites*! All of you untie your work animals and lead them to drink water every day—even on the Sabbath day*! ¹⁶This woman that I healed is our Jewish sister.* But Satan (*the devil*) has held her for 18 years. Surely it is not wrong for her to be made free from her sickness on a Sabbath day!" ¹⁷When Jesus said this, all the men that were criticizing him felt ashamed of themselves. And all the people were happy. They thanked God for the wonderful things Jesus was doing.

What Is God's Kingdom Like?

¹⁸Then Jesus said, "What is God's kingdom like? What can I compare it with? ¹⁹God's kingdom is like the seed of the mustard plant.* A person plants this seed in his garden. The seed grows and becomes a tree. The wild birds build nests on its branches."

²⁰Jesus said again, "What can I compare God's kingdom with? ²¹It is like yeast* that a woman mixes into a big bowl of flour to make bread. The yeast makes all the dough (*bread*) rise."

The Narrow Door

²²Jesus was teaching in every town and village. He continued to travel toward Jerusalem. ²³Someone said to Jesus, "Lord, how many people will be saved? Only a few?"

Jesus said, ²⁴"Try hard to enter through the narrow door *that opens the way to heaven*! Many people will try to enter there, but

---

synagogue Synagogues were places where Jews gathered to read and study the Scriptures.
Sabbath day Seventh day of the Jewish week. It was a special religious day for the Jews.
hypocrites People who act like they are good but are not.
Jewish sister Literally, "daughter of Abraham."
mustard plant The seed is very, very small, but the plant grows taller than a man.
yeast Used here as a symbol of good influence.

they will not be able to enter. ²⁵If a man locks the door of his house, then you can stand outside and knock on the door, but he won't open it. You can say, 'Sir, open the door for us!' But the man will answer, 'I don't know you! Where did you come from?' ²⁶Then you will say, 'We ate and drank with you. You taught in the streets of our town.' ²⁷Then he will say to you, 'I don't know you! Where did you come from? Go away from me! You are all people who do wrong!' ²⁸You will see Abraham, Isaac, Jacob,* and all the prophets* in God's kingdom. But you will be left outside. Then you will scream with fear and anger. ²⁹People will come from the east, west, north, and south. They will sit down at the table in the kingdom of God. ³⁰People who have the lowest place in life now will have the highest place in God's kingdom. And people who have the highest place now will have the lowest place in God's kingdom.''

Jesus Will Die in Jerusalem

³¹At that time some Pharisees* came to Jesus and said, "Go away from here and hide! Herod* wants to kill you!"

³²Jesus said to them, "Go tell that fox* (*Herod*), 'Today and tomorrow I am forcing demons* out of people and finishing my work of healing. Then, the next day, the work will be finished.' ³³After that, I must go, because all prophets* should die in Jerusalem.

³⁴"O Jerusalem, Jerusalem! You kill the prophets. You kill with rocks those men that God has sent you. Many, many times I wanted to help your people. I wanted to gather your people together like a hen gathers her chicks under her wings. But you did not let me. ³⁵Now your home will be left completely empty. I tell you, you will not see me again until that time when you will say, 'Blessed is the One who comes in the name of the Lord (*God*).' ''

Abraham, Isaac, Jacob   Three of the most important leaders in the Old Testament.
prophets   People who spoke for God. Their writings are part of the Old Testament.
Pharisees   Pharisees were a Jewish religious group that followed all the Old Testament and other
   Jewish laws and customs very carefully.
Herod   Herod Antipas, son of Herod the Great, tetrarch (ruler) of Galilee and Perea.
fox   Jesus says Herod is like a fox because foxes are clever and sly.
demons   Demons are evil spirits from the devil.

Is It Right to Heal on the Sabbath Day?

14 On a Sabbath day,* Jesus went to the home of a leading Pharisee* to eat with him. The people there were all watching Jesus very closely. ²A man with a bad disease* was put before Jesus. ³Jesus said to the Pharisees and teachers of the law, "Is it right or wrong to heal on the Sabbath day?" ⁴But they would not answer his question. So Jesus took the man and healed him. Then Jesus sent the man away. ⁵Jesus said to the Pharisees and teachers of the law, "If your son or work animal falls into a well on the Sabbath day, you know you would pull him out quickly." ⁶The Pharisees and teachers of the law could say nothing against what Jesus said.

Don't Make Yourself Important

⁷Then Jesus noticed that some of the guests were choosing the best places to sit. So Jesus told this story: ⁸"When a person invites you to a wedding, don't sit in the most important seat. The person may have invited someone more important than you. ⁹And if you are sitting in the most important seat, then the person who invited you will come to you and say, 'Give this man your seat!' Then you will begin to move down to the last place. And you will be very embarrassed. ¹⁰So when a person invites you, go sit in the seat that is not important. Then the person who invited you will come to you and say, 'Friend, move up here to a more important seat!' Then all the other guests will respect you. ¹¹Every person who makes himself important will be made humble. But the person who makes himself humble will be made important."

You Will Be Rewarded

¹²Then Jesus said to the Pharisee* who had invited him, "When you give a lunch or a dinner, don't invite only your friends, brothers, relatives, and rich neighbors. At another time

---

Sabbath day Seventh day of the Jewish week. It was a special religious day for the Jews.
Pharisees Pharisees were a Jewish religious group that followed all the Old Testament and other Jewish laws and customs very carefully.
disease The man had dropsy, a sickness that causes the body to swell larger and larger.

they will invite you to eat with them. Then you will have your reward. ¹³Instead, when you give a feast, invite the poor people, the crippled, and the blind. ¹⁴Then you will be blessed, because these people cannot pay you back. They have nothing. But you will be rewarded at the time when good people rise from death.''

Story About a Big Dinner Party

¹⁵One of the men sitting at the table with Jesus heard these things. The man said to Jesus, ''The people who eat a meal in God's kingdom will be very happy!''

¹⁶Jesus said to him, ''A man gave a big dinner. The man invited many people. ¹⁷When it was time to eat, the man sent his servant to tell the guests, 'Come! The food is ready!' ¹⁸But all the guests said they could not come. Each man made an excuse. The first man said, 'I have just bought a field, so I must go look at it. Please excuse me.' ¹⁹Another man said, 'I have just bought five pairs of work animals; I must go and try them. Please excuse me.' ²⁰A third man said, 'I just got married; I can't come.' ²¹So the servant returned. He told his master what had happened. Then the master became angry and said, 'Hurry! Go into the streets and alleys of the town. Bring me the poor people, the crippled, and the blind.' ²²Later the servant said to him, 'Master, I did what you told me to do, but we still have places for more people.' ²³The master said to the servant, 'Go out to the highways and country roads. Tell the people there to come. I want my house to be full! ²⁴None of those people that I invited first will ever eat with me!' ''

You Must First Plan

²⁵Many people were traveling with Jesus. Jesus said to the people, ²⁶''If a person comes to me but loves his father, mother, wife, children, brothers, or sisters more than he loves me, then that person cannot be my follower. A person must love me more than he loves himself! ²⁷If a person will not carry the cross (*suffering*) that is given to him when he follows me, then that person cannot be my follower. ²⁸If you wanted to build a building, you would first sit down and decide how much it would cost. You must see if you have enough money to finish the job.

²⁹If you don't do that, you might begin the work, but you would not be able to finish. And if you could not finish it, then all the people watching would laugh at you. ³⁰They would say, 'This man began to build, but was not able to finish!'

³¹"If a king is going to fight against another king, first he will sit down and plan. If the king has only 10,000 men, he will plan to see if he is able to defeat the other king who has 20,000 men. ³²If he cannot defeat the other king, then he will send some men to speak to the other king and ask for peace. ³³In the same way, all of you *must first plan*. You must give everything you have to follow me. If you don't, you cannot be my follower!"

Don't Lose Your Influence

³⁴"Salt is a good thing. But if the salt loses its salty taste, then it is worth nothing. You cannot make it salty again. ³⁵You can't even use it for soil or for plant food. People throw it away.

"You people who hear me, listen!"

Joy in Heaven

15 Many tax collectors* and bad people came to listen to Jesus. ²Then the Pharisees* and the teachers of the law began to complain, "Look! This man (*Jesus*) welcomes bad people and even eats with them!"

³Then Jesus told them this story: ⁴"Suppose one of you has 100 sheep, but he loses one of them. Then he will leave the other 99 sheep alone and go out and look for the lost sheep. The man will continue to search for the lost sheep until he finds it. ⁵And when he finds the sheep, the man is very happy. The man carries the sheep ⁶to his home. He goes to his friends and neighbors and says to them, 'Be happy with me because I found my lost sheep!' ⁷In the same way, I tell you, there is much joy in heaven when one sinner changes his heart. There is more joy for that one sinner than there is for 99 good people who don't need to change their hearts.

tax collectors   Jews hired by the Romans to collect taxes. They often cheated their people.
Pharisees   Pharisees were a Jewish religious group that followed all the Old Testament and other Jewish laws and customs very carefully.

[8]"Suppose a woman has ten silver coins,* but she loses one of them. The woman will take a light and clean the house. She will look carefully for the coin until she finds it. [9]And when she finds the lost coin, she will call her friends and neighbors and say to them, 'Be happy with me because I have found the coin that I lost!' [10]In the same way, there is joy before the angels of God when one sinner changes his heart.''

The Son Who Left Home

[11]Then Jesus said, "A man had two sons. [12]The younger son said to his father, 'Give me my part of all the things we own!' So the father divided the wealth with his two sons. [13]Then the younger son gathered up all that he had and left. He traveled far away to another country. There the son wasted his money like a fool. [14]He spent everything that he had. Soon after that, the land became very dry, and there was no rain. There was not enough food to eat anywhere in that country. The son was hungry and needed money. [15]So he went and got a job with one of the people of that country. The man sent the son into the fields to feed pigs. [16]The son was so hungry that he wanted to eat the food that the pigs were eating. But no person gave him anything. [17]The boy realized that he had been very foolish. He thought, 'All of my father's servants have plenty of food. But I am here, almost dead because I have nothing to eat. [18]I will leave and go to my father. I will say to him: Father, I sinned against God and have done wrong to you. [19]I am not good enough to be called your son. But let me be like one of your servants.' [20]So the son left and went to his father.''

The Son Returns

"While the son was still a long way off, his father saw him coming. The father felt sorry for his son. So the father ran to him. He hugged and kissed his son. [21]The son said, 'Father, I sinned against God and have done wrong to you. I am not good enough to be called your son.' [22]But the father said to his

---

silver coins One coin, a denarius, was the average pay for one day's work.

servants, 'Hurry! Bring the best clothes and dress him. Also, put a ring on his finger and good shoes on his feet. ²³Bring our fat calf. We will kill it and have plenty to eat. Then we can have a party! ²⁴My son was dead, but now he is alive again! He was lost, but now he is found!' So they began to have a party.''

The Older Son Comes

²⁵''The older son was in the field. He came closer to the house. He heard the sound of music and dancing. ²⁶So the older son called to one of the servant boys and asked, 'What does all this mean?' ²⁷The servant said, 'Your brother has come back. Your father killed the fat calf to eat. Your father is happy because your brother came home safely!' ²⁸The older son was angry and would not go in to the party. So his father went out to ask him to come in. ²⁹The son said to his father, 'I have served you like a slave for many years! I have always obeyed your commands. But you never even killed a goat for me. You never gave a party for me and my friends. ³⁰But your other son has wasted all your money on prostitutes.* Then he comes home, and you kill the fat calf for him!' ³¹But the father said to him, 'Son, you are always with me. All that I have is yours too. ³²We must be happy and have a party, because your brother was dead, but now he is alive. He was lost, but now he is found.' ''

True Wealth

16 Jesus said to his followers, ''Once there was a rich man. This rich man hired a manager to take care of his business. Later, the rich man learned that his manager was cheating him. ²So he called the manager in and said to him, 'I have heard bad things about you. Give me a report of what you have done with my money. You can't be my manager now!' ³Later, the manager thought to himself, 'What will I do? My master is taking my job away from me! I am not strong enough to dig ditches. I am too proud to beg. ⁴I know what I will do! I will do something so that when I lose my job, other people will welcome me into their homes.' ⁵So the manager called in each

---

prostitutes   Women who are paid by men who use them for sexual sin.

person who owed the master some money. He said to the first man, 'How much do you owe my master?' ⁶The man answered, 'I owe him 8,000 pounds of olive oil.' The manager said to him, 'Here is your bill; sit down quickly and make the bill less. Write 4,000 pounds.' ⁷Then the manager said to another man, 'How much do you owe my master?' The man answered, 'I owe him 60,000 pounds of wheat.' Then the manager said to him, 'Here is your bill; you can make it less. Write 50,000 pounds.' ⁸Later, the master told the dishonest manager that he had done a smart thing. Yes, worldly people are smarter with their own people than spiritual people are.

⁹"I tell you, use the things you have here in this world to make friends *with God*. Then, when those things are gone, you will be welcomed in that home that continues forever. ¹⁰If a person can be trusted with small things, then he can also be trusted with big things. If a person is dishonest in little things, then he will be dishonest in big things too. ¹¹If you cannot be trusted with worldly riches, then you will not be trusted with the true (*heavenly*) riches. ¹²And if you cannot be trusted with the things that belong to someone else, then you will not be given things of your own.

¹³"No servant can serve two masters at the same time. The servant will hate one master and love the other. Or he will be loyal to one and not care about the other. You cannot serve God and money at the same time."

God's Law Cannot Be Changed

¹⁴The Pharisees* were listening to all these things. The Pharisees criticized Jesus because they all loved money. ¹⁵Jesus said to the Pharisees, "You make yourselves look good in front of people. But God knows what is really in your hearts. The things that are important to people are worthless to God.

¹⁶"God wanted the people to live by the law *of Moses* and the writings of the prophets.* But since the time John* *the Baptizer*

Pharisees Pharisees were a Jewish religious group that followed all the Old Testament and other Jewish laws and customs very carefully.
prophets People who spoke for God. Their writings are part of the Old Testament.
John John the Baptizer, who preached to people about Christ's coming (Matt. 3, Luke 3).

came, the Good News about the kingdom of God is being told. Many people are trying hard to get into the kingdom of God. [17]Even the smallest part of a letter in the law cannot be changed. It would be easier for heaven and earth to pass away.''

Divorce and Remarriage

[18]''If a man divorces his wife and marries another woman, he is guilty of the sin of adultery.* And the man who marries a divorced woman is also guilty of adultery.''

The Rich Man and Lazarus

[19]Jesus said, ''There was a rich man who always dressed in the finest clothes. He was so rich that he was able to feast and have a party every day. [20]There was also a very poor man named Lazarus. Lazarus' body was covered with sores. Lazarus was often put at the rich man's gate. [21]Lazarus wanted only to eat the small pieces of food that fell from the rich man's table. And the dogs came and licked his sores! [22]Later, Lazarus died. The angels took Lazarus and placed him in the arms of Abraham.* The rich man also died and was buried. [23]He was sent to Hades* and had much pain. The rich man saw Abraham far away with Lazarus in his arms. [24]He called, 'Father Abraham, have mercy on me! Send Lazarus to me so that he can dip his finger in water and cool my tongue. I am suffering in this fire!' [25]But Abraham said, 'My child, remember when you lived? You had all the good things in life. But Lazarus was poor; he had nothing. All the bad things happened to him. Now Lazarus is comforted here, and you are suffering. [26]Also, there is a big pit (*hole*) between you and us. No person can cross over to help you. And no person can leave there and come here.' [27]The rich man said, 'Then please send Lazarus to my father's house on earth! [28]I have five brothers. Lazarus could warn my brothers so that they will not come to this place of pain.' [29]But Abraham said, 'They have the law of Moses and the

---

adultery   Breaking a marriage promise by doing sexual sin.
Abraham   Most respected ancestor of the Jews. Every Jew hoped to see Abraham.
Hades   Here, Hades means a place where bad people go after they die.

writings of the prophets* to read; let them learn from that!' ³⁰But the rich man said, 'No, father Abraham! If someone came to them from the dead, they would believe and change their hearts and lives.' ³¹But Abraham said to him, 'No! If your brothers won't listen to Moses and the prophets, then they won't listen to someone who comes back from death.' ''

Sin and Forgiveness

17 Jesus said to his followers, "Things will surely happen that will make people sin. But it will be very bad for the person who makes this happen. ²It will be very bad for a person if he makes one of these weak persons sin. It would be better for him to drown with a big rock around his neck. ³So be careful!

"If your brother sins, tell him he is wrong. But if he is sorry *and stops sinning*, forgive him. ⁴If your brother does something wrong to you seven times in one day, but he says that he is sorry each time, then you should forgive him."

How Big Is Your Faith?

⁵The apostles* said to the Lord (*Jesus*), "Give us more faith!"

⁶The Lord said, "If your faith is as big as a mustard seed,* then you can say to this mulberry tree, 'Dig yourself up and plant yourself in the ocean!' And the tree will obey you."

Be Good Servants

⁷"Suppose one of you has a servant who has been working in the field. The servant has been plowing the ground or caring for the sheep. When the servant comes in from working in the field, what would you say to him? Would you say, 'Come in and sit down to eat'? ⁸No! You would say to your servant, 'Prepare something for me to eat. Then get dressed and serve me. When I finish eating and drinking, then you can eat.' ⁹The servant should not get any special thanks for doing his job. He is only doing

---

prophets People who spoke for God. Their writings are part of the Old Testament.
apostles The men Jesus taught and chose to be his special helpers.
mustard seed This seed is very, very small, but the plant grows taller than a man.

what his master told him to do. ¹⁰It is the same with you. When you do all the things you are told to do, you should say, 'We are not worthy of any special thanks. We have only done the work we should do.' "

Be Thankful

¹¹Jesus was traveling to Jerusalem. He went from Galilee to Samaria. ¹²He came into a small town. Ten men met him there. These men did not come close to Jesus, because they all had leprosy.* ¹³But the men yelled to Jesus, "Jesus! Master! Please help us!"

¹⁴When Jesus saw the men, he said, "Go and show yourselves to the priests.*"

While the ten men were going to the priests, they were healed. ¹⁵When one of the men saw that he was healed, he went back to Jesus. He thanked God with a loud voice. ¹⁶He bowed down at Jesus' feet. The man thanked Jesus. (This man was a Samaritan,* *not a Jew*.) ¹⁷Jesus answered, "Ten men were healed; where are the other nine? ¹⁸Is this Samaritan man the only one who came back to thank God?" ¹⁹Then Jesus said to him, "Stand up! You can go. You were healed because you believed."

God's Kingdom Is Inside You

²⁰Some of the Pharisees* asked Jesus, "When will the kingdom of God come?"

Jesus answered, "God's kingdom is coming, but not in a way that you will be able to see with your eyes. ²¹People will not say, 'Look, God's kingdom is here!' Or, 'There it is!' No, God's kingdom is inside you."

²²Then Jesus said to his followers, "The time will come when you will want very much to see one of the days of the Son of

---

leprosy   A very bad skin disease.
show...priests   The law of Moses said a priest must say when a Jew with leprosy was well.
Samaritan   Samaritans were people from Samaria. These people were part Jew, but the Jews did not accept them as true Jews. Samaritans and Jews hated each other.
Pharisees   Pharisees were a Jewish religious group that followed all the Old Testament and other Jewish laws and customs very carefully.

208

Man,* but you will not be able. ²³People will say to you, 'Look, there it is!' or, 'Look, here it is!' Stay where you are; don't go away and search.''

When Jesus Comes Again

²⁴"The Son of Man* will come again. On the day when he comes he will shine like lightning flashes across the sky. ²⁵But first, the Son of Man must suffer many things and be killed by the people of this time. ²⁶It will be the same when the Son of Man comes again as it was when Noah lived. ²⁷In the time of Noah, people were eating, drinking, and getting married even on the day when Noah entered the ark (*boat*). Then the flood came and killed all the people. ²⁸It will be the same as during the time of Lot when God destroyed Sodom.* Those people were eating, drinking, buying, selling, planting, and building houses for themselves. ²⁹The people were doing these things even on the day when Lot left town. Then fire rained down from the sky and killed them all. ³⁰This is exactly how it will be when the Son of Man comes again.

³¹"On that day, if a man is on his roof, he will not have time to go inside and get his things. If a man is in the field, he cannot go back home. ³²Remember what happened to Lot's wife*? ³³The person who tries to save his life will lose it. But the person who gives his life away will save it. ³⁴At the time when I come again, there may be two men sleeping in one room. One man will be taken and the other man will be left. ³⁵There may be two women working together. One woman will be taken and the other woman will be left.'' ³⁶*

³⁷The followers asked Jesus, ''Where will this be, Lord?''

Jesus answered, ''People can always find a dead body by looking for the vultures.*''

Son of Man Jesus. Jesus was God's Son, but this name showed that Jesus was a man, too. In Daniel 7:13-14, this is the name for the Messiah (Christ).
Sodom A town where very bad people lived. God punished them by destroying their city.
Lot's wife The story about what happened to Lot's wife is found in Genesis 19:15-17, 26.
Verse 36 A few Greek copies of Luke add verse 36: "Two men will be in the same field. One man will be taken, but the other man will be left behind."
vultures Birds that eat dead animals.

God Will Answer His People

18 Then Jesus taught the followers that they should always pray and never lose hope. Jesus used this story to teach them: ²"Once there was a judge in a town. He did not care about God. The judge also did not care what people thought about him. ³In that same town there was a woman. Her husband was dead. The woman came many times to this judge and said, 'There is a man who is doing bad things to me. Give me my rights!' ⁴But the judge did not want to help the woman. After a long time, the judge thought to himself, 'I don't care about God. And I don't care about what people think. ⁵But this woman is bothering me. If I give her what she wants, then she will leave me alone. But if I don't give her what she wants, she will bother me until I am sick!' "

⁶The Lord (*Jesus*) said, "Listen! *There is meaning* in what the bad judge said. ⁷God's people shout to him night and day. God will always give his people what is right. God will not be slow to answer his people. ⁸I tell you, God will help his people quickly! But when the Son of Man* comes again, will he find people on earth who believe in him?"

Being Right with God

⁹There were some people who thought that they were very good. These people acted like they were better than other people. Jesus told this story to teach them: ¹⁰"One time there was a Pharisee* and a tax collector.* One day they both went to the temple* to pray. ¹¹The Pharisee stood alone, away from the tax collector. When the Pharisee prayed, he said, 'O God, I thank you that I am not as bad as other people. I am not like men who steal, cheat, or do other bad things. I thank you that I am better than this tax collector. ¹²*I am good*; I fast* twice a week, and I give one-tenth of everything I earn!'

Son of Man   Jesus. Jesus was God's Son, but this name showed that Jesus was a man, too. In Daniel 7:13-14, this is the name for the Messiah (Christ).

Pharisee   Pharisees were a Jewish religious group that followed all of the Old Testament and other Jewish laws and customs very carefully.

tax collector   A Jew hired by the Romans to collect taxes. Tax collectors often cheated people.

temple   The special building in Jerusalem where God commanded the Jews to worship him.

fast   To fast is to live without food for a special time of prayer and worship to God.

[13] "The tax collector* stood alone too. But when he prayed, he would not even look up to heaven. The tax collector felt very humble before God. He said, 'O God, have mercy on me. I am a sinner!' [14]I tell you, when this man finished his prayer and went home, he was right with God. But the Pharisee,* who felt that he was better than other people, was not right with God. Every person who makes himself important will be made humble. But the person who makes himself humble will be made important.''

Who Will Enter God's Kingdom?

[15]Some people brought their small children to Jesus so that Jesus could touch them. But when the followers saw this, they told the people not to do this. [16]But Jesus called the little children to him and said to his followers, "Let the little children come to me. Don't stop them, because the kingdom of God belongs to people who are like these little children. [17]I tell you the truth. You must accept God's kingdom like a little child accepts things, or you will never enter it!''

A Rich Man Asks Jesus a Question

[18]A *Jewish* leader asked Jesus, "Good teacher, what must I do to get the life that continues forever?''

[19]Jesus said to him, "Why do you call me good? No person is good. Only God is good. [20]*But I will answer your question.* You know the commandments: You must not do the sin of adultery,* you must not kill people, you must not steal, you must not lie, you must respect *and obey* your father and mother. . . .''*

[21]But the leader said, "I have obeyed all these commands since I was a boy!''

[22]When Jesus heard this, he said to the leader, "But there is still one more thing you need to do. Sell everything you have and give the money to the poor people. You will have a reward in heaven. Then come and follow me!'' [23]But when the man heard this, he

---

tax collector   A Jew hired by the Romans to collect taxes. Tax collectors often cheated people.
Pharisee   Pharisees were a Jewish religious group that followed all of the Old Testament and other Jewish laws and customs very carefully.
adultery   Breaking a marriage promise by doing sexual sin.
'You...mother'   Quotation from Exodus 20:12-16, Deuteronomy 5:16-20.

was very sad. The man was very rich *and wanted to keep his money*.

²⁴When Jesus saw that the man was sad, he said, "It will be very hard for rich people to enter the kingdom of God! ²⁵It would be easier for a camel to go through the eye of a needle than for a rich person to enter the kingdom of God!"

Who Can Be Saved?

²⁶When the people heard this, they said, "Then who can be saved?"

²⁷Jesus answered, "God can do things that are not possible for people to do!"

²⁸Peter said, "Look, we left everything we had and followed you!"

²⁹Jesus said, "I tell you the truth. Every person who has left his home, wife, brothers, parents, or children for God's kingdom ³⁰will get much more than he left. That person will get many times more in this life. And after that person dies, he will live with God forever."

Jesus Will Rise from Death

³¹Then Jesus talked to the twelve apostles* alone. Jesus said to them, "Listen! We are going to Jerusalem. Everything that God told the prophets* to write about the Son of Man* will happen! ³²His people will turn against him and give him to the non-Jewish people.* They will laugh at him and spit on him. He will be insulted and embarrassed. ³³They will beat him with whips and then kill him! But on the third day after his death, he will rise to life again." ³⁴The apostles tried to understand this, but they could not; the meaning was hidden from them.

Jesus Heals a Blind Man

³⁵Jesus came near the city of Jericho. There was a blind man sitting beside the road. The blind man was begging people for

apostles   The men Jesus taught and chose to be his special helpers.
prophets   People who spoke for God. Their writings are part of the Old Testament.
Son of Man   Jesus. Jesus was God's Son, but this name showed that Jesus was a man, too. In Daniel 7:13-14, this is the name for the Messiah (Christ).
non-Jewish people   Literally, "the nations," meaning the Romans.

money. [36]When this man heard the people coming down the road, he asked, "What is happening?"

[37]The people told him, "Jesus, the one from Nazareth, is coming here."

[38]The blind man was excited and said, "Jesus, Son of David*! Please help me!"

[39]The people who were in front, leading the group, criticized the blind man. They told him not to speak. But the blind man shouted more and more, "Son of David, please help me!"

[40]Jesus stopped there and said, "Bring that blind man to me!" When the blind man came near, Jesus asked him, [41]"What do you want me to do for you?"

The blind man said, "Lord, I want to see again."

[42]Jesus said to him, "See! You are healed because you believed."

[43]Then the man was able to see. The man followed Jesus, thanking God. All the people who saw this praised God for what happened.

Zaccheus

19 Jesus was going through the city of Jericho. [2]In Jericho there was a man named Zaccheus. He was a wealthy, very important tax collector.* [3]He wanted to see who Jesus was. There were many other people who wanted to see Jesus too. Zaccheus was too short to see above the people. [4]So he ran to a place where he knew Jesus would come. Then Zaccheus climbed a sycamore tree so he could see Jesus. [5]When Jesus came to that place, Jesus looked up and saw Zaccheus in the tree. Jesus said to him, "Zaccheus, hurry! Come down! I must stay at your house today."

[6]Then Zaccheus came down quickly. He was happy to have Jesus in his house. [7]All the people saw this. They began to complain, "Look at the kind of man Jesus stays with. Zaccheus is a sinner!"

Son of David   Name for the Christ, who was from the family of David, king of Israel.
tax collector   A Jew hired by the Romans to collect taxes. Tax collectors often cheated people.

[8]Zacchaeus said to the Lord (*Jesus*), "I want to do good. I will give half of my money to the poor. If I have cheated any person, I will pay that person back four times more!"

[9]Jesus said, "This man *is a good man—he* truly belongs to the family of Abraham . So today, Zacchaeus has been saved *from his sins*! [10]The Son of Man* came to find lost people and save them."

Use the Things God Gives You

[11]Jesus traveled closer to Jerusalem. Some of the people thought that God's kingdom would appear soon. [12]Jesus knew that the people thought this, so he told them this story: "A very important man was preparing to go to a country far away* to be made a king. Then the man planned to return home and rule his people. [13]So the man called ten of his servants together. He gave a bag of money* to each servant. The man said, 'Do business with this money until I come back.' [14]But the people in the kingdom hated the man. So the people sent a group to follow the man to the other country. In the other country, this group said, 'We don't want that man to be our king!'

[15]"But the man became king. When he came home, he said, 'Call those servants who have my money. I want to know how much more money they earned with it.' [16]The first servant came and said, 'Sir, I earned ten bags of money* with the one bag you gave me!' [17]The king said to the servant, 'Fine! You are a good servant. I see that I can trust you with small things. So now I will let you rule over ten of my cities!' [18]The second servant said, 'Sir, with your one bag of money I earned five bags!' [19]The king said to this servant, 'You can rule over five cities!' [20]Then another servant came in. The servant said to the king, 'Sir, here is your bag of money. I wrapped it in a piece of cloth and hid it. [21]I was afraid of you because you are powerful. I know you are a hard man. You even take money that you didn't earn and gather food that you didn't grow!' [22]Then the king said to the servant, 'You bad servant! I will use your own words to condemn you. You said

Son of Man   Jesus. Jesus was God's Son, but this name showed that Jesus was a man, too. In Daniel 7:13-14, this is the name for the Messiah (Christ).
country far away   Probably Rome. Kings were appointed by the Roman emperor.
bag(s) of money   One bag of money was a Greek "mina." One mina was enough money to pay a person for working three months.

that I am a hard man. You said that I even take money that I didn't earn and gather food that I didn't grow. ²³If that is true, then you should have put my money in the bank. Then, when I came back, my money would have earned some interest.' ²⁴Then the king said to the men who were watching, 'Take the bag of money away from this servant and give it to the servant who earned ten bags of money.' ²⁵The men said to the king, 'But sir, that servant already has ten bags of money!' ²⁶The king said, 'The person who uses what he has will get more. But the person who does not use what he has will have everything taken away from him! ²⁷Now where are my enemies? Where are the people who didn't want me to be king? Bring my enemies here and kill them. I will watch them die!' "

Jesus Enters Jerusalem

²⁸After Jesus said these things, he continued traveling toward Jerusalem. ²⁹Jesus came near Bethphage and Bethany, towns near the hill called the Mount of Olives.* Jesus sent out two of his followers. ³⁰He said, "Go into the town you can see there. When you enter the town, you will find a young donkey tied there. No person has ever ridden this donkey. Untie the donkey, and bring it here to me. ³¹If any person asks you why you are taking the donkey, you should say, 'The Master needs this donkey.' "

³²The two followers went into town. They found the donkey exactly like Jesus told them. ³³The followers untied the donkey. But the owners of the donkey came out. They said to the followers, "Why are you untying our donkey?"

³⁴The followers answered, "The Master needs it." ³⁵So the followers brought the donkey to Jesus. The followers put their coats on the donkey's back. Then they put Jesus on the donkey. ³⁶Jesus rode along the road toward Jerusalem. The followers spread their coats on the road before Jesus.

³⁷Jesus was coming close to Jerusalem. He was already near the bottom of the Mount of Olives.* The whole group of followers were happy. They were very excited and praised God. They thanked God for all the powerful things they had seen. They said,

Mount of Olives   A hill covered with olive trees near the city of Jerusalem.

³⁸"God bless the king who comes
in the name of the Lord (*God*)! *Psalm 118:26*
There is peace in heaven and glory to God!"

³⁹Some of the Pharisees* said to Jesus, "Teacher, tell your followers not to say these things!"

⁴⁰But Jesus answered, "I tell you, these things must be said. If my followers don't say these things, then these rocks will say them."

Jesus Cries for Jerusalem

⁴¹Jesus came near Jerusalem. He saw the city and began to cry for it. ⁴²Jesus spoke to Jerusalem. He said, "I wish you knew today what would bring you peace! But you can't know it, because it is hidden from you. ⁴³A time is coming when your enemies will build a wall around you. Your enemies will hold you on all sides. ⁴⁴They will destroy you and all your people. Not one stone will stay on top of another. All this will happen because you did not know the time when God came to save you."

Jesus Goes to the Temple

⁴⁵Jesus went into the temple.* He began to throw out the people who were selling things there. ⁴⁶Jesus said, "It is written *in the Scriptures*,* 'My house will be a house of prayer.'* But you have changed it into a 'hiding place for thieves'*!"

⁴⁷Jesus taught the people in the temple* every day. The leading priests, the teachers of the law, and some of the leaders of the people wanted to kill Jesus. ⁴⁸But all the people were listening closely to Jesus. They were very interested in the things Jesus said. So the leading priests, the teachers of the law, and the leaders did not know how they could kill Jesus.

Pharisees   Pharisees were a Jewish religious group that followed all the Old Testament and other Jewish laws and customs very carefully.
temple   The special building in Jerusalem where God commanded the Jews to worship him.
Scriptures   Holy Writings—the Old Testament.
'My house...prayer'   Quotation from Isaiah 56:7.
'hiding place for thieves'   Quotation from Jeremiah 7:11.

The Jewish Leaders Ask Jesus a Question

20 One day Jesus was in the temple.* He was teaching the people. Jesus told the people about the Good News of the kingdom of God. The leading priests, teachers of the law, and older Jewish leaders came to talk to Jesus. ²They said, "Tell us! What authority do you have to do these things? Who gave you this authority?"

³Jesus answered, "I will ask you a question too. Tell me: ⁴When John baptized* people, did that come from God or from man?"

⁵The priests, the teachers of the law, and the Jewish leaders all talked about this. They said to each other, "If we answer, 'John's baptism was from God,' then Jesus will say, 'Then why did you not believe John?' ⁶But if we say, 'John's baptism was from man,' then all the people will kill us. They will kill us because they believe that John was a prophet.*" ⁷So they answered, "We don't know the answer."

⁸So Jesus said to them, "Then I will not tell you what authority I use to do these things!"

God Sends His Son

⁹Then Jesus told the people this story: "A man planted a field with grapes. The man leased the land to some farmers. Then he went away for a long time. ¹⁰Later, it was time for the grapes to be picked. So the man sent a servant to those farmers so that they would give him his share of the grapes. But the farmers beat the servant and sent him away with nothing. ¹¹So the man sent another servant. The farmers beat this servant too. They showed no respect for him. The farmers sent the servant away with nothing. ¹²So the man sent a third servant to the farmers. The farmers hurt this servant badly and threw him out. ¹³The owner of the field said, 'What will I do now? I will send my son. I love my son very much. Maybe the farmers will respect my son!' ¹⁴When the farmers saw the son, they said to each other, 'This is the owner's son. This field will be his. If we kill him, then his field

---

temple   The special building in Jerusalem where God commanded the Jews to worship him.
baptized   A Greek word meaning to immerse, dip, or bury a person or thing briefly under water.
prophet   Person who spoke for God. He often told things that would happen in the future.

will be ours!' ¹⁵So the farmers threw the son out of the field and killed him.

"What will the owner of this field do? ¹⁶He will come and kill those farmers! Then he will give the field to some other farmers."

The people heard this story. They said, "No! Let this never happen!" ¹⁷But Jesus looked into their eyes and said, "Then what does this verse mean:

> 'The stone that the builders did not want
> became the cornerstone*'?   *Psalm 118:22*

¹⁸Every person who falls on that stone will be broken. If that stone falls on you, it will crush you!"

¹⁹The Jewish leaders heard this story that Jesus told. They knew this story was about them. So they wanted to arrest Jesus at that time. But they were afraid of what the people would do.

The Jewish Leaders Try to Trick Jesus

²⁰So the teachers of the law and the priests waited for the right time to get Jesus. They sent some men to Jesus. They told these men to act like they were good men. They wanted to find something wrong with the things Jesus said. (If they found something wrong, then they could give Jesus to the high priest* and the governor to be punished.) ²¹So the men asked Jesus, "Teacher, we know that what you say and teach is true. You teach the same to all people. You always teach the truth about God's way. ²²Tell us, is it right that we should pay taxes to Caesar*? Yes or No?"

²³But Jesus knew that these men were trying to trick him. Jesus said to them, ²⁴"Show me a coin. Whose name is on the coin? And whose picture is on it?"

They said, "Caesar's."

²⁵Jesus said to them, "Then give to Caesar the things that are Caesar's. And give to God the things that are God's."

²⁶The men were amazed at his wise answer. They could say nothing. The men were not able to trick Jesus before the people. Jesus said nothing they could use against him.

---

cornerstone   The first and most important rock of a building.
high priest   The most important Jewish priest and leader.
Caesar   The name or title given to the emperor (ruler) of Rome.

Some Sadducees Try to Trick Jesus

²⁷Some Sadducees* came to Jesus. (Sadducees believe that people will not rise from death.) They asked Jesus, ²⁸"Teacher, Moses wrote that if a married man dies and had no children, then his brother must marry the woman. Then they will have children for the dead brother. ²⁹One time there were seven brothers. The first brother married a woman, but died. He had no children. ³⁰Then the second brother married the woman, and he died. ³¹And then the third brother married the woman, and he died. The same thing happened with all the other brothers. They all died and had no children. ³²The woman was the last to die. ³³But all seven brothers married her. So when people rise from death, whose wife will this woman be?"

³⁴Jesus said to the Sadducees,* "On earth, people marry each other. ³⁵Some people will be worthy to be raised from death and live again after this life. In that life they will not marry. ³⁶In that life people are like angels and cannot die. They are children of God, because they have been raised from death. ³⁷Moses clearly showed that people are raised from death. When Moses wrote about the *burning* bush,* he said that the Lord *God* is 'the God of Abraham, the God of Isaac, and the God of Jacob.*'* ³⁸*This means that* God is the God of living people, not dead people. All people are alive to God."

³⁹Some of the teachers of the law said, "Teacher, your answer was very good." ⁴⁰No person was brave enough to ask him another question.

Is the Christ the Son of David?

⁴¹Then Jesus said, "Why do people say that the Christ* is the Son of David*? ⁴²In the book of Psalms, David himself says:

Sadducees   A leading Jewish religious group. They followed only the first five books of the Old Testament. They believed that people don't have another life after death.
burning bush   Read Exodus 3:1-12 in the Old Testament.
Abraham...Isaac...Jacob   Three of the most important leaders in the Old Testament.
'the God...Jacob'   These words are taken from Exodus 3:6.
Christ   The "anointed one" (the Messiah) or chosen one of God.
Son of David   Name for the Christ, who was from the family of David, king of Israel.

'The Lord (*God*) said to my Lord (*Christ*):
Sit by me at my right side.
⁴³I will put your enemies under your power.*'   *Psalm 110:1*
⁴⁴David calls the Christ 'Lord.' So how can the Christ be David's son?''

Jesus Warns Against the Teachers of the Law

⁴⁵All the people listened to Jesus. Jesus said to his followers, ⁴⁶''Be careful of the teachers of the law. They like to walk around wearing clothes that look important. And they love for people to show respect to them in the market places. They love to get the most important seats in the synagogues.* And they love to get the most important seats at the feasts. ⁴⁷But they are mean to widows* and steal their homes. Then they try to make themselves look good by saying long prayers. God will punish these people very much.''

True Giving

21 Jesus saw some rich people putting their gifts for God into the temple money box.* ²Then Jesus saw a poor widow.* She put two small copper coins into the box. ³Jesus said, ''I tell you the truth. This poor widow gave only two small coins. But she really gave more than all those rich people. ⁴The rich people have plenty; they gave only what they did not need. This woman is very poor. But she gave all she had. And she needed that money to help her live.''

The Destruction of the Temple

⁵Some of the followers were talking about the temple.* They said, ''This is a beautiful temple, built with the best stones. Look at the many good gifts that have been offered to God!''

I will put...power   Literally, ''I will make your enemies a footstool for your feet.''
synagogues   Synagogues were buildings where Jews gathered to read and study the Scriptures.
widows   A widow is a woman whose husband has died.
money box   A special box in the Jewish place for worship where people put their gifts to God.
temple   The special building in Jerusalem where God commanded the Jews to worship him.

⁶But Jesus said, "The time will come when all that you see here will be destroyed. Every stone *of these buildings* will be thrown down to the ground. Not one stone will be left on another!"

⁷Some followers asked Jesus, "Teacher, when will these things happen? What will show us that it is time for these things to happen?"

⁸Jesus said, "Be careful! Don't be fooled. Many people will come using my name. They will say, 'I am *the Christ*' and, 'The right time has come!' But don't follow them. ⁹When you hear about wars and riots, don't be afraid. These things must happen first. Then the end will come later."

¹⁰Then Jesus said to them, "Nations will fight against other nations. Kingdoms will fight against other kingdoms. ¹¹There will be great earthquakes, sicknesses, and other bad things in many places. In some places there will be no food for the people to eat. Great wonders* and amazing things will come from heaven.

¹²"But before all these things happen, people will arrest you and do bad things to you. People will judge you in their synagogues* and put you in jail. You will be forced to stand before kings and governors. People will do all these things to you because you follow me. ¹³But this will give you an opportunity to tell about me. ¹⁴Don't worry about what you will say. ¹⁵I will give you so much wisdom that all your enemies will not be able to show that you are wrong. ¹⁶Even your parents, brothers, relatives and friends will turn against you. They will kill some of you. ¹⁷All people will hate you because you follow me. ¹⁸But none of these things can really harm you. ¹⁹You will save yourselves by continuing strong in your faith through all these things."

The Destruction of Jerusalem

²⁰"You will see armies all around Jerusalem. Then you will know that the time for the destruction of Jerusalem has come. ²¹At that time, the people in Judea should run away to the mountains. The people in Jerusalem must leave quickly. If you are near the city, don't go in! ²²The prophets* wrote many things

---

wonders Powerful and amazing acts, done by the power of God.
synagogues Synagogues were buildings where Jews gathered to read and study the Scriptures.
prophets People who spoke for God. Their writings are part of the Old Testament.

about the time when God will punish his people. The time I am telling you about is the time when all these things must happen. [23]At that time, it will be bad for women who are pregnant or have small babies. Why? Because very bad times will come to this land. God will be angry with these people (*the Jews*). [24]Some of the people will be killed by soldiers. Other people will be made prisoners and taken to every country. The holy city of Jerusalem will be walked on by non-Jewish people until their time is finished."

Don't Fear

[25]"Amazing things will happen with the sun, moon, and stars. The people on earth will feel trapped. The oceans will be upset, and the people will not know why. [26]Men will become afraid. They will be very worried about the things that will happen to the whole world. Everything in the sky will be changed. [27]Then people will see the Son of Man* coming on a cloud with power and great glory. [28]When these things begin to happen, don't fear. Look up and be happy! Don't worry. Be happy, because you know that the time when God will free you is near!"

My Words Will Live Forever

[29]Then Jesus told this story: "Look at all the trees. The fig tree is a good example. [30]When it becomes green (*grows buds*), you know that summer is near. [31]It is the same with these things I told you would happen. When you see all these things happening, then you will know that God's kingdom is coming very soon.

[32]"I tell you the truth. All these things will happen while the people of this time are still living! [33]The whole world, earth and sky, will be destroyed; but the words I have said will never be destroyed!"

Be Ready All the Time

[34]"Be careful! Don't spend your time drinking and getting drunk. Or don't be too busy with worldly things. If you do that,

---

Son of Man Jesus. Jesus was God's Son, but this name showed that Jesus was a man, too. In Daniel 7:13-14, this is the name for the Messiah (Christ).

you will not be able to think right. And then the end might come when you are not ready. ³⁵It will come like a surprise to all people on earth. ³⁶So be ready all the time. Pray that you will be strong enough to continue safely through all these things that will happen. And pray that you will be able to stand before the Son of Man.*"

³⁷During the day, Jesus taught the people in the temple.* At night he went out of the city and stayed all night on the Mount of Olives.* ³⁸Every morning all the people got up early to go listen to Jesus in the temple.

The Jewish Leaders Want to Kill Jesus

22 It was almost time for the Jewish Feast of Unleavened Bread, called the Passover Feast.* ²The leading priests and teachers of the law were trying to find a way to kill Jesus. But they were afraid of the people.

Judas Makes Plans Against Jesus

³One of Jesus' twelve apostles* was named Judas Iscariot. Satan (*the devil*) went into Judas and made him do a bad thing. ⁴Judas went and talked with the leading priests and some of the soldiers who guarded the temple.* Judas talked to them about a way to give Jesus to them. ⁵The priests were very happy about this. They promised to give Judas money *if he would give Jesus to them*. ⁶Judas agreed. Then Judas waited for the best time to give Jesus to them. Judas wanted to do it when there were no people around to see him do it.

Son of Man   Jesus. Jesus was God's Son, but this name showed that Jesus was a man, too. In Daniel 7:13-14, this is the name for the Messiah (Christ).
temple   The special building in Jerusalem where God commanded the Jews to worship him.
Mount of Olives   A hill covered with olive trees near the city of Jerusalem.
Passover Feast   Important holy day for Jews. They ate a special meal on this day every year to remember that God freed them from slavery in Egypt in the time of Moses.
apostles   The men Jesus taught and chose to be his special helpers.

Preparation of the Passover Meal

[7]The Day of Unleavened Bread* came. This was the day when the Jews sacrificed* the Passover lambs.* [8]Jesus said to Peter and John, "Go and prepare the Passover meal* for us to eat."

[9]Peter and John said to Jesus, "Where do you want us to prepare the meal?"

Jesus said to them, [10]"Listen! After you go into the city (*Jerusalem*), you will see a man carrying a jar of water. Follow him. He will go into a house. You go with him. [11]Tell the person who owns that house, 'The Teacher asks that you please show us the room where he and his followers can eat the Passover meal.' hen the man who owns the house will show you a large room upstairs. This room is ready for you. Prepare the Passover meal there."

[13]So Peter and John left. Everything happened the way Jesus said. So they prepared the Passover meal.

The Lord's Supper

[14]The time came for them to eat the Passover meal.* Jesus and the apostles* were sitting at the table. [15]Jesus said to them, "I wanted very much to eat this Passover meal with you before I die. [16]I will never eat another Passover meal until it is given its true meaning in the kingdom of God."

[17]Then Jesus took a cup of wine. He gave thanks to God for it. Then he said, "Take this cup and give it to everyone here. [18]I will never drink wine again until God's kingdom comes."

[19]Then Jesus took some bread. He thanked God for the bread and divided it. He gave it to the apostles.* Then Jesus said, "This bread is my body that I am giving for you. Do this to remember me." [20]In the same way, after supper, Jesus took the cup of wine and said, "This wine shows the new agreement *from God to his*

Day of Unleavened Bread   Same as Passover Feast, the most important holy day for Jews. On this day they ate a special meal with bread that was made without yeast.

sacrificed   To offer a gift or kill an animal as an offering to God.

Passover lambs   Part of the celebration of the Passover Feast was the sacrifice of lambs.

Passover meal   This was the special meal the Jews ate for the Passover Feast.

apostles   The men Jesus taught and chose to be his special helpers.

people. This new agreement begins with my blood (*death*) that I am giving for you."*

Who Will Turn Against Jesus?

²¹Jesus said, "One of you will soon be against me. His hand is by my hand on the table. ²²The Son of Man* will do what God has planned. But it will be very bad for that person who gives the Son of Man *to be killed.*"

²³Then the apostles* asked each other, "Which one of us would do that to Jesus?"

Be Like a Servant

²⁴Later the apostles* began to argue about which one of them was the most important. ²⁵But Jesus said to them, "The kings of the world rule over their people. Men who have authority over other people are called 'very important.' ²⁶But you must not be like that. The greatest person should become like the youngest person! Leaders should be like servants. ²⁷Who is more important: the person sitting at the table or the person serving him? You think the person sitting at the table is more important. But I am like a servant among you!

²⁸"You men have stayed with me through many struggles. ²⁹My Father has given me a kingdom. I also give you authority to rule with me. ³⁰You will eat and drink at my table in my kingdom. You will sit on thrones and judge the twelve tribes (*family groups*) of Israel.*"

Don't Lose Your Faith!

³¹"Satan (*the devil*) has asked to test you like a farmer tests his wheat. O Simon, Simon (*Peter*), ³²I have prayed that you will not lose your faith! Help your brothers be stronger when you come back to me."

Verse 20   A few Greek copies do not have the last part of verse 19 and all of verse 20.
Son of Man   Jesus. Jesus was God's Son, but this name showed that Jesus was a man, too. In Daniel 7:13-14, this is the name for the Messiah (Christ).
apostles   The men Jesus taught and chose to be his special helpers.
Israel   First, Israel was the Jewish nation, but the name is also used to mean all of God's people.

³³But Peter said to Jesus, "Lord, I am ready to go to jail with you. I will even die with you!"

³⁴But Jesus said, "Peter, before the rooster crows tomorrow morning, you will say you don't know me. You will say this three times!"

Be Ready for Trouble

³⁵Then Jesus said to the apostles,* "I sent you *to preach to the people.* I sent you without money, a bag, or shoes. But did you need anything?"

The apostles said, " No."

³⁶Jesus said to them, "But now if you have money or a bag, carry that with you. If you don't have a sword, sell your coat and buy one. ³⁷The Scripture* says:

'People said he was a criminal.'   *Isaiah 53:12*

This verse must happen. It was written about me, and it is happening now."

³⁸The followers said, "Look, Lord, here are two swords!"

Jesus said to them, "Two will be enough."

Jesus Tells the Apostles to Pray

³⁹⁻⁴⁰Jesus left the city (*Jerusalem*) and went to the Mount of Olives.* His followers went with him. (Jesus went there often.) Jesus said to his followers, "Pray for strength against temptation."

⁴¹Then Jesus went about 50 yards away from them. He kneeled down and prayed, ⁴²"Father, if it is what you want, then let me not have this cup* *of suffering.* But *what you want is more important.* Do what you want, not what I want." ⁴³Then an angel from heaven appeared. The angel was sent to help Jesus. ⁴⁴Jesus was full of pain; he struggled hard in prayer. Sweat dripped from his face like he was bleeding. ⁴⁵When Jesus finished praying, he went to his followers. They were asleep. (Their sadness had made

apostles The men Jesus taught and chose to be his special helpers.
Scripture A part of the Holy Writings—the Old Testament.
Mount of Olives A hill covered with olive trees near the city of Jerusalem.
cup Jesus is talking about the bad things that will happen to him. Accepting these things will be very hard, like drinking a cup full of something that tastes very bad.

them very tired.) ⁴⁶Jesus said to them, "Why are you sleeping? Get up and pray for strength against temptation."

Jesus Is Arrested

⁴⁷While Jesus was speaking, a group of people came. One of the twelve apostles* was leading the group. He was Judas. Judas came close to Jesus so that he could kiss Jesus.

⁴⁸But Jesus said to him, "Judas, are you using the kiss *of friendship* to give the Son of Man* to his enemies?" ⁴⁹The followers of Jesus were standing there too. They saw what was happening. The followers said to Jesus, "Lord, should we use our swords?" ⁵⁰And one of the followers did use his sword. He cut off the right ear of the servant of the high priest.*

⁵¹Jesus said, "Stop!" Then Jesus touched the servant's ear and healed him.

⁵²The group that came to arrest Jesus were the leading priests, the older Jewish leaders, and the Jewish soldiers. Jesus said to them, "Why did you come out here with swords and sticks? Do you think I am a criminal? ⁵³I was with you every day in the temple.* Why didn't you try to arrest me there? But this is your time—the time when darkness (*sin*) rules."

Peter Is Afraid to Say He Knows Jesus

⁵⁴They arrested Jesus and took him away. They brought Jesus into the house of the high priest.* Peter followed them, but he did not come near Jesus. ⁵⁵The soldiers started a fire in the middle of the yard and sat together. Peter sat with them. ⁵⁶A servant girl saw Peter sitting there. She could see because of the light from the fire. The girl looked closely at Peter's face. Then she said, "This man was also with him (*Jesus*)!"

⁵⁷But Peter said this was not true. He said, "Lady, I don't know him." ⁵⁸A short time later, another person saw Peter and said, "You are also one of those people *that follow Jesus.*"

---

apostles   The men Jesus taught and chose to be his special helpers.
Son of Man   Jesus. Jesus was God's Son, but this name showed that Jesus was a man, too. In Daniel 7:13-14, this is the name for the Messiah (Christ).
high priest   The most important Jewish priest and leader.
temple   The special building in Jerusalem where God commanded the Jews to worship him.

But Peter said, "Man, I am not one of his followers!"

⁵⁹About an hour later, another man said, "It is true! This man was with him (*Jesus*). He is from Galilee!"

⁶⁰But Peter said, "Man, I don't know what you are talking about!"

Immediately, while Peter was still speaking, a rooster crowed. ⁶¹Then the Lord (*Jesus*) turned and looked into Peter's eyes. And Peter remembered what the Lord had said: "Before the rooster crows in the morning, you will say three times that you don't know me." ⁶²Then Peter went outside and cried with much pain in his heart.

The People Laugh at Jesus

⁶³⁻⁶⁴"Some men were holding (*guarding*) Jesus. They made fun of Jesus like this: They covered his eyes so that he could not see them. Then they hit him and said, "Be a prophet,* and tell us who hit you!" ⁶⁵The men said many very bad things to Jesus.

Jesus Before the Jewish Leaders

⁶⁶The next morning, the older leaders of the people, the leading priests, and the teachers of the law came together. They led Jesus away to their highest court. ⁶⁷They said, "If you are the Christ,* then tell us that you are!"

Jesus said to them, "If I tell you I am the Christ, you will not believe me. ⁶⁸And if I ask you, you will not answer. ⁶⁹But beginning now, the Son of Man* will sit at the right side of God's throne."

⁷⁰They all said, "Then are you the Son of God?" Jesus said to them, "Yes, you are right when you say that I am."

⁷¹They said, "Why do we need witnesses now? We ourselves heard him say this!"

---

prophet Person who spoke for God. He often told things that would happen in the future.
Christ The "anointed one" (the Messiah) or chosen one of God.
Son of Man Jesus. Jesus was God's Son, but this name showed that Jesus was a man, too. In Daniel 7:13-14, this is the name for the Messiah (Christ).

Governor Pilate Questions Jesus

23 Then the whole group stood up and led Jesus to Pilate.* ²They began to accuse Jesus. They told Pilate, "We caught this man telling things that were confusing our people. He (*Jesus*) says that we should not pay taxes to Caesar.* He (*Jesus*) calls himself the Christ,* a king."

³Pilate asked Jesus, "Are you the king of the Jews?"

Jesus answered, "Yes, that is right."

⁴Pilate said to the leading priests and the people, "I find nothing wrong with this man."

⁵They said again and again, "But Jesus is making trouble with the people! He teaches all around Judea. He began in Galilee, and now he is here!"

Pilate Sends Jesus to Herod

⁶Pilate heard this and asked if Jesus was from Galilee. ⁷Pilate learned that Jesus was under Herod's* authority. Herod was in Jerusalem at that time, so Pilate sent Jesus to him. ⁸When Herod saw Jesus, he was very happy. Herod had heard all about Jesus. So he had wanted to meet Jesus for a long time. Herod wanted to see a miracle.* So he hoped that Jesus would do a miracle. ⁹Herod asked Jesus many questions, but Jesus said nothing. ¹⁰The leading priests and teachers of the law were standing there. They were shouting things against Jesus. ¹¹Then Herod and his soldiers laughed at Jesus. They made fun of Jesus by dressing him in clothes like kings wear. Then Herod sent Jesus back to Pilate. ¹²In the past, Pilate and Herod had always been enemies. But on that day Herod and Pilate became friends.

Jesus Must Die

¹³Pilate called all the people together with the leading priests and the *Jewish* leaders. ¹⁴Pilate said to them, "You brought this

---

Pilate   Pontius Pilate was the Roman governor of Judea from 26 A.D. to 36 A.D.
Caesar   The name or title given to the emperor (ruler) of Rome.
Christ   The "anointed one" (the Messiah) or chosen one of God.
Herod   Herod Antipas, son of Herod the Great, tetrarch (ruler) of Galilee and Perea.
miracle   Miracles are powerful works or great things done by the power of God.

man (*Jesus*) to me. You said that he was making trouble among the people. But I judged him before you all. I found no wrong that he had done. Jesus is not guilty of the things you say. ¹⁵Also, Herod* found nothing wrong with him; Herod sent Jesus back to us. Look, Jesus has done nothing wrong. He should not be killed. ¹⁶So, after I punish him a little, I will let him go free." ¹⁷*

¹⁸But all the people yelled, "Kill him! Let Barabbas go free!" ¹⁹(Barabbas was a man who was in jail because he started a riot in the city. He had also killed some people.)

²⁰Pilate wanted to let Jesus go free. So again Pilate told them that he would let Jesus go. ²¹But they yelled again, "Kill him! Kill him on a cross!"

²²A third time Pilate said to the people, "Why? What wrong has he done? He is not guilty. I can find no reason to kill him. So I will let him go free after I punish him a little."

²³But the people continued to yell. They demanded that Jesus be killed on the cross. Their yelling became so loud that ²⁴Pilate decided to give them what they wanted. The people wanted Barabbas to go free. Barabbas was the man who had started a riot and had killed people. ²⁵Pilate let Barabbas go free. And Pilate gave Jesus to the people to be killed. This is what the people wanted.

Jesus Is Killed on a Cross

²⁶The soldiers led Jesus away *to be killed*. At that same time, there was a man coming into the city from the fields. His name was Simon. Simon was from the city of Cyrene. The soldiers forced Simon to carry Jesus' cross and walk behind Jesus.

²⁷Many, many people followed Jesus. Some of the women were sad and crying. They felt sorry for Jesus. ²⁸But Jesus turned and said to the women, "Women of Jerusalem, don't cry for me. Cry for yourselves and for your children too! ²⁹The time is coming when people will say, 'Happy are the women who cannot have babies! Happy are the women who have no children to care for.' ³⁰Then the people will say to the mountains, 'Fall on us!' The

Herod Herod Antipas, son of Herod the Great, tetrarch (ruler) of Galilee and Perea.
Verse 17 A few Greek copies of Luke add verse 17: "Every year at the Passover Feast, Pilate had
    to release one prisoner to the people."

people will say to the hills, 'Cover us!' [31]If people act like this now when life is good, what will happen when bad times come?*"

[32]There were also two criminals led out with Jesus to be killed. [33]Jesus and the two criminals were led to a place called "The Skull." There, the soldiers nailed Jesus to his cross. They also nailed the criminals to their crosses. They put one criminal beside Jesus on the right, and they put the other criminal beside Jesus on the left. [34]Jesus said, "Father, forgive these people *who are killing me*. They don't know what they are doing."

The soldiers gambled with dice to decide who would get Jesus' clothes. [35]The people stood there watching *Jesus*. The Jewish leaders laughed at Jesus. They said, "If he is God's Chosen One, the Christ,* then let him (*Jesus*) save himself. He saved other people, didn't he?"

[36]Even the soldiers laughed at Jesus and teased him. They came to Jesus and offered him some wine. [37]The soldiers said, "If you are the king of the Jews, save yourself!" [38](At the top of the cross these words were written: "THIS IS THE KING OF THE JEWS.")

[39]One of the criminals began to yell very bad things at Jesus: "Aren't you the Christ*? Then save yourself! And save us too!"

[40]But the other criminal stopped him. He said, "You should fear God! All of us will die soon! [41]You and I are guilty; we should be killed because we did wrong. But this man (*Jesus*) has done nothing wrong!" [42]Then this criminal said to Jesus, "Jesus, remember me when you begin your kingdom!"

[43]Then Jesus said to him, "Listen! What I say is true: Today you will be with me in Paradise*!"

Jesus Dies

[44]"It was about noon, but the whole area became dark until three o'clock in the afternoon. [45]There was no sun! The curtain in the temple* was torn into two pieces. [46]Jesus shouted, "Father, I give you my spirit." After Jesus said this, he died.

If...come Literally, "If they do these things in the green tree, what will happen in the dry?"
Christ The "anointed one" (the Messiah) or chosen one of God.
Paradise A happy place where good people go when they die.
curtain in the temple A curtain divided the "most holy place" from the other part of the temple, the special building in Jerusalem where God commanded the Jews to worship him.

⁴⁷The Roman army officer there saw what happened. He praised God, saying, "I know this man was a good man!"

⁴⁸Many people had come out of the city to see this thing. When the people saw it, they felt very sorry and left. ⁴⁹The people who were close friends of Jesus were there. Also, there were some women who had followed Jesus from Galilee. They all stood far away from the cross and watched these things.

Joseph of Arimathea

⁵⁰⁻⁵¹A man was there from the Jewish town of Arimathea. His name was Joseph. He was a good, religious man. He wanted the kingdom of God to come. Joseph was a member of the Jewish council. But he did not agree when the other Jewish leaders decided to kill Jesus. ⁵²Joseph went to Pilate to ask for the body of Jesus. *Pilate let Joseph have the body.* ⁵³So Joseph took the body down from the cross and wrapped it in cloth. Then he put Jesus' body in a tomb (*grave*) that was dug in a wall of rock. This tomb had never been used before. ⁵⁴This was late on Preparation day.* When the sun went down, the Sabbath day* would begin.

⁵⁵The women who had come from Galilee with Jesus followed Joseph. They saw the tomb. Inside they saw where the body of Jesus was put. ⁵⁶Then the women left to prepare some sweet-smelling things *to put on Jesus' body.*

On the Sabbath day* they rested. The law of Moses commanded all people to do this.

The Followers Learn That Jesus Has Risen from Death

24 Very early on Sunday morning, the women came to the tomb (*grave*) where Jesus' body was laid. They brought the sweet-smelling things they had prepared. ²*A heavy rock had been put in the doorway to close the tomb.* But the women found that the rock was rolled away. ³They went in, but they did not find the Lord Jesus' body. ⁴The women did not understand this. While they were wondering about it, two men (*angels*) in shining

---

Preparation day   Friday, the day before the Sabbath day.
Sabbath day   Seventh day of the Jewish week. It was a special religious day for the Jews.

clothes stood beside them. ⁵The women were very afraid; they bowed their heads down. The two men said to the women, "Why are you looking for a living person here? This is a place for dead people! ⁶Jesus is not here. He has risen from death! Do you remember what he said in Galilee? ⁷Jesus said that the Son of Man* must be given to evil men, be killed on a cross, and rise from death on the third day." ⁸Then the women remembered the things that Jesus said.

⁹The women left the tomb (*grave*) and went to the eleven apostles* and the other followers. The women told them everything that happened at the tomb. ¹⁰These women were Mary Magdalene, Joanna, Mary, the mother of James, and some other women. These women told the apostles everything that happened. ¹¹But the apostles did not believe what the women said. It sounded like crazy talk. ¹²But Peter got up and ran to the tomb to see if this was true. He looked in, but he saw only the cloth that Jesus' body had been wrapped in. The cloth was lying there alone. *Jesus was gone.* Peter went away to be alone, wondering what had happened.

On the Road to Emmaus

¹³That same day two of Jesus' followers were going to a town named Emmaus. It is about seven miles from Jerusalem. ¹⁴They were talking about everything that had happened. ¹⁵While they were discussing these things, Jesus himself came near and walked with them. ¹⁶(But the two men were not allowed to recognize Jesus.) ¹⁷Jesus walked with them for a while. Then he said, "What are these things you are talking about while you walk?"

The two men stopped. Their faces looked very sad. ¹⁸The one named Cleopas answered, "You must be the only man in Jerusalem who does not know what has just happened there."

¹⁹Jesus said to them, "What are you talking about?"

The men said to him, "It is about Jesus, the one from Nazareth. He was a prophet* from God to all the people. He said

---

Son of Man   Jesus. Jesus was God's Son, but this name showed that Jesus was a man, too. In Daniel 7:13-14, this is the name for the Messiah (Christ).
apostles   The men Jesus taught and chose to be his special helpers.
prophet   Person who spoke for God. He often told things that would happen in the future.

and did many powerful things. ²⁰Our leaders and the leading priests gave him away to be judged and killed. They nailed Jesus to a cross. ²¹But we were hoping that Jesus would free the Jews. It has been three days since this happened. ²²And today some of our women told us some amazing things. Early this morning the women went to the tomb (*grave*) where the body of Jesus was laid. ²³But they did not find his body there. The women came and told us that they had seen two angels in a vision.* The angels said that Jesus was alive! ²⁴So some of our group went to the tomb too. It was just like the women said—*the tomb was empty*. We looked, but none of us saw him (*Jesus*)."

²⁵Then Jesus said to the two men, "You are foolish and slow to realize what is true. You should believe everything the prophets* said. ²⁶The prophets said that the Christ* must suffer these things before he enters his glory." ²⁷Then Jesus began to explain everything that had been written about himself in the Scriptures.* Jesus started with the books of Moses and then he talked about what the prophets had said about him.

²⁸They came near the town of Emmaus and Jesus acted like he did not plan to stop there. ²⁹But they wanted him to stay. They begged him, "Stay with us. It is late; it is almost night." So he went in to stay with them.

³⁰Jesus sat down with them and took some bread. He gave thanks for the food and divided it. Then he gave it to them. ³¹At that time, the men were allowed to recognize Jesus. But when they saw who he was, he disappeared. ³²The two men said to each other, "When Jesus talked to us on the road, it felt like a fire burning in us. It was exciting when he explained the true meaning of the Scriptures.*"

³³So the two men got up then and went back to Jerusalem. In Jerusalem they found the followers of Jesus meeting together. The eleven apostles* and those people who were with them ³⁴said, "The Lord (*Jesus*) really has risen from death! He showed himself to Simon (*Peter*)."

vision A vision is something like a dream that God used to speak to people.
prophets Men who spoke for God. Some of them wrote books that are in the Old Testament.
Christ The "anointed one" (the Messiah) or chosen one of God.
Scriptures Holy Writings—the Old Testament.
apostles The men Jesus taught and chose to be his special helpers.

³⁵Then the two men told the things that had happened on the road. They talked about how they recognized Jesus when he divided the bread.

Jesus Appears to His Followers

³⁶While the two men were saying these things, Jesus himself stood among the group of followers. Jesus said to them, "Peace to you."

³⁷This surprised the followers. They became afraid. They thought they were seeing a ghost. ³⁸But Jesus said, "Why are you troubled? Why do you doubt what you see? ³⁹Look at my hands and my feet. It is really me! Touch me. You can see that I have a living body; a ghost does not have a body like this."

⁴⁰After Jesus told them this, he showed them *the holes in* his hands and feet. ⁴¹The followers were amazed and very, very happy to see that Jesus was alive. They still could not believe what they saw. Jesus said to them, "Do you have any food here?" ⁴²They gave him a piece of cooked fish. ⁴³While the followers watched, Jesus took the fish and ate it.

⁴⁴Jesus said to them, "Remember when I was with you before? I said that everything written about me must happen—everything written in the law of Moses, the books of the prophets,* and the Psalms."

⁴⁵Then Jesus explained all the Scriptures* to the followers. Jesus helped them understand the things written *about him*. ⁴⁶Then Jesus said to them, "It is written that the Christ* would be killed and rise from death on the third day. ⁴⁷⁻⁴⁸You saw these things happen—you are witnesses. You must go and tell people that their sins can be forgiven. Tell them that they must change their hearts and be sorry for their sins. If they will do this, then God will forgive them. You must start from Jerusalem and preach these things in my name. This Good News must be told to all people in the world. ⁴⁹Listen! My Father has promised you something; I will send it to you. But you must stay in Jerusalem until you have received that power from heaven."

---

prophets   Men who spoke for God. Some of them wrote books that are in the Old Testament.
Scriptures   Holy Writings—the Old Testament.
Christ   The "anointed one" (the Messiah) or chosen one of God.

Jesus Goes Back to Heaven

⁵⁰Jesus led his followers out of Jerusalem almost to Bethany. Jesus raised his hands and blessed his followers. ⁵¹While Jesus was blessing them, he was separated from them and carried into heaven. ⁵²The followers worshiped him there. Then they went back to the city. They were very happy. ⁵³They stayed at the temple* all the time, praising God.

---

temple The special building in Jerusalem where God commanded the Jews to worship him.

236

John

Christ Comes to the World

1 Before the world began, the Word* was there. The Word was there with God. The Word was God. ²He was there with God in the beginning. ³All things were made through him (*the Word*). Nothing was made without him. ⁴In him there was life. That life was light (*understanding, goodness*) for the people of the world. ⁵The Light shines in the darkness. But the darkness did not understand* the Light.

⁶There was a man named John.* He was sent by God. ⁷John came to tell people about the Light (*Christ*). Through John all people *could hear about the Light* and believe. ⁸John was not the Light. But John came to tell people about the Light. ⁹The true Light was coming into the world. This is the true Light that gives light to all people.

¹⁰The Word* was already in the world. The world was made through him. But the world (*people*) did not know him. ¹¹He came to the world that was his own. But his own people did not accept him. ¹²Some people did accept him. They believed in him. He gave something to those people who believed. He gave them the right to become children of God. ¹³These children were not born like little babies are born. They were not born from the wish or plan of a *mother and* father. These children were born from God.

¹⁴The Word* became a man and lived among us. We saw his glory—the glory that belongs to the only Son of the Father. The Word was full of grace (*kindness*) and truth. ¹⁵John told people

---

Word   The Greek word is "logos," meaning any kind of communication. It could be translated "message." Here, it means Christ. Christ was the way God told people about himself.
understand   This word in Greek could also mean "defeat."
John   John the Baptizer, who preached to people about Christ's coming (Matt. 3, Luke 3).

about him. John said, "This is the One I was talking about. I said, 'The One who comes after me is greater than I am. He was living before me.' "

¹⁶The Word (*Christ*) was full of grace and truth. From him we all received more and more blessings. ¹⁷The law was given through Moses. But grace and *the way of* truth came through Jesus Christ. ¹⁸No man has ever seen God. But the only Son (*Jesus*) is God. He is very close to the Father* (*God*). And the Son has shown us what God is like.

John Tells People About Jesus

¹⁹The Jews in Jerusalem sent some priests and Levites* to John. The Jews sent them to ask, "Who are you?"

²⁰John spoke freely. John did not refuse to answer. John said clearly, "I am not the Christ.*" That is what John told people.

²¹The Jews asked John, "Then who are you? Are you Elijah*?"

John answered, "No, I am not Elijah."

The Jews asked, "Are you the Prophet*?"

John answered, "No, I am not the Prophet."

²²Then the Jews said, "Who are you? Tell us about yourself. Give us an answer to tell the people who sent us. What do you say about yourself?"

²³John told them the words of the prophet Isaiah:

"I am the voice of a person shouting in the desert:
'Make a straight road ready for the Lord.' "   *Isaiah 40:3*

²⁴These Jews were sent from the Pharisees.* In the group of Jews there were some Pharisees. ²⁵These men said to John: "You

---

But...Father This could also be translated, "But the only God is very close to the Father." Also, some Greek copies say, "But the only Son is very close to the Father."

Levites Levites were men from the family group of Levi who helped the Jewish priests with their work in the temple. Read 1 Chronicles 23:24-32.

Christ The "anointed one" (the Messiah) or chosen one of God.

Elijah A man who spoke for God hundreds of years before Christ. The Jews were waiting for Elijah to return before the coming of the Messiah (Christ). Read Malachi 4:5-6.

Prophet They probably meant the prophet that God told Moses he would send (Deuteronomy 18:15-19).

Pharisees Pharisees were a Jewish religious group that followed all the Old Testament and other Jewish laws and customs very carefully.

say you are not the Christ.* You say you are not Elijah* or the Prophet.* Then why do you baptize* people?"

²⁶John answered, "I baptize people with water. But there is a person here with you that you don't know. ²⁷That person is the One who comes after me. I am not good enough to untie the strings on his shoes.*"

²⁸These things all happened at Bethany on the other side of the Jordan river. This is where John was baptizing people.

²⁹The next day John saw Jesus coming toward him. John said, "Look, the Lamb of God.* He takes away the sins of the world! ³⁰This is the One I was talking about. I said, 'A man will come after me, but he is greater than I am, because he was living before me—*he has always lived*.' ³¹Even I did not know who he was. But I came baptizing people with water so that God's people could know that Jesus is *the Christ*.*"

³²⁻³³Then John said, "I also did not know who the Christ was. But God sent me to baptize people with water. And God told me, 'You will see the Spirit come down and rest on a man. That man is the One who will baptize people with the Holy Spirit.*' " John said, "I have seen this happen. I saw the Spirit come down from heaven. The Spirit looked like a dove and sat on him (*Jesus*). ³⁴So this is what I tell people: 'He (*Jesus*) is the Son of God.' "

The First Followers of Jesus

³⁵The next day John was there again. John had two of his followers with him. ³⁶John saw Jesus walking by. John said, "Look, the Lamb of God*!"

³⁷The two followers heard John say this, so they followed Jesus. ³⁸Jesus turned and saw the two men following him. Jesus asked, "What do you want?"

Christ   The "anointed one" (the Messiah) or chosen one of God.
Elijah   A man who spoke for God hundreds of years before Christ. The Jews were waiting for Elijah to return before the coming of the Messiah (Christ). Read Malachi 4:5-6.
Prophet   They probably meant the prophet that God told Moses he would send (Deuteronomy 18:15-19).
baptize   A Greek word meaning to immerse, dip, or bury a person or thing briefly under water.
shoes   Literally, "sandals" or open shoes tied to the feet with leather strings.
Lamb of God   Name for Jesus. Jesus is like the lambs that were offered for a sacrifice to God.
Holy Spirit   Also called the Spirit of God, the Spirit of Christ, and the Comforter. He is joined with God and Christ. He does the work of God among people in the world.

The two men said, "Rabbi, where are you staying?" ("Rabbi" means "Teacher.")

³⁹Jesus answered, "Come with me and you will see." So the two men went with Jesus. They saw the place where Jesus stayed. They stayed there with Jesus that day. It was about four o'clock.

⁴⁰These two men followed Jesus after they heard about Jesus from John. One of these two men was named Andrew. Andrew was Simon Peter's brother. ⁴¹The first thing Andrew did was to go find his brother, Simon. Andrew said to Simon, "We have found the Messiah." ("Messiah" means "Christ."*)

⁴²Then Andrew brought Simon to Jesus. Jesus looked at Simon and said, "You are Simon, the son of John. You will be called Cephas." ("Cephas" means "Peter."*)

⁴³The next day Jesus decided to go to Galilee. Jesus found Philip and said to him, "Follow me." ⁴⁴Philip was from the town of Bethsaida, the same as Andrew and Peter. ⁴⁵Philip found Nathaniel and told him, "Remember what Moses wrote in the law. Moses wrote about a man that was coming. The prophets* wrote about him too. We have found him. His name is Jesus, the son of Joseph. He is from Nazareth."

⁴⁶But Nathaniel said to Philip, "Nazareth! Can anything good come from Nazareth?"

Philip answered, "Come and see."

⁴⁷Jesus saw Nathaniel coming toward him. Jesus said, "This man coming is truly one of God's people.* There is nothing false in him."

⁴⁸Nathaniel asked, "How do you know me?"

Jesus answered, "I saw you when you were under the fig tree. That was before Philip told you about me."

⁴⁹Then Nathaniel said to Jesus, "Rabbi (*Teacher*), you are the Son of God. You are the King of God's people.*"

⁵⁰Jesus said to Nathaniel, "I told you that I saw you under the fig tree. That is why you believe in me. But you will see much

Christ   The "anointed one" or chosen one of God.
Peter   The Greek name "Peter," like the Aramaic name "Cephas," means "rock."
prophets   People who spoke for God. Their writings are part of the Old Testament.
God's people   Literally, "Israel," the people God chose to bring his blessings to the world.

greater things than that!'' ⁵¹Jesus also said, ''I tell you the truth. You will all see heaven open. You will see 'angels of God going up and coming down'* on the Son of Man (*Jesus*).''

The Wedding at Cana

2 Two days later there was a wedding in the town of Cana in Galilee. Jesus' mother was there. ²Jesus and his followers were also invited to the wedding. ³At the wedding there was not enough wine. After the wine was all gone, Jesus' mother said to Jesus, ''They have no more wine.''

⁴Jesus answered, ''Dear woman, you should not tell me what to do. My time has not yet come.''

⁵Jesus' mother said to the servants, ''Do what Jesus tells you to do.''

⁶In that place there were six large waterpots made of stone. The Jews used waterpots like these in their washing ceremony.* Each waterpot held about 20 or 30 gallons.

⁷Jesus said to the servants, ''Fill those waterpots with water.'' So the servants filled the pots to the top.

⁸Then Jesus said to the servants, ''Now take out some water. Carry the water to the master of the feast.''

So the servants brought the water to the master. ⁹Then the man in charge of the wedding feast tasted it, but the water had become wine. The man did not know where the wine came from. But the servants who brought the water knew where it came from. The master of the wedding called the bridegroom.* ¹⁰He said to the bridegroom, ''People always serve the best wine first. Later, after the guests have become drunk, people serve the cheaper wine. But you have saved the best wine until now.''

¹¹This was the first miracle* that Jesus did. Jesus did this miracle in the town of Cana in Galilee. So Jesus showed his greatness. And his followers believed in him.

'angels...down'   These words are taken from Genesis 28:12.
washing ceremony   The Jews washed themselves in special ways before eating, before worshiping in the temple, and at other special times.
bridegroom   A man ready to be married.
miracle   Miracles are powerful works or great things done by the power of God.

JOHN 2

Jesus in the Temple

[12]Then Jesus went to the town of Capernaum. Jesus' mother and brothers and his followers went with him. They all stayed in Capernaum a few days. [13]It was almost time for the Jewish Passover Feast.* So Jesus went to Jerusalem. [14]In Jerusalem Jesus went to the temple.* In the temple Jesus found men selling cattle, sheep, and doves. Jesus saw other men sitting at tables. These men were exchanging and trading people's money. [15]Jesus made a whip with some pieces of rope. Then Jesus forced all these men and the sheep and cattle to leave the temple. Jesus turned over the tables and scattered the money of the men who exchange money. [16]Then Jesus said to the men who were selling pigeons, "Take these things out of here! Don't make my Father's house a place for buying and selling!"

[17]When this happened the followers of Jesus remembered what was written *in the Scriptures*:

> "My excitement for your house
> will destroy me."
> Psalm 69:9

[18]The Jews said to Jesus, "Show us a miracle* for a sign. Prove that you have the right to do these things."

[19]Jesus answered, "Destroy this temple and I will build it again in three days."

[20]The Jews answered, "People worked 46 years to build this temple! Do you really believe you can build it again in three days?"

([21]But the temple Jesus meant was his own body. [22]After Jesus was raised from death, his followers remembered that Jesus had said this. So his followers believed the Scripture* *about him*, and they believed the words Jesus said.)

[23]Jesus was in Jerusalem for the Passover Feast.* Many people believed in Jesus because they saw the miracles* he did. [24]But Jesus did not trust them. Why? Because Jesus knew the things people were thinking. [25]Jesus did not need any person to tell him about people. Jesus knew what was in a person's mind.

Passover Feast Important holy day for Jews. They ate a special meal on this day every year to
    remember that God freed them from slavery in Egypt in the time of Moses.
temple The special building in Jerusalem where God commanded the Jews to worship him.
Scripture(s) Holy Writings—the Old Testament.
miracle(s) Miracles are powerful works or great things done by the power of God.

242

Jesus and Nicodemus

3 There was a man named Nicodemus. Nicodemus was one of the Pharisees.* He was an important Jewish leader. ²One night Nicodemus came to Jesus. Nicodemus said, "Rabbi (*Teacher*), we know that you are a teacher sent from God. No person can do these miracles* that you do without God's help."

³Jesus answered, "I tell you the truth. A person must be born again. If a person is not born again, then that person cannot be in God's kingdom."

⁴Nicodemus said, "But if a man is already old, how can he be born again? A person cannot enter his mother's body again! So a person cannot be born a second time!"

⁵But Jesus answered, "I tell you the truth. A person must be born from water and the Spirit.* If a person is not born from water and the Spirit, then he cannot enter God's kingdom. ⁶A person's body is born from his human parents. But a person's spiritual life is born from the Spirit. ⁷Don't be surprised that I told you, 'You must be born again.' ⁸The wind blows where it wants to go. You hear the wind blow. But you don't know where the wind comes from or where the wind is going. It is the same with every person that is born from the Spirit."

⁹Nicodemus asked, "How can all this be possible?"

¹⁰Jesus said, "You are an important teacher of God's people.* But you still don't understand these things? ¹¹I tell you the truth. We talk about what we know. We tell about what we have seen. But you people don't accept what we tell you. ¹²I have told you about things here on earth. But you do not believe me. So surely you will not believe me if I tell you about the things of heaven! ¹³The only one who has ever gone up to heaven is the One who came down from heaven—the Son of Man.*

¹⁴"Moses lifted up the snake in the desert.* It is the same with

Pharisees   Pharisees were a Jewish religious group that followed all the Old Testament and other Jewish laws and customs very carefully.

miracles   Miracles are powerful works or great things done by the power of God.

Spirit   The Holy Spirit. Also called the Spirit of God, the Spirit of Christ, and the Comforter. He is joined with God and Christ. He does the work of God among people in the world.

God's people   Literally, "Israel," the people God chose to bring his blessings to the world.

Son of Man   Jesus. Jesus was God's Son, but this name showed that Jesus was a man, too. In Daniel 7:13-14, this is the name for the Messiah (Christ).

Moses...desert   The people of Israel were dying from snake bites. God told Moses to put a brass snake on a pole. The people who looked at the snake were healed (Numbers 21:4-9).

the Son of Man.* The Son of Man must be lifted up too. [15]Then every person who believes in the Son of Man can have life forever.''

[16]Yes, God loved the world so much that he gave his only Son. God gave his Son so that every person who believes in him would not be lost, but have life forever. [17]God sent his Son into the world. God did not send his Son to judge the world guilty. God sent his Son so that the world could be saved through his Son. [18]The person who believes in God's Son is not judged (condemned). But the person who does not believe is already judged. Why? Because that person has not believed in God's only Son. [19]People are judged by this fact: The Light (goodness) has come into the world. But men did not want light. They wanted darkness (sin). Why? Because they were doing evil things. [20]Every person who does evil hates the light. That person will not come to the light. Why? Because then the light will show all the bad things he has done. [21]But the person who follows the true way comes to the light. Then the light will show that the things that person has done were done through God.*

Jesus and John the Baptizer

[22]After this, Jesus and his followers went into the area of Judea. There Jesus stayed with his followers and baptized* people. [23]John was also baptizing people in Aenon. Aenon is near Salim. John was baptizing there because there was plenty of water. People were going there to be baptized. [24](This happened before John was put into prison.)

[25]Some of John's followers had an argument with another Jew. They were arguing about religious washing.* [26]So the followers came to John. They said, "Rabbi (Teacher), remember the man that was with you on the other side of the Jordan river? He is the man you were telling people about. That man is baptizing people, and many people are going to him.''

Son of Man Jesus. Jesus was God's Son, but this name showed that Jesus was a man, too. In Daniel 7:13-14, this is the name for the Messiah (Christ).
Verses 16-21 Some scholars think verses 16-21 are Jesus' words. Others think John wrote them.
baptized A Greek word meaning to immerse, dip, or bury a person or thing briefly under water.
religious washing The Jews washed themselves in special ways before eating, before worshiping in the temple, and at other special times.

²⁷John answered, "A man can get only what God gives him. ²⁸You yourselves heard me say, 'I am not the Christ.* I am only the one that God sent to prepare the way for him.' ²⁹The bride belongs only to the bridegroom.* The friend who helps the bridegroom waits and listens *for the bridegroom to come*. This friend is very happy when he hears the bridegroom's voice. That is the same pleasure I have. And my time of joy is now here. ³⁰He (*Jesus*) must become greater. And I must become less important."

The One Who Comes from Heaven

³¹"The One (*Jesus*) who comes from above is greater than all other people. The person who is from the earth belongs to the earth. That person talks about things that are on the earth. But the One (*Jesus*) who comes from heaven is greater than all other people. ³²He (*Jesus*) tells what he has seen and heard. But people don't accept what he says. ³³The person who accepts what he (*Jesus*) says has given proof that God is true. ³⁴God sent him (*Jesus*). And he tells the things that God says. God gives *him* the Spirit* fully. ³⁵The Father loves the Son. The Father has given the Son power over everything. ³⁶The person who believes in the Son has life forever. But the person who does not obey the Son will never have that life. God's anger stays with that person."

Jesus Talks to a Woman in Samaria

4 The Pharisees* heard that Jesus was making and baptizing* more followers than John. ²(But really Jesus himself did not baptize people. His followers baptized people for him.) Jesus knew that the Pharisees had heard about him. ³So Jesus left Judea and went back to Galilee. ⁴On the way to Galilee Jesus had to go through the country of Samaria.

Christ The "anointed one" (the Messiah) or chosen one of God.
bridegroom A man ready to be married.
Spirit The Holy Spirit. Also called the Spirit of God, the Spirit of Christ, and the Comforter. He is joined with God and Christ. He does the work of God among people in the world.
Pharisees Pharisees were a Jewish religious group that followed all the Old Testament and other Jewish laws and customs very carefully.
baptizing A Greek word meaning to immerse, dip, or bury a person or thing briefly under water.

⁵In Samaria Jesus came to the town called Sychar. This town is near the field that Jacob gave to his son Joseph. ⁶Jacob's well was there. Jesus was tired from his long trip. So Jesus sat down beside the well. It was about noon. ⁷A Samaritan* woman came to that well to get some water. Jesus said to her, "Please give me a drink of water." ⁸(This happened while Jesus' followers were in town buying some food.)

⁹The Samaritan woman answered, "I am surprised that you ask me for a drink! You are a Jew and I am a Samaritan woman!" (Jews are not friends with Samaritans.)*

¹⁰Jesus answered, "You don't know about the thing God gives. And you don't know who I am that asked you for a drink. If you knew these things, you would have asked me and I would have given you living water."

¹¹The woman said, "Sir, where will you get that living water? The well is very deep, and you have nothing to get water with. ¹²Are you greater than Jacob, our father (*ancestor*)? Jacob is the one who gave us this well. He drank from it himself. Also, his sons and all his animals drank water from this well."

¹³Jesus answered, "Every person who drinks this water will be thirsty again. ¹⁴But the person who drinks the water I give will never be thirsty again. That water I give will become like a spring of water flowing inside that person. That water will bring that person life forever."

¹⁵The woman said to Jesus, "Sir, give me this water. Then I will never be thirsty again. And I will not have to come back here to get more water."

¹⁶Jesus told her, "Go get your husband and come back here."

¹⁷The woman answered, "But I have no husband."

Jesus said to her, "You are right to say you have no husband. ¹⁸Really you have had five husbands. But the man you live with now is not your husband. You told me the truth."

¹⁹The woman said, "Sir, I can see that you are a prophet.* ²⁰Our fathers worshiped on this mountain. But you Jews say that Jerusalem is the place where people must worship."

Samaritan Samaritans were people from Samaria. These people were part Jew, but the Jews did not accept them as true Jews. Many Samaritans and Jews hated each other.
Jews...Samaritans This can also mean, "Jews don't use things that Samaritans have used."
prophet Person who spoke for God. He often told things that would happen in the future.

²¹Jesus said, "Believe me, woman! The time is coming when you will not have to be in Jerusalem or on that mountain to worship the Father (*God*). ²²You Samaritans worship something that you don't understand. We Jews understand what we worship. Salvation comes from the Jews. ²³The time is coming when the true worshipers will worship the Father in spirit and truth. That time is now here. And those are the kind of people the Father wants to be his worshipers. ²⁴God is spirit. So the people who worship God must worship in spirit and truth."

²⁵The woman said, "I know that the Messiah is coming." (Messiah is the One called Christ.*) "When the Messiah comes, he will explain everything to us."

²⁶Then Jesus said, "That person is talking to you now. I am *the Messiah.*"

²⁷At that time Jesus' followers came back from town. They were surprised because they saw Jesus talking with a woman. But none of them asked, "What do you want?" or "Why are you talking with her?"

²⁸Then the woman left her water and went back to town. She told the people in town, ²⁹"A man told me everything I have ever done. Come see him. Maybe he is the Christ*!" ³⁰So the people left the town and went to see Jesus.

³¹While the woman was in town Jesus' followers were begging him, "Teacher, eat something!"

³²But Jesus answered, "I have food to eat that you know nothing about."

³³So the followers asked themselves, "Did somebody already bring Jesus some food?"

³⁴Jesus said, "My food is to do what the One (*God*) who sent me wants me to do. My food is to finish the work that he gave me to do. ³⁵*When you plant* you always say, 'Four more months to wait before we gather the grain.' But I tell you, open your eyes. Look at the *people. They are like* fields ready for harvesting now. ³⁶Even now, the person who harvests the crop is being paid. He is gathering crops for eternal life. So now the person who plants can be happy together with the person who harvests. ³⁷It is true when

---

Christ   The "anointed one" or chosen one of God.

we say, 'One person plants, but another person harvests the crop.' ³⁸I sent you to harvest a crop that you did not work for. Other people did the work, and you get the profit from their work."

³⁹Many of the Samaritan people in that town believed in Jesus. They believed because of what the woman had told them about Jesus. She had told them, "He (*Jesus*) told me everything I have ever done." ⁴⁰The Samaritans went to Jesus. They begged Jesus to stay with them. So Jesus stayed there two days. ⁴¹Many more people believed because of the things Jesus said.

⁴²The people said to the woman, "First we believed in Jesus because of what you told us. But now we believe because we heard him ourselves. We know that this man really is the Savior* of the world."

Jesus Heals an Official's Son

⁴³Two days later Jesus left and went to Galilee. ⁴⁴(Jesus had said before that a prophet* is not respected in his own country.) ⁴⁵When Jesus arrived in Galilee, the people there welcomed him. These people had seen all the things Jesus did at the Passover Feast* in Jerusalem. These people had been at the Passover Feast too.

⁴⁶Jesus went to visit Cana in Galilee again. Cana is where Jesus had changed the water into wine. One of the king's important officials lived in the city of Capernaum. This man's son was sick. ⁴⁷The man heard that Jesus had come from Judea and was now in Galilee. So the man went to Jesus *in Cana*. He begged Jesus to come to Capernaum and heal his son. His son was almost dead. ⁴⁸Jesus said to him, "You people must see miracles* and wonderful works before you will believe in me."

⁴⁹The king's official said, "Sir, come *to my house* before my little son dies."

⁵⁰Jesus answered, "Go. Your son will live."

Savior   The one who will save the people of the world from punishment for their sins.
prophet   Person who spoke for God. He often told things that would happen in the future.
Passover Feast   Important holy day for Jews. They ate a special meal on this day every year to remember that God freed them from slavery in Egypt in the time of Moses.
miracles   Miracles are powerful works or great things done by the power of God.

The man believed what Jesus told him and went home. ⁵¹On the way home the man's servants came and met him. They told him, "Your son is well."

⁵²The man asked, "What time did my son begin to get well?"

The servants answered, "It was about one o'clock yesterday when the fever left him."

⁵³The father knew that one o'clock was the same time that Jesus had said, "Your son will live." So the man and all the people in his home believed in Jesus.

⁵⁴That was the second miracle* that Jesus did after coming from Judea to Galilee.

Jesus Heals a Man at a Pool

5 Later Jesus went to Jerusalem for a special Jewish feast. ²In Jerusalem there is a pool with five covered porches. In the Jewish language* it is called Bethzatha.* This pool is near the Sheep Gate. ³Many sick people were lying on the porches *beside the pool*. Some of the people were blind, some were crippled, and some were paralyzed.* ⁵There was a man lying there who had been sick for 38 years. ⁶Jesus saw the man lying there. Jesus knew that the man had been sick for a very long time. So Jesus asked the man, "Do you want to be well?"

⁷The sick man answered, "Sir, there is no person to help me get into the water when the water starts moving. I try to be the first person into the water. But when I try, another person always goes in before I can."

⁸Then Jesus said, "Stand up! Pick up your bed and walk." ⁹Then immediately the man was well. The man picked up his bed and walked.

The day all this happened was a Sabbath day.* ¹⁰So the Jews said to the man who had been healed, "Today is the Sabbath. It is against our law for you to carry your bed on the Sabbath day."

---

miracle   Miracles are powerful works or great things done by the power of God.
Jewish language   Aramaic, the "Hebrew" language in the first century.
Bethzatha   Also called Bethsaida or Bethesda, a pool of water north of the temple in Jerusalem.
Verse 3   Some Greek copies add "and they waited for the water to move." A few later copies add verse 4: "Sometimes an angel of the Lord came down to the pool and shook the water. After the angel did this, the first person to go into the pool was healed from any sickness he had."
Sabbath day   Seventh day of the Jewish week. It was a special religious day for the Jews.

¹¹But the man answered, "The person (*Jesus*) who made me well told me, 'Pick up your bed and walk.' "

¹²The Jews asked the man, "Who is the person who told you to pick up your bed and walk?"

¹³But the man who had been healed did not know who the person was. There were many people in that place, and Jesus had left.

¹⁴Later Jesus found the man at the temple.* Jesus said to him, "See, you are well now. But stop sinning or something worse may happen to you!"

¹⁵Then the man left and went back to those Jews. The man told them that Jesus was the one who made him well.

¹⁶Jesus was doing these things (*healing*) on the Sabbath day.* So the Jews began to do bad things to Jesus. ¹⁷But Jesus said to the Jews, "My Father never stops working. And so I work too."

¹⁸This made the Jews try harder to kill him. *The Jews said*, "First Jesus was breaking the law about the Sabbath day. Then he said that God is his Father! He is making himself equal with God!"

Jesus Has God's Authority

¹⁹But Jesus answered, "I tell you the truth. The Son can do nothing alone. The Son does only what he sees his Father doing. The Son does the same things that the Father does. ²⁰The Father loves the Son, and the Father shows the Son all the things he does. *This man was healed.* But the Father will show the Son greater things than this to do. Then you will all be amazed. ²¹The Father raises dead people and gives them life. In the same way, the Son gives life to the people he wants to. ²²Also, the Father judges no one. But the Father has given the Son power to do all the judging. ²³God did this so that all people will respect the Son the same as they respect the Father. If a person does not respect the Son, then that person does not respect the Father. The Father is the One who sent the Son.

²⁴"I tell you the truth: if a person hears what I say and believes in the One who sent me, that person has life forever. That person

---

temple The special building in Jerusalem where God commanded the Jews to worship him.
Sabbath day Seventh day of the Jewish week. It was a special religious day for the Jews.

will not be judged. He has already left death and has entered into life. ²⁵I tell you the truth: an *important* time is coming. That time is already here. People who are dead *in sin* will hear the voice of the Son of God. And the people who *accept the things they* hear *from the Son* will have life *forever*. ²⁶Life comes from the Father (*God*) himself. So the Father has also allowed the Son (*Jesus*) to give life. ²⁷And the Father has given the Son the power to judge *all people*. Why? Because that Son is the Son of Man.* ²⁸Don't be surprised at this. A time is coming when all people who are dead and in their graves will hear his voice. ²⁹Then they will come out of their graves. The people who did good *in life* will rise and have life forever. But the people who did evil will rise to be judged guilty."

Jesus Continues Talking to the Jews

³⁰"I can do nothing alone. I judge only the way I am told. So my judgment is right. Why? Because I don't try to please myself. But I want to please the One (*God*) who sent me.

³¹"If I tell people about myself, then people cannot accept those things I say about myself. ³²But there is another person who tells people about me. And I know that the things he says about me are true.

³³"You have sent men to John. And he has told you about the truth. ³⁴I don't need a man to tell people about me. But I tell you these things so that you can be saved. ³⁵John was like a lamp that burned and gave light. And you were happy to enjoy his light for a while.

³⁶"But I have a proof about myself that is greater than John. The things I do are my proof. These are the things my Father gave me to do. These things show that the Father sent me. ³⁷And the Father who sent me has given proof about me himself. But you have never heard his voice. You have never seen what he looks like. ³⁸The Father's teaching does not live in you. Why? Because you don't believe in the One that the Father sent. ³⁹You carefully

---

Son of Man   Jesus. Jesus was God's Son, but this name showed that Jesus was a man, too. In Daniel 7:13-14, this is the name for the Messiah (Christ).

study the Scriptures.* You think that those Scriptures give you life forever. Those same Scriptures tell about me! ⁴⁰But you refuse to come to me to have that life *you want*.

⁴¹"I don't want praise from men. ⁴²But I know you—I know that you don't have God's love in you. ⁴³I have come from my Father—I speak for him. But you don't accept me. But when another person comes speaking only for himself, you will accept him. ⁴⁴You like to have praise from each other. But you never try to get the praise that comes from the only God. So how can you believe? ⁴⁵Don't think that I will stand before the Father and say that you are wrong. Moses is the person who says that you are wrong. And Moses is the one that you hoped would save you. ⁴⁶If you really believed Moses, you would believe me. Why? Because Moses wrote about me. ⁴⁷But you don't believe what Moses wrote. So you cannot believe the things I say."

Jesus Feeds More Than 5,000 People

6 Later, Jesus went across Lake Galilee (or, Lake Tiberias). ²Many people followed Jesus. They followed him because they saw the ways Jesus showed his power by healing the sick people. ³Jesus went up on the side of the hill. He sat there with his followers. ⁴It was almost the time for the Jewish Passover Feast.*

⁵Jesus looked up and saw many people coming toward him. Jesus said to Philip, "Where can we buy *enough* bread for all these people to eat?" ⁶(Jesus asked Philip this question to test him. Jesus already knew what he planned to do.)

⁷Philip answered, "We would all have to work a month to buy enough bread for each person here to have only a little piece."

⁸Another follower there was Andrew. Andrew was Simon Peter's brother. Andrew said, ⁹"Here is a boy with five loaves of barley bread and two little fish. But that is not enough for so many people."

¹⁰Jesus said, "Tell the people to sit down." This was a very grassy place. There were about 5,000 men who sat down there. ¹¹Then Jesus held the loaves of bread. Jesus thanked God for the

Scriptures Holy Writings—the Old Testament.
Passover Feast Important holy day for Jews. They ate a special meal on this day every year to remember that God freed them from slavery in Egypt in the time of Moses.

bread and gave it to the people who were sitting down. He did the same with the fish. Jesus gave the people as much as they wanted.

¹²All the people had enough to eat. When they finished Jesus said to his followers, "Gather the pieces of fish and bread that were not eaten. Don't waste anything." ¹³So the followers gathered up the pieces that were left. The people had started eating with only five loaves of barley bread. But the followers filled twelve large baskets with the pieces of food that were left.

¹⁴The people saw this miracle* that Jesus did. The people said, "He must truly be the Prophet* who is coming into the world."

¹⁵Jesus knew that the people wanted him to become king. The people planned to come get Jesus and make him their king. So Jesus left and went into the hills alone.

Jesus Walks on the Water

¹⁶That evening Jesus' followers went down to the lake (*Lake Galilee*). ¹⁷It was dark now and Jesus had not yet come back to them. The followers got into a boat and started going across the lake to Capernaum. ¹⁸The wind was blowing very hard. The waves on the lake were becoming bigger. ¹⁹They rowed the boat about three or four miles. Then they saw Jesus. He was walking on the water. He was coming to the boat. The followers were afraid. ²⁰But Jesus said to them, "Don't be afraid. It's me." ²¹After Jesus said this, the followers were happy to take Jesus into the boat. Then the boat came to land at the place where they wanted to go.

The People Seek Jesus

²²The next day came. Some people had stayed on the other side of the lake. These people knew that Jesus did not go with his followers in the boat. The people knew that Jesus' followers had left in the boat alone. And they knew that it was the only boat that was there. ²³But then some boats from Tiberias came. The boats landed near the place where the people had eaten *the day before*. This was where they had eaten the bread after the Lord

---

miracle   Miracles are powerful works or great things done by the power of God.
Prophet   They probably meant the prophet that God told Moses he would send (Deut. 18:15-19).

(*Jesus*) gave thanks. ²⁴The people saw that Jesus and his followers were not there now. So the people got into the boats and went to Capernaum. They wanted to find Jesus.

Jesus, the Bread of Life

²⁵The people found Jesus on the other side of the lake. They asked Jesus, "Teacher, when did you come here?"

²⁶Jesus answered, "Why are you looking for me? Are you looking for me because you saw me do miracles* that prove my power? No! I tell you the truth. You are looking for me because you ate the bread and you were satisfied (*full*). ²⁷Earthly food spoils and ruins. So don't work to get that kind of food. But work to get the food that stays good always and gives you life forever. The Son of Man* will give you that food. God the Father showed that he is with the Son of Man."

²⁸The people asked Jesus, "What are the things God wants us to do?"

²⁹Jesus answered, "The work God wants you to do is this: to believe in the One that God sent."

³⁰So the people asked, "What miracle* will you do to prove *that you are the One God sent*? If we can see you do a miracle, then we will believe you. What will you do? ³¹Our fathers (*ancestors*) ate the manna (*food*) God gave them in the desert. This is written in the Scriptures*: 'God gave them bread from heaven to eat.'* "

³²Jesus said, "I tell you the truth. Moses was not the one who gave your people bread from heaven. But my Father gives you the true bread from heaven. ³³What is the bread of God? God's bread is the One who comes down from heaven and gives life to the world."

³⁴The people said, "Sir, give us this bread always."

---

miracle(s)   Miracles are powerful works or great things done by the power of God.

Son of Man   Jesus. Jesus was God's Son, but this name showed that Jesus was a man, too. In Daniel 7:13-14, this is the name for the Messiah (Christ).

Scriptures   Holy Writings—the Old Testament.

'God gave...eat'   Quotation from Psalm 78:24.

³⁵Then Jesus said, "I am the bread that gives life. The person who comes to me will never be hungry. The person who believes in me will never be thirsty. ³⁶I told you before that you have seen me, and still you don't believe. ³⁷The Father gives me my people. Every one of those people will come to me. I will always accept every person who comes to me. ³⁸I came down from heaven to do what God wants me to do. I did not come to do what I want to do. ³⁹I must not lose any person that God has given me. But I must raise up those people on the last day. This is what the One who sent me wants me to do. ⁴⁰Every person who sees the Son and believes in him has life forever. I will raise up that person on the last day. This is what my Father wants."

⁴¹The Jews began to complain about Jesus. They complained because Jesus said, "I am the bread that comes down from heaven." ⁴²The Jews said, "This is Jesus. We know his father and mother. Jesus is only Joseph's son. How can he say, 'I came down from heaven'?"

⁴³But Jesus answered, "Stop complaining to each other. ⁴⁴The Father is the One who sent me. And the Father is the One who brings people to me. I will raise up those people on the last day. If the Father does not bring a person to me, then that person cannot come to me. ⁴⁵It is written in the prophets,* 'God will teach all the people.'* People listen to the Father and learn from him. Those people come to me. ⁴⁶The only person who has seen the Father is the One who came from him. No other person has ever seen the Father. ⁴⁷I tell you the truth. If a person believes, then that person has life forever. ⁴⁸I am the bread that gives life. ⁴⁹Your ancestors ate the manna (*food*) God gave them in the desert. But *like all people*, they died. ⁵⁰*I am* that bread that comes down from heaven. If a person eats this bread, he will never die. ⁵¹I am the living bread that came down from heaven. If a person eats this bread, then that person will live forever. This bread is my body. I will give my body so that the people in the world can have life."

⁵²Then the Jews began to argue among themselves. They said, "How can this man give us his body to eat?"

---

prophets   People who spoke for God. Their writings are part of the Old Testament.
'God...people'   Quotation from Isaiah 54:13.

⁵³Jesus said, "I tell you the truth, you must eat the body of the Son of Man.* And you must drink his blood. If you don't do this, then you don't have real life in you. ⁵⁴The person who eats my body and drinks my blood has eternal life. I will raise up that person on the last day. ⁵⁵My body is true food. My blood is true drink. ⁵⁶If a person eats my body and drinks my blood, then that person lives in me, and I live in that person. ⁵⁷The Father sent me. The Father lives, and I live because of the Father. So the person who eats me will live because of me. ⁵⁸I am not like the bread that our ancestors ate *in the desert*. They ate that bread. But, *like all people*, they died. I am the bread that came down from heaven. The person who eats this bread will live forever." ⁵⁹Jesus said all these things while he was teaching in the synagogue* in the city of Capernaum.

The Words of Eternal Life

⁶⁰The followers of Jesus heard this. Many of the followers said, "This teaching is hard *to accept*. Who can accept this teaching?"

⁶¹Jesus knew that his followers were complaining about this. So Jesus said, "Does this teaching bother you? ⁶²Then will it also bother you to see the Son of Man* going back to the place where he came from? ⁶³It is not the body that gives a person life. It is the spirit that gives life. The things I told you are spirit. And so these things give life. ⁶⁴But some of you don't believe." (Jesus knew the people that did not believe. Jesus knew this from the beginning. And Jesus knew the person who would turn against him.) ⁶⁵Jesus said, "That is why I said, 'If the Father does not let a person come to me, then that person cannot come.' "

⁶⁶After Jesus said these things, many of his followers left him. They stopped following Jesus.

⁶⁷Jesus asked the twelve *apostles*,* "Do you want to leave too?"

⁶⁸Simon Peter answered Jesus, "Lord, where would we go? You have the things that give life forever. ⁶⁹We believe in you. We know that you are the Holy One from God."

Son of Man Jesus. Jesus was God's Son, but this name showed that Jesus was a man, too. In Daniel 7:13-14, this is the name for the Messiah (Christ).

synagogue Synagogues were places where Jews gathered to read and study the Scriptures.

apostles The men Jesus taught and chose to be his special helpers.

[70]Then Jesus answered, "I chose all twelve of you. But one of you is a devil."

[71]Jesus was talking about Judas, the son of Simon Iscariot. Judas was one of the twelve *apostles*.* But later Judas would turn against Jesus.

Jesus and His Brothers

7 After this, Jesus traveled around the country of Galilee. Jesus did not want to travel in Judea, because some of the Jews there wanted to kill him. [2]It was time for the Jewish Feast of Tabernacles.* [3]So Jesus' brothers said to him, "You should leave here and go to *the feast in* Judea. Then your followers there can see the miracles* you do. [4]If a person wants the people to know him, then that person must not hide the things he does. Show yourself to the world. *Let them see* these things (*miracles*) you do." [5](Even Jesus' brothers did not believe in him.) [6]Jesus said to his brothers, "The right time for me has not yet come. But any time is right for you *to go*. [7]The world cannot hate you. But the world hates me. Why? Because I tell the people in the world that they do evil things. [8]So you go to the feast. I will not go to the feast now. The right time for me has not yet come." [9]After Jesus said this, he stayed in Galilee.

[10]So Jesus' brothers left to go to the feast. After they left, Jesus went too. But Jesus did not let people see him. [11]At the feast the Jews were looking for Jesus. The Jews said, "Where is that man?"

[12]There was a large group of people there. Many of these people were talking to each other about Jesus. Some people said, "He is a good man."

But other people said, "No, he fools the people." [13]But none of the people were brave enough to talk about Jesus openly. The people were afraid of the Jewish leaders.

---

apostles   The men Jesus taught and chose to be his special helpers.
Feast of Tabernacles   A special week each year when the Jews lived in tents to remember the time their people wandered in the desert for 40 years during the time of Moses.
miracles   Miracles are powerful works or great things done by the power of God.

Jesus Teaches at the Feast in Jerusalem

¹⁴The feast* was about half finished. Then Jesus went to the temple* and began to teach. ¹⁵The Jews were amazed. They said, "This man has never studied in school. How did he learn so much?"

¹⁶Jesus answered, "The things I teach are not my own. My teaching comes from him (*God*) who sent me. ¹⁷If a person wants to do what God wants, then that person will know that my teaching comes from God. That person will know that this teaching is not my own. ¹⁸The person who teaches his own ideas is trying to get honor for himself. But the person who tries to bring honor to the one who sent him—that person speaks the truth. There is nothing false in him. ¹⁹Moses gave you the law.* Right? But none of you obey that law. Why are you trying to kill me?"

²⁰The people answered, "A demon* has come into you *and made you crazy*! We are not trying to kill you."

²¹Jesus said to them, "I did one miracle* and you are all amazed. ²²Moses gave you the law about circumcision.* (But really Moses did not give you circumcision. Circumcision came from our people *who lived before Moses*.) Sometimes you circumcise a baby on a Sabbath day.* ²³This shows that a person can be circumcised on a Sabbath day to obey the law of Moses. So why are you angry at me for healing a person's whole body on the Sabbath day? ²⁴Stop judging by the way things look. Be fair and judge by what is really right."

The People Wonder If Jesus Is the Christ

²⁵Then some of the people who lived in Jerusalem said, "This is the man they are trying to kill. ²⁶But he is teaching where everyone can see and hear him. And no person is trying to stop him from teaching. Maybe the leaders have decided that he really

---

feast   The Jewish Feast of Tabernacles. See note on previous page.
temple   The special building in Jerusalem where God commanded the Jews to worship him.
law   Moses gave God's people the law that God gave him on Mount Sinai (Exodus 34:29-32).
demon   Demons are evil spirits from the devil.
miracle   Miracles are powerful works or great things done by the power of God.
circumcision   The cutting off of the foreskin. This was done to every Jewish baby boy. It was a mark of the agreement that God made with Abraham (Genesis 17:9-14).
Sabbath day   Seventh day of the Jewish week. It was a special religious day for the Jews.

is the Christ.* ²⁷But we know where this man's home is. And when the real Christ comes, no person will know where he comes from.''

²⁸Jesus was still teaching in the temple.* Jesus said, "Yes, you know me and you know where I am from. But I have not come by my own authority. I was sent by the One (*God*) who is true. You don't know him. ²⁹But I know him. I am from him, and he sent me.''

³⁰When Jesus said this, the people tried to get him. But no person was able to touch Jesus. It was not yet the right time *for Jesus to be killed*. ³¹But many of the people believed in Jesus. The people said, "We are waiting for the Christ* to come. When the Christ comes, will he do more miracles* *than this* man (*Jesus*) has done? No! *So this man must be the Christ*.''

The Jews Try to Arrest Jesus

³²The Pharisees* heard these things the people were saying about Jesus. So the leading priests and the Pharisees sent some temple police to arrest Jesus. ³³Then Jesus said, "I will be with you people a little while longer. Then I will go back to the One (*God*) who sent me. ³⁴You will look for me, but you will not find me. And you cannot come where I am.''

³⁵The Jews said to each other, "Where will this man go that we cannot find him? Will he go to the Jews who live in the Greek cities? Will he teach the Greek people there? ³⁶This man (*Jesus*) says, 'You will look for me but you will not find me.' He also says, 'You cannot come where I am.' What does this mean?''

Jesus Talks About the Holy Spirit*

³⁷The last day of the feast came. It was the most important day. On that day, Jesus stood and said with a loud voice, "If a person is thirsty, let him come to me and drink. ³⁸If a person believes in

Christ   The "anointed one" (the Messiah) or chosen one of God.
temple   The special building in Jerusalem where God commanded the Jews to worship him.
miracles   Miracles are powerful works or great things done by the power of God.
Pharisees   Pharisees were a Jewish religious group that followed all the Old Testament and other Jewish laws and customs very carefully.
Holy Spirit   Also called the Spirit of God, the Spirit of Christ, and the Comforter. He is joined with God and Christ. He does the work of God among people in the world.

me, rivers of living water will flow out from his heart. That is what the Scripture* says." ³⁹Jesus was talking about the *Holy* Spirit.* The Spirit had not yet been given to people, because Jesus had not yet *died and* been raised to glory. But later, those people who believed in Jesus would receive the Spirit.

The People Argue About Jesus

⁴⁰The people heard these things that Jesus said. Some of the people said, "This man really is the Prophet.*"

⁴¹Other people said, "He is the Christ.*"

Other people said, "The Christ will not come from Galilee. ⁴²The Scripture* says that the Christ will come from David's family. And the Scripture says that the Christ will come from Bethlehem, the town where David lived." ⁴³So the people did not agree with each other because of Jesus. ⁴⁴Some of the people wanted to arrest Jesus. But no person tried to do this.

The Jewish Leaders Refuse to Believe in Jesus

⁴⁵The temple* police went back to the leading priests and the Pharisees.* The priests and the Pharisees asked, "Why didn't you bring Jesus?"

⁴⁶The temple police answered, "The things he says are greater than the words of any man!"

⁴⁷The Pharisees answered, "So Jesus has fooled you too! ⁴⁸Have any of the leaders believed in Jesus? No! Have any of us Pharisees* believed in him? No! ⁴⁹But those people *out there* know nothing about the law.* They are under God's curse!"

⁵⁰But Nicodemus was there in that group. Nicodemus was the one who had gone to see Jesus before.* Nicodemus said, ⁵¹"Our law will not let us judge a man without hearing him. We cannot

---

Scripture   A part of the Holy Writings—the Old Testament.
Holy Spirit   Also called the Spirit of God, the Spirit of Christ, and the Comforter. He is joined with God and Christ. He does the work of God among people in the world.
Prophet   They probably meant the prophet God told Moses he would send (Deut. 18:15-19).
Christ   The "anointed one" (the Messiah) or chosen one of God.
temple   The special building in Jerusalem where God commanded the Jews to worship him.
Pharisees   Pharisees were a Jewish religious group that followed all the Old Testament and other Jewish laws and customs very carefully.
law   The law of Moses.
Nicodemus...before   The story about Nicodemus going and talking to Jesus is in John 3:1-21.

judge him until we know what he has done." ⁵²The Jewish leaders answered, "Are you from Galilee too? Study the Scriptures.* You will learn that no prophet* comes from Galilee."

⁵³All the Jewish leaders left and went home.

The Woman Caught in Adultery

8 Jesus went to the Mount of Olives.* ²Early in the morning Jesus went back to the temple.* All the people came to Jesus. Jesus sat and taught the people. ³The teachers of the law and the Pharisees* brought a woman there. The woman had been caught doing the sin of adultery.* These Jews forced the woman to stand before the people. ⁴They said to Jesus, "Teacher, this woman was caught having sex with a man who is not her husband. ⁵The law of Moses commands that we kill with rocks every woman who does this. Jesus, what do you say we should do?" ⁶The Jews were using this question to trick Jesus. They wanted to catch Jesus saying something wrong. Then they could have a charge against him. But Jesus kneeled down and started writing on the ground with his finger. ⁷The Jewish leaders continued to ask Jesus their question. So Jesus looked up and said, "Is there any person here who has never sinned? That person without sin can throw the first rock at this woman." ⁸Then Jesus knelt down again and wrote on the ground.

⁹The people that heard Jesus began to leave one by one. The older men left first, and then the others. Jesus was left there alone with the woman. She was standing before him. ¹⁰Jesus looked up again and asked her, "Woman, all of those people are gone. None of them judged you guilty?"

¹¹The woman answered, "None of them judged me, sir."

Then Jesus said, "So I also don't judge you. You can go now, but don't sin again."*

Scriptures Holy Writings—the Old Testament.
prophet Person who spoke for God. He often told things that would happen in the future.
Mount of Olives A hill covered with olive trees near the city of Jerusalem.
temple The special building in Jerusalem where God commanded the Jews to worship him.
Pharisees Pharisees were a Jewish religious group that followed all the Old Testament and other
    Jewish laws and customs very carefully.
adultery Breaking a marriage promise by doing sexual sin.
Verses 7:53-8:11 The oldest and best Greek copies do not have these verses.

Jesus Is the Light of the World

¹²Later, Jesus talked to the people again. Jesus said, "I am the light of the world. The person who follows me will never live in darkness. That person will have the light that gives life."

¹³But the Pharisees* said to Jesus, "When you talk about yourself, you are the only one to say that these things are true. So we cannot accept these things you say."

¹⁴Jesus answered, "Yes, I am saying these things about myself. But people can believe these things I say. Why? Because I know where I came from. And I know where I am going. *I am not like you people*. You don't know where I came from or where I am going. ¹⁵You judge me the way you would judge any man. I don't judge any person. ¹⁶But if I judge, my judging is true. Why? Because when I judge I am not alone. The Father who sent me is with me. ¹⁷Your own law says that when two witnesses say the same thing, then you must accept what they say. ¹⁸I am one of the witnesses that speaks about myself. And the Father who sent me is my other witness."

¹⁹The people asked, "Where is your father?"

Jesus answered, "You don't know me or my Father. But if you knew me, then you would know my Father too." ²⁰Jesus said these things while he was teaching in the temple.* He was near the place where the money is kept that the people give. But no person arrested him. The right time for Jesus had not yet come.

The Jews Don't Understand About Jesus

²¹Again, Jesus said to the people, "I will leave you. You will look for me, but you will die with your sin. You cannot come where I am going."

²²So the Jews asked themselves, "Will Jesus kill himself? Is that why he said, 'You cannot come where I am going'?"

²³But Jesus said, "You people are from here below. But I am from above. You belong to this world, but I don't belong to this

---

Pharisees   Pharisees were a Jewish religious group that followed all the Old Testament and other Jewish laws and customs very carefully.

temple   The special building in Jerusalem where God commanded the Jews to worship him.

world. ²⁴I told you that you would die with your sins. Yes, you will die with your sins, if you don't believe that I AM.*"

²⁵The Jews asked, "Then who are you?"

Jesus answered, "I am what I have told you from the beginning. ²⁶I have many things to say about you. I could judge you. But I tell people only the things I have heard from the One who sent me. And he speaks the truth."

²⁷The people did not understand who Jesus was talking about. Jesus was telling them about the Father (*God*). ²⁸So Jesus said to the people, "You will lift up (*kill*) the Son of Man.* Then you will know that I AM.* You will know that these things I do are not by my own authority (*power*). You will know that I say only the things that the Father has taught me. ²⁹The One (*God*) who sent me is with me. I always do what pleases him. So he has not left me alone." ³⁰While Jesus was saying these things, many people believed in him.

Jesus Talks About Freedom from Sin

³¹So Jesus said to the Jews who believed in him, "If you continue to obey my teaching, then you are truly my followers. ³²Then you will know the truth. And the truth will make you free."

³³The Jews answered, "We are Abraham's people. And we have never been slaves. So why do you say that we will be free? "

³⁴Jesus answered, "I tell you the truth. Every person who sins is a slave. Sin is his master. ³⁵A slave does not stay with a family forever. But a son belongs to the family forever. ³⁶So if the Son makes you free, then you will be truly free. ³⁷I know you are Abraham's people. But you want to kill me. Why? Because you don't want to accept my teaching. ³⁸I am telling you what my Father has shown me. But you do the things that your father has told you."

³⁹The Jews answered, "Our father is Abraham."

Jesus said, "If you were really Abraham's children, then you

I AM   This is like the name of God used in Exodus 3:14, but it can also mean "I am he (the Christ)."

Son of Man   Jesus. Jesus was God's Son, but this name showed that Jesus was a man, too. In Daniel 7:13-14, this is the name for the Messiah (Christ).

would do the things that Abraham did. ⁴⁰I am a man who has told you the truth that I heard from God. But you are trying to kill me. Abraham did nothing like that. ⁴¹So you are doing the things that your own father did.''

But the Jews said, ''We are not like children who never knew who their father was. God is our Father. He is the only Father we have.''

⁴²Jesus said to those Jews, ''If God were really your Father, then you would love me. I came from God and now I am here. I did not come by my own authority. God sent me. ⁴³You don't understand these things I say. Why? It is because you cannot accept my teaching. ⁴⁴Your father is the devil. You belong to him. You want to do what he wants. The devil was a murderer from the beginning. The devil was against the truth. And there is no truth in the devil. He is like the lies he tells. The devil is a liar, and he is the father of lies. ⁴⁵I speak the truth. That is why you don't believe me. ⁴⁶Can any of you prove that I am guilty of sin? If I tell the truth, then why don't you believe me? ⁴⁷The person who belongs to God accepts what God says. But you don't accept what God says, because you don't belong to God.''

Jesus Talks About Himself and Abraham

⁴⁸The Jews answered, ''We say you are a Samaritan*! We say a demon* has come into you *and made you crazy*! Are we not right when we say these things?''

⁴⁹Jesus answered, ''I have no demon in me. I give honor to my Father. But you give no honor to me. ⁵⁰I am not trying to get honor for myself. There is One who wants this honor for me. He is the judge. ⁵¹I tell you the truth. If a person obeys my teaching, then that person will never die.''

⁵²The Jews said to Jesus, ''Now we know that you have a demon* in you! Even Abraham and the prophets* died. But you say, 'The person who obeys my teaching will never die.' ⁵³Do you think that you are greater than our father Abraham? Abraham died. And the prophets died too. Who do you think you are?''

Samaritan   Samaritans were people from Samaria. These people were part Jew, but the Jews did not accept them as true Jews. Most Samaritans and Jews hated each other.
demon   Demons are evil spirits from the devil.
prophets   People who spoke for God. Their writings are part of the Old Testament.

⁵⁴Jesus answered, "If I give honor to myself, then that honor is worth nothing. The One who gives me honor is my Father. And you say that he is your God. ⁵⁵But you don't really know him. I know him. If I said I did not know him, then I would be a liar like you are liars. But I do know him. And I obey what he says. ⁵⁶Your father Abraham was very happy that he would see the day when I came. He saw that day and was happy."

⁵⁷The Jews said to Jesus, "What? You have never seen Abraham! You are not even 50 years old!"

⁵⁸Jesus answered, "I tell you the truth. Before Abraham was born, I AM*!" ⁵⁹When Jesus said this, the people picked up rocks to throw at him. But Jesus hid, and then he left the temple.*

Jesus Heals a Man Born Blind

9 While Jesus was walking, he saw a blind man. This man had been blind since the time he was born. ²Jesus' followers asked him, "Teacher, this man was born blind. But whose sin made him be born blind? His own sin, or his parents' sin?"

³Jesus answered, "It is not this man's sin or his parents' sin that made him be blind. This man was born blind so that God's power could be shown to people *when I heal him*. ⁴While it is daytime, we must continue doing the work of the One who sent me. The night is coming. And no person can work at night. ⁵While I am in the world, I am the light of the world."

⁶After Jesus said this, Jesus spit on the dirt, and made some mud with it. Jesus put the mud on the man's eyes. ⁷Jesus told the man, "Go and wash in the pool of Siloam." (Siloam means "Sent".) So the man went to the pool. He washed and came back. Now he was able to see.

⁸Some people had seen this man begging before. These people and the man's neighbors said, "Look! Is this the same man who always sits and begs?"

I AM This is like the name of God used in Exodus 3:14, but it can also mean "I am he (the Christ)."
temple The special building in Jerusalem where God commanded the Jews to worship him.

⁹Some people said, "Yes! He is the one." But other people said, "No, he's not the same man. He only looks like him."

So the man himself said, "I am the man *who was blind before*."

¹⁰The people asked, "What happened? How did you get your sight?"

¹¹The man answered, "The man that people call Jesus made some mud. He put the mud on my eyes. Then Jesus told me to go to Siloam and wash. So I went to Siloam and washed. And then I could see."

¹²The people asked the man, "Where is this man (*Jesus*)?"

The man answered, "I don't know."

The Pharisees Ask About the Man Jesus Healed

¹³Then the people brought the man to the Pharisees.* This was the man who had been blind. ¹⁴Jesus had made mud and healed the man's eyes. The day Jesus did this was a Sabbath day.* ¹⁵So now the Pharisees asked the man, "How did you get your sight?"

The man answered, "He put mud on my eyes. I washed, and now I can see."

¹⁶Some of the Pharisees said, "This man (*Jesus*) does not obey the law about the Sabbath day. So he is not from God."

Other men said, "But a person who is a sinner can't do miracles* like these." These Jews could not agree with each other.

¹⁷The Jewish leaders asked the man again, "This man (*Jesus*) healed you, and you can see. What do you say about him?"

The man answered, "He is a prophet.*"

¹⁸The Jews still did not believe that this really happened to the man. They did not believe that this man was blind and was now healed. But later they sent for that man's parents. ¹⁹The Jews asked his parents, "Is this your son? You say that he was born blind. Then why can he see now?"

Pharisees   Pharisees were a Jewish religious group that followed all the Old Testament and other Jewish laws and customs very carefully.

Sabbath day   Seventh day of the Jewish week. It was a special religious day for the Jews.

miracles   Miracles are powerful works or great things done by the power of God.

prophet   Person who spoke for God. He often told things that would happen in the future.

²⁰The parents answered, "We know that this man is our son. And we know that he was born blind. ²¹But we don't know why he can see now. We don't know who healed his eyes. Ask him. He is old enough to answer for himself." ²²His parents said this because they were afraid of the Jewish leaders. The Jewish leaders had already decided that they would punish any person who said that Jesus was the Christ.* The Jewish leaders would put those people out of the synagogue.* ²³That is why his parents said, "He is old enough. Ask him."

²⁴So the Jewish leaders called the man who had been blind. They told the man to come in again. The Jewish leaders said, "You should give God the glory *for healing you*. We know that this man (*Jesus*) is a sinner."

²⁵The man answered, "I don't know if he is a sinner. But I do know this: I was blind, and now I can see."

²⁶The Jewish leaders asked, "What did he (*Jesus*) do to you? How did he heal your eyes?"

²⁷The man answered, "I have already told you that. But you would not listen to me. Why do you want to hear it again? Do you want to become his followers too?"

²⁸The Jewish leaders *became angry and* said some very bad things to the man. Then they said, "You are a follower of that man (*Jesus*). We are followers of Moses. ²⁹We know that God spoke to Moses. But we don't even know where this man (*Jesus*) comes from!"

³⁰The man answered, "This is a very strange thing. You don't know where Jesus comes from. But he healed my eyes. ³¹We all know that God does not listen to sinners. But God will listen to a person who worships and obeys him. ³²This is the first time that any person ever healed a man who was born blind. ³³This man (*Jesus*) must be from God. If he were not from God, he could not do anything *like this*."

³⁴The Jewish leaders answered, "You were born full of sin! Are you trying to teach us? " And the Jewish leaders forced the man to leave.

Christ   The "anointed one" (the Messiah) or chosen one of God.
synagogue   Synagogues were places where Jews gathered to read and study the Scriptures.

Spiritual Blindness

³⁵Jesus heard that the Jewish leaders had forced the man to leave. Jesus found the man and said, "Do you believe in the Son of Man*?"

³⁶The man asked, "Who is the Son of Man, sir? Tell me, so I can believe in him!"

³⁷Jesus said to him, "You have already seen him. The Son of Man is the one talking with you now."

³⁸The man answered, "Yes, I believe, Lord!" Then the man bowed and worshiped Jesus.

³⁹Jesus said, "I came into this world so that the world could be judged. I came so that blind people* could see. And I came so that people who *think they can* see will become blind."

⁴⁰Some of the Pharisees* were near Jesus. They heard Jesus say this. They asked, "What? Are you saying that we are blind too?"

⁴¹Jesus said, "If you were really blind (*without unde᷈ ʳanding*), you would not be guilty of sin. But you say that you   ᴇ (*know what you are doing*). So you are guilty."

The Shepherd and His Sheep

10 Jesus said, "I tell you the truth. When a man enters the sheep pen, he should use the gate. If he climbs in some other way, then he is a robber. He is trying to steal the sheep. ²But the man who takes care of the sheep enters through the gate. He is the shepherd. ³The man who guards the gate opens the gate for the shepherd. And the sheep listen to the voice of the shepherd. The shepherd calls his own sheep, using their names, and he leads them out. ⁴The shepherd brings all of his sheep out. Then he goes ahead of them and leads them. The sheep follow him because they know his voice. ⁵But sheep will never follow a person they don't know. They will run away from that person, because they don't know his voice." ⁶Jesus told the people this story. But the people did not understand what the story meant.

Son of Man Jesus. Jesus was God's Son, but this name showed that Jesus was a man, too. In Daniel 7:13-14, this is the name for the Messiah (Christ).

blind people Jesus is talking about people who are spiritually blind, not physically blind.

Pharisees Pharisees were a Jewish religious group that followed all the Old Testament and other Jewish laws and customs very carefully.

Jesus Is the Good Shepherd

⁷So Jesus said again, "I tell you the truth. I am the gate for the sheep. ⁸All the people who came before I came were thieves and robbers. The sheep did not listen to them. ⁹I am the gate. The person who enters through me will be saved. That person will be able to come in and go out. He will find everything he needs. ¹⁰A thief comes to steal and kill and destroy. But I came to give life—life that is full and good.

¹¹"I am the good shepherd. The good shepherd gives his life for the sheep. ¹²The worker who is paid to keep the sheep is different from the shepherd. The paid worker does not own the sheep. The shepherd owns the sheep. So when the worker sees a wolf coming, he runs away and leaves the sheep alone. Then the wolf attacks the sheep and scatters them. ¹³The man runs away because he is only a paid worker. He does not really care for the sheep.

¹⁴⁻¹⁵"I am the shepherd that cares for the sheep (*people*). I know my sheep, like the Father knows me. And my sheep know me, like I know the Father. I give my life for these sheep. ¹⁶I have other sheep too. They are not in this flock here. I must lead them also. They will listen to my voice. In the future there will be one flock and one shepherd. ¹⁷The Father loves me because I give my life. I give my life so that I can get it back again. ¹⁸No person takes my life away from me. I give my own life freely. I have the right to give my life. And I have the right to get it back again. This is what the Father commanded me to do."

¹⁹Again the Jews did not agree with each other because of these things Jesus said. ²⁰Many of these Jews said, "A demon* has come into him and made him crazy. Why listen to him?"

²¹But other Jews said, "A man who is crazy with a demon does not say things like this. Can a demon heal the eyes of blind people? No!"

²²The time came for the Feast of Dedication* at Jerusalem. This was during the winter. ²³Jesus was in the temple* at Solomon's Porch.* ²⁴The Jews gathered around Jesus. They said,

---

demon Demons are evil spirits from the devil.
Feast of Dedication A special week in December that the Jews celebrated.
temple The special building in Jerusalem where God commanded the Jews to worship him.
Solomon's Porch An area on the east side of the temple. It was covered by a roof.

"How long will you make us wonder about you? If you are the Christ,* then tell us clearly."

The Jews Against Jesus

²⁵Jesus answered, "I told you already, but you did not believe. I do miracles* in my Father's name. Those miracles show who I am. ²⁶But you don't believe. Why? Because you are not my sheep (*people*). ²⁷My sheep listen to my voice. I know them, and they follow me. ²⁸I give my sheep eternal life. They will never die. And no person can take them out of my hand. ²⁹My Father gave my sheep to me. He is greater than all. No person can steal my sheep out of my Father's hand. ³⁰The Father and I are one."

³¹Again the Jews picked up rocks to kill Jesus. ³²But Jesus said to them, "I have done many good things from the Father. You have seen those things. Which of those good things are you killing me for?"

³³The Jews answered, "We are not killing you for any good thing you did. But you say things that are against God. You are only a man, but you say you are the same as God! That is why we are trying to kill you with rocks!"

³⁴Jesus answered, "It is written in your law, 'I (*God*) said you are gods.'* ³⁵This was talking about those people that God had given his command to. This Scripture* called those people gods. And Scripture is always true. ³⁶I am the One that God chose for his work. God sent me into the world. I said that I am the Son of God. And you say that I am saying things that are against God. ³⁷If I don't do what my Father does, then don't believe what I say. ³⁸But if I do the same things my Father does, then you should believe in the things I do. You might not believe in me, but you should believe in the things that I do. Then you will know and understand that the Father is in me and I am in the Father."

³⁹The Jews tried to get Jesus again. But Jesus escaped from them.

Christ   The "anointed one" (the Messiah) or chosen one of God.
miracles   Miracles are powerful works or great things done by the power of God.
'I said...gods'   Quotation from Psalm 82:6.
Scripture   A part of the Holy Writings—the Old Testament.

⁴⁰Then Jesus went back across the Jordan river. Jesus went to the place where John* was baptizing* before. Jesus stayed there, ⁴¹and many people came to him. The people said, "John never did a miracle.* But everything John said about this man (*Jesus*) is true." ⁴²And in that place many people believed in Jesus.

The Death of Lazarus

11 There was a man named Lazarus who was sick. He lived in the town of Bethany. This is the town where Mary and her sister Martha lived. ²Mary is the same woman who later put perfume on the Lord (*Jesus*) and wiped his feet with her hair. Mary's brother was Lazarus, the man who was now sick. ³So Mary and Martha sent a person to tell Jesus, "Lord, your dear friend Lazarus is sick."

⁴When Jesus heard this he said, "The end of this sickness will not be death. But this sickness is for the glory of God. This has happened to bring glory to the Son of God." ⁵(Jesus loved Martha and her sister and Lazarus.) ⁶When Jesus heard that Lazarus was sick, he stayed where he was for two more days. ⁷Then Jesus said to his followers, "We should go back to Judea."

⁸The followers answered, "But teacher, the Jews in Judea tried to kill you with stones. That was only a short time ago. Now you want to go back there?"

⁹Jesus answered, "There are twelve hours of light in the day. Right? If a person walks in the day, then he will not stumble and fall. Why? Because he can see with the light of this world. ¹⁰But when a person walks at night he stumbles. Why? Because there is no light to help him see."

¹¹After Jesus said these things, he said, "Our friend Lazarus is now sleeping. But I am going there to wake him."

¹²The followers answered, "But Lord, if he can sleep, he will be well."

¹³Jesus meant that Lazarus was dead. But Jesus' followers thought that Jesus meant Lazarus was really sleeping. ¹⁴So then Jesus said clearly, "Lazarus is dead. ¹⁵And I am glad that I was

---

John   John the Baptizer, who preached to people about Christ's coming (Matthew 3, Luke 3).
baptizing   A Greek word meaning to immerse, dip, or bury a person or thing briefly under water.
miracle   Miracles are powerful works or great things done by the power of God.

not there. I am happy for you, because now you will believe *in me*. We will go to him now.''

¹⁶Then Thomas (the one called Didymus) said to the other followers, ''We will go too. We will die with Jesus *in Judea*.''

Jesus in Bethany

¹⁷Jesus arrived in Bethany. Jesus found that Lazarus had already been dead and in the tomb* for four days. ¹⁸Bethany was about two miles from Jerusalem. ¹⁹Many Jews had come to Martha and Mary. The Jews came to comfort Martha and Mary about their brother *Lazarus*.

²⁰Martha heard that Jesus was coming. She went out to greet Jesus. But Mary stayed at home. ²¹Martha said to Jesus, ''Lord, if you had been here, my brother would not have died. ²²But I know that even now God will give you anything you ask.''

²³Jesus said, ''Your brother will rise and be alive again.''

²⁴Martha answered, ''I know that he will rise and live again when people are resurrected (*raised from death*) on the last day.''

²⁵Jesus said to her, ''I am the resurrection.* I am life. The person who believes in me will have life *again* after he dies. ²⁶And the person who lives and believes in me will never really die. Martha, do you believe this?''

²⁷Martha answered, ''Yes, Lord. I believe that you are the Christ,* the Son of God. You are the One who was coming to the world.''

Jesus Cries

²⁸After Martha said these things, she went back to her sister Mary. Martha talked to Mary alone. Martha said, ''The Teacher (*Jesus*) is here. He is asking for you.'' ²⁹When Mary heard this, she stood up and went quickly to Jesus. ³⁰Jesus had not yet come into the village. He was still at the place where Martha met him. ³¹Some Jews were with Mary in the house. They were comforting her. They saw Mary stand and leave quickly. They thought that she was going to the tomb* *of Lazarus*. They thought she was

tomb Something like a cave dug in a wall of rock where dead people were buried.
resurrection Being raised from death to live again.
Christ The ''anointed one'' (the Messiah) or chosen one of God.

going there to cry. So they followed her. ³²Mary went to the place where Jesus was. When she saw Jesus, she bowed at his feet. Mary said, "Lord, if you had been here, my brother would not have died."

³³Jesus saw that Mary was crying. Jesus saw the Jews that came with her. They were crying too. Jesus felt very sad in his heart and was deeply troubled. ³⁴Jesus asked, "Where did you put him (*Lazarus*)?"

³⁵Jesus cried.

³⁶And the Jews said, "Look! Jesus loved Lazarus very much!"

³⁷But some of the Jews said, "Jesus healed the eyes of the blind man. Why didn't Jesus help Lazarus and stop him from dying?"

Jesus Makes Lazarus Alive Again

³⁸Again Jesus felt very sad in his heart. Jesus came to the tomb* *where Lazarus was*. The tomb was a cave with a large rock covering the entrance. ³⁹Jesus said, "Move the rock away."

Martha said, "But Lord, it has been four days since Lazarus died. There will be a bad smell." Martha was the sister of the dead man (*Lazarus*).

⁴⁰Then Jesus said to Martha, "Remember what I told you? I said that if you believed then you would see the glory of God."

⁴¹So they moved the rock away from the entrance. Then Jesus looked up and said, "Father, I thank you that you heard me. ⁴²I know that you always hear me. But I said these things because of the people here around me. I want them to believe that you sent me." ⁴³After Jesus said this he called in a loud voice, "Lazarus, come out!" ⁴⁴The dead man (*Lazarus*) came out. His hands and feet were wrapped with pieces of cloth. He had a handkerchief covering his face.

Jesus said to the people, "Take the cloth off of him and let him go."

The Jewish Leaders Plan to Kill Jesus

⁴⁵There were many Jews who came to visit Mary. These Jews saw what Jesus did. And many of these Jews believed in Jesus.

tomb Something like a cave dug in a wall of rock where dead people were buried.

⁴⁶But some of the Jews went to the Pharisees.* They told the Pharisees what Jesus did. ⁴⁷Then the leading priests and Pharisees called a meeting of the Jewish council. They asked, "What should we do? This man (*Jesus*) is doing many miracles.* ⁴⁸If we let him continue doing these things, all the people will believe in him. Then the Romans will come and take away our temple* and our nation."

⁴⁹One of the men there was Caiaphas. He was the high priest that year. Caiaphas said, "You people know nothing! ⁵⁰It is better for one man to die for the people than for the whole nation to be destroyed. But you don't realize this."

⁵¹Caiaphas did not think of this himself. He was high priest that year. So he was really prophesying* that Jesus would die for the Jewish people. ⁵²Yes, Jesus would die for the Jewish people. But Jesus would also die for God's other children who were scattered *in all the world*. He would die to bring them all together and make them one people.

⁵³That day the Jewish leaders began planning to kill Jesus. ⁵⁴So Jesus stopped traveling around openly among the Jews. Jesus left *Jerusalem* and went to a place near the desert.* Jesus went to the town called Ephraim. Jesus stayed there with his followers.

⁵⁵It was almost time for the Jewish Passover Feast.* Many people from the country went to Jerusalem before the Passover. They went to do the special things to make themselves pure *for the Passover*. ⁵⁶The people looked for Jesus. They stood in the temple* and asked each other, "Is he (*Jesus*) coming to the Feast? What do you think?" ⁵⁷But the leading priests and the Pharisees* had given a special order about Jesus. They said that if any person knew where Jesus was, the person must tell them. Then the leading priests and the Pharisees could arrest Jesus.

Pharisees   Pharisees were a Jewish religious group that followed all the Old Testament and other Jewish laws and customs very carefully.
miracles   Miracles are powerful works or great things done by the power of God.
temple   The special building in Jerusalem where God commanded the Jews to worship him.
prophesying   Here, to prophesy means to tell something that will happen in the future.
desert   The area is called a desert because no people lived there.
Passover Feast   Important holy day for Jews. They ate a special meal on this day every year to remember that God freed them from slavery in Egypt in the time of Moses.

Jesus in Bethany with His Friends

12 Six days before the Passover Feast,* Jesus went to Bethany. Bethany is the town where Lazarus lived. (Lazarus is the man Jesus raised from death.) ²In Bethany they had a dinner for Jesus. Martha served the food. Lazarus was one of the people eating with Jesus. ³Mary brought in a pint of very expensive perfume made from pure nard.* Mary poured the perfume on Jesus' feet. Then she wiped his feet with her hair. And the sweet smell from the perfume filled the whole house.

⁴Judas Iscariot was there. Judas was one of Jesus' followers. (He was the one who would later be against Jesus.) *Judas did not like what Mary did.* Judas said, ⁵"That perfume was worth 300 silver coins.* It should have been sold, and the money should have been given to the poor people." ⁶But Judas did not really care about poor people. Judas said this because he was a thief. Judas was the one who kept the money box *for the group of followers.* And Judas often stole money from the box.

⁷Jesus answered, "Don't stop her. It was right for her to save this perfume for today—the day for me to be prepared for burial. ⁸The poor people will always be with you. But you will not always have me."

The Plot Against Lazarus

⁹A large group of Jews heard that Jesus was in Bethany. So they went there to see Jesus. They also went there to see Lazarus. Lazarus was the one Jesus raised from death. ¹⁰So the leading priests made plans to kill Lazarus too. ¹¹Because of Lazarus many Jews were leaving *their leaders* and believing in Jesus. That is why the Jewish leaders wanted to kill Lazarus too.

Jesus Enters Jerusalem

¹²The next day the people in Jerusalem heard that Jesus was coming there. These were the many people that had come to the

---

Passover Feast   Important holy day for Jews. They ate a special meal on this day every year to remember that God freed them from slavery in Egypt in the time of Moses.
nard   A very expensive oil from the root of the nard plant. It was used like a perfume.
silver coins   One coin, a denarius, was the average pay for one day's work.

Passover Feast.* [13]The people took branches of palm trees and went out to meet Jesus. The people shouted,

> "Praise God!
> God bless the One who comes
> in the name of the Lord!
> God bless the King of Israel!"

Psalm 118:25-26

[14]Jesus found a donkey and rode on it. This was like the Scripture* says,

> [15]"Do not be afraid, city of Zion*!
> Look! Your king is coming.
> He is riding on a young donkey."

Zechariah 9:9

[16]The followers of Jesus did not understand this. But after Jesus was raised to glory, they understood that these things were written about him. Then the followers remembered that they had done these things for him.

People Tell About Jesus

[17]There were many people with Jesus when he raised Lazarus from death and told him to come out of the tomb.* Now those people were telling other people about what Jesus did. [18]Many people went out to meet Jesus, because they heard that Jesus did this miracle.* [19]So the Pharisees* said to each other, "Look! Our plan is not helping us. All the people are following him!"

Jesus Talks About His Death

[20]There were some Greek people there too. These were some of the people who went to Jerusalem to worship at the Passover Feast.* [21]These Greek people went to Philip. (Philip was from Bethsaida, in Galilee.) The Greek people said, "Sir, we want to meet Jesus." [22]Philip went and told Andrew. Then Andrew and Philip went and told Jesus.

Passover Feast   Important holy day for Jews. They ate a special meal on this day every year to remember that God freed them from slavery in Egypt in the time of Moses.
Scripture   A part of the Holy Writings—the Old Testament.
Zion   Literally, "daughter of Zion," meaning Jerusalem. Zion was an early name for Jerusalem.
tomb   Something like a cave dug in a wall of rock where dead people were buried.
miracle   Miracles are powerful works or great things done by the power of God.
Pharisees   Pharisees were a Jewish religious group that followed all the Old Testament and other Jewish laws and customs very carefully.

²³Jesus said to them, "Now is the time for the Son of Man* to receive his glory. ²⁴I tell you the truth. A grain of wheat must fall to the ground and die. Then it grows and makes many seeds. But if it never dies, then it will always be only a single seed. ²⁵The person who loves his own life will lose it. But the person who hates his life in this world will keep it. He will have life forever. ²⁶The person who serves me must follow me. Then my servant will be with me everywhere I am. My Father will give honor to people who serve me."

Jesus Speaks About His Death

²⁷"Now I am very troubled. What should I say? Should I say, 'Father save me from this time *of suffering*'? No, I came to this time so that I could suffer. ²⁸Father, bring glory to your name!"

Then a voice came from heaven, "I have brought glory to that name. I will do it again."

²⁹The people standing there heard the voice. Those people said it was thunder.

But other people said, "An angel spoke to Jesus!"

³⁰Jesus said to the people, "That voice was for you and not for me. ³¹Now is the time for the world to be judged. Now the ruler of this world (*the devil*) will be thrown out. ³²I will be lifted up from the earth. And when this happens, I will bring all people to me." ³³Jesus said this to show how he would die.

³⁴The people said, "But our law says that the Christ* will live forever. So why do you say, 'The Son of Man* must be lifted up'? Who is this 'Son of Man'?"

³⁵Then Jesus said, "The light will be with you for only a short time more. So walk while you have the light. Then the darkness (*sin*) will not catch you. The person who walks in the darkness does not know where he is going. ³⁶So put your trust in the light while you still have it. Then you will become sons of light." When Jesus finished saying these things, he left. Jesus went to a place where the people could not find him.

Son of Man Jesus. Jesus was God's Son, but this name showed that Jesus was a man, too. In Daniel 7:13-14, this is the name for the Messiah (Christ).
Christ The "anointed one" (the Messiah) or chosen one of God.

The Jews Refuse to Believe in Jesus

³⁷Jesus did all these many miracles.* The people saw these things, but they still did not believe in him. ³⁸They did not believe so that what Isaiah the prophet* said would happen:

"Lord, who believed the things we told them?
Who has seen the Lord's power?"   *Isaiah 53:1*

³⁹This is why the people could not believe. Because Isaiah also said,

⁴⁰"God made the people blind.
God closed their minds.
God did this so that they will not
see with their eyes,
understand with their hearts,
and then turn to me to heal them."   *Isaiah 6:10*

⁴¹Isaiah said this because he saw his (*Jesus'*) glory. So Isaiah spoke about him (*Jesus*).

⁴²But many people believed in Jesus. Even many of the Jewish leaders believed in Jesus. But they were afraid of the Pharisees.* So they did not say openly that they believed. They were afraid that they would be put out of the synagogue.* ⁴³These men loved praise from people more than praise from God.

People Will Be Judged by the Things Jesus Taught

⁴⁴Then Jesus said loudly, "The person who believes in me is really believing in the One (*God*) who sent me. ⁴⁵The person who sees me is really seeing the One who sent me. ⁴⁶I am light, and I came into this world. I came so that every person who believes in me would not stay in darkness.

⁴⁷"I did not come into the world to judge people. I came to save the people in the world. So I am not the one who judges the people who hear my teaching but don't obey. ⁴⁸There is one who will judge the person who refuses to believe in me and does not

miracles Miracles are powerful works or great things done by the power of God.
prophet A person who spoke for God to his people.
Pharisees Pharisees were a Jewish religious group that followed all the Old Testament and other Jewish laws and customs very carefully.
synagogue Synagogues were places where Jews gathered to read and study the Scriptures.

accept what I say. The words I have taught will judge that person on the last day. ⁴⁹Why? Because the things I taught were not from myself. The Father (*God*) who sent me told me what to say and what to teach. ⁵⁰And I know that eternal life comes from what the Father commands. So the things I say are what the Father told me to say.''

Jesus Washes His Followers' Feet

13 It was almost time for the Jewish Passover Feast.* Jesus knew that it was the time for him to leave this world. It was now time for Jesus to go back to the Father. Jesus had always loved those people in the world who were his. Now was the time Jesus showed them his love the most.

²Jesus and his followers were at the evening meal. The devil had already persuaded Judas Iscariot to turn against Jesus. (Judas was the son of Simon.) ³The Father had given Jesus power over everything. Jesus knew this. Jesus also knew that he had come from God. And he knew that he was going back to God. ⁴While they were eating, Jesus stood up and took off his robe. Jesus got a towel and wrapped the towel around his waist. ⁵Then Jesus poured water into a pitcher. He began to wash the followers' feet. He dried their feet with the towel that was wrapped around his waist.

⁶Jesus came to Simon Peter. But Peter said to Jesus, ''Lord, you should not wash my feet.''

⁷Jesus answered, ''You don't know what I am doing now. But later you will understand.''

⁸Peter said, ''No! You will never wash my feet.''

Jesus answered, ''If I don't wash your feet, then you cannot be one of my people.''

⁹Simon Peter answered, ''Lord, after you wash my feet, wash my hands and my head too!''

¹⁰Jesus said, ''After a person has a bath, his whole body is clean. He needs only to wash his feet. And you men are clean, but not every one of you.'' ¹¹Jesus knew who would turn against him. That is why Jesus said, ''Not every one of you is clean.''

Passover Feast Important holy day for Jews. They ate a special meal on this day every year to remember that God freed them from slavery in Egypt in the time of Moses.

¹²Jesus finished washing their feet. Then he put on his clothes and sat down again. Jesus asked, "Do you understand what I did for you? ¹³You call me 'Teacher.' And you call me 'Lord.' And this is right, because that is what I am. ¹⁴I am your Lord and Teacher. But I washed your feet *like a servant*. So you also should wash each other's feet. ¹⁵I did this as an example for you. So you should do *for each other* like I did for you. ¹⁶I tell you the truth. A servant is not greater than his master. The person who is sent to do something is not greater than the one who sent him. ¹⁷If you know these things, you will be happy if you do them.

¹⁸"I am not talking about all of you. I know the people I have chosen. But what the Scripture* said must happen: 'The man who shared my food has turned against me.'* ¹⁹I am telling you this now before it happens. Then when it happens you will believe that I AM.* ²⁰I tell you the truth. The person who accepts anyone I send, also accepts me. And the person who accepts me, also accepts the One who sent me."

Jesus Tells Who Will Give Him to be Killed

²¹After Jesus said these things, he felt very troubled. Jesus said openly, "I tell you the truth. One of you will be against me."

²²Jesus' followers all looked at each other. They did not understand who the person was that Jesus was talking about. ²³One of the followers was sitting* next to Jesus. This was the follower that Jesus loved. ²⁴Simon Peter made signs to this follower to ask Jesus who the person was that he was talking about.

²⁵That follower leaned closer to Jesus and asked, "Lord, who is it that will be against you?"

²⁶Jesus answered, "I will dip this bread into the dish. The man I give it to is the man who will turn against me." So Jesus took a piece of bread. He dipped it and gave it to Judas Iscariot, the son of Simon. ²⁷When Judas took the bread, Satan (*the devil*) entered him. Jesus said to Judas, "The thing that you will do—do it quickly!" ²⁸None of the men at the table understood why Jesus

Scripture A part of the Holy Writings—the Old Testament.
'The man...me' Literally, "The man...has lifted up his heel against me" (Psalm 41:9).
I AM This is like the name of God used in Exodus 3:14.
sitting Literally, "lying." The people of that time ate lying down and leaning on one arm.

said this to Judas. ²⁹Judas was the one who kept the money box *for the group*. So some of the followers thought that Jesus meant for Judas to go and buy some things they needed for the feast. Or they thought that Jesus wanted Judas to go give something to the poor people.

³⁰Judas accepted the bread Jesus gave him. Judas went out quickly. It was night.

Jesus Talks About His Death

³¹When Judas was gone, Jesus said, "Now the Son of Man* receives his glory. And God receives glory through the Son of Man. ³²If God receives glory through him, then God will give glory to the Son through himself. God will give him glory quickly."

³³Jesus said, "My children, I will be with you only a short time more. You will look for me. And what I told the Jews, I tell you now: Where I am going you cannot come.

³⁴"I give you a new commandment: Love each other. You must love each other like I loved you. ³⁵All people will know that you are my followers if you love each other."

Jesus Says that Peter Will Deny Him

³⁶Simon Peter asked Jesus, "Lord, where are you going?"

Jesus answered, "Where I am going you cannot follow now. But you will follow later."

³⁷Peter asked, "Lord, why can't I follow you now? I am ready to die for you!"

³⁸Jesus answered, "Will you really give your life for me? I tell you the truth. Before the rooster crows, you will say three times that you don't know me."

Jesus Comforts His Followers

14 Jesus said, "Don't let your hearts be troubled. Trust in God. And trust in me. ²There are many rooms in my Father's house. I would not tell you this if it were not true. I am

---

Son of Man   Jesus. Jesus was God's Son, but this name showed that Jesus was a man, too. In Daniel 7:13-14, this is the name for the Messiah (Christ).

going there to prepare a place for you. ³After I go and prepare a place for you, I will come back. Then I will take you with me, so that you can be where I am. ⁴You know the way to the place where I am going.''

⁵Thomas said to Jesus, ''Lord, we don't know where you are going. So how can we know the way?''

⁶Jesus answered, ''I am the way. I am the truth and the life. The only way to the Father is through me. ⁷If you really knew me, then you would know my Father too. But now you know the Father. You have seen him *in me*.''

⁸Philip said to Jesus, ''Lord, show us the Father. That is all we need.''

⁹Jesus answered, ''Philip, I have been with you for a long time. So you should know me. The person who has seen me has seen the Father too. So why do you say, 'Show us the Father'? ¹⁰Do you truly believe that I am in the Father and the Father is in me? The things I have told you don't come from me. The Father lives in me, and he is doing his own work. ¹¹Believe me when I say that I am in the Father and the Father is in me. Or believe because of the miracles* I have done. ¹²I tell you the truth. The person who believes in me will do the same things I have done. Yes! He will do even greater things than I have done. Why? Because I am going to the Father. ¹³And if you ask for anything in my name, I will do it for you. Then the Father's glory will be shown through the Son. ¹⁴If you ask me for anything in my name, I will do it.''

The Promise of the Holy Spirit

¹⁵''If you love me, then you will do the things I command. ¹⁶I will ask the Father, and he will give you another Helper.* He will give you this Helper to be with you forever. ¹⁷The Helper is the Spirit* of truth. The world cannot accept him. Why? Because the world does not see him or know him. But you know him. He lives with you and he will live in you.

¹⁸''I will not leave you all alone like children without parents. I will come back to you. ¹⁹In a very short time the people in the

miracles   Miracles are powerful works or great things done by the power of God.
Helper   ''Counselor,'' or ''Comforter.'' Jesus is talking about the Holy Spirit.
Spirit   The Holy Spirit. Also called the Spirit of God, the Spirit of Christ, and the Comforter. He is joined with God and Christ. He does the work of God among people in the world.

world will not see me any more. But you will see me, because I have life, and you will have life too. ²⁰On that day you will know that I am in the Father. You will know that you are in me and I am in you. ²¹If a person knows my commandments and obeys those commandments, then that person truly loves me. And my Father will love the person who loves me. And I will love that person. I will show myself to him."

²²Then Judas (not Judas Iscariot) said, "But Lord, why do you plan to show yourself to us, but not to the world?" ²³Jesus answered, "If any person loves me, then he will obey my teaching. My Father will love that person. My Father and I will come to that person and live with him. ²⁴But the person who does not love me does not obey my teaching. This teaching that you hear is not really mine. It is from my Father who sent me.

²⁵"I have told you all these things while I am with you. ²⁶But the Helper* will teach you everything. The Helper will cause you to remember all the things I told you. This Helper is the Holy Spirit* that the Father will send in my name.

²⁷"I leave you peace. It is my own peace I give you. I give you peace in a different way than the world does. So don't let your hearts be troubled. Don't be afraid. ²⁸You heard me say to you, 'I am leaving, but I will come back to you.' If you loved me, then you would be happy that I am going back to the Father. Why? Because the Father is greater than I am. ²⁹I have told you this now, before it happens. Then when it happens, you will believe. ³⁰I will not talk with you much longer. The ruler of this world (*the devil*) is coming. He has no power over me. ³¹But the world must know that I love the Father. So I do exactly what the Father told me to do.

"Come now. We will leave this place."

Jesus Is Like a Vine

15 "I am the true vine; my Father is the gardener. ²He cuts off every branch of mine that does not make fruit. And he trims and cleans every branch that makes fruit so that it will make even more fruit. ³You are already clean because of the

Helper "Counselor," or "Comforter." Jesus is talking about the Holy Spirit.
Holy Spirit Also called the Spirit of God, the Spirit of Christ, and the Comforter. He is joined with God and Christ. He does the work of God among people in the world.

teaching I have told you. ⁴Continue in me and I will continue in you. No branch can make fruit alone. It must continue in the vine. It is the same with you. You cannot make fruit alone. You must continue in me.

⁵"I am the vine and you are the branches. If a person continues in me and I continue in that person, then that person will make much fruit. But without me that person can do nothing. ⁶If a person does not continue in me, then he is like a branch that is thrown away. That branch dies. The dead branches are picked up, thrown into the fire, and burned. ⁷Continue in me and follow my teachings. If you do this, then you can ask for anything you want, and it will be given you. ⁸You should make much fruit and show that you are my followers. This brings glory to my Father. ⁹I loved you like the Father loved me. Now continue in my love. ¹⁰I have obeyed my Father's commands, and I continue in his love. In the same way, if you obey my commands, you will continue in my love. ¹¹I have told you these things so that you can have the same joy I have. I want your joy to be the fullest joy. ¹²This is what I command you: Love each other like I have loved you. ¹³The greatest love a person can show is to die for his friends. ¹⁴You are my friends if you do the things I command you. ¹⁵I don't call you servants now. A servant does not know what his master is doing. But now I call you friends because I have told you everything I heard from my Father. ¹⁶You did not choose me; I chose you. And I gave you this work: to go and make fruit. I want you to make fruit that will continue. Then the Father will give you anything you ask for in my name. ¹⁷This is my command: Love each other."

Jesus Warns His Followers About the World

"¹⁸If the world hates you, remember that the world hated me first. ¹⁹If you belonged to the world, then the world would love you like it loves its own people. But I have chosen you out of the world. So you don't belong to the world. That is why the world hates you. ²⁰Remember the lesson I told you: A servant is not greater than his master. If people did wrong to me, then they will do wrong to you too. And if people obeyed my teaching, then they will obey yours too. ²¹People will do all this to you because of me. They don't know the One who sent me. ²²If I had not come and spoken to the people of the world, then they would not be guilty of sin. But now I have spoken to them. So they have no excuse for their sin. ²³Any person who hates me also hates my Father. ²⁴I did things among those people that no other person has ever done. If I had not done those things, they would not be guilty of sin. But they have seen those things I did. And they hate me and my Father. ²⁵But this happened so that what is written in their law would be true: 'They hated me for no reason.'*

²⁶"I will send you the Helper* from the Father. The Helper is the Spirit* of truth who comes from the Father. When he comes, he will tell about me. ²⁷And you will tell people about me too, because you have been with me from the beginning."

16 "I have told you these things so that people will not be able to destroy your faith. ²People will make you leave their synagogues.* Yes, a time is coming when people will think that killing you would be doing service for God. ³People will do these things because they have not known the Father and they have not known me. ⁴I have told you these things now. So when the time comes for these things to happen, you will remember that I warned you."

The Work of the Holy Spirit

"I did not tell you these things at the beginning, because I was with you then. ⁵Now I am going back to the One who sent me. But none of you asks me, 'Where are you going?' ⁶Your hearts are filled with sadness because I have told you these things. ⁷But I tell you the truth: It is better for you that I go away. Why? Because when I go away I will send the Helper* to you. But if I did not go away, then the Helper would not come. ⁸When the Helper comes, he will prove to the people of the world the truth about these things: about sin, about being right with God, and about judgment. ⁹The Helper will prove that people have sin,

---

'They hated...reason' These words could be from Psalm 35:19 or Psalm 69:4.
Helper "Counselor," or "Comforter." Jesus is talking about the Holy Spirit.
Spirit The Holy Spirit. Also called the Spirit of God, the Spirit of Christ, and the Comforter. He is joined with God and Christ. He does the work of God among people in the world.
synagogues Synagogues were buildings where Jews gathered to read and study the Scriptures.

285

because they don't believe in me. [10]He will prove to them about *my* being right with God, because I am going to the Father. You will not see me then. [11]And the Helper will prove to the world the truth about judgment, because the ruler of this world (*the devil*) is already judged.

[12]"I have many more things to say to you. But those things are too much for you to accept now. [13]But when the Spirit* of truth comes he will lead you into all truth. The Spirit of truth will not speak his own words. He will speak only what he hears. He will tell you the things that will happen. [14]The Spirit of truth will bring glory to me. How? He will get things from me and tell them to you. [15]All the things that the Father has are mine. That is why I said that the Spirit will get things from me and tell them to you."

Sadness Will Change to Happiness

[16]"After a short time you will not see me. And then after another short time you will see me again."

[17]Some of the followers said to each other, "What does Jesus mean when he says, 'After a short time you will not see me. And then after another short time you will see me again'? And what does he mean when he says, 'Because I am going to the Father'?" [18]The followers asked, "What does he mean by 'a short time'? We don't understand what he is saying."

[19]Jesus saw that the followers wanted to ask him about this. So Jesus said to the followers, "Are you asking each other what I meant when I said, 'After a short time you will not see me. And then after another short time you will see me again'? [20]I tell you the truth, you will cry and be sad. But the world will be happy. You will be sad, but your sadness will become joy. [21]When a woman gives birth to a baby, she has pain, because her time has come. But when her baby is born, she forgets the pain. She forgets because she is so happy that a child has been born into the world. [22]It is the same with you. Now you are sad. But I will see you again and you will be happy. And no one will take away your

---

Spirit   The Holy Spirit. Also called the Spirit of God, the Spirit of Christ, and the Comforter. He is joined with God and Christ. He does the work of God among people in the world.

joy. ²³In that day you will not ask me for anything. I tell you the truth: My Father will give you anything you ask for in my name. ²⁴You have never asked for anything in my name. Ask and you will receive. And your joy will be the fullest joy.''

Victory over the World

²⁵"I have told you these things, using words that hide the meaning. But the time will come when I will not use words like that to tell you things. I will speak to you in plain words about the Father. ²⁶In that day you will ask the Father for things in my name. I am saying that I will not need to ask the Father for you. ²⁷No! The Father himself loves you. He loves you because you have loved me. And he loves you because you have believed that I came from God. ²⁸I came from the Father into the world. Now I am leaving the world and going back to the Father.''

²⁹Then the followers of Jesus said, "You are speaking clearly to us now. You are not using words that are hard to understand. ³⁰We can see now that you know all things. You can answer a person's question even before he asks it. This makes us believe that you came from God.''

³¹Jesus answered, "So now you believe? ³²Listen to me. A time is coming when you will be scattered. Each of you will be scattered to his own home. That time is now here. You will leave me. I will be alone. But I am never really alone. Why? Because the Father is with me.

³³"I told you these things so that you can have peace in me. In this world you will have trouble. But be brave! I have defeated the world!''

Jesus Prays for His Followers

17 After Jesus said these things he looked toward heaven. Jesus prayed, "Father, the time has come. Give glory to your Son so that the Son can give glory to you. ²You gave the Son power over all people so that the Son could give eternal life to all those people you have given to him. ³And this is eternal life: that men can know you, the only true God, and that men can know

Jesus Christ, the One you sent. ⁴I finished the work you gave me to do. I brought you glory on earth. ⁵And now, Father, give me glory with you. Give me the glory I had with you before the world was made.

⁶"You gave me some men from the world. I have shown them what you are like. Those men belonged to you, and you gave them to me. They have obeyed your teaching. ⁷Now they know that everything you gave me comes from you. ⁸I gave these men the teachings that you gave me. They accepted those teachings. They know that I truly came from you. ⁹I pray for them now. I am not praying for the people in the world. But I am praying for those men you gave me, because they are yours. ¹⁰All I have is yours, and all you have is mine. And my glory is shown through these men. ¹¹Now I am coming to you. I will not stay in the world now. But these men are still in the world. Holy Father, keep them safe. Keep them safe by the power of your name (the name you gave me), so that they will be one, the same as you and I are one. ¹²While I was with them, I kept them safe. I kept them safe by the power of your name—the name you gave me. I protected them. And only one of them, the child of hell (*Judas*), was lost. He was lost so that what was said in the Scripture* would happen.

¹³"I am coming to you now. But I pray these things while I am still in the world. I say these things so that these men can have my joy. I want them to have all of my joy. ¹⁴I have given them your teaching. And the world has hated them. The world hated these men, because they don't belong to the world, the same as I don't belong to the world. ¹⁵I am not asking you to take them out of the world. But I am asking that you keep them safe from the Evil One (*the devil*). ¹⁶They don't belong to the world, the same as I don't belong to the world. ¹⁷Make them ready for your service through your truth. Your teaching is truth. ¹⁸I have sent them into the world, the same as you sent me into the world. ¹⁹I am making myself ready to serve. I do this for them, so that they can truly be ready for your service.

²⁰"I pray for these men. But I am also praying for all people who will believe in me because of the teaching of these men. ²¹Father, I pray that all people who believe in me can be one. You

Scripture   A part of the Holy Writings—the Old Testament.

are in me and I am in you. I pray that these people can also be one in us, so that the world will believe that you sent me. ²²I have given these people the glory that you gave me. I gave them this glory so that they can be one, the same as you and I are one. ²³I will be in them and you will be in me. So they will be completely one. Then the world will know that you sent me. And the world will know that you loved these people the same as you loved me.

²⁴"Father, I want these people that you have given me to be with me in every place I am. I want them to see my glory. This is the glory you gave me because you loved me before the world was made. ²⁵Father, you are the One who is good. The world does not know you, but I know you. And these people know that you sent me. ²⁶I showed them what you are like. And again I will show them what you are like. Then they will have the same love that you have for me. And I will live in them."

Jesus Is Arrested

18 When Jesus finished praying, he left with his followers. They went across the Kidron Valley. On the other side there was a garden *of olive trees*. Jesus and his followers went there.

²Judas knew where this place was, because Jesus met there often with his followers. Judas was the one who turned against Jesus. ³So Judas led a group of soldiers to the garden. Judas also brought some guards from the leading priests and the Pharisees.* They were carrying torches, lanterns, and weapons.

⁴Jesus knew everything that would happen to him. Jesus went out and asked, "Who are you looking for?"

⁵The men answered, "Jesus from Nazareth."

Jesus said, "I am Jesus." (Judas, the one who turned against Jesus, was standing there with them.) ⁶When Jesus said, "I am Jesus," the men moved back and fell to the ground.

⁷Jesus asked them again, "Who are you looking for?"

The soldier said, "Jesus from Nazareth."

⁸Jesus said, "I told you that I am Jesus. So if you are looking for me, then let these other men go free." ⁹This happened so that

---

Pharisees Pharisees were a Jewish religious group that followed all the Old Testament and other Jewish laws and customs very carefully.

the words Jesus said before would be true: "I have not lost any of the men you gave me."

¹⁰Simon Peter had a sword. He took out the sword and struck the servant of the high priest.* Peter cut off the servant's right ear. (The servant's name was Malchus.) ¹¹Jesus said to Peter, "Put your sword back in its place! I must accept the cup* *of suffering* the Father has given me."

Jesus Is Brought Before Annas

¹²Then the soldiers with their commander and the Jewish guards arrested Jesus. They tied Jesus ¹³and brought him to Annas. Annas was the father-in-law of Caiaphas. Caiaphas was the high priest* that year. ¹⁴Caiaphas was the one who had told the Jews that it would be better if one man died for all the people.

Peter Says He Does Not Know Jesus

¹⁵Simon Peter and another one of Jesus' followers went with Jesus. This follower knew the high priest.* So he went into the high priest's courtyard with Jesus. ¹⁶But Peter waited outside near the door. The follower who knew the high priest came back outside. He spoke to the girl who opened the gate for people. Then he brought Peter inside. ¹⁷The girl at the gate said to Peter, "Are you also one of the followers of that man (*Jesus*)?"

Peter answered, "No, I am not!"

¹⁸It was cold, so the servants and guards had built a fire. They were standing around it and warming themselves. Peter was standing with these men.

The High Priest Questions Jesus

¹⁹The high priest* asked Jesus questions about his followers. He asked Jesus questions about the things Jesus taught. ²⁰Jesus answered, "I have always spoken openly to all people. I always taught in the synagogues* and in the temple.* All the Jews come

---

high priest The most important Jewish priest and leader.
cup Jesus is talking about the bad things that will happen to him. Accepting these things will be very hard, like drinking a cup full of something that tastes very bad.
synagogues Synagogues were buildings where Jews gathered to read and study the Scriptures.
temple The special building in Jerusalem where God commanded the Jews to worship him.

together there. I never said anything in secret. ²¹So why do you question me? Ask the people who heard my teaching. They know what I said."

²²When Jesus said this, one of the guards standing there hit him. The guard said, "You should not talk to the high priest* like that!"

²³Jesus answered, "If I said something wrong, then tell everyone here what was wrong. But if the things I said are right, then why do you hit me?"

²⁴So Annas sent Jesus to Caiaphas, the high priest. Jesus was still tied.

Peter Says Again That He Does Not Know Jesus

²⁵Peter was standing *at the fire*, keeping himself warm. The other men said to Peter, "Are you one of the followers of that man (*Jesus*)?"

But Peter denied it. He said, "No, I am not."

²⁶One of the servants of the high priest* was there. This servant was a relative to the man whose ear Peter had cut off. The servant said, "I think I saw you with him (*Jesus*) in the garden!"

²⁷But again Peter said, "No, I was not with him!" And at that same time a rooster crowed.

Jesus Is Brought Before Pilate

²⁸Then the Jews took Jesus from Caiaphas' house to the *Roman governor's* palace. It was early in the morning. The Jews would not go inside the palace. They did not want to make themselves unclean,* because they wanted to eat the Passover meal.* ²⁹So Pilate went outside to the Jews. He asked, "What do you say this man has done wrong?"

³⁰The Jews answered, "He is a bad man. That is why we brought him to you."

³¹Pilate said to the Jews, "You Jews take him yourselves and judge him by your own law."

---

high priest The most important Jewish priest and leader.
unclean Going into a non-Jewish place would ruin the cleansing they had done (John 11:55).
Passover meal This was the special meal the Jews ate for the Passover Feast.

The Jews answered, "But your law does not allow us to punish a person by killing him." ³²(This happened so that what Jesus said about how he would die would be true.)

³³Then Pilate went back inside the palace. Pilate called Jesus to him and asked Jesus, "Are you the king of the Jews?"

³⁴Jesus said, "Is that your own question, or did other people tell you about me?"

³⁵Pilate answered, "I am not a Jew! It was your own people and their leading priests who brought you before me. What have you done wrong?"

³⁶Jesus said, "My kingdom does not belong to this world. If it belonged to this world, then my servants would fight so that I would not be given to the Jews. But my kingdom is from another place."

³⁷Pilate said, "So you are a king!"

Jesus answered, "You say that I am a king. That is true. I was born for this: to tell people about the truth. That is why I came into the world. And every person who belongs to the truth listens to me."

³⁸Pilate said, "What is truth?" When Pilate said this, he went out to the Jews again. Pilate said to the Jews, "I can find nothing to charge against this man. ³⁹But it is one of your customs for me to free one prisoner to you at the time of the Passover.* Do you want me to free this 'king of the Jews'?"

⁴⁰The Jews yelled back, "No, not him! Let Barabbas go free!" (Barabbas was a robber.)

19 Then Pilate ordered that Jesus be taken away and be whipped. ²The soldiers used some thorny branches to make a crown. They put this crown of thorns on Jesus' head. Then the soldiers put a purple robe around Jesus. ³The soldiers came to Jesus many times and said, "Hello, O king of the Jews!" They hit Jesus in the face.

⁴Again Pilate came out and said to the Jews, "Look! I am bringing Jesus out to you. I want you to know that I find nothing I can charge against him." ⁵Then Jesus came out. He was wearing

Passover Important holy day for Jews. They ate a special meal on this day every year to remember that God freed them from slavery in Egypt in the time of Moses.

the crown of thorns and the purple robe. Pilate said to the Jews, "Here is the man!"

⁶When the leading priests and the Jewish guards saw Jesus they yelled, "Kill him on a cross! Kill him on a cross!"

But Pilate answered, "You take him and nail him to a cross yourselves. I find nothing I can charge against him."

⁷The Jews answered, "We have a law that says he must die, because he said that he is the Son of God."

⁸When Pilate heard this, he was more afraid. ⁹Pilate went back inside the palace. He asked Jesus, "Where are you from?" But Jesus did not answer him. ¹⁰Pilate said, "You refuse to speak to me? Remember, I have the power to make you free. I also have the power to kill you on a cross."

¹¹Jesus answered, "The only power you have over me is the power given to you by God. So the man who gave me to you is guilty of a greater sin."

¹²After this, Pilate tried to let Jesus go free. But the Jews yelled, "Any person who makes himself a king is against Caesar. So if you let this man (*Jesus*) go free, that means that you are not Caesar's friend."

¹³Pilate heard what the Jews said. So he brought Jesus out to the place called "The Stone Pavement." (In the Jewish language the name is "Gabbatha.") Pilate sat down on the judge's seat there. ¹⁴It was now almost noon on Preparation day* of Passover* week. Pilate said to the Jews, "Here is your king!"

¹⁵The Jews yelled, "Take him away! Take him away! Kill him on a cross!"

Pilate asked the Jews, "Do you want me to kill your king on a cross?"

The leading priests answered, "The only king we have is Caesar!"

¹⁶So Pilate gave Jesus to them to be killed on a cross.

Jesus Is Killed on a Cross

The soldiers took Jesus. ¹⁷Jesus carried his own cross. He went out to a place called "The Place of the Skull." (In the Jewish

Preparation day Friday, the day before the Sabbath day.
Passover Important holy day for Jews. They ate a special meal on this day every year to remember that God freed them from slavery in Egypt in the time of Moses.

language* the name of this place is "Golgotha.") ¹⁸At Golgotha they nailed Jesus to the cross. They also put two other men on crosses. They put the men on each side of Jesus with Jesus in the middle. ¹⁹Pilate wrote a sign and put it on the cross. The sign said, JESUS OF NAZARETH, THE KING OF THE JEWS. ²⁰The sign was written in the Jewish language, in Latin and in Greek. Many of the Jews read the sign, because this place where they killed Jesus on the cross was near the city. ²¹The leading Jewish priests said to Pilate, "Don't write, 'The King of the Jews.' But write, 'This man said, I am the King of the Jews.' "

²²Pilate answered, "I will not change what I have written."

²³After the soldiers nailed Jesus to the cross, they took his clothes. They divided his clothes into four parts. Each soldier got one part. They also took his tunic.* It was all one piece of cloth woven from top to bottom. ²⁴So the soldiers said to each other, "We should not tear this into parts *to divide it*. We should choose lots* to see who will get it." This happened so that it would be like the Scripture* said:

"They divided my clothes among them.
And they threw lots* for my clothing."   *Psalm 22:18*

So the soldiers did this.

²⁵Jesus' mother stood near his cross. His mother's sister was also standing there with Mary the wife of Clopas, and Mary of Magdala. ²⁶Jesus saw his mother. He also saw the follower that he loved standing there. He said to his mother, "Dear woman, here is your son." ²⁷Then Jesus said to the follower, "Here is your mother." So after that, this follower took Jesus' mother to live in his home.

Jesus Dies

²⁸Later, Jesus knew that everything had been done. To make the Scripture* happen he said, "I am thirsty."* ²⁹There was a jar full of vinegar there. So the soldiers soaked a sponge in it. They

---

Jewish language   Aramaic, the "Hebrew" language in the first century.
tunic   A piece of clothing like a long shirt, worn inside other clothes.
lots   Small rocks or sticks used like dice for making a choice.
Scripture   A part of the Holy Writings—the Old Testament.
"I am thirsty"   Read Psalms 22:15, 69:21.

put the sponge on a branch of a hyssop plant. Then they lifted it to Jesus' mouth. ³⁰Jesus tasted the vinegar. Then he said, "It is finished." Jesus bowed his head and died.

³¹This day was Preparation day.* The next day was a special Sabbath day.* The Jews did not want the bodies to stay on the cross on the Sabbath day. So they asked Pilate to order that the legs of the men be broken *to make them die sooner.* And they asked that the bodies of the men be taken down from the crosses. ³²So the soldiers came and broke the legs of the first man on the cross beside Jesus. Then they broke the legs of the other man beside Jesus. ³³But when the soldiers came close to Jesus, they saw that he was already dead. So they did not break his legs. ³⁴But one of the soldiers stuck his spear into Jesus' side. Blood and water came out. ³⁵(The one who saw this happen has told about it. He told about it so that you also can believe. The things he says are true. He knows that he tells the truth.) ³⁶These things happened so that it would be like the Scripture* said: "None of his bones will be broken."* ³⁷And another Scripture said, "People will look at the one they stuck *with the spear.*"*

Jesus Is Buried

³⁸Later, a man named Joseph from Arimathea asked Pilate for the body of Jesus. (Joseph was a follower of Jesus. But he did not tell people, because he was afraid of the Jews.) Pilate said that Joseph could take the body of Jesus. So Joseph came and took Jesus' body away. ³⁹Nicodemus went with Joseph. Nicodemus was the man who had come to Jesus before and talked to him at night. Nicodemus brought about 100 pounds* of spices. This was a mixture of myrrh and aloes.* ⁴⁰These two men took Jesus' body. They wrapped it in pieces of linen cloth with the spices. (This is how the Jews bury people.) ⁴¹In the place where Jesus was killed on the cross, there was a garden. In the garden there was a

Preparation day   Friday, the day before the Sabbath day.
Sabbath day   Seventh day of the Jewish week. It was a special religious day for the Jews.
Scripture   A part of the Holy Writings—the Old Testament.
"None...broken"   Quotation from Psalm 34:20. The idea is from Exodus 12:46, Numbers 9:12.
"People...spear"   Quotation from Zechariah 12:10.
100 pounds   100 Roman pounds were equal to about 75 pounds today.
myrrh and aloes   Sweet-smelling spices used for perfume and also to prepare a body to be buried.

new tomb.* No person had ever been buried there before. ⁴²The men put Jesus in that tomb because it was near, and the Jews were preparing to start their Sabbath day.*

Some Followers Find Jesus' Tomb Empty

20 Early on Sunday morning Mary Magdalene went to the tomb (*grave*) *where Jesus' body was*. It was still dark. Mary saw that the large stone *that covered the entrance* was moved away. ²So Mary ran to Simon Peter and the other follower (the one Jesus loved). Mary said, "They have taken the Lord out of the tomb. We don't know where they put him."

³So Peter and the other follower started going to the tomb. ⁴They were both running, but the other follower ran faster than Peter. So the other follower reached the tomb first. ⁵The follower bent down and looked in. He saw the pieces of linen cloth lying there, but he did not go in. ⁶Then Simon Peter came from behind him. Peter went into the tomb. He saw the pieces of linen lying there. ⁷He also saw the cloth that had been around Jesus' head. The cloth was folded up and laid in a different place from the pieces of linen. ⁸Then the other follower went in. This was the follower who had reached the tomb first. He saw what had happened and believed. ⁹(These followers did not yet understand from the Scriptures* that Jesus must rise from death.)

Jesus Appears to Mary Magdalene

¹⁰Then the followers went back home. ¹¹But Mary stood outside the tomb, crying. While she was crying, she bent down and looked inside the tomb. ¹²Mary saw two angels dressed in white. They were sitting where Jesus' body had been. One angel was sitting where Jesus' head had been, and the other angel was sitting where Jesus' feet had been.

¹³The angels asked Mary, "Woman, why are you crying?"

Mary answered, "Some people have taken away *the body of* my Lord. I don't know where they put him." ¹⁴When Mary said

---

tomb   Something like a cave dug in a wall of rock where dead people were buried.
Sabbath day   Seventh day of the Jewish week. It was a special religious day for the Jews.
Scriptures   Holy Writings—the Old Testament.

this she turned around and saw Jesus standing there. But she did not know that it was Jesus.

¹⁵Jesus asked her, "Woman, why are you crying? Who are you looking for?"

Mary thought that this was the man who takes care of the garden. So Mary said to him, "Did you take Jesus away, sir? Tell me where you put him. I will go and get him."

¹⁶Jesus said to her, "Mary."

Mary turned toward Jesus and said in the Jewish language,* "Rabboni." (This means "Teacher.")

¹⁷Jesus said to her, "Don't hold me. I have not yet gone back up to the Father. But go to my brothers (*followers*) and tell them this: 'I am going back to my Father and your Father. I am going back to my God and your God.' " ¹⁸Mary Magdalene went to the followers and told them, "I saw the Lord!" And she told them the things Jesus said to her.

Jesus Appears to His Followers

¹⁹The day was Sunday. That same evening the followers were together. The doors were locked, because they were afraid of the Jews. Then Jesus came and stood among them. Jesus said, "Peace be with you!" ²⁰After Jesus said this, he showed the followers his hands and his side. The followers were very happy when they saw the Lord.

²¹Then Jesus said again, "Peace be with you! The Father sent me. In the same way, I now send you." ²²After Jesus said that, he breathed *on the followers*. Jesus said, "Receive the Holy Spirit.* ²³If you forgive people's sins, then their sins are forgiven. If you don't forgive people's sins, then their sins are not forgiven."

Jesus Appears to Thomas

²⁴Thomas (called Didymus) was not with the followers when Jesus came. Thomas was one of the twelve. ²⁵The other followers told Thomas, "We saw the Lord." Thomas said, "I will not

---

Jewish language Aramaic, the "Hebrew" language in the first century.
Holy Spirit Also called the Spirit of God, the Spirit of Christ, and the Comforter. He is joined with God and Christ. He does the work of God among people in the world.

believe it until I see the nail holes in his hands. And I will not believe until I put my finger where the nails were and put my hand into his side.''

²⁶A week later the followers were in the house again. Thomas was with them. The doors were locked, but Jesus came and stood among them. Jesus said, ''Peace be with you!'' ²⁷Then Jesus said to Thomas, ''Put your finger here. Look at my hands. Put your hand here in my side. Stop doubting and start believing.''

²⁸Thomas said to Jesus, ''My Lord and my God!''

²⁹Jesus said to Thomas, ''You believe because you see me. Those people who believe without seeing me will be truly blessed.''

Why John Wrote This Book

³⁰Jesus did many other miracles* that his followers saw. Those miracles are not written in this book. ³¹But these things are written so that you can believe that Jesus is the Christ,* the Son of God. Then, by believing, you can have life through his name.

Jesus Appears to Seven Followers

21 Later, Jesus showed himself to his followers. This was by the sea of Tiberias. This is how it happened: ²Some of the followers were together. They were Simon Peter, Thomas (called Didymus), Nathanael from Cana in Galilee, the two sons of Zebedee, and two other followers. ³Simon Peter said, ''I am going out to fish.''

The other followers said, ''We will go with you.'' So all the followers went out and got into the boat. They fished that night, but caught nothing.

⁴Early the next morning Jesus stood on the shore. But the followers did not know that it was Jesus. ⁵Then Jesus said to the followers, ''Friends, have you caught any fish?''

The followers answered, ''No.''

⁶Jesus said, ''Throw your net into the water on the right side of your boat. You will find some fish there.'' So the followers did

---

miracles Miracles are powerful works or great things done by the power of God.
Christ The ''anointed one'' (the Messiah) or chosen one of God.

this. They caught so many fish that they could not pull the net back into the boat.

⁷The follower that Jesus loved said to Peter, "That man is the Lord (*Jesus*)!" Peter heard him say, "That man is the Lord." Peter put his coat around himself. (Peter had taken his clothes off *to work*.) Then he jumped into the water. ⁸The other followers went to shore in the boat. They pulled the net full of fish. They were not very far from shore, only about 100 yards. ⁹When the followers stepped out of the boat and onto the shore, they saw a fire of hot coals. There were fish on the fire and some bread there too. ¹⁰Then Jesus said, "Bring some of the fish that you caught."

¹¹Simon Peter went into the boat and pulled the net to the shore. It was full of big fish. There were 153. The fish *were very heavy*, but the net did not tear. ¹²Jesus said to them, "Come and eat." None of the followers would ask him, "Who are you?" They knew he was the Lord. ¹³Jesus walked to the food. He took the bread, and gave it to them. Jesus also got the fish and gave it to them.

¹⁴This was now the third time Jesus showed himself to his followers after he was raised from death.

Jesus Talks to Peter

¹⁵When they finished eating, Jesus said to Simon Peter, "Simon, son of John, do you love me more than these *other men love me*?"

Peter answered, "Yes, Lord, you know that I love you."

Jesus said to Peter, "Take care of my lambs.*"

¹⁶Again Jesus said to Peter, "Simon, son of John, do you love me?"

Peter answered, "Yes, Lord, you know that I love you."

Jesus said to Peter, "Take care of my sheep.*"

¹⁷A third time Jesus said, "Simon, son of John, do you love me?"

---

lambs, sheep   Jesus uses these words to mean his followers, as in John 10.

Peter was sad because Jesus asked him three times, "Do you love me?" Peter said, "Lord, you know everything. You know that I love you!"

Jesus said to Peter, "Take care of my sheep. [18]I tell you the truth: When you were young, you tied your own belt and went where you wanted. But when you are old, you will put out your hands and another person will tie you. That person will lead you where you don't want to go." [19](Jesus said this to show how Peter would die to give glory to God.) Then Jesus said to Peter, "Follow me!"

[20]Peter turned and saw the follower that Jesus loved walking behind them. (This was the follower who had leaned against Jesus at the supper and said, "Lord, who will turn against you?") [21]When Peter saw this follower behind them he asked Jesus, "Lord, what about him?"

[22]Jesus answered, "Maybe I want him to live until I come. That should not be important to you. You follow me!"

[23]So a story spread among the brothers (*followers*). They were saying that this follower *that Jesus loved* would not die. But Jesus did not say that he would not die. He only said, "Maybe I want him to live until I come. That should not be important to you."

[24]"That follower is the one who is telling these things. He is the one who has now written these things. We know that what he says is true.

[25]There are many other things that Jesus did. If every one of these things were written down, I think the whole world would not be big enough for all the books that would be written.

Acts

Luke Writes Another Book

1 Dear Theophilus,
The first book I wrote was about everything that Jesus did and taught. ²I wrote about the whole life of Jesus, from the beginning until the day he was carried up into heaven. Before this happened, Jesus talked to the apostles* he had chosen. With the help of the Holy Spirit,* Jesus told the apostles what they should do. ³This was after Jesus' death, but he showed the apostles that he was alive. Jesus proved this by doing many powerful things. The apostles saw Jesus many times during the 40 days after he was raised from death. Jesus spoke to the apostles about the kingdom of God. ⁴One time when he was together with them, he told them not to leave Jerusalem. Jesus said, "The Father has promised you something; I told you about it before. Wait here *in Jerusalem* to receive this promise. ⁵John baptized* people with water, but in a few days you will be baptized with the Holy Spirit.*"

Jesus Is Carried Up into Heaven

⁶The apostles* were all together. They asked Jesus, "Lord, is this the time for you to give the Jews their kingdom again?"

⁷Jesus said to them, "The Father is the only One who has the authority to decide dates and times. You cannot know these things. ⁸But the Holy Spirit will come to you. Then you will receive power. You will be my witnesses—*you will tell people about me*. First, you will tell people in Jerusalem. Then you will

---

apostles Men that Jesus chose to be his special helpers for telling his Good News to the world.
Holy Spirit Also called the Spirit of God, the Spirit of Christ, and the Comforter. He is joined with God and Christ. He does the work of God among people in the world.
baptized A Greek word meaning to immerse, dip, or bury a person or thing briefly under water.

tell people in all of Judea, in Samaria, and in every part of the world.''

⁹After Jesus told the apostles* these things, he was lifted up into the sky. While the apostles were watching, Jesus went into a cloud and they could not see him. ¹⁰Jesus was going away, and the apostles were looking into the sky. Suddenly, two men (*angels*) wearing white clothes stood beside them. ¹¹The two men said to the apostles, ''Men from Galilee, why are you standing here looking into the sky? You saw Jesus carried away from you into heaven. He will come back in the same way you saw him go.''

A New Apostle Is Chosen

¹²Then the apostles* went back to Jerusalem from the Mount of Olives. (This mountain is about one-half mile from Jerusalem.) ¹³The apostles entered the city. They went to the place where they were staying; this was in a room upstairs. The apostles were: Peter, John, James, Andrew, Philip, Thomas, Bartholomew, Matthew, James (the son of Alphaeus), Simon (known as the Zealot*), and Judas (the son of James).

¹⁴The apostles were all together. They were constantly praying with the same purpose. Some women, Mary, the mother of Jesus, and his brothers were there with the apostles.*

¹⁵After a few days there was a meeting of the believers. (There were about 120 of them.) Peter stood up and said, ¹⁶⁻¹⁷''Brothers, in the Scriptures* the Holy Spirit* said through David that something must happen. He was talking about Judas, one of our own group. Judas served together with us. The Spirit said that Judas would lead men to arrest Jesus. ¹⁸Judas was paid money for doing this. His money was used to buy him a field. (But Judas fell on his head, and his body broke open. All his intestines poured out.) ¹⁹All the people of Jerusalem learned about this. That is why they named that field Akeldama. (In their language

---

apostles Men that Jesus chose to be his special helpers for telling his Good News to the world.
Zealot The Zealots or ''Enthusiasts'' were a Jewish political group.
Scriptures Holy Writings—the Old Testament.
Holy Spirit Also called the Spirit of God, the Spirit of Christ, and the Comforter. He is joined with God and Christ. He does the work of God among people in the world.

Akeldama means "field of blood.") [20]In the book of Psalms, this is written *about Judas*:

> 'People should not go
>   near his land (*property*);
> No one should live there!'   *Psalm 69:25*

And it is also written:

> 'Let another man have his work.'   *Psalm 109:8*

[21-22]So now another man must join us and become a witness of Jesus' resurrection (*rising from death*). This man must be one of those men who were part of our group during all the time when the Lord Jesus was with us. This man must have been with us from the time John began to baptize* people until the day when Jesus was carried up from us into heaven."

[23]The apostles* put two men before the group. One was Joseph Barsabbas. He was also called Justus. The other man was Matthias. [24-25]The apostles prayed, "Lord, you know the minds of all men. Show us which one of these two men you choose to do this work. Judas turned away from it and went where he belongs. Lord, show us which man should take his place as an apostle!" [26]Then the apostles used lots* to choose one of the two men. The lots showed that Matthias was the one that the Lord wanted. So he became an apostle with the other eleven.

The Coming of the Holy Spirit

2 The apostles* were all together in one place when the day of Pentecost* came. [2]Suddenly a noise came from the sky. It sounded like a strong wind blowing. This noise filled the whole house where they were sitting. [3]They saw something that looked like flames of fire. The flames were separated and stood over each person there. [4]They were all filled with the Holy Spirit,* and they began to speak different languages. The Holy Spirit was giving them the power to do this.

---

baptize   A Greek word meaning to immerse, dip, or bury a person or thing briefly under water.
apostles   Men that Jesus chose to be his special helpers for telling his Good News to the world.
lots   Small rocks or sticks used like dice for making a choice.
Pentecost   Jewish feast day (50 days after Passover) celebrating the harvest of wheat.
Holy Spirit   Also called the Spirit of God, the Spirit of Christ, and the Comforter. He is joined with God and Christ. He does the work of God among people in the world.

⁵There were some very religious Jewish men in Jerusalem at this time. These men were from every country in the world. ⁶A large group of these men came together because they heard the noise. The apostles* were speaking, and every man heard in his own language. ⁷The Jews were all amazed at this. They did not understand how the apostles could do this. They said, "Look! These men (*the apostles*) that we hear speaking are all from Galilee*! ⁸But we hear them in our own languages. How is this possible? We are from different places: ⁹Parthia, Media, Elam, Mesopotamia, Judea, Cappadocia, Pontus, Asia,* ¹⁰Phrygia, Pamphylia, Egypt, Cyrene in Libya, Rome, ¹¹Crete and Arabia. Some of us were born Jews. Others are converts.* We are from these different countries. But we can hear these men in our own languages! We can all understand the great things they are saying about God." ¹²The people were all amazed and confused. They asked each other, "What is happening?" ¹³Other people were laughing at the apostles. These people thought the apostles were drunk from too much wine.

Peter Speaks to the People

¹⁴Then Peter stood up with the other eleven apostles.* He spoke loudly so that all the people could hear. He said, "My Jewish brothers and all of you who live in Jerusalem, listen to me. I will tell you something you need to know. Listen carefully. ¹⁵These men are not drunk like you think; it is only nine o'clock in the morning! ¹⁶But Joel the prophet* wrote about the things you see happening here today. This is what Joel wrote:

¹⁷'God says: In the last days,
   I will pour out (*give*) my Spirit* to all people.
Your sons and daughters will prophesy.*
   Your young men will see visions.*
   Your old men will have special dreams.

apostles   Men that Jesus chose to be his special helpers for telling his Good News to the world.
from Galilee   The people thought men from Galilee could speak only their own language.
Asia   The western part of Asia Minor.
converts   People who have changed their religion to become Jews.
prophet, prophesy   A prophet was a person who prophesied (spoke for God).
Spirit   The Holy Spirit. Also called the Spirit of God, the Spirit of Christ, and the Comforter. He is joined with God and Christ. He does the work of God among people in the world.
visions   A vision is something like a dream that God used to speak to people.

304

¹⁸At that time I will pour out (*give*) my Spirit*
    to my servants, men and women,
    and they will prophesy.*
¹⁹I will show amazing things in the sky above.
    I will give proofs on the earth below.
    There will be blood, fire, and thick smoke.
²⁰The sun will be changed into darkness,
    and the moon will become red like blood.
  Then the great and glorious day of the Lord
    will come.
²¹And every person who trusts in the Lord
    will be saved.'

Joel 2:28-32

²²"My Jewish brothers, listen to these words: Jesus from Nazareth was a very special man. God clearly showed this to you. God proved this by the powerful and amazing things he did through Jesus. You all saw these things. So you know this is true. ²³Jesus was given to you, and you killed him. With the help of bad men, you nailed Jesus to a cross. But God knew all this would happen. This was God's plan. God made this plan long ago. ²⁴Jesus suffered the pain of death, but God made him free. God raised Jesus from death. Death could not hold Jesus. ²⁵David said this about Jesus:

'I always saw the Lord before me;
    because he is at my right side
      to keep me safe.
²⁶So my heart was glad,
    and my mouth spoke with joy.
    Yes, even my body will live with hope;
²⁷because you will not leave my soul in death.
    You will not let the body of your Holy One
      rot in the grave.
²⁸You taught me how to live.
    You came close to me,
    and I felt great joy.'

Psalm 16:8-11

²⁹"My brothers, I can tell you truly about David, our ancestor. He died and was buried. His grave is still here with us today.

Spirit The Holy Spirit. Also called the Spirit of God, the Spirit of Christ, and the Comforter. He is joined with God and Christ. He does the work of God among people in the world.
prophesy To prophesy means to speak or teach things from God.

305

30David was a prophet* and knew something God said. God promised David that he would make a person from David's family to be a king like David. 31David knew this before it happened. That is why David said this about that person:

'He was not left in death.
His body did not rot in the grave.'

David was talking about the Christ* rising from death. 32So Jesus is the One God raised from death, *not David*! We are all witnesses of this. We saw him! 33Jesus was lifted up to heaven. Now Jesus is with God, at God's right side. The Father (*God*) has now given the Holy Spirit* to Jesus. The Holy Spirit is what God promised to give. So now Jesus has poured out (*has given*) that Spirit. This is what you see and hear. 34David was not the one who was lifted up to heaven. It was Jesus who was lifted up to heaven. David himself said:

'The Lord (*God*) said to my Lord (*Christ*):
  Sit at my right side.
35I will put your enemies under your power.*'   *Psalm 110:1*

36"So, all the people of Israel should know this truly: God has made Jesus to be Lord and Christ.* He is the man you nailed to the cross!"

37When the people heard this, they felt very, very sorry. They asked Peter and the other apostles,* "What should we do?"

38Peter said to them, "Change your hearts and lives! And each one of you must be baptized* in the name of Jesus Christ. Then God will forgive your sins, and you will receive the gift of the Holy Spirit.* 39This promise is for you. It is also for your children and for people who are far away. It is for every person that the Lord our God calls to himself."

40Peter warned them with many other words; he begged them, "Be saved from the evil people who live now!" 41Then those people who accepted (*believed*) what Peter said were baptized.*

---

prophet Person who spoke for God. He often told things that would happen in the future.
Christ The "anointed one" (the Messiah) or chosen one of God.
Holy Spirit Also called the Spirit of God, the Spirit of Christ, and the Comforter. He is joined with God and Christ. He does the work of God among people in the world.
I will put...power Literally, "I will make your enemies a footstool for your feet."
apostles Men that Jesus chose to be his special helpers for telling his Good News to the world.
baptized A Greek word meaning to be immersed, dipped, or buried briefly under water.

On that day about 3,000 people were added to the group of believers. ⁴²*The believers continued to meet together*. They used their time to learn the teaching of the apostles.* The believers shared with each other. They ate* together and prayed together.

The Believers Share

⁴³The apostles* were doing many powerful and amazing things; and every person felt great respect for God. ⁴⁴All the believers stayed together. They shared everything. ⁴⁵The believers sold their land and the things they owned. Then they divided the money and gave it to those people who needed it. ⁴⁶The believers met together in the temple* every day. They all had the same purpose. They ate together in their homes. They were happy to share their food and ate with joyful hearts. ⁴⁷The believers praised God, and all the people liked them. More and more people were being saved every day; the Lord was adding those people to the group of believers.

Peter Heals a Crippled Man

3 One day Peter and John went to the temple.* It was three o'clock in the afternoon. This was the time for the daily temple prayer service. ²When they were going into the temple yard, a man was there. This man had been crippled all his life. He could not walk, so some friends carried him. His friends brought him to the temple every day. They put the crippled man by one of the gates outside the temple. It was called Beautiful Gate. There the man begged for money from the people going into the temple. ³*That day* the man saw Peter and John going into the temple. He asked them for money. ⁴Peter and John looked at the crippled man and said, "Look at us!" ⁵The man looked at them; he thought they would give him some money. ⁶But Peter said, "I don't have any silver or gold, but I do have something else I can give you: By the power of Jesus Christ from Nazareth—stand up and walk!" ⁷Then Peter held the man's right hand and lifted him

apostles Men that Jesus chose to be his special helpers for telling his Good News to the world.
ate Literally, "broke bread." This may mean a meal like in verse 46, or the Lord's Supper, the special meal Jesus told his followers to eat to remember him (Luke 22:14-20).
temple The special building in Jerusalem where God commanded the Jews to worship him.

307

up. Immediately the man's feet and legs became strong. [8]The man jumped up, stood on his feet, and began to walk. He went into the temple with them. The man was walking and jumping, and he was praising God. [9-10]All the people recognized him. The people knew he was the crippled man who always sat by Beautiful Gate to beg for money. Now they saw this same man walking and praising God. The people were amazed. They could not understand how this could happen.

Peter Speaks to the People

[11]The man was holding on to Peter and John. All the people were amazed *because the man was healed*. They ran to Peter and John at Solomon's Porch.* [12]When Peter saw this, he said to the people, "My Jewish brothers, why are you surprised at this? You are looking at us like it was our power that made this man walk. Do you think this was done because we are good? [13]No! God did it! He is the God of Abraham, the God of Isaac, and the God of Jacob.* He is the God of all our fathers (*ancestors*). He gave glory to Jesus, his special servant. But you gave Jesus to be killed. Pilate decided to let Jesus go free. But you told Pilate you did not want Jesus. [14]Jesus was pure and good (*innocent*), but you said you did not want him. You told Pilate to give you a murderer* instead of Jesus. [15]And so you killed the One that gives life! But God raised him from death. We are witnesses of this—we saw this with our own eyes. [16]It was the power of Jesus that made this crippled man well. This happened because we trusted in the power of Jesus. You can see this man and you know him. He was made completely well because of trust in Jesus. You all saw it happen!

[17]"My brothers, I know you did those things to Jesus because you did not understand what you were doing. Your leaders also did not understand. [18]God said that these things would happen. God said through the prophets* that his Christ* would suffer and die. I have told you how God made this happen. [19]So you must

Solomon's Porch An area on the east side of the temple. It was covered by a roof.
Abraham...Isaac...Jacob Three of the most important leaders of the Old Testament.
murderer Barabbas, the man the Jews asked Pilate to let go free instead of Jesus (Luke 23:18).
prophet People who spoke for God. Their writings are part of the Old Testament.
Christ The "anointed one" (the Messiah) or chosen one of God.

change your hearts and lives! Come back to God and he will forgive your sins. ²⁰Then the Lord (*God*) will give you times of spiritual rest. He will give you Jesus, the One he chose to be the Christ.* ²¹But Jesus must stay in heaven until the time when all things will be made right again. God told about these things long ago when he spoke through his holy prophets.* ²²Moses said, 'The Lord your God will give you a prophet* like me. That prophet will come from among your own people (*the Jews*). You must obey everything he tells you. ²³And if any person refuses to obey that prophet, then that person will die, separated from God's people.'* ²⁴Samuel, and all the other prophets who spoke for God after Samuel, talked about this time now. ²⁵You have received the things the prophets talked about. You have received the agreement that God made with your fathers (*ancestors*). God said to your father Abraham, 'I will bless all people on earth. I will use one of your children (*descendants*) to do this.'* ²⁶God has sent his special servant (*Jesus*). God sent him to you first. God sent Jesus to bless you. He does this by making each of you turn away from doing bad things.''

Peter and John Before the Jewish Council

4 While Peter and John were speaking to the people, some men came to them. There were some Jewish priests, the captain of the soldiers that guarded the temple,* and some Sadducees.* ²They were upset because the two apostles* were teaching the people. Peter and John were preaching that people will rise from death through the power of Jesus. ³The Jewish leaders grabbed Peter and John and put them in jail. It was already night, so they kept Peter and John in jail until the next day. ⁴But many of the people that heard Peter and John preach believed the things they said. There were now about 5,000 men in the group of believers.

Christ   The "annointed one" (the Messiah) or chosen one of God.
prophet   People who spoke for God. Their writings are part of the Old Testament.
'The Lord...people'   Quotation from Deuteronomy 18:15,19.
'I...this'   Quotation from Genesis 22:18, 26:24.
temple   The special building in Jerusalem where God commanded the Jews to worship him.
Sadducees   A leading Jewish religious group. They followed only the first five books of the Old Testament. They believed that people don't have another life after death.
apostles   Men that Jesus chose to be his special helpers for telling his Good News to the world.

⁵The next day the Jewish leaders, the older Jewish leaders, and the teachers of the law met in Jerusalem. ⁶Annas (the high priest*), Caiaphas, John, and Alexander were there. Everyone from the high priest's family was there. ⁷They made Peter and John stand before all the people there. The Jewish leaders asked them many times, "How did you make this crippled man well? What power did you use? With whose authority did you do this?"

⁸Then Peter was filled with the Holy Spirit.* He said to them, "Leaders of the people and you older leaders: ⁹Are you questioning us about the good thing that was done to this crippled man? Are you asking us who made him well? ¹⁰We want all of you and all the Jewish people to know that this man was made well by the power of Jesus Christ from Nazareth! You nailed Jesus to a cross. God raised him from death. This man was crippled, but he is now well and able to stand here before you because of the power of Jesus! ¹¹Jesus is

> 'the stone* that you builders
>> thought was not important.
> But this stone has become
>> the cornerstone.*'
>
> *Psalm 118:22*

¹²Jesus is the only One who can save people. His name is the only power in the world that has been given to save people. We must be saved through Jesus!"

¹³The Jewish leaders understood that Peter and John had no special training or education. But the leaders also saw that Peter and John were not afraid to speak. So the leaders were amazed. Then they realized that Peter and John had been with Jesus. ¹⁴They saw the crippled man standing there beside the two apostles.* They saw that the man was healed. So they could say nothing against the apostles. ¹⁵The Jewish leaders told them to leave the meeting. Then the leaders talked to each other about

---

high priest   The most important Jewish priest and leader.
Holy Spirit   Also called the Spirit of God, the Spirit of Christ, and the Comforter. He is joined with God and Christ. He does the work of God among people in the world.
stone   A picture or symbol meaning Jesus.
cornerstone   The first and most important rock of a building.
apostles   Men that Jesus chose to be his special helpers for telling his Good News to the world.

what they should do. [16]They said, "What shall we do with these men (*the apostles*)? Every person in Jerusalem knows that they have done a great miracle*! This is clear. We cannot say it is not true. [17]But we must make them afraid to talk to people about this man (*Jesus*). Then this problem will not spread among the people."

[18]So the Jewish leaders called Peter and John in again. They told the apostles* not to say anything or to teach anything in the name of Jesus. [19]But Peter and John answered them, "What do you think is right? What would God want? Should we obey you or God? [20]We cannot be quiet. We must tell people about the things we saw and heard." [21-22]The Jewish leaders could not find a way to punish the apostles, because all the people were praising God for what had been done. (This miracle* was a proof from God. The man that was healed was more than 40 years old!) So the Jewish leaders warned the apostles again and let them go free.

Peter and John Return to the Believers

[23]Peter and John left the meeting of Jewish leaders and went to their own group. They told the group everything that the leading priests and the older Jewish leaders had said to them. [24]When the believers heard this, they prayed to God with one purpose—they all felt the same. They prayed, "Master, you are the One who made the sky, the earth, the sea, and everything in the world. [25]Our father (*ancestor*), David, was your servant. With the help of the Holy Spirit* he wrote these words:

'Why were the nations so mad?
Why did the people of the world
plan things *against God*?
It is hopeless!
[26]The kings of the earth prepared themselves to fight,
and the rulers all came together
against the Lord (*God*)
and against his Christ.*'

Psalm 2:1-2

miracle   Miracles are powerful works or great things done by the power of God.
apostles   Men that Jesus chose to be his special helpers for telling his Good News to the world.
Holy Spirit   Also called the Spirit of God, the Spirit of Christ, and the Comforter. He is joined
   with God and Christ. He does the work of God among people in the world.
Christ   The "anointed one" (the Messiah) or chosen one of God.

311

²⁷These things really happened when Herod,* Pontius Pilate, the nations, and the Jewish people all 'came together' against Jesus here in Jerusalem. Jesus is your holy Servant. He is the One you (*God*) made to be the Christ.* ²⁸These people that 'came together' against Jesus made your plan happen; it happened because of your power and your will. ²⁹And now, Lord, listen to what they are saying. They are trying to make us afraid! Lord, we are your servants. Help us to speak the things you want us to say without fear. ³⁰Help us to be brave by showing us your power; make sick people well, give proofs, and make miracles* happen by the power of Jesus, your holy servant.''

³¹After the believers prayed, the place where they were meeting shook. They were all filled with the Holy Spirit,* and they continued to speak God's message* without fear.

The Believers Share

³²The group of believers were joined in their hearts and they had the same spirit. No person in the group said that the things he had were his own. Instead, they shared everything. ³³With great power the apostles* told the people that the Lord Jesus was truly raised from death. And God blessed all the believers very much. ³⁴They all received the things they needed. Everyone that owned fields (*land*) or houses sold them for money. They brought the money ³⁵and gave it to the apostles. Then each person was given the things he needed.

³⁶One of the believers was named Joseph. The apostles* called him Barnabas. (This name means ''a person who helps others.'') He was a Levite* born in Cyprus. ³⁷Joseph owned a field. He sold the field, brought the money, and gave it to the apostles.

Herod   Herod Antipas, son of Herod the Great, tetrarch (ruler) of Galilee and Perea.
Christ   The ''anointed one'' (the Messiah) or chosen one of God.
miracles   Miracles are powerful works or great things done by the power of God.
Holy Spirit   Also called the Spirit of God, the Spirit of Christ, and the Comforter. He is joined with God and Christ. He does the work of God among people in the world.
God's message   The news that God has made a way through Christ for people to have their sins forgiven and live with God. When people accept this truth, God accepts them.
apostles   Men that Jesus chose to be his special helpers for telling his Good News to the world.
Levite   Levites were men from the family group of Levi who helped the Jewish priests with their work in the temple. Read 1 Chronicles 23:24-32.

Ananias and Sapphira

5 There was a man named Ananias. His wife's name was Sapphira. Ananias sold some land that he had. ²But he gave only part of the money to the apostles.* He secretly kept some of the money for himself. His wife knew this and she agreed with it. ³Peter said, "Ananias, why did you let Satan (*the devil*) rule your heart? You lied and tried to deceive (*fool*) the Holy Spirit.* You sold your field, but why did you keep part of the money for yourself? ⁴Before you sold the field, it belonged to you. And even after you sold it, you could have used the money any way you wanted. Why did you think of doing this bad thing? You lied to God, not to men!" ⁵⁻⁶When Ananias heard this, he fell down and died. Some young men came and wrapped his body. They carried it out and buried it. And every person that heard about this was filled with fear.

⁷About three hours later his wife (*Sapphira*) came in. Sapphira did not know about this thing that had happened to her husband. ⁸Peter said to her, "Tell me how much money you got for your field. Was it this much (*the amount Ananias had said*)?"

Sapphira answered, "Yes, that was all we got for the field."

⁹Peter said to her, "Why did you and your husband agree to test the Spirit of the Lord? Listen! Do you hear those footsteps? The men that buried your husband are at the door! They will carry you out in the same way." ¹⁰At that moment Sapphira fell down by his feet and died. The young men came in and saw that she was dead. The men carried her out and buried her beside her husband. ¹¹All the believers and all the other people who heard about these things were filled with fear.

Proofs from God

¹²The apostles* did many miracles* and powerful things. All the people saw these things. The apostles were together in Solomon's Porch*; they all had the same purpose. ¹³None of the

---

apostles Men that Jesus chose to be his special helpers for telling his Good News to the world.
Holy Spirit Also called the Spirit of God, the Spirit of Christ, and the Comforter. He is joined with God and Christ. He does the work of God among people in the world.
miracles Miracles are powerful works or great things done by the power of God.
Solomon's Porch An area on the east side of the temple. It was covered by a roof.

other people felt worthy to stand with them. All the people were saying good things about the apostles.* ¹⁴And more and more people believed in the Lord (*Jesus*)—many men and women were added to the group of believers. ¹⁵So the people brought their sick people into the streets. *The people heard that* Peter was coming by. So the people put their sick on little beds and mattresses. They thought that if the sick people could be close enough for Peter's shadow to touch them, it would be enough to heal them. ¹⁶People came from all the towns around Jerusalem. They brought their sick people and those that were bothered by evil spirits *from the devil*. All of these people were healed.

The Jews Try to Stop the Apostles

¹⁷The high priest* and all his friends (a group called the Sadducees*) became very jealous. ¹⁸They grabbed the apostles* and put them in jail. ¹⁹But during the night, an angel of the Lord opened the door of the jail. The angel led the apostles outside and said, ²⁰"Go and stand in the temple.* Tell the people everything about this new life *in Jesus*." ²¹When the apostles heard this, they obeyed and went into the temple. It was early in the morning. The apostles began to teach the people.

The high priest* and his friends came to the temple. They called a meeting of the Jewish leaders and all the important older men of the Jews. They sent some men to the jail to bring the apostles* to them. ²²When the men went to the jail, they could not find the apostles there. So they went back and told the Jewish leaders about this. ²³The men said, "The jail was closed and locked. The guards were standing at the doors. But when we opened the doors, the jail was empty!" ²⁴The captain of the temple guards and the leading priests heard this. They were confused. They wondered, "What will happen because of this?" ²⁵Then another man came and told them, "Listen! The men you put in jail are standing in the temple.* They are teaching the people!" ²⁶Then the captain and his men went out and brought

apostles   Men that Jesus chose to be his special helpers for telling his Good News to the world.
high priest   The most important Jewish priest and leader.
Sadducees   A leading Jewish religious group. They followed only the first five books of the Old Testament. They believed that people don't have another life after death.
temple   The special building in Jerusalem where God commanded the Jews to worship him.

the apostles* back. But the soldiers did not use force, because they were afraid of the people. The soldiers were afraid that the people would *become angry and* kill them (*the soldiers*) with rocks.

²⁷The soldiers brought the apostles* to the meeting and made them stand before the Jewish leaders. The high priest* questioned the apostles. ²⁸He said, "We told you never to teach about this man (*Jesus*)! But look what you have done! You have filled Jerusalem with your teaching. You are trying to make us responsible (*guilty*) for the death of this man (*Jesus*)."

²⁹Peter and the other apostles* answered, "We must obey God, not you! ³⁰You killed Jesus. You hung him on a cross. But God, the same God our fathers (*ancestors*) had, raised Jesus up from death! ³¹Jesus is the One that God raised to his right side. God made Jesus our Leader and Savior. God did this so that all Jews could change their hearts and lives. Then God can forgive their sins. ³²We saw all these things happen, and we can say these things are true. The Holy Spirit* also shows that these things are true. God has given the Spirit to all people who obey him."

³³The Jewish leaders heard these words. They became very angry. They began to plan a way to kill the apostles.* ³⁴One of the Pharisees* in the meeting stood up. His name was Gamaliel. He was a teacher of the law, and all the people respected him. He told the men to make the apostles leave the meeting for a few minutes. ³⁵Then he said to them, "Men of Israel, be careful of what you are planning to do to these men! ³⁶Remember when Theudas appeared? He said that he was an important man. About 400 men joined him. But he was killed. And all who followed him were scattered and ran away. They were able to do nothing. ³⁷Later, a man named Judas came from Galilee. It was at the time of the registration.* He led a group of followers, too. He was also killed. And all his followers were scattered and ran away. ³⁸And so now I tell you: Stay away from these men. Leave

apostles   Men that Jesus chose to be his special helpers for telling his Good News to the world.
high priest   The most important Jewish priest and leader.
Holy Spirit   Also called the Spirit of God, the Spirit of Christ, and the Comforter. He is joined with God and Christ. He does the work of God among people in the world.
Pharisees   Pharisees were a Jewish religious group that followed all the Old Testament and other Jewish laws and customs very carefully.
registration   A census or counting of all the people and the things they own.

315

them alone. If their plan comes from men, it will fail. ³⁹But if this is from God, then you will not be able to stop them. You might even be fighting against God himself!''

The Jewish leaders agreed with the things that Gamaliel said. ⁴⁰They called the apostles* in again. They beat the apostles and told them not to talk to people about Jesus again. Then they let the apostles go free. ⁴¹The apostles left the meeting. The apostles were happy because they were given the honor of suffering dishonor (*shame*) for the name *of Jesus*. ⁴²The apostles did not stop teaching people. The apostles continued to tell the people the Good News—that Jesus is the Christ.* They did this every day in the temple* and in people's homes.

Seven Men Chosen for a Special Work

6 More and more people were becoming followers of Jesus. But during this same time, the Greek-speaking followers had an argument with the other Jewish followers. They said that their widows* were not getting their share of the things that the followers received every day. ²The twelve apostles* called the whole group of followers together. The apostles said to them, ''Our work of teaching God's word has stopped. That's not good! It is better for us to continue teaching God's word than to help people have something to eat. ³So, brothers, choose seven of your own men. They must be men that people say are good. They must be full of wisdom and full of the Spirit.* We will give them this work to do. ⁴Then we can use all our time to pray and to teach the word *of God*.''

⁵The whole group liked the idea. So they chose these seven men: Stephen (a man with great faith and full of the Holy Spirit*), Philip,* Prochorus, Nicanor, Timon, Parmenas, and Nicolaus (a man from Antioch, who had become a Jew). ⁶Then

---

apostles   Men that Jesus chose to be his special helpers for telling his Good News to the world.
Christ   The ''anointed one'' (the Messiah) or chosen one of God.
temple   The special building in Jerusalem where God commanded the Jews to worship him.
widows   A widow is a woman whose husband has died.
Spirit, Holy Spirit   Also called the Spirit of God, the Spirit of Christ, and the Comforter. He is joined with God and Christ. He does the work of God among people in the world.
Philip   Not the apostle named Philip.

they put these men before the apostles.* The apostles prayed and put their hands on* the men.

⁷The word of God was influencing more and more people. The group of followers in Jerusalem became larger and larger. Even a big group of Jewish priests believed and obeyed.

The Jews Against Stephen

⁸Stephen (*one of the seven men*) received a great blessing. God gave Stephen power to do miracles* and to show proofs from God to the people. ⁹But some Jews came and argued with Stephen. These Jews were from a synagogue.* It was called a synagogue for Libertines.* (This synagogue was also for Jews from Cyrene, and for Jews from Alexandria.) Jews from Cilicia and Asia were with them. They all came and argued with Stephen. ¹⁰But the Spirit* was helping Stephen speak with wisdom. His words were so strong that the Jews could not argue with him. ¹¹So the Jews paid some men to say, "We heard Stephen say bad things against Moses and against God!" ¹²By doing this, these Jews upset the people, the older Jewish leaders, and the teachers of the law. They became so angry that they came and grabbed Stephen. They took him to a meeting of the Jewish leaders. ¹³The Jews brought some men into the meeting. They told these men to tell lies about Stephen. The men said, "This man (*Stephen*) always says bad things about this holy place (*the temple**). And he always says bad things against the law *of Moses*. ¹⁴This is true because we heard him say that Jesus from Nazareth will destroy this place. He also said that Jesus will change the things that Moses told us to do." ¹⁵All the people sitting in the meeting watched Stephen closely. His face looked like the face of an angel, and they saw it.

---

apostles Men that Jesus chose to be his special helpers for telling his Good News to the world.
put their hands on Here, doing this showed that these men were given a special work of God.
miracles Miracles are powerful works or great things done by the power of God.
synagogue Synagogues were places where Jews gathered to read and study the Scriptures.
Libertines Jews who had been slaves or whose fathers had been slaves, but were now free.
Spirit The Holy Spirit. Also called the Spirit of God, the Spirit of Christ, and the Comforter. He
   is joined with God and Christ. He does the work of God among people in the world.
temple The special building in Jerusalem where God commanded the Jews to worship him.

Stephen's Speech

7 The high priest* said to Stephen, "Are these things true?"
²Stephen answered, "My Jewish fathers and brothers, listen
to me. Our glorious God appeared to Abraham, our father
(*ancestor*). Abraham was in Mesopotamia. This was before he
lived in Haran. ³God said to Abraham, 'Leave your country and
your relatives! Go to another country. I will show you where to
go.'* ⁴So Abraham left the country of Chaldea. He went to live in
Haran. After Abraham's father died, God sent him to this place
here, where you live now. ⁵But God did not give Abraham any of
this land. God did not give him even a foot of it. But God
promised that in the future he would give Abraham this land for
himself and for his children. (This was before Abraham had any
children.) ⁶This is what God said to him: 'Your children
(*descendants*) will live in another country. They will be strangers.
The people there will make them slaves and do bad things to them
for 400 years. ⁷But I will judge (*condemn*) that nation which
made them slaves.'* And God also said, 'After those things
happen, your children will come out of that country. Then your
children will worship me in this place here.'* ⁸God made an
agreement with Abraham; the sign for this agreement was
circumcision.* And so when Abraham had a son, he circumcised
his son when he was eight days old. His son's name was Isaac.
Isaac also circumcised his son Jacob. And Jacob did the same for
his sons. These sons later became the twelve fathers.*

⁹"These fathers* became jealous of Joseph (*their younger
brother*). They sold Joseph to be a slave in Egypt. But God was
with Joseph. ¹⁰Joseph had many troubles there, but God saved
him from all those troubles. Pharaoh was the king of Egypt. He
liked Joseph and respected him because of the wisdom that God
gave Joseph. Pharaoh gave Joseph the job of being a governor of
Egypt. He even let Joseph rule over all the people in Pharaoh's

high priest   The most important Jewish priest and leader.
'Leave...go'   Quotation from Genesis 12:1.
'Your children...slaves'   Quotation from Genesis 15:13-14.
'After...here'   Quotation from Genesis 15:14 and Exodus 3:12.
circumcision   The cutting off of the foreskin. This was done to every Jewish baby boy. It was a
    mark of the agreement that God gave to Abraham (Genesis 17:9-14).
twelve fathers   Important ancestors of the Jews; the leaders of the twelve Jewish family groups.

house. ¹¹But all the land of Egypt and of Canaan became dry. It became so dry that food could not grow there. This made the people suffer very much. Our fathers* could not find anything to eat. ¹²But Jacob heard that there was food *stored* in Egypt. So he sent our fathers (*Jacob's sons*) there. (This was their first trip to Egypt.) ¹³Then they went there a second time. This time, Joseph told his brothers who he was. And Pharaoh learned about Joseph's family. ¹⁴Then Joseph sent some men to invite Jacob, his father, to come to Egypt. He also invited all his relatives (75 persons altogether). ¹⁵So Jacob went down to Egypt. Jacob and our fathers (*ancestors*) *lived there until they* died. ¹⁶Later their bodies were moved to Shechem. They were put in a grave there. (It was the same grave that Abraham had bought in Shechem from the sons of Hamor. He paid them with silver.)

¹⁷"The number of Jewish people in Egypt grew. There were more and more of our people there. (The promise that God made to Abraham was soon to come true.) ¹⁸Then a different king began to rule Egypt. He knew nothing about Joseph. ¹⁹This king tricked (*deceived*) our people. He was bad to our fathers (*ancestors*). The king made them put their children outside to die. ²⁰This was the time when Moses was born. He was a very fine child. For three months they took care of Moses in his father's house. ²¹When they put Moses outside, Pharaoh's daughter took him. She raised him like he was her own son. ²²The Egyptians taught Moses about all the things they knew. He was powerful in the things he said and did.

²³"When Moses was about 40 years old, he thought it would be good to visit his brothers, the Jewish people. ²⁴Moses saw an Egyptian man doing wrong to a Jew. So he defended the Jew. Moses punished the Egyptian for hurting the Jew; Moses hit him so hard that he died. ²⁵Moses thought that his Jewish brothers would understand that God was using him to save them. But they did not understand. ²⁶The next day, Moses saw two Jewish men fighting. He tried to make peace between them. He said, 'Men, you are brothers! Why are you doing wrong to each other?' ²⁷The man who was doing wrong to the other man pushed Moses away. He said to Moses, 'Who made you our ruler and judge? ²⁸Will

twelve fathers Important ancestors of the Jews; the leaders of the twelve Jewish family groups.

319

you kill me like you killed the Egyptian man yesterday?' ²⁹When Moses heard him say this, he left Egypt. He went to live in the land of Midian. He was a stranger there. While Moses lived in Midian, he had two sons.

³⁰"After 40 years, Moses was in the desert on Mount Sinai. An angel appeared to him in the flame of a burning bush. ³¹When Moses saw this, he was amazed. He went near to look closer at it. Moses heard a voice; it was the Lord's (*God's*). ³²The Lord said, 'I am the same God your fathers (*ancestors*) had—the God of Abraham, Isaac, and Jacob.*'* Moses began to shake with fear. He was afraid to look at the bush. ³³The Lord said to him, 'Take off your shoes, because the place where you are now standing is holy ground. ³⁴I saw my people suffer much in Egypt. I heard my people crying. I have come down to save them. And now, Moses, I am sending you back to Egypt.'*

³⁵"This Moses was the same man the Jews said they did not want. They had said to him, 'Who made you a ruler and judge?' Moses is the same man that God sent to be a ruler and savior. God sent Moses with the help of an angel. This was the angel Moses saw in the *burning* bush. ³⁶So Moses led the people out. He did powerful things and miracles.* Moses did these things in Egypt, at the Red Sea, and then in the desert for 40 years. ³⁷This is the same Moses that said these words to the Jewish people: 'God will give you a prophet* like me. He will come from among your own people.'* ³⁸This is the same Moses who was with the gathering of the Jews in the desert. He was with the angel that spoke to him at Mount Sinai, and he was with our fathers (*ancestors*). Moses received commandments *from God* that give life. Moses gave us those commandments.

³⁹"But our fathers (*ancestors*) did not want to obey Moses. They rejected him. They wanted to go back to Egypt again. ⁴⁰Our fathers said to Aaron, 'Make us some gods to lead us! Moses brought us out of Egypt, but we don't know what has happened

---

Abraham, Isaac, and Jacob   Three of the most important leaders of the Old Testament.
'I am...Jacob'   Quotation from Exodus 3:6.
'Take...Egypt'   Quotation from Exodus 3:5-10.
miracles   Miracles are powerful works or great things done by the power of God.
prophet   Person who spoke for God. He often told things that would happen in the future.
'God...people'   Quotation from Deuteronomy 18:15.

to him.' ⁴¹So the people made an idol that looked like a calf. Then they brought sacrifices (*gifts*) to it. The people were very happy with what they had made with their own hands! ⁴²But God turned against them. God finished trying to stop them from worshiping the army *of false gods* in the sky. This is what is written in the book of the prophets*: God says,

'You Jewish people did not give me sacrifices*
    and offerings in the desert for 40 years;
You carried with you the tent (*place of worship*)
⁴³   for Moloch (*a false god*)
    and the image of the star of your god Rephan.
These were the idols you made to worship.
So I will send you away beyond Babylon.'   *Amos 5:25-27*

⁴⁴"The tent* where God spoke to our fathers (*ancestors*) was with these Jews in the desert. God told Moses how to make this tent. He made it like the plan that God showed him. ⁴⁵Later, Joshua led our fathers to capture the lands of the other nations. Our people went in and God made the other people go out. When our people went into this new land, they took with them this same tent. Our people received this tent from their fathers, and our people kept it until the time of David. ⁴⁶God was very pleased with David. David asked God to let him build a house (*temple*) for him, the God of Jacob. ⁴⁷But Solomon (*David's son*) was the person who built the temple.

⁴⁸"But the Most High (*God*) does not live in houses that men build with their hands. This is what the prophet* writes:

'The Lord says,
Heaven is my throne.
⁴⁹   The earth is a place to rest my feet.
What kind of house can you build for me?
    There is no place where I need to rest!
⁵⁰Remember, I made all these things!' "   *Isaiah 66:1-2*

⁵¹Stephen continued speaking: "You stubborn Jewish leaders! You have not given your hearts to God! You won't listen to him!

---

prophet(s) People who spoke for God. Their writings are part of the Old Testament.
sacrifices Offerings or gifts to God.
tent This tent, which could be moved, was used like the temple, that was built later.
temple The special building in Jerusalem where God commanded the Jews to worship him.

You are always against what the Holy Spirit* is trying to tell you. Your fathers (*ancestors*) did this, and you are just like them! ⁵²Your fathers persecuted (*did bad things to*) every prophet* that ever lived. Those prophets said long ago that the Righteous One (*Jesus*) would come. But your fathers killed those prophets. And now you have turned against the Righteous One and killed him. ⁵³You are the people that received the law *of Moses*. God gave you this law through his angels. But you don't obey this law!''

Stephen Is Killed

⁵⁴The Jewish leaders heard Stephen say these things. They became very angry. The Jewish leaders were so mad that they were grinding their teeth at Stephen. ⁵⁵But Stephen was full of the Holy Spirit.* Stephen looked up into the sky. He saw the glory of God. He saw Jesus standing at God's right side. ⁵⁶Stephen said, ''Look! I see heaven open. And I see the Son of Man (*Jesus*) standing at God's right side!''

⁵⁷Then the Jewish leaders all shouted with a loud voice. They closed (*covered*) their ears with their hands. They all ran at Stephen together. ⁵⁸They took him out of the city and threw rocks at him until he was dead. The men who told lies against Stephen gave their coats to a young man named Saul. ⁵⁹Then they threw rocks at Stephen. But Stephen was praying. He said, ''Lord Jesus, receive my spirit!'' ⁶⁰He fell on his knees and shouted, ''Lord, don't blame them for this sin!'' After Stephen said this, he died.

8 Saul agreed that the killing of Stephen was a good thing.

Trouble for the Believers

¹⁻³Some good (*religious*) men buried Stephen. They cried very loudly for him. On that day the Jews began to persecute (*do bad things to*) the group of believers in Jerusalem. The Jews made them suffer very much. Saul was also trying to destroy the group. Saul went into their houses. He dragged out men and women and

---

Holy Spirit   Also called the Spirit of God, the Spirit of Christ, and the Comforter. He is joined with God and Christ. He does the work of God among people in the world.
prophet   Person who spoke for God. He often told things that would happen in the future.

put them in jail. All the believers left Jerusalem. Only the apostles* stayed. The believers went to different places in Judea and Samaria. ⁴The believers were scattered everywhere. In every place the believers went they told people the Good News.*

Philip Preaches in Samaria

⁵Philip* went to the city of Samaria. He preached about the Christ.* ⁶The people there heard Philip and saw the miracles* he was doing. They all listened carefully to the things Philip said. ⁷Many of these people had evil spirits *from the devil* inside them. But Philip made the evil spirits leave them. The spirits made a loud noise when they came out. There were also many weak and crippled people there. Philip made these people well, too. ⁸The people in that city were very happy because of this.

⁹But there was a man named Simon in that city. Before Philip came there, Simon did magic tricks. He amazed all the people of Samaria with his tricks. Simon boasted and called himself a great man. ¹⁰All the people—the least important and the most important—believed the things Simon said. The people said, "This man has the power of God that is called 'the Great Power'!" ¹¹Simon amazed the people with his magic tricks so long that the people became his followers. ¹²But Philip told the people the Good News* about the kingdom of God and the power of Jesus Christ. Men and women believed Philip. They were baptized.* ¹³Simon himself also believed and was baptized. Simon stayed very close to Philip. He saw the miracles* and the very powerful things that Philip did. Simon was amazed.

¹⁴The apostles* were still in Jerusalem. They heard that the people of Samaria had accepted the word of God. So the apostles sent Peter and John to the people in Samaria. ¹⁵When Peter and John arrived, they prayed for the Samaritan believers to receive the Holy Spirit.* ¹⁶These people had been baptized* in the name

apostles Men that Jesus chose to be his special helpers for telling his Good News to the world.
Good News The news that God has made a way through Christ for people to have their sins
forgiven and live with God. When people accept this truth, God accepts them.
Philip Not the apostle named Philip.
Christ The "anointed one" (the Messiah) or chosen one of God.
miracles Miracles are powerful works or great things done by the power of God.
baptized A Greek word meaning to immerse, dip, or bury a person or thing briefly under water.
Holy Spirit Also called the Spirit of God, the Spirit of Christ, and the Comforter. He is joined
with God and Christ. He does the work of God among people in the world.

of the Lord Jesus. But the Holy Spirit* had not yet come down on any of them. This is why Peter and John prayed. ¹⁷The two apostles* put their hands on* the people. Then the people received the Holy Spirit.

¹⁸Simon saw that the Spirit* was given to people when the apostles* put their hands on them. So Simon offered the apostles money. ¹⁹Simon said, "Give me this power so that when I put my hands on a person, he will receive the Holy Spirit.*"

²⁰Peter said to Simon, "You and your money should both be destroyed! You thought you could buy God's gift with money. ²¹You cannot share with us in this work. Your heart is not right before God. ²²Change your heart! Turn away from this bad thing you have done. Pray to the Lord (*God*). Maybe he will forgive you for thinking this. ²³I see that you are full of bitter jealousy and ruled by sin."

²⁴Simon answered, "Both of you pray for me to the Lord (*God*). Pray that the things you have said will not happen to me!"

²⁵Then the two apostles* told the people the things they had seen *Jesus do*. The apostles told the people the message* of the Lord. Then they went back to Jerusalem. On the way they went through many Samaritan towns and preached the Good News* to the people.

Philip Teaches a Man from Ethiopia

²⁶An angel of the Lord spoke to Philip.* The angel said, "Get ready and go south. Go to the road that leads down to Gaza from Jerusalem—the road that goes through the desert." ²⁷So Philip got ready and went. On the road he saw a man from Ethiopia. This man was a eunuch.* He was an important officer in the service of Candace, the queen of the Ethiopians. He was responsible for taking care of all her money. This man had gone

---

Holy Spirit   Also called the Spirit of God, the Spirit of Christ, and the Comforter. He is joined with God and Christ. He does the work of God among people in the world.

apostles   Men that Jesus chose to be his special helpers for telling his Good News to the world.

put their hands on   Here, doing this showed that the apostles had God's authority or power to give people special powers of the Holy Spirit. Only the apostles had this authority.

message, Good News   The news that God has made a way through Christ for people to have their sins forgiven and live with God. When people accept this truth, God accepts them.

Philip   Not the apostle named Philip.

eunuch   Man who cannot have sexual relations. Rulers often gave them important work.

to Jerusalem to worship. ²⁸Now he was on his way home. He was sitting in his chariot* and reading from the book of Isaiah, the prophet.* ²⁹The Spirit* said to Philip, "Go to that chariot and stay near it." ³⁰So Philip went toward the chariot and he heard the man reading. He was reading from Isaiah, the prophet. Philip said to him, "Do you understand what you are reading?"

³¹The man answered, "How can I understand? I need some person to explain it to me!" Then he invited Philip to climb in and sit with him. ³²The verse of Scripture* that he was reading was this:

"He was like a sheep when it is taken to be killed.
He was like a lamb that makes no sound
    when someone cuts off its wool.
He says nothing.
³³He was shamed; and all his rights
    were taken away.
His life on earth was ended;
    There will be no story
        about his family (*descendants*)."   *Isaiah 53:7-8*

³⁴The officer said to Philip, "Please, tell me, who is the prophet* talking about? Is he talking about himself or about someone else?" ³⁵Philip began to speak. He started with this same Scripture and told the man the Good News* about Jesus.

³⁶While they were traveling down the road, they came to some water. The officer said, "Look! Here is water! What is stopping me from being baptized*?" ³⁷* ³⁸Then the officer commanded the chariot to stop. Both Philip and the officer went down into the water, and Philip baptized him. ³⁹When they came up out of the water, the Spirit* of the Lord took Philip away; the officer never saw him again. The officer continued on his way home. He was

chariot Something like a wagon pulled by horses.
prophet Person who spoke for God. He often told things that would happen in the future.
Spirit The Holy Spirit. Also called the Spirit of God, the Spirit of Christ, and the Comforter. He is joined with God and Christ. He does the work of God among people in the world.
Scripture A part of the Holy Writings—the Old Testament.
Good News The news that God has made a way through Christ for people to have their sins forgiven and live with God. When people accept this truth, God accepts them.
baptized A Greek word meaning to be immersed, dipped, or buried briefly under water.
Verse 37 Some late copies of Acts add verse 37: "Philip answered, 'If you believe with all your heart, you can.' The officer said, 'I believe that Jesus Christ is the Son of God.'"

very happy. ⁴⁰But Philip appeared in a city called Azotus. He was going to the city of Caesarea. He preached the Good News* in all the towns on the way from Azotus to Caesarea.

Saul Is Converted

9 *In Jerusalem* Saul was still trying to scare and kill the followers of the Lord (*Jesus*) all the time. So he went to the high priest.* ²Saul asked him to write letters to the Jews of the synagogues* in the city of Damascus. Saul wanted the high priest to give him the authority to find people in Damascus who were followers of *Christ's* Way. If he found any believers there, men or women, he would arrest them and bring them back to Jerusalem.

³So Saul went to Damascus. When he came near the city, a very bright light from the sky suddenly shined around him. ⁴Saul fell to the ground. He heard a voice saying to him: "Saul, Saul! Why are you doing these bad things to me?"

⁵Saul said, "Who are you, Lord?"

The voice answered, "I am Jesus. I am the One you are persecuting. ⁶Get up now and go into the city. Someone there will tell you what you must do."

⁷The men traveling with Saul stood there. They said nothing. The men heard the voice, but they saw no one. ⁸Saul got up from the ground. He opened his eyes, but he could not see. So the men with Saul held his hand and led him into Damascus. ⁹For three days Saul could not see; he did not eat or drink.

¹⁰There was a follower *of Jesus* in Damascus. His name was Ananias. The Lord (*Jesus*) spoke to Ananias in a vision*: "Ananias!"

Ananias answered, "Here I am, Lord."

¹¹The Lord said to Ananias, "Get up and go to the street called Straight Street. Find the house of Judas.* Ask for a man named Saul from the city of Tarsus. He is there now, praying. ¹²Saul has

---

Good News   The news that God has made a way through Christ for people to have their sins forgiven and live with God. When people accept this truth, God accepts them.
high priest   The most important Jewish priest and leader.
synagogues   Synagogues were buildings where Jews gathered to read and study the Scriptures.
vision   A vision is something like a dream that God used to speak to people.
Judas   This is not either of the apostles named Judas.

seen a vision.* In this vision, a man named Ananias came to him and put his hands on him. Then Saul could see again.''

[13]But Ananias answered, ''Lord (*Jesus*), many people have told me about this man (*Saul*). They told me about the many bad things this man did to your saints* (*believers*) in Jerusalem. [14]Now he (*Saul*) has come here to Damascus. The leading priests have given him the power to arrest all people who believe in you.*''

[15]But the Lord (*Jesus*) said to Ananias, ''Go! I have chosen Saul for an important work. He must tell about me to kings, to the Jewish people, and to other nations. [16]I will show Saul the things he must suffer for my name.''

[17]So Ananias left and went to the house of Judas. He put his hands on Saul and said, ''Saul, my brother, the Lord Jesus sent me. He is the One you saw on the road when you came here. Jesus sent me so that you can see again and so that you can be filled with the Holy Spirit.*'' [18]Immediately, something that looked like fish scales fell off Saul's eyes. Saul was able to see again! Saul got up and was baptized.* [19]Then he ate some food and began to be strong again.

Saul Preaches in Damascus

Saul stayed with the followers *of Jesus* in Damascus for a few days. [20]Soon he began to preach about Jesus in the synagogues.* He told the people, ''Jesus is the Son of God!''

[21]All the people who heard Saul were amazed. They said, ''This is the same man that was in Jerusalem. He was trying to destroy the people that trust in this name (*Jesus*)! He (*Saul*) has come here to do the same thing. He came here to arrest the followers *of Jesus* and take them back *to Jerusalem* to the leading priests.''

---

vision   A vision is something like a dream that God used to speak to people.
saints   The followers of Jesus are also called saints, which means ''holy people.''
believe in you   Literally, ''call on your name,'' meaning to show faith in Jesus by worshiping him.
Holy Spirit   Also called the Spirit of God, the Spirit of Christ, and the Comforter. He is joined with God and Christ. He does the work of God among people in the world.
baptized   A Greek word meaning to be immersed, dipped, or buried briefly under water.
synagogues   Synagogues were buildings where Jews gathered to read and study the Scriptures.

²²But Saul became more and more powerful. He proved that Jesus is the Christ.* His proofs were so strong that the Jews who lived in Damascus could not argue with him.

Saul Escapes from the Jews

²³After many days, the Jews made plans to kill Saul. ²⁴The Jews were watching the city gates day and night, *waiting for Saul*. They wanted to kill him. But Saul learned about their plan. ²⁵One night some followers that Saul had taught helped him leave the city. The followers put Saul in a basket. They put the basket through a hole in the city wall and lowered him down.

Saul in Jerusalem

²⁶Then Saul went to Jerusalem. He tried to join the group of followers (*believers*), but they were all afraid of him. They did not believe that Saul was really a follower *of Jesus*. ²⁷But Barnabas accepted Saul and brought him to the apostles.* Barnabas told the apostles that Saul had seen the Lord (*Jesus*) on the road *to Damascus*. Barnabas explained to the apostles how the Lord had spoken to Saul. Then he told the apostles that Saul preached for the Lord (*Jesus*) without fear to the people in Damascus.

²⁸And so Saul stayed with the followers. He went everywhere in Jerusalem, preaching for the Lord (*Jesus*) without fear. ²⁹Saul often talked with the Jews that spoke Greek. He had arguments with them. But they were trying to kill him. ³⁰When the brothers (*believers*) learned about this, they took Saul to the city of Caesarea. From Caesarea they sent Saul to the city of Tarsus.

³¹The church (*believers*) everywhere in Judea, Galilee, and Samaria had a time of peace. With the help of the Holy Spirit,* the group became stronger. The believers showed that they respected the Lord by the way they lived. Because of this, the group of believers grew larger and larger.

Christ   The "anointed one" (the Messiah) or chosen one of God.
apostles   Men that Jesus chose to be his special helpers for telling his Good News to the world.
Holy Spirit   Also called the Spirit of God, the Spirit of Christ, and the Comforter. He is joined with God and Christ. He does the work of God among people in the world.

Peter Heals Aeneas

³²The apostle* Peter traveled through all the towns *around Jerusalem*. He visited the saints* (*believers*) who lived in Lydda. ³³In Lydda he met a paralyzed (*crippled*) man named Aeneas. Aeneas had not been able to leave his bed for the past eight years. ³⁴Peter said to him, "Aeneas, Jesus Christ heals you. Stand up and make your bed! You can do this for yourself now!" Aeneas stood up immediately. ³⁵All the people living in Lydda and on the plain of Sharon saw him. These people turned to (*believed in*) the Lord *Jesus*.

Peter in Joppa

³⁶In the city of Joppa there was a follower *of Jesus* named Tabitha. (Her Greek name, Dorcas, means "a deer.") She always did good things for people. She always gave money to people who needed it. ³⁷While Peter was in Lydda, Tabitha became sick and died. They washed her body and put it in a room upstairs. ³⁸The followers in Joppa heard that Peter was in Lydda. (Lydda is near Joppa.) So they sent two men to Peter. They begged him, "Hurry, please come quickly!" ³⁹Peter got ready and went with them. When he arrived, they took him to the room upstairs. All the widows* stood around Peter. They were crying. They showed Peter the coats and other clothes that Dorcas (*Tabitha*) had made when she was still alive. ⁴⁰Peter sent all the people out of the room. He kneeled and prayed. Then he turned to Tabitha's body and said, "Tabitha, stand up!" She opened her eyes. When she saw Peter, she sat up. ⁴¹He gave her his hand and helped her stand up. Then he called the saints* (*believers*) and the widows into the room. He showed them Tabitha; she was alive! ⁴²People everywhere in Joppa learned about this. Many of these people believed in the Lord (*Jesus*). ⁴³Peter stayed in Joppa for many days. He stayed with a man named Simon who was a leatherworker.*

---

apostle Person Jesus chose to be a special helper for telling the Good News to the world.
saints The followers of Jesus are also called saints, which means "holy people."
widows A widow is a woman whose husband has died.
leatherworker A worker who makes leather from the skins of animals.

Peter and Cornelius

10 In the city of Caesarea there was a man named Cornelius. He was an officer in the "Italian" group *of the Roman army*. ²Cornelius was a good (*religious*) man. He and all the other people who lived in his home worshiped the true God. He gave much of his money to the poor people. Cornelius prayed to God always. ³One afternoon about three o'clock, Cornelius saw a vision.* He saw it clearly. In the vision, an angel came to him and said, "Cornelius!"

⁴Cornelius looked at the angel. He became afraid and said, "What do you want, sir?"

The angel said to Cornelius, "God has heard your prayers. He has seen the things you give to the poor people. God remembers you. ⁵Send some men now to the city of Joppa. Send your men to bring back a man named Simon. Simon is also called Peter. ⁶Simon is staying with a man, also named Simon, who is a leatherworker.* He has a house beside the sea." ⁷The angel who spoke to Cornelius left. Then Cornelius called two of his servants and a soldier. This soldier was a good (*religious*) man. The soldier always stayed close to Cornelius. ⁸Cornelius explained everything to these three men. Then he sent them to Joppa.

⁹The next day these men came near Joppa. At that time, Peter was going up to the roof to pray. It was about noon. ¹⁰Peter was hungry. He wanted to eat. But while they were preparing the food for Peter to eat, a vision* came to him. ¹¹He saw something coming down through the open sky. It looked like a big sheet coming down to the ground. It was being lowered to the ground by its four corners. ¹²Every kind of animal was in it—animals that walk, animals that crawl on the ground, and birds that fly in the air. ¹³Then a voice said to Peter, "Get up, Peter; kill any of these animals and eat it."

¹⁴But Peter said, "I would never do that, Lord! I have never eaten food that is unholy or not pure."

¹⁵But the voice said to him again, "God has made these things clean (*pure*). Don't call them 'unholy'!" ¹⁶This happened three times. Then the whole thing was taken back up into the sky.

---

vision A vision is something like a dream that God used to speak to people.
leatherworker A worker who makes leather from the skins of animals.

¹⁷Peter wondered what this vision* meant. The men that Cornelius sent had found Simon's house. They were standing at the door. ¹⁸They asked, "Is Simon Peter staying here?"

¹⁹Peter was still thinking about the vision.* But the Spirit* said to him, "Listen! Three men are looking for you. ²⁰Get up and go downstairs. Go with these men and don't ask questions. I have sent them to you." ²¹So Peter went downstairs to the men. He said, "I am the man you are looking for. Why did you come here?"

²²The men said, "A holy angel told Cornelius to invite you to his house. Cornelius is a *Roman army* officer. He is a good (*righteous*) man; he worships God. All the Jewish people respect him. The angel told Cornelius to invite you to his house so that he can listen to the things you have to say." ²³Peter asked the men to come in and stay for the night.

The next day Peter got ready and went away with the three men. Some of the brothers (*believers*) from Joppa went with Peter. ²⁴The next day they came into the city of Caesarea. Cornelius was waiting for them. He had already gathered his relatives and close friends *at his house*. ²⁵When Peter entered the house, Cornelius met him. Cornelius fell down at Peter's feet and worshiped him. ²⁶But Peter told him to get up. Peter said, "Stand up! I am only a man like you." ²⁷Peter continued talking with Cornelius. Then Peter went inside and saw a large group of people together there. ²⁸Peter said to the people, "You people understand that it is against our Jewish law for a Jew to associate with or visit any person who is not a Jew. But God has shown me that I should not call any person 'unholy' or 'not clean.' ²⁹That is why I did not argue when the men asked me to come here. Now, please tell me why you sent for me."

³⁰Cornelius said, "Four days ago, I was praying in my house. It was at this same time—three o'clock in the afternoon. Suddenly, there was a man (*angel*) standing before me. He was wearing bright, shiny clothes. ³¹The man said, 'Cornelius! God has heard your prayer. God has seen the things you give to the poor people. God remembers you. ³²So send some men to the city of Joppa. Ask Simon Peter to come. Peter is staying in the house of a man,

vision A vision is something like a dream that God used to speak to people.
Spirit The Holy Spirit. Also called the Spirit of God, the Spirit of Christ, and the Comforter. He is joined with God and Christ. He does the work of God among people in the world.

331

also named Simon, who is a leatherworker.* His house is beside the sea.' ³³So I sent for you immediately. It was very good of you to come here. Now we are all here before God to hear everything the Lord has commanded you to tell us.''

Peter Speaks in the House of Cornelius

³⁴Peter began to speak, ''I really understand now that to God every person is the same. ³⁵And God accepts any person who worships him and does what is right. It is not important what country a person comes from. ³⁶God has spoken to the Jewish people. God sent them the Good News* that peace has come through Jesus Christ. Jesus is the Lord (*Ruler*) of all people! ³⁷You know what has happened all over Judea. It began in Galilee after John* preached to the people about baptism.* ³⁸You know about Jesus from Nazareth. God made him the Christ* by giving him the Holy Spirit* and power. Jesus went everywhere doing good things for people. Jesus healed the people who were ruled by the devil. This showed that God was with Jesus. ³⁹We saw all the things that Jesus did in Judea and in Jerusalem. We are witnesses. But Jesus was killed. They put him on a cross made of wood. ⁴⁰But, on the third day *after his death*, God raised Jesus to life! God let people see Jesus clearly. ⁴¹But Jesus was not seen by all the people. Only the witnesses that God had already chosen saw him. We are those witnesses! We ate and drank with Jesus after he was raised from death. ⁴²Jesus told us to preach to the people. He told us to tell people that he is the One that God chose to be the Judge of all people who are living and all people who are dead. ⁴³Every person who believes (*trusts*) in Jesus will be forgiven. God will forgive the sins of that person through the name of Jesus. All the prophets* say this is true.''

leatherworker A worker who makes leather from the skins of animals.
Good News The news that God has made a way through Christ for people to have their sins forgiven and live with God. When people accept this truth, God accepts them.
John John the Baptizer, who preached to people about Christ's coming (Matt. 3, Luke 3).
baptism A Greek word meaning to be immersed, dipped, or buried briefly under water.
Christ The ''anointed one'' (the Messiah) or chosen one of God.
Holy Spirit Also called the Spirit of God, the Spirit of Christ, and the Comforter. He is joined with God and Christ. He does the work of God among people in the world.
prophets People who spoke for God. Their writings are part of the Old Testament.

The Holy Spirit Comes to Non-Jews

⁴⁴While Peter was still speaking these words, the Holy Spirit* came down on all those people who were listening to his speech. ⁴⁵The Jewish believers who came with Peter were amazed. They were amazed that the Holy Spirit was poured out (*given*) to the non-Jewish people too. ⁴⁶These Jewish believers heard them speaking different languages and praising God. Then Peter said, ⁴⁷"We cannot refuse to allow these people to be baptized* in water. They have received the Holy Spirit the same as we did!" ⁴⁸So Peter commanded that Cornelius and his relatives and friends be baptized in the name of Jesus Christ. Then the people asked Peter to stay with them for a few days.

Peter Returns to Jerusalem

11 The apostles* and the brothers in Judea heard that non-Jewish people had accepted God's teaching too. ²But when Peter came to Jerusalem, some Jewish believers* argued with him. ³They said, "You went into the homes of people that are not Jews and are not circumcised*! You even ate with them!"

⁴So Peter explained the whole story to them. ⁵Peter said, "I was in the city of Joppa. While I was praying, a vision* came to me. In the vision, I saw something coming down from the sky. It looked like a big sheet. It was being lowered to the ground by its four corners. It came down and stopped very close to me. ⁶I looked inside it. I saw animals, both tame and wild. I saw animals that crawl and birds that fly in the air. ⁷I heard a voice say to me, 'Get up, Peter. Kill any of these animals and eat it!' ⁸But I said, 'I would never do that, Lord! I have never eaten anything that is unholy or not pure.' ⁹But the voice from the sky answered again, 'God has made these things clean (*pure*). Don't call them unholy!' ¹⁰This happened three times. Then the whole thing was

Holy Spirit   Also called the Spirit of God, the Spirit of Christ, and the Comforter. He is joined with God and Christ. He does the work of God among people in the world.

baptized   A Greek word meaning to be immersed, dipped, or buried briefly under water.

apostles   Men that Jesus chose to be his special helpers for telling his Good News to the world.

Jewish believers   Literally, "those of the circumcision." This may mean Jews who thought that all Christians must be circumcised and obey all the law of Moses (Galatians 2:12, Titus 1:10).

circumcised   To have the foreskin cut off. This was done to every Jewish baby boy. It was a mark of the agreement that God gave to Abraham (Genesis 17:9-14).

vision   A vision is something like a dream that God used to speak to people.

taken back into the sky. ¹¹Then three men came to the house where I was staying. These three men were sent to me from the city of Caesarea. ¹²The Spirit* told me to go with them without doubting. These six brothers (*believers*) here also went with me. We went to the house of Cornelius. ¹³Cornelius told us about the angel he saw standing in his house. The angel said to Cornelius, 'Send some men to Joppa. Invite Simon Peter to come. ¹⁴He will speak to you. The things he will say will save you and all your family.' ¹⁵When I began my speech, the Holy Spirit* came down on them the same as he (*the Spirit*) came on us at the beginning.* ¹⁶Then I remembered the words of the Lord (*Jesus*). The Lord said, 'John baptized* people in water, but you will be baptized in the Holy Spirit!' ¹⁷God gave to these people the same gift that he gave to us who believed in the Lord Jesus Christ. So could I stop the work of God? No!''

¹⁸When the Jewish believers heard these things, they stopped arguing. They praised God and said, "So God is allowing the non-Jewish people to change their hearts and have life the same as us!''

The Good News Comes to Antioch

¹⁹The believers were scattered by the persecution* that happened after Stephen was killed. Some of the believers went to places far away like Phoenicia, Cyprus, and Antioch. The believers told the Good News* in these places; but they told it only to Jews. ²⁰Some of these believers were men from Cyprus and Cyrene. When these men came to Antioch, they also spoke to Greeks (*non-Jews*). They told these Greek people the Good News about the Lord Jesus. ²¹The Lord was helping the believers. And a large group of people believed and started following the Lord (*Jesus*).

Spirit, Holy Spirit Also called the Spirit of God, the Spirit of Christ, and the Comforter. He is joined with God and Christ. He does the work of God among people in the world.
beginning The beginning of the church on the day of Pentecost. (Read Acts 2.)
baptized A Greek word meaning to be immersed, dipped, or buried briefly under water.
persecution A time when the Jews were punishing the people who believed in Christ (Acts 8:1-4).
Good News The news that God has made a way through Christ for people to have their sins forgiven and live with God. When people accept this truth, God accepts them.

²²The church (*group of believers*) in Jerusalem heard about these new believers *in Antioch*. So the believers in Jerusalem sent Barnabas to Antioch. ²³⁻²⁴Barnabas was a good man. He was full of the Holy Spirit* and full of faith. When Barnabas went to Antioch, he saw that God had blessed those people very much. This made Barnabas very happy. He encouraged all the believers in Antioch. He told them, "Never lose your faith. Always obey the Lord with all your hearts." Many, many people became followers of the Lord *Jesus*.

²⁵Then Barnabas went to the city of Tarsus. He was looking for Saul. ²⁶When he found Saul, Barnabas brought him to Antioch. Saul and Barnabas taught many people. In Antioch the followers *of Jesus* were called "Christians" for the first time.

²⁷About that same time some prophets* went from Jerusalem to Antioch. ²⁸One of these prophets was named Agabus. In Antioch, Agabus stood up and spoke. With the help of the Holy Spirit,* he said, "A very bad time is coming to the whole world. There will be no food for people to eat." (This time without food happened when Claudius was emperor.*) ²⁹The believers decided that they would all try to help their brothers and sisters who lived in Judea. Each believer planned to send them as much as he could. ³⁰They gathered the money and gave it to Barnabas and Saul. Then Barnabas and Saul brought it to the elders* in Judea.

Herod Agrippa Hurts the Church

12 During that same time King Herod* began to persecute (*do bad things to*) some of the people who belonged to the church (*group of believers*). ²Herod ordered James to be killed with a sword. James was the brother of John. ³Herod saw that the Jews liked this. So he decided to arrest Peter, too. (This happened during the time of the Jewish holiday called the

---

Antioch An important city in the country of Syria.
Holy Spirit Also called the Spirit of God, the Spirit of Christ, and the Comforter. He is joined with God and Christ. He does the work of God among people in the world.
prophets People who spoke for God.
emperor The ruler (leader) of the Roman empire (almost all the world).
elders A group of men chosen to lead a church. Also called "overseers" and "pastors" (shepherds), they have the work of caring for God's people (Acts 20:28, Ephesians 4:11).
Herod Herod Agrippa I, grandson of Herod the Great.

Passover.*) ⁴Herod arrested Peter and put him in jail. A group of 16 soldiers guarded Peter. Herod wanted to wait until after the Passover feast. Then he planned to bring Peter before the people. ⁵So Peter was kept in jail. But the church was constantly praying to God for Peter.

Peter Leaves the Jail

⁶Peter was sleeping between two of the soldiers. He was bound with two chains. More soldiers were guarding the door of the jail. It was at night, and Herod planned to bring Peter out before the people the next day. ⁷Suddenly, an angel of the Lord stood there. A light shined in the room. The angel touched Peter on the side and woke him up. The angel said, "Hurry, Get up!" The chains fell off Peter's hands. ⁸The angel said to Peter, "Get dressed and put on your shoes." And so Peter did this. Then the angel said, "Put on your coat and follow me." ⁹So the angel went out and Peter followed. Peter did not know if the angel was really doing this. He thought he might be seeing a vision.* ¹⁰Peter and the angel went past the first guard and the second guard. Then they came to the iron gate that separated them from the city. The gate opened itself for them. Peter and the angel went through the gate and walked about a block. Then the angel suddenly left.

¹¹Peter realized then what had happened. He thought, "Now I know that the Lord really sent his angel to me. He rescued (*saved*) me from Herod. The Jewish people thought that bad things would happen to me. But the Lord saved me from all these things."

¹²When Peter realized this, he went to the home of Mary. She was the mother of John. (John was also called Mark.) Many people were gathered there. They were all praying. ¹³Peter knocked on the outside door. A servant girl named Rhoda came to answer it. ¹⁴Rhoda recognized Peter's voice, and she was very happy. She even forgot to open the door. But she ran inside and told the group, "Peter is at the door!"

Passover Important holy day for Jews. They ate a special meal on this day every year to remember that God freed them from slavery in Egypt in the time of Moses.
vision A vision is something like a dream that God used to speak to people.

¹⁵The believers said to Rhoda, "You are crazy!" But she continued to say that it was true. So they said, "It must be Peter's angel."

¹⁶But Peter continued to knock. When the believers opened the door, they saw Peter. They were amazed. ¹⁷Peter made a sign with his hand to tell them to be quiet. He explained to them how the Lord led him out of the jail. He said, "Tell James and the other brothers what happened." Then Peter left to go to another place.

¹⁸The next day the soldiers were very upset. They wondered what happened to Peter. ¹⁹Herod looked everywhere for Peter, but could not find him. So Herod questioned the guards. Then he ordered that the guards be killed.

The Death of Herod Agrippa

Later Herod* moved from Judea. He went to the city of Caesarea and stayed there a while. ²⁰Herod was very angry with the people from the cities of Tyre and Sidon. Those people all came in a group to Herod. They were able to get Blastus on their side. Blastus was the king's personal servant. The people asked Herod for peace because their country needed food from Herod's country.

²¹Herod decided a day to meet with them. On that day Herod was wearing a beautiful royal robe. He sat on his throne and made a speech to the people. ²²The people shouted, "This is the voice of a god, not a man!" ²³Herod *accepted this praise and* did not give the glory to God. So an angel of the Lord caused him to become sick. He was eaten by worms inside him, and he died.

²⁴The message* of God was spreading and influencing more and more people. The group of believers became larger and larger.

²⁵After Barnabas and Saul finished their work in Jerusalem, they returned to Antioch. John Mark was with them.

Herod   Herod Agrippa I, grandson of Herod the Great.
message   The news that God has made a way through Christ for people to have their sins
   forgiven and live with God. When people accept this truth, God accepts them.

Barnabas and Saul Chosen for a Special Work

13 In the church (*group of believers*) at Antioch there were some prophets* and teachers. They were: Barnabas, Simeon (also called Niger), Lucius (from the city of Cyrene), Manaen (who had grown up with Herod,* the ruler) and Saul. ²These men were all serving the Lord and fasting.* The Holy Spirit* said to them, "Give Barnabas and Saul to me to do a special work. I have chosen them to do this work."

³So the church fasted* and prayed. They put their hands on* Barnabas and Saul and sent them out.

Barnabas and Saul in Cyprus

⁴Barnabas and Saul were sent out by the Holy Spirit.* They went to the city of Seleucia. Then they sailed from Seleucia to the island of Cyprus. ⁵When Barnabas and Saul came to the city of Salamis, they preached the message* of God in the Jewish synagogues.* (John *Mark* was with them to help.)

⁶They went across the whole island to the city of Paphos. In Paphos they met a Jewish man who did magic tricks. His name was Barjesus. He was a false prophet.* ⁷Barjesus always stayed close to Sergius Paulus, the governor. Sergius Paulus was a wise man. He asked Barnabas and Saul to come to him. He wanted to hear the message* of God. ⁸But Elymas, the magician, was against Barnabas and Saul. (Elymas is the name for Barjesus in the Greek language.) Elymas tried to stop the governor from believing *in Jesus*. ⁹But Saul was filled with the Holy Spirit.* (Saul's other name was Paul.) Paul looked at Elymas (*Barjesus*) ¹⁰and said, "You son of the devil! You are an enemy of everything that is right! You are full of evil tricks and lies. You

---

prophets   People who spoke for God.
Herod   Herod Agrippa I, grandson of Herod the Great.
fasting, fasted   To fast is to live without food for a special time of prayer and worship to God.
Holy Spirit   Also called the Spirit of God, the Spirit of Christ, and the Comforter. He is joined with God and Christ. He does the work of God among people in the world.
put their hands on   Here, this was a sign to show that these men were given a special work of God.
message   The news that God has made a way through Christ for people to have their sins forgiven and live with God. When people accept this truth, God accepts them.
synagogues   Synagogues were buildings where Jews gathered to read and study the Scriptures.
false prophet   A person who says he speaks for God, but does not really speak God's truth.

always try to change the Lord's truths into lies! ¹¹Now the Lord will touch you and you will be blind. For a time you will not be able to see anything—not even the light from the sun.''

Then everything became dark for Elymas. He walked around lost. He was trying to find someone to lead him by the hand. ¹²When the governor (*Sergius Paulus*) saw this, he believed. He was amazed at the teaching of the Lord.

Paul and Barnabas Leave Cyprus

¹³Paul and those people with him sailed away from Paphos. They came to Perga, a city in Pamphylia. But John *Mark* left them; he returned to Jerusalem. ¹⁴They continued their trip from Perga and went to Antioch, a city near Pisidia. In Antioch, on the Sabbath day,* they went into the Jewish synagogue* and sat down. ¹⁵The law of Moses and the writings of the prophets* were read. Then the leaders of the synagogue sent a message to Paul and Barnabas: "Brothers, if you have something to say that will help the people here, please speak!"

¹⁶Paul stood up. He raised his hand* and said, "My Jewish brothers and you other people who also worship the true God, please listen to me! ¹⁷The God of the Jewish people chose our fathers (*ancestors*). God helped his people to have success during the time they lived in Egypt as strangers. God brought them out of that country with great power. ¹⁸And God was patient with them for 40 years in the desert. ¹⁹God destroyed seven nations in the land of Canaan. He gave their land to his people. ²⁰All this happened in about 450 years.

"After this, God gave *our people* judges (*leaders*) until the time of Samuel the prophet.* ²¹Then the people asked for a king. God gave them Saul, the son of Kish. Saul was from the family group of Benjamin. He was king for 40 years. ²²After God took Saul away, God made David their king. This is what God said about David: 'David, the son of Jesse, is the man I like. He will do all the things I want him to do.' ²³God has brought one of David's

---

Sabbath day   Seventh day of the Jewish week. It was a special religious day for the Jews.
synagogue   Synagogues were places where Jews gathered to read and study the Scriptures.
prophet(s)   People who spoke for God. Their writings are part of the Old Testament.
raised his hand   This was a sign to make the people pay attention.

descendants to the Jewish people to be their Savior.* That descendant is Jesus. God promised to do this. ²⁴Before Jesus came, John* preached to all the Jewish people. John told the people to change their hearts and lives and be baptized.* ²⁵When John was finishing his work, he said, 'Who do you think I am? I am not the Christ.* He is coming later. I am not worthy to untie his shoes.'

²⁶"My brothers, sons in the family of Abraham, and you non-Jews who also worship the true God, listen! The news about this salvation has been sent to us. ²⁷The *Jews* living in Jerusalem and the Jewish leaders did not realize that *Jesus* was the Savior. The words that the prophets* wrote *about Jesus* were read to the Jews every Sabbath day,* but they did not understand. The Jews condemned Jesus. When they did this, they made the words of the prophets come true! ²⁸They could not find any real reason why Jesus should die, but they asked Pilate to kill him. ²⁹These Jews did all the things that the Scriptures* said about Jesus. Then they took Jesus down from the cross and put him in a grave. ³⁰But God raised him up from death! ³¹After this, for many days, the people who had gone with Jesus from Galilee to Jerusalem saw Jesus. These people are now his witnesses to the people. ³²We tell you the Good News* about the promise God made to our fathers (*ancestors*). ³³We are their children (*descendants*), and God has made this promise come true for us. God did this by raising Jesus from death. We also read about this in Psalm 2:

'You are my Son.
Today I have become your Father.'   *Psalm 2:7*

³⁴God raised Jesus from death. Jesus will never go back to the grave and become dust. So God said:

'I will give you the true and holy promises
that I made to David.'   *Isaiah 55:3*

Savior   The One God promised to send to save his people from punishment for their sins.
John   John the Baptizer, who preached to people about Christ's coming (Matt. 3, Luke 3).
baptized   A Greek word meaning to be immersed, dipped, or buried briefly under water.
Christ   The "anointed one" (the Messiah) or chosen one of God.
prophets   People who spoke for God. Their writings are part of the Old Testament.
Sabbath day   Seventh day of the Jewish week. It was a special religious day for the Jews.
Scriptures   Holy Writings—the Old Testament.
Good News   The news that God has made a way through Christ for people to have their sins forgiven and live with God. When people accept this truth, God accepts them.

³⁵But in another place God says:

'You will not let *the body of* your Holy One
rot in the grave.' *Psalm 16:10*

³⁶David did God's will during the time when he lived. Then he died. David was buried with his fathers. And his body did rot in the grave! ³⁷But the One (*Jesus*) that God raised from death did not rot in the grave. ³⁸⁻³⁹Brothers, you must understand what we are telling you: You can have forgiveness of your sins through this One (*Jesus*). The law of Moses could not free you from your sins. But every person who believes *in Jesus* is free from all his sins through him (*Jesus*). ⁴⁰The prophets* said some things would happen. Be careful! Don't let these things happen to you. The prophets said:

⁴¹'Listen, you people who doubt!
You can wonder, but then go away and die;
because during your time, I (*God*) will do
something that you will not believe.
You will not believe it,
even if someone explains it to you!' " *Habakkuk 1:5*

⁴²While Paul and Barnabas were leaving *the synagogue*,* the people asked Paul and Barnabas to *come again* on the next Sabbath day* and tell them more about these things. ⁴³After the meeting, many of the Jews followed Paul and Barnabas from that place. With the Jews there were many converts* to the Jewish religion. These converts also worshiped the true God. Paul and Barnabas were persuading them to continue trusting in God's grace (*kindness*).

⁴⁴On the next Sabbath day,* almost all the people in the city came together to hear the word of the Lord. ⁴⁵The Jews saw all these people there. So the Jews became very jealous. They said some very bad things and argued against the words that Paul said. ⁴⁶But Paul and Barnabas spoke very boldly. They said, "We must speak the message* of God to you Jews first. But you refuse

---

prophets People who spoke for God. Their writings are part of the Old Testament.
synagogue Synagogues were places where Jews gathered to read and study the Scriptures.
Sabbath day Seventh day of the Jewish week. It was a special religious day for the Jews.
converts People who have changed their religion to become Jews.
message The news that God has made a way through Christ for people to have their sins forgiven and live with God. When people accept this truth, God accepts them.

to listen. You are making yourselves lost—not worthy of having eternal life! So we will now go to the people of other nations! ⁴⁷This is what the Lord (*God*) told us to do. The Lord said:

> 'I have made you a light for other nations,
> so that you can show the way of salvation
> to people all over the world.' "

Isaiah 49:6

⁴⁸When the non-Jewish people heard Paul say this, they were happy. They gave honor to the message* of the Lord. And many of the people believed the message. These were the people chosen to have life forever.

⁴⁹And so the message* of the Lord was being told through the whole country. ⁵⁰But the Jews caused some of the important religious women and the leaders of the city to become angry and to be against Paul and Barnabas. These people did things against Paul and Barnabas and threw them out of town. ⁵¹So Paul and Barnabas shook the dust off their feet.* Then they went to the city of Iconium. ⁵²But the followers *of Jesus in Antioch* were happy and full of the Holy Spirit.*

Paul and Barnabas in Iconium

14 Paul and Barnabas went to the city of Iconium. They entered the Jewish synagogue.* (This is what they did in every city.) They spoke to the people there. Paul and Barnabas spoke so well that many Jews and Greeks (*non-Jews*) believed what they said. ²But some of the Jews did not believe. These Jews excited the non-Jewish people and made them think bad things about the brothers (*believers*). ³But Paul and Barnabas spoke bravely for the Lord, and they stayed in Iconium a long time. Paul and Barnabas preached about God's grace (*kindness*). The Lord proved that what they said was true by helping the apostles* (*Paul and Barnabas*) do miracles and wonders.* ⁴But some of the

message The news that God has made a way through Christ for people to have their sins forgiven and live with God. When people accept this truth, God accepts them.
shook...feet A warning. It showed that they were finished talking to these people.
Holy Spirit Also called the Spirit of God, the Spirit of Christ, and the Comforter. He is joined with God and Christ. He does the work of God among people in the world.
synagogue Synagogues were places where Jews gathered to read and study the Scriptures.
apostles Men that Jesus chose to be his special helpers for telling his Good News to the world.
miracles and wonders Powerful works or great things done by the power of God.

people in the city agreed with the Jews. Other people in the city believed Paul and Barnabas. So the city was divided.

⁵Some non-Jewish people, some Jews, and their Jewish leaders tried to hurt Paul and Barnabas. These people wanted to kill them with rocks. ⁶When Paul and Barnabas learned about this, they left that city. They went to Lystra and Derbe, cities in Lycaonia, and to the areas around those cities. ⁷They told the Good News* there too.

Paul in Lystra and Derbe

⁸In Lystra there was a man who had something wrong with his feet. He had been born crippled; he had never walked. ⁹This man was sitting and listening to Paul speak. Paul looked at him. Paul saw that the man believed that God could heal him. ¹⁰So Paul shouted, "Stand up on your feet!" The man jumped up and began walking around. ¹¹When the people saw what Paul did, they shouted in their own Lycaonian language. They said, "The gods have become like men! They have come down to us!" ¹²The people began to call Barnabas "Zeus."* They called Paul "Hermes,"* because he was the main speaker. ¹³The temple of Zeus was near the city. The priest of this temple brought some bulls and flowers to the city gates. The priest and the people wanted to give an offering to *worship* Paul and Barnabas.

¹⁴But when the apostles,* Barnabas and Paul, understood what the people were doing, they tore their own clothes.* Then they ran in among the people and shouted to them, ¹⁵"Men, why are you doing these things? We are not gods! We have the same feelings as you have! We came to tell you the Good News.* We are telling you to turn away from these worthless things. Turn to the true living God. He is the One who made the sky, the earth, the sea, and everything that is in them. ¹⁶In the past, God let all the nations do what they wanted. ¹⁷But God did things that prove

---

Good News   The news that God has made a way through Christ for people to have their sins forgiven and live with God. When people accept this truth, God accepts them.

Zeus   The Greeks believed in many gods. Zeus was their most important god.

Hermes   Another Greek god. The Greeks believed he was a messenger for the other gods.

apostles   Men that Jesus chose to be his special helpers for telling the Good News to the world.

tore...clothes   This showed that they were very angry because of what the people did.

that he is real: He does good things for you. He gives you rain from the sky. He gives you good harvests at the right times. He gives you plenty of food and he fills your hearts with joy." [18]Paul and Barnabas told the people these things. But still Paul and Barnabas almost could not stop the people from offering sacrifices to *worship* them.

[19]Then some Jews came from Antioch and Iconium. They persuaded the people to be against Paul. And so the people threw rocks at Paul and dragged him out of the town. The people thought that they had killed Paul. [20]The followers *of Jesus* gathered around Paul and he got up and went back into the town. The next day, he and Barnabas left and went to the city of Derbe.

The Return to Antioch in Syria

[21]Paul and Barnabas told the Good News* in the city of Derbe too. Many people became followers *of Jesus*. Paul and Barnabas returned to the cities of Lystra, Iconium, and Antioch. [22]In those cities Paul and Barnabas made the followers *of Jesus* stronger. They helped them to stay in the faith. Paul and Barnabas said, "We must suffer many things on our way into God's kingdom." [23]Paul and Barnabas chose elders* for each church (*group of believers*). They fasted* and prayed for these elders. These elders were men who had trusted the Lord *Jesus*. So Paul and Barnabas put them in the Lord's care.

[24]Paul and Barnabas went through the country of Pisidia. Then they came to the country of Pamphylia. [25]They preached the message* *of God* in the city of Perga and then they went down to the city of Attalia. [26]And from there Paul and Barnabas sailed away to Antioch *in Syria*. This is the city where the believers had given them to God's care and sent them to do this work. Now they had finished the work.

[27]When Paul and Barnabas arrived, they gathered the church (*group of believers*) together. Paul and Barnabas told them about

---

Good News, message   The news that God has made a way through Christ for people to have their sins forgiven and live with God. When people accept this truth, God accepts them.

elders   A group of men chosen to lead a church. Also called "overseers" and "pastors" (shepherds), they have the work of caring for God's people (Acts 20:28; Ephesians 4:11).

fasted   To fast is to live without food for a special time of prayer and worship to God.

all the things God had done with them. They said, "God opened a door so that the people of other nations (*non-Jews*) could also believe!" ²⁸Paul and Barnabas stayed there a long time with the followers *of Christ*.

The Meeting at Jerusalem

15 Then some men came *to Antioch* from Judea. They began teaching the non-Jewish brothers: "You cannot be saved if you are not circumcised.* Moses taught us to do this." ²Paul and Barnabas were against this teaching. They argued with these men about it. So the group decided to send Paul, Barnabas, and some other men to Jerusalem. These men were going there to talk more about this with the apostles* and elders.*

³The church helped the men leave on the trip. These men went through the countries of Phoenicia and Samaria. In these countries they told all about how the non-Jewish people had turned to the true God. This made all the brothers very happy. ⁴Paul, Barnabas, and the others arrived in Jerusalem. The apostles,* the elders,* and the whole group of believers welcomed them. Paul, Barnabas, and the others told about all of the things that God had done with them. ⁵Some of the believers *in Jerusalem* had belonged to the Pharisee group.* They stood up and said, "The non-Jewish believers must be circumcised.* We must tell them to obey the law of Moses!"

⁶Then the apostles* and the elders* gathered to study this problem. ⁷There was a long debate. Then Peter stood up and said to them, "My brothers, I know that you remember what happened in the early days. God chose me then from among you to preach the Good News* to the non-Jewish people. They heard the Good News from me and they believed. ⁸God knows the thoughts of all men and he accepted these non-Jewish people.

circumcised   To have the foreskin cut off. This was done to every Jewish baby boy. It was a physical mark of the agreement that God gave to Abraham (Genesis 17:9-14).

apostles   Men that Jesus chose to be his special helpers for telling the Good News to the world.

elders   A group of men chosen to lead a church. Also called "overseers" and "pastors" (shepherds), they have the work of caring for God's people (Acts 20:28; Ephesians 4:11).

Pharisee group   A Jewish religious group that followed all the Old Testament and other Jewish laws and customs very carefully.

Good News   The news that God has made a way through Christ for people to have their sins forgiven and live with God. When people accept this truth, God accepts them.

God showed this to us by giving them the Holy Spirit* the same as he did to us. ⁹To God, those people are not different from us. When they believed, God made their hearts pure. ¹⁰So now, why are you testing God? You are putting a heavy burden around the necks of the non-Jewish brothers. We and our fathers (*ancestors*) were not strong enough to carry it! ¹¹No, we believe that we and these people will be saved by the grace (*mercy*) of the Lord Jesus!''

¹²Then the whole group became quiet. They listened to Paul and Barnabas speak. Paul and Barnabas told about all the miracles and wonders* that God did through them among the non-Jewish people. ¹³Paul and Barnabas finished speaking. Then James spoke. He said, ''My brothers, listen to me. ¹⁴Simon (*Peter*) has told us how God showed his love for the non-Jewish people. For the first time, God accepted the non-Jewish people and made them his people. ¹⁵The words of the prophets* agree with this too:

¹⁶'I (*God*) will return after this.
    I will build David's house again.
        It has fallen down.
    But I will build again the parts of his house
        that have been pulled down.
    I will make his house new.
¹⁷Then all other people will look for the Lord (*God*)—
    all the non-Jewish people that
        are my people too.
    The Lord (*God*) said this.
        And he is the One who does all these things.
¹⁸These things have been known
        from the beginning of time.'   *Amos 9:11-12*

¹⁹''So I think we should not bother the non-Jewish brothers who have turned to God. ²⁰Instead, we should write a letter to

---

Holy Spirit   Also called the Spirit of God, the Spirit of Christ, and the Comforter. He is joined
    with God and Christ. He does the work of God among people in the world.
miracles and wonders   Powerful works or great things done by the power of God.
prophets   People who spoke for God. Their writings are part of the Old Testament.

them. We should tell them these things:

> Don't eat food that has been given to idols.*
>
> > (This makes the food unclean.)
>
> Don't do any kind of sexual sin.
> Don't taste (*eat*) blood.
> Don't eat animals that have been strangled (*choked*).

²¹They should not do these things, because there are still men (*Jews*) in every city who teach the law of Moses. The words of Moses have been read in the synagogue* every Sabbath day* for many years."

The Letter to the Non-Jewish Believers

²²The apostles,* the elders,* and the whole church (*group of believers*) wanted to send some men with Paul and Barnabas to Antioch. The group decided to choose some of their own men. They chose Judas Barsabbas and Silas. These men were respected by the brothers *in Jerusalem*. ²³The group sent the letter with these men. The letter said:

> "From the apostles and elders, your brothers.
> To all the non-Jewish brothers in the city of Antioch
> > and in the countries of Syria and Cilicia:
>
> Dear Brothers,
>
> ²⁴We have heard that some men have come to you from our group. The things they said troubled and upset you. But we did not tell them to do this! ²⁵We have all agreed to choose some men and send them to you. They will be with our dear friends, Barnabas and Paul. ²⁶Barnabas and Paul have given their lives to serve our Lord Jesus Christ. ²⁷So we have sent Judas and Silas with them. They will tell you the same things. ²⁸The Holy Spirit* thinks that you should have no more burdens and we agree. You need to do only these things:
>
> > ²⁹Don't eat any food that has been given to idols.
> > Don't taste (*eat*) blood.

idols   The false gods that the non-Jewish people worshiped.
synagogue   Synagogues were places where Jews gathered to read and study the Scriptures.
Sabbath day   Seventh day of the Jewish week. It was a special religious day for the Jews.
apostles   Men that Jesus chose to be his special helpers for telling the Good News to the world.
elders   A group of men chosen to lead a church. Also called "overseers" and "pastors" (shepherds), they have the work of caring for God's people (Acts 20:28; Ephesians 4:11).
Holy Spirit   Also called the Spirit of God, the Spirit of Christ, and the Comforter. He is joined with God and Christ. He does the work of God among people in the world.

Don't eat any animals that have been strangled (*choked*).
Don't do any kind of sexual sin.
If you stay away from these things, you will do well.
We say good-bye now.''

³⁰So Paul, Barnabas, Judas, and Silas left Jerusalem. They went to Antioch. In Antioch, they gathered the group of believers and gave them the letter. ³¹When the believers read it, they were happy. The letter comforted them. ³²Judas and Silas were also prophets.* They said many things to help the brothers (*believers*) and make them stronger. ³³After Judas and Silas stayed there for a while, they left. They received a blessing of peace from the brothers. Judas and Silas went back to the brothers *in Jerusalem* who had sent them. ³⁴*

³⁵But Paul and Barnabas stayed in Antioch. They and many others told the Good News* and taught the people the message* of the Lord.

Paul and Barnabas Separate

³⁶A few days later, Paul said to Barnabas, ''We told the message* of the Lord in many towns. We should go back to all of those towns to visit the brothers and sisters and see how they are doing.'' ³⁷Barnabas wanted to bring John Mark with them too. ³⁸But, *on their first trip*, John Mark had left them at Pamphylia; he did not continue with them in the work. So, Paul did not think it was a good idea to take him. ³⁹Paul and Barnabas had a big argument about this. They separated and went different ways. Barnabas sailed to Cyprus and took Mark with him. ⁴⁰Paul chose Silas to go with him. The brothers *in Antioch* put Paul into the Lord's care and sent him out. ⁴¹Paul and Silas went through the countries of Syria and Cilicia, helping the churches* grow stronger.

prophets People who spoke for God. They often told things that would happen in the future.
Verse 34 Some Greek copies of Acts add verse 34: ''...but Silas decided to remain there.''
Good News, message The news that God has made a way through Christ for people to have their sins forgiven and live with God. When people accept this truth, God accepts them.
churches Groups of believers in the towns where Paul and Barnabas went before.

Timothy Goes with Paul and Silas

16 Paul went to the cities of Derbe and Lystra. A follower *of Christ* named Timothy was there. Timothy's mother was a Jewish believer. His father was a Greek (*not a Jew*). ²The believers in the cities of Lystra and Iconium respected Timothy. They said good things about him. ³Paul wanted Timothy to travel with him. But all the Jews living in that area knew that Timothy's father was Greek (*not Jewish*). So Paul circumcised* Timothy to please the Jews. ⁴Then Paul and the men with him traveled through other cities.* They gave the believers the rules and decisions from the apostles* and elders* in Jerusalem. They told the believers to obey these rules. ⁵So the churches (*groups of believers*) were becoming stronger in the faith and were growing bigger every day.

Paul Is Called out of Asia

⁶Paul and the men with him went through the countries of Phrygia and Galatia. The Holy Spirit* did not allow them to preach the Good News* in the country of Asia.* ⁷Paul and Timothy went near the country of Mysia. They wanted to go into the country of Bithynia. But the Spirit of Jesus did not let them go in. ⁸So they passed by Mysia and went to the city of Troas. ⁹That night Paul saw a vision.* In this vision, a man from the country of Macedonia came to Paul. The man stood there and begged, "Come across to Macedonia. Help us!" ¹⁰After Paul had seen the vision, we immediately prepared to leave for Macedonia. We understood that God had called us to tell the Good News* to those people.

---

circumcised   To have the foreskin cut off. This was done to every Jewish baby boy. It was a physical mark of the agreement that God gave to Abraham (Genesis 17:9-14).
cities   The cities where there were groups of believers.
apostles   Men that Jesus chose to be his special helpers for telling the Good News to the world.
elders   A group of men chosen to lead a church. Also called "overseers" and "pastors" (shepherds), they have the work of caring for God's people (Acts 20:28; Ephesians 4:11).
Holy Spirit   Also called the Spirit of God, the Spirit of Christ, and the Comforter. He is joined with God and Christ. He does the work of God among people in the world.
Good News   The news that God has made a way through Christ for people to have their sins forgiven and live with God. When people accept this truth, God accepts them.
Asia   The western part of Asia Minor.
vision   A vision is something like a dream that God used to speak to people.

The Conversion of Lydia

[11]We left Troas in a ship and sailed to the island of Samothrace. The next day, we sailed to the city of Neapolis.* [12]Then we went to Philippi. Philippi is an important city in that part of Macedonia. It is a city for Romans. We stayed in that city for a few days.

[13]On the Sabbath day,* we went out the city gate to the river. At the river we thought we might find a special place for prayer. Some women had gathered there. So we sat down and talked with them. [14]There was a woman named Lydia from the city of Thyatira. Her job was selling purple cloth. She worshiped the true God. Lydia listened to Paul. The Lord opened her heart. She believed the things Paul said. [15]She and all the people living in her home were baptized.* Then Lydia invited us into her home. She said, "If you think I am truly a believer in the Lord Jesus, then come stay in my house." She persuaded us to stay with her.

Paul and Silas in Jail

[16]One time, something happened to us while we were going to the place for prayer. A servant girl met us. She had a special spirit* in her. This spirit gave her the power to tell what would happen in the future. By doing this, she earned a lot of money for the men who owned her. [17]This girl followed Paul and us. She said loudly, "These men are servants of the Most High God! They are telling you how you can be saved!" [18]She continued doing this for many days. This bothered Paul, so he turned and said to the spirit, "By the power of Jesus Christ, I command you to come out of her!" Immediately, the spirit came out.

[19]The men that owned the servant girl saw this. These men knew that now they could not use her to make money. So they grabbed Paul and Silas and dragged them into the meeting place of the city. The city officials were there. [20]The men brought Paul and Silas to the leaders and said, "These men are Jews. They are

Neapolis   City in Macedonia. It was the first city Paul visited on the continent of Europe.
Sabbath day   Seventh day of the Jewish week. It was a special religious day for the Jews.
baptized   A Greek word meaning to be immersed, dipped, or buried briefly under water.
spirit   This was a spirit from the devil that gave this girl special knowledge.

making trouble in our city. ²¹They are telling the people to do things that are not right for us. We are Roman citizens and cannot do these things." ²²The people were against Paul and Silas. Then the leaders tore the clothes off Paul and Silas and told some men to beat Paul and Silas with rods. ²³The men beat Paul and Silas many times. Then the leaders put Paul and Silas in jail. The leaders told the jailer, "Guard them very carefully!" ²⁴The jailer heard this special order. So he put Paul and Silas far inside the jail. He tied their feet between large blocks of wood.

²⁵About midnight Paul and Silas were praying and singing songs to God. The other prisoners were listening to them. ²⁶Suddenly, there was a big earthquake. It was so strong that it shook the foundation of the jail. Then all the doors of the jail opened. All the prisoners were freed from their chains. ²⁷The jailer woke up. He saw that the jail doors were open. He thought that the prisoners had already escaped. So the jailer got his sword and was ready to kill himself.* ²⁸But Paul shouted, "Don't hurt yourself! We are all here!"

²⁹The jailer told someone to bring a light. Then he ran inside. He was shaking. He fell down in front of Paul and Silas. ³⁰Then he brought them outside and said, "Men, what must I do to be saved?"

³¹They said to him, "Believe in the Lord Jesus and you will be saved—you and all the people living in your house." ³²So Paul and Silas told the message* of the Lord to the jailer and all the people in his house. ³³It was late at night, but the jailer took Paul and Silas and washed their wounds. Then the jailer and all his people were baptized.* ³⁴After this, the jailer took Paul and Silas home and gave them some food. All the people were very happy because they now believed in God.

³⁵The next morning, the leaders sent some soldiers to tell the jailer, "Let these men (*Paul and Silas*) go free!"

³⁶The jailer said to Paul, "The leaders have sent these soldiers to let you go free. You can leave now."

---

kill himself He thought the leaders would kill him for letting the prisoners escape.
message The news that God has made a way through Christ for people to have their sins forgiven and live with God. When people accept this truth, God accepts them.
baptized A Greek word meaning to be immersed, dipped, or buried briefly under water.

³⁷But Paul said to the soldiers, "Your leaders did not prove that we did wrong. But they beat us in front of the people and put us in jail. We are Roman citizens,* *so we have rights.* Now the leaders want to make us go away quietly. No! The leaders must come and bring us out!"

³⁸The soldiers told the leaders what Paul said. When the leaders heard that Paul and Silas were Roman citizens,* they were afraid. ³⁹So the leaders came and told Paul and Silas they were sorry. The leaders took Paul and Silas out of jail and asked them to leave the city. ⁴⁰But when Paul and Silas came out of the jail, they went to Lydia's house. They saw some of the believers there and comforted them. Then Paul and Silas left.

Paul and Silas in Thessalonica

17 Paul and Silas traveled through the cities of Amphipolis and Apollonia. They came to the city of Thessalonica. In that city there was a Jewish synagogue.* ²Paul went into this synagogue to see the Jews. This is what he always did. Every Sabbath day* for three weeks, Paul talked with the Jews about the Scriptures.* ³Paul explained these Scriptures to the Jews. He showed that the Christ* must die and then rise from death. Paul told them about Jesus. He showed them that Jesus is the Christ. ⁴In the synagogue there were some Greek men who worshiped the true God. There were also some important women. Many of these people also joined Paul and Silas.

⁵But the Jews *that did not believe* became jealous. They hired some bad men from the city. These bad men gathered many people and made trouble in the city. The people went to Jason's house, looking for Paul and Silas. The men wanted to bring Paul and Silas out before the people. ⁶But they did not find Paul and Silas. So the people dragged Jason and some of the other believers to the leaders of the city. The people all yelled, "These men (*Paul and Silas*) have made trouble everywhere in the world.

Roman citizens   Roman law said that Roman citizens must not be beaten before they had a trial.
synagogue   Synagogues were places where Jews gathered to read and study the Scriptures.
Sabbath day   Seventh day of the Jewish week. It was a special religious day for the Jews.
Scriptures   Holy Writings—the Old Testament.
Christ   The "anointed one" (the Messiah) or chosen one of God.

And now they have come here too! [7]Jason is keeping them in his house. All of them do things against the laws of Caesar.* They say that there is another king called Jesus."

[8]The leaders of the city and the other people heard these things. They became very upset. [9]They made Jason and the other believers pay a fine. Then they let the believers go free.

Paul and Silas Go to Berea

[10]That same night the believers sent Paul and Silas to another city named Berea. In Berea, Paul and Silas went to the Jewish synagogue.* [11]These Jews were better people than the Jews in Thessalonica. These Jews were very happy to listen to the things Paul and Silas said. These Jews in Berea studied the Scriptures* every day. They wanted to know if these things were true. [12]Many of these Jews believed. Many important Greek men and Greek women also believed. [13]But when the Jews in Thessalonica learned that Paul was telling the word of God in Berea, they came to Berea too. The Jews from Thessalonica upset the people in Berea and made trouble. [14]So the believers sent Paul away quickly to the sea. But Silas and Timothy stayed in Berea. [15]The believers that went with Paul took him to the city of Athens. These brothers carried a message from Paul back to Silas and Timothy. The message said, "Come to me as soon as you can!"

Paul in Athens

[16]Paul was waiting for Silas and Timothy in Athens. Paul was troubled because he saw that the city was full of idols.* [17]In the synagogue,* Paul talked with the Jews and the Greeks who worshiped the true God. Paul also talked with some people in the business area of the city. Paul did this every day. [18]Some of the Epicurean and Stoic philosophers* argued with him.

Some of them said, "This man doesn't really know what he is talking about. What is he trying to say?" Paul was telling them

Caesar   The name or title given to the emperor (ruler) of Rome.
synagogue   Synagogues were places where Jews gathered to read and study the Scriptures.
Scriptures   Holy Writings—the Old Testament.
idols   The false gods that the non-Jewish people worshiped.
philosophers   People who study and talk about the ideas of other men.

the Good News of Jesus' rising from death. So they said, "He seems to be telling us about some other gods." ¹⁹They got Paul and took him to a meeting of the Areopagus council.* They said, "Please explain to us this new idea that you have been teaching. ²⁰The things that you are saying are new to us. We have never heard these things before. We want to know what this teaching means." ²¹(All the people of Athens and the people from other countries who lived there always used their time talking about all the newest ideas.)

²²Then Paul stood before the meeting of the Areopagus council.* Paul said, "Men of Athens, I can see that you are very religious in all things. ²³I was going through your city and I saw the things you worship. I found an altar that had these words written on it: 'TO THE GOD WHO IS NOT KNOWN.' You worship a god that you don't know. This is the God I am telling you about! ²⁴He is the God who made the whole world and everything in it. He is the Lord (*Ruler*) of the land and the sky. He does not live in temples* that men build! ²⁵This God is the One who gives life, breath, and everything else to people. He does not need any help from people. God has everything he needs. ²⁶God started with one man (*Adam*). He made all the different people to live everywhere in the world. God decided exactly when and where they must live. ²⁷God wanted the people to look for him. Maybe they could search all around for him and find him. But he is not far from any of us:

> ²⁸'We live with him.
> We walk with him.
> We are with him.'

Some of your own writers have said:

> 'For we are his children.'

²⁹We are God's children. So, you must not think that God is like something that people imagine or make. He is not like gold, silver, or rock. ³⁰In the past, people did not understand God, but God ignored this. But now, God tells every person in the world to

---

Areopagus council   A group of important leaders in Athens. They were like judges.
temples   Buildings where people go to worship.

change his heart and life. ³¹God has decided a day when he will judge all the people in the world. He will be fair. He will use a man (*Jesus*) to do this. God chose this man long ago. And God has proved this to every person; God proved it by raising that man from death!"

³²When the people heard about *Jesus* being raised from death, some of them laughed. The people said, "We will hear more about this from you later." ³³Paul went away from them. ³⁴But some of the people believed Paul and joined him. One of the people who believed was Dionysius. He was a member of the Areopagus council.* Another person who believed was a woman named Damaris. There were also some other people who believed.

Paul in Corinth

18 Later, Paul left Athens and went to the city of Corinth. ²In Corinth Paul met a Jewish man named Aquila. Aquila was born in the country of Pontus. But Aquila and his wife, Priscilla, had recently moved *to Corinth* from Italy. They left Italy because Claudius* commanded that all Jews must leave Rome. Paul went to visit Aquila and Priscilla. ³They were tentmakers, the same as Paul. Paul stayed with them and worked with them. ⁴Every Sabbath day* Paul talked with the Jews and Greeks in the synagogue.* Paul tried to persuade these people *to believe in Jesus*.

⁵Silas and Timothy came from Macedonia to Paul in Corinth. After this, Paul used all his time telling people the Good News.* He showed the Jews that Jesus is the Christ.* ⁶But the Jews would not accept Paul's teaching. The Jews said some very bad things. So Paul shook off the dust from his clothes.* He said to the Jews, "If you are not saved, it will be your own fault! I have done all I can do! After this, I will go only to non-Jewish people!" ⁷Paul

---

Areopagus council A group of important leaders in Athens. They were like judges.
Claudius The Emperor (ruler) of Rome, A.D. 41-54.
Sabbath day Seventh day of the Jewish week. It was a special religious day for the Jews.
synagogue Synagogues were places where Jews gathered to read and study the Scriptures.
Good News The news that God has made a way through Christ for people to have their sins forgiven and live with God. When people accept this truth, God accepts them.
Christ The "anointed one" (the Messiah) or chosen one of God.
shook...clothes This was a warning. It showed that Paul was finished talking to the Jews.

left the synagogue and moved into the home of Titius Justus. This man worshiped the true God. His house was next to the synagogue.* ⁸Crispus was the leader of that synagogue. Crispus and all the people living in his house believed in the Lord (*Jesus*). Many other people in Corinth also listened to Paul. They too believed and were baptized.*

⁹During the night, Paul had a vision.* The Lord said to him, "Don't be afraid! Continue talking to people and don't stop! ¹⁰I am with you. No one will be able to hurt you. Many of my people are in this city." ¹¹Paul stayed there for a year and a half, teaching God's truth to the people.

Paul Is Brought Before Gallio

¹²Gallio became the governor of the country of Achaia. At that time, some of the Jews came together against Paul. They took Paul to the court. ¹³The Jews said to Gallio, "This man is teaching people to worship God in a way that is against our *Jewish* law!"

¹⁴Paul was ready to say something, but Gallio spoke to the Jews. Gallio said, "I would listen to you Jews if you were complaining about a bad crime or some wrong. ¹⁵But the things you Jews are saying are only questions about words and names— arguments about your own *Jewish* law. So you must solve this problem yourselves. I don't want to be a judge of these things." ¹⁶Then Gallio made them leave the court.

¹⁷Then they all grabbed Sosthenes. (Sosthenes was *now* the leader of the synagogue.*) They beat Sosthenes before the court. But this did not bother Gallio.

Paul Returns to Antioch

¹⁸Paul stayed with the brothers for many days. Then he left and sailed for Syria. Priscilla and Aquila were also with him. At Cenchrea, Paul cut off his hair.* *This showed that* he had made a

---

synagogue Synagogues were places where Jews gathered to read and study the Scriptures.
baptized A Greek word meaning to be immersed, dipped, or buried briefly under water.
vision A vision is something like a dream that God used to speak to people.
cut...hair Jews did this to show that the time of a special promise to God was finished.

promise (*vow*) to God. ¹⁹Then they went to the city of Ephesus. This is where Paul left Priscilla and Aquila. While Paul was in Ephesus, he went into the synagogue* and talked with the Jews. ²⁰The Jews asked Paul to stay longer, but he refused. ²¹Paul left them and said, "I will come back to you again if God wants me to." And so Paul sailed away from Ephesus.

²²Paul went to the city of Caesarea. Then he went and said hello to the church (*group of believers*) *in Jerusalem*. After that, Paul went to the city of Antioch. ²³Paul stayed in Antioch for a while. Then he left Antioch and went through the countries of Galatia and Phrygia. Paul traveled from town to town in these countries. He made all the followers *of Jesus* stronger.

Apollos in Ephesus and Achaia (Corinth)

²⁴A Jew named Apollos came to Ephesus. Apollos was born in the city of Alexandria. He was an educated man. He knew very much about the Scriptures.* ²⁵Apollos had been taught about the Lord (*Jesus*). Apollos was always very excited when he talked to people about Jesus. The things Apollos taught about Jesus were right. But the only baptism* that Apollos knew about was the baptism that John* taught. ²⁶Apollos began to speak very boldly in the synagogue.* Priscilla and Aquila heard him speak. They took him to their home and helped him understand the way of God better. ²⁷Apollos wanted to go to the country of Achaia. So, the brothers *in Ephesus* helped him. They wrote a letter to the followers *of Jesus in Achaia*. In the letter, they asked these followers to accept Apollos. These followers *in Achaia* had believed in Jesus because of God's grace (*kindness*). When Apollos went there, he helped them very much. ²⁸He argued very strongly against the Jews before all the people. Apollos clearly proved that the Jews were wrong. He used the Scriptures* and showed that Jesus is the Christ.*

---

synagogue   Synagogues were places where Jews gathered to read and study the Scriptures.
Scriptures   Holy Writings—the Old Testament.
baptism   A Greek word meaning to be immersed, dipped, or buried briefly under water.
John   John the Baptizer, who preached to people about Christ's coming (Matt. 3, Luke 3).
Christ   The "anointed one" (the Messiah) or chosen one of God.

Paul in Ephesus

19 While Apollos was in the city of Corinth, Paul was visiting some places on the way to the city of Ephesus. In Ephesus Paul found some followers *of John*.* ²Paul asked them, "Did you receive the Holy Spirit* when you believed?"

These followers said to him, "We have never even heard of a Holy Spirit!"

³So Paul asked them, "What kind of baptism* did you have?"

They said, "It was the baptism that John* taught."

⁴Paul said, "John baptized people when they decided to change their hearts and lives. John told people to believe in the One who would come after him. That person is Jesus."

⁵When these followers *of John* heard this, they were baptized in the name of the Lord Jesus. ⁶Then Paul put his hands on them* and the Holy Spirit* came into them. They began speaking different languages and prophesying.* ⁷There were about twelve men in this group.

⁸Paul went into the synagogue* and spoke very boldly. Paul continued doing this for three months. He talked with the Jews and persuaded them to accept the things he said about the kingdom of God. ⁹But some of the Jews became stubborn. They refused to believe. These Jews said some very bad things about the Way *of God*. All the people heard these things. So Paul left those Jews and took the followers *of Jesus* with him. Paul went to a place where a man named Tyrannus had a school. There Paul talked with people every day. ¹⁰Paul did this for two years. Because of this work, every Jew and Greek (*non-Jews*) in the country of Asia* heard the word of the Lord.

John John the Baptizer, who preached to people about Christ's coming (Matt. 3, Luke 3).
Holy Spirit Also called the Spirit of God, the Spirit of Christ, and the Comforter. He is joined with God and Christ. He does the work of God among people in the world.
baptism A Greek word meaning to be immersed, dipped, or buried briefly under water.
put his hands on them Here, doing this was a sign to show that Paul had God's authority or power to give these people special powers of the Holy Spirit. Only apostles had this authority.
prophesying Speaking or teaching things from God.
synagogue Synagogues were places where Jews gathered to read and study the Scriptures.
Asia The western part of Asia Minor.

The Sons of Sceva

[11]God used Paul to do some very special miracles.* [12]Some people carried handkerchiefs and clothes that Paul had used. The people put these things on sick people. When they did this, the sick people were healed and evil spirits *from the devil* left them.

[13-14]Some Jews were also making evil spirits go out of people. The seven sons of Sceva were doing this. (Sceva was a leading Jewish priest.*) These Jews tried to use the name of the Lord Jesus to make the evil spirits go out of people. They all said, "By the same Jesus that Paul talks about, I order you to come out!"

[15]But one time an evil spirit said to these Jews, "I know Jesus, and I know about Paul, but who are you?"

[16]Then the man, who had the evil spirit *from the devil* inside him, jumped on these Jews. He was much stronger than all of them. He beat them up and tore their clothes off. These Jews ran away from that house. [17]All the people in Ephesus, Jews and Greeks (*non-Jews*), learned about this. They all began to have great respect *for God*. And the people gave great honor to the name of the Lord Jesus. [18]Many of the believers began to confess and tell all the bad things they had done. [19]Some of the believers had used magic. These believers brought their magic books and burned them before everyone. Those books were worth about 50,000 silver coins.* [20]This is how the word of the Lord was influencing more and more people in a powerful way. And more and more people believed.

Paul Plans a Trip

[21]After these things, Paul made plans to go to Jerusalem. Paul planned to go through the countries of Macedonia and Achaia, and then go to Jerusalem. Paul thought, "After I visit Jerusalem, I must also visit Rome." [22]Timothy and Erastus were two of Paul's helpers. Paul sent them ahead to the country of Macedonia. Paul stayed in Asia* for a while.

---

miracles   Miracles are powerful works or great things done by the power of God.
leading Jewish priest   The most important Jewish priest and leader.
50,000 silver coins   Probably drachmas. One coin was enough to pay a man for working one day.
Asia   The western part of Asia Minor.

Trouble in Ephesus

²³But during that time, there was some bad trouble in Ephesus. This trouble was about the Way *of God*. This is how it all happened: ²⁴There was a man named Demetrius. He worked with silver. He made little silver models that looked like the temple* of the goddess Artemis.* The men that did this work made much money. ²⁵Demetrius had a meeting with these men and some other men who did the same kind of work. Demetrius told them, "Men, you know that we make much money from our business. ²⁶But look at what this man Paul is doing! Listen to what he is saying! Paul has influenced and changed many people. He has done this in Ephesus and all over the whole country of Asia*! Paul says the gods that men make are not real. ²⁷These things that Paul says might turn the people against our work. But there is also another problem: People will begin to think that the temple of the great goddess Artemis is not important! Her greatness will be destroyed. Artemis is the goddess that everyone in Asia and the whole world worships."

²⁸When the men heard this, they became very angry. The men shouted, "Artemis,* the goddess of the city of Ephesus, is great!" ²⁹All the people in the city became upset. The people grabbed Gaius and Aristarchas. (These two men were from Macedonia and were traveling with Paul.) Then all the people ran to the stadium. ³⁰Paul wanted to go in and talk to the people, but the followers *of Jesus* did not let him go. ³¹Also, some leaders of the country were friends of Paul. These leaders sent him a message. They told Paul not to go into the stadium. ³²Some people were yelling one thing and other people were yelling other things. The meeting was very confused. Most of the people did not know why they had come there. ³³The Jews made a man named Alexander stand before the people. The people told him what to do. Alexander waved his hand because he wanted to explain things to the people. ³⁴But when the people saw that Alexander was a Jew, they all began shouting the same thing.

---

temple   The special building in Ephesus where the people worshiped the false goddess, Artemis.
Artemis   A Greek goddess that the people of Asia Minor worshiped.
Asia   The western part of Asia Minor.

They continued shouting for two hours. The people said, "Great is Artemis* of Ephesus! Great is Artemis of Ephesus! Great is Artemis...!"

³⁵Then the city clerk persuaded the people to be quiet. He said, "Men of Ephesus, all people know that Ephesus is the city that keeps the temple* of the great goddess Artemis.* All people know that we also keep her holy rock.* ³⁶No person can say that this is not true. So you should be quiet. You must stop and think before you do anything. ³⁷You brought these men,* but they have not said anything bad against our goddess. They have not stolen anything from her temple. ³⁸We have courts of law and there are judges. Do Demetrius and those men that work with him have a charge against anyone? They should go to the courts! That is where they can argue with each other! ³⁹Is there something else you want to talk about? Then come to the regular town meeting of the people. It can be decided there. ⁴⁰I say this because some person might see this trouble today and say that we are rioting (*making trouble*). We could not explain all this trouble, because there is no real reason for this meeting." ⁴¹After the city clerk said these things, he told the people to go home. And all the people left.

Paul Goes to Macedonia and Greece

20 When the trouble stopped, Paul invited the followers *of Jesus* to come visit him. He said things to comfort them and then told them good-bye. Paul left and went to the country of Macedonia. ²He said many things to strengthen the followers *of Jesus* in the different places on his way through Macedonia. Then Paul went to Greece (*Achaia*). ³He stayed there three months. He was ready to sail for Syria, but some Jews were planning something against him. So Paul decided to go back through Macedonia to Syria. ⁴Some men were with him. They were: Sopater, the son of Pyrrhus, from the city of Berea, Aristarchus and Secundus, from the city of Thessalonica, Gaius, from the city

---

Artemis A Greek goddess that the people of Asia Minor worshiped.
temple The special building in Ephesus where the people worshiped the false goddess, Artemis.
holy rock Probably a meteorite or rock that the people thought looked like Artemis.
men Gaius and Aristarchus, the men traveling with Paul.

of Derbe, Timothy, and Tychicus and Trophimus, two men from Asia.* ⁵These men went first, ahead of Paul. They waited for us in the city of Troas. ⁶We sailed from the city of Philippi after the Jewish Feast of Unleavened Bread.* We met these men in Troas five days later. We stayed there for seven days.

Paul's Last Visit to Troas

⁷On Sunday,* we all met together to eat the Lord's Supper.* Paul spoke to the group. He was planning to leave the next day. Paul continued talking until midnight. ⁸We were all together in a room upstairs, and there were many lights in the room. ⁹There was a young man named Eutychus sitting in the window. Paul continued talking, and Eutychus became very, very sleepy. Finally, Eutychus went to sleep and fell out of the window. He fell to the ground from the third floor. When the people *went and lifted him up*, he was dead. ¹⁰Paul went down to Eutychus. He kneeled down and hugged Eutychus. Paul said to the other believers, "Don't worry. He is alive now." ¹¹Paul went upstairs again. He divided the bread and ate. Paul spoke to them a long time. When he finished talking, it was early morning. Then Paul left. ¹²The people took the young man (*Eutychus*) home. He was alive, and the people were very much comforted.

The Trip from Troas to Miletus

¹³We sailed for the city of Assos. We went first, ahead of Paul. He planned to meet us in Assos and join us on the ship there. Paul told us to do this because he wanted to go to Assos by land. ¹⁴Later, we met Paul at Assos and then he came on the ship with us. We all went to the city of Mitylene. ¹⁵The next day, we sailed away from Mitylene. We came to a place near the island of Chios. Then the next day, we sailed to the island of Samos. A day later, we came to the city of Miletus. ¹⁶Paul had already decided not to stop at Ephesus. He did not want to stay too long in Asia.* He

---

Asia The western part of Asia Minor.

Feast of Unleavened Bread Same as Passover Feast, the most important holy day for Jews. On this day they ate a special meal with bread that was made without yeast.

Sunday Literally, "first day of the week," which for the Jews began at sunset on Saturday. But if Luke is not using Jewish time, then the meeting was Sunday night.

Lord's Supper The meal Jesus told his followers to eat to remember him (Luke 22:14-20).

was hurrying because he wanted to be in Jerusalem on the day of Pentecost,* if that was possible.

Paul Speaks to the Elders from Ephesus

¹⁷In Miletus, Paul sent a message back to Ephesus. Paul invited the elders* (*leaders*) of the church in Ephesus to come to him. ¹⁸When the elders came, Paul said to them, "You know about my life from the first day I came to Asia.* You know the way I lived all the time I was with you. ¹⁹The Jews planned things against me. This troubled me very much. But you know that I always served the Lord. I never thought about myself first. And I often cried. ²⁰I always did what was best for you. I told you the Good News* about Jesus in public before the people and also in your homes. ²¹I told all people—Jewish people and Greek (*non-Jewish*) people—to change their hearts and turn to God. I told them all to believe in our Lord Jesus. ²²But now I must obey the Holy Spirit* and go to Jerusalem. I don't know what will happen to me there. ²³I know only that in every city the Holy Spirit tells me that troubles and even jail wait for me *in Jerusalem*. ²⁴I don't care about my own life. The most important thing is that I finish my work. I want to finish the work that the Lord Jesus gave me to do—to tell people the Good News about God's grace (*kindness*).

²⁵"And now listen to me. I know that none of you will ever see me again. All the time I was with you, I told you the Good News* about the kingdom of God. ²⁶So today I can tell you one thing that I am sure of: God will not blame me if some of you are not saved! ²⁷I can say this because I know that I told you everything that God wants you to know. ²⁸Be careful for yourselves and for all the people that God has given you. The Holy Spirit* gave you the work of caring for this flock (*God's people*). You must be like shepherds to the church (*people*) of God.* This is the church that

---

Pentecost Jewish feast day (50 days after Passover) celebrating the harvest of wheat.

elders A group of men chosen to lead a church. Also called "overseers" and "pastors" (shepherds), they have the work of caring for God's people (Eph. 4:11; 1 Tim. 3:1-7).

Asia The western part of Asia Minor.

Good News The news that God has made a way through Christ for people to have their sins forgiven and live with God. When people accept this truth, God accepts them.

Holy Spirit Also called the Spirit of God, the Spirit of Christ, and the Comforter. He is joined with God and Christ. He does the work of God among people in the world.

of God Some Greek copies say, "of the Lord."

God bought with his own blood.* ²⁹I know that after I leave, some men will come into your group. They will be like wild wolves. They will try to destroy the flock (*group*). ³⁰Also, men from your own group will become bad leaders. They will begin to teach things that are wrong. They will lead some followers *of Jesus* away from the truth. ³¹So be careful! Always remember this: I was with you for three years. During this time, I never stopped warning you. I taught you night and day. I often cried for you.

³²"Now I am giving you to God. I am depending on the message* about God's grace (*kindness*) to make you strong. That message is able to give you the blessings that God gives to all his holy people. ³³When I was with you, I never wanted anyone's money or fine clothes. ³⁴You know that I always worked to take care of my own needs and the needs of the people that were with me. ³⁵I always showed you that you should work like I did and help people that are weak. I taught you to remember the words of Jesus. Jesus once said, 'You will be happier when you give than when you receive.' "

³⁶When Paul finished saying these things, he kneeled down and they all prayed together. ³⁷⁻³⁸They all cried and cried. The men were very sad because Paul had said that they would never see him again. They hugged Paul and kissed him. They went with him to the ship to say good-bye.

Paul Goes to Jerusalem

21 We all said good-bye to the elders.* Then we sailed away. We sailed straight to Cos island. The next day, we went to the island of Rhodes. From Rhodes we went to Patara. ²At Patara, we found a ship that was going to the area of Phoenicia. We went on the ship and sailed away. ³We sailed near the island of Cyprus. We could see it on the north side, but we did not stop. We sailed to the country of Syria. We stopped at the city of Tyre because the ship needed to unload its cargo there. ⁴We found

his own blood This can also mean, "the blood of his own son."
message The news that God has made a way through Christ for people to have their sins forgiven and live with God. When people accept this truth, God accepts them.
elders A group of men chosen to lead a church. Also called "overseers" and "pastors" (shepherds), they have the work of caring for God's people (Acts 20:17,28; Eph. 4:11).

some followers *of Jesus* in Tyre, and we stayed with them for seven days. They warned Paul not to go to Jerusalem because of what the Holy Spirit* had told them. ⁵But when we finished our visit, we left. We continued our trip. All the followers *of Jesus*, even the women and children, came outside the city with us to say good-bye. We all kneeled down on the beach and prayed. ⁶Then we said good-bye and got on the ship. The followers went home.

⁷We continued our trip from Tyre and went to the city of Ptolemais. We greeted the brothers (*believers*) there and stayed with them one day. ⁸The next day, we left Ptolemais and went to the city of Caesarea. We went into the home of Philip and stayed with him. Philip had the work of telling the Good News.* He was one of the seven helpers.* ⁹He had four daughters who were not married. These daughters had the gift of prophesying.* ¹⁰After we had been there for many days, a prophet* named Agabus came from Judea. ¹¹He came to us and borrowed Paul's belt. Then Agabus used the belt to tie his own hands and feet. Agabus said, "The Holy Spirit* tells me, 'This is how the Jews in Jerusalem will tie the man who wears this belt.* Then they will give him to the non-Jewish people.' "

¹²We all heard these words. So we and the other followers *of Jesus* there begged (*asked*) Paul not to go to Jerusalem. ¹³But Paul said, "Why are you crying? Why are you making me so sad? I am ready to be tied in Jerusalem. I am also ready to die for the name of the Lord Jesus!"

¹⁴We could not persuade him to stay away from Jerusalem. So we stopped begging him and said, "We pray that what the Lord wants will be done."

¹⁵After this, we got ready and left for Jerusalem. ¹⁶Some of the followers *of Jesus* from Caesarea went with us. These followers took us to the home of Mnason, a man from Cyprus. Mnason

---

Holy Spirit Also called the Spirit of God, the Spirit of Christ, and the Comforter. He is joined with God and Christ. He does the work of God among people in the world.

Good News The news that God has made a way through Christ for people to have their sins forgiven and live with God. When people accept this truth, God accepts them.

helpers The seven men chosen for a special work in Acts 6:1-6.

prophesying To prophesy means to speak or teach things from God.

prophet Person who spoke for God. He often told things that would happen in the future.

belt Paul's belt; so Agabus means that the Jews in Jerusalem will tie (arrest) Paul.

was one of the first people to be a follower *of Jesus*. They took us to his home so that we could stay with him.

Paul Visits James

[17]In Jerusalem, the believers were very happy to see us. [18]The next day, Paul went with us to visit James. All the elders (*church leaders*) were there too. [19]Paul greeted all of them. Then he told them about how God used him to do many things among the non-Jewish people. He told them all the things that God did through him. [20]When the leaders heard these things, they praised God. Then they said to Paul, "Brother, you can see that thousands of Jews have become believers. But they think it is very important to obey the law of Moses. [21]These Jews have heard about your teaching. They heard that you tell the Jews who live in other countries among non-Jews to leave the law of Moses. They heard that you tell those Jews not to circumcise* their children and not to obey Jewish customs. [22]What should we do? The Jewish believers here will learn that you have come. [23]So we will tell you what to do: Four of our men have made a vow* (*promise*) to God. [24]Take these men with you and share in their cleansing (*washing*) ceremony.* Pay their expenses. Then they can shave their heads.* Do this and it will prove to everyone that the things they have heard about you are not true. They will see that you obey the law of Moses in your own life. [25]We have already sent a letter to the non-Jewish believers. The letter said:

> 'Don't eat food that has been given to idols.*
> Don't taste (*eat*) blood.
> Don't eat animals that have been strangled (*choked*).
> Don't do any kind of sexual sin.' "

[26]Then Paul took the four men with him. The next day, Paul shared in the cleansing (*washing*) ceremony.* Then he went to the temple.* Paul announced the time when the days of the cleansing

---

circumcise   To cut off the foreskin. This was done to every Jewish baby boy. It was a physical mark of the agreement that God gave to Abraham (Genesis 17:9-14).
vow   probably a Nazirite vow, a time of special service that Jews promised to give God.
cleansing ceremony   The special things Jews did to end the Nazirite vow.
shave their heads   The Jews did this to show that their vow was finished.
idols   The false gods that the non-Jewish people worshiped.
temple   The special building in Jerusalem where God commanded the Jews to worship him.

ceremony would be finished. On the last day, an offering would be given for each of the men.

²⁷The seven days were almost finished. But some Jews from Asia* saw Paul at the temple.* They caused all the people to be upset, and they grabbed Paul. ²⁸They shouted, "You Jewish men, help us! This is the man who is teaching things that are against the law of Moses, against our people, and against this place (*the temple*). This man is teaching these things to all people everywhere. And now he has brought some Greek (*non-Jewish*) men into the temple! He has made this holy place unclean!" ²⁹(The Jews said this because they had seen Trophimus with Paul in Jerusalem. Trophimus was a *Greek* man from Ephesus. The Jews thought that Paul had taken him into the temple.)

³⁰All the people in Jerusalem became very upset. They all ran and grabbed Paul. They dragged him out of the temple.* The temple doors were closed immediately. ³¹The people were trying to kill Paul. The commander of the Roman army in Jerusalem learned that there was trouble in the whole city. ³²Immediately the commander went to the place where the people were. He brought some officers and soldiers with him. The people saw the commander and his soldiers. So they stopped beating Paul. ³³The commander went to Paul and arrested him. The commander told his soldiers to tie Paul with two chains. Then the commander asked, "Who is this man? What has he done wrong?" ³⁴Some people there were yelling one thing and other people were yelling other things. Because of all this confusion and shouting, the commander could not learn the truth about what had happened. So the commander told the soldiers to take Paul to the army building. ³⁵⁻³⁶All the people were following them. When the soldiers came to the steps, they had to carry Paul. They did this *to protect Paul*, because the people were ready to hurt him. The people shouted, "Kill him!"

³⁷The soldiers were ready to take Paul into the army building. But Paul spoke to the commander. Paul asked, "Do I have the right to say something to you?"

Asia   The western part of Asia Minor.
temple   The special building in Jerusalem where God commanded the Jews to worship him.

The commander said, "Oh! You speak Greek? ³⁸Then you are not the man I thought you were? I thought you were the Egyptian man who started some trouble against the government not long ago. That Egyptian man led 4,000 killers out to the desert."

³⁹Paul said, "No, I am a Jewish man from Tarsus. Tarsus is in the country of Cilicia. I am a citizen of that important city. Please, let me speak to the people."

⁴⁰The commander let Paul speak to the people. So Paul stood on the steps. He made signs with his hands so that the people would be quiet. The people became quiet and Paul spoke to them. He used the Jewish language.*

Paul Speaks to the People

22 Paul said, "My brothers and fathers, listen to me! I will make my defense to you." ²The Jews heard Paul speaking the Jewish language.* So they became very quiet. Paul said, ³"I am a Jew. I was born in Tarsus in the country of Cilicia. I grew up in this city (*Jerusalem*). I was a student of Gamaliel.* He carefully taught me everything about the law of our fathers (*ancestors*). I was very serious about serving God, the same as all of you here today. ⁴I persecuted (*did bad things to*) the people who followed the Way *of Jesus*. Some of them were killed because of me. I arrested men and women. I put them in jail. ⁵The high priest* and the whole council of older Jewish leaders can tell you that this is true! One time these leaders gave me some letters. The letters were to the Jewish brothers in the city of Damascus. I was going there to arrest the followers of Jesus and bring them back to Jerusalem for punishment."

Paul Tells About His Conversion

⁶"But something happened to me on my way to Damascus. It was about noon when I came close to Damascus. Suddenly, a bright light from the sky shined all around me. ⁷I fell to the ground. I heard a voice saying to me: 'Saul, Saul, why are you

---

Jewish language   Aramaic, the "Hebrew" language in the first century.
Gamaliel   A very important teacher of the Pharisees, a Jewish religious group (Acts 5:34).
high priest   The most important Jewish priest and leader.

doing these bad things to me?' ⁸I asked, 'Who are you, Lord?' The voice said, 'I am Jesus from Nazareth. I am the One you are persecuting.' ⁹The men who were with me did not understand the voice. But the men saw the light. ¹⁰I said, 'What shall I do, Lord?' The Lord (*Jesus*) answered, 'Get up and go into Damascus. There you will be told about all the things I have planned for you to do.' ¹¹I could not see, because the bright light had made me blind. So the men led me into Damascus.

¹²"In Damascus, a man named Ananias* came to me. Ananias was a religious man; he obeyed the law of Moses. All the Jews who lived there respected him. ¹³Ananias came to me and said, 'Brother Saul, see again!' Immediately, I was able to see him. ¹⁴Ananias told me, 'The God of our fathers (*ancestors*) chose you long ago. God chose you to know his plan. He chose you to see the Righteous One (*Jesus*) and to hear words from him. ¹⁵You will be his witness to all people. You will tell men about the things you have seen and heard. ¹⁶Now, don't wait any longer. Get up, be baptized* and wash your sins away. Do this, trusting in him (*Jesus*) *to save you*.'

¹⁷"Later, I came back to Jerusalem. I was praying in the temple* yard, and I saw a vision.* ¹⁸I saw Jesus, and Jesus said to me: 'Hurry! Leave Jerusalem now! The people here will not accept the truth about me.' ¹⁹I said, 'But Lord, the people know that I was the one who put the believers in jail and beat them. I went through all the synagogues* to find and arrest the people who believe in you. ²⁰The people also know that I was there when Stephen, your witness, was killed. I stood there and agreed that they should kill Stephen. I even held the coats of the men who were killing him!' ²¹But Jesus said to me, 'Leave now. I will send you far away to the non-Jewish people.' "

²²The people stopped listening when Paul said this last thing *about going to the non-Jewish people*. They all shouted, "Kill him! Get him out of the world! A man like this should not be

---

Ananias   In Acts there are three men with this name. Read Acts 5:1 and 23:2 for the other two.
baptized   A Greek word meaning to be immersed, dipped, or buried briefly under water.
temple   The special building in Jerusalem where God commanded the Jews to worship him.
vision   A vision is something like a dream that God used to speak to people.
synagogues   Synagogues were buildings where Jews gathered to read and study the Scriptures.

allowed to live!'' ²³They yelled and threw off their coats.* They threw dust into the air.* ²⁴Then the commander told the soldiers to take Paul into the army building. He told the soldiers to beat Paul. The commander wanted to make Paul tell why the people were shouting against him like this. ²⁵So the soldiers were tying Paul, preparing to beat him. But Paul said to an officer there, ''Do you have the right to beat a Roman citizen* who has not been proven guilty?''

²⁶When the officer heard this, he went to the commander and told him about it. The officer said, ''Do you know what you are doing? This man (*Paul*) is a Roman citizen!''

²⁷The commander came to Paul and said, ''Tell me, are you really a Roman citizen?''

Paul answered, ''Yes.''

²⁸The commander said, ''I paid much money to become a Roman citizen.''

But Paul said, ''I was born a citizen.''

²⁹The men who were preparing to question Paul moved away from him immediately. The commander was afraid because he had already tied Paul, and Paul was a Roman citizen.*

Paul Speaks to the Jewish Leaders

³⁰The next day the commander decided to learn why the Jews were speaking against Paul. So he commanded the leading priests and the Jewish council to meet together. The commander took Paul's chains off. Then he brought Paul out and stood Paul before their meeting.

23 Paul looked at the Jewish council meeting and said, ''Brothers, I have lived my life in a good way before God. I have always done what I thought was right.'' ²Ananias,* the high priest,* was there. Ananias heard Paul and told the men who were standing near Paul to hit him on his mouth. ³Paul said to Ananias, ''God will hit you too! You are like a *dirty* wall that has been painted white! You sit there and judge me, using the law *of*

---

threw off their coats   This showed that the Jews were very angry at Paul.
threw dust into the air   In this way they showed that they were very, very angry.
Roman citizen   Roman law said that Roman citizens must not be beaten before their trial.
Ananias   This is not the same man named Ananias in Acts 22:12.
high priest   The most important Jewish priest and leader.

Moses. But you are telling them to hit me, and that is against the law *of Moses*."

⁴The men standing near Paul said to him, "You cannot talk like that to God's high priest*! You are insulting him!"

⁵Paul said, "Brothers, I did not know this man was the high priest. It is written in the Scriptures,* 'You must not say bad things about a ruler of your people.'* "

⁶Some of the men in the meeting were Sadducees* and some others were Pharisees.* So Paul had an idea: He shouted to them, "My brothers, I am a Pharisee and my father was a Pharisee! I am on trial here because I hope (*believe*) that people will rise from death!"

⁷When Paul said this, there was a big argument between the Pharisees* and the Sadducees.* The group was divided. ⁸(The Sadducees believe that after people die, they cannot live again. The Sadducees also teach that there are no angels or spirits. But the Pharisees believe in all these things.) ⁹All these Jews began shouting louder and louder. Some of the teachers of the law, who were Pharisees, stood up and argued, "We find nothing wrong with this man! Maybe an angel or a spirit did speak to him *on the road to Damascus*!"

¹⁰The argument became a fight. The commander was afraid that the Jews would tear Paul to pieces. So the commander told the soldiers to go down and take Paul away from these Jews and to put him in the army building.

¹¹The next night, the Lord *Jesus* came and stood by Paul. He said, "Be brave! You have told people in Jerusalem about me. You must also go to Rome to tell people there about me!"

¹²The next morning, some of the Jews made a plan. They wanted to kill Paul. The Jews made a promise (*vow*) to themselves that they would not eat or drink anything until they had killed Paul. ¹³There were more than 40 Jews who made this plan. ¹⁴These Jews went and talked to the leading priests and the

---

high priest   The most important Jewish priest and leader.
Scriptures   Holy Writings—the Old Testament.
'You...people'   Quotation from Exodus 22:28.
Sadducees   A leading Jewish religious group. They followed only the first five books of the Old Testament. They believed that people don't have another life after death.
Pharisees   Pharisees were a Jewish religious group that followed all the Old Testament and other Jewish laws and customs very carefully.

older Jewish leaders. The Jews said, "We have made a serious promise to ourselves. We promised that we will not eat or drink until we have killed Paul! ¹⁵So this is what we want you to do: Send a message to the commander from you and all the Jewish leaders. Tell the commander you want him to bring Paul out to you. Tell the commander that you want to ask Paul more questions. We will be waiting to kill Paul while he is on the way here."

¹⁶But Paul's nephew heard about this plan. He went to the army building and told Paul about the plan. ¹⁷Then Paul called one of the officers and said to him, "Take this young man to the commander. He has a message for him." ¹⁸So the officer brought Paul's nephew to the commander. The officer said, "The prisoner, Paul, asked me to bring this young man to you. He wants to tell you something."

¹⁹The commander led the young man to a place where they could be alone. The commander asked, "What do you want to tell me?"

²⁰The young man said, "The Jews have decided to ask you to bring Paul down to their council meeting tomorrow. The Jews want you to think that they plan to ask Paul more questions. ²¹But don't believe them! There are more than 40 Jews who are hiding and waiting to kill Paul. They have all promised (*vowed*) not to eat or drink until they have killed him! Now they are waiting for you to say yes."

²²The commander sent the young man away. The commander told him, "Don't tell anyone that you have told me about their plan."

Paul Is Sent to Caesarea

²³Then the commander called two officers. He said to them, "I need some men to go to Caesarea. Get 200 soldiers ready. Also, get 70 soldiers on horses and 200 men to carry spears. Be ready to leave at nine o'clock tonight. ²⁴Get some horses for Paul to ride. He must be taken to Governor Felix safely." ²⁵The commander wrote a letter. This is what the letter said:

²⁶From Claudius Lysias

To the Most Excellent Governor Felix:

Greetings.

²⁷ The Jews had taken this man (*Paul*), and they planned to kill him. But I learned that he is a Roman citizen, so I went with my soldiers and saved him. ²⁸I wanted to know why they were accusing him. So I brought him before their council meeting. ²⁹This is what I learned: The Jews said Paul did some things that were wrong. But these charges were about their own Jewish laws. And none of these things were worthy of jail or death. ³⁰I was told that some of the Jews were making a plan to kill Paul. So I send him to you. I also told those Jews to tell you the things they have against him.

³¹The soldiers did the things they were told. The soldiers got Paul and took him to the city of Antipatris that night. ³²The next day, the soldiers on horses went with Paul to Caesarea. But the other soldiers and the spearmen went back to the army building *in Jerusalem*. ³³The soldiers on horses entered Caesarea and gave the letter to the governor (*Felix*). Then they gave Paul to him. ³⁴The governor read the letter. Then he asked Paul, "What country are you from?" The governor learned that Paul was from Cilicia. ³⁵The governor said, "I will hear your case when the Jews who are against you come here too." Then the governor gave orders for Paul to be kept in the palace. (This building had been built by Herod.*)

The Jews Accuse Paul

24 Five days later, Ananias went to the city of Caesarea. Ananias was the high priest.* Ananias also brought some of the older Jewish leaders and a lawyer named Tertullus. They went to Caesarea to make charges against Paul before the governor. ²Paul was called into the meeting, and Tertullus began to make his charges.

Tertullus said, "Most Excellent Felix! Our people enjoy much peace because of you, and many wrong things in our country are being made right through your wise help. ³We are very thankful

---

Herod   Herod I (Herod the Great), ruler (king) of Judea 40-4 B.C.
high priest   The most important Jewish priest and leader.

to accept these things from you. We accept these things always and in every place. ⁴But I don't want to take any more of your time. So I will say only a few words. Please be patient. ⁵This man (*Paul*) is a troublemaker. He makes trouble with the Jews everywhere in the world. He is a leader of the Nazarene group. ⁶Also, he was trying to make the temple* unclean, but we stopped him.* ⁸You can decide if all these things are true. Ask him some questions yourself." ⁹The other Jews agreed. They said, "These things are really true!"

¹⁰The governor made a sign for Paul to speak. So Paul answered, "Governor Felix, I know that you have been a judge over this nation (*Israel*) for a long time. So I am happy to defend myself before you. ¹¹I went to worship in Jerusalem only twelve days ago. You can learn for yourself that this is true. ¹²These Jews who are accusing me did not find me arguing with anyone in the temple.* I was not making trouble with the people. And I was not making trouble or arguing in the synagogues* or any other place in the city. ¹³These Jews cannot prove the things they are saying against me now. ¹⁴But I will tell you this: I worship the God of our fathers (*ancestors*) as a follower of the Way *of Jesus*. The Jews say that the Way *of Jesus* is not the right way. But I believe everything that is taught in the law of Moses. And I believe everything that is written in the books of the Prophets.* ¹⁵I have the same hope in God that these Jews have—the hope that all people, good and bad, will be raised from death. ¹⁶This is why I always try to do what I believe is right before God and men.

¹⁷"I was away *from Jerusalem* for many years. I went back there to bring money to my people and to give some offerings (*gifts*). ¹⁸I was doing this when some Jews found me in the temple.* I had finished the cleansing (*washing*) ceremony.* I had not made any trouble; no people were gathering around me. ¹⁹But some Jews from Asia* were there. They should be here, standing before you. If I have really done anything wrong, those Jews

---

temple   The special building in Jerusalem where God commanded the Jews to worship him.
Verse 6   Some Greek copies add 6b-8a: "And we wanted to judge him by our own law. ⁷But the officer Lysias came and used much force to take him from us. ⁸And Lysias commanded his people to come to you to accuse us."
synagogues   Synagogues were buildings where Jews gathered to read and study the Scriptures.
Prophets   People who spoke for God. Their writings are part of the Old Testament.
cleansing ceremony   The special things Jews did to end the Nazirite vow.
Asia   The western part of Asia Minor.

from Asia are the ones who should accuse me. They were there! [20]Ask these Jews here if they found any wrong in me when I stood before the Jewish council meeting in Jerusalem. [21]I did say one thing when I stood before them: I said, 'You are judging me today because I believe that people will rise from death!' "

[22]Felix already understood a lot about the Way *of Jesus*. He stopped the trial and said, "When commander Lysias comes here, I will decide about these things." [23]Felix told the officer to keep Paul guarded. But he told the officer to give Paul some freedom and to let Paul's friends bring the things that Paul needed.

Paul Speaks to Felix and His Wife

[24]After a few days, Felix came with his wife, Drusilla. She was a Jew. Felix asked for Paul to be brought to him. Felix listened to Paul talk about believing in Christ Jesus. [25]But Felix became afraid when Paul spoke about things like living right, self-control, and the judgment that will come in the future. Felix said, "Go away now! When I have more time, I will call you." [26]But Felix had another reason for talking with Paul. Felix hoped that Paul would pay him a bribe.* So Felix sent for Paul often and talked with him.

[27]But after two years, Porcius Festus became governor. So, Felix was no longer governor. But Felix left Paul in prison, because Felix wanted to do something to please the Jews.

Paul Asks to See Caesar

25 Festus became governor, and three days later he went from Caesarea to Jerusalem. [2]The leading priests and the important Jewish leaders made charges against Paul before Festus. [3]They asked Festus to do something for them; the Jews wanted Festus to send Paul back to Jerusalem. They had a plan to kill Paul on the way. [4]But Festus answered, "No! Paul will be kept in Caesarea. I myself will go to Caesarea soon. [5]Some of your leaders should go with me. They can accuse the man (*Paul*) there in Caesarea, if he has really done something wrong."

---

bribe   Money to pay for Paul's freedom.

⁶Festus stayed in Jerusalem another eight or ten days. Then he went back to Caesarea. The next day, Festus told the soldiers to bring Paul before him. Festus was seated on the judgment seat. ⁷Paul came into the room. The Jews who had come from Jerusalem stood around him. The Jews said that Paul had done many wrong things. But they could not prove any of these things. ⁸This is what Paul said to defend himself: "I have done nothing wrong against the Jewish law, against the temple,* or against Caesar*!"

⁹But Festus wanted to please the Jews. So he asked Paul, "Do you want to go to Jerusalem? Do you want me to judge you there on these charges?"

¹⁰Paul said, "I am standing at Caesar's* judgment seat now. This is where I should be judged! I have done nothing wrong to the Jews; you know this is true. ¹¹If I have done something wrong, and the law says I must die, then I agree that I should die. I don't ask to be saved from death. But if these charges are not true, then no person can give me to these Jews. No! I want Caesar* to hear my case!"

¹²Festus talked about this with his advisers. Then he said, "You have asked to see Caesar,* so you will go to Caesar!"

Paul Before Herod Agrippa

¹³A few days later, King Agrippa* and Bernice* came to Caesarea to visit Festus. ¹⁴They stayed there many days. Festus told the king about Paul's case. Festus said, "There is a man that Felix left in prison. ¹⁵When I went to Jerusalem, the leading priests and the older Jewish leaders there made charges against him. These Jews wanted me to order his death. ¹⁶But I answered, 'When a man is accused of doing something wrong, Romans don't give the man to other people to judge. First, the man must face the people who are accusing him. And he must be allowed to defend himself against their charges.' ¹⁷So these Jews came here *to Caesarea* for the trial. And I did not waste time. The next day I

---

temple   The special building in Jerusalem where God commanded the Jews to worship him.
Caesar, Caesar's   The name or title given to the emperor (ruler) of Rome.
Agrippa   Herod Agrippa II, great-grandson of Herod the Great.
Bernice   Agrippa's sister. She was the oldest daughter of Herod Agrippa II.

sat on the judgment seat and commanded that the man (*Paul*) be brought in. ¹⁸The Jews stood up and accused him. But the Jews did not accuse him of any bad crimes. I thought they would. ¹⁹The things they said were about their own religion and about a man named Jesus. Jesus died, but Paul said that he is still alive. ²⁰I did not know much about these things, so I did not ask questions. But I asked Paul, 'Do you want to go to Jerusalem and be judged there?' ²¹But Paul asked to be kept in Caesarea. He wants a decision from the Emperor (*Caesar**). So I commanded that Paul be held until I could send him to Caesar *in Rome*."

²²Agrippa* said to Festus, "I would like to hear this man, too." Festus said, "Tomorrow you can hear him!"

²³The next day, Agrippa* and Bernice* appeared. They dressed and acted like very important people. Agrippa and Bernice, the army leaders, and the important men of Caesarea went into the judgment room. Festus commanded the soldiers to bring Paul in. ²⁴Festus said, "King Agrippa and all of you men gathered here with us, you see this man (*Paul*). All the Jewish people, here and in Jerusalem, have complained to me about him. When they complain about him, they shout that he should be killed. ²⁵When I judged him, I could find nothing wrong. I found no reason to order his death. But he asked to be judged by Caesar.* So, I decided to send him *to Rome*. ²⁶But I don't really know what to tell Caesar that this man has done wrong. So, I have brought him before all of you—especially you, King Agrippa. I hope that you can question him, and give me something to write to Caesar. ²⁷I think it is foolish to send a prisoner *to Caesar* without making some charges against him."

Paul Before King Agrippa

26 Agrippa* said to Paul, "You may now speak to defend yourself."

Then Paul raised his hand* and began to speak. ²He said, "King Agrippa, I will answer all the charges that the Jews say against me. I think it is a blessing that I can stand here before you

---

Caesar   The name or title given to the emperor (ruler) of Rome.
Agrippa   Herod Agrippa II, great-grandson of Herod the Great.
Bernice   Agrippa's sister. She was the oldest daughter of Herod Agrippa I.
raised his hand   This was a sign to make the people pay attention.

today and do this. ³I am very happy to talk to you, because you know much about all the Jewish customs and the things that the Jews argue about. Please listen to me patiently.

⁴"All the Jews know about my whole life. They know the way I lived from the beginning in my own country and later in Jerusalem. ⁵These Jews have known me for a long time. If they want to, they can tell you that I was a good Pharisee.* And the Pharisees obey the laws of the Jewish religion more carefully than any other group of Jewish people. ⁶Now I am on trial because I hope for the promise that God made to our fathers (*ancestors*). ⁷This is the promise that all the twelve tribes (*family groups*) of our people hope to receive. For this hope the Jews serve God day and night. My king, the Jews have accused me because I hope for this same promise! ⁸Why do you people think it is impossible for God to raise people from death?

⁹"*When I was a Pharisee*, even I thought I should do many things against the name of Jesus from Nazareth. ¹⁰And in Jerusalem I did many things against the saints* (*believers*). The leading priests gave me the power to put many of these people (*believers*) in jail. When the followers of Jesus were being killed, I agreed that it was a good thing. ¹¹In every synagogue,* I punished them. I tried to make them say bad things against* *Jesus*. I was so angry against these people (*believers*) that I went to other cities to find them and hurt them."

Paul Tells About Seeing Jesus

¹²"One time, the leading priests gave me permission and the power to go to the city of Damascus. ¹³I was on the way to Damascus. It was noon. I saw a light from the sky. The light was brighter than the sun. The light shined all around me and the men who were traveling with me. ¹⁴We all fell to the ground. Then I heard a voice talking to me in the Jewish language.* The voice said, 'Saul, Saul, why are you doing these bad things to me? You

Pharisee   Pharisees were a Jewish religious group that followed all of the Old Testament and other Jewish laws and customs very carefully.
saints   The followers of Jesus are also called saints, which means "holy people."
synagogue   Synagogues were places where Jews gathered to read and study the Scriptures.
say...against   Literally, "blaspheme," the same as saying they did not believe in Jesus.
Jewish language   Aramaic, the "Hebrew" language in the first century.

are only hurting yourself by fighting me.' ¹⁵I said, 'Who are you, Lord?' The Lord said, 'I am Jesus. I am the One you are persecuting. ¹⁶Stand up! I have chosen you to be my servant. You will be my witness—you will tell people the things that you have seen and the things that I will show you. This is why I have come to you today. ¹⁷I will not let *your own* people (*the Jews*) hurt you. But I am sending you to the non-Jewish people. I will keep you safe from these people too. ¹⁸You will show the people the Truth. The non-Jewish people will turn away from darkness (*sin*) to the light (*good*). They will turn away from the power of Satan, and they will turn to God. Then their sins can be forgiven. They can have a share with those people who have been made holy* by believing in me.' ''

Paul Tells About His Work

¹⁹Paul continued speaking, ''King Agrippa,* after I had this vision* from heaven, I obeyed it. ²⁰I began telling people that they should change their hearts and lives and turn back to God. I told the people to do things that show that they really changed their hearts. I told these things first to people in Damascus. Then I went to Jerusalem and to every part of Judea and told these things to the people there. I also went to the non-Jewish people. ²¹This is why the Jews grabbed me and were trying to kill me in the temple.* ²²But God helped me, and he is still helping me today. With God's help I am standing here today and telling all people the things I have seen. But I am saying nothing new. I am saying the same things that Moses and the prophets* said would happen. ²³They said that the Christ* would die and be the first to rise from death. Moses and the prophets said that the Christ would bring light to the Jewish people and to the non-Jewish people.''

---

holy   A holy person is pure, belongs only to God, and does only the things that God wants.
Agrippa   Herod Agrippa II, great-grandson of Herod the Great.
vision   A vision is something like a dream that God used to speak to people.
temple   The special building in Jerusalem where God commanded the Jews to worship him.
prophets   People who spoke for God. Their writings are part of the Old Testament.
Christ   The ''anointed one'' (the Messiah) or chosen one of God.

Paul Tries to Persuade Agrippa

²⁴While Paul was saying these things to defend himself, Festus shouted, "Paul, you are crazy! Too much study has made you crazy!"

²⁵Paul said, "Most Excellent Festus, I am not crazy. The things I say are true. My words are not the words of a foolish man; I am serious. ²⁶King Agrippa* knows about these things. I can speak freely to him. I know that he has heard about all of these things. Why? Because these things happened where all people could see. ²⁷King Agrippa, do you believe the things the prophets* wrote? I know you believe!"

²⁸King Agrippa said to Paul, "Do you think you can persuade me to become a Christian so easily?"

²⁹Paul said, "It is not important if it is easy or if it is hard; I pray to God that not only you but every person listening to me today could be saved and be like me—except for these chains I have!"

³⁰King Agrippa,* Governor Festus, Bernice,* and all the people sitting with them stood up ³¹and left the room. They were talking to each other. They said, "This man should not be killed or put in jail; he has done nothing really bad!" ³²And Agrippa said to Festus, "We could let this man go free, but he has asked to see Caesar.*"

Paul Sails for Rome

27 It was decided that we would sail for Italy. A Roman officer named Julius guarded Paul and some other prisoners. Julius served in the emperor's* army. ²We got on a ship and left. The ship was from the city of Adramyttium and was ready to sail to different places in Asia. Aristarchus went with us. He was a man from the city of Thessalonica in Macedonia. ³The

---

Agrippa Herod Agrippa II, great-grandson of Herod the Great.
prophets People who spoke for God. Their writings are part of the Old Testament.
Bernice King Agrippa's sister. She was the oldest daughter of Herod Agrippa I.
Caesar The name or title given to the emperor (ruler) of Rome.
emperor's The ruler (leader) of the Roman empire (almost all the world).

next day we came to the city of Sidon. Julius was very good to Paul. He gave Paul freedom to go visit his friends. These friends took care of Paul's needs. ⁴We left the city of Sidon. We sailed south of the island of Cyprus because the wind was blowing against us. ⁵We went across the sea by Cilicia and Pamphylia. Then we came to the city of Myra in Lycia. ⁶In Myra, the Roman officer found a ship from the city of Alexandria. This ship was going to Italy. So he put us on it.

⁷We sailed slowly for many days. It was hard for us to reach the city of Cnidus because the wind was blowing against us. We could not go any farther that way. So we sailed by the south side of the island of Crete near Salmone. ⁸We sailed along the coast, but the sailing was hard. Then we came to a place called Safe Harbors. The city of Lasea was near there.

⁹But we had lost much time. It was now dangerous to sail, because it was already after the Jewish day of fasting.* So Paul warned them, ¹⁰"Men, I can see that there will be much trouble on this trip. The ship and the things in the ship will be lost. Our lives may even be lost!" ¹¹But the captain and the owner of the ship did not agree with Paul. So the officer did not believe Paul. Instead, the officer believed what the captain and owner of the ship said. ¹²And that harbor (*Safe Harbors*) was not a good place for the ship to stay for the winter. So most of the men decided that the ship should leave there. The men hoped we could go to Phoenix. The ship could stay there for the winter. (Phoenix was a city on the island of Crete. It had a harbor which faced southwest and northwest.)

The Storm

¹³Then a good wind began to blow from the south. The men on the ship thought, "This is the wind we wanted and now we have it!" So they pulled up the anchor. We sailed very close to the island of Crete. ¹⁴But then a very strong wind named the "Northeaster" came from the island. ¹⁵This wind took the ship and carried it away. The ship could not sail against the wind. So

---

day of fasting The Day of Atonement, an important Jewish holy day in the fall of the year. This was the time of year that bad storms happened on the sea.

we stopped trying and let the wind blow us. ¹⁶We went below a small island named Cauda. Then* we were able to bring in the lifeboat, but it was very hard to do. ¹⁷After the men took the lifeboat in, they tied ropes around the ship to hold the ship together. The men were afraid that the ship would hit the sandbanks of Syrtis.* So they lowered the sail and let the wind carry the ship. ¹⁸The next day, the storm was blowing us so hard that the men threw some things out of the ship.* ¹⁹A day later, they threw out the ship's equipment. ²⁰For many days we could not see the sun or the stars. The storm was very bad. We lost all hope of staying alive—we thought we would die.

²¹The men did not eat for a long time. Then one day Paul stood up before them and said, "Men, I told you not to leave Crete. You should have listened to me. Then you would not have all this trouble and loss. ²²But now I tell you to be happy. None of you will die! But the ship will be lost. ²³Last night an angel came to me from God. This is the God I worship. I am his. ²⁴God's angel said, 'Paul, don't be afraid! You must stand before Caesar.* And God *has promised* to give you something good: He will save the lives of all those men sailing with you.' ²⁵So men, be happy! I trust in God. Everything will happen like his angel told me. ²⁶But we will crash on an island."

²⁷On the 14th night, we were floating around in the Adriatic Sea.* The sailors thought we were close to land. ²⁸They threw a rope into the water with a weight on the end of it. They found that the water was 120 feet deep. They went a little further and threw the rope in again. It was 90 feet deep. ²⁹The sailors were afraid that we would hit the rocks. So they threw four anchors into the water. Then they prayed for daylight to come. ³⁰Some of the sailors wanted to leave the ship. They lowered the lifeboat to the water. The sailors wanted the other men to think that they were throwing more anchors from the front of the ship. ³¹But Paul told the officer and the other soldiers, "If these men do not stay in the ship, then your lives cannot be saved!" ³²So the

Then While the island protected them from the wind.
Syrtis Shallow area in the sea near the Libyan coast.
out of the ship The men did this to make the ship lighter so that it would not sink easily.
Caesar The name or title given to the emperor (ruler) of Rome.
Adriatic Sea The sea between Greece and Italy, including the central Mediterranean.

soldiers cut the ropes and let the lifeboat fall into the water.

³³Just before dawn, Paul began persuading all the people to eat something. He said, "For the past two weeks you have been waiting and watching. You have not eaten for 14 days. ³⁴Now I beg (*ask*) you to eat something. You need it to stay alive. None of you will lose even one hair off your heads." ³⁵After he said this, Paul took some bread and thanked God for it before all of them. He broke off a piece and began eating. ³⁶All the men felt better. They all started eating too. ³⁷(There were 276 people on the ship.) ³⁸We ate all we wanted. Then we began making the ship lighter by throwing the grain into the sea.

The Ship Is Destroyed

³⁹When daylight came, the sailors saw land. But they did not know where we were. We saw a bay with a beach. The sailors wanted to sail the ship to the beach if they could. ⁴⁰So the men cut the ropes to the anchors and left the anchors in the sea. At the same time, the men untied the ropes that were holding the rudders. Then the men raised the front sail into the wind and sailed toward the beach. ⁴¹But the ship hit a sandbank. The front of the ship stuck there. The ship could not move. Then the big waves began to break the back of the ship to pieces.

⁴²The soldiers decided to kill the prisoners so that none of the prisoners could swim away and escape. ⁴³But the officer (*Julius*) wanted to let Paul live. So he did not allow the soldiers to kill the prisoners. Julius told the people who could swim to jump into the water and swim to land. ⁴⁴The other people used wooden boards or pieces of the ship. And this is how all the people went to land. None of the people died.

Paul on the Island of Malta

28 When we were safe on land, we learned that the island was called Malta. ²It was raining and very cold. But the people who lived there were very good to us. They made a fire for us and welcomed all of us. ³Paul gathered a pile of sticks for the fire. Paul was putting the sticks on the fire. A poisonous snake came out because of the heat and bit Paul on the hand. ⁴The people living on the island saw the snake hanging from Paul's hand. They said, "This man must be a murderer! He did not die in the sea, but Justice* does not want him to live." ⁵But Paul shook the snake off into the fire. Paul was not hurt. ⁶The people thought that Paul would swell up or fall down dead. The people waited and watched Paul for a long time, but nothing bad happened to him. So the people changed their opinion of Paul. They said, "He is a god!"

⁷There were some fields around that same area. A very important man on the island owned these fields. His name was Publius. He welcomed us into his home. Publius was very good to us. We stayed in his house for three days. ⁸Publius' father was very sick. He had a fever and dysentery.* But Paul went to him and prayed for him. Paul put his hands on the man and healed him. ⁹After this happened, all the other sick people on the island came to Paul. Paul healed them too. ¹⁰⁻¹¹The people on the island gave us many honors. We stayed there three months. When we were ready to leave, the people gave us the things we needed.

Paul Goes to Rome

We got on a ship from the city of Alexandria. The ship had stayed on the island of Malta during the winter. On the front of the ship was the sign for the twin gods.* ¹²We stopped at the city of Syracuse. We stayed in Syracuse three days and then left. ¹³We came to the city of Rhegium. The next day, a wind began to blow from the southwest, so we were able to leave. A day later, we came to the city of Puteoli. ¹⁴We found some brothers (*believers*) there. They asked us to stay with them a week. Finally, we came to Rome. ¹⁵The believers in Rome heard that we were there. They came out to meet us at the Market of Appius* and at the Three Inns.* When Paul saw these believers, he felt better. Paul thanked God.

Justice The people thought there was a god named Justice who would punish bad people.
dysentery A very bad sickness like diarrhea.
twin gods Statues of Castor and Pollux, mythological Greek gods.
Market of Appius A town about 27 miles from Rome.
Three Inns A town about 30 miles from Rome.

Paul in Rome

¹⁶Then we went to Rome. In Rome, Paul was allowed to live alone. But a soldier stayed with Paul to guard him.

¹⁷Three days later, Paul sent for some of the most important Jews. When they came together, Paul said, "My Jewish brothers, I have done nothing against our people (*the Jews*). I have done nothing against the customs of our fathers (*ancestors*). But I was arrested in Jerusalem and given to the Romans. ¹⁸The Romans asked me many questions. But they could not find any reason why I should be killed. So they wanted to let me go free. ¹⁹But the Jews there did not want that. So I had to ask *to come to Rome* to have my trial before Caesar.* But I am not saying that my people (*the Jews*) have done anything wrong. ²⁰That is why I wanted to see you and talk with you. I am bound with this chain because I believe in the hope of Israel.*"

²¹The Jews answered Paul, "We have received no letters from Judea about you. None of our Jewish brothers who have traveled from there (*Judea*) brought news about you or told us anything bad about you. ²²We want to hear your ideas. We know that people everywhere are speaking against this group (*Christians*)."

²³Paul and the Jews chose a day for a meeting. On that day, many more of these Jews met with Paul at his house. Paul spoke to them all day long. Paul explained the kingdom of God to them. Paul tried to persuade them to believe the things about Jesus. He used the law of Moses and the writings of the prophets* to do this. ²⁴Some of the Jews believed the things Paul said, but others did not believe. ²⁵They had an argument. The Jews were ready to leave, but Paul said one more thing to them: "The Holy Spirit* spoke the truth to your fathers (*ancestors*) through Isaiah the prophet.* He said,

²⁶"Go to this people (*the Jews*) and tell them:
　　You will listen and you will hear,
　　　　but you will not understand!

Caesar　The name or title given to the emperor (ruler) of Rome.
Israel　The Jewish nation (people).
prophet(s)　People who spoke for God. Their writings are part of the Old Testament.
Holy Spirit　Also called the Spirit of God, the Spirit of Christ, and the Comforter. He is joined with God and Christ. He does the work of God among people in the world.

> You will look and you will see,
> > but you will not understand what you see!
> ²⁷ Yes, the hearts (*minds*) of these people (*the Jews*)
> > are now hard.
> > These people have ears, but they don't listen.
> > And these people refuse to see *the truth*.
> This has happened so that these people will not
> > see with their eyes,
> > hear with their ears,
> > understand with their minds.
> This has happened so that they will not
> > turn to me to heal them.'   *Isaiah 6:9-10*

²⁸"I want you Jews to know that God has sent his salvation to the non-Jewish people. They will listen!" ²⁹*

³⁰Paul stayed two full years in his own rented house. He welcomed all people who came and visited him. ³¹Paul preached about the kingdom of God. He taught about the Lord Jesus Christ. He was very bold (*brave*), and no one tried to stop him from speaking.

Verse 29 Some late copies of Acts add verse 29: "After Paul said this, the Jews left. They were arguing very much with each other."

Romans

1 From Paul, a servant of Christ Jesus. God called me to be an apostle.* I was chosen to tell God's Good News* to all people.

²God promised long ago to give this Good News to his people. God used his prophets* to promise this. That promise is written in the Holy Scriptures.* ³⁻⁴The Good News is about God's Son, Jesus Christ our Lord. As a person, he was born from the family of David. But through the Spirit* of holiness Jesus was shown to be God's Son. He was shown to be God's Son with great power by rising from death. ⁵Through Christ, God gave me the special work of an apostle.* God gave me this work to lead people of all nations to believe and obey. And I do this work for Christ. ⁶And you people in Rome were also called to belong to Jesus Christ.

⁷This letter is to all people in Rome that God has called to be his holy* people. You are people that God loves.

Grace (*kindness*) and peace to you from God our Father and from the Lord Jesus Christ.

A Prayer of Thanks

⁸First I want to say that I thank my God through Jesus Christ for all of you. I thank God because people everywhere in the world are talking about your great faith. ⁹⁻¹⁰Every time I pray I always remember you. God knows this is true. God is the One I

---

apostle   Person Jesus chose to be a special helper for telling the Good News to the world.
Good News   The news that God has made a way through Christ for people to have their sins
    forgiven and live with God. When people accept this truth, God accepts them.
prophets   People who spoke for God. Their writings are part of the Old Testament.
Scriptures   Holy Writings—the Old Testament.
Spirit   Probably the Holy Spirit.
holy   A holy person is pure, belongs only to God, and does only the things that God wants.

worship (*serve*) in my spirit by telling people the Good News* about his Son. I pray that I will be allowed to come to you. It will happen if God wants it. [11]I want very much to see you. I want to give you some spiritual gift to make you strong. [12]I mean that I want us to help each other with the faith that we have. Your faith will help me, and my faith will help you. [13]Brothers *and sisters*, I want you to know that I planned many times to come to you. But I have not been allowed to come to you. I wanted to come so that I could help you grow spiritually. I want to help you like I have helped the other non-Jewish people.

[14]I must serve all people—Greeks and non-Greeks, wise people and foolish people. [15]That is why I want so much to preach the Good News* to you there in Rome.

[16]I am proud of the Good News. The Good News is the power God uses to save every person who believes—to save the Jews first, and also to save the non-Jews. [17]The Good News shows how God makes people right with himself. God's way of making people right begins and ends with faith. Like the Scripture* says, "The person who is right with God by faith will live forever."*

All People Have Done Wrong

[18]God's anger is shown from heaven. God is angry with all the evil and wrong things that people do against God. People have the truth, but by their evil lives they hide the truth. [19]Everything that is known about God has been made clear to people. Yes, God has clearly shown people everything that is known about him. [20]There are things about God that people cannot see—his eternal power and all the things that make him God. But since the beginning of the world those things have been easy for people to understand. Those things are made clear in the things that God has made. So people have no excuse for the bad things they do. [21]People knew God. But they did not give glory to God and they did not thank him. People's thinking became useless. Their foolish minds were filled with darkness (*sin*). [22]People said they

---

Good News The news that God has made a way through Christ for people to have their sins forgiven and live with God. When people accept this truth, God accepts them.
Scripture A part of the Holy Writings—the Old Testament.
"The person...forever" Quotation from Habakkuk 2:4.

were wise, and they became fools. [23]People gave up the glory of God who lives forever. People traded that glory for the worship of idols* made to look like earthly people. People traded God's glory for things that look like birds, animals, and snakes.

[24]People were full of sin, wanting only to do evil things. So God left them and let them go their sinful way. And so they became full of sexual sins, using their bodies wrongly with each other. [25]Those people traded the truth of God for a lie. Those people worshiped and served things that were made. But people did not worship and serve the God who made those things. God should be praised forever. Amen.

[26]Because people did those things, God left them and let them do the shameful things they wanted to do. Women stopped having natural sex with men. They started having sex with other women. [27]In the same way, men stopped having natural sex with women. The men began wanting each other all the time. Men did shameful things with other men. And in their bodies they received the punishment for those wrong things they did.

[28]People did not think it was important to have a true knowledge of God. So God left them and allowed those people to have their own worthless minds. And so those people do the things that they should not do. [29]Those people are filled with every kind of sin, evil, selfishness, and hatred. Those people are full of jealousy, murder, fighting, lying, and thinking the worst things about each other. Those people gossip [30]and say evil things about each other. Those people hate God. They are rude and conceited and boast about themselves. Those people invent ways of doing evil. They don't obey their parents, [31]they are foolish, they don't keep their promises, and they show no kindness or mercy to other people. [32]Those people know God's law. They know that God's law says that people who live like this should die. But they continue to do these wrong things. And they also feel that people who do these things are doing right.

---

idols Statues made from wood, stone, or metal that people worshiped as gods.

You People Also Are Sinful

2 If you think that you can judge those other people, then you are wrong. You too are guilty of sin. You judge those people, but you do the same bad things they do. So when you judge them, you are really judging yourself guilty. ²God judges the people who do those wrong things. And we know that God's judgment is right. ³You also judge the people that do those wrong things. But you do those wrong things too. So surely you understand that God will judge you. You will not be able to escape. ⁴God has been very kind to you. And he has been patient with you. God has been waiting for you to change. But you think nothing of his kindness. Maybe you don't understand that God is kind to you so that you will change your hearts and lives. ⁵But you people are hard and stubborn. You refuse to change. So you are making your own punishment greater and greater. You will get that punishment on the day when God will show his anger. On that day people will see God's right judgments. ⁶God will reward or punish every person for the things that person has done. ⁷Some people live for God's glory, for honor, and for life that cannot be destroyed. Those people live for those things by always continuing to do good. God will give life forever to those people. ⁸But other people are selfish and refuse to follow truth. Those people follow evil. God will give those people his punishment and anger. ⁹God will give trouble and suffering to every person who does evil—to the Jews first and also to the non-Jews. ¹⁰But God will give glory, honor, and peace to every person who does good—to the Jews first and also to the non-Jews. ¹¹God judges all people the same.

¹²People who have the law* and people who have never heard of the law are all the same when they sin. People who don't have the law and are sinners will be lost. And in the same way people who have the law and are sinners will be judged by the law. ¹³Hearing the law does not make people right with God. The law makes people right with God only if those people always obey everything the law says. ¹⁴(The non-Jews don't have the law. But when they freely do things that the law commands without even knowing the law, then they are the law for themselves. This is true

law God's law. The law of Moses is a good example of this law.

even though they don't have the law. ¹⁵They show that in their hearts they know what is right and wrong the same as the law commands. And those people also show this by the way they feel about right and wrong. Sometimes their thoughts tell them that they did wrong, and this makes them guilty. And sometimes their thoughts tell them that they did right, and this makes them not guilty.) ¹⁶All these things will happen on the day when God will judge the secret things inside of people. The Good News* that I tell people says that God will judge people through Christ Jesus. That is the gospel* that I preach.

The Jews and the Law

¹⁷What about you? You say that you are a Jew. You trust in the law *of Moses* and boast that you are close to God. ¹⁸You know what God wants you to do. And you know the things that are important because you have learned the law. ¹⁹You think you are a guide for people who don't know the right way. You think you are a light for people who are in darkness (*sin*). ²⁰You think you can show foolish people what is right. And you think you are a teacher for people that still need to learn. You have the law and so you think that you know everything and have all truth. ²¹You teach other people. So why don't you teach yourself? You tell people not to steal. But you yourselves steal. ²²You say that people must not do the sin of adultery.* But you yourselves are guilty of that sin. You hate idols.* But you steal from temples.* ²³You boast about God's law. But you bring shame to God by breaking his law. ²⁴It is written in the Scriptures*: "The non-Jews speak against God's name because of you Jews."*

²⁵If you follow the law,* then your circumcision* has meaning. But if you break the law, then it is like you were never

---

Good News, gospel   The Good News that God has made a way through Christ for people to have their sins forgiven and live with God. When people accept this truth, God accepts them.

adultery   Breaking a marriage promise by doing sexual sin.

idols   The false gods that the non-Jewish people worshiped.

temples   Places where people worship.

Scriptures   Holy Writings—the Old Testament.

"The non-Jews...Jews"   Quotation from Isaiah 52:5, Ezekiel 36:20.

law   The law of Moses.

circumcision   The cutting off of the foreskin. This was done to every Jewish baby boy. It was a mark of the agreement that God made with Abraham (Genesis 17:9-14).

circumcised.* ²⁶The non-Jews are not circumcised. But if they do what the law* says, then it is like they were circumcised. ²⁷You Jews have the written law and circumcision,* but you break the law. So the people who are not circumcised in their bodies but still obey the law will show that you people are guilty.

²⁸A person is not a true Jew if he is only a Jew in his physical body. True circumcision* is not only on the outside of the body. ²⁹A person is a true Jew only if he is a Jew inside. True circumcision is done in the heart. It is done by the Spirit,* not by the written law. And a person who is circumcised in the heart by the Spirit gets praise from God, not from other people.

3 So, do Jews have anything that other people don't have? Is there anything special about being circumcised*? ²Yes, the Jews have many special things. The most important thing is this: God trusted the Jews with his teachings. ³It is true that some Jews were not faithful to God. But will that stop God from doing what he promised? ⁴No! God will continue to be true even when every person is false. Like the Scriptures* say:

"You will be proved right in your words,
    and you will win when you are being judged."   *Psalm 51:4*

⁵When we do wrong, that shows more clearly that God is right. So can we say that God does wrong when he punishes us? (I am using an idea that some people might have.) ⁶No! If God could not punish us, then God could not judge the world.

⁷A person might say, "When I lie it really gives God glory, because my lie shows God's truth. So why am I judged a sinner?" ⁸It would be the same to say, "We should do evil so that good will come." Many people criticize us and say that we teach those things. People who say those things about us are wrong, and they should be condemned.

---

circumcised, circumcision   To have the foreskin cut off. This was done to every Jewish baby boy.
    It was a physical mark of the agreement that God made with Abraham (Genesis 17:9-14).
law   God's law. The law of Moses is a good example of this law.
Spirit   The Holy Spirit. Also called the Spirit of God, the Spirit of Christ, and the Comforter. He
    is joined with God and Christ. He does the work of God among people in the world.
Scriptures   Holy Writings—the Old Testament.

All People Are Guilty

[9]So are we Jews better than other people? No! We have already said that Jews and non-Jews are the same. They are all guilty of sin. [10]Like the Scriptures* say:

"There is no person without sin. None!
[11] There is no person who understands.
There is no person who really wants to be with God.
[12]All people have turned away,
and all people have become worthless.
There is no person who does good. None!"   *Psalm 14:1-3*
[13]"People's mouths are like open graves;
they use their tongues for telling lies."   *Psalm 5:9*
"The things they say are like the poison of snakes"; *Psalm 140:3*
[14] "their mouths are full of cursing and bitterness." *Psalm 10:7*
[15]"People are always ready to hurt and kill;
[16] everywhere they go they cause ruin and sadness.
[17]People don't know the way of peace."   *Isaiah 59:7-8*
[18] "They have no fear or respect for God."   *Psalm 36:1*

[19]The law* commands many things. We know that those commands are for the people who live under the law. This stops all people's excuses and brings the whole world under God's judgment. [20]Why? Because no person can be made right with God by following the law. The law only shows us our sin.

How God Makes Men Right

[21]But God has a way to make people right without the law. And God has now shown us that new way. The law and the prophets* told us about this new way. [22]God makes people right through their faith in Jesus Christ. God does this for all people who believe in Christ. All people are the same. [23]All people have sinned and are not good enough for God's glory. [24]People are made right with God by his grace (*kindness*). This is a free gift. People are made right with God by being made free from sin through Jesus Christ. [25]God gave Jesus as a way to forgive

Scriptures Holy Writings—the Old Testament.
law God's law. The law of Moses is a good example of this law.
prophets People who spoke for God. Their writings are part of the Old Testament.

393

people's sins through faith. God does this by the blood (*death*) of Jesus. This showed that God always does what is right and fair. God was right in the past when he was patient and did not punish people for their sins. ²⁶And God gave Jesus to show today that God does what is right. God did this so that he could judge rightly and also make right any person who has faith in Jesus.

²⁷So do we have a reason to boast about ourselves? No! And why not? It is the way of faith that stops all boasting, not the way of following the law. ²⁸Why? Because a person is made right with God through faith, not through the things he has done to follow the law. This is what we believe. ²⁹God is not only the God of the Jews. He is also the God of the non-Jews. ³⁰There is only one God. He will make Jews* right with him by their faith. And he will also make non-Jews* right with him through their faith. ³¹So do we destroy the law by following the way of faith? No! Faith causes us to be what the law truly wants.

The Example of Abraham

4 So what can we say about Abraham,* the father of our people? What did he learn about faith? ²If Abraham was made right by the things he did, then he had a reason to boast. But Abraham could not boast before God. ³The Scripture* says, "Abraham believed God. And God accepted Abraham's faith. That made Abraham right with God."*

⁴When a person works, his pay is not given to him as a gift. He earns the pay he gets. ⁵But a person cannot do any work that will make him right with God. So that person must trust in God. Then God accepts that person's faith (*trust*), and that makes him right with God. God is the One who makes even evil people right. ⁶David said the same thing. David said that a person is truly happy when God does not look at the things that person has done but accepts him like a good person:

⁷ "People are truly blessed (*happy*)
    when their wrongs are forgiven,

Jews   Literally, "the circumcised people."
non-Jews   Literally, "people who are not circumcised."
Abraham   Most respected ancestor of the Jews. Every Jew hoped to see Abraham.
Scripture   A part of the Holy Writings—the Old Testament.
"Abraham...right with God"   Quotation from Genesis 15:6.

and when their sins are covered!

⁸ And when the Lord accepts a person like he was without sin,
that person is truly blessed!''

Psalm 32:1-2

⁹Is this happiness only for those people who are circumcised*?
Or is this happiness also for people who are not circumcised? We
have already said that God accepted Abraham's* faith, and that
faith made him right with God. ¹⁰So how did this happen? Did
God accept Abraham before or after he was circumcised?
God accepted him before his circumcision.* ¹¹Abraham was
circumcised later to show that God accepted him. His
circumcision was proof that he was right with God through faith
before he was circumcised. So Abraham is the father of all people
who believe but are not circumcised. Those people believe and are
accepted like people who are right with God. ¹²And Abraham is
also the father of people who have been circumcised. But it is not
their circumcision that makes Abraham their father. He is their
father only if they live following the faith that our father
Abraham had before he was circumcised.

God's Promise Received Through Faith

¹³Abraham* and his descendants* received the promise that
they would get the whole world. But Abraham did not receive
that promise through the law.* Abraham received that promise
because he was right with God through his faith. ¹⁴If people could
get the things that God promised by following the law, then faith
is worthless. And God's promise to Abraham is worthless.
¹⁵Why? Because the law can only bring God's anger *when the law
is not obeyed*. But if there is no law, then there is nothing to
disobey.

¹⁶So people get God's promise by having faith. This happens so
that the promise can be a free gift. And if the promise is a free
gift, then all of Abraham's people can have that promise. The
promise is not only for those people that live under the law *of*

---

circumcised, circumcision To have the foreskin cut off. This was done to every Jewish baby boy.
It was a physical mark of the agreement that God made with Abraham (Genesis 17:9-14).
Abraham Most respected ancestor of the Jews. Every Jew hoped to see Abraham.
descendants All the people born in a person's family after that person dies.
law God's law. The law of Moses is a good example of this law.

Moses. The promise is for any person who lives with faith like Abraham. Abraham is the father of us all. ¹⁷Like it is written *in the Scriptures**: "I have made you (*Abraham*) a father of many nations."* This is true before God. Abraham believed in God—the God who gives life to dead people and decides that things will happen that have not yet happened.

¹⁸There was no hope *that Abraham would have children*. But Abraham believed God and continued hoping. And that is why he became the father of many nations. Like God told him, "You will have many descendants (*children*)."* ¹⁹Abraham was almost 100 years old, so his body was much past the age for having children. Also, Sarah could not have children. Abraham thought about this. But his faith in God did not become weak. ²⁰Abraham never doubted that God would do the thing that God promised. Abraham never stopped believing. He grew stronger in his faith and gave praise to God. ²¹Abraham felt sure that God was able to do the thing that God promised. ²²So, "God accepted Abraham's faith. That made him right with God."* ²³Those words ("God accepted Abraham's faith") were written not only for Abraham. ²⁴Those words were also written for us. God will also accept us because we believe. We believe in the One (*God*) that raised Jesus our Lord from death. ²⁵Jesus was given to die for our sins. And he was raised from death to make us right with God.

Right with God

5 We have been made right with God because of our faith. So we have peace with God through our Lord Jesus Christ. ²Through our faith, Christ has brought us into that blessing of God's grace (*kindness*) that we now enjoy. And we are very happy because of the hope we have of sharing God's glory. ³And we are also happy with the troubles we have. Why are we happy with troubles? Because we know that these troubles make us more patient. ⁴And this patience is proof that we are strong. And this proof gives us hope. ⁵And this hope will never disappoint us—it will never fail. Why? Because God has poured out his love to fill

Scriptures   Holy Writings—the Old Testament.
"I...nations"   Quotation from Genesis 17:5.
"You...descendants"   Quotation from Genesis 15:5.
"God...right with God"   Quotation from Genesis 15:6.

our hearts. God gave us his love through the Holy Spirit.* That Holy Spirit was a gift to us from God.

⁶Christ died for us while we were still weak people. We were living against God, but at the right time, Christ died for us. ⁷Very few people will die to save the life of another person, even if that other person is a good person. If the person is a very good person, then someone might be willing to die for that person. ⁸But Christ died for us while we were still sinners. In that way God showed us that he loves us very much.

⁹We have been made right with God by Christ's blood (*death*). So through Christ we will surely be saved from God's anger. ¹⁰I mean that while we were God's enemies, God made friends with us through the death of his Son. So surely, now that we are God's friends, God will save us through his Son's life. ¹¹And not only will we be saved, but we are also very happy now. We are happy in God through our Lord Jesus Christ. It is because of Jesus that we are now God's friends.

Adam and Christ

¹²Sin came into the world because of what one man (*Adam*) did. And with sin came death. So this is why all people must die—because all people sinned. ¹³Sin was in the world before the law *of Moses*. But God does not make people guilty for sin if there is no law. ¹⁴But from the time of Adam to the time of Moses, all people had to die. Adam died because he sinned by not obeying God's command. But even those people who did not sin the way Adam sinned had to die.

Adam was like the One (*Christ*) who was coming in the future. ¹⁵But God's free gift is not like Adam's sin. Many people died because of the sin of that one man (*Adam*). But the grace (*kindness*) that people received from God was much greater. Many people received God's gift *of life* by the grace of the one man, Jesus Christ. ¹⁶After Adam sinned once, he was judged guilty. But the gift of God is different. God's free gift came after many sins. And the gift makes people right with God. ¹⁷One man sinned, and so death ruled all people because of that one man.

Holy Spirit Also called the Spirit of God, the Spirit of Christ, and the Comforter. He is joined with God and Christ. He does the work of God among people in the world.

But now some people accept God's full grace (*kindness*) and his great gift of being made right. Surely those people will have true life and rule through the one man, Jesus Christ.

¹⁸So one sin *of Adam* brought the punishment *of death* to all people. But in the same way, one good thing *that Christ did* makes all people right with God. And that brings true life for those people. ¹⁹One man (*Adam*) disobeyed God and many people became sinners. But in the same way, one man (*Christ*) obeyed God and many people will be made right. ²⁰The law came to make people have more sin. But when people had more sin, God gave them more of his grace (*kindness*). ²¹Sin once used death to rule us. But God gave people more of his grace so that grace could rule by making people right with him. This brings life forever through Jesus Christ our Lord.

Dead to Sin but Alive in Christ

6 So do you think that we should continue sinning so that God will give us more and more grace (*kindness*)? ²No! We died to (*quit living*) our old sinful lives. So how can we continue living with sin? ³Did you forget that all of us became part of Christ when we were baptized*? We shared his death in our baptism.* ⁴So when we were baptized, we were buried with Christ and shared his death. We were buried with Christ so that we could *be raised up and* live a new life. This happened the same as Christ was raised from death by the wonderful power of the Father.

⁵Christ died, and we have been joined with Christ by dying too. So we will also be joined with him by rising from death like Christ rose from death. ⁶We know that our old life died with Christ on the cross. This happened so that our sinful selves would have no power over us. And then we would not be slaves to sin. ⁷Any person who has died is made free from sin's control (*power*).

⁸If we died with Christ, we know that we will also live with him. ⁹Christ was raised from death. And we know that he cannot die again. Death has no power over him now. ¹⁰Yes, when Christ died, he died to *defeat the power of* sin one time—enough for all time. He now has a new life, and his new life is with God. ¹¹In the

---

baptized, baptism A Greek word meaning to be immersed, dipped, or buried briefly under water.

same way, you should see yourselves as being dead to the power of sin. And see yourselves as being alive for God through Christ Jesus.

[12]But don't let sin control you in your life here on earth. You must not be ruled by the things your sinful self makes you want to do. [13]Don't offer the parts of your body to serve sin. Don't use your bodies as things to do evil with. But you should offer yourselves to God. Be like people who have died and now live. Offer the parts of your body to God to be used for doing good. [14]Sin will not be your master. Why? Because you are not under law. You now live under God's grace (*kindness*).

Slaves of Righteousness

[15]So what should we do? Should we sin because we are under grace (*kindness*) and not under law? No! [16]Surely you know that when you give yourselves like slaves to obey someone, then you are really slaves of that person. The person you obey is your master. You can follow sin, or obey God. Sin brings spiritual death. But obeying God makes you right with him. [17]In the past you were slaves to sin—sin controlled you. But thank God, you fully obeyed the things that were taught to you. [18]You were made free from sin. And now you are slaves to goodness (*right living*). [19]I explain this by using an example that people know. I explain it this way because it is hard for you to understand. In the past you offered the parts of your body to be slaves to sin and evil. You lived only for evil. In the same way now you must give yourselves to be slaves of goodness. Then you will live only for God.

[20]In the past you were slaves to sin, and goodness (*right living*) did not control you. [21]You did evil things. Now you are ashamed of those things. Did those things help you? No. Those things only bring *spiritual* death. [22]But now you are free from sin. You are now slaves of God. And this brings you a life that is only for God. And from that you will get life forever. [23]When people sin, they earn what sin pays—death. But God gives his people a free gift—life forever in Christ Jesus our Lord.

An Example from Marriage

7 Brothers *and sisters*, all of you understand the law *of Moses*. So surely you know that the law rules over a man only while he is alive. ²*I will give you an example*: A woman must stay married to her husband as long as he is alive. But if her husband dies, then she is made free from the law of marriage. ³But if that woman marries another man while her husband is still alive, the law says she is guilty of adultery.* But if the woman's husband dies, then that woman is made free from the law of marriage. So if that woman marries another man after her husband dies, she is not guilty of adultery.

⁴In the same way, my brothers *and sisters*, your old selves died and you became free from the law through the body of Christ. Now you belong to someone else. You belong to the One (*Christ*) that was raised from death. We belong to Christ so that we can be used in service to God. ⁵In the past, we were ruled by our sinful selves. The law made us want to do sinful things. And those sinful things we wanted to do controlled our bodies, so that the things we did were only bringing us spiritual death. ⁶In the past, the law held us like prisoners. But our old selves died and we were made free from the law. So now we serve God in a new way, not in the old way with the written rules. Now we serve God in the new way with the Spirit.*

Our Fight Against Sin

⁷You might think that I am saying that sin and the law* are the same thing. That is not true. But the law was the only way I could learn what sin means. I would never have known what it means to want something wrong. But the law said, "Don't want wrong things."* ⁸And sin found a way to use that commandment and make me want every kind of wrong thing. So sin came to me because of that commandment. But without the law, sin has no

---

adultery Breaking a marriage promise by doing sexual sin.
Spirit The Holy Spirit. Also called the Spirit of God, the Spirit of Christ, and the Comforter. He is joined with God and Christ. He does the work of God among people in the world.
law God's law. The law of Moses is a good example of this law.
"Don't...things" Quotation from Exodus 20:17, Deuteronomy 5:21.

power. ⁹I was alive without the law before I knew the law. But when the law's commandment came to me, then sin began to live. ¹⁰And I died *spiritually* because of sin. The commandment was meant to bring life, but for me that commandment brought death. ¹¹Sin found a way to fool me by using the commandment. Sin used the commandment to make me die *spiritually*.

¹²So the law is holy, and the commandment is holy and right and good. ¹³Does this mean that something that is good brought death to me? No! But sin used something that is good to bring death to me. This happened so that I could see what sin is really like. It happened to show that sin is something very, very bad. And the commandment was used to show this.

The Conflict in Man

¹⁴We know that the law* is spiritual. But I am not spiritual. Sin rules me like I am its slave. ¹⁵I don't understand the things I do. I don't do the *good* things I want to do. And I do the *bad* things I hate to do. ¹⁶And if I don't want to do the *bad* things I do, then that means that I agree that the law is good. ¹⁷But it is not really me that is doing these *bad* things. It is sin living in me that does these things. ¹⁸Yes, I know that nothing good lives in me—I mean nothing good lives in the part of me that is earthly and sinful. I want to do the things that are good. But I don't do those things. ¹⁹I don't do the good things that I want to do. I do the bad things that I don't want to do. ²⁰So if I do things I don't want to do, then it is not really me doing those things. It is sin living in me that does those bad things.

²¹So I have learned this rule: When I want to do good, evil is there with me. ²²In my mind, I am happy with God's law. ²³But I see another law working in my body. That law makes war against the law that my mind accepts. That other law working in my body is the law of sin, and that law makes me its prisoner. ²⁴This is terrible! Who will save me from this body that brings me death? ²⁵God *will save me*! I thank him *for his salvation* through Jesus Christ our Lord!

So in my mind I am a slave to God's law. But in my sinful self I am a slave to the law of sin.

law God's law. The law of Moses is a good example of this law.

Life in the Spirit

8 So now people who are in Christ Jesus are not judged guilty. [2]Why am I not judged guilty? Because in Christ Jesus the law of the Spirit* that brings life made me free. It made me free from the law that brings sin and death. [3]The law* was without power because the law was made weak by our sinful selves. But God did what the law could not do. God sent his own Son to earth with the same human life that other people use for sin. God sent his Son to be an offering for sin. So God used a human life to condemn (*destroy*) sin. [4]God did this so that we could be right like the law said we must be. Now we don't live following our sinful selves. We live following the Spirit.*

[5]People who live following their sinful selves think only about things that their sinful selves want. But those people who live following the Spirit* are thinking about the things that the Spirit wants them to do. [6]If a person's thinking is controlled by his sinful self, then there is spiritual death. But if a person's thinking is controlled by the Spirit, then there is life and peace. [7]Why is this true? Because if a person's thinking is controlled by his sinful self, then that person is against God. That person refuses to obey God's law. And really that person is not able to obey God's law. [8]Those people who are ruled by their sinful selves cannot please God.

[9]But you are not ruled by your sinful selves. You are ruled by the Spirit,* if that Spirit of God lives in you. But if any person does not have the Spirit of Christ, then that person does not belong to Christ. [10]Your body will always be dead because of sin. But if Christ is in you, then the Spirit gives you life because Christ made you right with God. [11]God raised Jesus from death. And if God's Spirit is living in you, then he will also give life to your bodies that die. God is the One who raised Christ from death. And he will give life to your bodies through his Spirit that lives in you.

[12]So, my brothers *and sisters*, we must not be ruled by our sinful selves. We must not live the way our sinful selves want. [13]If you use your lives to do the wrong things your sinful selves want,

---

Spirit The Holy Spirit. Also called the Spirit of God, the Spirit of Christ, and the Comforter. He is joined with God and Christ. He does the work of God among people in the world.
law God's law. The law of Moses is a good example of this law.

then you will die spiritually. But if you use the Spirit's* help to stop doing the wrong things you do with your body, then you will have *true* life.

¹⁴The true children of God are those people who let God's Spirit* lead them. ¹⁵The Spirit that we received is not a spirit that makes us slaves again to fear. The Spirit that we have makes us children of God. And with that Spirit we say, "Father, dear Father."* ¹⁶And the Spirit himself joins with our spirits to say that we are God's children. ¹⁷If we are God's children, then we will get the blessings God has for his people. We will get these things from God. We will receive those blessings together with Christ. But we must suffer like Christ suffered. Then we will have glory like Christ has glory.

We Will Have Glory in the Future

¹⁸We have sufferings now. But the sufferings we have now are nothing compared to the great glory that will be given to us. ¹⁹Everything that God made is waiting with excitement for the time when God will show the world who his children are. The whole world wants very much for that to happen. ²⁰Everything that God made was changed to be like it was worth nothing. It did not want to change, but God decided to change it. But there was this hope: ²¹that everything God made would be made free from ruin (*decay*). There was hope that everything God made would have the freedom and glory that belong to God's children.

²²We know that everything God made has been waiting until now in pain like a woman ready to give birth to a child. ²³Not only the world, but we also have been waiting with pain inside us. We have the Spirit* as the first part of God's promise. So we are waiting for God to finish making us his own children. I mean we are waiting for our bodies to be made free. ²⁴We were saved and we have this hope. If we can see what we are waiting for, then that is not really hope. People don't hope for something they already have. ²⁵But we are hoping for something that we don't have yet. We are waiting for it patiently.

Spirit's, Spirit The Holy Spirit, called the Spirit of God, the Spirit of Christ, and the Comforter. He is joined with God and Christ. He does the work of God among people in the world.
"Father, dear Father" Literally, "Abba, Father." Jewish children called their fathers "Abba," a name that means "daddy."

²⁶Also, the Spirit* helps us. We are very weak, but the Spirit helps us with our weakness. We don't know how to pray like we should. But the Spirit himself speaks to God for us. The Spirit begs God for us. The Spirit speaks to God with deep feelings that words cannot explain. ²⁷God can see what is in people's hearts. And God knows what is in the mind of the Spirit, because the Spirit speaks to God for his people in the way that God wants.

²⁸We know that in everything God works for the good of those people who love him. These are the people God called (*chose*), because that was his plan. ²⁹God knew those people before he made the world. And God decided that those people would be like his Son (*Jesus*). Then Jesus would be the firstborn* of many brothers *and sisters*. ³⁰God planned for those people to be like his Son. And he called (*chose*) those people. God called those people and made them right with him. And God gave his glory to those people that he made right.

God's Love in Christ Jesus

³¹So what should we say about this? If God is with us, then no person can defeat us. ³²*God will do anything for us.* God even let his own Son suffer for us. God gave his Son for us all. So with Jesus now, God will surely give us all things. ³³Who can accuse the people that God has chosen? No one! God is the One who makes his people right. ³⁴Who can say that God's people are guilty? No one! Christ Jesus died *for us*, but that is not all. He was also raised from death. And now he is on God's right side and is begging God for us. ³⁵Can anything separate us from the love of Christ? No! Can trouble separate us from Christ's love? No! Can problems or persecution* separate us from Christ's love? No! If we have no food or clothes, will that separate us from Christ's love? No! Will danger or even death separate us from Christ's love? No! ³⁶Like it is written in the Scriptures*:

Spirit The Holy Spirit. Also called the Spirit of God, the Spirit of Christ, and the Comforter. He is joined with God and Christ. He does the work of God among people in the world.
firstborn This probably means that Christ was the first in God's family to share God's glory.
persecution Being hurt by other people or suffering bad things from them.
Scriptures Holy Writings—the Old Testament.

> "For you (*Christ*) we are in danger of death all the time.
> People think we are worth no more
> than sheep to be killed."

Psalm 44:22

[37]But in all these things we have full victory through God who showed his love for us. [38-39]Yes, I am sure that nothing can separate us from the love of God. Not death, not life, not angels, not ruling spirits, nothing now or nothing in the future, no powers, nothing above us, nothing below us, or anything else in the whole world will ever be able to separate us from the love of God that is in Christ Jesus our Lord.

God and the Jewish People

9 I am in Christ and I am telling you the truth. I don't lie. My feelings are ruled by the Holy Spirit.* And those feelings tell me that I am not lying: [2]I have great sorrow and always feel much sadness *for the Jewish people*. [3]They are my brothers *and sisters*, my earthly family. I wish I could help them. I would even have a curse on me and cut myself off from Christ if that would help them. [4]They are the people of Israel.* Those people (*the Jews*) are God's chosen children. Those people have the glory of God, and the agreements that God made between himself and his people. God gave them the law and the right way of worship. And God gave his promises to those people (*the Jews*). [5]Those people are the descendants of our great fathers (*ancestors*). And they are the earthly family of Christ. Christ is God over all things. Praise him forever!* Amen.

[6]*Yes, I feel sorry for the Jewish people*. I don't mean that God failed to keep his promise to them. But only some of the people of Israel (*the Jews*) are truly God's people.* [7]And only some of Abraham's* descendants* are true children of Abraham (*God's people*). *This is what God said to Abraham*: "Only the family of

---

Holy Spirit   Also called the Spirit of God, the Spirit of Christ, and the Comforter. He is joined with God and Christ. He does the work of God among people in the world.
Israel   The Jewish nation (people).
Christ...forever   This can also mean, "May God, who rules over all things, be praised forever!"
God's people   Literally. "Israel," the people God chose to bring his blessings to the world.
Abraham   Most respected ancestor of the Jews. Every Jew hoped to see Abraham.
descendants   All the people born in a person's family after that person dies.

Isaac will be called your people."* [8]This means that not all of Abraham's descendants* (*family*) are God's true children. Abraham's true children are those people that become God's children because of the promise God made to Abraham. [9]God's promise to Abraham was like this: "At the right time I will come back, and Sarah will have a son."*

[10]And that is not all. Rebecca also had sons. And those sons had the same father. He is our father (*ancestor*) Isaac. [11-12]But before the two boys were born, God told Rebecca, "The older boy will serve the younger."* This was before the boys had done anything good or bad. God said this before they were born so that the boy God chose would be chosen because of God's own plan. He was chosen because he was the one God wanted to call, and not because of anything the boys did. [13]Like the Scripture* says, "I loved Jacob, but I hated Esau."*

[14]So what should we say about this? Is God not fair? We cannot say that. [15]God said to Moses, "I will show mercy to the person that I want to show mercy to. I will show pity to the person that I want to show pity to."* [16]So God will choose the person he decides to show mercy to. And his choice does not depend on what people want or try to do. [17]*In* the Scripture* *God* says to Pharaoh: "I made you king so you could do this for me. I wanted to show my power in you. I wanted my name to be announced in all the world."* [18]So God shows mercy to the people he wants to show mercy to. And God makes the people stubborn that he wants to make stubborn.

[19]So one of you will ask me: "If God controls the things we do, then why does God blame us *for our sins*?" [20]*Don't ask that.* You are only people. And people have no right to question God. A clay jar does not question the man who made it. The jar does not say, "Why did you make me like this?" [21]The man who makes

"Only...people"   Quotation from Genesis 21:12.
descendants   All the people born in a person's family after that person dies.
"At...son"   Quotation from Genesis 18:10,14.
"The older...younger"   Quotation from Genesis 25:23.
Scripture   A part of the Holy Writings—the Old Testament.
"I...Esau"   Quotation from Malachi 1:2-3.
"I will show mercy...pity to"   Quotation from Exodus 33:19.
"I made...world"   Quotation from Exodus 9:16.

the jar can make anything he wants to make. He can use the same clay to make different things. He can make one thing for special purposes and another thing for daily use.

²²It is the same way with what God has done. God wanted to show his anger and to let people see his power. But God endured patiently those people he was angry with—people that were ready to be destroyed. ²³God waited with patience so that he could make known his rich glory. God wanted to give that glory to the people who receive his mercy. God has prepared these people to have his glory. ²⁴We are those people. We are the people God called (*chose*). God called us from the Jews and from the non-Jews. ²⁵Like the Scripture* says in *the book of* Hosea:

> "The people who are not mine—
> I will say that they are my people.
> And the people that I did not love—
> I will say that they are the people I love."   *Hosea 2:23*

²⁶"And in the same place that God said,
> 'You are not my people'—
> in that place they will be called
> sons of the living God."   *Hosea 1:10*

²⁷And Isaiah cries out about Israel*:

> "There are so many people of Israel that they are like the grains of sand by the sea. But only a few of those people will be saved. ²⁸Yes, the Lord will quickly finish judging the people on the earth."*

²⁹It is like Isaiah said:

> "The Lord has all power. The Lord saved some of his people for us. If he had not done that, then we would now be like Sodom,* and we would now be like Gomorrah.*"*

Scripture   A part of the Holy Writings—the Old Testament.
Israel   The Jewish nation (people).
"There...earth"   Quotation from Isaiah 10:22-23.
Sodom, Gomorrah   Cities where evil people lived. God punished them by destroying their cities.
"The Lord...Gomorrah"   Quotation from Isaiah 1:9.

³⁰So what does all this mean? It means this: that the non-Jews were not trying to make themselves right with God. But they were made right with God. They became right because of their faith. ³¹And the people of Israel* tried to follow a law to make themselves right with God. But they did not succeed. ³²Why not? Because they tried to make themselves right by the things they did. They did not trust in God to make them right. They fell over the stone that makes people fall. ³³The Scripture* talks about that stone:

"Look, I put in Zion* a stone
        that will make people fall.
    It is a rock that will make people sin.
But the person who trusts in that rock
        will never be made ashamed."

Isaiah 28:16

10 Brothers *and sisters*, the thing I want most is for all the Jews to be saved. That is my prayer to God. ²I can say this about them: They really try to follow God. But they don't know the right way. ³They did not know the way that God makes people right with him. And they tried to make themselves right in their own way. So they did not accept God's way of making people right. ⁴Christ ended the law so that every person who believes in him is made right with God.

⁵Moses writes about being made right by following the law. Moses says, "A person who wants to find life by following these things (*the law*) must do the things the law says."* ⁶But this is what the Scripture* says about being made right through faith: "Don't say to yourself, 'Who will go up into heaven?' "* (That means, "Who will go up to heaven to get Christ and bring him down to earth?") ⁷"And don't say, 'Who will go down into the world below?' "* (That means, "Who will go down to get Christ and bring him up from death?") ⁸This is what the Scripture says: "God's teaching is near you; it is in your mouth and in your heart."* That teaching is the teaching of faith that we tell people.

Israel   The Jewish nation (people).
Scripture   A part of the Holy Writings—the Old Testament.
Zion   An early name for Jerusalem, the city of God's people.
"A person...says"   Quotation from Leviticus 18:5.
Verses 6-8   Quotations from Deuteronomy 30:12-14.

⁹If you use your mouth to say, "Jesus is Lord," and if you believe in your mind that God raised Jesus from death, then you will be saved. ¹⁰Yes, we believe with our hearts, and so we are made right with God. And we use our mouths to say that we believe, and so we are saved. ¹¹Yes, the Scripture* says, "Any person who believes in him (*Christ*) will not be made sorry."* ¹²That Scripture* says "any person" because there is no difference between Jew and non-Jew. The same Lord is the Lord of all people. The Lord gives many blessings to all people that trust in him. ¹³Yes, *the Scripture says*, "Every person who trusts in the Lord will be saved."*

¹⁴But before people can trust in the Lord for help they must believe in him. And before people can believe in the Lord they must hear about him. And for people to hear about the Lord, another person must tell them. ¹⁵And before a person can go and tell them, that person must be sent. It is written, "Beautiful are the feet of those people who come to tell good news."*

¹⁶But not all *the Jews* accepted the good news. Isaiah said, "Lord, who believed the things we told them?"* ¹⁷So faith comes from hearing *the Good News.** And people hear *the Good News* when a person tells them about Christ.

¹⁸But I ask, "Did people not hear *the Good News*?" Yes, they heard—*like the Scripture* says*:

> "Their voices went out all around the world.
> Their words went everywhere in the world."   *Psalm 19:4*

¹⁹Again I ask, "Did the people of Israel* not understand?" Yes, they did understand. First, Moses says this *for God*:

> "I will use a people that is not really a nation
>   to make you jealous.
> I will use a nation that does not understand
>   to make you angry."   *Deuteronomy 32:21*

Scripture   A part of the Holy Writings—the Old Testament.
"Any...sorry"   Quotation from Isaiah 28:16.
"Every...saved"   Quotation from Joel 2:32.
"Beautiful...news"   Quotation from Isaiah 52:7.
"Lord...them"   Quotation from Isaiah 53:1.
Good News   The news that God has made a way through Christ for people to have their sins forgiven and live with God. When people accept this truth, God accepts them.
Israel   The Jewish nation (people).

²⁰Then Isaiah is bold enough to say this *for God*:

> "The people that were not looking for me—
>   those people found me.
> I showed myself to people that did not ask for me." *Isaiah 65:1*

²¹*God said this through Isaiah about the non-Jewish people*. But about the Jewish people God says, "All day long I have waited for those people, but they refuse to obey and refuse to follow me."*

God Has Not Forgotten His People

11 So I ask, "Did God throw out his people?" No! I myself am an Israelite (*Jew*). I am from the family of Abraham,* from the family group (*tribe*) of Benjamin. ²God chose the Israelites to be his people before *they were born*. And God did not throw out those people. Surely you know what the Scripture* says about Elijah.* The Scripture tells about Elijah praying to God against the people of Israel. Elijah said, ³"Lord, the people have killed your prophets* and destroyed your altars.* I am the only prophet still living. And the people are trying to kill me now."* ⁴But what answer did God give Elijah? God said, "I have kept for myself 7,000 men who still worship me. These 7,000 men have not given worship to Baal.*"* ⁵It is the same now. There are a few people that God has chosen by his grace (*kindness*). ⁶And if God chose his people by grace, then it is not the things they have done that made them God's people. If they could be made God's people by the things they did, then God's gift of grace would not really be a gift.

⁷So this is what has happened: The people of Israel (*the Jews*) tried *to be right with God*. But they did not succeed. But the people God chose did *become right with him*. The other people

---

"All...me" Quotation from Isaiah 65:2.
Abraham Most respected ancestor of the Jews. Every Jew hoped to see Abraham.
Scripture A part of the Holy Writings—the Old Testament.
Elijah A man who spoke for God about 800 years before Christ.
prophets People who spoke for God. Their writings are part of the Old Testament.
altars An altar is a place where sacrifices or gifts are offered to God.
"Lord...now" Quotation from I Kings 19:10,14.
Baal The name of a false god.
"I...Baal" Quotation from I Kings 19:18.

became hard and refused to listen to God. ⁸Like it is written *in the Scriptures**:

> "God caused the people to not understand,
>   God closed their eyes so they could not see *the truth*,
>   and God closed their ears so they could not hear *the truth*.
> This continues until now."
>
> *Deuteronomy 29:4*

⁹And David says:

> "Let those people be caught and trapped at their own feasts.
>   Let those people fall and be punished.
> ¹⁰Let their eyes be closed so they
>   cannot see *the truth*.
> And let them be troubled forever."
>
> *Psalm 69:22-23*

¹¹So I ask: When the Jews fell, did that fall destroy them? No! But their mistake brought salvation to the non-Jews. This happened to make Jews jealous. ¹²The Jews' mistake brought rich blessings for the world. And what the Jews lost brought rich blessings for the non-Jewish people. So surely the world will get much richer blessings when enough Jews become the kind of people God wants.

¹³Now I am speaking to you people who are not Jews. I am an apostle* to the non-Jews. So while I have that work, I will do the best I can. ¹⁴I hope I can make my own people (*the Jews*) jealous. That way, maybe I can help some of them to be saved. ¹⁵God turned away from the Jews. When that happened, God became friends with the other people in the world. So when God accepts the Jews, then surely that will bring to people life after death.

¹⁶If the first piece of bread is offered to God, then the whole loaf is made holy. If the roots of a tree are holy, then the tree's branches are holy too.

¹⁷Some of the branches from an olive tree have been broken off, and the branch of a wild olive tree has been joined to that first tree. You non-Jews are the same as that wild branch, and you now share the strength and life of the first tree (*the Jews*). ¹⁸So don't boast about those branches that were broken off. You have no reason to boast. Why? You don't give life to the root.

Scriptures   Holy Writings—the Old Testament.
apostle   Person Jesus chose to be a special helper for telling the Good News to the world.

The root gives life to you. ¹⁹You will say, "Branches were broken off so that I could be joined to their tree." ²⁰That is true. But those branches were broken off because they did not believe. And you continue to be part of the tree only because you believe. Don't be proud, but be afraid. ²¹If God did not let the natural branches of that tree stay, then he will not let you stay *if you don't believe*.

²²So you see that God is kind, but he can also be very strict. God punishes those people who stop following him. But God is kind to you, if you continue following in his kindness. If you don't continue following him, you will be cut off *from the tree*. ²³And if the Jews will believe in God again, then God will accept the Jews back again. God is able to put them back where they were. ²⁴It is not natural for a wild branch to become part of a good tree. But you non-Jews are like a branch cut from a wild olive tree. And you were joined to a good olive tree. Those Jews are like a branch that grew from the good tree. So surely they can be joined to their own tree again.

²⁵I want you to understand this secret truth, brothers *and sisters*. This truth will help you understand that you don't know everything. The truth is this: Part of Israel* has been made stubborn. But that will change when enough non-Jews have come to God. ²⁶And that is how all Israel will be saved. It is written *in the Scriptures**:

"The Savior will come from Zion*;
   He will take away all evil from the family of Jacob.*
²⁷And I will make this agreement with those people
   when I take away their sins."   *Isaiah 59:20-21; 27:9*

²⁸The Jews refuse to accept the Good News,* so they are God's enemies. This has happened to help you non-Jews. But the Jews are still God's chosen people. So God loves them very much. God loves them because of *the promises he made to* their fathers. ²⁹God never changes his mind about the people he calls and the

---

Israel   The Jewish nation (people).
Scriptures   Holy Writings—the Old Testament.
Zion   An early name for Jerusalem, the city of God's people.
Jacob   Father of the twelve family groups of Israel, the people God chose to be his people.
Good News   The news that God has made a way through Christ for people to have their sins forgiven and live with God. When people accept this truth, God accepts them.

things he gives them. And God never takes back his call to the people. ³⁰At one time you refused to obey God. But now you have received mercy because those people (*the Jews*) refused to obey. ³¹And now the Jews refuse to obey because God showed mercy to you. But this happened so that they can also receive mercy from God. ³²All people have refused to obey God. God has put all people together as people who don't obey him, so that God can show mercy to all people.

Praise to God

³³Yes, God's riches are very great! God's wisdom and knowledge have no end! No person can explain the things God decides. No person can understand God's ways. ³⁴Like the Scripture* says,

> "Who knows the mind of the Lord?
> Who is able to give God advice?"   *Isaiah 40:13*
> ³⁵"Who has ever given God anything?
> God owes nothing to any person."   *Job 41:11*

³⁶Yes, God made all things. And everything continues through God and for God. To God be the glory forever! Amen.

Give Your Lives to God

12 So brothers *and sisters*, I beg you to do something. God has shown us great mercy. So offer your lives as a living sacrifice* to God. Your offering must be only for God and will be pleasing to him. This offering of yourselves is the spiritual way for you to worship (*serve*) God. ²Don't change yourselves to be like the people of this world. But be changed inside yourselves with a new way of thinking. Then you will be able to decide and accept what God wants for you. You will be able to know what things are good and pleasing to God and what things are perfect.

³God has given me a special gift. That is why I have something to say to every person among you. Don't think that you are better than you really are. You must see yourself like you really are.

Scripture   A part of the Holy Writings—the Old Testament.
sacrifice   An offering or gift to God.

Decide what you are by the kind of faith God has given you.
⁴Each one of us has one body and that body has many parts.
These parts don't all do the same thing. ⁵In the same way, we are
many people, but in Christ we are all one body. We are the parts
of that body. And each part of that body belongs to all the other
parts. ⁶We all have different gifts. Each gift came because of the
grace (*kindness*) that God gave us. If a person has the gift of
prophecy,* then that person should use that gift with the faith he
has. ⁷If a person has the gift of serving, then that person should
serve. If a person has the gift of teaching, then that person should
teach. ⁸If a person has the gift of comforting other people, then
that person should comfort. If a person has the gift of giving to
help other people, then that person should give freely. If a person
has the gift of being a leader, then that person should work hard
when he leads. If a person has the gift of showing kindness to
other people, then that person should do that with joy.

⁹Your love must be real. Hate the things that are evil. Do only
the things that are good. ¹⁰Love each other in a way that you feel
close to each other like brothers and sisters. You should want to
give your brothers and sisters more honor than you want for
yourself. ¹¹Don't be lazy when you need to be working for the
Lord. Be spiritually excited about serving him. ¹²Be happy
because you have hope. Be patient when you have troubles. Pray
all the time. ¹³Share with God's people who need help. Look for
people that need help, and welcome those people into your
homes.

¹⁴Say only good things to those people who do bad things to
you. Say good things to them and don't curse them. ¹⁵When other
people are happy, you should be happy with them. And when
other people are sad, you should be sad with them. ¹⁶Live
together in peace with each other. Don't be proud. Be willing to
be friends with people who are not important to other people.
Don't be conceited.

¹⁷If someone does wrong to you, don't pay him back by doing
wrong to him. Try to do the things that all people think are good.
¹⁸Do the best you can to live in peace with all people. ¹⁹My
friends, don't try to punish people when they do wrong to you.
Wait for God to punish them with his anger. It is written: "I am

gift of prophecy The ability that God gives a person to speak for him.

the One who punishes; I will pay people back,"* says the Lord. [20]But you should do this: "If your enemy is hungry, feed him; if your enemy is thirsty, give him something to drink. Doing this will be like pouring burning coals on his head (*you will make him ashamed*)."* [21]Don't let evil defeat you. You should defeat evil by doing good.

Christians Should Obey the Law

13 All of you must obey the government rulers. Every person who rules was given the power to rule by God. And all the people that rule now were given that power by God. [2]So the person who is against the government is really against something God has commanded. People who are against the government cause themselves to be punished. [3]People who do right don't have to fear the rulers. But those people who do wrong must fear the rulers. Do you want to be free from fearing the rulers? Then you should do right. If you do right, then the rulers will praise you. [4]A ruler is God's servant to help you. But if you do wrong, then be afraid. The ruler has the power to punish and he will use that power. He is God's servant to punish people who do wrong. [5]So you must obey the government. You should obey because you might be punished if you don't obey. And you should also obey because you know that is the right thing to do.

[6]And this is why you pay taxes too. Those rulers are working for God and give all their time to the work of ruling. [7]Give all people what you owe them. If you owe them any kind of tax, then pay it. Show respect to the people you should respect. And show honor to the people you should honor.

Love Other People

[8]Don't owe people anything. But you will always owe love to each other. The person who loves other people has obeyed all the law.* [9]Why is this true? Because the law says, "Don't do the sin of adultery*; don't kill; don't steal; don't want things that are wrong."* All these commandments and all other commandments

"I...back"   Quotation from Deuteronomy 32:35.
"If...ashamed"   Quotation from Proverbs 25:21-22.
law   God's law. The law of Moses is a good example of this law.
adultery   Breaking a marriage promise by doing sexual sin.
"Don't...wrong"   Quotation from Exodus 20:13-15,17— (four of the Ten Commandments).

are really only one rule: "Love other people the same as you love yourself."* ¹⁰Love doesn't hurt other people. So loving is the same as obeying all the law.*

¹¹I say these things because you know that we live in an important time. Yes, it is now time for you to wake up from your sleep. Our salvation is nearer now than when we first believed. ¹²The "night"* is almost finished. The "day"* is almost here. So we should stop doing things that belong to darkness (*sin*). We should prepare ourselves with the things that belong to light (*good*). ¹³Let us live in a right way, like people who belong to the day. We should not have wild and wasteful parties. We should not be drunk. We should not do sexual sins or sin in any way with our bodies. We should not cause arguments and trouble or be jealous. ¹⁴But clothe yourselves with the Lord Jesus Christ. Don't think about how to satisfy your sinful self and the bad things you want to do.

Don't Criticize Other People

14 Don't refuse to accept into your group a person who is weak in faith. And don't argue with that person about his different ideas. ²One person believes that he can eat any kind of food* he wants. But if another person's faith is weak, then that person believes he can eat only vegetables. ³The person who knows that he can eat any kind of food must not feel that he is better than the person who eats only vegetables. And the person who eats only vegetables must not decide that the person who eats all foods is wrong. God has accepted that person who eats all foods. ⁴You cannot judge another person's servant. His own master decides if he is doing right or wrong. And the Lord's servant will be right because the Lord is able to make him right.

⁵One person might believe that one day is more important than another. And another person might believe that every day is the same. Each person should be sure about his own beliefs in his

---

"**Love...yourself**" Quotation from Leviticus 19:18.
law God's law. The law of Moses is a good example of this law.
"**night**" This is used as a symbol of the sinful world we live in. This world will soon end.
"**day**" This is used as a symbol of the good time that is coming, when we will be with God.
any...food The Jewish law said there were some foods Jews should not eat. When Jews became Christians, some of them did not understand they could now eat all foods.

own mind. ⁶The person who thinks one day is more important than other days is doing that for the Lord. And the person who eats all kinds of food is doing that for the Lord. Yes, he gives thanks to God *for that food*. And the person who refuses to eat some foods does that for the Lord. And he gives thanks to God. ⁷Yes, *we all live for the Lord*. We don't live or die for ourselves. ⁸If we live, we are living for the Lord. And if we die, we are dying for the Lord. So living or dying, we belong to the Lord.

⁹That is why Christ died and rose from death to live again. Christ did this so that he could be Lord (*ruler*) over people that have died and people that are living. ¹⁰So why do you judge your brother *in Christ*? And why do you think that you are better than your brother? We will all stand before God, and he will judge us all. ¹¹Yes, it is written in the Scriptures*:

"Every person will bow before me;
  every person will say that I am God.
As surely as I live, these things will happen,
  says the Lord (*God*)."   *Isaiah 45:23*

¹²So each of us will have to explain to God about his life.

Don't Cause Other People to Sin

¹³So we should stop judging each other. We must decide not to do anything that will make a brother *or sister* weak or fall into sin. ¹⁴I am in the Lord Jesus. And I know that there is no food that is wrong to eat. But if a person believes that something is wrong, then that thing is wrong for him. ¹⁵If you hurt your brother's faith because of something you eat, then you are not really doing what love would lead you to do. Don't destroy a person's faith by eating something *that he thinks is wrong*. Christ died for that person. ¹⁶Don't allow something that you think is good to become something that other people say is evil. ¹⁷In the kingdom of God, eating and drinking are not important. In the kingdom of God, the important things are living right with God, peace, and joy in the Holy Spirit.* ¹⁸Any person who serves

---

Scriptures Holy Writings—the Old Testament.
Holy Spirit Also called the Spirit of God, the Spirit of Christ, and the Comforter. He is joined
  with God and Christ. He does the work of God among people in the world.

Christ by living this way is pleasing God. And that person will be accepted by other people.

¹⁹So let us try as hard as we can to do the things that make peace. And let us try to do the things that will help each other. ²⁰Don't let the eating of food destroy the work of God. All food is right to eat. But it is wrong for a person to eat something that makes another person fall into sin. ²¹It is better not to eat meat or drink wine if that makes your brother *or sister* fall into sin. It is better not to do anything that will make your brother *or sister* sin.

²²Your beliefs about these things should be kept secret between yourself and God. A person is blessed (*happy*) if he can do the things he thinks are right without feeling guilty. ²³But if a person eats something without being sure that it is right, then that person makes himself wrong. Why? Because that person did not believe that it was right. And if a person does anything without believing that it is right, then it is sin.

15 We are strong with faith. So we should help the people who are weak. We should help them with their weaknesses. We should not try to please ourselves. ²Each of us should please other people. We should do this to help them. We should try to help them be stronger in faith. ³Even Christ did not live trying to please himself. It was like the Scriptures* said *about him*: "Those people who insulted you have also insulted me."* ⁴Everything that was written in the past was written to teach us. Those things were written so that we could have hope. That hope comes from the patience and strength that the Scriptures give us. ⁵Patience and strength come from God. And I pray that God will help you all agree together the way Christ Jesus wants. ⁶Then you will all be joined together. And all together you will give glory (*praise*) to God the Father of our Lord Jesus Christ. ⁷Christ accepted you. So you should accept each other. This will bring glory to God. ⁸I tell you that Christ became a servant of the Jews to show that what God promises is true. Christ did this to prove that God will do the things he promised the Jewish fathers.

Scriptures Holy Writings—the Old Testament.
"Those...me" Quotation from Psalm 69:9.

⁹Christ also did this so that the non-Jews could give glory to God for the mercy he gives to them. It is written *in the Scriptures**:

> "So I will give thanks to you among the non-Jewish people,
> I will sing praise to your name." *Psalm 18:49*

¹⁰The Scripture* also says,

> "You non-Jews should be happy
> together with God's people." *Deuteronomy 32:43*

¹¹The Scripture* also says,

> "Praise the Lord, all you non-Jews;
> all people should praise the Lord." *Psalm 117:1*

¹²And Isaiah says,

> "A person will come from Jesse's family.*
> That person will come to rule over the non-Jews;
> and the non-Jews will have hope
> because of that person." *Isaiah 11:10*

¹³I pray that the God who gives hope will fill you with much joy and peace while you trust in him. Then you will be full of hope and it will flow out of you by the power of the Holy Spirit.*

Paul Talks About This Letter and About His Work

¹⁴My brothers *and sisters*, I am sure that you are full of good. I know that you have all the knowledge you need and that you are able to teach each other. ¹⁵But I have written to you very openly about some things that I wanted you to remember. I did this because God showed his grace (*kindness*) to me ¹⁶by making me a minister of Christ Jesus. God made me a minister to help the non-Jewish people. I served God by teaching his Good News.* I did this so that the non-Jewish people could be an offering that God would accept. Those people are made holy* for God by the Holy Spirit.*

Scripture(s)   Holy Writings—the Old Testament.
Jesse's family   Jesse was the father of David, king of Israel. Jesus was from their family.
Holy Spirit   Also called the Spirit of God, the Spirit of Christ, and the Comforter. He is joined with God and Christ. He does the work of God among people in the world.
Good News   The news that God has made a way through Christ for people to have their sins forgiven and live with God. When people accept this truth, God accepts them.
holy   A holy person is pure, belongs only to God and does only the things that God wants.

¹⁷So I am proud of the things I have done for God in Christ Jesus. ¹⁸I will not talk about anything I did myself. I will talk only about the things that Christ has done with me in leading the non-Jewish people to obey God. They have obeyed God because of the things I have said and done. ¹⁹And they obeyed God because of the power of the miracles* and the great things they saw, and because of the power of the Holy Spirit.* I preached the Good News* from Jerusalem all the way around to Illyricum. And so I have finished that part of my work. ²⁰I always want to preach the Good News in places where people have never heard of Christ. I do this because I don't want to build on the work that another person has already started. ²¹But it is written *in the Scriptures**:

> "Those people who were not told
> > about him (*the Christ*) will see,
> and those people who have not heard about him
> > will understand."
> > > > > > > *Isaiah 52:15*

Paul's Plan to Visit Rome

²²That is why many times I was stopped from coming to you.

²³Now I have finished my work in these areas here. And for many years I have wanted to visit you. ²⁴So I will visit you when I go to Spain. Yes, I hope to visit you while I am traveling to Spain, and I will stay and enjoy being with you. Then you can help me on my trip. ²⁵Now I am going to Jerusalem to help God's people. ²⁶Some of God's people in Jerusalem are poor. *The believers in* Macedonia and Achaia were happy to give. They gave to help those people in Jerusalem. ²⁷*The believers in* Macedonia and Achaia were happy to do this. And really they should help those believers in Jerusalem. They should help because they are non-Jews and have shared in the Jews' spiritual blessings. So they should use the things they have to help the Jews. They owe this to the Jews. ²⁸I must be sure that the poor people in Jerusalem get all

---

miracles Miracles are powerful works or great things done by the power of God.
Holy Spirit Also called the Spirit of God, the Spirit of Christ, and the Comforter. He is joined with God and Christ. He does the work of God among people in the world.
Good News The news that God has made a way through Christ for people to have their sins forgiven and live with God. When people accept this truth, God accepts them.
Scriptures Holy Writings—the Old Testament.

this money that has been given for them. After I finish this work, then I will leave for Spain. While I am traveling to Spain, I will stop and visit you. ²⁹I know that when I visit you, I will bring you Christ's full blessing.

³⁰Brothers *and sisters*, I beg you to help me in my work by praying for me to God. Do this because of our Lord Jesus and the love that the Holy Spirit* gives us. ³¹Pray that I will be saved from the non-believers in Judea. And pray that this help I bring to Jerusalem will please God's people there. ³²Then, if God wants me to, I will come to you. I will come with joy, and together you and I will have a time of rest. ³³The God that gives peace be with you all. Amen.

Paul Has Things to Say to Many Christians in Rome

16 I want you to know that you can trust our sister *in Christ*, Phoebe. She is a helper* in the church in Cenchreae. ²I ask you to accept her in the Lord. Accept her the way God's people should. Help her with anything she needs from you. She has helped me very much, and many other people too.

³Say hello to Priscilla and Aquila. They work together with me in Christ Jesus. ⁴They risked their own lives to save my life. I am thankful to them, and all the non-Jewish churches are thankful to them. ⁵Also, say hello to the church that meets at their house.

Say hello to my dear friend Epaenetus. He was the first person to follow Christ in Asia.* ⁶Say hello to Mary. She worked very hard for you. ⁷Say hello to Andronicus and Junias. They are my relatives and they were in prison with me. They are some of God's most important workers.* They were believers in Christ before I was. ⁸Say hello to Ampliatus, my dear friend in the Lord. ⁹Say hello to Urbanus. He is a worker together with me for Christ. And say hello to my dear friend Stachys. ¹⁰Say hello to Apelles. He was tested and proved that he truly loves Christ. Say hello to all those people who are in the family of Aristobulus. ¹¹Say hello

---

Holy Spirit Also called the Spirit of God, the Spirit of Christ, and the Comforter. He is joined with God and Christ. He does the work of God among people in the world.

helper Literally, "deacon." This might mean the same as one of the special women helpers in Timothy 3:11.

Asia The western part of Asia Minor.

most important workers Literally, "important among (or to) the apostles."

to Herodion, my relative. Say hello to all the people in the family of Narcissus who belong to the Lord. ¹²Say hello to Tryphaena and Tryphosa. Those women work very hard for the Lord. Say hello to my dear friend Persis. She has also worked very hard for the Lord. ¹³Say hello to Rufus. He is a special person in the Lord. Say hello to his mother. She has been a mother to me also. ¹⁴Say hello to Asyncritus, Phlegon, Hermes, Patrobas, Hermas, and all the brothers *in Christ* that are with them. ¹⁵Say hello to Philologus, Julia, Nereus and his sister. Say hello to Olympas and all the saints (*believers*) with them. ¹⁶When you see each other, say hello with a holy kiss. All of Christ's churches (*groups of believers*) say hello to you.

¹⁷Brothers *and sisters*, I ask you to be very careful of those people who cause people to be against each other. Be very careful of those people who upset other people's faith. Those people are against the true teaching you learned. Stay away from those people. ¹⁸People like that are not serving our Lord Christ. They are only doing things to please themselves. They use fancy talk and say nice things to fool the minds of people who don't know about evil. ¹⁹All the believers have heard that you obey. So I am very happy because of you. But I want you to be wise about the things that are good. And I want you to know nothing about things that are evil.

²⁰The God that brings peace will soon defeat Satan (*the devil*) and give you power over him.

The grace (*kindness*) of our Lord Jesus be with you.

²¹Timothy, a worker together with me, says hello to you. Also Lucius, Jason, and Sosipater (these are my relatives) say hello to you.

²²I am Tertius, and I am writing these things that Paul says. I say hello to you in the Lord.

²³Gaius is letting me and the whole church here use his home. He also says hello to you. Erastus and our brother Quartus say hello to you. Erastus is the city treasurer here. ²⁴*

Verse 24 Some Greek copies add verse 24: "The grace (*kindness*) of our Lord Jesus Christ be with all of you. Amen."

²⁵Glory to God. God is the One who can make you strong in faith. God can use the Good News* that I teach to make you strong. That is the Good News about Jesus Christ that I tell people. That Good News is the secret truth that God has made known. That secret truth was hidden since the beginning. ²⁶But that secret truth has now been shown to us. And that truth has been made known to all people. It has been made known by the things the prophets* wrote. This is what God commanded. And that secret truth has been made known to all people, so that they can believe and obey God. God lives forever. ²⁷Glory forever to the only wise God through Jesus Christ. Amen.

Good News The news that God has made a way through Christ for people to have their sins forgiven and live with God. When people accept this truth, God accepts them.
prophets People who spoke for God. Their writings are part of the Old Testament.

1 Corinthians

1 From Paul. I was called (*chosen*) to be an apostle* of Christ Jesus. I was called because that is what God wanted. Our brother Sosthenes also sends greetings.

²To the church of God in Corinth, to those people who have been made holy* in Christ Jesus. You were called to be God's holy people. You were called with all the people everywhere who trust in the name of the Lord Jesus Christ—their Lord and ours:

³Grace (*kindness*) and peace to you from God our Father and the Lord Jesus Christ.

Paul Gives Thanks to God

⁴I always thank my God for you because of the grace (*kindness*) that God has given you through Christ Jesus. ⁵In Jesus you have been blessed in every way. You have been blessed in all your speaking and all your knowledge. ⁶The truth about Christ has been proved in you. ⁷So you have every spiritual gift while you wait for our Lord Jesus Christ to come again. ⁸Jesus will keep you strong always until the end. He will keep you strong, so that there will be no wrong in you on the day when our Lord Jesus Christ comes again. ⁹God is faithful. He is the One who has called you to share life with his Son, Jesus Christ our Lord.

Problems in the Church at Corinth

¹⁰I beg you brothers *and sisters* in the name of our Lord Jesus Christ. I beg that all of you agree with each other so that there will be no divisions among you. I beg that you be completely joined together by having the same kind of thinking and the same purpose. ¹¹My brothers *and sisters*, some people from Chloe's

apostle Person Jesus chose to be a special helper for telling the Good News to the world.
holy A holy person is pure, belongs only to God, and does only the things that God wants.

424

family told me about you. I heard that there are arguments among you. ¹²This is what I mean: One of you says, "I follow Paul"; another person says, "I follow Apollos"; another person says, "I follow Cephas (*Peter*)"; and another person says, "I follow Christ." ¹³Christ cannot be divided *into different groups*! Did Paul die on the cross for you? No! Were you baptized* in the name of Paul? No! ¹⁴I am thankful that I did not baptize any of you except Crispus and Gaius. ¹⁵I am thankful, because now no one can say that you people were baptized in my name. ¹⁶(I also baptized the family of Stephanas. But I don't remember that I myself baptized any others.) ¹⁷Christ did not give me the work of baptizing people. Christ gave me the work of telling the Good News.* But Christ sent me to tell the Good News without using words of worldly wisdom. If I used worldly wisdom to tell the Good News, then the cross* of Christ would lose its power.

Christ Is the Power and the Wisdom of God

¹⁸The teaching about the cross seems foolish to those people who are lost. But to us who are being saved it is the power of God. ¹⁹It is written *in the Scriptures*:

"I will destroy the wisdom of the
     wise people.
I will make the intelligence of the intelligent
     people worth nothing."   *Isaiah 29:14*

²⁰Where is the wise person? Where is the educated person? Where is the philosopher* of this time? God has made the wisdom of the world foolish. ²¹This is what God with his wisdom wanted: The world did not know God through the world's own wisdom. So God used the message* that sounds foolish to save the people who believe it. ²²The Jews ask for miracles* as proofs. The Greeks want wisdom. ²³But we preach this: Christ was killed

---

baptized   A Greek word meaning to be immersed, dipped, or buried briefly under water.
Good News, message   The news that God has made a way through Christ for people to have their sins forgiven and live with God. When people accept this truth, God accepts them.
cross   Paul uses the cross as a picture of the gospel, the story of Christ's death and rising from death to pay for men's sins. The cross or Christ's death was God's way to save men.
Scriptures   A part of the Holy Writings—the Old Testament.
philosopher   A person who studies and talks about his own ideas and the ideas of other people.
miracles   Miracles are powerful works or great things done by the power of God.

on a cross. This is a big problem to the Jews. And it seems foolish to the non-Jews. [24]But Christ is the power of God and the wisdom of God to those people that God has called—Jews and Greeks (*non-Jews*). [25]Even the foolishness of God is wiser than men. Even the weakness of God is stronger than men.

[26]Brothers *and sisters*, God called (*chose*) you. Think about that! And not many of you were wise in the way the world judges wisdom. Not many of you had great influence. Not many of you came from important families. [27]But God chose the foolish things of the world to give shame to the wise people. God chose the weak things of the world to give shame to the strong people. [28]And God chose what the world thinks is not important. He chose what the world hates and thinks is nothing. God chose these to destroy what the world thinks is important. [29]God did this so that no man can boast before him. [30]It is God that has made you part of Christ Jesus. Christ has become wisdom for us from God. Christ is the reason we are holy* and right with God, and have freedom. [31]So, like the Scripture* says, "If a person boasts, that person should boast only in the Lord."

The Message About Christ on the Cross

2 Dear brothers *and sisters*, when I came to you I told you the truth of God. But I did not use fancy words or great wisdom. [2]I decided that while I was with you I would forget about everything except Jesus Christ and his death on the cross. [3]When I came to you I was weak and I shook with fear. [4]My teaching and my speaking were not with wise words that persuade people. But the proof of my teaching was the power that the Spirit* gives. [5]I did this so that your faith would be in God's power, not in the wisdom of a man.

God's Wisdom

[6]We teach wisdom to people who are mature. But this wisdom we teach is not from this world. It is not the wisdom of the rulers

---

holy   A holy person is pure, belongs only to God, and does only the things that God wants.
Scripture   A part of the Holy Writings—the Old Testament.
Spirit   The Holy Spirit. Also called the Spirit of God, the Spirit of Christ, and the Comforter. He is joined with God and Christ. He does the work of God among people in the world.

of this world. Those rulers are losing their power. ⁷But we speak God's secret wisdom. This wisdom has been hidden *from people*. God planned this wisdom for our glory. He planned it before the world began. ⁸None of the rulers of this world understood this wisdom. If they had understood it, then they would not have killed the Lord of glory on a cross. ⁹But like it is written *in the Scriptures**:

> "No eye has seen,
> no ear has heard,
> no person has imagined,
> what God has prepared for those people
> who love him."

Isaiah 64:4

¹⁰But God has shown us these things through the Spirit.*

The Spirit* knows all things. The Spirit even knows the deep secrets of God. ¹¹It is like this: No person knows the thoughts that another person has. Only that person's spirit that lives inside him knows those thoughts. It is the same with God. No one knows the thoughts of God. Only the Spirit of God knows those thoughts. ¹²We did not receive the spirit of the world. But we received the Spirit* that is from God. We received this Spirit so that we can know the things that God has given us. ¹³When we speak these things we don't use words taught to us by the wisdom that men have. We use words taught to us by the Spirit. We use spiritual words to explain spiritual things. ¹⁴A person who is not spiritual does not accept the things that come from the Spirit of God. That person thinks that those things are foolish. That person cannot understand the things of the Spirit, because those things can only be judged spiritually. ¹⁵But the spiritual person is able to make judgments about all things. Other people cannot judge that person. *The Scripture* says*:

> ¹⁶"Who knows the mind of the Lord?
> Who can tell the Lord what to do?"

Isaiah 40:13

But we have the mind of Christ.

Scripture(s)   Holy Writings—the Old Testament.
Spirit   The Holy Spirit. Also called the Spirit of God, the Spirit of Christ, and the Comforter. He is joined with God and Christ. He does the work of God among people in the world.

Following Men Is Wrong

3 Brothers *and sisters*, in the past, I could not talk to you like I talk to spiritual people. I had to talk to you like worldly people—like babies in Christ. ²The teaching I gave you was like milk, not solid food. I did this because you were not ready for solid food. And even now you are not ready for solid food. ³You are still not spiritual people. You have jealousy and arguing among you. This shows that you are not spiritual. You are acting the same as people of the world. ⁴One of you says, "I follow Paul," and another person says, "I follow Apollos." When you say things like that, you are acting like *worldly* people.

⁵Is Apollos important? No! Is Paul important? No! We are only servants of God who helped you believe. Each one of us did the work God gave us to do. ⁶I planted the seed (*teaching*) and Apollos watered it. But God is the One who made the seed grow. ⁷So the person who plants is not important, and the person who waters is not important. Only God is important, because he is the One who makes things grow. ⁸The person who plants and the person who waters have the same purpose. And each person will be rewarded for his own work. ⁹We are workers together for God. And you are like a farm that belongs to God.

And you are a house that belongs to God. ¹⁰Like an expert builder I built the foundation* of that house. I used the gift that God gave me to do this. Other people are building on that foundation. But each person should be careful how he builds. ¹¹The foundation has already been built. No person can build any other foundation. The foundation that has already been built is Jesus Christ. ¹²A person can build on that foundation, using gold, silver, jewels, wood, grass, or straw. ¹³But the work that each person does will be clearly seen, because the Day* will make it plain. That Day will appear with fire, and the fire will test every man's work. ¹⁴If the building that a person puts on the foundation still stands, then that person will get his reward. ¹⁵But if that person's building is burned up, then he will suffer loss. The person will be saved, but it will be like he escaped from a fire.

---

foundation The bottom part or first part of a house that the rest of the house is built on.
Day The day Christ will come to judge all people and take his people to live with him.

¹⁶You should know that you yourselves are God's temple.* God's Spirit* lives in you. ¹⁷If any person destroys God's temple, then God will destroy that person. Why? Because God's temple is holy.* You yourselves are God's temple.

¹⁸Don't fool yourselves. If any person among you thinks that he is wise in this world, then he should become a fool. Then that person can become truly wise. ¹⁹Why? Because the wisdom of this world is foolishness to God. It is written *in the Scriptures,** "He (*God*) catches the wise (*smart*) people when they use their sneaky ways."* ²⁰It is also written *in the Scriptures*, "The Lord knows the thoughts of the wise people. He knows that their thoughts are worth nothing."* ²¹So you should not boast about men. All things are yours: ²²Paul, Apollos, and Cephas (*Peter*); the world, life, death, the present and the future—all these things are yours. ²³And you belong to Christ, and Christ belongs to God.

Apostles of Christ

4 This is what people should think about us: We are servants of Christ. We are the people that God has trusted with his secret truths. ²A person who is trusted with something must show that he is worthy of that trust. ³I don't care if I am judged by you. And I don't care if I am judged by any human court. I don't even judge myself. ⁴I don't know of any wrong that I have done. But that does not make me innocent (*without guilt*). The Lord is the One who judges me. ⁵So don't judge before the right time; wait until the Lord comes. He will shine light on the things that are hidden in darkness. He will make known the secret purposes of people's hearts. Then God will give every person the praise he should get.

⁶Brothers *and sisters*, I have used Apollos and myself as examples for you in these things. I did this so that you could learn from us the meaning of "Follow only what is written *in the Scriptures.*" Then you will not be proud of one man and hate

temple God's house—the place where God's people worship and serve him.
Spirit The Holy Spirit. Also called the Spirit of God, the Spirit of Christ, and the Comforter. He is joined with God and Christ. He does the work of God among people in the world.
holy A holy person is pure, belongs only to God, and does only the things that God wants.
Scriptures Holy Writings—the Old Testament.
"He...ways" Quotation from Job 5:13.
"The Lord...nothing" Quotation from Psalm 94:11.

another. ⁷Who says that you are better than other people? Everything you have was given to you. So, if everything you have was given to you, then why do you boast like you got those things by your own power?

⁸*You think* you have everything you need. *You think* you are rich. *You think* you have become kings without us. I wish you really were kings! Then we could be kings together with you. ⁹But it seems to me that God has given me and the other apostles* the last place. We are like men condemned to die *with all the people watching*. We are like a show for the whole world to see—angels and people. ¹⁰We are fools for Christ. But *you think* you are very wise in Christ. We are weak, but *you think* you are strong. People give you honor, but they don't honor us. ¹¹Even now we still don't have *enough* to eat or drink, and we don't have *enough* clothes. We often get beatings. We have no homes. ¹²We work hard with our own hands *to feed ourselves*. People curse us, but we speak a blessing for them. People persecute* us, and we accept it. ¹³People say bad things about us, but we say good things to them. At this time people still treat us like we are the garbage of the earth—the dirt of the world.

¹⁴I am not trying to make you feel ashamed. But I am writing these things to give you a warning like you were my own dear children. ¹⁵You may have 10,000 teachers in Christ, but you don't have many fathers. Through the gospel* I became your father in Christ Jesus. ¹⁶So I beg you to please be like me. ¹⁷That is why I am sending Timothy to you. He is my son in the Lord. I love Timothy and he is faithful. He will help you remember the way I live in Christ Jesus. That way of life is what I teach in all the churches everywhere.

¹⁸Some of you have become boasters. You boast, thinking that I will not come to you again. ¹⁹But I will come to you very soon. I will come if the Lord wants me to. Then I will see what these boasters can do, not what they can say. ²⁰I will want to see this because the kingdom of God is not talk but power. ²¹Which do you want:

apostles Men that Jesus chose to be his special helpers for telling his Good News to the world.
persecute To hurt other people and cause them to suffer bad things.
gospel The Good News that God has made a way through Christ for people to have their sins forgiven and live with God. When people accept this truth, God accepts them.

that I come to you with punishment, or
that I come with love and gentleness?

Immorality in the Church

5 People are really saying that there is sexual sin among you. And it is such a bad kind of sexual sin that it does not happen even among those people who don't know God. People say that a man there has his father's wife. ²And still you are proud of yourselves! You should have been filled with sadness. And the man who did that sin should be put out of your group. ³My body is not there with you, but I am with you in spirit. And I have already judged the man who did that sin. I judged him the same as I would if I were really there. ⁴Come together in the name of our Lord Jesus. I will be with you in spirit, and you will have the power of our Lord Jesus with you. ⁵Then give this man to Satan (*the devil*), so that his sinful self* will be destroyed. Then his spirit can be saved on the day of the Lord.

⁶Your proud boasting is not good. You know the saying, "Just a little yeast* makes the whole batch of dough rise." ⁷So take out all the old yeast so that you will be a new batch of dough. And you really are new dough without yeast. Why? Because Christ, our Passover lamb,* was killed *to cleanse us*. ⁸So let us continue to eat our feast, but not with *the bread that has* the old yeast. That old yeast is the yeast of sin and wrongdoing. But let us eat the bread that has no yeast. This is the bread of goodness and truth.

⁹I wrote to you in my letter that you should not associate with people that sin sexually. ¹⁰But I did not mean that you should not associate with the sinful people of this world. Those people of the world do sin sexually, or they are selfish and they cheat each other, or they worship idols (*false gods*). But to get away from those people you would have to leave this world. ¹¹I am writing to tell you that the person you must not associate with is this: any person who calls himself a brother in Christ but who sins

---

sinful self   Literally, "flesh." This could also mean his body.
yeast   Used as a symbol of evil or bad influence.
Passover lamb   Jesus was a sacrifice for his people, like a lamb killed for the Passover Feast.

sexually, or is selfish, or worships idols, or talks bad to people, or gets drunk, or cheats people. Don't even eat with a person like that.

¹²⁻¹³It is not my business to judge those people who are not part of the church (*group of believers*). God will judge those people. But you must judge the people who are part of the church. The Scripture* says, "Take the evil person out of your group."*

Judging Problems Between Christians

6 When one of you has something against another person, why do you go to *the judges in the law courts*? Those people are not right with God. So why do you let those people decide who is right? You should be ashamed! Why don't you let God's people decide who is right? ²Surely you know that God's people will judge the world. So if you will judge the world, then surely you are able to judge small things *like this*. ³You know that, in the future, we will judge angels. So surely we can judge things in this life. ⁴So if you have those disagreements that must be judged, why do you take those things to people who are not part of the church? Those people mean nothing to the church. ⁵I say this to shame you. Surely there is some person in your group wise enough to judge a complaint between two brothers (*believers*)! ⁶But now one brother goes to court against another brother. You let men who are not believers judge their case!

⁷The lawsuits that you have against each other show that you are already defeated. It would be better for you to let someone do wrong against you! It would be better for you to let someone cheat you! ⁸But you yourselves do wrong and cheat! And you do this to your own brothers *in Christ*!

⁹⁻¹⁰Surely you know that the people who do wrong will not get God's kingdom. Don't be fooled. These people will not get God's kingdom: people who sin sexually, people who worship idols,* people who commit adultery,* men who let other men use them for sex or who have sex with other men, people who steal, people

---

Scripture A part of the Holy Writings—the Old Testament.
"Take...group" Quotation from Deuteronomy 17:7; 19:19; 22:21,24; 24:7.
idols The false gods that the non-Jewish people worshiped.
adultery Breaking a marriage promise by doing sexual sin.

who are selfish, people who get drunk, people who say bad things to other people, and people who cheat. ¹¹In the past, some of you were like that. But you were washed clean, you were made holy,* and you were made right with God in the name of the Lord Jesus Christ and by the Spirit of our God.

Use Your Bodies for God's Glory

¹²"All things are allowed for me." But not all things are good. "All things are allowed for me." But I will not let anything be my master. ¹³"Food is for the stomach, and the stomach for food." Yes. But God will destroy them both. The body is not for sexual sin. The body is for the Lord, and the Lord is for the body. ¹⁴By God's power, God raised the Lord *Jesus* from death. God will also raise us from death. ¹⁵Surely you know that your bodies are parts of Christ himself. So I must never take the parts of Christ and join those parts to a prostitute*! ¹⁶It is written *in the Scriptures*,* "The two will become one body."* So you should know that a person who *sexually* joins himself with a prostitute becomes one with her in body. ¹⁷But the person who joins himself with the Lord is one with the Lord in spirit.

¹⁸So run away from sexual sin. Every other sin that a man does is outside his body. But the person who sins sexually sins against his own body. ¹⁹You should know that your body is a temple* for the Holy Spirit.* The Holy Spirit is in you. You have received the Holy Spirit from God. You don't own yourselves. ²⁰You were bought *by God* at a price. So honor God with your bodies.

About Marriage

7 Now *I will discuss* the things you wrote to me about. It is good for a man not to marry. ²But sexual sin is a danger. So each man should have his own wife. And each woman should have her own husband. ³The husband should give his wife all that

holy   A holy person is pure, belongs only to God, and does only the things that God wants.
prostitute   A woman who is paid by men who use her for sexual sin.
Scriptures   Holy Writings—the Old Testament.
"The two...body"   Quotation from Genesis 2:24.
temple   God's house—the place where God's people worship and serve him.
Holy Spirit   Also called the Spirit of God, the Spirit of Christ, and the Comforter. He is joined with God and Christ. He does the work of God among people in the world.

she should have as his wife. And the wife should give her husband all that he should have as her husband. ⁴The wife does not have power over her own body. Her husband has the power over her body. And the husband does not have power over his own body. His wife has the power over his body. ⁵Don't refuse to give your bodies to each other. But you might both agree to stay away *from sex* for a time. You might do this so that you can give your time to prayer. Then come together again. This is so that Satan (*the devil*) cannot tempt you in your weakness. ⁶I say this to give you permission *to be separated for a time*. It is not a command. ⁷I wish all people were like me. But each person has his own gift from God. One person has one gift, another person has another gift.

⁸Now to the people who are not married and to the widows* I say this: It is good for them to stay single like me. ⁹But if they cannot control their bodies, then they should marry. It is better to marry than to burn *with sexual desire*.

¹⁰Now I give this command to the married people. (The command is not from me; it is from the Lord.) A wife must not leave her husband. ¹¹But if a wife leaves her husband she must not marry again. Or she should go back together with her husband. Also the husband must not divorce his wife.

¹²To all the other people I say this (I am saying these things, not the Lord). A brother *in Christ* might have a wife who is not a believer. If she will live with him, then he must not divorce her. ¹³And a woman might have a husband who is not a believer. If he will live with her, then she must not divorce him. ¹⁴The husband who is not a believer is made holy through his *believing* wife. And the wife who is not a believer is made holy through her *believing* husband. If this were not true, then your children would not be clean. But now your children are holy.

¹⁵But if the person who is not a believer decides to leave, let that person leave. When this happens, the brother or sister *in Christ* is free. God called us to a life of peace. ¹⁶Wives, maybe you will save your husband, and husbands, maybe you will save your wife. You don't know now what will happen later.

---

widows   A widow is a woman whose husband has died.

Live as God Called You

[17]But each person should continue to live the way God has given him to live—the way you were when God called you. This is a rule I make in all the churches. [18]If a man was already circumcised* when he was called, then he should not change his circumcision.* If a man was without circumcision when he was called, then he should not be circumcised. [19]It is not important if a person is circumcised or not circumcised. The important thing is obeying God's commands. [20]Each person should stay the way he was when God called him. [21]If you were a slave when God called you, don't let that bother you. But if you can be free, then become free. [22]The person who was a slave when the Lord called him is free in the Lord. That person belongs to the Lord. In the same way, the person who was free when he was called is now Christ's slave. [23]You people were bought with a price. So don't become slaves of men. [24]Brothers *and sisters*, in your new life with God each one of you should continue the way you were when you were called.

Paul Answers Questions About Getting Married

[25]Now I write about people who are not married.* I have no command from the Lord about this. But I give my opinion. And I can be trusted, because the Lord has given me mercy. [26]This is a time of trouble. So I think that it is good for you to stay the way you are (*not married*). [27]If you have a wife, then don't try to become free from her. If you are not married, then don't try to find a wife. [28]But if you decide to marry, that is not a sin. And it is not a sin for a girl that has never married to get married. But those people who marry will have trouble in this life. I want you to be free from this trouble.

[29]Brothers *and sisters*, this is what I mean: We don't have much time left. So starting now, people who have wives should use their time *to serve the Lord* like they don't have wives. [30]People who

---

circumcised, circumcision To have the foreskin cut off. This was done to every Jewish baby boy. It was a physical mark of the agreement that God made with Abraham (Genesis 17:9-14).
people...not married Literally, "virgins."

are sad should live like they are not sad. People who are happy should live like they are not happy. People who buy things should live like they own nothing. [31]People who use the things of the world should live like those things are not important to them. You should live like this, because this world, the way it is now, will soon be gone.

[32]I want you to be free from worry. A man who is not married is busy with the Lord's work. He is trying to please the Lord. [33]But a man who is married is busy with things of the world. He is trying to please his wife. [34]He must think about two things—*pleasing his wife and pleasing the Lord*. A woman who is not married or a girl who has never married is busy with the Lord's work. She wants to give herself fully—body and soul—to the Lord. But a married woman is busy with things of the world. She is trying to please her husband. [35]I am saying these things to help you. I am not trying to limit you. But I want you to live in the right way. And I want you to give yourselves fully to the Lord without giving your time to other things.

[36]A man might think that he is not doing the right thing with his virgin* *daughter* if she is almost past the best age to marry. So he might think that marriage is necessary. He should do what he wants. He should let them marry. It is no sin. [37]But another man might be more sure in his mind. There may be no need for marriage, so that he is free to do what he wants. If this person has decided in his own heart to keep his virgin *unmarried*, then he is doing the right thing. [38]So the person who gives his virgin *daughter* in marriage does right. And the person who does not give his virgin *daughter* in marriage does better.*

[39]A woman must stay with her husband as long as he lives. But if the husband dies the woman is free to marry any man she wants. But she must marry in the Lord. [40]The woman is happier if

---

virgin A pure girl who is not married.

Verses 36-38 Another possible translation is: "[36]A person might think that he is not doing the right thing with his virgin (*the girl he is engaged to*). The girl might be almost past the best age to marry. So the man might feel that he should marry her. He should do what he wants. They should get married. It is no sin. [37]But another person might be more sure in his mind. There may be no need for marriage, so he is free to do what he wants. If this person has decided in his own heart to keep his virgin *unmarried*, then he is doing the right thing. [38]So the person who marries his virgin does right. And the person who does not marry does better."

she does not marry again. This is my opinion, and I believe that I have God's Spirit.*

About Food Offered to Idols

8 Now *I will write* about meat that has been sacrificed* to idols.* We know that "we all have knowledge." "Knowledge" puffs you up full of pride. But love makes *you help* others grow stronger. ²The person who thinks he knows something does not yet know anything like he should. ³But the person who loves God is known by God.

⁴So *this is what I say* about eating meat: We know that an idol* is really nothing in the world. And we know that there is only one God. ⁵It's really not important if there are things called gods, in heaven or on earth. (And there are many *things that people call* "gods" and "lords.") ⁶But for us there is only one God. He is our Father. All things came from him and we live for him. And there is only one Lord. He is Jesus Christ. All things were made through Jesus and we also have life through him.

⁷But not all people know this. Some people have had the habit of worshiping idols* until now. So now when those people eat meat, they still feel like it belongs to an idol. They are not sure that it is right to eat this meat. So when they eat it, they feel guilty. ⁸But food will not make us closer to God. Refusing to eat does not make us less *pleasing to God*. And eating does not make us better.

⁹But be careful with your freedom. Your freedom may make those people who are weak in faith fall into sin. ¹⁰You have understanding (*knowledge*), so you might be eating in an idol's* temple. A person who is weak in faith might see you eating there. This will encourage him to eat meat sacrificed* to idols, too. But he really thinks it is wrong. ¹¹So this weak brother is ruined (*destroyed*) because of your knowledge. And Christ died for this brother. ¹²When you sin against your brothers *and sisters in Christ* like this and you hurt them by causing them to do things they feel are wrong, then you are also sinning against Christ. ¹³So

Spirit The Holy Spirit. Also called the Spirit of God, the Spirit of Christ, and the Comforter. He is joined with God and Christ. He does the work of God among people in the world.
sacrificed Killed and offered as a gift to show worship.
idol(s), idol's The false gods made from wood or stone and worshiped by the non-Jewish people.

if the food I eat makes my brother fall into sin, then I will never eat meat again. I will stop eating meat so that I will not make my brother sin.

Paul Is Like the Other Apostles

9 I am a free man! I am an apostle*! I have seen Jesus our Lord. You people are *an example of* my work in the Lord. [2]Other people may not accept me as an apostle. But surely you accept me as an apostle. You people are proof that I am an apostle in the Lord.

[3]Some people want to judge me. So this is the answer I give them: [4]We have the right to eat and drink, don't we? [5]We have the right to bring a believing wife with us when we travel, don't we? The other apostles* and the Lord's brothers and Cephas all do this. [6]And are Barnabas and I the only ones who must work to earn our living? [7]No soldier ever serves in the army and pays his own salary. No person ever plants a garden of grapes without eating some of the grapes himself. No person takes care of a flock of sheep without drinking some of the milk himself.

[8]These things are not only what men think. The law *of Moses* says the same things. [9]It is written in the law of Moses: "When a work animal is being used to separate grain, don't cover its mouth *and stop it from eating the grain.*"* Was God thinking only about work animals? No. [10]He was really talking about us. Yes, that Scripture* was written for us. The person who plows and the person who separates the grain should hope (*expect*) to get some of the grain for their work. [11]We planted spiritual seed among you. So we should be able to harvest (*get*) some things for this life from you. Surely that is not asking too much. [12]Other men have this right to get things from you. So surely we have this right too. But we don't use this right. No, we endure everything ourselves so that we will not stop *anyone from obeying* the Good News* of Christ. [13]Surely you know that people who work at the temple* get their food from the temple. And people who serve at

apostle(s)   The men Jesus taught and chose to be his special helpers.
"When...grain"   Quotation from Deuteronomy 25:4.
Scripture   A part of the Holy Writings—the Old Testament.
Good News   The news that God has made a way through Christ for people to have their sins forgiven and live with God. When people accept this truth, God accepts them.
temple   The special building in Jerusalem where God commanded the Jews to worship him.

the altar* get part of what is offered at the altar. ¹⁴It is the same with people who preach the Good News.* The Lord has commanded that those people who preach the Good News should get their living from it.

¹⁵But I have not used any of these rights. And I am not trying to get these things. That is not my purpose for writing this to you. I would rather die than to have my reason for boasting taken away.

¹⁶But preaching the Good News* is no reason for me to boast. Preaching the Good News is my duty—something I must do. It will be bad for me if I don't preach the Good News. ¹⁷If I preach the Good News because it is my own choice, then I deserve a reward. But I have no choice. I must preach the Good News. I am only doing the duty that was given to me. ¹⁸So what reward do I get? This is my reward: that when I preach the Good News I can offer it freely. In this way I don't use the right *to be paid* that I have in *preaching* the Good News.

¹⁹I am free. I belong to no man. But I make myself a slave to all people. I do this to help save as many people as I can. ²⁰To the Jews I became like a Jew. I did this to help save the Jews. I myself am not ruled by the law.* But to people who are ruled by the law I became like a person who is ruled by the law. I did this to help save those people who are ruled by the law. ²¹To those who are without the law I became like a person that is without the law. I did this to help save those people who are without the law. (But really, I am not without God's law—I am ruled by Christ's law.) ²²To the people who are weak I became weak so that I could help save them. I have become all things to all people. I did this so that I could save people in any way possible. ²³I do all these things because of the Good News.* I do these things so that I can share in *the blessings of* the Good News.

²⁴You know that in a race all the runners run. But only one runner gets the prize. So run like that. Run to win! ²⁵All people who compete in the games use strict training. They do this so that they can win a crown (*reward*). But that crown is an earthly thing

---

altar Place where sacrifices or gifts are offered to God.
Good News The news that God has made a way through Christ for people to have their sins forgiven and live with God. When people accept this truth, God accepts them.
law Probably the laws God gave to Moses on Mount Sinai. (Read Exodus 19-20.)

that lasts only a short time. But our crown (*reward*) will continue forever. ²⁶So I run like a person who has a goal. I fight like a boxer who is hitting something—not just the air. ²⁷It is my own body that I hit. I make it my slave. I do this so that I myself will not be rejected (*thrown out by God*) after I preached to other people.

Don't Be Like the Jews

10 Brothers *and sisters*, I want you to know what happened to our ancestors *who followed Moses*. They were all under the cloud and they all walked through the sea. ²Those people were all baptized* into Moses in the cloud and in the sea. ³They all ate the same spiritual food. ⁴And they all drank the same spiritual drink. They drank from that spiritual rock that was with them. That rock was Christ. ⁵But God was not pleased with most of those people. They were killed (*destroyed*) in the desert.

⁶And these things that happened are examples for us. These examples should stop us from wanting evil things like those people did. ⁷Don't worship idols* like some of those people did. It is written *in the Scriptures**: "The people sat down to eat and drink. The people stood up to dance."* ⁸We should not do sexual sins like some of those people did. In one day 23,000 of them died *because of their sin*. ⁹We should not test the Lord like some of those people did. They were killed by snakes *because they tested the Lord*. ¹⁰And don't complain like some of those people did. Those people were killed by the angel that destroys.

¹¹The things that happened to those people are examples. And those things were written to be warnings for us. We live in a time when all those past histories have come to their end. ¹²So the person who thinks he is standing strong should be careful that he doesn't fall. ¹³The only temptations that you have are the same temptations that all people have. But you can trust God. He will not let you be tempted more than you can bear. But when you are

baptized   A Greek word meaning to be immersed, dipped, or buried briefly under water.
idols   The false gods made from wood or stone and worshiped by the non-Jewish people.
Scriptures   Holy Writings—the Old Testament.
"The...dance"   Quotation from Exodus 32:6.

tempted, God will also give you a way to escape that temptation. Then you will be able to endure it.

¹⁴So, my dear friends, stay away from worshiping idols.* ¹⁵I am speaking to you like you are intelligent people; judge for yourselves what I say. ¹⁶The cup of blessing* that we give thanks for is a sharing in the blood (*death*) of Christ, isn't it? And the bread that we break is a sharing in the body of Christ, isn't it? ¹⁷There is one loaf of bread. And we are many people. But we all share from that one loaf. So we are really one body.

¹⁸Think about the people of Israel*: Those people who eat the sacrifices* share in the altar, don't they? ¹⁹I don't mean that the food sacrificed to an idol* is something important. And I don't mean that an idol is anything at all. No! ²⁰But I say that the things people sacrifice *to idols* are offered to demons,* not to God. And I don't want you to share anything with demons. ²¹You cannot drink the cup of the Lord and the cup of demons too. You cannot share in the Lord's table and the table of demons too. ²²Do we want to make the Lord jealous? Are we stronger than he is? No!

Use Your Freedom for God's Glory

²³"All things are allowed." Yes. But not all things are good. "All things are allowed." Yes. But some things don't help *others* grow stronger. ²⁴No person should try to do the things that will help *only* himself. He should try to do what is good for other people.

²⁵Eat any meat that is sold in the meat market. Don't ask questions *about the meat* to see if it is something you think is wrong to eat. ²⁶*You can eat it*, "because the earth and everything in it belong to the Lord."*

²⁷A person who is not a believer might invite you to eat with him. If you want to go, then eat anything that is put before you. Don't ask questions to see if it is something you think is wrong to eat. ²⁸But if a person tells you, "That food was offered to

idol(s)   The false gods that the non-Jewish people worshiped.
cup of blessing   The cup of wine that Christians thank God for and drink at the Lord's Supper.
Israel   The Jewish nation (people).
sacrifices   Offerings or gifts to God.
demons   Demons are evil spirits from the devil.
"because...Lord"   Quotation from Psalms 24:1; 50:12; 89:11.

idols,*'' then don't eat that food. Don't eat it because *you don't want to hurt the faith* of that person who told you and because eating that meat is something that people think is wrong. ²⁹I don't mean that you think it is wrong. But the other person might think it is wrong. *That is the only reason I would not eat the meat.* My own freedom should not be judged by what another person thinks. ³⁰I eat the meal with thankfulness. So I don't want to be criticized because of something I thank God for.

³¹So if you eat or if you drink or if you do anything, do everything for the glory of God. ³²Never do anything that might make other people do wrong—Jews, Greeks (*non-Jews*), or God's church. ³³I do the same thing. I try to please everybody in every way. I am not trying to do what is good for me. I try to do what is good for the most people. I do this so that they can be saved.

11 Follow my example, like I follow the example of Christ.

Being Under Authority

²I praise you because you remember me in all things. You follow closely the teachings that I gave you. ³But I want you to understand this: The head (*authority*) of every man is Christ. And the head of a woman is the man.* And the head of Christ is God. ⁴Every man who speaks for God or prays with his head covered brings shame to his head. ⁵But every woman who prays or speaks for God should have her head covered. If her head is not covered, then she brings shame to her head. Then she is the same as a woman who has her head shaved. ⁶If a woman does not cover her head, then it is the same as cutting off all her hair. But it is shameful for a woman to cut off her hair or to shave her head. So she should cover her head. ⁷But a man should not cover his head. Why? Because he is made like God and is God's glory. But woman is man's glory. ⁸Man did not come from woman. Woman came from man. ⁹And man was not made for woman. Woman was made for man. ¹⁰So that is why a woman should have her head covered with *something to show that she is under* authority. And also she should do this because of the angels.

idols   False gods that the non-Jewish people worshiped.
the man   This could also mean "her husband."

¹¹But in the Lord, the woman is important to the man, and the man is important to the woman. ¹²This is true because woman came from man, but also man is born from woman. Really, everything comes from God. ¹³Decide this for yourselves: Is it right for a woman to pray to God without something on her head? ¹⁴Even nature itself teaches you that wearing long hair is shameful for a man. ¹⁵But wearing long hair is a woman's honor. Long hair is given to the woman to cover her head. ¹⁶Some people may still want to argue *about this*. But we and the churches of God don't accept what those people are doing.

The Lord's Supper

¹⁷In the things I tell you now I don't praise you. Your meetings hurt you more than they help you. ¹⁸First, I hear that when you meet together as a church you are divided. And I believe some of this. ¹⁹(It is necessary for there to be differences among you. That is the way to make it clear which ones of you are really doing right.) ²⁰When you all come together, you are not really eating the Lord's Supper.* ²¹Why? Because when you eat, each person eats without waiting for the others. Some people don't get enough to eat while other people *have so much that they* become drunk. ²²You can eat and drink in your own homes! It seems that you think God's church (*people*) is not important. You embarrass those people who are poor. What should I tell you? Should I praise you for doing this? I don't praise you.

²³The teaching that I gave you is the same teaching that I received from the Lord: On the night when Jesus was given to be killed, he took bread ²⁴and gave thanks for it. Then he divided the bread and said, "This is my body; it is for you. Do this to remember me." ²⁵In the same way, after they ate, Jesus took the cup of wine. Jesus said, "This wine shows the new agreement *from God to his people*. This new agreement begins with my blood (*death*). When you drink this, do it to remember me." ²⁶Every time you eat this bread and drink this cup, you make known the Lord's death until he comes.

²⁷So if a person eats the bread or drinks the cup of the Lord in a way that is not worthy of it, then that person is sinning against

Lord's Supper The special meal Jesus told his followers to eat to remember him (Luke 22:14-20).

the body and the blood of the Lord. ²⁸Every person should look into his own heart before he eats the bread and drinks the cup. ²⁹If a person eats *the bread* and drinks *the cup* without recognizing the body, then that person is judged guilty by eating and drinking. ³⁰That is why many in your group are sick and weak. And many have died. ³¹But if we judged ourselves in the right way, then God would not judge us. ³²But when the Lord judges us, he punishes us to show us the right way. He does this so that we will not be condemned with *the other people in* the world.

³³So my brothers *and sisters*, when you come together to eat, wait for each other. ³⁴If a person is *too* hungry, then he should eat at home. Do this so that your meeting together will not bring God's judgment on you. I will tell you what to do about the other things when I come.

Gifts from the Holy Spirit

12 Now, brothers *and sisters*, I want you to understand about spiritual gifts. ²You remember the lives you lived before you were believers. You let yourselves be influenced and led away to *worship* idols*—things that have no life. ³So I tell you that no person who is speaking with the help of God's Spirit says, "Jesus be cursed." And no person can say, "Jesus is Lord" without the help of the Holy Spirit.*

⁴There are different kinds of spiritual gifts, but *they are all from* the same Spirit.* ⁵There are different ways to serve, but *all these ways are from* the same Lord. ⁶And there are different ways that God works in people, but *all these ways are from* the same God. God works in us all to do everything. ⁷Something from the Spirit can be seen in each person. The Spirit gives this to each person to help other people. ⁸The Spirit gives one person the ability to speak with wisdom. And the same Spirit gives another person the ability to speak with knowledge. ⁹The same Spirit* gives faith to one person. And that one Spirit gives another person gifts of healing. ¹⁰The Spirit gives to another person the

---

idols   The false gods that the non-Jewish people worshiped.
Holy Spirit, Spirit   Also called the Spirit of God, the Spirit of Christ, and the Comforter. He is joined with God and Christ. He does the work of God among people in the world.

power to do miracles,* to another person the ability to prophesy,* to another person the ability to know the difference between good and evil spirits. The Spirit* gives one person the ability to speak in different kinds of languages, and to another person the ability to interpret those languages. ¹¹One Spirit, the same Spirit, does all these things. The Spirit decides what to give each person.

The Body of Christ

¹²A person's body is only one thing, but it has many parts. Yes, there are many parts to a body, but all those parts make only one body. Christ is like that too: ¹³Some of us are Jews and some of us are Greeks (non-Jews); some of us are slaves and some of us are free. But we were all baptized* into one body through one Spirit.* And we were all given* the one Spirit.

¹⁴And a person's body has more than one part. It has many parts. ¹⁵The foot might say, "I am not a hand. So I don't belong to the body." But saying this would not stop the foot from being a part of the body. ¹⁶The ear might say, "I am not an eye. So I don't belong to the body." But saying this would not make the ear stop being a part of the body. ¹⁷If the whole body were an eye, then the body would not be able to hear. If the whole body were an ear, then the body would not be able to smell anything. ¹⁸⁻¹⁹If each part of the body were the same part, then there would be no body. But truly God put the parts in the body like he wanted them. He made a place for each one of them. ²⁰And so there are many parts, but only one body.

²¹The eye cannot say to the hand, "I don't need you!" And the head cannot say to the foot, "I don't need you!" ²²No! Those parts of the body that seem to be weaker are really very important. ²³And the parts of the body that we think are not worth very much are the parts that we give the most care to. And

---

miracles Miracles are powerful works or great things done by the power of God.
prophesy To prophesy means to speak or teach things from God.
Spirit The Holy Spirit. Also called the Spirit of God, the Spirit of Christ, and the Comforter. He is joined with God and Christ. He does the work of God among people in the world.
baptized A Greek word meaning to be immersed, dipped, or buried briefly under water.
given Literally, "given to drink."

we give special care to the parts of the body that we don't want to show. ²⁴The more beautiful parts of our body don't need this special care. But God put the body together and gave more honor to the parts that need it. ²⁵God did this so that our body would not be divided. God wanted the different parts to care the same for each other. ²⁶If one part of the body suffers, then all the other parts suffer with it. Or if one part of our body is honored, then all the other parts share its honor too.

²⁷All of you together are the body of Christ. Each one of you is a part of that body. ²⁸And in the church God has given a place first to apostles,* second to prophets,* and third to teachers. Then God has given a place to those people that do miracles,* those people that have gifts of healing, those people that can help others, those people who are able to lead, and those people who can speak in different kinds of languages. ²⁹Not all people are apostles. Not all people are prophets. Not all people are teachers. Not all people do miracles. ³⁰Not all people have gifts of healing. Not all people speak in *different kinds of* languages. Not all people interpret those languages. ³¹But you should truly want to have the greater gifts *of the Spirit.**

Love

And now I will show you the best way of all.

13 I may speak in different languages of men or even angels. But if I don't have love, then I am only a noisy bell or a ringing cymbal. ²I may have the gift of prophecy*; I may understand all the secret things *of God* and all knowledge; and I may have faith so great that I can move mountains. But even with all these things, if I don't have love then I am nothing. ³I may give everything I have to feed people. And I may even give my body *as an offering* to be burned. But I gain nothing by doing these things if I don't have love.

---

apostles   Men that Jesus chose to be his special helpers for telling his Good News to the world.
prophets   People who speak for God.
miracles   Miracles are powerful works or great things done by the power of God.
Spirit   The Holy Spirit. Also called the Spirit of God, the Spirit of Christ, and the Comforter. He is joined with God and Christ. He does the work of God among people in the world.
prophecy   Speaking for God.

⁴Love is patient and love is kind. Love is not jealous, it does not boast, and it is not proud. ⁵Love is not rude, love is not selfish, and love does not become angry easily. Love does not remember wrongs done against it. ⁶Love is not happy with evil, but love is happy with the truth. ⁷Love patiently accepts all things. Love always trusts, always hopes, and always continues strong.

⁸Love never ends. There are *gifts of* prophecy,* but they will be ended. There are *gifts of speaking in different kinds of* languages, but those gifts will end. There is *the gift of* knowledge, but it will be ended. ⁹These things will end, because this knowledge and these prophecies we have are not complete (*not perfect*). ¹⁰But when perfection comes, the things that are not complete will end. ¹¹When I was a child, I talked like a child; I thought like a child; I made plans like a child. When I became a man, I stopped those childish ways. ¹²It is the same with us. Now we see like we are looking into a dark mirror. But at that time, in the future, we shall see clearly. Now I know only a part. But at that time I will know fully, like God has known me. ¹³So these three things continue: faith, hope, and love. And the greatest of these is love.

Use Spiritual Gifts to Help the Church

14 Love is the thing you should try for. And you should truly want to have the spiritual gifts. And the gift you should want most is to be able to prophesy.* ²I will explain why: A person *who has the spiritual gift of* speaking in a *different* language is not speaking to people. He is speaking to God. No one understands that person—he is speaking secret things through the Spirit.* ³But a person who prophesies* is speaking to people. He gives people strength, encouragement, and comfort. ⁴The person who speaks in a *different* language is helping only himself. But the person who prophesies is helping the whole

---

prophecy, prophesy, prophesies To prophesy means to speak a prophecy, a teaching from God.
Spirit The Holy Spirit. Also called the Spirit of God, the Spirit of Christ, and the Comforter. He is joined with God and Christ. He does the work of God among people in the world.

church. ⁵I would like all of you *to have the spiritual gift of* speaking in *different kinds of* languages. But more, I want you to prophesy.* The person who prophesies is greater than the person who can only speak *in different kinds of* languages. But the person speaking in *different kinds of* languages is the same as the person who prophesies if he can also interpret those languages. Then the church can be helped *by what he says*.

⁶Brothers *and sisters*, will it help you if I come to you speaking in *different* languages? No! It will help you only if I bring you some message from God, or some knowledge, or some prophecy,* or some teaching. ⁷It is the same as with non-living things that make sounds—like a flute or a harp. If the different musical notes are not made clear, then you can't understand what song is being played. Each note must be played clearly to be able to understand the tune. ⁸And *in a war*, if the trumpet does not sound clearly, then the soldiers will not know it is time to prepare for fighting. ⁹It is the same with you. The words you speak with your tongue must be clear. If you don't speak clearly, then no person can understand what you are saying. You will be talking to the air! ¹⁰It is true that there are many kinds of speech in the world. And they all have meaning. ¹¹So if I don't understand the meaning of what a person says to me, then I think that he talks strange, and he thinks that I talk strange. ¹²It is the same with you. You want spiritual gifts very much. So try most to have those things that help the church grow stronger.

¹³So the person who has the gift of speaking in a *different* language should pray that he can also interpret the things he says. ¹⁴If I pray in a *different* language, then my spirit is praying. But my mind does nothing. ¹⁵So what should I do? I will pray with my spirit, but I will also pray with my mind. I will sing with my spirit, but I will also sing with my mind. ¹⁶You might be praising God with your spirit. But a person there without understanding cannot say ''Amen''* to your prayer of thanks. Why? Because he does not know what you are saying. ¹⁷You may be thanking God in a good way, but the other person is not helped.

---

prophesy, prophecy   To prophesy means to speak a prophecy, a teaching from God.
''Amen''   When a person says ''Amen,'' it means he agrees with the things that were said.

¹⁸I thank God that my gift of speaking in *different kinds of* languages is greater than any of yours. ¹⁹But in the church meetings I would rather speak five words that I understand than thousands of words in a *different* language. I would rather speak with my understanding so that I can teach other people.

²⁰Brothers *and sisters*, don't think like children. In evil things, be like babies. But in your thinking you should be like full grown people. ²¹It is written in the Scriptures*:

> "Using people that speak different
>   kinds of languages
>   and using the lips of foreigners,
> I will speak to these people;
>   but even then these people
>   will not obey me."   *Isaiah 28:11-12*

That is what the Lord says.

²²So *the gift of speaking in different kinds of* languages is a proof for people who don't believe, not for people who believe. And prophecy* is for people who believe, not for people who don't believe. ²³Suppose the whole church meets together and all the people speak in *different* languages. If some people come in who are without understanding or don't believe, then those people will say you are crazy. ²⁴But suppose all the people are prophesying* and a person comes in who does not believe or a person without understanding comes in. If all the people are prophesying, then that person's sin will be shown to him, and he will be judged by all the things the people there say. ²⁵The secret things in that person's heart will be made known. So that person will bow down and worship God. He will say, "Truly, God is with you."

Your Meetings Should Help the Church Grow Strong

²⁶So, brothers *and sisters*, what should you do? When you meet together, one person has a song, another person has a teaching, another person has a message from God, another person speaks in a *different* language, and another person interprets that

---

Scriptures Holy Writings—the Old Testament.
prophecy, prophesying Speaking or teaching a prophecy—things from God.

language. The purpose of all these things should be to help *the church* grow strong. ²⁷When you meet together, if any person speaks to the group in a *different* language, then it should be only two or not more than three people that do this. And they should speak one after the other. And another person should interpret *what they say*. ²⁸But if there is no interpreter, then any person who speaks in a *different* language should be quiet in the church meeting. That person should speak only to himself and to God.

²⁹And only two or three prophets* should speak. The others should judge what they say. ³⁰And if a message from God comes to another person who is sitting, then the first speaker should stop. ³¹You can all prophesy* one after the other. In that way all the people can be taught and encouraged. ³²The spirits of prophets are under the control of the prophets themselves. ³³God is not a God of confusion, but a God of peace.

³⁴Women should keep quiet in the church meetings. This is the same as in all the churches of God's people. Women are not allowed to speak. They must be under control. This is also what the law *of Moses* says. ³⁵If there is something the women want to know, then they should ask their own husbands at home. It is shameful for a woman to speak in the church meeting. ³⁶Did God's teaching come from you? No! Or are you the only ones who have received that teaching? No!

³⁷If any person thinks that he is a prophet* or that he has a spiritual gift, then that person should understand that what I am writing to you is the Lord's command. ³⁸If that person does not know this, then he is not known *by God*.

³⁹So my brothers *and sisters*, you should truly want to prophesy.* And don't stop people from *using the gift of* speaking in *different kinds of* languages. ⁴⁰But everything should be done in a way that is right and orderly.

prophet(s) People who spoke for God. They often told things that would happen in the future.
prophesy To prophesy means to speak or teach things from God.

The Good News About Christ

15 Now, brothers *and sisters*, I want you to remember the gospel* I preached to you. You received this gospel and you continue strong in it. [2] You are saved by this gospel. But you must continue believing the things that I preached to you. If you don't do that, then you believed for nothing.

[3] I preached to you the things that I received. Those things were the most important things: that Christ died for our sins, like the Scriptures* say; [4] that Jesus was buried, and was raised to life on the third day, like the Scriptures say; [5] and that Jesus showed himself to Peter, and then to the twelve *apostles* together*. [6] After that, Jesus showed himself to more than 500 of the brothers at the same time. Most of these brothers are still living today. But some have died. [7] Then Jesus showed himself to James and later to all the apostles *again*. [8] Last of all Jesus showed himself to me—like to a person not born at the normal time. [9] All the other apostles are greater than I am. This is because I persecuted (*did bad things to*) the church of God. That is why I am not even good enough to be called an apostle. [10] But because of God's grace that is what I am. And his grace that he gave me was not wasted. I worked harder than all the other apostles. (But I was not really the one working. It was God's grace that was with me.) [11] So then *it is not important* if I *preached to you* or if the other apostles *preached to you*—we all preach the same thing, and this is what you believed.

We Will Be Raised from Death

[12] It is preached that Christ was raised from death. So why do some of you say that people will not be raised from death? [13] If people will never be raised from death, then Christ has never been raised from death. [14] And if Christ has never been raised, then our preaching is worth nothing. And your faith is worth nothing. [15] And also we will be guilty of lying about God. Why? Because

gospel The Good News that God has made a way through Christ for people to have their sins forgiven and live with God. When people accept this truth, God accepts them.
Scriptures Holy Writings—the Old Testament.
apostles Men that Jesus chose to be his special helpers for telling his Good News to the world.

we have preached about God by saying that he raised Christ from death. And if people are not raised from death, then God never raised Christ from death. ¹⁶If dead people are not raised, then Christ has not been raised either. ¹⁷And if Christ has not been raised from death, then your faith is for nothing; you are still guilty of your sins. ¹⁸And also those people in Christ who have already died are lost. ¹⁹If our hope in Christ is only for this life *here on earth*, then people should feel more sorry for us than for anyone else.

²⁰But Christ has truly been raised from death—the first one of all those *believers* who are asleep in death. ²¹Death happens to people because of what one man (*Adam*) did. But the rising from death also happens because of one man (*Christ*). ²²In Adam all of us die. In the same way, in Christ all of us will be made alive again. ²³But every man will be raised to life in the right order. Christ was first to be raised. Then when Christ comes again the people who belong to Christ will be raised to life. ²⁴Then the end will come. Christ will destroy all rulers, authorities, and powers. Then Christ will give the kingdom to God the Father. ²⁵Christ must rule until God puts all enemies under Christ's control.* ²⁶The last enemy to be destroyed will be death. ²⁷*The Scripture** *says*, "God put all things under his control."* When it says that "all things" are put under him (*Christ*), it is clear that this does not include God himself. God is the one putting everything under Christ's control. ²⁸After everything has been put under Christ, then the Son (*Christ*) himself will be put under God. God is the One who put all things under Christ. Christ will be put under God so that God will be the complete ruler over everything.

²⁹If people will never be raised from death, then what will people do who are baptized* for those who have died? If dead people are never raised, then why are people baptized for them?

³⁰And what about us? Why do we put ourselves in danger every hour? ³¹I die every day. That is true, brothers, the same as it is true that I boast about you in Christ Jesus our Lord. ³²If I fought wild animals in Ephesus only for human reasons, to satisfy my

---

control   Literally, "feet." Being under a person's feet means being under his control.
Scripture   A part of the Holy Writings—the Old Testament.
"God...control"   Quotation from Psalm 8:6.
baptized   A Greek word meaning to be immersed, dipped, or buried briefly under water.

own pride, then I have gained nothing. If people are not raised from death, then "Let us eat and drink, because tomorrow we die."*

³³Don't be fooled: "Bad friends will ruin good habits." ³⁴Come back to your right way of thinking and stop sinning. I say this to shame you—some of you don't know God.

What Kind of Body Will We Have?

³⁵But some person may ask, "How are dead people raised? What kind of body will they have?" ³⁶Those are stupid questions. When you plant something, it must die *in the ground* before it can live and grow. ³⁷And when you plant something, the thing you plant does not have the same "body" that it will have later. The thing you plant is only a seed, maybe wheat or something else. ³⁸But God gives it a body that he has planned for it. And God gives each kind of seed its own body. ³⁹All things made of flesh (*bodies*) are not the same kind of flesh: People have one kind of flesh (*body*), animals have another kind, birds have another kind, and fish have another kind. ⁴⁰Also there are heavenly bodies and earthly bodies. But the beauty of the heavenly bodies is one kind. The beauty of the earthly bodies is another kind. ⁴¹The sun has one kind of beauty. The moon has another kind of beauty, and the stars have another. And each star is different in its beauty.

⁴²It is the same with the dead people who are raised to life. The body that is "planted" will ruin and decay. But that body is raised to a life that cannot be destroyed. ⁴³When the body is "planted," it is without honor. But it is raised in glory. When the body is "planted," it is weak. But when it is raised, it has power. ⁴⁴The body that is "planted" is a physical body. When it is raised, it is a spiritual body.

There is a physical body. So there is also a spiritual body. ⁴⁵It is written *in the Scriptures**: "The first man (Adam) became a living person.*"* But the last Adam (*Christ*) became a spirit that gives life. ⁴⁶The spiritual *man* did not come first. It was the

"Let...die" Quotation from Isaiah 22:13; 56:12.
Scriptures Holy Writings—the Old Testament.
person Literally, "soul."
"The first...person" Quotation from Genesis 2:7.

physical *man* that came first, then came the spiritual. [47]The first man came from the dust of the earth. The second man (*Christ*) came from heaven. [48]People belong to the earth. They are like that first man of earth. But those people who belong to heaven are like that man of heaven. [49]We were made like that man of earth. So we will also be made like that man of heaven.

[50]I tell you this, brothers *and sisters*: Flesh and blood (*a physical body*) cannot have a part in the kingdom of God. A thing that will ruin cannot have a part in something that never ruins. [51]But listen, I tell you this secret: We will not all die, but we will all be changed. [52]It will take only the time of a second. We will be changed as quickly as an eye blinks. This will happen when the last trumpet blows. The trumpet will blow and those *believers* who have died will be raised to live forever. And we *also* will all be changed. [53]This *body* that will ruin must clothe itself with something that will never ruin. And this *body* that dies must clothe itself with something that will never die. [54]So this *body* that ruins will clothe itself with that which never ruins. And this body that dies will clothe itself with that which never dies. When this happens, then this Scripture* will be made true:

> "Death is swallowed (*defeated*) in victory." *Isaiah 25:8*
> [55]"Death, where is your victory?
> Death, where is your power to hurt?" *Hosea 13:14*

[56]Death's power to hurt is sin. The power of sin is the law. [57]But we thank God! He gives us the victory through our Lord Jesus Christ.

[58]So my dear brothers *and sisters*, stand strong. Don't let anything change you. Always give yourselves fully to the work of the Lord. You know that your work in the Lord is never wasted.

The Offering for Other Believers

16 Now *I will write* about the collection *of money* for God's people. Do the same thing that I told the Galatian churches to do: [2]On the first day of every week each one of you should save as much money as you can from what you are blessed

---

Scripture   A part of the Holy Writings—the Old Testament.

with. You should put this money in a special place and keep it there. Then you will not have to gather your money after I come. ³When I come I will send some men to take your gift to Jerusalem. These men will be the men that you all agree should go. I will send them with letters of introduction. ⁴If it seems good for me to go also, then those men will go with me.

Paul's Plans

⁵I plan to go through Macedonia. So I will come to you after I go through Macedonia. ⁶Maybe I will stay with you for a time. I might even stay all winter. Then you can help me on my trip, wherever I go. ⁷I don't want to come see you now, because I would have to leave to go to other places. I hope to stay a longer time with you if the Lord allows it. ⁸But I will stay at Ephesus until Pentecost.* ⁹I will stay, because a good opportunity for a great and growing work has been given to me now. And there are many people working against me.

¹⁰Timothy might come to you. Try to make him feel comfortable with you. He is working for the Lord the same as I am. ¹¹So none of you should refuse to accept Timothy. Help him on his trip in peace so that he can come back to me. I am expecting him to come back with the brothers.

¹²Now about our brother Apollos: I strongly encouraged him to visit you with the other brothers. But he was sure that he did not want to go now. But when he has the opportunity, he will go to you.

Paul Ends His Letter

¹³Be careful. Continue strong in the faith. Have courage, and be strong. ¹⁴Do everything in love.

¹⁵You know that the family of Stephanas were the first believers in Achaia. They have given themselves to the service of God's people. I ask you, brothers *and sisters*, ¹⁶to follow the leading of people like these, and any other person who works and serves with them.

Pentecost   Jewish feast day (50 days after Passover) celebrating the harvest of wheat.

¹⁷I am happy that Stephanas, Fortunatus, and Achaicus have come. You are not here, but they have filled your place. ¹⁸They have given rest to my spirit and to yours. You should recognize the value of men like these.

¹⁹The churches in Asia* say hello to you. Aquila and Priscilla say hello to you in the Lord. Also the church that meets in their house says hello to you. ²⁰All the brothers *and sisters* here say hello to you. Give each other a holy kiss when you meet.

²¹I am Paul, and I am writing this greeting with my own hand.

²²If any person does not love the Lord, then let that person be separated from God—lost forever!

Come, O Lord*!

²³The grace of the Lord Jesus be with you.

²⁴My love be with all of you in Christ Jesus.

Asia   The western part of Asia Minor.
Come, O Lord   The Aramaic word "marana tha." This could also mean, "Our Lord has come."

2 Corinthians

1 From Paul, an apostle* of Christ Jesus. I am an apostle because that is what God wanted.

Also from Timothy our brother *in Christ*,

To the church of God that lives in Corinth and to all of God's people in the whole country of Achaia:

²Grace (*kindness*) and peace to you from God our Father and the Lord Jesus Christ.

Paul Gives Thanks to God

³Praise be to the God and Father of our Lord Jesus Christ. God is the Father who is full of mercy. He is the God of all comfort. ⁴He comforts us every time we have trouble, so that we can comfort other people any time they have trouble. We can comfort them with the same comfort that God gives us. ⁵We share in the many sufferings of Christ. In the same way, much comfort comes to us through Christ. ⁶If we have troubles, those troubles are for our comfort and salvation. If we have comfort, it is for your comfort. This helps you to patiently accept the same sufferings that we have. ⁷Our hope for you is strong. We know that you share in our sufferings. So we know that you also share in our comfort.

⁸Brothers *and sisters*, we want you to know about the trouble we suffered in the country of Asia.* We had great burdens there. The burdens were greater than our own strength. We even gave up hope for life. ⁹Truly in our own hearts we believed that we would die. But this happened so that we would not trust in ourselves. It happened so that we would trust in God, who raises

apostle   Person Jesus chose to be a special helper for telling the Good News to the world.
Asia   The western part of Asia Minor.

people from death. ¹⁰God saved us from these great dangers of death. And God will continue to save us. We have put our hope in him, and he will continue to save us. ¹¹And you can help us with your prayers. Then many people will give thanks for us—that God blessed us because of their many prayers.

The Change in Paul's Plans

¹²This is what we are proud of, and I can say with all my heart that it is true: In all the things we have done in the world, we have done everything with an honest and pure heart from God. And this is even more true in the things we have done with you. We did this by God's grace (*kindness*), not by the kind of wisdom the world has. ¹³The only things we write to you are things that you can read and understand. And I hope that you will always understand, ¹⁴like you have already understood some things about us. I hope that you will understand that you can be proud of us, like we will be proud of you on the day our Lord Jesus Christ comes again.

¹⁵I was very sure of all this. That is why I made plans to visit you first. Then you could be blessed twice. ¹⁶I planned to visit you on my way to Macedonia. Then I planned to visit you again on my way back. I wanted to get help from you for my trip to Judea. ¹⁷Do you think that I made those plans without really thinking? Or maybe you think I make plans like the world makes plans, so that I say "Yes, yes," and at the same time "No, no."

¹⁸But if you can believe God, then you can believe that what we tell you is never both "Yes" and "No." ¹⁹The Son of God, Jesus Christ, that Silas and Timothy and I preached to you was not "Yes" and "No." In Christ it has always been "Yes." ²⁰The "Yes" to all of God's promises is in Christ. And that is why we say "Amen"* through Christ to the glory of God. ²¹And God is the One who makes you and us strong in Christ. God gave us his special blessing.* ²²He put his mark on us to show that we are his. And he put his Spirit* in our hearts to be a guarantee—*a proof that he will give us what he promised.*

"Amen" To say "Amen" means to agree strongly.
gave...blessing Literally, "anointed us."
Spirit The Holy Spirit. Also called the Spirit of God, the Spirit of Christ, and the Comforter. He is joined with God and Christ. He does the work of God among people in the world.

²³I tell you this, and I ask God to be my witness that this is true: The reason I did not come back to Corinth was that I did not want to punish or hurt you. ²⁴I don't mean that we are trying to control your faith. You are strong in faith. But we are workers with you for your own happiness.

2 So I decided that my next visit to you would not be another visit to make you sad. ²If I make you sad, then who will make me happy? Only you can make me happy—you that I made sad. ³I wrote you a letter for this reason: so that when I came to you I would not be made sad by those people who should make me happy. I felt sure of all of you. I felt sure that all of you would share my joy. ⁴When I wrote to you before, I was very troubled and unhappy in my heart. I wrote with many tears. I did not write to make you sad. I wrote so that you could know how much I love you.

Forgive the Person Who Did Wrong

⁵A person *in your group* has caused sadness. He has caused this sadness not only to me, but to all of you—I mean he has caused sadness in some way. (I don't want to make it sound worse than it really is.) ⁶The punishment that most of your group gave him is enough for him. ⁷But now you should forgive him and comfort him. This will keep him from having too much sadness and giving up completely. ⁸So I beg you to show him that you love him. ⁹This is why I wrote to you. I wanted to test you and see if you obey in everything. ¹⁰If you forgive a person, then I also forgive that person. And what I have forgiven—if I had anything to forgive—I forgave it for you, and Christ was with me. ¹¹I did this so that Satan (*the devil*) would not win anything from us. We know very well what Satan's plans are.

Paul's Anxiety in Troas

¹²I went to Troas to preach the Good News* of Christ. The Lord gave me a good opportunity there. ¹³But I had no peace

---

Good News The news that God has made a way through Christ for people to have their sins forgiven and live with God. When people accept this truth, God accepts them.

because I did not find my brother Titus there. So I said good-bye and went to Macedonia.

Victory Through Christ

¹⁴But thanks be to God. God always leads us in victory through Christ. God uses us to spread his knowledge everywhere like a sweet-smelling perfume. ¹⁵Our offering to God is this: We are the sweet smell of Christ among people who are being saved and among people who are being lost. ¹⁶To the people who are being lost, we are the smell of death that brings death. But to the people who are being saved, we are the smell of life that brings life. So who is good enough to do this work? ¹⁷We don't sell the word of God for a profit like many other people do. No! But in Christ we speak in truth before God. We speak like men sent from God.

Servants of the New Covenant

3 Are we starting to boast about ourselves again? Do we need letters of introduction to you or from you, like some other people? ²You yourselves are our letter. That letter is written on our hearts. It is known and read by all people. ³You show that you are a letter from Christ that he sent through us. This letter is not written with ink, but with the Spirit* of the living God. It is not written on stone tablets.* It is written on human hearts.

⁴We can say these things because through Christ we feel sure before God. ⁵I don't mean that we are able to say that we can do anything *good* ourselves. It is God who makes us able to do all that we do. ⁶God made us able to be servants of a new agreement *from God to his people*. This new agreement is not a written law. It is of the Spirit.* The written law brings death, but the Spirit gives life.

Spirit The Holy Spirit. Also called the Spirit of God, the Spirit of Christ, and the Comforter. He is joined with God and Christ. He does the work of God among people in the world.
stone tablets Meaning the law of Moses that was written on stone tablets (Exodus 24:12; 25:16).

Paul's Service Is Greater than Moses' Service

⁷The service that brought death (*the law*) was written with words on stone.* It came with *God's* glory. Moses' face was so bright with glory that the people of Israel (*the Jews*) could not continue looking at his face. And that glory later disappeared. ⁸So surely the service that brings the Spirit* has even more glory. ⁹This is what I mean: That service (*the law*) judged people guilty of sin, but it had glory. So surely the service that makes people right *with God* has much greater glory. ¹⁰That *old service* had glory. But it really loses its glory when it is compared to the much greater glory *of this new service*. ¹¹If *the service* that disappeared came with glory, then *the service* that continues *forever* has much greater glory.

¹²We have this hope, so we are very brave. ¹³We are not like Moses. He put a covering over his face. Moses covered his face so that the people of Israel (*the Jews*) would not see it. The glory (*brightness*) was disappearing, and Moses did not want them to see it end. ¹⁴But their minds were closed—*they could not understand*. Even today that same covering hides the meaning when they (*the Jews*) read the old testament. That covering has not been removed. It is taken away only through Christ. ¹⁵But even today, when these people read *the law of* Moses there is a covering over their minds. ¹⁶But when a person changes and follows the Lord, that covering is taken away. ¹⁷The Lord is the Spirit. And where the Spirit of the Lord is, there is freedom. ¹⁸And our faces are not covered. We all show the Lord's glory. We are being changed to be like him. This change in us brings more and more glory. This glory comes from the Lord who is the Spirit.

Spiritual Treasure in Clay Jars

4 God, with his mercy, gave us this work to do. So we don't give up. ²But we have turned away from secret and shameful ways. We don't use trickery, and we don't change the teaching of

---

stone The law God gave Moses on Mt. Sinai was written on tablets of stone.
Spirit The Holy Spirit. Also called the Spirit of God, the Spirit of Christ, and the Comforter. He is joined with God and Christ. He does the work of God among people in the world.

God. No! But we teach the truth plainly. This is how we show people who we are. And this is how they can know in their hearts what kind of people we are before God. ³The Good News* that we preach may be hidden. But it is hidden only to those people who are lost. ⁴The ruler* of this world (*the devil*) has blinded the minds of people who don't believe. They cannot see the light (*truth*) of the Good News—the Good News about the glory of Christ. Christ is the One who is exactly like God. ⁵We don't preach about ourselves. But we preach that Jesus Christ is Lord; and we preach that we are your servants for Jesus. ⁶God once said, "The light will shine out of the darkness!" And this is the same God who made his light shine in our hearts. He gave us light by letting us know the glory of God that is in the face of Christ.

⁷We have this treasure *from God*. But we are only like clay jars that hold the treasure. This shows that this great power is from God, not from us. ⁸We have troubles all around us, but we are not defeated. We often don't know what to do, but we don't give up. ⁹We are persecuted, but God does not leave us. We are hurt sometimes, but we are not destroyed. ¹⁰We have the death of Jesus in our own bodies. We carry this death so that the life of Jesus can also be seen in our bodies (*lives*). ¹¹We are alive, but for Jesus we are always in danger of death. This happens to us so that the life of Jesus can be seen in our bodies that die. ¹²So death is working in us, but life is working in you.

¹³It is written *in the Scriptures*,* "I believed, so I spoke."* Our faith is like that too. We believe, and so we speak. ¹⁴God raised the Lord Jesus from death. And we know that God will also raise us with Jesus. God will bring us together with you and we will stand before him. ¹⁵All these things are for you. And so the grace (*kindness*) of God is being given to more and more people. This will bring more and more thanks to God for his glory.

Good News The news that God has made a way through Christ for people to have their sins forgiven and live with God. When people accept this truth, God accepts them.
the ruler Literally, "the god."
Scriptures Holy Writings—the Old Testament.
"I...spoke" Quotation from Psalm 116:10.

Living by Faith

[16]That is why we never become weak. Our physical body is becoming older and weaker, but our spirit inside us is made new every day. [17]We have small troubles for a while now, but those troubles are helping us gain an eternal glory. That eternal glory is much greater than the troubles. [18]So we think about the things we cannot see, not what we see. The things we see continue only a short time. And the things we cannot see will continue forever.

5 We know that *our body*—the tent we live in here on earth— will be destroyed. But when that happens, God will have a home for us to live in. It will not be a home made by men. It will be a home in heaven that will continue forever. [2]But now we are tired of this body. We want God to give us our heavenly home. [3]This will clothe us and we will not be naked. [4]While we live in this tent (*body*), we have burdens and we complain. We don't want to be naked. We want to be clothed *with our heavenly home*. Then this body that dies will be fully covered with life. [5]This is what God made us for. And he has given us the Spirit* to be a guarantee—a proof *that he will give us this new life.*

[6]So we always have courage (*confidence*). We know that while we live in this body, we are away from the Lord. [7]We live by what we believe, not by what we can see. [8]So I say that we have confidence. And we really want to be away from this body and be at home with the Lord. [9]Our only goal is to please God. We want to please him when we are living here *in our body*, or there *with the Lord*. [10]We must all stand before Christ to be judged. Each person will get what he should. Each person will be paid for the things he did—good or bad—when he lived in the earthly body.

Helping People Become God's Friends

[11]We know what it means to fear the Lord. So we try to help people accept the truth. God knows what we really are. And I hope that in your hearts you know us too. [12]We are not trying to prove ourselves to you again. But we are telling you about

---

Spirit   The Holy Spirit. Also called the Spirit of God, the Spirit of Christ, and the Comforter. He is joined with God and Christ. He does the work of God among people in the world.

ourselves. We are giving you reasons to be proud of us. Then you will have an answer for those people who are proud about things that can be seen. Those people don't care about what is in a person's heart. [13]If we are crazy, then it is for God. If we have our right mind, then it is for you. [14]The love of Christ controls us. Why? Because we know that One (*Christ*) has died for all people. So all have died. [15]Christ died for all people so that the people who live would not continue to live for themselves. He died for them and was raised from death so that those people would live for him.

[16]From this time on we don't think of any person like the world thinks of people. It is true that in the past we thought of Christ like the world thinks. But we don't think that way now. [17]If any person is in Christ, then that person is made new. The old things have gone; everything is made new! [18]All this is from God. Through Christ, God made peace between us and himself. And God gave us the work of bringing people into peace with him. [19]I mean that God was in Christ, making peace between the world and himself. God did not hold people guilty of their sins. And he gave us this message of peace *to tell people*. [20]So we have been sent to speak for Christ. It is like God is calling to people through us. We speak for Christ when we beg you to be at peace with God. [21]Christ had no sin. But God made him become sin. God did this for us, so that, in Christ, we could become right with God.

6 We are workers together with God. So we beg you: Don't let the grace (*kindness*) that you received from God be for nothing. [2]God says,

> "I heard you at the right time,
>   and I gave you help on the
>   day of salvation."

Isaiah 49:8

I tell you that the "right time" is now. The "day of salvation" is now.

[3]We don't want people to find anything wrong with our work. So we do nothing that will be a problem to other people. [4]But in every way we show that we are servants of God: in accepting many hard things, in troubles, in difficulties, and in great

problems. ⁵We are beaten and thrown into prison. People become upset and fight us. We work hard and sometimes we get no sleep or food. ⁶*We show that we are servants of God* by our understanding, by our patience, by our kindness, and by living pure. *We show this* by the Holy Spirit,* by true love, ⁷by speaking the truth, and by God's power. We use our right living to defend ourselves against everything. ⁸Some people honor us, but other people shame us. Some people say good things about us, but other people say bad things. Some people say we are liars, but we speak the truth. ⁹To some people we are not known (*not important*), but we are well known. We seem to be dying, but look! We continue to live. We are punished, but we are not killed. ¹⁰We have much sadness, but we are always rejoicing. We are poor, but we are making many people rich *in faith*. We have nothing, but really we have everything.

¹¹We have spoken freely to you people in Corinth. We have opened our hearts to you. ¹²Our feelings of love for you have not stopped. It is you that have stopped your feelings of love for us. ¹³I speak to you like you are my children. Do the same as we have done—open your hearts also.

Warning About Living with Non-Christians

¹⁴You are not the same as those people who don't believe. So don't join yourselves to them. Good and bad don't belong together. Light and darkness cannot have fellowship (*sharing*). ¹⁵How can Christ and Belial (*the devil*) have any agreement? What can a believer have together with a non-believer? ¹⁶The temple* of God cannot have any agreement with idols.* And we are the temple of the living God. Like God said:

"I will live with them and walk with them,
I will be their God,
and they will be my people." *Leviticus 26:11-12*

Holy Spirit Also called the Spirit of God, the Spirit of Christ, and the Comforter. He is joined with God and Christ. He does the work of God among people in the world.
temple God's house—the place where people worship and serve him.
idols The false gods that the non-Jewish people worshiped.

465

¹⁷"So come away from those people
  and separate yourselves from them,
    says the Lord.
  Touch nothing that is not clean,
    and I will accept you."   *Isaiah 52:11*

¹⁸"I will be your father,
  and you will be my sons and daughters,
    says the Lord All-Powerful."   *2 Samuel 7:14; 7:8*

7 Dear friends, we have these promises *from God*. So we should make ourselves pure—free from anything that makes our body or our soul unclean. We should try to become perfect in the way we live because we respect God.

Paul's Joy

²Open your hearts to us. We have not done wrong to any person. We have not ruined *the faith of* any person, and we have not cheated any person. ³I am not blaming you. I told you before that we love you so much that we would live or die with you. ⁴I feel very sure of you. I am very proud of you. You give me much courage. And in all of our troubles I have great joy.

⁵When we came into Macedonia we had no rest. We found trouble all around us. We had fighting on the outside and fear on the inside. ⁶But God comforts people who are troubled. And God comforted us when Titus came. ⁷We were comforted by his coming and also by the comfort that you gave him. Titus told us about your wish to see me. He told us that you are very sorry for the things you did. And Titus told me about your great care for me. When I heard this, I was much happier.

⁸Even if the letter I wrote you made you sad, I am not sorry I wrote it. I know that letter made you sad, and I was sorry for that. But it made you sad only for a short time. ⁹Now I am happy. My happiness is not because you were made sad. I am happy because your sorrow made you change your hearts. You became sad like God wanted. So you were not hurt by us in any way. ¹⁰Being sorry like God wants makes a person change his heart and life. This leads a person to salvation, and we cannot be sorry for that. But the kind of sorrow the world has will bring death. ¹¹You

had the kind of sorrow God wanted you to have. Now see what that sorrow has brought you: That sorrow has made you very serious. It made you want to prove that you were not wrong. It made you angry and afraid. It made you want *to see me*. It made you care. It made you want the right thing to be done. You proved that you were not guilty in any part of that problem. ¹²I wrote that letter, but not because of the one who did the wrong. And it was not written because of the person who was hurt. But I wrote that letter so that you could see, before God, the great care that you have for us. ¹³That is why we were comforted.

We were very comforted. And we were even happier to see that Titus was so happy. All of you made him feel good. ¹⁴I boasted to Titus about you. And you showed that I was right. Everything that we said to you was true. And also the things that we boasted to Titus about you have proven to be true. ¹⁵And his love for you is stronger when he remembers that you were all ready to obey. You welcomed him with respect and fear. ¹⁶I am very happy that I can trust you fully.

Christian Giving

8 And now, brothers *and sisters*, we want you to know about the grace (*kindness*) that God gave the churches (*groups of believers*) in Macedonia. ²Those believers have been tested by great troubles. And they are very poor people. But they gave much because of their great joy. ³I can tell you that they gave as much as they were able. Those believers gave even more than they could afford. They did this freely. No person told them to do this. ⁴But they asked us again and again—they begged us to let them share in this service for God's people. ⁵And they gave in a way that we did not expect: They gave themselves to the Lord and to us before *they gave their money*. This is what God wants. ⁶So we asked Titus to help you finish this special work of grace (*kindness*). Titus is the one who started this work. ⁷You are rich in everything—in faith, in speaking, in knowledge, in truly wanting to help, and in the love you learned from us. And so we want you to also be rich in this gift of giving.

⁸I am not commanding you to give. But I want to see if your love is true love. I do this by showing you that other people really

want to help. ⁹You know the grace (*kindness*) of our Lord Jesus Christ. You know that Christ was rich *with God*, but for you he became poor. Christ did this so that you could become rich by his becoming poor.

¹⁰This is what I think you should do: Last year you were the first to want to give. And you were the first that gave. ¹¹So now finish the work *that you started*. Then your "doing" will be equal to your "wanting to do." Give from what you have. ¹²If you want to give, then your gift will be accepted. Your gift will be judged by what you have, not by what you don't have. ¹³We don't want you to have troubles while other people are comforted. We want everything to be equal. ¹⁴At this time you have plenty. These things you have can help other people to have the things they need. Then later, when they have plenty, they can help you to have the things you need. Then all will be equal. ¹⁵Like it is written in the Scriptures,*

> "The person that gathered much
>   did not have too much,
>   and the person that gathered little
>   did not have too little."

Exodus 16:18

Titus and His Companions

¹⁶I thank God because he gave Titus the same love for you that I have. ¹⁷Titus accepted the things we asked him to do. He wanted very much to go to you. This was his own idea. ¹⁸We are sending with Titus the brother who is praised by all the churches (*groups of believers*). This brother is praised because of his service in the gospel.* ¹⁹Also, this brother was chosen by the churches to go with us when we carry this gift (*the money*). We are doing this service to bring glory to the Lord and to show that we really want to help.

²⁰We are being careful so that no person will criticize us about the way we are caring for this large gift. ²¹We are trying to do what is right. We want to do what the Lord accepts as right and what people think is right.

Scriptures   Holy Writings—the Old Testament.
gospel   The Good News that God has made a way through Christ for people to have their sins forgiven and live with God. When people accept this truth, God accepts them.

²²Also, we are sending with them our brother who is always ready to help. He has proved this to us in many ways. And he wants to help even more now because he has much faith in you.

²³Now about Titus—he is my partner. He is working together with me to help you. And about the other brothers—they are sent from the churches (*groups of believers*), and they bring glory to Christ. ²⁴So show these men that you really have love. Show them why we are proud of you. Then all the churches can see it.

Help for Fellow Christians

9 I really don't need to write to you about this help for God's people. ²I know that you want to help. I have been boasting about this to the people in Macedonia. I have told them that you people in Achaia were ready to give since last year. And your wanting to give has made most of the people here ready to give also. ³But I am sending the brothers to you. I don't want our boasting about you in this to be for nothing. I want you to be ready like I said you would be. ⁴If any of the people from Macedonia come with me, and they find that you are not ready, then we will be ashamed. We will be ashamed that we were so sure of you. (And you will be ashamed too!) ⁵So I thought that I should ask these brothers to go to you before we come. They will finish making ready the gift you promised. Then the gift will be ready when we come, and it will be a gift you wanted to give—not a gift that you hated to give.

⁶Remember this: The person who plants little will harvest only little. But the person who plants much will harvest much. ⁷Each person should give what he has decided in his heart to give. A person should not give if it makes him sad. And a person should not give if he thinks he is forced to give. God loves the person who gives happily. ⁸And God can give you more blessings than you need. Then you will always have plenty of everything. You will have enough to give to every good work. ⁹It is written *in the Scriptures**:

> "He gives generously to the poor;
> his kindness will continue forever." *Psalm 112:9*

Scriptures Holy Writings—the Old Testament.

¹⁰God is the One who gives seed to the person who plants. And he gives bread for food. And God will give you *spiritual* seed and make your seed grow. He will make a great harvest from your goodness (*giving*). ¹¹God will make you rich in every way so that you can always give freely. And your giving through us will make people give thanks to God. ¹²This service that you do helps the needs of God's people. But that is not all your service does. It is also bringing more and more thanks to God. ¹³This service you do is a proof *of your faith*. People will praise God because of this. They will praise God because you follow the gospel* of Christ—the gospel you say you believe. People will praise God because you freely share with them and with all people. ¹⁴And when those people pray, they will wish they could be with you. They will feel this because of the great grace (*kindness*) that God gave you. ¹⁵Thanks be to God for his gift that is too wonderful to explain.

Paul Defends His Ministry

10 I am Paul, and I am begging you. I beg you with the gentleness and the kindness of Christ. *Some people say that* I am humble when I am with you, and brave when I am away. ²Some people think that we live in a worldly way. I plan to be very bold against those people when I come. I beg you that when I come I will not need to use that same boldness *with you*. ³We do live in the world. But we don't fight in the same way that the world fights. ⁴We fight with weapons that are different from the weapons the world uses. Our weapons have power from God. These weapons can destroy *the enemy's* strong places. We destroy *people's* arguments. ⁵And we destroy every proud thing that raises itself against the knowledge of God. And we capture (*catch*) every thought and make it give up and obey Christ. ⁶We are ready to punish any person there who does not obey. But first we want you to obey fully.

⁷You must look at the facts before you. If a person feels sure that he belongs to Christ, then he must remember that we belong

---

gospel The Good News that God has made a way through Christ for people to have their sins forgiven and live with God. When people accept this truth, God accepts them.

to Christ the same as that person. ⁸It is true that we boast freely about the authority (*power*) the Lord gave us. But he gave us this power to strengthen you, not to hurt you. So I will not be ashamed of that boasting we do. ⁹I don't want you to think that I am trying to scare you with my letters. ¹⁰Some people say, "Paul's letters are powerful and sound important. But when he is with us, he is weak. And his speaking is nothing." ¹¹Those people should know this: We are not there with you now, so we say these things in letters. But when we are there with you, we will show the same power that we show in our letters.

¹²We don't dare to put ourselves in the same group with those people who think that they are very important. We don't compare ourselves to them. They are stupid, because they use themselves to measure themselves, and they judge themselves by what they themselves are. ¹³But we will not boast about things outside the work that was given us to do. We will limit our boasting to the work that God gave us. But this work includes our work with you. ¹⁴We are not boasting too much. We would be boasting too much if we had not already come to you. But we have come to you. We came to you with the Good News* of Christ. ¹⁵We limit our boasting to the work that is ours. We don't boast in the work other people have done. We hope that your faith will continue to grow. We hope that you will help our work to grow much larger. ¹⁶We want to tell the Good News* in the areas beyond your city. We don't want to boast about work that has already been done in another man's area. ¹⁷But, "The person who boasts should boast in the Lord." ¹⁸It is not the person who says that he is good who is accepted. It is the person that the Lord thinks is good who is accepted.

Paul and the False Apostles

11 I wish you would be patient with me even when I am a little foolish. But you are already patient with me. ²I feel jealousy for you. And this jealousy is a jealousy that comes from God. I promised to give you to Christ. Christ must be your only

---

Good News The news that God has made a way through Christ for people to have their sins forgiven and live with God. When people accept this truth, God accepts them.

husband. I want to give you to Christ to be his pure bride.* ³But I am afraid that your minds will be led away from your true and pure following of Christ. This might happen the same as Eve was tricked (*fooled*) by the snake (*the devil*) with his evil ways. ⁴You are very patient with any person who comes to you and preaches things about Jesus that are different from the things we told you. You are very willing to accept a spirit or a gospel that is different from the Spirit* and gospel* that you received from us. *So you should be patient with me.*

⁵I don't think that those "great apostles" are any better than I am. ⁶It is true that I am not a trained speaker. But I do have knowledge. We have shown this to you clearly in every way.

⁷I preached God's Good News* to you without pay. I humbled myself to make you important. Do you think that was wrong? ⁸I accepted pay from other churches. I took their money so that I could serve you. ⁹If I needed something when I was with you, I did not trouble any of you. The brothers who came from Macedonia gave me all that I needed. I did not allow myself to be a burden to you in any way. And I will never be a burden to you. ¹⁰No person in Achaia* will stop me from boasting about that. I say this with the truth of Christ in me. ¹¹And why *do I not burden you*? Do you think it is because I don't love you? No. God knows that I love you.

¹²And I will continue doing what I am doing now. I will continue this because I want to stop those people from having a reason to boast. They would like to say that the work they boast about is the same as ours. ¹³These people are not true apostles.* They are workers who lie. And they change themselves to *make people think they are* apostles of Christ. ¹⁴That does not surprise us. Why? Even Satan (*the devil*) changes himself to *make people think he is* an angel of light.* ¹⁵So it does not surprise us if

---

bride   Literally, "virgin."
Spirit   The Holy Spirit. Also called the Spirit of God, the Spirit of Christ, and the Comforter. He is joined with God and Christ. He does the work of God among people in the world.
gospel, Good News   The news that God has made a way through Christ for people to have their sins forgiven and live with God. When people accept this truth, God accepts them.
Achaia   The southern part of Greece where Corinth was.
apostles   The men Jesus chose to be his special helpers for telling his Good News to the world.
angel of light   Messenger from God. The devil fools people so that they think he is from God.

Satan's servants make themselves look like servants who work for what is right. But in the end those people will be paid (*punished*) for the things they do.

Paul Tells About His Sufferings

[16]I tell you again: No person should think that I am a fool. But if you think that I am a fool, then accept me like you accept a fool. Then I can boast a little too. [17]I boast because I feel sure of myself. But I am not talking like the Lord would talk. I am boasting like a fool. [18]Many people are boasting about their lives in the world. So I will boast too. [19]You are wise, so you will gladly be patient with fools! [20]*I know you will be patient,* because you are even patient with a person who forces you to do things, and uses you! You are patient with people that trick you, or think they are better than you, or hit you in the face! [21]It is shameful to me to say this, but we were too "weak" *to do those things to you*!

But if any person is brave enough to boast, then I also will be brave and boast. (I am talking like a fool.) [22]Are those people Hebrews*? I am too. Are they Israelites*? I am too. Are they from Abraham's* family? I am too. [23]Are those people serving Christ? I am serving him more. (I am crazy to talk like this.) I have worked much harder than those people. I have been in prison more often. I have been hurt more in beatings. I have been near death many times. [24]Five times the Jews have given me their punishment of 39 hits with a whip. [25]Three different times I was beaten with rods. One time I was almost killed with rocks. Three times I was in ships that were wrecked, and one of those times I spent the night and the next day in the sea. [26]I have traveled many, many times. And I have been in danger from rivers, from thieves, from my own people (*the Jews*), and from people who are not Jews. I have been in danger in cities, in places where no people live, and on the sea. And I have been in danger with people who say they are brothers, but are really not brothers. [27]I have done hard and tiring work, and many times I did not sleep. I have been hungry and thirsty. Many times I have been without

Hebrews   A name for the Jews that some Jews were very proud of.
Israelites   The Jewish people. They were from the twelve sons of Jacob, who is also called Israel.
Abraham   Most respected ancestor of the Jews. Every Jew hoped to see Abraham.

food. I have been cold and without clothes. ²⁸And there are many other problems. One of these is the care I have for all the churches. I worry about them every day. ²⁹I feel weak every time another person is weak. I feel upset (*angry*) inside myself every time another person is led into sin.

³⁰If I must boast, then I will boast about the things that show that I am weak. ³¹God knows that I am not lying. He is the God and Father of the Lord Jesus Christ, and he is to be praised forever. ³²When I was in Damascus, the governor under King Aretas wanted to arrest me. So he put guards around the city. ³³But *some friends* put me in a basket. Then they put the basket through a hole in the wall and lowered me down. So I escaped from the governor.

A Special Blessing in Paul's Life

12 I must continue to boast. It won't help, but I will talk now about visions* and revelations* from the Lord. ²I know a man* in Christ who was taken up to the third heaven. This happened 14 years ago. I don't know if the man was in his body, or out of his body. But God knows. ³⁻⁴And I know that this man was taken up to paradise.* I don't know if he was in his body or away from his body. But he heard things which he is not able to explain. He heard things that no man is allowed to tell. ⁵I will boast about a man like that. But I will not boast about myself. I will boast only about my weaknesses. ⁶But if I wanted to boast about myself, I would not be a fool. I would not be a fool, because I would be telling the truth. But I won't boast about myself. Why? Because I don't want people to think more of me than what they see me do or hear me say.

⁷But I must not become too proud of the wonderful things that were shown to me. So a painful problem* was given to me. That problem is an angel from Satan (*the devil*). It is sent to beat me and keep me from being too proud. ⁸I begged the Lord three times to take this problem away from me. ⁹But the Lord said to

---

visions   A vision is something like a dream that God used to speak to people.
revelations   A revelation is an opening up (making known) of truth that was hidden.
man   Paul is probably talking about himself.
paradise   A happy place where good people go when they die.
painful problem   Literally, "thorn in the flesh."

me, "My grace (*kindness*) is enough for you. When you are weak, then my power is made perfect in you." So I am very happy to boast about my weaknesses. Then Christ's power can live in me. [10]So I am happy when I have weaknesses. I am happy when people say bad things to me. I am happy when I have hard times. I am happy when people treat me badly. And I am happy when I have problems. All these things are for Christ. And I am happy with these things, because when I am weak, then I am truly strong.

Paul's Love for the Christians in Corinth

[11]I have been *talking like* a fool. But you made me do it. You people are the ones who should say good things about me. I am worth nothing, but those "great apostles" are not worth any more than I am! [12]When I was with you, I did the things that prove that I am an apostle*—I did signs, wonders, and miracles.* I did these things with much patience. [13]So you received everything that the other churches have received. Only one thing was different: I was not a burden to you. Forgive me for this!

[14]I am now ready to visit you the third time. And I will not be a burden to you. I don't want any of the things you own. I want only you. Children should not have to save things to give to their parents. Parents should save to give to their children. [15]So I am happy to give everything I have for you. I will even give myself for you. If I love you more, will you love me less?

[16]It is clear that I was not a burden to you. But *you think that* I was tricky, and used lies to catch you. [17]Did I cheat you by using any of the men I sent to you? No! You know I didn't. [18]I asked Titus to go to you. And I sent our brother with him. Titus did not cheat you, did he? No! You know that Titus and I did the same things and with the same spirit.

[19]Do you think that we have been defending ourselves to you all this time? No. We say these things in Christ. And we say these things before God. You are our dear friends. And everything that

---

apostle   Person Jesus chose to be a special helper for telling the Good News to the world.
signs, wonders, miracles   Powerful works from God that men cannot do without God's help.

we do is to make you stronger. ²⁰I do this because I am afraid that when I come you will not be what I want you to be. And I am afraid that I will not be what you want me to be. I am afraid that in your group there may be arguing, jealousy, anger, selfish fighting, evil talk, gossip, pride, and confusion. ²¹I am afraid that when I come to you again, my God will make me humble before you. I may be saddened by many of you who have sinned. I may be saddened because those people have not changed their hearts to be sorry for their evil lives, for their sexual sins and the shameful things they have done.

Final Warnings and Greetings

13 I will come to you again. This will be the third time. And remember, "For every complaint there must be two or three people to say that they know it is true."* ²When I was with you the second time, I gave a warning to those people who had sinned. Now I am away from you, and I give a warning to all the other people *who have sinned*: When I come to you again, I will punish you *for your sin*. ³You want proof that Christ is speaking through me. *My proof is that* Christ is not weak in *punishing* you. But Christ is powerful among you. ⁴It is true that Christ was weak when he was killed on the cross. But he lives now by God's power. And it is true that we are weak in Christ. But for you we will be alive in Christ by God's power.

⁵Look closely at yourselves. Test yourselves to see if you are *living* in the faith. You know that Christ Jesus is in you. But if you fail the test (*if you find that you are not living in the faith*), then Christ is not living in you. ⁶But I hope you will see that we have not failed the test. ⁷We pray to God that you will not do anything wrong. It is not important that people see that we have passed the test. But it is important that you do what is right, even if *people think* that we have failed the test. ⁸We cannot do things that are against the truth. We can only do things that are for the truth. ⁹We are happy to be weak, if you are strong. And we pray that you will grow stronger and stronger. ¹⁰I am writing these things while I am not with you. I am writing so that when I come I

"For...true" Quotation from Deuteronomy 19:15.

will not have to use my power to punish you. The Lord gave me that power to use to make you stronger, not to destroy you.

[11]Now, brothers *and sisters*, I say good-bye. Try to be perfect. Do the things I have asked you to do. Agree in your minds with each other, and live in peace. Then the God of love and peace will be with you.

[12]Give each other a holy kiss when you greet each other. [13]All of God's holy people say hello to you.

[14]The grace (*kindness*) of the Lord Jesus Christ, the love of God, and the fellowship* of the Holy Spirit* be with you all.

---

fellowship   Associating with people and sharing things together with them. Christians share love, joy, sorrow, faith, and other things with each other and with God.
Holy Spirit   Also called the Spirit of God, the Spirit of Christ, and the Comforter. He is joined with God and Christ. He does the work of God among people in the world.

Galatians

1 From Paul, an apostle.*
I was not chosen to be an apostle by men. I was not sent from men. No! It was Jesus Christ and God the Father who made me an apostle. God is the One who raised Jesus from death.

²This letter is also from all the brothers *in Christ* who are with me.

To the churches (*groups of believers*) in Galatia*:

³I pray that God our Father and the Lord Jesus Christ will be good to you and give you peace. ⁴Jesus gave himself for our sins. Jesus did this to free us from this evil world we live in. This is what God the Father wanted. ⁵The glory belongs to God forever and ever. Amen.

There Is Only One True Gospel

⁶A short time ago, God called you to follow him. He called you through his grace (*kindness*) that came through Christ. But now I am amazed at you people! You are already turning away and believing a different gospel. ⁷Really, there is no other true gospel.* But some people are confusing you. They want to change the gospel of Christ. ⁸We told you the true gospel. So if we ourselves or even an angel from heaven tells you a different gospel, he should be condemned! ⁹I said this before. Now I say it again: You have already accepted the true gospel. If any person tells you another way to be saved, he should be condemned!

¹⁰Now do you think I am trying to make people accept me? No! God is the One I am trying to please. Am I trying to please men?

---

apostle Person Jesus chose to be a special helper for telling the Good News to the world.
Galatia Probably the same country where Paul preached and began churches on his first missionary trip. Read the book of Acts, chapters 13 and 14.
gospel The Good News that God has made a way through Christ for people to have their sins forgiven and live with God. When people accept this truth, God accepts them.

If I wanted to please men, I would not be a servant of Jesus Christ.

Paul's Authority Is from God

[11]Brothers, I want you to know that the gospel* I preached to you was not made by men. [12]I did not get the gospel from men. No man taught me the gospel. Jesus Christ gave it to me. He showed me the gospel that I should tell people.

[13]You have heard about my past life. I was in the Jewish religion. I persecuted the church of God very much. I tried to destroy the church (*believers*). [14]I was becoming a leader in the Jewish religion. I did better than most other Jews my own age. I tried harder than anyone else to follow the old rules. These rules were the customs we got from our ancestors.

[15]But God had special plans for me even before I was born. So God called me with his grace (*kindness*). God wanted me [16]to tell the Good News* about his Son (*Jesus*) to the non-Jewish people. So God showed (*taught*) me about his Son. When God called me, I did not get advice or help from any man. [17]I did not go to see the apostles* in Jerusalem. These men were apostles before I was. But, without waiting, I went away to Arabia. Later, I went back to the city of Damascus.

[18]Three years later, I went to Jerusalem; I wanted to meet Peter.* I stayed with Peter 15 days. [19]I met no other apostles*— only James, the brother of the Lord (*Jesus*). [20]God knows that these things I write are not lies. [21]Later, I went to the areas of Syria and Cilicia.

[22]In Judea, the churches (*groups of believers*) in Christ had never met me before. [23]They had only heard this about me: "This man was persecuting us. But now he is telling people about the same faith that he once tried to destroy." [24]These believers praised God because of me.

---

gospel, Good News   The Good News that God has made a way through Christ for people to have their sins forgiven and live with God. When people accept this truth, God accepts them.
apostles   Men that Jesus chose to be his special helpers for telling his Good News to the world.
Peter   The text says Cephas, the Jewish name for Peter. He was one of Jesus' twelve apostles.

The Other Apostles Accepted Paul

2 After 14 years, I went to Jerusalem again. I went with Barnabas, and I took Titus with me. ²I went because God showed me that I should go. I went to those men who were the leaders *of the believers*. When we were alone, I told these men the gospel* I preach to the non-Jewish people. *I wanted these men to understand my work*, so that my past work and the work I do now would not be wasted. ³⁻⁴Titus was with me. Titus is a Greek (*non-Jew*). But these leaders did not force even Titus to be circumcised.* *We needed to talk about these problems*, because some false brothers had come into our group secretly. They came in like spies to find out about the freedom we have in Christ Jesus. ⁵But we did not agree with anything those false brothers wanted! We wanted the truth of the gospel to continue for you.

⁶Those men who seemed to be important did not change the gospel* I preach. (It doesn't matter to me if they were "important" or not. To God all men are the same.) ⁷But these leaders saw that God had given me a special work, the same as Peter.* God gave Peter the work of telling the Good News* to the Jews. But God gave me the work of telling the Good News to the non-Jewish people. ⁸God gave Peter the power to work as an apostle.* Peter is an apostle for the Jewish people. God gave me the power to work as an apostle too. But I am an apostle for the people who are not Jews. ⁹James, Peter, and John seemed to be the leaders. They saw that God had given me special grace. So they accepted Barnabas and me. Peter, James, and John said, "Paul and Barnabas, we agree that you should go to the people who are not Jews. We will go to the Jews." ¹⁰They asked us to do only one thing—to remember to help the poor people. And this was something that I really wanted to do.

---

gospel, Good News   The Good News that God has made a way through Christ for people to have
their sins forgiven and live with God. When people accept this truth, God accepts them.
circumcised   To have the foreskin cut off. This was done to every Jewish baby boy. It was a
physical mark of the agreement that God made with Abraham (Genesis 17:9-14).
Peter   The text says, "Cephas," the Jewish name for Peter. He was one of Jesus' twelve apostles.
apostle   Person Jesus chose to be a special helper for telling the Good News to the world.

Paul Shows that Peter Was Wrong

[11]Peter came to Antioch. He did something that was not right. I was against Peter, because he was wrong. [12]This is what happened: When Peter first came to Antioch, he ate and associated with the non-Jewish people. But then some Jewish men were sent from James. When these Jewish men came, Peter stopped eating with the non-Jewish people. Peter separated himself from the non-Jews. He was afraid of the Jews who believe that all non-Jewish people must be circumcised.* [13]So Peter was a hypocrite.* The other Jewish believers joined with Peter. So they were hypocrites too. Even Barnabas was influenced by the things these Jewish believers did. [14]I saw what these Jews did. They were not following the truth of the gospel.* So I spoke to Peter in a way that all the other Jews could hear what I said. This is what I said: "Peter, you are a Jew. But you don't live like a Jew. You live like the non-Jewish people. So why do you now force the non-Jewish people to live like Jews?"

[15]We Jews were not born as non-Jews and sinners. We were born as Jews. [16]We know that a person is not made right with God by following the law.* No! It is trusting in Jesus Christ that makes a person right with God. So we have put our faith in Christ Jesus, because we wanted to be made right with God. And we are right with God because we trusted in Christ—not because we followed the law. *This is true* because no person can be made right with God by following the law.

[17]We Jews came to Christ to be made right with God. So it is clear that we were sinners too. Does this mean that Christ makes us sinners? No! [18]But I would really be wrong to begin teaching again those things (*the law*) that I gave up. [19]I stopped living for the law. It was the law that killed me. I died to the law so that I can now live for God. I (*my old life*) was killed on the cross with

---

circumcised   To have the foreskin cut off. This was done to every Jewish baby boy. It was a
    physical mark of the agreement that God made with Abraham (Genesis 17:9-14).
hypocrite   A person who acts like he is good but is not.
gospel   The Good News that God has made a way through Christ for people to have their sins
    forgiven and live with God. When people accept this truth, God accepts them.
law   God's law. The law of Moses is a good example of this law.

Christ. ²⁰So the life that I live now is not really me—it is Christ living in me. I still live in my body, but I live by faith in the Son of God (*Jesus*). Jesus is the One who loved me. He gave himself to save me. ²¹This gift is from God, and it is very important to me. Why? Because if the law could make us right with God, then Christ did not have to die.

God's Blessing Comes Through Faith

3 You people in Galatia were told very clearly about the death of Jesus Christ on the cross. But you were very foolish. You let someone trick you. ²Tell me this one thing: How did you receive the *Holy* Spirit*? Did you receive the Spirit by following the law*? No! You received the Spirit because you heard *the Good News** and believed it. ³You began *your life in Christ* with the Spirit. Now do you try to continue it by your own power? That is foolish. ⁴You have experienced many things. Were all those experiences wasted? I hope they were not wasted! ⁵Does God give you the Spirit because you follow the law? No! Does God work miracles* among you because you follow the law? No! God gives you his Spirit and works miracles among you because you heard *the Good News* and believed it.

⁶*The Scriptures** *say* the same thing about Abraham*: "Abraham believed God. And God accepted Abraham's faith. That made Abraham right with God." ⁷So you should know that the true children of Abraham are the people who have faith. ⁸The Scriptures told what would happen in the future. These writings said that God would make the non-Jewish people right through their faith. This Good News* was told to Abraham before, like the Scripture says: "God will use you, *Abraham*, to bless all the people on earth." ⁹Abraham believed this. Because Abraham believed, he was blessed. *It is the same today*. All people who believe are blessed the same as Abraham was blessed. ¹⁰But

Holy Spirit Also called the Spirit of God, the Spirit of Christ, and the Comforter. He is joined with God and Christ. He does the work of God among people in the world.
law God's law. The law of Moses is a good example of this law.
Good News The news that God has made a way through Christ for people to have their sins forgiven and live with God. When people accept this truth, God accepts them.
miracles Miracles are powerful works or great things done by the power of God.
Scriptures Holy Writings—the Old Testament.
Abraham Most respected ancestor of the Jews. Every Jew hoped to see Abraham.

482

people who depend on following the law *to make them right* are under a curse. Why? Because the Scriptures* say, "A person must do all the things that are written in the law.* If he does not always obey, then that person is under a curse!" ¹¹So it is clear that no person can be made right with God by the law. *The Scriptures say*, "The person who is right with God by faith will live *forever*." ¹²The law does not use faith; *it uses a different way*. The law says, "A person who wants to find life by following these things (*the law*) must do the things the law says." ¹³The law put a curse on us. But Christ took away that curse. He changed places with us. Christ put himself under that curse. It is written in the Scriptures, "When a person's body is put (*hung*) on a tree,* that person is under a curse." ¹⁴Christ did this so that God's blessing could be given to all people. God promised this blessing to Abraham. The blessing comes through Jesus Christ. *Jesus died* so that we could have the *Holy* Spirit* that God promised. We receive this promise by believing.

The Law and the Promise

¹⁵Brothers *and sisters*, let me give you an example: Think about an agreement that one person makes with another person. After that agreement is made official, no person can stop that agreement or add anything to it. And no person can ignore that agreement. ¹⁶God made promises to Abraham* and his Descendant. God did not say, "and to your descendants." That would mean many people. But God said, "and to your Descendant." That means only one person; that person is Christ. ¹⁷This is what I mean: God gave an agreement to Abraham. God promised to do the things that he told Abraham. The law* came 430 years later. The law does not change God's promise to Abraham. ¹⁸Can following the law give us the things God promised? No! If we could receive those things by following the

---

Scriptures Holy Writings—the Old Testament.
law The law of Moses.
put...tree Deuteronomy 21:22-23 says that when a person was killed for doing wrong, his body was hung on a tree to show shame. Paul means that the cross of Jesus was like that.
Holy Spirit Also called the Spirit of God, the Spirit of Christ, and the Comforter. He is joined with God and Christ. He does the work of God among people in the world.
Abraham Most respected ancestor of the Jews. Every Jew hoped to see Abraham.

law, then it is not God's promise that brings us those things. But God freely gave *his blessings* to Abraham through the promise God made.

[19]So what was the law* for? The law was given *to show people the wrong things they do.* The law continued until the special Descendant (*Christ*) of Abraham came. God's promise was about this Descendant. The law was given through angels. The angels used *Moses* for a mediator* to give the law to men. [20]A mediator is not needed when there is only one side, but God is only one.

The Purpose of the Law of Moses

[21]Does this mean that the law* is against God's promises? No! If there was a law that could give men life, then we could be made right by following the law. [22]But this is not true, because the Scriptures* showed that all people are bound by sin. Why did the Scriptures do this? So that the promise would be given to people through faith. The promise is given to people who believe in Jesus Christ.

[23]Before this faith came, we were all held prisoners by the law. We had no freedom until God showed us the way of faith that was coming. [24]So the law was our master until Christ came. After Christ came, we could be made right with God through faith. [25]Now the way of faith has come. So we don't live under the law now.

[26-27]You were all baptized* into Christ. So you were all clothed with Christ. This shows that you are all children of God through faith in Christ Jesus. [28]Now, in Christ, there is no difference between Jew and Greek (*non-Jew*). There is no difference between slaves and free men. There is no difference between male and female. You are all the same in Christ Jesus. [29]You belong to Christ. So you are Abraham's* descendants. You get all of God's blessings because of the promise *that God made to Abraham.*

---

law   The law of Moses.
mediator   A person who helps one person talk to or give something to another person.
Scriptures   Holy Writings—the Old Testament.
baptized   A Greek word meaning to be immersed, dipped, or buried briefly under water.
Abraham   Most respected ancestor of the Jews. Every Jew hoped to see Abraham.

4 I want to tell you this: While the heir* is still a child, he is no different from a slave. It doesn't matter that the heir owns everything. Why? ²Because while he is a child, he must obey the people who are chosen to care for him. But when the child reaches the age his father set, he is free. ³It is the same for us. We were once like children. We were slaves to the useless rules of this world. ⁴But when the right time came, God sent his Son. God's Son was born from a woman. God's Son lived under the law.* ⁵God did this so that he could buy the freedom of the people who were under the law. God's purpose was to make us his children.

⁶You are God's children. That is why God sent the Spirit of his Son into your hearts. The Spirit* cries out, "Father, dear Father."* ⁷So now you are not a slave like before. You are God's child. God will give you the things he promised because you are his child.

Paul's Love for the Galatian Christians

⁸In the past, you did not know God. You were slaves to gods that were not real. ⁹But now you know the true God. Really, it is God who knows you. So why do you turn back to those weak and useless rules you followed before? Do you want to be slaves to those things again? ¹⁰You still follow *the teaching of the law about* special days, months, seasons, and years. ¹¹I am afraid for you. I fear that my work for you has been wasted.

¹²Brothers *and sisters*, I was like you; so please become like me. You were very good to me before. ¹³You remember why I came to you the first time. It was because I was sick. That was when I preached the Good News* to you. ¹⁴My sickness was a burden to you. But you did not show hate for me. You did not make me leave. You welcomed me like I was an angel from God. You accepted me like I was Jesus Christ himself! ¹⁵You were very happy then. Where is that joy now? I remember that *you wanted to do anything possible to help me.* You would have taken out

heir   A person who gets his father's things when his father dies.
law   The law of Moses.
Spirit   The Holy Spirit. Also called the Spirit of God, the Spirit of Christ, and the Comforter. He is joined with God and Christ. He does the work of God among people in the world.
Good News   The news that God has made a way through Christ for people to have their sins forgiven and live with God. When people accept this truth, God accepts them.

your own eyes and given them to me if that were possible. [16]Now am I your enemy because I tell you the truth?

[17]Those people* are working hard to persuade you. But this is not good for you. Those people want to persuade you to turn against us. They want you to follow only them and no other people. [18]It is good for people to show interest in you, but only if their purpose is good. This is always true. It is true when I am with you and when I am away. [19]My little children, again I feel pain for you like a mother feels when she gives birth. I will feel this until you truly become like Christ. [20]I wish I could be with you now. Then maybe I could change the way I am talking to you. Now I don't know what to do about you.

The Example of Hagar and Sarah

[21]Some of you people still want to be under the law *of Moses*. Tell me, do you know what the law says? [22]The Scriptures* say that Abraham* had two sons. The mother of one son was a slave woman. The mother of the other son was a free woman. [23]Abraham's son from the slave woman was born in the normal human way. But the son from the free woman was born because of the promise *God made to Abraham*.

[24]This true story makes a picture for us. The two women are like the two agreements (*covenants*) between God and men. One agreement is *the law that God made* on Mount Sinai.* The people who are under this agreement are like slaves. The mother named Hagar is like that agreement. [25]So Hagar is like Mount Sinai in Arabia. She is a picture of the earthly *Jewish* city of Jerusalem. This city is a slave, and all its people (*the Jews*) are slaves *to the law*. [26]But the heavenly Jerusalem that is above is like the free woman. This is our mother. [27]It is written in the Scriptures*:

"Be happy, woman who cannot have children!
    You never gave birth.
Shout and cry with joy! You never felt the pain
    of giving birth.

Those people   These are the false teachers who were bothering the believers in Galatia (Gal. 1:7).
Scriptures   Holy Writings—the Old Testament.
Abraham   Most respected ancestor of the Jews. Every Jew hoped to see Abraham.
Mount Sinai   Mountain in Arabia where God gave his laws to Moses (Exodus 19 and 20).

> The woman who is alone* will have more children
> than the woman who has a husband." *Isaiah 54:1*

²⁸⁻²⁹One son *of Abraham** was born in the normal way. *Abraham's* other son (*Isaac*) was born by the power of the Spirit,* *because of God's promise*. My brothers *and sisters*, you are also children of promise like Isaac was then. The son who was born in the normal way treated the other son (*Isaac*) badly. It is the same today. ³⁰But what does the Scripture* say? "Throw out the slave woman and her son! The son of the free woman will receive everything his father has. But the son of the slave woman will receive nothing." ³¹So, my brothers *and sisters*, we are not children of the slave woman. We are children of the free woman.

Keep Your Freedom

5 We have freedom now. Christ made us free. So stand strong. Don't change and go back into the slavery *of the law.* ²Listen! I am Paul. I tell you that if you *go back to the law* by being circumcised,* then Christ is no good for you. ³Again, I warn every man: If you allow yourselves to be circumcised, then you must follow all the law. ⁴If you try to be made right with God through the law, then your life with Christ is finished—you have left God's grace (*kindness*). ⁵But we have a hope. We wait for this anxiously. We will be made right with God through the Spirit.* How? By our faith. ⁶When a person is in Christ Jesus, it is not important if he is circumcised or not. The only thing that is important is faith—the kind of faith that works through love.

⁷You were running a good race. You were obeying the truth. Who persuaded you to stop following the true way? ⁸That persuasion does not come from the One (*God*) who chose you. ⁹*Be careful!* "Just a little yeast makes the whole batch of dough rise"—*a small thing can make a big problem.* ¹⁰I trust in the Lord that you will not believe those different ideas. Some person is

---

woman...alone   The woman is alone because her husband has left her.
Abraham   Most respected ancestor of the Jews. Every Jew hoped to see Abraham.
Spirit   The Holy Spirit. Also called the Spirit of God, the Spirit of Christ, and the Comforter. He is joined with God and Christ. He does the work of God among people in the world.
Scripture   A part of the Holy Writings—the Old Testament.
circumcised   To have the foreskin cut off. This was done to every Jewish baby boy. It was a physical mark of the agreement that God made with Abraham (Genesis 17:9-14).

confusing you with those ideas. That person will be punished, whoever he is.

[11]My brothers *and sisters*, I don't teach that people must be circumcised.* If I do teach circumcision,* then why am I still being persecuted? If I still taught that people must be circumcised, then my preaching about the cross would not be a problem. [12]I wish those people who are bothering you would add castration* *to their circumcision.*

[13]My brothers *and sisters*, God called you to be free. But don't use your freedom as an excuse to do the things that please your sinful self. But serve each other with love. [14]The whole law* is made complete in this one command: "Love other people like you love yourself." [15]If you continue hurting each other and tearing each other apart, be careful! You will completely destroy each other.

The Spirit and Human Nature

[16]So I tell you: Live by following the Spirit.* Then you will not do the evil things your sinful selves want. [17]Our sinful selves want things that are against the Spirit. The Spirit wants things that are against our sinful selves. These two different things are against each other. So you don't do the things you really want to do. [18]But if you let the Spirit lead you, then you are not under the law.*

[19]The wrong things our sinful self does are clear: being sexually unfaithful, not being pure, doing sexual sins, [20]worshiping false gods, doing witchcraft,* hating, making trouble, having jealousy, being very angry, being selfish, making people mad at each other, making divisions, [21]having envy, being drunk, having wild and wasteful parties, and doing other things like this. I warn you now like I warned you before: The people who do these

---

circumcised, circumcision To have the foreskin cut off. This was done to every Jewish baby boy. It was a physical mark of the agreement that God made with Abraham (Genesis 17:9-14).

castration To cut off part of the male sex organs. Paul uses this word because it is like "circumcision." Paul wants to show that he is very upset with the false teachers.

law God's law. The law of Moses is a good example of this law.

Spirit The Holy Spirit. Also called the Spirit of God, the Spirit of Christ, and the Comforter. He is joined with God and Christ. He does the work of God among people in the world.

witchcraft Using magic or the power of Satan to do things.

things will not be in God's kingdom. ²²But the Spirit* gives love, joy, peace, patience, kindness, goodness, faithfulness, ²³gentleness, self-control. There is no law that can say these things are wrong. ²⁴Those people who belong to Christ Jesus have crucified (*killed*) their own sinful selves. They have given up their old selfish feelings and the evil things they wanted to do. ²⁵We get our new life from the Spirit. So we should follow the Spirit. ²⁶We must not be vain (*conceited*). We must not make trouble with each other. And we must not be jealous of each other.

Help Each Other

6 Brothers *and sisters*, a person in your group might do something wrong. You people who are spiritual should go to the person who is sinning. You should help to make him right again. You should do this in a gentle way. But be careful! You might be tempted to sin too. ²Help each other with your troubles. When you do this, you truly obey the law of Christ. ³If a person thinks that he is important when he is really not important, he is only fooling himself. ⁴A person should not compare himself with other people. Each person should judge his own actions. Then he can be proud for what he himself has done. ⁵Each person must accept his own responsibility.

⁶The person who is learning the teaching of God should share all the good things he has with the person who is teaching him.

Life Is Like Planting a Field

⁷Don't be fooled: You cannot cheat God. A person harvests only the things he plants.* ⁸If a person plants (*lives*) to satisfy his sinful self, then his sinful self will bring him eternal death. But if a person plants to please the Spirit,* he will get eternal life from the Spirit. ⁹We must not become tired of doing good. We will

---

Spirit The Holy Spirit. Also called the Spirit of God, the Spirit of Christ, and the Comforter. He is joined with God and Christ. He does the work of God among people in the world.

harvests...plants Paul uses these words about farming to show that life is like a farmer planting a field. A farmer will get from the field only what he plants. Life is like that.

receive our harvest *of eternal life* at the right time. We must not give up! ¹⁰When we have the opportunity to do good to any person, we should do it. But we should give special attention to the people that are in the family of believers (*the church*).

Paul Ends His Letter

¹¹I am writing this myself. See what big letters I use. ¹²Some men are trying to force you to be circumcised.* They do these things so that other people (*the Jews*) will accept them. Those men fear that they will be persecuted if they follow only the cross of Christ* (*the gospel*). ¹³Those men who are circumcised don't obey the law* themselves. But they want you to be circumcised. Then they can boast about what they forced you to do. ¹⁴I hope I will never boast about things like that. The cross of our Lord Jesus Christ is my only reason for boasting. Through the cross of Jesus my world has died (was crucified); and I died to the world. ¹⁵It is not important if a person is circumcised or not circumcised. The important thing is being the new people God has made. ¹⁶Peace and mercy to the people who follow this rule—to all of God's people.

¹⁷So don't give me any more trouble. I have scars on my body. These scars show* that I belong to Christ Jesus.

¹⁸My brothers *and sisters*, I pray that the grace (*kindness*) of our Lord Jesus Christ will be with your spirits. Amen.

---

circumcised   To have the foreskin cut off. This was done to every Jewish baby boy. It was a physical mark of the agreement that God made with Abraham (Genesis 17:9-14).
cross of Christ   Paul uses the cross as a picture of the gospel, the story of Christ's death to pay for men's sins. The cross (Christ's death) was God's way to save men.
law   The law of Moses.
These scars show   Many times Paul was beaten and whipped by people who were against him because he was teaching about Christ. The scars were from these beatings.

Ephesians

1 From Paul, an apostle* of Christ Jesus. I am an apostle because that is what God wanted.

To God's holy people living in Ephesus, believers in Christ Jesus.

²Grace (*kindness*) and peace to you from God our Father and the Lord Jesus Christ.

Spiritual Blessings in Christ

³Praise be to the God and Father of our Lord Jesus Christ. In Christ, God has given us every spiritual blessing in heaven. ⁴In Christ, God chose us before the world was made. God chose us in love to be his holy people—people without blame before him. ⁵And before the world was made, God decided to make us his own children through Jesus Christ. That was what God wanted to do. That pleased him. ⁶And this brings praise to God because of his wonderful grace (*kindness*). God gave that grace to us freely. He gave us that grace in *Christ*, the One he loves. ⁷In Christ we are made free by Christ's blood (*death*). We have forgiveness of sins because of God's rich grace. ⁸God gave us that grace fully and freely. ⁹God, with full wisdom and understanding, let us know his secret plan. This was what God wanted. And he planned to do it through Christ. ¹⁰God's goal was to finish his plan when the right time came. God planned that all things in heaven and on earth be joined together with Christ as the head.

¹¹In Christ we were chosen *to be God's people*. God had already planned for us to be his people, because that is what God wanted. And God is the One who makes everything agree with

apostle Person Jesus chose to be a special helper for telling the Good News to the world.

what he decides and wants. [12]We are the first people who hoped in Christ. And we were chosen so that we would bring praise to God's glory. [13]It is the same with you people. You heard the true teaching—the Good News* about your salvation. When you heard that Good News, you believed in Christ. And in Christ, God put his special mark on you by giving you the Holy Spirit* that he promised. [14]That Holy Spirit is the guarantee that we will get the things God promised for his people. This will bring full freedom to those people who belong to God. The goal of all this is to bring praise to God's glory.

Paul's Prayer

[15-16]That is why I always remember you in my prayers and always thank God for you. I have always done this since the time I heard about your faith in the Lord Jesus and your love for all God's people. [17]I always pray to the God of our Lord Jesus Christ—to the glorious Father. I pray that he will give you a spirit that will make you wise with the knowledge of God—the knowledge that he has shown you. [18]I pray that you will have greater understanding in your heart. Then you will know the hope that God has chosen us to have. You will know that the blessings God has promised his holy people are rich and glorious. [19]And you will know that God's power is very great for us who believe. That power is the same as the great strength [20]that God used to raise Christ from death. God put Christ at his right side in the heavenly places. [21]God made Christ more important than all rulers, authorities, powers, and kings. Christ is more important than anything that has power in this world or in the next world. [22]God put everything under Christ's power. And God gave him to be the head (*ruler*) over everything for the church. [23]The church is Christ's body. The church is filled with Christ. He makes everything complete in every way.

Good News The news that God has made a way through Christ for people to have their sins forgiven and live with God. When people accept this truth, God accepts them.

Holy Spirit Also called the Spirit of God, the Spirit of Christ, and the Comforter. He is joined with God and Christ. He does the work of God among people in the world.

From Death to Life

2 In the past your spiritual lives were dead because of your sins and the things you did wrong against God. ²Yes, in the past you lived doing those sins. You lived the way the world lives. You followed the ruler of the evil powers over the earth. That same spirit is now working in those people who refuse to obey God. ³In the past all of us lived like those people. We lived trying to please our sinful selves. We did all the things our bodies and minds wanted. We were *evil* people. We should have suffered God's anger because of the way we were. We were the same as all other people.

⁴But God's mercy is very great, and God loved us very much. ⁵We were *spiritually* dead. We were dead because of the things we did wrong against God. But God gave us new life with Christ. You have been saved by God's grace (*kindness*). ⁶And God raised us up with Christ and gave us a seat with him in the heavenly places. God did this for us who are in Christ Jesus. ⁷God did this so that for all future time he could show the very great riches of his grace. God shows that grace by being kind to us in Christ Jesus. ⁸I mean that you are saved by grace. And you got that grace by believing. You did not save yourselves. It was a gift from God. ⁹No! You are not saved by the things you have done. So no person can boast *that he saved himself*. ¹⁰God has made us what we are. In Christ Jesus, God made us new people so that we would do good things. God had already planned those good things for us. God had planned for us to live our lives doing those good things.

One in Christ

¹¹You were born non-Jews. You are the people the Jews call "uncircumcised.*" Those Jews who call you "uncircumcised" call themselves "circumcised.*" (Their circumcision* is only something they themselves do on their bodies.) ¹²Remember that

---

uncircumcised   People not having the mark of circumcision like the Jews have.
circumcised   People having the mark of circumcision.
circumcision   The cutting off of the foreskin. This was done to every Jewish baby boy. It was a mark of the agreement that God made with Abraham (Genesis 17:9-14).

in the past you were without Christ. You were not citizens of Israel.* And you did not have the agreements* with the promise *that God made to his people*. You had no hope and you did not know God. ¹³Yes, at one time you were far away *from God*. But now in Christ Jesus you are brought near to him. You are brought near *to God* through the blood (*death*) of Christ. ¹⁴Because of Christ we now have peace. Christ made us both (*Jews and non-Jews*) one people. The Jews and the non-Jews were separated like there was a wall between them. They hated each other. But Christ broke down that wall of hate by *giving* his own body. ¹⁵The Jewish law had many commandments and rules. But Christ ended that law. Christ's purpose was to make the two groups of people (*Jew and non-Jew*) become one new people in him. By doing this Christ would make peace. ¹⁶And after the two groups became one body, Christ wanted to bring them both back to God. Christ did this with his death on the cross. Through the cross Christ ended the hate between the two groups. ¹⁷Christ came and preached peace to you people (*non-Jews*) who were far away *from God*. And he preached peace to the people (*Jews*) who were near *to God*. ¹⁸Yes, through Christ we all have the right to come to the Father in one Spirit.*

¹⁹So now you *non-Jews* are not visitors or strangers. Now you are citizens together with God's holy people. You belong to God's family. ²⁰You believers are like a building that God owns. That building was built on the foundation that the apostles* and prophets* prepared. Christ Jesus himself is the most important stone* in that building. ²¹That whole building is joined together in Christ. And Christ makes it grow and become a holy temple* in the Lord. ²²And in Christ you people are being built together with the other people (*the Jews*). You are being made into a place where God lives through the Spirit.*

Israel The Jewish nation (people).
agreements The agreements that God gave to his people in the Old Testament.
Spirit The Holy Spirit. Also called the Spirit of God, the Spirit of Christ, and the Comforter. He is joined with God and Christ. He does the work of God among people in the world.
apostles Men that Jesus chose to be his special helpers for telling his Good News to the world.
prophets People who spoke for God.
most important stone Literally, "cornerstone." The first and most important rock in a building.
temple God's house—the place where God's people worship and serve him.

Paul's Work for the Gentiles

3 So I (*Paul*) am a prisoner of Christ Jesus. I am a prisoner for you people who are not Jews. [2]Surely you know that God gave me this work through his grace (*kindness*). God gave me this work to help you. [3]God let me know his secret plan. He showed it to me. I have already written a little about this. [4]And if you read these things I wrote, then you can see that I truly understand the secret truth about the Christ. [5]People who lived in other times were not told that secret truth. But now, through the Spirit,* God has shown that secret truth to his holy apostles* and prophets.* [6]This is that secret truth: that the non-Jews will get the things God has for his people, the same as the Jews. The non-Jews are together with the Jews in the same body. And they share together in the promise that God made in Christ Jesus. The non-Jews have all these things because of the Good News.*

[7]By God's grace (*kindness*), I became a servant to tell that Good News.* God gave me that grace by using his power. [8]I am the least important of all of God's people. But God gave me this gift—to tell the non-Jewish people the Good News about the riches Christ has. Those riches are too great to understand fully. [9]And God gave me the work of telling all people about the plan for God's secret truth. That secret truth has been hidden in God since the beginning of time. God is the One who created everything. [10]God's purpose was that all the rulers and powers in the heavenly places will now know the wisdom of God. They will know this because of the church.* [11]This agrees with the plan God had since the beginning of time. God did what he planned. He did it through Christ Jesus our Lord. [12]In Christ we can come before God with freedom and without fear. We can do this through faith in Christ. [13]So I ask you not to become discouraged *and lose hope* because of the sufferings I am having for you. My sufferings bring honor to you.

Spirit   The Holy Spirit. Also called the Spirit of God, the Spirit of Christ, and the Comforter. He
    is joined with God and Christ. He does the work of God among people in the world.
apostles   Men that Jesus chose to be his special helpers for telling his Good News to the world.
prophets   People who spoke for God.
Good News   The news that God has made a way through Christ for people to have their sins
    forgiven and live with God. When people accept this truth, God accepts them.
church   God's church—his people in Christ.

The Love of Christ

¹⁴So I bow in prayer before the Father. ¹⁵Every family in heaven and on earth gets its true name from him. ¹⁶I ask the Father with his great glory to give you the power to be strong in your spirits. He will give you that strength through his Spirit.* ¹⁷I pray that Christ will live in your hearts because of your faith. I pray that your life will be strong in love and be built on love. ¹⁸And I pray that you and all God's holy people will have the power to understand the greatness of Christ's love. I pray that you can understand how wide and how long and how high and how deep that love is. ¹⁹Christ's love is greater than any person can ever know. But I pray that you will be able to know that love. Then you can be filled with the fullness of God.

²⁰With God's power working in us, God can do much, much more than anything we can ask or think of. ²¹To him be glory in the church and in Christ Jesus for all time, for ever and ever. Amen.

The Unity of the Body

4 I am in prison because I belong to the Lord. And God chose you to be his people. I tell you now to live the way God's people should live. ²Always be humble and gentle. Be patient and accept each other with love. ³You are joined together with peace through the Spirit.* Do all you can to continue together in this way. Let peace hold you together. ⁴There is one body and one Spirit. And God called you to have one hope. ⁵There is one Lord, one faith, and one baptism.* ⁶There is one God and Father of everything. He rules everything. He is everywhere and in everything.

⁷Christ gave each one of us a special gift. Each person received what Christ wanted to give that person. ⁸That is why it says *in the Scriptures,**

Spirit   The Holy Spirit. Also called the Spirit of God, the Spirit of Christ, and the Comforter. He is joined with God and Christ. He does the work of God among people in the world.

baptism   A Greek word meaning the burying of a person briefly under water. This happens when a person begins his new life in Christ.

Scriptures   Holy Writings—the Old Testament.

"He went up high into the sky;
he took prisoners with him,
and he gave gifts to people."

Psalm 68:18

⁹When it says, "He went up," what does it mean? It means that he first came down low to earth. ¹⁰So Jesus came down, and he is the same One who went up. He went up above all the sky. Christ did that to fill everything with himself. ¹¹And that same Christ gave gifts to people—he made some people to be apostles,* some people to be prophets,* some people to go and tell the Good News,* and some people to have the work of caring for and teaching God's people. ¹²Christ gave those gifts to prepare God's holy people for the work of serving. He gave those gifts to make the body of Christ stronger. ¹³*This work must continue* until we are all joined together in the same faith and in the same knowledge about the Son of God. We must become like a mature (*perfect*) person—we must grow until we become like Christ and have all his perfection.

¹⁴Then we will not still be babies. We will not be people who change like a ship that the waves carry one way and then another. We will not be influenced (*changed*) by every new teaching we hear from men who try to fool us. Those men make plans and try any kind of trick to fool people into following the wrong way. ¹⁵No! We will speak the truth with love. We will grow to be like Christ in every way. Christ is the head *and we are the body.* ¹⁶The whole body depends on Christ. And all the parts of the body are joined and held together. Each part of the body does its own work. And this makes the whole body grow and be strong with love.

The Way You Should Live

¹⁷For the Lord I tell you this. I warn you: Don't continue living like those people who don't believe. Their thoughts are worth nothing. ¹⁸Those people don't understand. They know nothing because they refuse to listen. So they cannot have the life that God gives. ¹⁹They have lost their feeling of shame. And they use

apostles Men that Jesus chose to be his special helpers for telling his Good News to the world.
prophets People who spoke for God. Their writings are part of the Old Testament.
Good News The news that God has made a way through Christ for people to have their sins forgiven and live with God. When people accept this truth, God accepts them.

their lives for doing evil. More and more they want to do all kinds of bad things. ²⁰But the things you learned in Christ were not like those bad things. ²¹I know that you heard about him. And you are in him, so you were taught the truth. Yes, the truth is in Jesus. ²²You were taught to leave your old self—to stop living the evil way you lived before. That old self becomes worse and worse because people are fooled by the evil things they want to do. ²³But you were taught to be made new in your hearts. ²⁴You were taught to become a new person. That new person is made to be like God—made to be truly good and holy.*

²⁵So you must stop telling lies. You must always speak the truth to each other, because we all belong to each other in the same body. ²⁶When you become angry, don't let that anger make you sin. And don't continue to be angry all day. ²⁷Don't give the devil a way to defeat you. ²⁸If a person is stealing, he must stop stealing. That person must start working. He must use his hands for doing something good. Then he will have something to share with those people who are poor.

²⁹When you talk, don't say any bad things. But say things that people need—things that will help other people become stronger. Then the things you say will help the people who listen to you. ³⁰And don't make the Holy Spirit* sad. The Spirit is God's proof that you belong to God. God gave you that Spirit to show that God will make you free at the right time. ³¹Never be bitter or angry or mad. Never shout angrily or say things to hurt other people. Never do anything evil. ³²Be kind and loving to each other. Forgive each other the same as God forgave you in Christ.

Living in the Light

5 You are God's children that he loves. So try to be like God. ²Live a life of love. Love other people the same as Christ loved us. Christ gave himself for us—he was a sweet-smelling offering and sacrifice* to God.

³But there must be no sexual sin among you. There must not be any kind of evil or greed (*selfishness*). Why? Because those things

---

holy   A holy person is pure, belongs only to God, and does only the things that God wants.
Holy Spirit   Also called the Spirit of God, the Spirit of Christ, and the Comforter. He is joined with God and Christ. He does the work of God among people in the world.
sacrifice   An offering or gift to God.

are not right for God's holy* people. ⁴Also, there must be no evil talk among you. You must not speak foolishly or tell evil jokes. These things are not right for you. But you should be giving thanks to God. ⁵You can be sure of this: No person will have a place in the kingdom of Christ and of God if that person does sexual sins, or does evil things, or is a person who always wants more and more for himself. A person who always wants more and more for himself is serving a false god.

⁶Don't let any person fool you by telling you things that are not true. Those evil things make God angry with the people who don't obey. ⁷So don't do those things with them. ⁸In the past you were *full of* darkness (*sin*) but now you are *full of* light (*goodness*) in the Lord. So live like children who belong to the light. ⁹Light brings every kind of goodness, right living, and truth. ¹⁰Try to learn what pleases the Lord. ¹¹Don't do the things that people in darkness do. Doing those things brings nothing good. But *do the good things to* show that those things in darkness are wrong. ¹²It is really very shameful to even talk about the things those people in darkness do in secret. ¹³But when we show that those things are wrong, the light makes all those things easy to see. ¹⁴And everything that is made easy to see can become light. This is why we say:

> "Wake up, you sleeping person!
>   Rise from death,
> and Christ will shine on you."

¹⁵So be very careful how you live. Don't live like people who are not wise. But live wisely. ¹⁶I mean that you should use every chance you have for doing good, because these are evil times. ¹⁷So don't be foolish with your lives. But learn what the Lord wants you to do. ¹⁸Don't be drunk with wine. That will ruin (*destroy*) you spiritually. But be filled with the Spirit.* ¹⁹Communicate to each other with psalms, hymns, and spiritual songs. Sing and make music in your hearts to the Lord. ²⁰Always give thanks to God the Father for everything. Give him thanks in the name of our Lord Jesus Christ.

---

holy   Holy people are pure, belong only to God and do only the things that God wants.
Spirit   The Holy Spirit. Also called the Spirit of God, the Spirit of Christ, and the Comforter. He is joined with God and Christ. He does the work of God among people in the world.

Wives and Husbands

²¹Be willing to obey each other. Do this because you respect Christ.

²²Wives, be under the authority of (*obey*) your husbands the same as the Lord. ²³The husband is the head of the wife the same as Christ is the head of the church. The church is Christ's body— Christ is the Savior of the body. ²⁴The church is under the authority of Christ. So it is the same with you wives. You should be under the authority of your husbands in everything.

²⁵Husbands, love your wives the same as Christ loved the church. Christ died for the church. ²⁶He died to make the church holy.* Christ used the telling of the Good News* to make the church clean by washing it with water. ²⁷Christ died so that he could give the church to himself *like a bride* full of glory (*beauty*). He died so that the church could be pure and without fault, with no evil or sin or any other thing wrong in the church. ²⁸And husbands should love their wives like that. They should love their wives like they love their own bodies. The man who loves his wife loves himself. ²⁹Why? Because no person ever hates his own body. Every person feeds and takes care of his body. And that is what Christ does for the church, ³⁰because we are parts of his body. ³¹*The Scripture* says*, "So a man will leave his father and mother and join his wife. And the two will become one body."* ³²That secret truth is very important—I am talking about Christ and the church. ³³But each one of you must love his wife like he loves himself. And a wife must respect her husband.

Children and Parents

6 Children, obey your parents the way the Lord wants. That is the right thing to do. ²The commandment says, "You must respect *and obey* your father and mother."* That is the first commandment that has a promise with it. ³That promise is:

---

holy   Holy people are pure, belong only to God and do only the things that God wants.
Good News   The news that God has made a way through Christ for people to have their sins forgiven and live with God. When people accept this truth, God accepts them.
Scripture   A part of the Holy Writings—the Old Testament.
"So...body"   Quotation from Genesis 2:24.
"You...mother"   Quotation from Exodus 20:12, Deuteronomy 5:16.

"Then everything will be fine with you. And you will have a long life on the earth."*

⁴Fathers, don't make your children angry. But raise your children with the training and teaching of the Lord.

Slaves and Masters

⁵Slaves, obey your masters here on earth. Obey with fear and respect. And do that with a heart that is true, the same as you obey Christ. ⁶You must do more than just obey your masters to please them while they are watching you. You must obey them like you are obeying Christ. With all your heart you must do what God wants. ⁷Do your work and be happy to do it. Work like you are serving the Lord, not like you are serving only men. ⁸Remember that the Lord will give every person a reward for doing good. Every person, slave or free, will get a reward for the good things he does.

⁹Masters, in the same way, be good to your slaves. Don't say things to scare them. You know that the One who is your Master and their Master is in heaven. And that Master (*God*) judges every person the same.

Wear the Full Armor of God

¹⁰To end my letter I tell you, be strong in the Lord and in his great power. ¹¹Wear the full armor (*protection*) of God. Wear God's armor so that you can fight against the devil's evil tricks. ¹²Our fight is not against people on earth. We are fighting against the rulers and authorities and the powers of this world's darkness. We are fighting against the spiritual powers of evil in the heavenly places. ¹³That is why you need to get God's full armor. Then on the day of evil you will be able to stand strong. And when you have finished the whole fight, you will still be standing. ¹⁴So stand strong, with the belt of truth tied around your waist. And on your chest wear the protection of right living. ¹⁵And on your feet wear the Good News* of peace to help you

---

"Then...earth" Quotation from Exodus 20:12, Deuteronomy 5:16.
Good News The news that God has made a way through Christ for people to have their sins forgiven and live with God. When people accept this truth, God accepts them.

stand strong. ¹⁶And also use the shield of faith. With that you can stop all the burning arrows of the evil one (*the devil*). ¹⁷Accept God's salvation to be your helmet. And take the sword of the Spirit*—that sword is the teaching of God. ¹⁸Pray in the Spirit at all times. Pray with all kinds of prayers and ask for everything you need. To do this you must always be ready. Never give up. Always pray for all of God's people.

¹⁹Also pray for me. Pray that when I speak, God will give me words so that I can tell the secret truth of the gospel* without fear. ²⁰I have the work of speaking for that gospel. I am doing that now, here in prison. Pray that when I preach that gospel I will speak without fear, like I should.

Final Greetings

²¹I am sending to you Tychicus our brother that we love. He is a faithful servant of the Lord's work. He will tell you everything that is happening with me. Then you will know how I am and what I am doing. ²²I send him to you so that he can tell you these things about me. I want you to know how we are. And I send him so that he can comfort you.

²³Peace and love with faith to you from God the Father and the Lord Jesus Christ. ²⁴God's grace (*kindness*) to all of you who love our Lord Jesus Christ with love that never ends.

Spirit   The Holy Spirit. Also called the Spirit of God, the Spirit of Christ, and the Comforter. He is joined with God and Christ. He does the work of God among people in the world.
gospel   The Good News that God has made a way through Christ for people to have their sins forgiven and live with God. When people accept this truth, God accepts them.

Philippians

1 From Paul and Timothy, servants of Jesus Christ. To all of God's people in Christ Jesus that live in Philippi. And to all your elders* and deacons.*

²Grace (*kindness*) and peace to you from God our Father and the Lord Jesus Christ.

Paul's Prayer

³I thank God every time I remember you. ⁴And I always pray for all of you with joy. ⁵I thank God for the help you gave me while I preached the gospel.* You helped from the first day you believed until now. ⁶God began doing good things with you. And God is continuing that work in you. God will finish that work in you when Jesus Christ comes again. I am sure of that.

⁷And I know that I am right to think like this about all of you. I am sure because I have you in my heart—I feel very close to you. I feel close to you because all of you share in God's grace (*kindness*) with me. You share in God's grace with me while I am in prison, while I am defending the gospel,* and while I am proving the truth of the gospel. ⁸God knows that I want to see you very much. I love all of you with the love of Christ Jesus.

⁹This is my prayer for you:

that your love will grow more and more;
that you will have knowledge and understanding with
    your love;
¹⁰that you will see the difference between good and bad
    and choose the good;

elders A group of men chosen to lead a church. Also called "overseers" and "pastors" (shepherds), they have the work of caring for God's people (Acts 20:28; Ephesians 4:11).
deacons People chosen to serve the church in special ways.
gospel The Good News that God has made a way through Christ for people to have their sins forgiven and live with God. When people accept this truth, God accepts them.

that you will be pure and without wrong for the coming
of Christ;
¹¹that you will do many good things with the help of
Christ, to bring glory and praise to God.

Paul's Troubles Help the Lord's Work

¹²Brothers *and sisters*, I want you to know that those bad things
that happened to me have helped to spread the gospel.* ¹³It is
clear why I am in prison. I am in prison because I am a believer in
Christ. All the guards know this and so do all the other people. ¹⁴I
am still in prison, but most of the believers feel better about it
now. And so they are much braver about telling people the
message* *about Jesus*.

¹⁵Some people preach about Christ because they are jealous
and bitter. Other people preach about Christ because they want
to help. ¹⁶These people preach because they have love. They know
that God gave me the work of defending the gospel.* ¹⁷But those
other people preach about Christ because they are selfish. Their
reason for preaching is wrong. They want to make trouble for me
in prison.

¹⁸I don't care if they make trouble for me. The important thing
is that they are telling people about Christ. I want them to tell
people about Christ. They should do it for the right reasons. But I
am happy even if they do it for false and wrong reasons. I am
happy because they tell people about Christ, and I will continue
to be happy. ¹⁹You are praying for me, and the Spirit of Jesus
Christ helps me. So I know that this trouble will bring my
freedom. ²⁰The thing I want and hope for is that I will not fail
Christ in anything. I hope that I will have the courage now, like
always, to show the greatness of Christ in my life here on earth. I
want to do that if I die or if I live. ²¹I mean that to me the only
important thing about living is Christ. And even death would be
profit for me, *because death would bring me nearer to Christ*. ²²If
I continue living in the body, then I will be able to work for the

gospel, message   The Good News that God has made a way through Christ for people to have
their sins forgiven and live with God. When people accept this truth, God accepts them.

Lord. But what would I choose—living or dying? I don't know.
²³It is hard to choose between living or dying. I want to leave this
life and be with Christ. That is much better. ²⁴But you people
need me here in my body. ²⁵I know that you need me. And so I
know that I will stay with you. I will help you grow and have joy
in your faith. ²⁶You will be very happy in Christ when I am with
you again.

²⁷Be sure that you live in a way that brings honor to the gospel*
of Christ. Then if I come and visit you or if I am away from you,
I will hear good things about you. I will hear that you continue
strong with the same purpose and work together like a team for
the faith (*truth*) of the gospel. ²⁸And you will not be afraid of
those people who are against you. All of these things are proof
from God that you are being saved and that your enemies will be
lost. ²⁹God gave you the honor of believing in Christ. But that is
not all. God also gave you the honor of suffering for Christ. Both
these things bring glory to Christ. ³⁰When I was with you, you
saw the struggles I had *with people who were against the gospel*.
And now you hear about the struggles I am having. You
yourselves are having the same kind of struggles.

Be United and Care for Each Other

2 Is there any way in Christ that I can ask you to do
something? Does your love make you want to comfort me?
Do we share together in the Spirit*? Do you have mercy and
kindness? ²If you have these things, then I ask you to do
something for me. This will make me very happy. I ask that all
your minds be joined together by believing the same things. Be
joined together in your love for each other. Live together by
agreeing with each other and having the same goals. ³When you
do things, don't let selfishness or pride be your guide. Be humble
and give more honor to other people than to yourselves. ⁴Don't
be interested only in your own life, but be interested in the lives of
other people, too.

gospel The Good News that God has made a way through Christ for people to have their sins
    forgiven and live with God. When people accept this truth, God accepts them.
Spirit The Holy Spirit. Also called the Spirit of God, the Spirit of Christ, and the Comforter. He
    is joined with God and Christ. He does the work of God among people in the world.

Learn from Christ to Be Unselfish

[5]In your lives you must think and act like Christ Jesus.

[6]Christ himself was like God in everything. Christ was equal with God. But Christ did not think that being equal with God was something that he must keep.

[7]He gave up his place with God, and agreed to be like a servant. He was born to be a man and became like a servant.

[8]When he was living as a man, he humbled himself by being fully obedient to God. He obeyed even when that caused him to die. And he died on a cross.

[9]Christ obeyed God, so God raised Christ to the most important place. God made the name of Christ greater than every other name.

[10]God wants every person to bow for the name of Jesus. Every person in heaven, on the earth, and under the earth will bow.

[11]Every person will confess (say), "Jesus Christ is Lord (Master)." When they say this, it will bring glory to God the Father.

Be the People God Wants You to Be

[12]My dear friends, you have always obeyed. You obeyed God when I was with you. It is even more important that you obey now while I am not with you. Without my help you must make sure that you get your salvation. Do this with respect and fear for God. [13]Yes, God is working in you. God makes you want to do the things that please him. And he helps you do these things.

[14]Do everything without complaining or arguing. [15]Then you will be innocent and without anything wrong in you. You will be God's children without fault. But you are living with evil people all around you who have become very bad. Among those people you shine like lights in the dark world. [16]You offer those people the teaching that gives life. So I can be happy when Christ comes again. I can be happy because my work was not wasted. I ran in the race and won.

[17]Your faith makes you give your lives as a sacrifice* in serving God. Maybe I will have to offer my own blood (death) with your

---

sacrifice An offering or gift to God.

sacrifice. But if that happens, I will be happy and full of joy with all of you. ¹⁸You also should be happy and full of joy with me.

News About Timothy and Epaphroditus

¹⁹I hope in the Lord Jesus to send Timothy to you soon. I will be happy to learn how you are. ²⁰I have no other person like Timothy. He truly cares for you. ²¹Other people are interested only in their own lives. They are not interested in the work of Christ Jesus. ²²You know the kind of person **Timothy** is. You know that he has served with me in telling the Good News* like a son serves his father. ²³I plan to send him to you quickly. I will send him when I know what will happen to me. ²⁴I am sure that the Lord will help me to come to you soon.

²⁵Epaphroditus is my brother in Christ. He works and serves with me in the army of Christ. When I needed help, you sent him to me. I think now that I must send him back to you. ²⁶I send him because he wants very much to see all of you. He is worried because you heard that he was sick. ²⁷He was sick and was near death. But God helped him and me too, so that I would not have more sadness. ²⁸So I want very much to send him to you. When you see him, you can be happy. And I can stop worrying about you. ²⁹Welcome him in the Lord with much joy. Give honor to people like Epaphroditus. ³⁰He should be honored because he almost died for the work of Christ. He put his life in danger so that he could help me. This was help that you could not give me.

Christ Is More Important Than All Other Things

3 My brothers *and sisters*, be happy in the Lord. It is no trouble for me to write the same things to you again, and it will help you to be more ready. ²Be careful of those people who do evil. They are like dogs. They demand to cut* the body. ³But we are the people who are truly circumcised.* We worship (*serve*) God through his Spirit.* We are proud to be in Christ Jesus. And

Good News The news that God has made a way through Christ for people to have their sins forgiven and live with God. When people accept this truth, God accepts them.

cut The word in Greek is like the word "circumcise," but it means "to cut completely off."

circumcised To have the foreskin cut off. This was done to every Jewish baby boy. It was a physical mark of the agreement that God made with Abraham (Genesis 17:9-14).

Spirit The Holy Spirit. Also called the Spirit of God, the Spirit of Christ, and the Comforter. He is joined with God and Christ. He does the work of God among people in the world.

we don't trust in ourselves or anything we can do. ⁴Even if I am able to trust in myself, still I don't trust in myself. If any other person thinks that he has a reason to trust in himself, then he should know that I have a greater reason for trusting in myself. ⁵I was circumcised* eight days after my birth. I am from the people of Israel* and the family group of Benjamin. I am a Hebrew (*Jew*) and my parents were Hebrews. The law *of Moses* was very important to me. That is why I became a Pharisee.* ⁶I was so excited *about my Jewish religion* that I persecuted* the church (*the believers*). No person could find fault with the way I always obeyed the law *of Moses*. ⁷At one time all these things were important to me. But now I think those things are worth nothing because of Christ. ⁸Not only those things, but I think that all things are worth nothing compared with the greatness of knowing Christ Jesus my Lord. Because of Christ, I lost all those things *I thought were important*. And now I know that all those things are worthless trash. This allows me to have Christ. ⁹It allows me to be in Christ. In Christ, I am right with God. And this does not come from my following the law. It comes from God through faith. God uses my faith in Christ to make me right with him. ¹⁰All I want is to know Christ and the power of his rising from death. I want to share in Christ's sufferings and become like him in his death. ¹¹If I have these things, then I have hope that I myself will be raised from death.

We Must Continue Trying to Reach Our Goal

¹²I don't mean that I am already exactly like God wants me to be. I have not yet reached that goal. But I continue trying to reach that goal and to make it mine. Christ wants me to do that. That is the reason Christ made me his. ¹³Brothers *and sisters*, I know that I have not yet reached that goal. But there is one thing I always do: I forget the things that are past. I try as hard as I can to reach

---

circumcised   To have the foreskin cut off. This was done to every Jewish baby boy. It was a
    physical mark of the agreement that God made with Abraham (Genesis 17:9-14).
Israel   The Jewish nation (people).
Pharisee   Pharisees were a Jewish religious group that followed all of the Old Testament and
    other Jewish laws and customs very carefully.
persecuted   To persecute is to punish or hurt other people.

the goal that is before me. ¹⁴I keep trying to reach the goal and get the prize. That prize is mine because God called me through Christ to the life above.

¹⁵All of us who have grown spiritually to be mature (*perfect*) should think this way too. And if there is any of these things you don't agree with, God will make it clear to you. ¹⁶But we should continue following the *truth* we already have.

¹⁷Brothers *and sisters*, all of you should try to live like me. And copy those people who live the way we showed you. ¹⁸Many people live like enemies of the cross of Christ. I have often told you about these people. And it makes me cry to tell you about them now. ¹⁹The way these people live is leading them to destruction. They don't serve God. Those people live only to please themselves. They do shameful things, and they are proud of those things. They think only about earthly things. ²⁰But our home is in heaven. We are waiting for our Savior to come from heaven. Our Savior is the Lord Jesus Christ. ²¹He will change our humble bodies and make them like his own glorious body. Christ can do this by his power. With that power Christ is able to rule all things.

Paul Tells the Philippian Christians Some Things to Do

4 My dear brothers *and sisters*, I love you and want to see you. You bring me joy and make me proud of you. Continue following the Lord like I have told you.

²I ask Euodia and Syntyche to agree in the Lord. ³And because you serve faithfully with me, my friend, I ask you to help these women do this. These women served with me in telling people the Good News.* They served together with Clement and the other people who worked with me. Their names are written in the book of life.*

⁴Be full of joy in the Lord always. I will say again, be full of joy.

⁵Let all people know that you are gentle and kind. The Lord is coming soon. ⁶Don't worry about anything. But pray and ask God for everything you need. And when you pray, always give

Good News The news that God has made a way through Christ for people to have their sins forgiven and live with God. When people accept this truth, God accepts them.
book of life God's book that has the names of all God's chosen people (Revelation 3:5; 21:27).

thanks. [7]And God's peace will keep your hearts and minds in Christ Jesus. That peace which God gives is so great that we cannot understand it.

[8]Brothers *and sisters*, continue to think about the things that are good and worthy of praise. Think about the things that are true and honorable and right and pure and beautiful and respected. [9]And do the things that you learned and received from me. Do the things I told you and the things you saw me do. And the God who gives peace will be with you.

Paul Thanks the Philippian Christians for a Gift

[10]I am very happy in the Lord that you have shown your care for me again. You continued to care about me, but there was no way for you to show it. [11]I am telling you these things, but it is not because I need something. I have learned to be satisfied with the things I have and with everything that happens. [12]I know how to live when I am poor. And I know how to live when I have plenty. I have learned the secret of being happy at any time in everything that happens. I have learned to be happy when I have enough to eat and when I don't have enough to eat. I have learned to be happy when I have all the things I need and when I don't have the things I need. [13]I can do all things through Christ, because he gives me strength.

[14]But it was good that you helped me when I needed help. [15]You people in Philippi remember when I first preached the Good News* there. When I left Macedonia, you were the only church that gave me help. [16]Several times you sent me things I needed when I was in Thessalonica. [17]Really, it is not that I want to get gifts from you. But I want you to have the good that comes *from giving*. [18]I have all the things I need. I have even more than I need. I have all I need because Epaphroditus brought your gift to me. Your gift is like a sweet-smelling sacrifice* offered to God. God accepts that sacrifice and it pleases him. [19]My God is very

---

Good News The news that God has made a way through Christ for people to have their sins forgiven and live with God. When people accept this truth, God accepts them.
sacrifice An offering or gift to God.

rich with the glory of Christ Jesus. God will use his riches in Christ Jesus to give you everything you need. [20]Glory to our God and Father forever and ever. Amen.

[21]Say hello to each of God's people in Christ. God's people who are with me say hello to you. [22]All of God's people say hello to you. And those believers from Caesar's* palace say hello, too.

[23]The grace (*kindness*) of the Lord Jesus Christ be with you all.

Caesar The name or title given to the emperor (ruler) of Rome.

Colossians

1 From Paul, an apostle* of Christ Jesus.
I am an apostle because that is what God wanted.
This letter is also from Timothy, our brother in Christ.

²To the holy* and faithful brothers *and sisters* in Christ that live in Colossae. Grace (*kindness*) and peace from God our Father.

³In our prayers we always thank God for you. God is the Father of our Lord Jesus Christ. ⁴We thank God because we have heard about the faith you have in Christ Jesus, and the love you have for all of God's people. ⁵You have faith in Christ and love God's people because of the hope you have. You know that the things you hope for are saved for you in heaven. You learned about this hope when you heard the true teaching, the Good News* ⁶that was told to you. Everywhere in the world that Good News is bringing blessings and growing. This same thing has happened with you since the time you heard that Good News and understood the truth about the grace (*kindness*) of God. ⁷You learned about the grace of God from Epaphras. Epaphras works together with us and we love him. He is a faithful servant of Christ for us. ⁸Epaphras also told us about the love you have from the *Holy* Spirit.*

⁹Since the day we heard these things about you, we have continued praying for you. We pray these things for you:

> that you will know fully the things that God wants;
> that with your knowledge you will also have great
> wisdom and understanding in spiritual things;

---

apostle   Person Jesus chose to be a special helper for telling the Good News to the world.
holy   A holy person is pure, belongs only to God, and does only the things that God wants.
Good News   The news that God has made a way through Christ for people to have their sins forgiven and live with God. When people accept this truth, God accepts them.
Holy Spirit   Also called the Spirit of God, the Spirit of Christ, and the Comforter. He is joined with God and Christ. He does the work of God among people in the world.

512

¹⁰that you will use these things to live in a way that
brings honor to the Lord and pleases him in every way;
that you will do all kinds of good things and grow in the
knowledge of God;
¹¹that God will strengthen you with his own great power;
that God will strengthen you so that you will not quit when
troubles come, and so that you will be patient and happy.

¹²Then you can give thanks to the Father. He has made you able to have the things he prepared for you. He has prepared these things for all his people who live in the light (*good*). ¹³God made us free from the power of darkness (*evil*). And he brought us into the kingdom of his dear Son (*Jesus*). ¹⁴The Son paid for our sins. In him we have forgiveness of our sins.

When We Look at Christ, We See God

¹⁵No person can see God. But Jesus is exactly like God. Jesus is ruler over all the things that have been made. ¹⁶Through his power all things were made—things in heaven and on earth, things seen and not seen, all *spiritual* powers, authorities, lords, and rulers. All things were made through Christ and for Christ. ¹⁷Christ was there before anything was made. And all things continue because of him. ¹⁸Christ is the head of the body. (The body is the church.) Everything comes from him. And he is the Lord who was raised from death. So in all things Jesus is most important. ¹⁹God was pleased for all of himself to live in Christ. ²⁰And through Christ, God was happy to bring all things back to himself again—things on earth and things in heaven. God made peace by using Christ's blood (*death*) on the cross.

²¹At one time you were separated from God. You were God's enemies in your minds because the evil things you did were against God. ²²But now Christ has made you God's friends again. Christ did this by his death while he was in his body. Christ did this so that he could bring you before God. He brings you before God as people who are holy,* with no wrong in you, and with nothing that God can judge you guilty of. ²³Christ will do this if

---

holy A holy person is pure, belongs only to God, and does only the things that God wants.

you continue to believe in the Good News* you heard. You must continue strong and sure in your faith. You must not be moved away from the hope that Good News gave you. That same Good News has been told to all people in the world. I, Paul, help in telling that Good News.

Paul's Work for the Church

[24]I am happy in my sufferings for you. There are many things that Christ must still suffer through his body, the church. I am accepting my part of these things that must be suffered. I accept these sufferings in my body. I suffer for his body, the church. [25]I became a servant of the church because God gave me a special work to do. This work helps you. My work is to tell fully the teaching of God. [26]This teaching is the secret truth that was hidden since the beginning of time. This truth was hidden from all people. But now that secret truth is made known to God's people. [27]God decided to let his people know that rich and glorious truth. That great truth is for all people. That truth is Christ himself, who is in you. He is our only hope for glory. [28]So we continue to tell people about Christ. We use all wisdom to strengthen every person and teach every person. We are trying to bring all people before God as people who have grown to be spiritually mature (*perfect*) in Christ. [29]To do this, I work and struggle using the great strength that Christ gives me. That strength is working in my life.

2 I want you to know that I am trying very hard to help you. And I am trying to help the people in Laodicea and other people who have never seen me. [2]I want them to be strengthened and joined together with love. I want them to be rich in the strong belief that comes from understanding. I mean I want you to know fully the secret truth that God has made known. That truth is Christ himself. [3]In Christ all the treasures of wisdom and knowledge are safely kept.

Good News The news that God has made a way through Christ for people to have their sins forgiven and live with God. When people accept this truth, God accepts them.

⁴I tell you these things so that no person can fool you by telling you ideas that seem good, but are false. ⁵I am not there with you, but my heart is with you. I am happy to see your good lives and your strong faith in Christ.

Continue to Live in Christ

⁶You received Christ Jesus the Lord. So continue to live following him without changing anything. ⁷You must depend on Christ only. Life and strength come from him. You were taught the truth. You must continue to be sure of that true teaching. And always be thankful.

⁸Be sure that no person leads you away with false ideas and words that mean nothing. Those ideas come from people, not Christ. Those ideas are the worthless ideas of people in the world. ⁹All of God lives in Christ fully (even in Christ's life on earth). ¹⁰And in Christ you are full. You need nothing else. Christ is ruler over all rulers and powers.

¹¹In Christ you had a different kind of circumcision.* That circumcision was not done by the hands of any person. I mean you were made free from the power of your sinful self. That is the kind of circumcision Christ does. ¹²When you were baptized,* *your old self died and* you were buried with Christ. And in that baptism* you were raised up with Christ because of your faith in God's power. God's power was shown when he raised Christ from death. ¹³You were spiritually dead because of your sins and because you were not free from the power of your sinful self. But God made you alive with Christ. And God forgave all our sins. ¹⁴We owed a debt because we broke God's laws. That debt listed all the rules we failed to follow. But God forgave us of that debt. God took away that debt and nailed it to the cross. ¹⁵God defeated the spiritual rulers and powers. With the cross God won the victory and defeated those rulers and powers. God showed the world that they were powerless.

---

circumcision   The cutting off of the foreskin. This was done to every Jewish baby boy. It was a mark of the agreement that God made with Abraham (Genesis 17:9-14).
baptized, baptism   Greek words meaning to be immersed, dipped, or buried briefly under water.

Don't Follow Teachings and Rules That Men Make

[16]So don't let any person make rules for you about eating and drinking or about Jewish customs (feasts, new moon celebrations,* or Sabbath days*). [17]In the past, these things were like a shadow that showed what was coming. But the new things that were coming are found in Christ. [18]Some people enjoy acting like they are humble and love to worship angels. Those people always talk about the visions* they have seen. Don't let those people say, "You don't do these things, so you are wrong." Those people are full of foolish pride because they think only the thoughts of people, *not the thoughts of God*. [19]Those people don't keep themselves under the control of the head (*Christ*). The whole body depends on Christ. Because of Christ all the parts of the body care for each other and help each other. This strengthens the body and holds it together. And so the body grows in the way God wants.

[20]You died with Christ and were made free from the worthless rules of the world. So why do you act like you still belong to this world? I mean, why do you follow rules like these: [21]"Don't eat this," "Don't taste that," "Don't touch that thing"? [22]These rules are talking about earthly things that are gone after they are used. These rules are only commands and teachings from people, *not God*. [23]These rules seem to be wise. But these rules are only part of a man-made religion that makes people pretend to be humble and makes them punish their bodies. But these rules don't help people to stop doing the evil things their sinful selves want to do.

Your New Life in Christ

3 You were raised from death with Christ. So try to get the things in heaven. I mean the things where Christ is, sitting at the right hand of God. [2]Think only about the things in heaven, not the things on earth. [3]Your old sinful self has died, and your new life is kept with Christ in God. [4]Christ is your life. When he comes again, you will share in his glory.

new moon celebrations Special days that some people thought were holy days.
Sabbath days The Sabbath day (seventh day of the week) was a special religious day for the Jews.
visions A vision is something like a dream that God used to speak to people.

⁵So put all evil things out of your life: sexual sinning, doing evil, letting evil thoughts control you, wanting things that are evil, and always selfishly wanting more and more. This wanting really means to live serving a false god. ⁶These things make God angry.* ⁷In your evil life in the past, you also did these things.

⁸But now put these things out of your life: anger, being very mad, doing or saying things to hurt other people, and using evil words when you talk. ⁹Don't lie to each other. Why? Because you have left your old sinful life and the things you did before. ¹⁰You have begun to live the new life. In your new life you are being made new. You are becoming like the One who made you. This new life brings you the true knowledge of God. ¹¹In the new life there is no difference between Greeks and Jews. There is no difference between people that are circumcised* and people that are not circumcised, or people that are from some foreign country, or Scythians.* There is no difference between slaves and free people. But Christ is in all those believers. And Christ is all that is important.

¹²God has chosen you and made you his holy* people. He loves you. So always do these things: Show mercy to people; be kind, humble, gentle, and patient. ¹³Don't be angry with each other, but forgive each other. If another person does something wrong against you, then forgive that person. Forgive other people because the Lord forgave you. ¹⁴Do all these things; but most important, love each other. Love is the thing that holds you all together in perfect unity. ¹⁵Let the peace that Christ gives control your thinking. You were all called together in one body* to have peace. Always be thankful. ¹⁶Let the teaching of Christ live inside you richly. Use all wisdom to teach and strengthen each other. Sing psalms, hymns, and spiritual songs with thankfulness in your hearts to God. ¹⁷Everything you say and everything you do should all be done for Jesus your Lord (*Master*). And in all you do, give thanks to God the Father through Jesus.

These...angry Some Greek copies add: "against the people who don't obey God."
circumcised To have the foreskin cut off. This was done to every Jewish baby boy. It was a physical mark of the agreement that God made with Abraham (Genesis 17:9-14).
Scythians The Scythians were known as very wild and uncivilized people.
holy A holy person is pure, belongs only to God, and does only the things that God wants.
body The spiritual body of Christ, meaning the church or his people.

Your New Life with Other People

¹⁸Wives, be under the authority of (*obey*) your husbands. This is the right thing to do in the Lord.

¹⁹Husbands, love your wives, and be gentle to them.

²⁰Children, obey your parents in all things. This pleases the Lord.

²¹Fathers, don't frustrate your children. If you are too hard to please, they might want to quit trying.

²²Servants, obey your masters in all things. Obey all the time, even when your masters can't see you. But it is not people you are really trying to please—*you are trying to please the Lord*. So obey honestly because you respect the Lord. ²³In all the work you are doing, work the best you can. Work like you are working for the Lord, not for people. ²⁴Remember that you will receive your reward from the Lord. He will give you what he promised his people. You are serving the Lord Christ. ²⁵Remember that any person who does wrong will be punished for that wrong. And the Lord treats every person the same.

4 Masters, give the things that are good and fair to your servants. Remember that you have a Master in heaven.

Paul Tells Christians Some Things to Do

²Continue praying. And when you pray, always thank God. ³Also pray for us. Pray that God will give us an opportunity to tell people his message.* Pray that we can preach the secret truth that God has made known about Christ. I am in prison because I preach this truth. ⁴Pray that I can make this truth clear to people. That is what I should do.

⁵Be wise in the way you act with those people who are not believers. Use your time in the best way you can. ⁶When you talk, you should always be kind and wise. Then you will be able to answer every person in the way you should.

---

message   The Good News that God has made a way through Jesus for people to have their sins forgiven and live with God. When people accept this truth, God accepts them.

News About the People with Paul

[7]Tychicus is my dear brother in Christ. He is a faithful minister and servant with me in the Lord. He will tell you all the things that are happening to me. [8]I send Tychicus to tell you how we are. And I send him to strengthen you. [9]I send him with Onesimus. Onesimus is a faithful and dear brother in Christ. He is from your group. Tychicus and Onesimus will tell you all that has happened here.

[10]Aristarchus says hello. He is a prisoner with me. And Mark, the cousin of Barnabas, also says hello. (I have already told you what to do about Mark. If he comes, welcome him.) [11]Jesus (he is also called Justus) also says hello. These are the only Jewish believers who work with me for the kingdom of God. They have been a comfort to me.

[12]Epaphras also says hello. He is a servant of Jesus Christ. And he is from your group. He always prays for you. He prays that you will grow to be spiritually mature (*perfect*) and have everything that God wants for you. [13]I know that he has worked hard for you and the people in Laodicea and in Hierapolis. [14]Demas and our dear friend Luke, the doctor, say hello.

[15]Say hello to the brothers *and sisters* in Laodicea. And say hello to Nympha and to the church that meets in her house. [16]After this letter is read to you, be sure that it is also read to the church in Laodicea. And you read the letter that I wrote to Laodicea. [17]Tell Archippus, "Be sure to do the work the Lord gave you."

[18]I say hello and write this with my own hand—Paul. Remember me in prison. God's grace (*kindness*) be with you.

1 Thessalonians

1 From Paul, Silvanus, and Timothy.
To the church (*group of believers*) that lives in Thessalonica.
That church is in God the Father and the Lord Jesus Christ.
God's grace (*kindness*) and peace be yours.

The Life and Faith of the Thessalonians

²We always remember you when we pray and we thank God for all of you. ³When we pray to God our Father we always thank him for the things you have done because of your faith. And we thank him for the work you have done because of your love. And we thank him that you continue to be strong because of your hope in our Lord Jesus Christ. ⁴Brothers *and sisters*, God loves you. And we know that he has chosen you to be his. ⁵We brought the Good News* to you. But we did not use only words. We brought that Good News with power. We brought it with the Holy Spirit* and with sure knowledge that it was true. Also you know how we lived when we were with you. We lived that way to help you. ⁶And you became like us and like the Lord. You suffered much, but still you accepted the teaching with joy. The Holy Spirit gave you that joy. ⁷You became an example to all the believers in Macedonia and Achaia. ⁸The Lord's teaching spread from you in Macedonia and Achaia. And also your faith in God has become known everywhere. So we don't need to say anything about your faith. ⁹People everywhere tell about the good way you accepted us when we were there with you. Those people tell about

Good News   The news that God has made a way through Christ for people to have their sins forgiven and live with God. When people accept this truth, God accepts them.
Holy Spirit   Also called the Spirit of God, the Spirit of Christ, and the Comforter. He is joined with God and Christ. He does the work of God among people in the world.

how you stopped worshiping idols* and changed to serve the living and true God. ¹⁰And you stopped worshiping idols to wait for God's Son to come from heaven. God raised that Son from death. He is Jesus who saves us from God's angry judgment that is coming.

Paul's Work in Thessalonica

2 Brothers *and sisters*, you know that our visit to you was not a failure. ²Before we came to you, we suffered in Philippi. People there said bad things against us. You know all about that. And when we came to you, many people were against us. But our God helped us to be brave. He helped us to tell you his Good News.* ³We encourage (*teach*) people. No person has fooled us. We are not evil. We are not trying to trick people. Those are not our reasons for doing what we do. ⁴No. We speak the Good News* because God tested us and trusted us to tell the Good News. So when we speak, we are not trying to please men. We are trying to please God. God is the One who tests (*looks closely at*) our hearts. ⁵You know that we never tried to influence you by saying nice things about you. We were not trying to get your money. We had no selfishness to hide from you. God knows that this is true. ⁶We were not looking for praise from people. We were not looking for praise from you or any other people.

⁷We are apostles* of Christ. And so when we were with you, we could have used our authority to make you do things. But we were very gentle with you. We were like a mother caring for her little children. ⁸We loved you very much. So we were happy to share God's Good News* with you; but not only that—we were also happy to share even our own lives with you. ⁹Brothers *and sisters*, I know that you remember how hard we worked. We worked night and day. We did not want to burden you *by making you pay us* while we preached God's Good News to you.

¹⁰When we were with you believers, we lived in a holy and right way, without fault. You know that this is true, and God knows that this is true. ¹¹You know that we treated each one of you like a

idols   The false gods that the non-Jewish people worshiped.
Good News   The news that God has made a way through Christ for people to have their sins forgiven and live with God. When people accept this truth, God accepts them.
apostles   Men that Jesus chose to be his special helpers for telling his Good News to the world.

521

father treats his own children. ¹²We strengthened you, we comforted you, and we told you to live good lives for God. God calls you to his kingdom and glory.

¹³Also, we always thank God because of the way you accepted God's message (*teaching*). You heard that message from us, and you accepted it like it was God's words, not the words of men. And it really is God's message (*teaching*). And that message works in you people who believe. ¹⁴Brothers *and sisters*, you are like God's churches (*people*) in Christ that are in Judea.* God's people in Judea suffered bad things from the other Jews there. And you suffered the same bad things from the people of your own country. ¹⁵Those Jews killed the Lord Jesus. And they killed the prophets.* And those Jews forced us to leave that country (*Judea*). God is not pleased with them. They are against all people. ¹⁶Yes. They try to stop us from teaching the non-Jews. We teach the non-Jews so that the non-Jews can be saved. But those Jews are adding more and more sins to the sins they already have. The anger of God has fully come to them now.

Paul's Desire to Visit Them Again

¹⁷Brothers *and sisters*, we were separated from you for a short time. (We were not there with you, but our thoughts were still with you.) We wanted very much to see you, and we tried very hard to do this. ¹⁸Yes. We wanted to come to you. Truly I, Paul, tried to come many times, but Satan (*the devil*) stopped us. ¹⁹You are our hope, our joy, and the crown we will be proud of when our Lord Jesus Christ comes. ²⁰Truly you are our joy and our glory.

3 We couldn't come to you, but it was very hard to wait any longer. So we decided to send Timothy to you and stay in Athens alone. Timothy is our brother. He works with us for God. He helps us tell people the Good News* about Christ. We sent Timothy to strengthen and comfort you in your faith. ³We sent Timothy so that none of you would be upset by these troubles we

---

Judea   The Jewish land where Jesus lived and taught, and where the church first began.
prophets   People who spoke for God. Their writings are part of the Old Testament.
Good News   The news that God has made a way through Christ for people to have their sins forgiven and live with God. When people accept this truth, God accepts them.

have now. You yourselves know that we must have these troubles. ⁴Even when we were with you, we told you that we all would have to suffer. And you know that it happened the way we said. ⁵This is why I sent *Timothy* to you, so that I could know about your faith. I sent him when I could not wait any more. I was afraid that the one (*the devil*) who tempts people might have defeated you with temptations. Then our hard work would have been wasted.

⁶But Timothy came back to us from you. He told us good news about your faith and love. Timothy told us that you always remember us in a good way. He told us that you want very much to see us again. And it is the same with us—we want very much to see you. ⁷So, brothers *and sisters*, we are comforted about you, because of your faith. We have much trouble and suffering, but still we are comforted. ⁸Our life is really full if you stand strong in the Lord. ⁹We have so much joy before our God because of you! So we thank God for you. But we cannot thank him enough for all the joy we feel. ¹⁰We continue praying very strongly for you night and day. We pray that we can be there and see you again, and give you all the things you need to make your faith strong.

¹¹We pray that our God and Father and our Lord Jesus will prepare the way for us to come to you. ¹²We pray that the Lord will make your love grow. We pray that he will give you more and more love for each other and for all people. We pray that you will love all people like we love you. ¹³We pray this so that your hearts will be made strong. Then you will be holy* and without fault before our God and Father when our Lord Jesus comes with all his holy people.

A Life That Pleases God

4 Brothers *and sisters*, now I have some other things to tell you. We taught you how to live in a way that will please God. And you are living that way. Now we ask you and encourage you in the Lord Jesus to live that way more and more. ²You know the things we told you to do. We told you those things by the authority (*power*) of the Lord Jesus. ³God wants you to be

---

holy   A holy person is pure, belongs only to God, and does only the things that God wants.

holy.* He wants you to stay away from sexual sins. ⁴God wants each one of you to learn to control your own body.* Use your body in a way that is holy and that gives honor to God. ⁵Don't use your body for sexual sin. The people who don't know God use their bodies for that. ⁶None of you should do wrong to your brother *in Christ* or cheat him in this way. The Lord will punish people that do those things. We have already told you and warned you about that. ⁷God called us to be holy.* He does not want us to live in sin. ⁸So the person who refuses to obey this teaching is refusing to obey God, not man. And God is the One who gives us his Holy Spirit.*

⁹We don't need to write to you about having love for your brothers and sisters in Christ. God has already taught you to love each other. ¹⁰And truly you do love the brothers *and sisters* in all of Macedonia. Brothers *and sisters*, now we encourage you to love them more and more.

¹¹Do all you can to live a peaceful life. Take care of your own business. Do your own work. We have already told you to do these things. ¹²If you do these things, then people who are not believers will respect the way you live. And you will not have to depend on other people for what you need.

The Lord's Coming

¹³Brothers *and sisters*, we want you to know about those people who have died. We don't want you to be sad like other people—people who have no hope. ¹⁴We believe that Jesus died. But we believe that Jesus rose again. So, because of Jesus, God will bring together with Jesus those people who have died. ¹⁵What we tell you now is the Lord's own message. We who are living now might still be living when the Lord comes again. We who are living at that time will be with the Lord, but not before those people who have already died. ¹⁶The Lord himself will come down from heaven. There will be a loud command. That command will be given with the voice of the archangel* and with

holy   A holy person is pure, belongs only to God, and does only the things that God wants.
body   Literally, "vessel." This might also mean "wife."
Holy Spirit   Also called the Spirit of God, the Spirit of Christ, and the Comforter. He is joined
    with God and Christ. He does the work of God among people in the world.
archangel   The leader among God's angels or messengers.

the trumpet call of God. And the people who have died and were in Christ will rise first. [17]After that, we people who are still alive at that time will be gathered up with those people who have died. We will be taken up in the clouds and meet the Lord in the air. And we will be with the Lord forever. [18]So comfort each other with these words.

Be Ready for the Lord's Coming

5 Now, brothers *and sisters*, we don't need to write to you about times and dates. [2]You know very well that the day the Lord comes again will be *a surprise* like a thief that comes in the night. [3]People will say, "We have peace and we are safe." At that time, destruction will come to them quickly. Destruction will come like the pains of a woman who is having a baby. And those people will not escape. [4]But you, brothers *and sisters*, are not living in darkness (*sin*). And so that day will not surprise you like a thief. [5]You are all people who belong to the light (*goodness*). You belong to the day. We don't belong to the night or to darkness (*evil*). [6]So we should not be like other people. We should not be sleeping. We should be awake and have self-control. [7]People who sleep, sleep at night. People who get drunk, get drunk at night. [8]But we belong to the day (*goodness*), so we should control ourselves. We should wear faith and love to protect us. And the hope of salvation should be our helmet. [9]God did not choose us to suffer his anger. God chose us to have salvation through our Lord Jesus Christ. [10]Jesus died for us so that we can live together with him. It is not important if we are alive or dead *when Jesus comes*. [11]So comfort each other and give each other strength. And you are doing that now.

Final Instructions and Greetings

[12]Now brothers *and sisters*, we ask you to respect those people who work hard with you—those who lead you in the Lord and teach you. [13]Respect those people with a very special love because of the work they do *with you*. Live in peace with each other. [14]We ask you, brothers *and sisters*, to warn those people who don't work. Encourage the people who are afraid. Help the people who

are weak. Be patient with every person. ¹⁵Be sure that no person pays back wrong for wrong. But always try to do what is good for each other and for all people.

¹⁶Always be happy. ¹⁷Never stop praying. ¹⁸Give thanks *to God* at all times. That is what God wants for you in Christ Jesus.

¹⁹Don't stop the work of the *Holy* Spirit.* ²⁰Don't treat prophecy* like it is not important. ²¹But test everything. Keep what is good. ²²And stay away from everything that is evil.

²³We pray that God himself, the God of peace, will make you pure—belonging only to him. We pray that your whole self—spirit, soul, and body—will be kept safe, and be without wrong when our Lord Jesus Christ comes. ²⁴The One (*God*) who calls you will do that for you. You can trust him.

²⁵Brothers *and sisters*, please pray for us.

²⁶Give all the brothers *and sisters* a holy kiss when you meet. ²⁷I tell you by the authority (*power*) of the Lord to read this letter to all the brothers *and sisters*.

²⁸The grace (*kindness*) of our Lord Jesus Christ be with you.

Holy Spirit Also called the Spirit of God, the Spirit of Christ, and the Comforter. He is joined with God and Christ. He does the work of God among people in the world.
prophecy Teaching from God, given by a person who speaks for God.

2 Thessalonians

1 From Paul, Silvanus, and Timothy.
To the church (*group of believers*) that lives in Thessalonica. You people are in God our Father and the Lord Jesus Christ.

²Grace (*kindness*) and peace to you from God the Father and the Lord Jesus Christ.

Paul Gives Thanks and Talks About God's Judgment

³We thank God for you always. And we should do that because that is right for us to do. It is right because your faith is growing more and more. And the love that every one of you has for each other is also growing. ⁴So we boast about you to the other churches of God. We tell the other churches the way you continue to be strong and have faith. You are being persecuted and are suffering many troubles, but you continue with strength and faith.

⁵That is proof that God is right in his judgment. God wants you to be worthy of his kingdom. Your suffering is for that kingdom. ⁶God will do what is right. He will give trouble to those people who trouble you. ⁷And God will give peace to you people who are troubled. And he will give peace to us. God will give us this help when the Lord Jesus is shown to us. Jesus will come from heaven with his powerful angels. ⁸He will come from heaven with burning fire to punish those people who don't know God. He will punish those people who don't obey the gospel* of our Lord Jesus Christ. ⁹Those people will be punished with a destruction that continues forever. They will not be allowed to be with the Lord. Those people will be kept away from his great power. ¹⁰This will happen on the day when the Lord *Jesus* comes. Jesus

---

gospel   The Good News that God has made a way through Christ for people to have their sins forgiven and live with God. When people accept this truth, God accepts them.

will come to receive glory with his holy* people. And all the people who have believed will be amazed at Jesus. You will be in that group of believers because you believed the things we told you.

¹¹That is why we always pray for you. We ask our God to help you live the good way that he called you to live. The goodness you have makes you want to do good. And the faith you have makes you work. We pray that with his power God will help you do these things more and more. ¹²We pray all this so that the name of our Lord Jesus Christ can have glory in you. And you can have glory in him. That glory comes from the grace (*kindness*) of our God and the Lord Jesus Christ.

Evil Things Will Happen Before the Lord Comes

2 Brothers *and sisters*, we have something to say about the coming of our Lord Jesus Christ. We want to talk to you about that time when we will meet together with him. ²Don't become easily upset in your thinking or afraid if you hear that the day of the Lord has already come. Some person may say this in a prophecy* or in some message. Or you may read it in a letter that some person tells you came from us. ³Don't let any person fool you in any way. *That day of the Lord will not come* until the turning away *from God* happens. And *that day will not come* until the Man of Evil appears (*comes*). That Man of Evil belongs to hell.* ⁴That Man of Evil is against anything called God or anything that people worship. And that Man of Evil puts himself above anything called God or anything that people worship. That Man of Evil even goes into God's temple* and sits there. Then he says that he is God.

⁵I told you before that all these things would happen. Remember? ⁶And you know what is stopping that Man of Evil now. He is being stopped now so that he will appear (*come*) at the right time. ⁷The secret power of evil is already working in the world now. But there is one who is stopping that secret power of evil. And he will continue to stop it until he is removed (*taken out of the way*). ⁸Then that Man of Evil will appear (*come*). And the

holy   God's people are called holy because they are made pure and belong only to God.
prophecy   Teaching from God, given by a person who speaks for God.
That...hell   Literally, "He is the son of destruction."
temple   Probably the special building in Jerusalem where God commanded the Jews to worship.

Lord Jesus will kill that Man of Evil with the breath that comes from his mouth. The Lord Jesus will destroy that Man of Evil with the glory of his coming. ⁹The Man of Evil will come by the power of Satan (*the devil*). He will have great power, and he will do many different false miracles, signs, and wonders.* ¹⁰The Man of Evil will use every kind of evil to trick those people who are lost. Those people are lost because they refused to love the truth. (If they loved the truth, they would be saved.) ¹¹But those people refused to love the truth, so God sends them something powerful that leads them away from the truth. God sends them that power so that they will believe something that is not true. ¹²So all those people who don't believe the truth will be condemned (*judged guilty*). They did not believe the truth, and they enjoyed doing evil things.

You Are Chosen for Salvation

¹³Brothers *and sisters*, the Lord loves you. God chose you from the beginning to be saved. So we should always thank God for you. You are saved by the Spirit* making you holy* and by your faith (*believing*) in the truth. ¹⁴God called you to have that salvation. He called you by using the Good News* that we preached. God called you so that you can share in the glory of our Lord Jesus Christ. ¹⁵So, brothers *and sisters*, stand strong and continue to believe the teachings we gave you. We taught you those things in our speaking, and in our letter to you.

¹⁶⁻¹⁷We pray that the Lord Jesus Christ himself and God our Father will comfort you and strengthen you in every good thing you do and say. God loved us. Through his grace (*kindness*) he gave us a good hope and comfort that lasts forever.

Pray for Us

3 And now, brothers *and sisters*, pray for us. Pray that the Lord's teaching will continue to spread quickly. And pray that people will give honor to that teaching, the same as happened

---

false miracles, signs, and wonders These are powerful acts done by the devil's power.
Spirit The Holy Spirit. Also called the Spirit of God, the Spirit of Christ, and the Comforter. He is joined with God and Christ. He does the work of God among people in the world.
holy God's people are called holy, because they are made pure and belong only to God.
Good News The news that God has made a way through Christ for people to have their sins forgiven and live with God. When people accept this truth, God accepts them.

with you. ²And pray that we will be protected from bad and evil people. (Not all people believe *in the Lord*.)

³But the Lord is faithful. He will give you strength and protect you from the Evil One (*the devil*). ⁴The Lord makes us feel sure that you are doing the things we told you. And we know that you will continue to do those things. ⁵We pray that the Lord will lead your hearts into God's love and Christ's patience.

The Obligation to Work

⁶Brothers *and sisters*, by the authority (*power*) of our Lord Jesus Christ we command you to stay away from any believer who refuses to work. People who refuse to work are not following the teaching that we gave them. ⁷You yourselves know that you should live like we live. We were not lazy when we were with you. ⁸And when we ate another person's food, we always paid for it. We worked and worked so that we would not be trouble to any of you. We worked night and day. ⁹We had the right *to ask you to help us*. But *we worked to take care of ourselves* so that we would be an example for you to follow. ¹⁰When we were with you, we gave you this rule: "If a person will not work, then he will not eat."

¹¹We hear that some people in your group refuse to work. They do nothing. And they make themselves busy in other people's lives. ¹²We command those people to stop bothering other people. We command them to work and earn their own food. In the Lord Jesus Christ we beg them to do this. ¹³Brothers *and sisters*, never become tired of doing good.

¹⁴If any person does not obey what we tell you in this letter, then remember who that person is. Don't associate with that person. Then maybe that person will feel ashamed. ¹⁵But don't treat him like an enemy—warn him like a brother.

Final Words

¹⁶We pray that the Lord of peace will give you peace. We pray that he will give you peace at all times and in every way. The Lord be with all of you.

[17]I am Paul, and I end this letter now with my own writing. All my letters have this to show they are from me. This is the way I write.

[18]The grace (*kindness*) of our Lord Jesus Christ be with you all.

1 Timothy

1 From Paul, an apostle* of Christ Jesus. I am an apostle by the command of God our Savior and Christ Jesus our hope.
²To Timothy. You are *like* a true son to me because you believe.

Grace (*kindness*), mercy, and peace from God the Father and Christ Jesus our Lord.

Warnings Against False Teachings

³I want you to stay in Ephesus. I asked you to do that when I went into Macedonia. Some people there in Ephesus are teaching false things. Stay there so that you can command those people not to teach those false things. ⁴Tell those people not to give their time to stories that are not true and to long lists of names in family histories. Those things only bring arguments. Those things don't help God's work. God's work is done by faith. ⁵The goal of this command is for people to have love. To have this love people must have a pure heart, they must do what they know is right, and they must have true faith. ⁶Some people have not done these things. They have wandered away, and now they talk about things that are worth nothing. ⁷Those people want to be teachers of the law.* But they don't know what they are talking about. They don't even understand the things that they say they are sure about.

⁸We know that the law* is good if a man uses it right. ⁹We also know that the law is not made for good men. The law is made for people who are against the law and for people who refuse to follow the law. The law is for people who are against God and are sinful, people who are not holy and have no religion, people who

---

apostle Person Jesus chose to be a special helper for telling the Good News to the world.
law Probably the Jewish law that God gave to Moses on Mount Sinai. (Read Exodus 19-20.)

kill their fathers and mothers, murderers, [10]people who do sexual sins, homosexuals, people who sell slaves, people who tell lies, people who speak falsely, and people who do anything that is against the true teaching *of God*. [11]That teaching is part of the Good News* that God gave me to tell. That glorious Good News is from the blessed God.

Thanks for God's Mercy

[12]I thank Christ Jesus our Lord because he trusted me and gave me this work of serving him. And he gives me strength. [13]In the past I spoke against Christ and persecuted him and did things to hurt him. But God gave me mercy because I did not know what I was doing. I did those things when I did not believe. [14]But the grace (*kindness*) of our Lord was fully given to me. And with that grace came the faith and love that are in Christ Jesus.

[15]What I say is true and you should fully accept it: Christ Jesus came into the world to save sinners. And I am the worst of those sinners. [16]But I was given mercy. I was given mercy so that in me Christ Jesus could show that he has patience without limit. Christ showed his patience with me, the worst of all sinners. Christ wanted me to be an example for those people who would believe in him and have life forever. [17]Honor and glory to the King that rules forever. He cannot be destroyed and cannot be seen. Honor and glory for ever and ever to the only God. Amen.

[18]Timothy, you are *like* a son to me. I am giving you a command. This command agrees with the prophecies* that were told about you in the past. I tell you these things so that you can follow those prophecies and fight the good fight *of faith*. [19]Continue to have faith and do what you know is right. Some people have not done this. Their faith has been destroyed. [20]Hymenaeus and Alexander are men who have done that. I have given those men to Satan (*the devil*) so that they will learn not to speak against God.

Good News   The news that God has made a way through Christ for people to have their sins forgiven and live with God. When people accept this truth, God accepts them.

prophecies   Things that prophets said about Timothy's life before those things happened.

Some Rules for Men and Women

2 First, I tell you to pray for all people. Talk to God about all people. Ask him for the things people need, and be thankful to him. ²You should pray for kings and for all people who have authority (*power*). Pray for those leaders so that we can have quiet and peaceful lives—lives full of worship and respect for God. ³This is good and it pleases God our Savior. ⁴God wants all people to be saved. And he wants all people to know the truth. ⁵There is only one God. And there is only one way that people can reach God. That way is through Jesus Christ, who is also a man. ⁶Jesus gave himself to pay for *the sins of* all people. Jesus is proof *that God wants all people to be saved.* And he came at the right time. ⁷That is why I was chosen to tell the Good News.* That is why I was chosen to be an apostle.* (I am telling the truth. I am not lying.) I was chosen to be a teacher of the non-Jewish people. I teach them to believe and know the truth.

⁸I want men everywhere to pray. These men who lift up their hands in prayer must be holy.* They must not be men who become angry and have arguments.

⁹I also want women to wear clothes that are right for them. Women should dress with respect and right thinking. They should not use fancy braided hair or gold or pearls or expensive clothes to make themselves beautiful. ¹⁰But they should make themselves beautiful by doing good things. Women who say they worship God should make themselves beautiful in that way.

¹¹A woman should learn while listening quietly and while being fully ready to obey. ¹²I don't allow a woman to teach a man. And I don't allow a woman to have authority (*power*) over a man. The woman must continue in quietness. Why? ¹³Because Adam was made first. Eve was made later. ¹⁴Also, Adam was not the one who was tricked *by the devil.* It was the woman who was tricked and became a sinner. ¹⁵But women will be saved in their work of having children. They will be saved if they continue in faith, love, and holiness, and control themselves in the right way.

Good News The news that God has made a way through Christ for people to have their sins forgiven and live with God. When people accept this truth, God accepts them.
apostle Person Jesus chose to be a special helper for telling the Good News to the world.
holy A holy person is pure, belongs only to God, and does only the things that God wants.
Adam...devil The devil tricked Eve, and Eve caused Adam to sin (Genesis 3:1-13).

Leaders in the Church

3 What I say is true: If any person is trying hard to become an elder,* that person is wanting a good work. ²An elder must be good enough that people cannot rightly criticize him. He must have only one wife. An elder must have self-control and be wise. He must be respected by other people. He must be ready to help people by accepting them into his home. He must be a good teacher. ³He must not drink too much wine, and he must not be a person who likes to fight. He must be gentle and peaceful. He must not be a person who loves money. ⁴He must be a good leader of his own family. This means that his children obey him with full respect. ⁵(If a man does not know how to be a leader over his own family, then he will not be able to take care of God's church.) ⁶But an elder* must not be a new believer. It might make a new believer be too proud of himself *if he were made an elder*. Then he would be judged (*condemned*) for his pride the same as the devil was. ⁷An elder must also have the respect of people who are not in the church. Then he will not be criticized by other people and be caught in the devil's trap.

Helpers in the Church

⁸In the same way, deacons* (*men who serve*) must be men that people can respect. Deacons must not say things they don't mean. They must not use their time drinking too much wine, and they must not be men who are always trying to get rich by cheating others. ⁹They must follow the faith (*truth*) that God made known to us and always do what they know is right. ¹⁰You should test those men first. If you find nothing wrong in them, then they can serve as deacons. ¹¹In the same way, their wives* must have the respect of other people. They must not be women who talk evil about other people. They must have self-control and be women who can be trusted in everything. ¹²Deacons (*men who serve*) must have only one wife. They must be good leaders of their

---

elder One of a group of men chosen to lead a church. Called "overseers" and "pastors" (shepherds), they have the work of caring for God's people (Acts 20:28; Ephesians 4:11).
deacons People chosen to serve the church in special ways.
wives Literally, "women." It might mean women who serve in the same way as deacons.

children and their own families. ¹³Those persons who serve in a good way are making an honorable place for themselves. And they will feel very sure of their faith in Christ Jesus.

The Secret of Our Life

¹⁴I hope I can come to you soon. But I am writing these things to you now. ¹⁵Then, even if I cannot come soon, you will know about the things that people must do in the family* of God. That family is the church of the living God. And God's church is the support and foundation of the truth. ¹⁶Without any doubt, the secret of our life of worship is great:

> He (*Christ*) was shown to us in a human body,
>> the Spirit* proved that he was right,
>>> he was seen by angels.
> *The Good News about him* was preached
>> to the nations (*non-Jews*),
>> people in the world believed in him,
>>> he was taken up to heaven in glory.

Warning About False Teachers

4 The Holy Spirit* clearly says that in the later times some people will stop believing the *true* faith (*teaching*). Those people will obey spirits that tell lies. And those people will follow the teachings of demons.* ²Those teachings come through men who tell lies and trick people. Those men cannot see what is right and what is wrong. It is like their understanding was destroyed by a hot iron. ³Those men tell people that it is wrong to marry. And those men tell people that there are some foods that people must not eat. But God made those foods. And those people who believe and who know the truth can eat those foods with thanks. ⁴Everything that God made is good. Nothing that God made should be refused if it is accepted with thanks to God. ⁵Everything God made is made holy by what God has said and by prayer.

family   Literally, "house." This could mean that God's people are like God's temple.
Spirit, Holy Spirit   Also called the Spirit of God, the Spirit of Christ, and the Comforter. He is joined with God and Christ. He does the work of God among people in the world.
demons   Demons are evil spirits from the devil.

Be a Good Servant of Christ Jesus

⁶Tell these things to the brothers *and sisters* there. This will show that you are a good servant of Christ Jesus. You will show that you are made strong by the words of faith and good teaching that you have followed. ⁷People tell silly stories that don't agree with God's truth. Don't follow *what* those stories *teach*. But teach yourself to truly serve God. ⁸Training (*teaching*) your body helps you in some ways. But serving God helps you in every way. Serving God brings you blessings in this life and in the future life too. ⁹What I say is true, and you should fully accept it. ¹⁰This is why we work and struggle: We hope in the living God. He is the Savior of all people. And in a special way, he is the Savior of all those people who believe in him.

¹¹Command and teach these things. ¹²You are young, but don't let any person treat you like you are not important. But be an example to show the believers how they should live. Show them with the things you say, with the way you live, with your love, with your faith, and with your pure life. ¹³Continue to read the Scriptures* to the people, strengthen them, and teach them. Do those things until I come. ¹⁴Remember to use the gift that you have. That gift was given to you through a prophecy* when the group of elders* put their hands on* you. ¹⁵Continue to do those things. Give your life to doing those things. Then all the people can see that your work is progressing (*continuing*). ¹⁶Be careful in your life and in your teaching. Continue to live and teach rightly. Then you will save yourself and those people who listen to your teaching.

Some Rules for Living with Other People

5 Don't speak angrily to an older man. But talk to him like he was your father. Treat the younger men like brothers. ²Treat the older women like mothers. And treat the younger women like sisters. Always treat them in a good way.

Scriptures   Holy Writings—the Old Testament.
prophecy   Something said about Timothy's life before that thing happened.
elders   A group of men chosen to lead a church. Also called "overseers" and "pastors" (shepherds), they have the work of caring for God's people (Acts 20:28; Ephesians 4:11).
put their hands on   A sign to show that Timothy was being given a special work of God.

³Give honor to (*take care of*) widows* who are really alone. ⁴But if a widow has children or grandchildren, the first thing they need to learn is this: to show respect for their own family *by helping their parents*. When they do this, they will be repaying their parents or grandparents. That pleases God. ⁵If a widow is really alone and without help, then she hopes in God *to take care of her*. That woman prays all the time, night and day. She asks God for help. ⁶But the widow who uses her life to please herself is really dead while she is still living. ⁷Tell the believers there to do these things (*take care of their family*) so that no other person can say they are doing wrong. ⁸A person should take care of all his own people. Most important, he should take care of his own family. If a person does not do that, then he does not accept the *true* faith (*teaching*). That person is worse than a person who does not believe.

⁹To be added to your list of widows,* a woman must be 60 years old or older. She must have been faithful to her husband. ¹⁰She must be known as a woman who has done good things. I mean good things like raising her children, accepting visitors in her home, washing the feet of God's people, helping people in trouble, and using her life to do all kinds of good things.

¹¹But don't put younger widows* on that list. After they give themselves to Christ they are often pulled away from him by their strong physical needs. And then they want to marry again. ¹²And they will be judged for that. They will be judged for not doing what they first promised to do. ¹³Also, those younger widows begin to waste their time by going from house to house. They also begin to gossip and be busy with other people's lives. They say things that they should not say. ¹⁴So I want the younger widows to marry, have children, and take care of their homes. If they do this, then our enemy will not have any reason to criticize them. ¹⁵But some of the younger widows have already turned away to follow Satan (*the devil*).

¹⁶If any woman who is a believer has widows* in her family, then she should care for them herself. The church should not be troubled to care for them. Then the church will be able to care for the widows who have no living family.

---

widows A widow is a woman whose husband has died.

[17]The elders* who lead the church in a good way should receive great honor. Those elders who work by speaking and teaching are the men who should have that great honor. [18]Why? Because the Scripture* says, "When a work animal is doing the work of separating grain, don't cover its mouth *and stop it from eating the grain.*"* And the Scripture also says, "The man who works has earned the pay he gets."*

[19]Don't listen to a person who accuses an elder.* You should listen to that person only if there are two or three other people who can say what the elder did wrong. [20]Tell those people who sin that they are wrong. Do this in front of the whole church. In that way, the others will have a warning.

[21]Before God and Jesus Christ and the chosen angels I command you to do these things. But don't judge people before you know the truth. And do these things equally to every person.

[22]Think carefully before you put your hands on* any person, *making him an elder.* Don't share in the sins of other people. Keep yourself pure.

[23]Timothy, you have been drinking only water. Stop doing that, and drink a little wine. This will help your stomach, and you will not be sick so often.

[24]The sins of some people are easy to see. Their sins show that they will be judged. But the sins of some other people are seen only later. [25]It is the same with the good things people do. The good things people do are easy to see. But even when those good things are not easy to see, they cannot stay hidden.

6 All people who are slaves should show full respect to their masters. When they do that, then God's name and our teaching will not be criticized. [2]Some slaves have masters who are believers. So those slaves and those masters are brothers. But the slaves should not show them any less respect. No! Those slaves should serve those believing masters even better. Why? Because those slaves are helping believers that they love.

---

elder(s) Elders are men chosen to lead a church. Also called "overseers" and "pastors" (shepherds), they have the work of caring for God's people (Acts 20:28; Ephesians 4:11).
Scripture Part of the Holy Writings—God's message to people through the writers of the Bible.
"When...grain" Quotation from Deuteronomy 25:4.
"The man...gets" Quotation from Luke 10:7.
put your hands on A sign of giving authority or power to another person.

False Teaching and True Riches

You must teach and tell the people to do these things. ³Some people will teach things that are false. Those people will not agree with the true teaching of our Lord Jesus Christ. And they will not accept the teaching that agrees with the true way to serve God. ⁴That person who teaches falsely is full of pride and understands nothing. That person is sick with a love for arguing and fighting about words. And that brings jealousy, making trouble, insults, and evil mistrust. ⁵And also that brings arguments from men who have evil minds. Those people have lost the truth. They think that serving God is a way to get rich.

⁶It is true that serving God makes a person very rich, if that person is satisfied with what he has. ⁷When we came into the world, we brought nothing. And when we die, we can take nothing out. ⁸So, if we have food and clothes, we will be satisfied with that. ⁹People who want to become rich bring temptations to themselves. They are caught in a trap. They begin to want many foolish things that will hurt them. Those things ruin and destroy people. ¹⁰The love of money causes all kinds of evil. Some people have left the *true* faith (*teaching*) because they want to get more and more money. But they have caused themselves to be very, very sad.

Some Things You Should Remember

¹¹But you are a man of God. So you should stay away from all those things. Try to live in the right way, serve God, have faith, love, patience, and gentleness. ¹²Keeping your faith is like running a race. Try as hard as you can to win that race. Be sure you get that life that continues forever. You were called to have that life. And you confessed the great truth *about Christ* in a way that many people heard you. ¹³Before God and Christ Jesus I give you a command. Christ Jesus is the One that confessed that same great truth when he stood before Pontius Pilate. And God is the One that gives life to everything. Now I tell you: ¹⁴Do the things you were commanded to do. Do those things without wrong or blame until the time when our Lord Jesus Christ comes again. ¹⁵God will make that happen at the right time. God is the blessed

and only Ruler. God is the King of all kings and the Lord of all lords (*rulers*). ¹⁶God is the only One who never dies. God lives in light so bright that men cannot go near it. No person has ever seen God. No person is able to see God. Honor to God and power forever. Amen.

¹⁷Give this command to the people who are rich with the things this world has. Tell them not to be proud. Tell those rich people to hope in God, not their money. Money cannot be trusted. But God takes care of us richly. He gives us everything to enjoy. ¹⁸Tell the rich people to do good. Tell them to be rich in doing good things. And tell them to be happy to give and ready to share. ¹⁹By doing that they will be saving a treasure for themselves *in heaven*. That treasure will be a strong foundation*—their future life can be built on that treasure. Then they will be able to have the life that is true life.

²⁰Timothy, God has trusted you with many things. Keep those things safe. Stay away from people who say foolish things that are not from God. Stay away from people who argue against *the truth*. Those people use something they call "knowledge"—but it is really not knowledge. ²¹Some people say that they have that "knowledge." Those people have left the *true* faith (*teaching*).

God's grace (*kindness*) be with you all.

---

foundation   The bottom part or first part of a house that the rest of the house is built on.

2 Timothy

1 From Paul, an apostle* of Christ Jesus. I am an apostle because God wanted me to be. God sent me to tell people about the promise of life that is in Christ Jesus.

²To Timothy. You are *like* a dear son to me. Grace (*kindness*), mercy, and peace to you from God the Father and from Christ Jesus our Lord.

Thanksgiving and Encouragement

³I always remember you in my prayers day and night. And I thank God for you in those prayers. He is the God my ancestors served. And I have always served him, doing what I know is right. ⁴I remember that you cried for me. And I want very much to see you so that I can be filled with joy. ⁵I remember your true faith. That kind of faith first belonged to your grandmother Lois and to your mother Eunice. And I know that you now have that same faith. ⁶That is why I want you to remember the gift God gave you. God gave you that gift when I put my hands on* you. Now I want you to use that gift and let it grow more and more, like a small flame grows into a fire. ⁷God did not give us a spirit that makes us afraid. God gave us a spirit of power and love and self-control.

⁸So don't be ashamed to tell people about our Lord *Jesus*. And don't be ashamed of me—I am in prison for the Lord. But suffer with me for the gospel.* God gives us the strength to do that. ⁹God saved us and made us his holy people.* And that happened not because of anything we did ourselves. No! God saved us and

apostle   Person Jesus chose to be a special helper for telling the Good News to the world.
put...hands on   A sign to show that Paul had power from God to give Timothy a special blessing.
gospel   The Good News that God has made a way through Christ for people to have their sins
forgiven and live with God. When people accept this truth, God accepts them.
holy people   God's people are called holy because they are made pure and belong only to God.

made us his people because that was what he wanted and because of his grace (*kindness*). That grace was given to us through Christ Jesus before time began. [10]That grace was not shown to us until now. It was shown to us when our Savior Christ Jesus came. Jesus destroyed death and showed us the way to have life. Yes! Through the Good News* Jesus showed us the way to have life that cannot be destroyed. [11]And I was chosen to tell that Good News. I was chosen to be an apostle* and a teacher of that Good News. [12]And I suffer now because I tell that Good News. But I am not ashamed. I know the One (*Jesus*) that I have believed. And I am sure that he is able to protect the things that he has trusted me with until that Day.* [13]Follow the true teachings you heard from me. Follow those teachings with the faith and love we have in Christ Jesus. Those teachings are an example *that shows you what you should teach*. [14]Protect the truth that you were given. Protect those things with the help of the Holy Spirit.* That Holy Spirit lives inside us.

[15]You know that every person in the country of Asia has left me. Even Phygelus and Hermogenes have left me. [16]I pray that the Lord will show mercy to the family of Onesiphorus. Many times Onesiphorus helped me. He was not ashamed that I was in prison. [17]No. He was not ashamed. When he came to Rome, he looked and looked for me until he found me. [18]I pray that the Lord will allow Onesiphorus to have mercy from the Lord on that Day.* You know how many ways Onesiphorus helped me in Ephesus.

A Loyal Soldier of Christ Jesus

2 Timothy, you are *like* a son to me. Be strong in the grace (*kindness*) that we have in Christ Jesus. [2]You have heard the things that I have taught. Many other people heard those things too. You should teach those same things. Give those teachings to some people you can trust. Then they will be able to teach those

---

Good News The news that God has made a way through Christ for people to have their sins forgiven and live with God. When people accept this truth, God accepts them.

apostle Person Jesus chose to be a special helper for telling the Good News to the world.

Day The day Christ will come to judge all people and take his people to live with him.

Holy Spirit Also called the Spirit of God, the Spirit of Christ, and the Comforter. He is joined with God and Christ. He does the work of God among people in the world.

things to other people. ³Share in the troubles that we have. Accept those troubles like a true soldier of Christ Jesus. ⁴A person that is a soldier wants to please his commanding officer. So, that soldier does not use his time doing the things that most people do. ⁵If an athlete is running a race, he must obey all the rules to win. ⁶The farmer who works hard should be the first person to get some of the food that he grew. ⁷Think about these things that I am saying. The Lord will give you the ability to understand all these things.

⁸Remember Jesus Christ. He is from the family of David. After Jesus died, he was raised from death. This is the Good News* that I tell people. ⁹And I am suffering because I tell that Good News. I am even bound with chains like a person who has really done wrong. But God's teaching is not bound. ¹⁰So I patiently accept all these troubles. I do this to help all the people that God has chosen. I accept these troubles so that those people can have the salvation that is in Christ Jesus. With that salvation comes glory that never ends.

¹¹This teaching is true:

If we died with him (*Jesus*),
then we will also live with him.
¹²If we accept suffering,
then we will also rule with him.
If we refuse to accept him,
then he will refuse to accept us.
¹³If we are not faithful,
he will still be faithful,
because he cannot be false to himself.

An Approved Worker

¹⁴Continue telling the people these things. And warn those people before God not to argue about words. Arguing about words does not help any person. And it ruins those people who listen. ¹⁵Do the very best you can to be the kind of person that God will accept and give yourself to him. Be a worker who is not

---

Good News The news that God has made a way through Christ for people to have their sins forgiven and live with God. When people accept this truth, God accepts them.

ashamed of his work—a worker who uses the true teaching in the right way. ¹⁶Stay away from people who talk about useless things that are not from God. That kind of talk will lead a person more and more against God. ¹⁷Their *evil* teaching will spread like a sickness inside the body. Hymenaeus and Philetus are men like that. ¹⁸They have left the true teaching. They say that the rising from death *of all people* has already happened. And those two men are destroying the faith of some people. ¹⁹But God's strong foundation* continues to be the same. These words are written on that foundation: "The Lord knows those people who belong to him."* And also these words are written on that foundation, "Every person who says that he believes in the Lord must stop doing wrong."

²⁰In a large house, there are things made of gold and silver. But also there are things made of wood and clay. Some things are used for special purposes. Other things are made for dirty jobs. ²¹If any person will make himself clean from all the evil things, then that person will be used for special purposes. That person will be made holy,* and the master can use him. That person will be ready to do any good work.

²²Stay away from the evil things a young person wants to do. Try very hard to live right and to have faith, love, and peace. Do these things together with those people who have pure hearts and trust in the Lord. ²³Stay away from foolish and stupid arguments. You know that those arguments grow into bigger arguments. ²⁴And a servant of the Lord must not argue! He must be kind to every person. A servant of the Lord must be a good teacher. He must be patient. ²⁵The Lord's servant must gently teach those people who don't agree with him. Maybe God will let those people change their hearts so that they can accept the truth. ²⁶The devil has trapped those people and makes them do what he wants. But maybe they can wake up *and see that the devil is using them*, and free themselves from the devil's trap.

---

foundation   The bottom part or first part of a house that the rest of the house is built on.
"The Lord...him"   Quotation from Numbers 16:5.
holy   A holy person is pure, belongs only to God, and does only the things that God wants.

The Last Days

3 Remember this! There will be many troubles in the last days. [2]In those times people will love only themselves and money. They will be boastful, and proud. People will say bad things against other people. People will not obey their parents. People will not be thankful. They will not be the kind of people God wants. [3]People will not have love for other people. They will refuse to forgive other people and they will speak bad things. People will not control themselves. They will be angry and mean, and will hate things that are good. [4]In the last days, people will turn against their friends. They will do foolish things without thinking. They will be conceited and proud. People will love pleasure—they will not love God. [5]Those people will continue to act like they serve God. But the way they live shows that they don't really serve God. Timothy, stay away from those people. [6]Some of those people go into homes and get women who are weak. Those women are full of sin. Those women are led to sin by the many evil things they want to do. [7]Those women always try to learn *new teachings*, but they are never able to fully understand the truth. [8]Remember Jannes and Jambres. They were against Moses. It is the same with these people. They are against the truth. They are people whose thinking has been confused. They have failed in trying to follow the faith. [9]But they will not be successful in the things they do. All the people will see that they are foolish. That is what happened to Jannes and Jambres.

Last Instructions

[10]But you know all about me. You know what I teach and the way I live. You know my goal in life. You know my faith, my patience, and my love. You know that I never stop trying. [11]You know about my persecutions (*troubles*), and my sufferings. You know all the things that happened to me in Antioch, Iconium, and Lystra. You know the persecutions I suffered in those places. But the Lord saved me from all those troubles. [12]Every person who wants to live the way God wants, in Christ Jesus, will be persecuted. [13]People who are evil and cheat other people will

become worse and worse. They will fool other people, but they will also be fooling themselves.

[14]But you should continue following the teachings that you learned. You know that those teachings are true. And you know you can trust the people who taught you those things. [15]You have known the Holy Scriptures* since you were a child. Those Scriptures are able to make you wise. And that wisdom leads to salvation through faith in Christ Jesus. [16]All Scripture is given by God. And all Scripture is useful for teaching and for showing people the things that are wrong in their lives. It is useful for correcting faults, and teaching how to live right. [17]Using the Scriptures, the person who serves God will be ready and will have everything he needs to do every good work.

4 Before God and Jesus Christ I give you a command. Christ Jesus is the One who will judge the people who are living and the people who have died. Jesus has a kingdom, and he is coming again. So I give you this command: [2]Tell people the Good News.* Be ready at all times. Tell people the things they need to do, tell them when they are wrong, and encourage them. Do these things with great patience and careful teaching. [3]The time will come when people will not listen to the true teaching. But people will find more and more teachers that please them. People will find teachers that say the things those people want to hear. [4]People will stop listening to the truth. They will begin to follow the teaching in false stories. [5]But you should control yourself at all times. When troubles come, accept those troubles. Do the work of telling the Good News. Do all the duties of a servant of God.

[6]My life is being given as an offering for God. The time has come for me to leave this life here. [7]I have fought the good fight. I have finished the race. I have kept the faith. [8]Now, a crown (reward) is waiting for me. I will get that crown for being right with God. The Lord is the judge who judges rightly. He will give me the crown on that Day.* Yes! He will give that crown to me. He will give that crown to all people who have wanted him to come again, and have waited for him.

Scriptures Holy Writings—the Old Testament.
Good News The news that God has made a way through Christ for people to have their sins forgiven and live with God. When people accept this truth, God accepts them.
Day The day Christ will come to judge all people and take his people to live with him.

Personal Words

⁹Do your best to come to me as soon as you can. ¹⁰Demas loved this world too much. That is why he left me. He went to Thessalonica. Crescens went to Galatia. And Titus went to Dalmatia. ¹¹Luke is the only one still with me. Get Mark and bring him with you when you come. He can help me in my work here. ¹²I sent Tychicus to Ephesus.

¹³When I was in Troas, I left my coat there with Carpus. So when you come, bring it to me. Also, bring my books. The books written on parchment* are the ones I need most.

¹⁴Alexander the metalworker did many bad things against me. The Lord will punish Alexander for the things he did. ¹⁵You should be careful that he doesn't hurt you too. He fought strongly against our teaching.

¹⁶The first time I defended myself, no person helped me. Every person left me. I pray that God will forgive them. ¹⁷But the Lord stayed with me. The Lord gave me strength so that I could fully tell the Good News* to the non-Jews. The Lord wanted all the non-Jews to hear that Good News. I was saved from the lion's (enemy's) mouth. ¹⁸The Lord will save me when any person tries to hurt me. The Lord will bring me safely to his heavenly kingdom. Glory for ever and ever be the Lord's.

Final Greetings

¹⁹Say hello to Priscilla and Aquila and to the family of Onesiphorus. ²⁰Erastus stayed in Corinth. And I left Trophimus in Miletus—he was sick. ²¹Try as hard as you can to come to me before winter.

Eubulus says hello to you. Also Pudens, Linus, Claudia, and all the brothers in Christ say hello to you.

²²The Lord be with your spirit. Grace (kindness) be with you.

---

parchment   Something like paper made from the skins of sheep and used for writing on.
Good News   The news that God has made a way through Christ for people to have their sins forgiven and live with God. When people accept this truth, God accepts them.

Titus

1 From Paul, a servant of God and an apostle* of Jesus Christ. I was sent to help the faith of God's chosen people. I was sent to help those people to know the truth. And that truth shows people how to serve God. ²That faith and that knowledge come from our hope for life forever. God promised that life to us before time began—and God does not lie. ³At the right time, God let the world know about that life. God told the world through my preaching. God trusted me with that work. I preached those things because God our Savior commanded me to.

⁴To Titus. You are *like* a true son to me in the faith we share together.

Grace (*kindness*) and peace to you from God the Father and Christ Jesus our Savior.

Titus' Work in Crete

⁵I left you in Crete so that you could finish doing the things that still needed to be done. And I also left you there so that you could choose men to be elders* in every town. ⁶To be an elder, a man must not be guilty of doing anything wrong. He must have only one wife. His children must be believers. They must not be known as children who are wild and who don't obey. ⁷An elder has the job of taking care of God's work. So he must not be guilty of doing anything wrong. He must not be a person who is proud and selfish or who becomes angry quickly. He must not drink too much wine. He must not be a person who likes to fight. And he must not be a person who always tries to get rich by cheating people. ⁸An elder must be ready to help people by accepting them

---

apostle Person Jesus chose to be a special helper for telling the Good News to the world.
elders A group of men chosen to lead a church. Also called "overseers" and "pastors" (shepherds), they have the work of caring for God's people (Acts 20:28; Ephesians 4:11).

into his home. He must love what is good. He must be wise. He must live right. He must be holy.* And he must be able to control himself. *⁹An elder** must faithfully follow the truth the same as we teach it. An elder must be able to help people by using true and right teaching. And he must be able to show the people who are against the true teaching that they are wrong.

¹⁰There are many people who refuse to obey—people who talk about worthless things and lead other people into the wrong way. I am talking mostly about those people who say that all non-Jewish people must be circumcised.* ¹¹An elder* must *be able to show that those people are wrong and* stop them from talking *about those worthless things*. Those people are destroying whole families by teaching things that they should not teach. They teach those things only to cheat people and make money. ¹²Even one of their own prophets (*teachers*) *from Crete* said, "Cretan people are always liars. They are evil animals and lazy people who do nothing but eat." ¹³The words that prophet said are true. So tell those people that they are wrong. You must be strict with them. Then they will become strong in the faith. ¹⁴Then those people will stop accepting Jewish stories. And they will stop following the commands of those people who don't accept the truth. ¹⁵To people that are pure, all things are pure. But to people who are full of sin and don't believe, nothing is pure. Really, those people's thinking has become evil and their knowledge of what is right has been ruined. ¹⁶Those people say they know God. But the *evil* things those people do show that they don't accept God. They are terrible people, they refuse to obey, and they are not useful for doing anything good.

Following the True Teaching

2 You must tell people the things they must do to follow the true teaching. ²Teach the older men to have self-control, to be serious, and to be wise. They should be strong in the faith, strong in love, and strong in patience.

---

holy   A holy person is pure, belongs only to God, and does only the things that God wants.
elder   One of a group of men chosen to lead a church. Called "overseers" and "pastors" (shepherds), they have the work of caring for God's people (Acts 20:28; Ephesians 4:11).
circumcised   To have the foreskin cut off. This was done to every Jewish baby boy. It was a physical mark of the agreement that God made with Abraham (Genesis 17:9-14).

³Also, teach the older women to be holy* in the way they live. Teach them not to speak against other people, or have the habit of drinking too much wine. Those women should teach what is good. ⁴In that way they can teach the younger women to love their husbands and children. ⁵They can teach the younger women to be wise and to be pure, to take care of their homes, to be kind, and to obey their husbands. Then no person will be able to criticize the teaching God gave us.

⁶In the same way, tell the young men to be wise. ⁷You should do good things to be an example in every way for the young men. When you teach, be honest and serious. ⁸And when you speak, speak the truth so that you cannot be criticized. Then any person who is against you will be ashamed because he has nothing bad that he can say against us.

⁹And tell these things to the people who are slaves: They should obey their masters at all times; they should try to please their masters; they should not argue with their masters; ¹⁰they should not steal from their masters; and they should show their masters that they can be trusted. The slaves should do these things so that in everything they do, they will show that the teaching of God our Savior is good.

¹¹God's grace (*kindness*) has come. That grace can save every person. And that grace has been given to us. ¹²That grace teaches us not to live against God and not to do the bad things the world wants to do. That grace teaches us to live on earth now in a wise and right way—a way that shows that we serve God. ¹³We should live like that while we are waiting for the coming of our great God and Savior Jesus Christ. He is our great hope, and he will come with glory. ¹⁴He gave himself for us. He died to free us from all evil. He died to make us pure people that belong only to him—people that are always wanting to do good things.

¹⁵Tell the people these things. You have full authority (*power*). So use that authority to strengthen the people and tell them what they should do. And don't let any person treat you like you are not important.

---

holy   A holy person is pure, belongs only to God, and does only the things that God wants.

The Right Way to Live

3 Tell the people to remember always to do these things: to be under the authority of rulers and government leaders; to obey those leaders and be ready to do good; ²to speak no evil against any person; to live in peace with other people; to be gentle to other people; and to be polite to other people. Tell the believers to do these things to all people.

³In the past we were foolish people too. We did not obey, we were wrong, and we were slaves to the many things our bodies wanted and enjoyed. We lived doing evil and being jealous. People hated us and we hated each other. ⁴But then God our Savior showed kindness and love to us. ⁵He saved us because of his mercy (*love*)—not because of the good things we did to be right with God. He saved us through the washing that made us new people. He saved us by making us new through the Holy Spirit.* ⁶God gave us that Holy Spirit fully through Jesus Christ our Savior. ⁷We were made right with God by his grace (*kindness*). And God gave us the Spirit so that we could receive the life that never ends. That is what we hope for. ⁸This teaching is true.

And I want you to be sure that the people understand these things. Then the people who believe in God will be careful to use their lives for doing good. These things are good and will help all people.

⁹Stay away from people who have foolish arguments, people who talk about useless family histories, people who make trouble and fight about what the law *of Moses* teaches. Those things are worth nothing and will not help people. ¹⁰If a person causes arguments, then give him a warning. If that person continues to cause arguments, then warn him again. If he continues causing arguments, then don't associate with him. ¹¹You know that a person like that is evil and sinful. His sins prove that he is wrong.

Holy Spirit   Also called the Spirit of God, the Spirit of Christ, and the Comforter. He is joined with God and Christ. He does the work of God among people in the world.

Some Things to Remember

¹²I will send Artemas and Tychicus to you. When I send them, try hard to come to me at Nicopolis. I have decided to stay there this winter. ¹³Zenas the lawyer and Apollos will be traveling from there. Do all that you can to help them on their trip. Be sure that they have everything they need. ¹⁴Our people must learn to use their lives for doing good things. They should do good for people who need it. Then our people will not have empty lives.

¹⁵All the people with me here say hello to you. Say hello to those people who love us in the faith.

Grace (*kindness*) be with you all.

Philemon

From Paul, a prisoner of Jesus Christ, and from Timothy, our brother.

To Philemon, our dear friend and worker with us. ²Also to Apphia, our sister, to Archippus, a worker with us, and to the church that meets in your home.

³Grace (*kindness*) and peace to you from God our Father and the Lord Jesus Christ.

Philemon's Love and Faith

⁴I remember you in my prayers. And I always thank my God for you. ⁵I hear about the love you have for all God's holy people* and the faith you have in the Lord Jesus. And I thank God for that love and faith you have. ⁶I pray that the faith you share will make you understand every good thing that we have in Christ. ⁷My brother, you have shown love to God's people. You have made them feel happy. This has given me great joy and comfort.

Accept Onesimus Like a Brother

⁸There is something that you should do. And because of your love in Christ I feel free to command you to do that. ⁹But *I am not commanding you*; I am asking you to do it. I am Paul. I am an old man now, and I am a prisoner for Christ Jesus. ¹⁰I am asking you for my son Onesimus. He became my son while I was in prison. ¹¹In the past he was useless to you. But now he has become useful for both you and me.

---

holy people God's people are called holy because they are made pure and belong only to God.

¹²I am sending him back to you. With him, I am sending my own heart. ¹³I wanted to keep him with me to help me while I am in prison for the gospel.* By helping me he would be serving you. ¹⁴But I did not want to do anything without asking you first. Then the good thing you do for me will be because you wanted to do it, not because I forced you to do it.

¹⁵Onesimus was separated from you for a short time. Maybe that happened so that you could have him back forever—¹⁶not to be a slave, but better than a slave, to be a loved brother. I love him very much. But you will love him even more. You will love him as a man, and as a brother in the Lord.

¹⁷If you accept me to be your friend, then accept Onesimus back. Welcome him like you would welcome me. ¹⁸If Onesimus has done anything wrong to you, charge that to me. If he owes you anything, charge that to me. ¹⁹I am Paul, and I am writing this with my own hand. I will pay back anything Onesimus owes. And I will say nothing about what you owe me for your own life. ²⁰So, my brother, I ask that you do something for me in the Lord. Comfort my heart in Christ. ²¹I write this letter, knowing that you will do what I ask you. I know that you will do even more than I ask.

²²Also, please prepare a room for me to stay in. I hope that God will answer your prayers, and that I will be able to come to you.

Final Greetings

²³Epaphras is a prisoner with me for Christ Jesus. He says hello to you. ²⁴And also Mark, Aristarchus, Demas, and Luke say hello to you. They are workers together with me.

²⁵The grace (*kindness*) of our Lord Jesus Christ be with your spirit.

---

gospel   The Good News that God has made a way through Christ for people to have their sins forgiven and live with God. When people accept this truth, God accepts them.

Hebrews

God Has Spoken Through His Son

1 In the past God spoke to our people through the prophets.*
God spoke to them many times and in many different ways.
²And now in these last days God has spoken to us again. God has
spoken to us through his Son. God made the whole world
through his Son. And God has chosen his Son to have all things.
³The Son shows the glory of God. He is a perfect copy of God's
nature. The Son holds everything together with his powerful
words. The Son made people clean from their sins. Then he sat
down at the right side of the Great One (*God*) in heaven. ⁴God
gave him a name that is a much greater name than any of the
angels have. And he became that much greater than the angels.

⁵God never said these things to any of the angels:

> "You are my Son;
>   Today I have become your Father."   *Psalm 2:7*

God also never said to an angel,

> "I will be his Father,
>   And he will be my Son."   *2 Samuel 7:14*

⁶And when God brings his firstborn* Son into the world, he says,

> "Let all God's angels worship the Son.*"   *Deuteronomy 32:43*

⁷This is what God said about the angels:

> "God makes his angels become like winds,
>   and God makes his servants become
>   like flames of fire."   *Psalm 104:4*

---

prophets People who spoke for God. Their writings are part of the Old Testament.
firstborn Christ was the first and most important of all God's children.
"Let...Son" These words are found in Deuteronomy 32:43 in the Septuagint, the Greek version
of the Old Testament, and in a Hebrew copy among the Dead Sea Scrolls.

⁸But God said this about his Son:

"Your throne, O God, will continue forever and ever,
You will rule your kingdom with right judgments.
⁹ You love the right and you hate the wrong.
So God, your God has given you a greater joy
than he gave those people with you."   *Psalm 45:6-7*

¹⁰God also says,

"O Lord, in the beginning you made the earth.
And your hands made the sky.
¹¹These things will disappear, but you will stay.
All things will become old like clothes.
¹²You will fold them like a coat.
And they will be changed like clothes.
But you never change.
And your life will never end."   *Psalm 102:25-27*

¹³And God never said this to an angel:

"Sit at my right side
and I will put your enemies
under your power.*"   *Psalm 110:1*

¹⁴All the angels are spirits who serve God and are sent to help those people who will receive salvation.

Our Salvation Is Greater Than
the Law Brought by Angels

2 So we must be more careful to follow the things that we were taught. We must be careful so that we will not be pulled away from *the true way*. ²The teaching (*the law*) that God spoke through angels was shown to be true. And every time the *Jewish* people did something against that teaching they were punished for what they did. They were punished when they did not obey that teaching. ³The salvation *that was given to us* is very great. So surely we also will be punished if we live like this salvation is not important. It was the Lord (*Jesus*) who first told people about this salvation. And the people who heard him proved to us that this salvation is true. ⁴God also proved it by using wonders, great

I will put...power   Literally, "I will make your enemies a footstool for your feet."

signs, and many kinds of miracles.* And he proved it by giving people gifts through the Holy Spirit.* He gave those gifts the way he wanted.

Christ Became Like Men to Bring Them Salvation

⁵God did not choose angels to be the rulers over the new world that was coming. That future world is the world we have been talking about. ⁶It is written some place *in the Scriptures,**

> "*God*, why do you care about people?
>> Why do you care about the son of man*?
>> Is he so important?
> ⁷ For a short time you made him lower
>> than the angels.
>> You gave him glory and honor to be his crown.
> ⁸   You put everything under his control.*"   *Psalm 8:4-6*

If God put everything under his control, then there was nothing left that he did not rule. But we don't yet see him ruling over everything. ⁹For a short time Jesus was made lower than the angels, but now we see him wearing a crown of glory and honor because he suffered and died. Because of God's grace (*kindness*) Jesus died for every person.

¹⁰God is the One who made all things. And all things are for his glory. God wanted to have many sons (*people*) to share his glory. So God did what he needed to do. He made perfect the One (*Jesus*) who leads those people to salvation. God made Jesus *a* perfect *Savior* through Jesus' suffering.

¹¹The One (*Jesus*) who makes people holy* and those people who are made holy are from the same family. So he (*Jesus*) is not ashamed to call those people his brothers *and sisters*. ¹²Jesus says,

> "God, I will tell my brothers *and sisters* about you.
>> Before all your people I will sing your praises."   *Psalm 22:22*

---

miracles   Miracles are powerful works or great things done by the power of God.
Holy Spirit   Also called the Spirit of God, the Spirit of Christ, and the Comforter. He is joined with God and Christ. He does the work of God among people in the world.
Scriptures   Holy Writings—the Old Testament.
son of man   This can mean any man (person), but the name "Son of Man" is often used to mean Jesus. When Jesus became a man, he showed what God planned for all men (people) to be.
control   Literally, "feet." To be under a person's feet means to be under his control.
holy   God's people are holy because they are made pure and belong only to God.

[13]He also says,

"I will trust in God." *Isaiah 8:17*

And he also says,

"I am here. And with me are the children
that God has given me." *Isaiah 8:18*

[14]Those children are people with physical bodies. So Jesus himself became like those people and had the same experiences people have. Jesus did this so that, by dying, he could destroy the one who has power of death. That one is the devil. [15]Jesus became like those people and died so that he could free them. They were like slaves all their lives because of their fear of death. [16]Clearly, it is not angels that Jesus helps. Jesus helps the people who are from Abraham.* [17]For this reason Jesus had to be made like his brothers *and sisters* (*people*) in every way. Jesus became like people so that he could be their merciful and faithful high priest* in service to God. Then Jesus could bring forgiveness for the people's sins. [18]And now Jesus can help those people who are tempted. Jesus is able to help because he himself suffered and was tempted.

Jesus Is Greater Than Moses

3 So all of you should think about Jesus. God sent Jesus to us and he is the high priest* of our faith. I tell this to you, my holy brothers *and sisters*. You were all called by God. [2]God sent Jesus to us and made him our high priest. And Jesus was faithful to God like Moses was. He did everything God wanted him to do in God's house (*family*). [3]When a man builds a house, people will honor the man more than the house. It is the same with Jesus. Jesus should have more honor than Moses. [4]Every house is built by some person. But God built everything. [5]Moses was faithful in all God's house (*family*) like a servant. He told people the things that God would say in the future. [6]But Christ is faithful in ruling God's house like a Son. We *believers* are God's house (*family*). We are God's house if we continue to be sure and proud of the great hope we have.

Abraham Most respected ancestor of the Jews. Every Jew hoped to see Abraham.
high priest The most important priest for God's people.

We Must Continue to Follow God

⁷So it is like the Holy Spirit* says:

"If you hear God's voice today,
⁸ don't be stubborn like in the past,
    when you were against God.
That was the day you tested God in the desert.
⁹ For 40 years in the desert your people
    saw the things I did.
But they tested me and my patience.
¹⁰So I was angry with those people.
I said, 'Those people's thoughts
    are always wrong.
Those people have never understood my ways.'
¹¹So I was angry and made a promise:
'Those people will never enter
    and have my rest.*' "

Psalm 95:7-11

¹²So brothers *and sisters*, be careful that none of you is sinful, and refuses to believe, and stops following the living God. ¹³But comfort each other every day. Do this while it is "today."* Help each other so that none of you will become hardened because of sin and the way sin fools people. ¹⁴We all share together with Christ. This is true if we continue until the end to have the sure faith we had in the beginning. ¹⁵This is what that Scripture* said:

"If you hear God's voice today,
    don't be stubborn like in the past
        when you were against God."

Psalm 95:7-8

¹⁶Who were those people who heard God's voice and were against him? It was all those people that Moses led out of Egypt. ¹⁷And who was God angry with for 40 years? God was angry with those people who sinned. Those people died in the desert. ¹⁸And what people was God talking to when he promised that they would never enter and have his rest*? God was talking about those people who did not obey him. ¹⁹So we see that those people were

Holy Spirit Also called the Spirit of God, the Spirit of Christ, and the Comforter. He is joined with God and Christ. He does the work of God among people in the world.
rest The place of rest God promised to give his people.
"today" This word is taken from verse 7. It means that it is important to do these things now.
Scripture A part of the Holy Writings—the Old Testament.

not allowed to enter and have God's rest. Why? Because they did not believe.

4 And we still have that promise God gave those people. That promise is that we can enter and have God's rest. So we should be very careful, so that none of you fail to get that promise. ²A way to be saved* was told to us the same as to those people. But the teaching those people heard did not help them. They heard that teaching but did not accept it with faith. ³We people who believe are able to enter and have God's rest. Like God said,

> "I was angry and made a promise:
> 'Those people will never enter
> and have my rest.*' "   *Psalm 95:11*

God said this. But God's work was finished from the time he made the world. ⁴Some place *in the Scriptures** God talked about the seventh day of the week: "And on the seventh day God rested from all his work."* ⁵And in that other Scripture God also said, "Those people will never enter and have my rest.*"

⁶It is still true that some people will enter and have God's rest. But those people who first heard the way to be saved* did not enter. They did not enter because they did not obey. ⁷So God planned another special day. It is called "today." God spoke about that day through David a long time later. It is the same Scripture* we used before:

> "If you hear God's voice today,
> don't be stubborn like in the past,

⁸We know that Joshua* did not lead the people into the rest* *God promised*. We know this, because God spoke later about another day *for rest* (*"today"*). ⁹This shows that the seventh-day rest* for God's people is still coming. ¹⁰God rested after he finished his work. So the person who enters and has God's rest is the person who has finished his work like God did. ¹¹So let us try as hard as

---

a way to be saved Literally, "the Good News" or "the gospel." See Romans 1:16.
rest The place of rest God promised to give his people.
Scriptures Holy Writings—the Old Testament.
"And...work" Quotation from Genesis 2:2.
Joshua After Moses died, Joshua became leader of the Jewish people. Joshua led them into the land that God promised to give them.
seventh-day rest Literally, "sabbath rest," meaning a sharing in the rest that God began after he created the world.

we can to enter God's rest. We must try hard so that none of us will be lost by following the example of those people who refused to obey God.

[12]God's word* (*message*) is alive and working. His word is sharper than the sharpest sword. God's word cuts all the way into us *like a sword*. It cuts deep to the place where the soul and the spirit are joined. God's word cuts to the center of our joints and our bones. God's word judges the thoughts and feelings in our hearts. [13]Nothing in all the world can be hidden from God. He can clearly see all things. Everything is open before him. And to him we must explain the way we have lived.

Jesus Helps Us Come Before God

[14]We have a great high priest* who has gone to live with God in heaven. He is Jesus the Son of God. So let us continue strongly in the faith we have. [15]Jesus, the high priest that we have, is able to understand our weaknesses. When Jesus lived on earth, he was tempted in every way. He was tempted in the same ways that we are tempted, but he never sinned. [16]With Jesus as our high priest we can feel free to come before God's throne where there is grace (*forgiveness*). There we receive mercy and kindness to help us when we need it.

5 Every Jewish high priest* is chosen from among men. That priest is given the work of helping people with the things they must do for God. That priest must offer to God gifts and sacrifices* for sins. [2]The high priest himself is weak *like all people*. So he is able to be gentle with those people who don't understand and who are doing wrong things. [3]The high priest offers sacrifices for the sins of the people. But the high priest has weaknesses himself. So he also must offer sacrifices for his own sins.

[4]To be a high priest* is an honor. But no person chooses himself for this work. That person must be called by God like Aaron* was. [5]It is the same with Christ. He did not choose

---

God's word   God's teachings and commands.
high priest   The most important priest for God's people.
sacrifices   A sacrifice is a gift or offering to God. The Jewish priests killed animals and offered
   them to God. Jesus Christ gave his own life as a sacrifice to pay for people's sins.
Aaron   Aaron was the first Jewish high priest. He was Moses' brother.

himself to have the glory of becoming a high priest. But God chose him. God said to Christ,

"You are my Son;
    today I have become your Father." *Psalm 2:7*

⁶And in another Scripture* God says,

"You will be a priest forever,
    the same as Melchizedek.*" *Psalm 110:4*

⁷While Christ lived on earth he prayed to God and asked God for help. God is the One who could save him from death, and Jesus prayed to God with loud cries and tears. And God answered Jesus' prayers because Jesus was humble and did everything God wanted. ⁸Jesus was the Son of God. But Jesus suffered and learned to obey by the things that he suffered. ⁹Then Jesus was perfect. And Jesus is the reason that all those people who obey him can have salvation forever. ¹⁰And God made Jesus the high priest,* the same as Melchizedek.

Warning Against Falling Away

¹¹We have many things to tell you about this. But it is hard to explain because you have stopped trying to understand. ¹²You have had enough time that by now you should be teachers. But you need some person to teach you again the first lessons of God's teaching. You still need the teaching that is like milk. You are not ready for solid food. ¹³Any person who lives on milk is still a baby. That person knows nothing about right teaching. ¹⁴But solid food is for people who have stopped being like babies. It is for people who are grown-up in their spirits. Those people have practiced and taught themselves to know the difference between good and evil.

6 So we should be finished with the beginning lessons about Christ. We should not go back to the things we started with. We began *our life in Christ* by turning away from the evil things

---

Scripture   A part of the Holy Writings—the Old Testament.
Melchizedek   A priest and king who lived in the time of Abraham. (Read Genesis 14:17-24.)
high priest   The most important priest for God's people.
Holy Spirit   Also called the Spirit of God, the Spirit of Christ, and the Comforter. He is joined with God and Christ. He does the work of God among people in the world.

we did before and by believing in God. ²At that time we were taught about baptisms,* and about the special act of a person putting his hands on people.* We were taught about people rising from death and about the judgment that will continue forever. But now we need to go forward to more mature (*advanced*) teaching.* ³And we will do this if God allows.

⁴⁻⁶After people have left *the way of Christ*, can you make them change their life again? I am talking about people who have learned the truth. They received God's gift and also shared in the Holy Spirit.* Those people heard the things God said and they saw the great powers of God's new world. And they saw for themselves that those things are very good. But then those people left *the way of Christ*. It is not possible to make those people change their lives *and come to Christ* again. Why? Because those people *that leave Christ's way* are really nailing Christ to the cross again. Those people bring shame to Christ before all people.

⁷*Those people are like* land that gets plenty of rain. A farmer plants and cares for that land so that it will give food for people. If that land grows plants that help people, then that land has the blessing of God. ⁸But if that land grows thorns and weeds, it is worthless. That land is in danger that it will be cursed by God. And that land will be destroyed by fire.

⁹Dear friends, we are saying these things to you. But really we expect better things from you. We feel sure that you will do the things that are a part of salvation. ¹⁰God is fair. God will remember all the work you have done. And God will remember that you showed your love to him by helping his people. And God will remember that you continue to help his people. ¹¹We want each of you to continue with the same hard work all your lives. Then you will surely get that great thing you hope for. ¹²We don't want you to become lazy. We want you to be like those people who get the things that God promised. Those people get God's promises because they have faith and patience.

baptisms The word here may mean Christian baptism (a brief burial in water), or it may mean the Jewish ceremonial washings.
putting his hands on people Putting the hands on people showed that they were being given some special work or some spiritual gift or blessing.
now...teaching In the Greek text, these words are in verse 1.
Holy Spirit Also called the Spirit of God, the Spirit of Christ, and the Comforter. He is joined with God and Christ. He does the work of God among people in the world.

¹³God made a promise to Abraham. And there is no one greater than God, so God used himself to vow (*promise*) that he would do what he said. ¹⁴God said, "I will surely bless you and give you many descendants.*"* ¹⁵Abraham waited patiently for this to happen. And later Abraham received what God promised.

¹⁶People always use the name of someone greater than themselves to make a vow (*promise*). The vow proves that what they say is true. *Then other people accept what they say.* And this ends all arguing. ¹⁷God wanted to prove that his promise was true. God wanted to prove this to those people who would get what he promised. God wanted those people to understand clearly that his purposes (*plans*) never change. So God said something would happen, and he proved what he said by also making a vow (*promise*). ¹⁸Those two things cannot change. God cannot lie when he says something and he cannot lie when he makes a vow. So those things give great comfort to us who came to God for safety. Those two things give us comfort and strength to continue in the hope that God gives us. ¹⁹We have this hope. And it is like an anchor. It is strong and sure and keeps our soul safe. That hope enters into *the most holy place* behind the curtain *in the heavenly temple.* ²⁰Jesus has already entered there and opened the way for us. Jesus has become the high priest* forever the same as Melchizedek.*

The Priest Melchizedek

7 Melchizedek was the king of Salem and a priest for God the Most High. Melchizedek met Abraham when Abraham was coming back after defeating the kings. When they met, Melchizedek blessed Abraham. ²And Abraham gave Melchizedek one tenth of everything Abraham had. (The name Melchizedek means "king of goodness." Also, "king of Salem" means "king of peace.") ³No person knows who Melchizedek's father or mother was.* No person knows where he came from. And no person knows when he was born or when he died. Melchizedek* is

descendants   The people born into a person's family after that person has died.
"I will...descendants"   Quotation from Genesis 22:17.
high priest   The most important priest for God's people.
Melchizedek   A priest and king who lived in the time of Abraham. (Read Genesis 14:17-24.)
No...was   Literally, "Melchizedek was without father, without mother, without genealogy."

like the Son of God and he continues being a priest forever.

⁴You can see that Melchizedek was very great. Abraham, the great father, gave Melchizedek one tenth of everything that Abraham won in battle. ⁵Now the law says that people in the family group of Levi who become priests must get one tenth from the people. The priests collect it from their own people (*the Jews*), even though the priests and their people are both from the family of Abraham. ⁶Melchizedek was not from the family group of Levi. But he got one tenth from Abraham. And he blessed Abraham—the man who had God's promises. ⁷And all people know that the more important person blesses the less important person. ⁸Those priests get one tenth, but they are only men who live and then die. But Melchizedek, who got one tenth *from Abraham*, continues living, like the Scripture* says. ⁹It is Levi who gets one tenth *from the people*. But we can say that when Abraham paid Melchizedek one tenth, then Levi also paid it. ¹⁰Levi was not yet born. But Levi was in the body of his ancestor Abraham when Melchizedek met Abraham.

¹¹People were given the law* under the system of priests from the Levi family group.* But people could not be made spiritually perfect through that system of priests. So there was a need for another priest to come. I mean a priest that is like Melchizedek, not Aaron. ¹²And when a different kind of priest comes, then the law must be changed too. ¹³We are saying these things about Christ. He belonged to a different family group. No person from that family group ever served *as a priest* at the altar.* ¹⁴It is clear that our Lord (*Christ*) came from the family group of Judah. And Moses said nothing about priests belonging to that family group.

Jesus Is a Priest like Melchizedek

¹⁵And these things become even more clear. We see that another priest (*Jesus*) comes who is like Melchizedek. ¹⁶He was

---

Melchizedek   A priest and king who lived in the time of Abraham. (Read Genesis 14:17-24.)
Scripture   A part of the Holy Writings—the Old Testament.
law   The law of Moses.
family group   One of the twelve "tribes" of the Jewish people, named after Jacob's twelve sons.
altar   Place where the Jews sacrificed animals and gifts to God for worship.

not made a priest by human rules and laws. He became a priest through the power of his life which continues forever. [17]*In the Scriptures,** this is said about him: "You will be a priest forever, the same as Melchizedek."*

[18]The old rule (*law*) is now ended because it was weak and worthless. [19]The law *of Moses* could not make anything perfect. And now a better hope has been given to us. And with that hope we can come near to God.

[20]Also, it is important that God made a vow (*promise*) when he made Jesus high priest.* When those other men became priests, there was no vow. [21]But Jesus became a priest with God's vow. God said to him:

> "The Lord has made a vow (*promise*)
>   and will not change his mind:
> 'You are a priest forever.' "   *Psalm 110:4*

[22]So this means that Jesus is the guarantee of a better agreement* *from God to his people.*

[23]Also, when one of those other priests died, he could not continue being a priest. So there were many of those priests. [24]But Jesus lives forever. He will never stop serving as priest. [25]So Christ can save those people who come to God through him. Christ can do this forever, because he always lives, ready to help people when they come before God.

[26]So Jesus is the kind of high priest* that we need. He is holy— he has no sin in him. He is pure and not influenced by sinners. And he is raised above the heavens. [27]He is not like those other priests. Those other priests had to offer (*give*) sacrifices* every day. They had to offer sacrifices first for their own sins and then for the sins of the people. But Christ doesn't need to do that. Christ offered only one sacrifice for all time. Christ offered himself. [28]The law chooses high priests who are people and have the same weaknesses as people. But God made a promise that came after the law. God spoke those words with a vow (*promise*),

Scriptures   Holy Writings—the Old Testament.
"You...Melchizedek"   Quotation from Psalm 110:4.
high priest   The most important priest for God's people.
agreement   God gives a contract or agreement to his people. For the Jews, this agreement was the law of Moses. But now God has given a better agreement to his people through Christ.
sacrifices   A sacrifice is a gift or offering to God. The Jewish priests killed animals and offered them to God. Jesus Christ gave his own life as a sacrifice to pay for people's sins.

and those words made the Son of God to be the high priest.* And that Son has been made perfect forever.

Jesus Our High Priest

8 Here is the point of what we are saying: We have a high priest* like we have been telling you about. That high priest now sits on the right side of God's throne in heaven. ²Our high priest serves in the Most Holy Place.* He serves in the true place of worship* that was made by God, not by people.

³Every high priest has the work of offering gifts and sacrifices* to God. So our high priest must also offer something to God. ⁴If our high priest were now living on earth, then he would not be a priest. I say this because there are already priests here who follow the law by offering gifts to God. ⁵The work that these priests do is really only a copy and a shadow of the things that are in heaven. That is why God warned Moses when Moses was ready to build the place of worship: "Be sure to make everything exactly like the pattern I showed you on the mountain." ⁶But the work that has been given to Jesus is much greater than the work that was given to those priests. In the same way, the new agreement* that Jesus brought from God to his people is much greater than the old one. And the new agreement is based on promises of better things.

⁷If there were nothing wrong with the first agreement, then there would be no need for a second agreement. ⁸But God found something wrong with the people. God said:

"The time is coming, says the Lord,
    when I will give a new agreement
        to the people of Israel,*
    and to the people of Judah.*
⁹ It will not be like the agreement I gave
        to their fathers (*ancestors*).

---

high priest   The most important priest for God's people.
Most Holy Place   Literally, "holy of holies," the spiritual place where God lives and is worshiped.
true place of worship   Literally, "true tabernacle (*tent*)."
sacrifices   A sacrifice is a gift or offering to God. The Jewish priests killed animals and offered them to God. Jesus Christ gave his own life as a sacrifice to pay for people's sins.
new agreement   This is the "better agreement" that God has given to his people through Jesus.
Israel   The Jewish nation was divided into two parts. The northern part was called Israel.
Judah   The southern part of the Jewish nation was called Judah.

> That is the agreement I gave
>> when I took them by the hand
>> and led them out of Egypt.
> They did not continue following the agreement
>> I gave them,
>> and I turned away from them, says the Lord.
> [10]This is the new agreement I will give
>> the people of Israel.*
> I will give this agreement in the future,
>> says the Lord:
> I will put my laws in their minds,
>> and I will write my laws on their hearts.
> I will be their God,
>> and they will be my people.
> [11]Never again will a person have to teach
>> his brother or God's other people.
> He will not need to tell them to know the Lord.
> Why? Because all people—the greatest people
>> and the least important people—will know me.
> [12]And I will forgive the wrong things they do against me,
>> and I will not remember their sins."   *Jeremiah 31:31-34*

[13]God called this a new agreement, so God has made the first agreement old. And anything that is old and useless is ready to disappear.

Worship Under the Old Agreement

9 The first agreement* had rules for worship. And it had a man-made place for worship. [2]This place was inside a tent. The first area in the tent was called the Holy Place. In the Holy Place were the lamp and the table with the special bread offered to God. [3]Behind the second curtain was a room called the Most Holy Place.* [4]In the Most Holy Place was a golden altar* for burning incense.* And also there was the holy box that held the

---

Israel The Jewish nation—God's chosen people.
first agreement The contract God gave to the Jewish people when he gave them the law of Moses.
Most Holy Place Literally, "holy of holies," the place where God met with the high priest.
altar Place where gifts and offerings were made to God for worship.
incense Special dried tree sap used for a sacrifice. It was burned to make a sweet-smelling smoke.

old agreement.* The box was covered with gold. Inside this box were a golden jar of manna* and Aaron's rod (*stick*)—the rod that once grew leaves. Also in the box were the flat rocks *with the Commandments* of the old agreement *written on them*. ⁵Above the box were the cherubim* (*statues*) that showed God's glory. These cherubim were over the mercy seat.* But we cannot say everything about these things now.

⁶Everything in the tent was made ready in the way I have explained. Then the priests went into the first room every day to do their worship. ⁷But only the high priest* could go into the second room. And the high priest went into that room only once a year. And the high priest could never enter that room without taking blood with him. The priest offered that blood to God for himself and for the people's sins. Those sins were the sins the people did without knowing that they were sinning. ⁸The Holy Spirit* uses those two separate rooms to teach us this: that the way into the Most Holy Place* was not open while that first room was still there. ⁹This is an example for us today. This shows that the gifts and sacrifices* that were offered to God were not able to fully cleanse the person who was worshiping God. Those sacrifices could not make that person perfect in his heart. ¹⁰Those gifts and sacrifices were only about food and drink and special washings. Those things were only rules about the body—*not about things inside people's hearts*. God gave those rules *for his people to follow* until the time of God's new way.

Worship Under the New Agreement

¹¹But Christ has already come to be the high priest.* He is the high priest of the good things we now have. But Christ does not serve in a place like the tent that those other priests served in. Christ serves in a place that is better than that tent. It is more

holy box...agreement Wooden box covered with gold that had in it God's law on two flat stones.
manna The food that God gave the Jewish people in the desert.
cherubim Cherubim are angels. Two images or statues of angels were in the Most Holy Place.
mercy seat The place on top of "the holy box that held the agreement," where the high priest put the blood of an animal once a year to pay for the sins the people had done.
high priest The most important priest for God's people.
Holy Spirit Also called the Spirit of God, the Spirit of Christ, and the Comforter. He is joined with God and Christ. He does the work of God among people in the world.
Most Holy Place Literally, "holy of holies," the spiritual place where God lives and is worshiped.
sacrifices The Jewish priests killed animals and offered them as sacrifices to God.

perfect. And that place is not made by men. It does not belong to this world. [12]Christ entered the Most Holy Place* only one time—enough for all time. Christ entered the Most Holy Place by using his own blood (*death*), not the blood of goats or young bulls. Christ entered there and got for us freedom forever. [13]The blood of goats and bulls and the ashes of a cow were sprinkled on those people who were no longer pure *enough to enter that tent (place of worship)*. That blood and those ashes made those people pure again—but only their bodies. [14]So surely the blood of Christ can do much, much more. Christ offered himself through the eternal Spirit* as a perfect sacrifice* to God. His blood will make us fully clean from the evil things we have done. His blood will make us pure even in our hearts. We are made pure so that we can worship (*serve*) the living God.

[15]So Christ brings a new agreement* from God to his people. Christ brings this new agreement so that those people that are called by God can have the things that God promised. God's people can have those things forever. They can have those things because Christ died to pay for the sins that people did under the first agreement.* Christ died to make people free from those sins.

[16]When a man dies, he leaves a will* (*agreement*). But people must prove that the man who wrote that will is dead. [17]A will means nothing while the man who wrote it is still living. The will can be used only after the man dies. [18]It is the same with the first agreement *between God and his people*. There had to be blood (*death*) before the agreement could be made good. [19]First, Moses told all the people every commandment in the law. Then Moses took the blood of calves and mixed it with water. Then he used red wool and a branch of hyssop* to sprinkle the blood and water on the book of the law and on all the people. [20]Then Moses said, "This is the blood that makes the agreement good—the

---

Most Holy Place   Literally, "holy of holies," the spiritual place where God lives and is worshiped.
Spirit   Probably the Holy Spirit. Called the Spirit of God, the Spirit of Christ, and the Comforter, he is joined with God and Christ. He does the work of God among people in the world.
sacrifice   A gift offered to God. Jesus Christ gave his life to pay for people's sins.
new agreement   This is the "better agreement" that God has given to his people through Jesus.
first agreement   The contract God gave to the Jewish people when he gave them the law of Moses.
will   The paper a person signs to show which people he wants to have his things after he dies.
    "Will" is the same Greek word as the word for "agreement" or "contract."
hyssop   A special plant.

agreement that God commanded you to follow." ²¹In the same way, Moses sprinkled the blood on the tent. He sprinkled the blood over all the things used in worship. ²²The law says that almost everything must be made clean by blood. And sins cannot be forgiven without blood (*death*).

Christ's Sacrifice Takes Away Sins

²³These things are copies of the real things that are in heaven. These copies had to be made clean by animal sacrifices.* But the real things in heaven must have much better sacrifices. ²⁴Christ went into the Most Holy Place.* But Christ did not go into the Most Holy Place that was made by men. That Most Holy Place is only a copy of the real one. Christ went into heaven. Christ is now there before God to help us. ²⁵The high priest* enters the Most Holy Place once every year. He takes with him blood to offer. But he does not offer his own blood *like Christ did*. Christ went into heaven, but not to offer himself many times like the high priest *offers blood again and again*. ²⁶If Christ had offered himself many times, then he would have needed to suffer many times since the time the world was made. But Christ came *and offered himself* only once. And that once is enough for all time. Christ came at a time when the world is nearing an end. Christ came to take away all sin by sacrificing* himself. ²⁷Every person must die once. After a person dies he is judged. ²⁸So Christ was offered as a sacrifice* one time to take away the sins of many people. And Christ will come a second time, but not for people's sin. Christ will come the second time to bring salvation to those people who are waiting for him.

Christ's Sacrifice Makes Us Perfect

10 The law* gave us only an unclear picture of the good things coming in the future. The law is not a perfect picture of the real things. The law tells people to offer the same

sacrifice(s) A sacrifice is a gift or offering to God. The Jewish priests killed animals and offered them to God. Jesus Christ gave his own life as a sacrifice to pay for people's sins.
Most Holy Place Literally, "holy of holies," the place where God met the high priest.
high priest The most important priest for God's people.
sacrificing Offering a gift to God. Jesus Christ gave his life to pay for people's sins.
law The law of Moses.

sacrifices* every year. The people who come to worship God continue to offer those sacrifices. But the law can never make those people perfect. ²If the law could make people perfect, then those sacrifices would have already stopped. Those people would already be clean *from their sins*. And they would not still feel guilty for their sins. *But the law cannot do that*. ³Those people's sacrifices make them remember their sins every year, ⁴because it is not possible for the blood of bulls and goats to take away sins.

⁵So when Christ came into the world he said:

> "You (*God*) don't want sacrifices* and offerings,
>> but you have prepared a body for me.
> ⁶ You are not pleased with the sacrifices
>> of animals killed and burned.
> And you are not pleased with sacrifices
>> to take away sins.
> ⁷ Then I said, 'Here I am, God.
> It is written about me in the book of the law.
> I have come to do the things you want.' "   *Psalm 40:6-8*

⁸*In this Scripture** he (*Christ*) first said, "You don't want sacrifices* and offerings, and you are not pleased with sacrifices and offerings. You are not pleased with animals killed and burned or with sacrifices to take away sin." (These are all sacrifices that the law* commands.) ⁹Then he (*Christ*) said, "Here I am, God. I have come to do the things you want." So God ends that first system of sacrifices and starts his new way. ¹⁰Jesus Christ did the things God wanted him to do. And because of that, we are made holy through the sacrifice* of Christ's body. Christ made that sacrifice one time—enough for all time.

¹¹Every day, the priests stand and do their religious service. Again and again the priests offer the same sacrifices.* But those sacrifices can never take away sins. ¹²But Christ offered only one sacrifice for sins, and that sacrifice is enough for all time. Then Christ sat down at the right side of God. ¹³And now Christ waits

---

sacrifice(s)   A sacrifice is a gift or offering to God. The Jewish priests killed animals and offered them to God. Jesus Christ gave his own life as a sacrifice to pay for people's sins.
Scripture   A part of the Holy Writings—the Old Testament.
law   The law of Moses.

there for his enemies to be put under his power.* [14]With one sacrifice Christ made his people perfect forever. Those people are the ones who are being made holy.*

[15]The Holy Spirit* also tells us about this. First he says:

> [16]"This is the agreement* I will make with my people
>   in the future, says the Lord.
> I will put my laws in my people's hearts.
>   I will write my laws in their minds."   *Jeremiah 31:33*

[17]Then he says:

> "I will forgive their sins
>   and the evil things they do—
> I will never remember those things again."   *Jeremiah 31:34*

[18]And after all these things are forgiven, there is no more need for a sacrifice* for sins.

Let Us Come Near to God

[19]And so, brothers *and sisters*, we are completely free to enter the Most Holy Place.* We can do this without fear because of the blood (*death*) of Jesus. [20]We can enter through a new way that Jesus opened for us. It is a living way. This new way leads through the curtain—Christ's body. [21]And we have a great priest who rules the house (*people*) of God. [22]We have been cleansed and made free from feelings of guilt. And our bodies have been washed with pure water. So come near to God with a sincere (*true*) heart, feeling sure because of our faith. [23]We should hold strongly to the hope that we have. And we should never fail to tell people about our hope. We can trust God to do what he promised. [24]We should think about each other and see how we can help each other to show love and do good things. [25]We should not quit meeting together. That's what some people are doing. But we should *meet together and* strengthen each other. You should do this more and more as you see the Day* coming.

---

to be put...power Literally, "to be made a footstool for his feet."
holy God's people are called holy because they are made pure and belong only to God.
Holy Spirit Also called the Spirit of God, the Spirit of Christ, and the Comforter. He is joined with God and Christ. He does the work of God among people in the world.
agreement The new and better agreement that God has given to his people through Jesus.
sacrifice A gift offered to God. Jesus Christ gave his life to pay for people's sins.
Most Holy Place Literally, "holy of holies," the spiritual place where God lives and is worshiped.
the Day Probably the Day when Christ will come again.

²⁶If we decide to continue sinning after we have learned the truth, then there is no other sacrifice* that will take away sins. ²⁷If we continue sinning, all we have is fear in waiting for the judgment and the angry fire that will destroy all people who live against God. ²⁸Any person who refused to obey the law of Moses was found guilty from the proof given by two or three witnesses. That person was not forgiven. He was killed. ²⁹So what do you think should be done to a person who shows his hate for the Son of God? Surely that person should have a much worse punishment. Yes, that person should have a worse punishment for not showing respect for the blood (*Jesus' death*) of the new agreement.* That blood once made that person holy. And that person should have a worse punishment for showing his hate against the Spirit* of God's grace (*kindness*). ³⁰We know that God said, "I will punish people *for the wrong things they do*; I will repay them."* And God also said, "The Lord will judge his people."* ³¹It is a terrible thing *for a sinful person* to fall into the hands of the living God.

³²Remember those days when you first learned the truth. You had a hard struggle with many sufferings, but you continued strong. ³³Sometimes people said hateful things to you and persecuted you before many people. And sometimes you helped other people who were being treated that same way. ³⁴Yes, you helped those people in prison and shared in their suffering. And you still had joy when all the things you owned were taken away from you. You continued with joy because you knew that you had something much better that would continue forever.

³⁵So don't lose the courage that you had in the past. Your courage will be rewarded richly. ³⁶You must be patient. After you have done what God wants, then you will get the things that he promised you. ³⁷In a very short time,

"The One who is coming will come.
He will not be late.

---

sacrifice   A gift offered to God.
new agreement   This is the "better agreement" that God has given to his people through Jesus.
Spirit   The Holy Spirit. Also called the Spirit of God, the Spirit of Christ, and the Comforter. He
   is joined with God and Christ. He does the work of God among people in the world.
"I will...them"   Quotation from Deuteronomy 32:35.
"The Lord...people"   Quotation from Psalm 135:14.

> [38]The person who is right with me (*God*)
> will have life because of his faith.
> But if that person turns back with fear,
> I will not be pleased with him."*
>   *Habakkuk 2:3-4*

[39]But we are not those people who turn back and are lost. No. We are the people who have faith and are saved.

Faith

11 Faith means being sure of the things we hope for. And faith means knowing that something is real even if we don't see it. [2]God was pleased with those people who lived a long time ago because they had faith like this.

[3]Faith helps us understand that God created the whole world with his command. This means that the things we see were made by something that cannot be seen.

[4]Cain and Abel both offered sacrifices* to God. But Abel offered a better sacrifice to God because Abel had faith. God said he was pleased with the things Abel offered. And so God called Abel a good man because Abel had faith. Abel died, but through his faith he is still speaking.

[5]Enoch was carried away from this earth. He never died. Before Enoch was carried off, the Scripture* says, Enoch was a man who truly pleased God. Later, people could not find Enoch, because God brought Enoch to be with him. This happened to Enoch because he had faith. [6]Without faith, a person cannot please God. Any person who comes to God must believe that God is real. And any person who comes to God must believe that God rewards those people who truly want to find him.

[7]Noah was warned by God about things that Noah could not yet see. But Noah had faith and respect for God. So Noah built a large boat to save his family. With his faith, Noah showed that the world was wrong. And Noah became one of those people who are made right with God through faith.

[8]God called Abraham to travel to another place that God promised to give Abraham. Abraham did not know where that

"The One...him"   This quotation is from the Septuagint, Greek version of the Old Testament.
sacrifices   A sacrifice is a gift or offering to God.
Scripture   A part of the Holy Writings—the Old Testament.

other place was. But Abraham obeyed God and started traveling, because Abraham had faith. ⁹Abraham lived in that country that God promised to give him. Abraham lived there like a visitor who did not belong. Abraham did this because he had faith. Abraham lived in tents with Isaac and Jacob. Isaac and Jacob also received that same promise from God. ¹⁰Abraham was waiting for the city* that has real foundations. He was waiting for the city that is planned and built by God.

¹¹Abraham was too old to have children. And Sarah was not able to have children. But Abraham had faith in God, and so God made them able to have children. Abraham trusted God to do the things he promised. ¹²This man was so old that he was almost dead. But from that one man came as many descendants (*people*) as there are stars in the sky. So many people came from that one man that they are like grains of sand on the seashore.

¹³All those great men continued living with faith until they died. Those men did not get the things that God promised his people. The men only saw those things coming far in the future and were glad. Those men accepted the fact that they were like visitors and strangers on earth. ¹⁴When people accept something like that, then those people show that they are waiting for a country that will be their own country. ¹⁵If those men were thinking about that country they had left, then they could have gone back. ¹⁶But those men were waiting for a better country—a heavenly country. So God is not ashamed to be called their God. And God has prepared a city for those men.

¹⁷⁻¹⁸God tested Abraham's faith. God told Abraham to offer Isaac as a sacrifice.* Abraham obeyed because he had faith. Abraham already had the promises from God. And God had already said to Abraham, "The descendants I promised you will come through Isaac." But Abraham was ready to offer his only son (*Isaac*). Abraham did this because he had faith. ¹⁹Abraham believed that God could raise people from death. And really, *when God stopped Abraham from killing Isaac*, it was like Abraham got Isaac back from death.

---

city The spiritual "city" where God's people live with him. Also called "the heavenly Jerusalem." (See Hebrews 12:22.)
sacrifice A gift offered to God.

²⁰Isaac blessed the future of Jacob and Esau. Isaac did that because he had faith. ²¹And Jacob blessed each one of Joseph's sons. Jacob did this while he was dying. He was leaning on his rod and worshiping God. Jacob did those things because he had faith.

²²And when Joseph was almost dead, he spoke about the Israelites* (*Jews*) leaving Egypt. And Joseph told the people what they should do with his body. Joseph said those things because he had faith.

²³And the mother and father of Moses hid Moses for three months after he was born. They did this because they had faith. They saw that Moses was a beautiful baby. And they were not afraid to disobey the king's (*Pharaoh's*) order.

²⁴Moses grew up and became a man. Moses refused to be called the son of Pharaoh's daughter. ²⁵Moses chose not to enjoy the pleasures of sin. Those pleasures end quickly. Instead, Moses chose to suffer bad things with God's people. Moses did this because he had faith. ²⁶Moses thought that it was better to suffer for the Christ* than to have all the treasures of Egypt. Moses was waiting for the reward *that God would give him*. ²⁷Moses left Egypt. He left because he had faith. Moses was not afraid of the king's (*Pharaoh's*) anger. Moses continued strong like he could see the God that no person can see. ²⁸Moses prepared the Passover* and spread the blood *on the doors*. This blood was spread *on the doors* so that the Angel of Death* would not kill the firstborn* sons of the Israelites (*the Jews*). Moses did this because he had faith.

²⁹And the people *that Moses led* all walked through the Red Sea like it was dry land. They were able to do this because they had faith. The Egyptians also tried to walk through the Red Sea, but they were all drowned.

Israelite(s)   The Jewish people were from the twelve sons of Jacob, who is also called "Israel."
Christ   The "anointed one" (the Messiah) or chosen one of God.
Passover   A special meal that God told Moses and his people to eat. A lamb was killed for this meal, and the blood from the lamb was spread around the door of each house.
Angel of Death   Literally, "the destroyer." To punish the Egyptian people, God sent an angel to kill the oldest son in each home (Exodus 12:29-32).
firstborn   The first child born into a family.

³⁰And the walls of Jericho fell because of the faith of God's people. The people marched around the walls of Jericho for seven days, and then the walls fell.

³¹And Rahab, the prostitute,* welcomed the *Israelite* spies and helped them like friends. And because of her faith she was not killed with those other people who refused to obey.

³²Do I need to give you more examples? I don't have enough time to tell you about Gideon, Barak, Samson, Jephthah, David, Samuel and the prophets.* ³³All those people had great faith. And with that faith they defeated kingdoms. They did the things that are right and they got the things that God promised. With their faith some people closed the mouths of lions. ³⁴Some people stopped great fires, and other people were saved from being killed with swords. They did those things because they had faith. Weak people were made strong because of their faith. They became powerful in battle and defeated other armies. ³⁵People that had died were raised from death, and they were given back to the women in their families. Other people were tortured* and refused to accept their freedom. They did this so that they could be raised from death to a better life. ³⁶Some people were laughed at and beaten. Other people were tied and put into prison. ³⁷They were killed with stones and cut in half. They were killed with swords. Some of these people wore the skins of sheep and goats. They were poor, persecuted, and treated badly by other people. ³⁸The world was not good enough for these great people. These people wandered in deserts and mountains, living in caves and holes in the ground.

³⁹All these people are known for their faith. But none of these people got God's great promise. ⁴⁰God planned to give us something better. Then those people could be made perfect, but only together with us.

We Should Also Follow Jesus' Example

12 We have those many people *of faith* around us. Their lives tell us what faith means. So we should be like them. We too should run the race that is before us and never stop

prostitute   A woman who is paid by men who use her for sexual sin.
prophets   People who spoke for God. Their writings are part of the Old Testament.
tortured   To be bound or tied and then hurt or punished by another person.

trying. We should take away *from our lives* anything that would stop us. And we should take away the sin that so easily catches us. ²We should always follow the example of Jesus. Jesus is the leader in our faith. And he makes our faith perfect. He suffered the cross because of the joy that God put before him. Jesus accepted the shame of the cross like it was nothing. And now he is sitting at the right side of God's throne. ³Think about Jesus. He was patient while sinful men were doing bad things against him. Jesus did this so that you also will be patient and not stop trying.

God Is Like a Father Who Punishes His Children

⁴You are struggling against sin, but your struggles have not yet caused you to be killed. ⁵You are sons of God, and he speaks words of comfort to you. You have forgotten these words:

"My son, don't think it is worth nothing
 when the Lord punishes you,
 and don't stop trying when the Lord corrects you.
⁶ The Lord punishes every person that he loves,
 and he punishes every person
  that he accepts as a son."

Proverbs 3:11-12

⁷So accept sufferings like those sufferings are a father's punishment. God does these things to you like a father punishing his sons. All sons are punished by their fathers. ⁸If you are never punished (and every son must be punished), then you are not true children and not really sons. ⁹We have all had fathers here on earth who punished us. And we respected our fathers. So it is even more important that we accept punishment from the Father of our spirits. If we do this we will have life. ¹⁰Our fathers on earth punished us for a short time. They punished us the way that they thought was best. But God punishes us to help us, so that we can become holy* like him. ¹¹We don't enjoy punishment when we get it. Being punished is painful. But later, after we have learned from being punished, we have peace, because we start living right.

---

holy   A holy person is pure, belongs only to God, and does only the things that God wants.

Be Careful How You Live

¹²You have become weak. So make yourselves strong again. ¹³Walk (*live*) in the right way, so that you will be saved and your weakness will not cause you to be lost.

¹⁴Try to live in peace with all people. And try to live lives free from sin. If a person's life is not holy, then he will never see the Lord. ¹⁵Be careful that no person fails to get God's grace (*kindness*). Be careful that no person becomes like a bitter weed growing among you. A person like that can ruin your whole group. ¹⁶Be careful that no person does sexual sin. And be careful that no person is like Esau and never thinks about God. Esau was the oldest son and he would have inherited (*received*) everything from his father. But Esau sold all that for a single meal. ¹⁷You remember that after Esau did this, he wanted to get his father's blessing. Esau wanted that blessing so much that he cried. But his father refused to give him the blessing, because Esau could find no way to change the thing he had done.

¹⁸You have come to a new place. It is not a place like the mountain that the people of Israel* came to. You have not come to a mountain that can be touched and that is burning with fire. You have not come to darkness, sadness, and storms. ¹⁹You have not come to the sound of a trumpet or to a voice speaking words to you. When the people heard the voice, they begged to never hear another word. ²⁰They did not want to hear the command: "If anything, even an animal, touches the mountain, it must be killed with stones."* ²¹The things those people saw were so terrible that Moses said, "I am shaking with fear."*

²²But you have not come to that kind of place. The new place you have come to is Mount Zion.* You have come to the city of the living God, the heavenly Jerusalem.* You have come to thousands of angels gathered together with joy. ²³You have come to the meeting of God's firstborn* children. Their names are written in heaven. You have come to God, the judge of all people.

Israel   The Jewish nation—God's chosen people.
"If...stones"   Quotation from Exodus 19:12-13.
"I...fear"   Quotation from Deuteronomy 9:19.
Mount Zion   Another name for Jerusalem, here meaning the spiritual city of God's people.
heavenly Jerusalem   The spiritual place where God's people live with him.
firstborn   The first son born in a Jewish family was given the most important place in the family and received special blessings. All of God's children are like that.

And you have come to the spirits of good people who have been made perfect. ²⁴You have come to Jesus—the One that brought the new agreement* from God to his people. You have come to the sprinkled blood* that tells us about better things than the blood of Abel.*

²⁵Be careful and don't refuse to listen when God speaks. Those people (*Israelites*) refused to listen to him when he warned them on earth. And those people did not escape. Now God is speaking from heaven. So now it will be worse for those people who refuse to listen to him. ²⁶When he spoke before, his voice shook the earth. But now he has promised, "Once again I will shake the earth. But I will also shake heaven."* ²⁷The words "once again" clearly show us that everything that was made will be destroyed. Those are the things that can be shaken. And only the things that cannot be shaken will continue.

²⁸So we should be thankful because we have a kingdom that cannot be shaken. We should be thankful and worship God in a way that will please him. We should worship him with respect and fear, ²⁹because our God is like a fire that can destroy.

The Way to Worship God

13 You are brothers *and sisters* in Christ, so continue loving each other. ²Always remember to help people by accepting them into your home. Some people have done that and have helped angels without knowing it. ³Don't forget those people in prison. Remember them like you are in prison with them. And don't forget those people who are suffering. Remember them like you are suffering with them.

⁴Marriage should be honored by all people. And every marriage should be kept pure between only two people. God will judge guilty those people who do sexual sins and adultery.* ⁵Keep your lives free from the love of money. And be satisfied with the things you have. God has said,

---

new agreement This is the "better agreement" that God has given to his people through Jesus.
sprinkled blood The blood (death) of Jesus.
Abel The son of Adam and Eve, who was killed by his brother Cain (Genesis 4:8).
"Once...shake heaven" Quotation from Haggai 2:6.
adultery Breaking a marriage promise by doing sexual sin.

"I will never leave you;
I will never run away from you."

Deuteronomy 31:6

⁶So, we can feel sure and say,

"The Lord is my helper;
I will not be afraid.
People can do nothing to me."

Psalm 118:6

⁷Remember your leaders. They taught God's message to you. Remember how they lived and died, and copy their faith. ⁸Jesus Christ is the same yesterday, today, and forever.

⁹Don't let all kinds of strange teachings lead you in the wrong way. Your hearts should be strengthened by God's grace (*kindness*), not by obeying rules about foods. Obeying those rules doesn't help people.

¹⁰We have a sacrifice.* And those priests who serve in the tent* cannot eat from our sacrifice. ¹¹The high priest* carries the blood of animals into the Most Holy Place.* He offers that blood for sins. But the bodies of those animals are burned outside the camp. ¹²So Jesus also suffered outside of the city. Jesus died to make his people holy* with his own blood (*death*). ¹³So we should go to Jesus outside the camp. We should accept the same shame that Jesus had. ¹⁴Here on earth we don't have a city that continues forever. But we are waiting for the city that we will have in the future. ¹⁵So through Jesus we should never stop offering our sacrifice to God. That sacrifice is our praise, coming from lips that speak his name. ¹⁶And don't forget to do good for other people. And share with other people. These are the sacrifices that please God.

¹⁷Obey your leaders and be under their authority. Those men are responsible for you. So they are always watching to protect your souls. Obey those men so that they will do this work with joy, not sadness. It will not help you to make their work hard.

¹⁸Continue praying for us. We feel right about the things we do, because we always try to do the best thing. ¹⁹And I beg you to

---

sacrifice   A gift offered to God. Jesus Christ gave his life to pay for people's sins.
tent   The special tent or "tabernacle" where the Jewish priests worshiped God.
high priest   The most important priest for God's people.
Most Holy Place   Literally, "holy of holies," the place where God met the high priest.
holy   God's people are called holy because they are made pure and belong only to God.

pray that God will send me back to you soon. I want this more than anything else.

²⁰⁻²¹I pray that the God of peace will give you every good thing you need to do the things he wants. God is the One who raised our Lord Jesus from death. He raised Jesus, the Great Shepherd of the sheep. God raised Jesus because of his blood (*death*). His blood began the new agreement* that continues forever. I pray that God will do the things in us that please him. I ask that he will do those things through Jesus Christ. To Jesus be glory forever. Amen.

²²My brothers *and sisters*, I beg you to listen patiently to these things I have said. I said these things to strengthen you. And this letter is not very long. ²³I want you to know that our brother Timothy is out of prison. If he comes to me soon, we will both come to see you.

²⁴Say hello to all your leaders and to all God's people. All *the brothers and sisters* in Italy say hello to you.

²⁵God's grace (*kindness*) be with you all.

---

new agreement   This is the "better agreement" that God has given to his people through Jesus.

James

1 From James, a servant of God and of the Lord Jesus Christ.
To all of God's people that are scattered everywhere in the
world:

Greetings.

Faith and Wisdom

²My brothers *and sisters*, you will have many kinds of troubles.
But when these things happen, you should be very happy. ³Why?
Because you know that these things are testing your faith. And
this will give you patience. ⁴Let your patience make you stronger
and stronger. Then you will be perfect. You will have everything
you need. ⁵But if any of you needs wisdom, then you should ask
God for it. God is generous. He enjoys giving to all people. So
God will give you wisdom. ⁶But when you ask God, you must
believe. Don't doubt God. The person who doubts is like a wave
in the sea. The wind blows the wave up and down. The person
who doubts is like that wave. ⁷⁻⁸The person who doubts is
thinking two different things at the same time. He cannot decide
about anything he does. A person like that should not think that
he will receive anything from the Lord.

True Riches

⁹If a believer is poor, he should be proud because God has
made him *spiritually* rich. ¹⁰If a believer is rich, he should be
proud because *God has shown him that* he is *spiritually* poor. The
rich person will die like a wild flower in the grass. ¹¹The sun rises
and becomes hotter and hotter. The heat from the sun makes the
plants very dry. The flower falls off. The flower was beautiful,
but now it is dead. It is the same with a rich person. While he is
still making plans for his business, he will die.

Temptation Does Not Come from God

¹²When a person is tempted and still continues strong, he should be happy. Why? Because after he has proved *his faith*, God will give him the reward of life forever. God promised this to all people who love him. ¹³When a person is being tempted, he should not say, "God is tempting me." Evil cannot tempt God. And God himself does not tempt any person. ¹⁴It is the evil things a person wants that tempt that person. His own evil desire leads him away and holds him. ¹⁵This desire causes sin. Then the sin grows and brings death.

¹⁶My dear brothers *and sisters*, don't be fooled about this. ¹⁷Everything good comes from God. And every perfect gift is from God. These good gifts come down from the Father (*Maker*) of all light (*sun, moon, stars*). God does not change. He is always the same. ¹⁸God decided to give us life through the word of truth. He wanted us to be the most important of all the things he made.

Listening and Obeying

¹⁹My dear brothers *and sisters*, always be more willing to listen than to speak. Don't become angry easily. ²⁰A person's anger does not help him live right like God wants. ²¹So put out of your life every evil thing and every kind of wrong thing you do. Be humble and accept God's teaching that is planted in your hearts. This teaching can save your souls.

²²Do what God's teaching says; don't just listen and do nothing. Why? Because when you only sit and listen, you are fooling yourselves. ²³If a person hears God's teaching and does nothing, he is like this: He is like a man who looks at his face in the mirror. ²⁴The man sees himself, then goes away and quickly forgets what he looked like. ²⁵But the truly happy person is the person who carefully studies God's perfect law that makes people free. He continues to study it. He listens to God's teaching and does not forget what he heard. Then he obeys what God's teaching says. When that person does this, it makes that person happy.

The True Way to Worship God

²⁶Some person might think he is religious (*good*). But if that person says things he should not say, then he is fooling himself. His "religion" is worth nothing. ²⁷This is the kind of religion (*worship*) that God accepts: caring for orphans* or widows* who need help, and keeping yourself free from the world's *evil* influence. This is the kind of religion (*worship*) that God accepts as pure and good.

Love All People

2 My dear brothers *and sisters*, you are believers in our glorious Lord Jesus Christ. So don't think that some people are more important than other people. ²Suppose a person comes into your group. He is wearing very nice clothes and a gold ring. At the same time, a poor man comes in wearing old, dirty clothes. ³You show special attention to the man wearing nice clothes. You say, "Sit here in this good seat." But you say to the poor man, 'Stand there!" or, "Sit on the floor by our feet!" ⁴What are you doing? You are making some people more important than others. With evil thoughts you are deciding which person is better.

⁵Listen, my dear brothers *and sisters*! Don't forget: God chose the poor people in the world to have some special blessings: to be rich with faith and to receive the kingdom God promised to people who love him. ⁶But you show no respect to the poor man. And you know that the rich people are the people who always try to control your lives. And they are the people who take you to court. ⁷And the rich people are the people who say bad things against the good name of the One (*Jesus*) who owns you.

⁸One law rules over all other laws. This royal law is found in the Scriptures*: "Love other people as much as you love yourself."* If you obey this law, then you are doing right. ⁹But if you are treating one person like he is more important than another person, then you are sinning. That *royal* law proves that you are guilty of breaking *God's* law. ¹⁰A person might follow all

orphans Children whose mother and father have died.
widows A widow is a woman whose husband has died.
Scriptures Holy Writings—the Old Testament.
"Love...yourself" Quotation from Leviticus 19:18.

of *God's* law. But if that person fails to obey only one command, then he is guilty of breaking all the commands in that law. ¹¹God said, "Don't do the sin of adultery.*"* The same God also said, "Don't kill."* So, if you don't do the sin of adultery, but you kill a person, then you are guilty of breaking all of *God's* law. ¹²You will be judged by the law that makes people free. You should remember this in everything you say and do. ¹³Yes, you must show mercy to other people or God will not show mercy to you when he judges you. But the person who shows mercy can stand without fear when he is judged.

Faith and Good Works

¹⁴My brothers *and sisters*, if a person says that he has faith, but does nothing, then that faith is worth nothing. Can faith like that save him? No! ¹⁵A brother or sister *in Christ* might need clothes or might need food to eat. ¹⁶And you say to that person, "God be with you! I hope you stay warm and get plenty to eat." You say these things, but you don't give that person those things he needs. If you don't help that person, your words are worth nothing. ¹⁷It is the same with faith. If faith does nothing, then that faith is dead, because it is alone.

¹⁸A person might say, "You have faith, but I do things. Show me your faith! Your faith does nothing. I will show you my faith by the things I do." ¹⁹You believe there is one God. Good! But the demons* believe, too! And they shake with fear.

²⁰You foolish person! Must you be shown that faith that does nothing is worth nothing? ²¹Abraham is our father (*ancestor*). Abraham was made right with God by the things he did. He offered (*gave*) his son Isaac to God on the altar.* ²²So you see that Abraham's faith and the things he did worked together. His faith was made perfect by the things he did. ²³This shows the full meaning of the Scripture* that says: "Abraham believed God. And God accepted Abraham's faith. That faith made Abraham

---

adultery Breaking a marriage promise by doing sexual sin.
"Don't...adultery" Quotation from Exodus 20:14 and Deuteronomy 5:18.
"Don't kill" Quotation from Exodus 20:13 and Deuteronomy 5:17.
demons Demons are evil spirits from the devil.
altar An altar is a place where sacrifices or gifts are offered to God.
Scripture A part of the Holy Writings—the Old Testament.

right with God."* Abraham was called "God's friend."* ²⁴So you see that a person is made right with God by the things he does. He cannot be made right by faith only.

²⁵Another example is Rahab. Rahab was a prostitute.* But she was made right with God by something she did: She helped the spies *for God's people*. She welcomed them into her home and helped them escape by a different road.*

²⁶A person's body that does not have a spirit is dead. It is the same with faith—faith that does nothing is dead!

Controlling the Things We Say

3 My brothers *and sisters*, not many of you should become teachers. Why? Because you know that we who teach will be judged more strictly than other people. ²We all make many mistakes. If there were a person who never said anything wrong, then that person would be perfect. He would be able to control his whole body, too. ³We put bits into the mouths of horses to make them obey us. With these bits in the horses' mouths, we can control their whole body. ⁴It is the same with ships. A ship is very big, and it is pushed by strong winds. But a very small rudder controls that big ship. The man who controls the rudder decides where the ship will go. The ship goes where the man wants. ⁵It is the same with our tongue. It is a small part of the body, but it boasts about doing great things.

A big forest fire can be started with only a little flame. ⁶The tongue is like a fire. It is a world of evil among the parts of our body. How? The tongue spreads its evil through our whole body. It starts a fire that influences all of life. The tongue gets this fire from hell. ⁷People can tame every kind of wild animal, bird, reptile, and fish. People have already tamed all these things. ⁸But no person can tame (*control*) the tongue. It is wild and evil. It is full of poison that can kill. ⁹We use our tongues to praise our Lord and Father (*God*), but then we curse (*say bad things to*) people. And God made those people like himself. ¹⁰Praises and

"**Abraham...God**" Quotation from Genesis 15:6.
"**God's friend**" These words about Abraham are found in 2 Chronicles 20:7 and Isaiah 41:8.
prostitute A woman who is paid by men who use her for sexual sin.
She helped...road The story about Rahab is found in Joshua 2:1-21.

curses come from the same mouth! My brothers *and sisters*, this should not happen. ¹¹Do good water and bad water flow from the same spring? No! ¹²My brothers *and sisters*, can a fig tree make olives? No! Can a grapevine make figs? No! And a well full of salty water cannot give good water.

True Wisdom

¹³Is there any person among you who is truly wise and understanding? Then he should show his wisdom by living right. He should do good things with humility. A wise person does not boast. ¹⁴If you are selfish and have bitter jealousy in your hearts, then you have no reason to boast. Your boasting is a lie that hides the truth. ¹⁵That kind of "wisdom" does not come from God. That "wisdom" comes from the world. It is not spiritual. It is from the devil. ¹⁶Where there are jealousy and selfishness, there will be confusion and every kind of evil. ¹⁷But the wisdom that comes from God is like this: First, it is pure. It is also peaceful, gentle, and easy to please. This wisdom is always ready to help people who have trouble and to do good things for other people. This wisdom is always fair and honest. ¹⁸People who work for peace in a peaceful way get the good things that come from right living.

Give Yourselves to God

4 Do you know where your fights and arguments come from? Your fights and arguments come from the selfish desires that make war inside you. ²You want things, but you don't get them. So you kill and are jealous of other people. But you still cannot get what you want. So you argue and fight. You don't get the things you want because you don't ask *God*. ³Or when you ask, you don't receive. Why? Because the reason you ask is wrong. You only want things so that you can use those things for your own pleasures.

⁴You people are not faithful to God! You should know that loving the world is the same as hating God. So, if a person wants to be a part* of the world, then he makes himself God's enemy.

part Literally, "friend."

590

⁵Do you think the Scripture* means nothing? The Scripture says, "The Spirit* that *God* made to live in us wants us only for himself."* ⁶But the grace (*kindness*) that God gives is greater. Like the Scripture says, "God is against proud people, but he gives grace (*kindness*) to people who are humble."* ⁷So give yourselves to God. Be against the devil and the devil will run away from you. ⁸Come near to God and God will come near to you. You are sinners. So clean sin out of your lives.* You are trying to follow God and the world at the same time. Make your thinking pure. ⁹Be sad, be sorry, and cry! Change your laughter into crying. Change your joy into sadness. ¹⁰Be humble before the Lord and he will make you great.

You Are Not the Judge

¹¹Brothers *and sisters*, don't say things against each other. If you criticize your brother *in Christ* or judge him, then you are criticizing the law *he follows*. When you judge a brother *in Christ*, you are really judging the law *he follows*. And when you are judging the law, you are not a follower of the law. You have become a judge! ¹²God is the only One who makes laws. He is the only Judge. God is the only One who can save and destroy. So it is not right for you to judge another person.

Let God Plan Your Life

¹³Some of you say, "Today or tomorrow we will go to some city. We will stay there a year, do business, and make money." Listen! Think about this: ¹⁴You don't know what will happen tomorrow! Your life is like a fog. You can see it for a short time, but then it goes away. ¹⁵So you should say, "If the Lord wants, we will live and do this or that." ¹⁶But now you are proud and you boast. All of this boasting is wrong. ¹⁷And when a person knows how to do good, but does not do good, then he is sinning.

Scripture   A part of the Holy Writings—the Old Testament.
Spirit   The Holy Spirit. Also called the Spirit of God, the Spirit of Christ, and the Comforter. He
   is joined with God and Christ. He does the work of God among people in the world.
"The Spirit...himself"   These words may be from Exodus 20:5.
"God...humble"   Quotation from Proverbs 3:34.
So clean...lives   Literally, "So wash your hands and make your hearts pure."

Selfish Rich People Will Be Punished

5 You rich people, listen! Cry and be very sad because much trouble will come to you. ²Your riches will rot and be worth nothing. Your clothes will be eaten by moths.* ³Your gold and silver will rust, and that rust will be a proof that you were wrong. This rust will eat your bodies like fire. You saved your treasure in the last days. ⁴People worked in your fields, but you did not pay them. Those people are crying out against you. Those people harvested your crops. Now the Lord (*God*) of heaven's armies* has heard the things they are shouting. ⁵Your life on earth was full of rich living. You pleased yourselves with everything you wanted. You made yourselves fat, like an animal ready for the day of slaughter.* ⁶You showed no mercy to good people. They were not against you, but you killed them.

Be Patient

⁷Brothers *and sisters*, be patient; the Lord *Jesus* will come. So be patient until that time. Farmers are patient. A farmer waits for his valuable crop to grow up from the earth. A farmer waits patiently for his crop to receive the first rain and the last rain.* ⁸You must be patient, too. Don't stop hoping. The Lord *Jesus* is coming soon. ⁹Brothers *and sisters*, don't complain against each other. If you don't stop complaining, you will be judged guilty. And the Judge is ready to come! ¹⁰Brothers *and sisters*, follow the example of the prophets* who spoke for the Lord (*God*). They suffered many bad things, but they were patient. ¹¹We say that those people who accepted their troubles with patience are now happy. You have heard about Job's patience.* You know that after all Job's trouble, the Lord helped him. This shows that the Lord is full of mercy and is kind.

moths   Moths are flying insects that eat clothes.
heaven's armies   Literally, "Lord Sabaoth," meaning ruler of all heavenly powers.
You made...slaughter   Literally, "You fattened your hearts for the day of slaughter."
first rain...last rain   The "first rain" came in the Fall and the "last rain" in the Spring.
prophets   People who spoke for God. Their writings are part of the Old Testament.
Job's patience   Read the book of Job in the Old Testament.

Be Careful What You Say

¹²My brothers *and sisters*, it is very important that you not use an oath when you make a promise. Don't use the name of heaven, earth, or anything else to prove what you say. When you mean yes, say only "yes." When you mean no, say only "no." Do this so that you will not be judged guilty.

The Power of Prayer

¹³If one of you is having troubles, he should pray. If one of you is happy, he should sing. ¹⁴If one of you is sick, he should call the church's elders.* The elders should rub oil on him* in the name of the Lord and pray for him. ¹⁵And the prayer that is said with faith will make the sick person well. The Lord will heal him. And if this person has sinned, then God will forgive him. ¹⁶Always tell each other the wrong things you have done. Then pray for each other. Do this so that God can heal you. When a good person prays hard, great things happen. ¹⁷Elijah* was a person the same as us. He prayed that it would not rain. And it did not rain on the land for three and a half years! ¹⁸Then Elijah prayed that it would rain. And the rain came down from the sky, and the land grew crops again.

Saving a Soul

¹⁹My brothers *and sisters*, one of you may wander away from the truth. And another person may help him come back to the truth. ²⁰Remember this: Any person who brings a sinner back from the wrong way will save that sinner's soul from death (*hell*). By doing this, that person will cause many sins to be forgiven.

---

elders   A group of men chosen to lead a church. Also called "overseers" and "pastors" (shepherds), they have the work of caring for God's people (Acts 20:28; Ephesians 4:11).
rub oil on him   Oil was used like a medicine, so that is probably how the believers used it.
Elijah   A man who spoke for God hundreds of years before Christ.

1 Peter

1 From Peter, an apostle* of Jesus Christ.

To God's chosen people who are away from their homes. You are scattered all around the areas of Pontus, Galatia, Cappadocia, Asia, and Bithynia. ²God planned long ago to choose you by making you his holy* people. Making you holy is the Spirit's* work. God wanted you to obey him and to be made clean by the blood (*death*) of Jesus Christ. Grace (*kindness*) and peace be yours more and more.

A Living Hope

³Praise be to the God and Father of our Lord Jesus Christ. God has great mercy, and because of his mercy he gave us a new life. This new life brings us a living hope through Jesus Christ's rising from death. ⁴Now we hope for the blessings God has for his children. Those blessings are kept for you in heaven. Those blessings cannot ruin or be destroyed or lose their beauty. ⁵God's power protects you through your faith and it keeps you safe until your salvation comes. That salvation is ready to be given to you at the end of time. ⁶This makes you very happy. But now for a short time different kinds of troubles may make you sad. ⁷Why do these troubles happen? To prove that your faith is pure (*true*). This purity of faith is worth more than gold. Gold can be proved to be pure by fire, but gold will ruin. The purity of your faith will bring you praise and glory and honor when Jesus Christ appears (*comes*). ⁸You have not seen Christ, but still you love him. You can't see him now, but you believe in him. You are filled with a joy that cannot be explained. And that joy is full of glory. ⁹Your

apostle Person Jesus chose to be a special helper for telling the Good News to the world.
holy God's people are called holy because they are pure and belong only to God.
Spirit's The Holy Spirit. Also called the Spirit of God, the Spirit of Christ, and the Comforter. He is joined with God and Christ. He does the work of God among people in the world.

faith has a goal. That goal is to save your souls. And you are receiving that goal—your salvation.

[10]The prophets* studied carefully and tried to learn about this salvation. Those prophets spoke about the grace (*kindness*) that was coming to you. [11]The Spirit of Christ was in those prophets. And the Spirit was telling about the sufferings that would happen to Christ and about the glory that would come after those sufferings. Those prophets tried to learn about what the Spirit was showing them. They tried to learn when those things would happen and what the world would be like at that time. [12]It was shown to those prophets that their service was not for themselves. The prophets were serving you. They were serving you when they told about the things that you have heard. The men who preached the gospel* to you told you those things. They told you with the help of the Holy Spirit* that was sent from heaven. The things you were told are things that even the angels want very much to know about.

A Call to Holy Living

[13]So prepare your minds for service, and have self-control. All your hope should be for the gift of grace (*kindness*) that will be yours when Jesus Christ appears (*comes*). [14]In the past you did not understand about these things, so you did the evil things you wanted. But now you are children *of God* who obey. So don't live like you lived in the past. [15]But be holy* in all the things you do, the same as God is holy. God is the One who called you. [16]It is written *in the Scriptures**: "Be holy, because I (*God*) am holy."*

[17]You pray to God and call him Father. God judges each man's work equally. So while you are visiting *here on earth*, you should live with fear (*respect*) for God. [18]You know that *in the past* you were living in a worthless way. You got that way of living from the people who lived before you. But you were saved from that

---

prophets People who spoke for God. Their writings are part of the Old Testament.
gospel The Good News that God has made a way through Christ for people to have their sins forgiven and live with God. When people accept this truth, God accepts them.
Holy Spirit Also called the Spirit of God, the Spirit of Christ, and the Comforter. He is joined with God and Christ. He does the work of God among people in the world.
holy A holy person is pure, belongs only to God, and does only the things that God wants.
Scriptures Holy Writings—the Old Testament.
"Be...holy" Quotation from Leviticus 11:45, 19:2, 20:7.

way of living. You were bought, but not with things that ruin like gold or silver. ¹⁹But you were bought with the precious blood (*death*) of Christ—a pure and perfect lamb. ²⁰Christ was chosen before the world was made. But he was shown *to the world* in these last times for you. ²¹You believe in God through Christ. God raised Christ from death. Then God gave glory to him. So your faith and your hope are in God.

²²Now you have made yourselves pure by obeying the truth. Now you can have true love for your brothers and sisters. So love each other deeply—with all your heart. ²³You have been born again. This new life did not come from something that dies. That life came from something that cannot die. You were born again through God's living message* that continues forever. ²⁴"The Scripture* says,

> "All people are like the grass,
> and all their glory is like the flower on the grass.
> The grass dies,
> and the flower falls,
> ²⁵but the word of God will live forever."

Isaiah 40:6-8

And this is the word (*teaching*) that was told to you.

The Living Stone and the Holy Nation

2 So don't do anything to hurt *other people*, don't lie, don't do things to fool people, don't be jealous, don't say bad things about people. Put all these things out of your life. ²Be like babies that are newly born. Be hungry for the pure milk (*teaching*) that feeds your spirit. By drinking that you can grow up and be saved. ³You have already tasted the goodness of the Lord.

⁴The Lord *Jesus* is the "stone"* that lives. The people *of the world* decided they did not want that stone (*Jesus*). But he was the stone God chose. To God he was worth much. So come to him. ⁵You also are like living stones. Let yourselves be used to build a

---

message The news that God has made a way through Christ for people to have their sins forgiven and live with God. When people accept this truth, God accepts them.

Scripture A part of the Holy Writings—the Old Testament.

"stone" The most important stone in God's spriritual temple or house (his people).

spiritual temple*—to be holy priests who give spiritual sacrifices* to God that he will accept. You give those sacrifices through Jesus Christ. ⁶The Scripture* says:

> "Look, I have chosen a precious (*valuable*) cornerstone,*
> and I put that stone (*Jesus*) in Zion*;
> the person who trusts in him
> will never be ashamed."   *Isaiah 28:16*

⁷That stone (*Jesus*) is worth much to you people who believe. But to the people who don't believe, he is

> "the stone that the builders decided they did not want.
> That stone became the most important stone.*"   *Psalm 118:22*

⁸To people who don't believe, he is

> "a stone that makes people stumble (*trip*),
> a stone that makes people fall."   *Isaiah 8:14*

People stumble because they don't obey what God says. This is what God planned to happen to those people.

⁹But you are chosen people. You are the King's priests. You are a holy nation of people. You are people who belong to God. God chose you to tell about the wonderful things he has done. He called (*brought*) you out of darkness (*sin*) into his wonderful light. ¹⁰At one time you were not God's people. But now you are God's people. In the past you had never received mercy. But now you have received mercy *from God.*

Live for God

¹¹Dear friends, you people are like visitors and strangers *in this world.* So I beg you to stay away from the evil things your bodies want to do. These things fight against your soul. ¹²People who don't believe are living all around you. Those people may say that you are doing wrong. So live good lives. Then they will see the good things you do. And they will give glory to God on that day when he comes.

---

temple God's house—the place where God's people worship and serve him.
sacrifices A sacrifice is a gift or offering for God.
Scripture A part of the Holy Writings—the Old Testament.
cornerstone, most important stone The first and most important rock of a building.
Zion Another name for Jerusalem, the city of God's chosen people.

Obey Every Human Authority

[13]Obey the people who have authority* in this world. Do this for the Lord. Obey the king, who is the highest authority. [14]And obey the leaders who are sent by the king. They are sent to punish people who do wrong and to praise those people who do good. [15]So when you do good, you stop foolish people from saying stupid things about you. This is what God wants. [16]Live like free men. But don't use your freedom as an excuse to do evil. Live like you are serving God. [17]Show respect for all people. Love all the brothers and sisters of God's family. Fear (respect) God, and honor the king.

The Example of Christ's Suffering

[18]Slaves, accept the authority of your masters. Do this with all respect. You should obey the masters that are good and kind, and also the masters that are bad. [19]A person might have to suffer even when he has done nothing wrong. If that person thinks of God and bears the pain, then this pleases God. [20]But if you are punished for doing wrong, there is no reason to praise you for bearing that punishment. But if you suffer for doing good, and you are patient, then that pleases God. [21]That is what you were called to do. Christ gave you an example to follow. You should do the same as he did. *You should be patient when you suffer*, because Christ suffered for you.

[22]"He (*Christ*) did no sin,
   and no lies were found in his mouth." *Isaiah 53:9*

[23]People said bad things to Christ, but he did not say bad things to them. Christ suffered, but he did not threaten (*speak against*) the people. No! Christ let God take care of him. God is the One who judges rightly. [24]Christ carried our sins in his body on the cross. He did this so that we would stop living for sin and live for what is right. By his (*Christ's*) wounds you were healed. [25]You were like sheep that went the wrong way. But now you have come back to the Shepherd and Protector of your souls.

---

people...authority   Rulers, governors, presidents, or other government leaders.

Wives and Husbands

3 In the same way, you wives should accept the authority of your husbands. Then, if some of your husbands have not obeyed *God's* teaching, they will be persuaded to believe. You will not need to say anything. They will be persuaded by the way their wives live. ²Your husbands will see the pure lives that you live with your respect *for God*. ³It is not fancy hair, gold jewelry, or fine clothes that should make you beautiful. ⁴No, your beauty should come from inside you—the beauty of a gentle and quiet spirit. That beauty will never disappear. It is worth very much to God. ⁵It was the same with the holy women who lived long ago and followed God. They made themselves beautiful in that same way. They accepted the authority of their husbands. ⁶*I am talking about women* like Sarah. She obeyed Abraham, her husband, and called him her master. And you women are true children of Sarah if you always do what is right and are not afraid.

⁷In the same way, you husbands should live with your wives in an understanding way. You should show respect to your wives. They are weaker than you. But God gives your wives the same blessing that he gives you—the grace (*kindness*) that gives true life. Do these things, so that nothing will trouble your prayers.

Suffering for Doing Right

⁸So all of you should live together in peace. Try to understand each other, love each other like brothers, be kind and humble. ⁹Don't do wrong to a person to pay him back for doing wrong to you. Or don't say something bad to a person to pay him back for saying something bad to you. But *ask God to* bless that person. Do this, because you yourselves were called to receive a blessing. ¹⁰*The Scripture* says*,

> "The person who wants to love life
> and wants to enjoy good days
> must stop speaking evil,
> and he must stop telling lies.
> ¹¹That person must stop doing evil and do good;
> that person should look for peace and try to get it.

Scripture   A part of the Holy Writings—the Old Testament.

> ¹²"The Lord sees the good people,
>   and the Lord listens to their prayers;
>   but the Lord is against those people
>   who do evil."

Psalm 34:12-16

¹³If you are always trying to do good, then no person can really hurt you. ¹⁴But you may suffer for doing right. If that happens, then you are blessed (*happy*). "Don't be afraid of those people *who make you suffer*; don't be worried." ¹⁵But you should keep the Lord Christ holy in your hearts. Always be ready to answer every person who asks you to explain about the hope you have. ¹⁶But answer those people in a gentle way with respect. Always be able to feel that you are doing right. When you do that, the people who say bad things about you will be made ashamed. They say these bad things about the good way you live in Christ. They will be made ashamed for the bad things they said about you. ¹⁷It is better to suffer for doing good than for doing wrong. Yes, it is better, if that is what God wants. ¹⁸Christ himself died for you. And that one death paid for your sins. He was not guilty, but he died for people who are guilty. He did this to bring you all to God. His body was killed, but he was made alive in the spirit. ¹⁹And in the spirit he went and preached to the spirits in prison. ²⁰Those were the spirits who refused to obey God long ago, in the time of Noah. God was waiting patiently for them while Noah was building the ark (*boat*). Only a few people—eight in all— were saved in that ark. Those people were saved by water. ²¹That water is like baptism* that now saves you. Baptism is not the washing of dirt from the body. Baptism is asking God for a pure heart. It saves you because Jesus Christ was raised from death. ²²Now Jesus has gone into heaven. He is at God's right side. He rules over angels, authorities, and powers.

Changed Lives

4 Christ suffered while he was in his body. So you should strengthen yourselves with the same kind of thinking Christ had. The person who suffered in his body is finished with sin. ²*Strengthen yourselves* so that you will live your lives here on

---

baptism A Greek word meaning to be immersed, dipped, or buried briefly under water.

earth doing what God wants, not doing the evil things that people want. ³In the past you wasted too much time doing the things that the non-believers like to do. You were doing sexual sins. You were doing the *evil* things you wanted. You were becoming drunk, having wild and wasteful parties, having drunken parties, and doing wrong by worshiping idols (*false gods*). ⁴Those non-believers think that it is strange that you don't do the many wild and wasteful things that they do. And so they say bad things about you. ⁵But those people will have to explain about the things they have done. They will have to explain to the One (*Christ*) who is ready to judge the people who are living and the people who are dead. ⁶The gospel* was preached to those people who are now dead, because those people will be judged like all people are judged. They will be judged for the things they did while they were living. But the gospel* was preached to them so that they could live in the spirit like God lives.

Be Good Managers of God's Gifts

⁷The time is near when all things will end. So keep your minds clear, and control yourselves. This will help you to pray. ⁸Most important, love each other deeply. Love hides many, many sins. ⁹Share your homes with each other without complaining. ¹⁰Each of you received a spiritual gift *from God*. God has shown you his grace (*kindness*) in many different ways. And you are like servants who are responsible for using God's gifts. So be good servants and use your gifts to serve each other. ¹¹The person who speaks should speak words from God. The person who serves should serve with the strength that God gives. You should do these things so that in everything God will be praised through Jesus Christ. Power and glory belong to him forever and ever. Amen.

Suffering as a Christian

¹²My friends, don't be surprised at the painful things that you are now suffering. Those things are testing your faith. Don't

gospel   The Good News that God was making a way for people to be saved.

think that something strange is happening to you. [13]But you should be happy that you are sharing in Christ's sufferings. You will be happy and full of joy when Christ shows his glory. [14]When people say bad things to you because you follow Christ, then you are blessed (*happy*). You are blessed because the Spirit* of glory is with you. That is the Spirit of God. [15]Don't be like a criminal, or a person who kills, steals, or bothers other people. A person will suffer for doing those things. None of you should ever suffer like that. [16]But if you suffer because you are a Christian, then don't be ashamed. You should praise (*thank*) God for that name (*Christian*). [17]It is time for judging to begin. That judging will begin with God's family. If that judgment begins with us, then what will happen to those people who don't obey the gospel* of God? [18]"It is very hard for a good person to be saved. So what will happen to the person who is against God and is full of sin?"* [19]So those people who suffer like God wants them to should trust their souls to him. God is the One who made them, and they can trust him. So they should continue to do good.

The Flock of God

5 Now I have something to say to the elders* in your group. I am also an elder. I myself have seen Christ's sufferings. And I will share in the glory that will be shown to us. I beg you, [2]take care of the group of people that you are responsible for. They are God's flock.* Watch over that flock because you want to, not because you are forced to do it. That is how God wants it. Do it because you are happy to serve, not because you want money. [3]Don't be like a hard ruler over those people you are responsible for. But be good examples to those people. [4]Then when the Ruling Shepherd (*Christ*) comes you will get a crown. That crown will be very glorious, and it will never lose its beauty. [5]Young men, I have something to say to you too. You should accept the

Spirit The Holy Spirit. Also called the Spirit of God, the Spirit of Christ, and the Comforter. He is joined with God and Christ. He does the work of God among people in the world.
gospel The Good News that God has made a way through Christ for people to have their sins forgiven and live with God. When people accept this truth, God accepts them.
"It is...sin?" Quotation from Proverbs 11:31 in the Septuagint, the Greek version of the Old Testament.
elders A group of men chosen to lead a church. Also called "overseers" and "pastors" (shepherds), they have the work of caring for God's people (Acts 20:28; Ephesians 4:11).
God's flock God's people. They are like a flock (group) of sheep that need to be cared for.

authority of the elders.* All of you should be very humble with each other.

> "God is against the proud people,
>   but he gives grace (*kindness*)
>   to the humble people."

Proverbs 3:34

⁶So be humble under God's powerful hand. Then he will lift you up when the right time comes. ⁷Give all your worries to him, because he cares for you.

⁸Control yourselves and be careful! The devil is your enemy. And he goes around like a roaring lion looking for some person to eat. ⁹Refuse to follow the devil. Stand strong in your faith. You know that your brothers *and sisters* all over the world are having the same sufferings that you have.

¹⁰Yes, you will suffer for a short time. But after that, God will make everything right. He will make you strong. He will support you and keep you from falling. He is the God that gives all grace (*kindness*). He called you to share in his glory in Christ. That glory will continue forever. ¹¹All power is his forever and ever. Amen.

Final Greetings

¹²I wrote this short letter with the help of Silas. I know that he is a faithful brother *in Christ*. I wrote to comfort and encourage you. I wanted to tell you that this is the true grace (*kindness*) of God. Stand strong in that grace.

¹³The church* in Babylon says hello to you. Those people were chosen the same as you. Mark, my son *in Christ*, also says hello. ¹⁴Give each other a kiss of love when you meet.

Peace to all of you who are in Christ.

---

elders A group of men chosen to lead a church. Also called "overseers" and "pastors" (shepherds), they have the work of caring for God's people (Acts 20:28; Ephesians 4:11).
The church Literally, "She in Babylon."

2 Peter

1 From Simon Peter, a servant and apostle* of Jesus Christ.
To all you people who have a faith that is valuable like ours.
You received that faith because our God and Savior Jesus Christ
is fair. He does what is right.

²Grace (*kindness*) and peace be given to you more and more.
You will have grace and peace because you truly know God and
Jesus our Lord.

God Has Given Us Everything We Need

³Jesus has the power of God. His power has given us everything
we need to live and to serve God. We have these things because
we know him. Jesus called us by his glory and goodness.
⁴Through his glory and goodness Jesus gave us the very great and
rich gifts that he promised us. With those gifts you can share in
being like God. And so the world will not ruin you with the evil
things it wants.

⁵Because you have these blessings you should try as much as
you can to add these things *to your life*: to your faith add
goodness; and to your goodness add knowledge; ⁶and to your
knowledge add self-control; and to your self-control add
patience; and to your patience add service for God; ⁷and to your
service for God add kindness for your brothers and sisters *in
Christ*; and to this kindness for your brothers and sisters add
love. ⁸If all these things are in you and they are growing, then
these things will help you to never be useless. These things will
help you to never be worthless in the knowledge of our Lord
Jesus Christ. ⁹But if a person does not have these things, then he
cannot see clearly. That person is blind. He has forgotten that he
was cleansed (*forgiven*) from his past sins.

apostle   Person Jesus chose to be a special helper for telling the Good News to the world.

604

[10]My brothers *and sisters*, God called you and chose you to be his. Try hard to show that you really are God's called and chosen people. If you do all those things, you will never fall. [11]And you will be given a very great welcome into the kingdom of our Lord and Savior Jesus Christ. That kingdom continues forever.

[12]You know these things. You are very strong in the truth you have. But I will always help you to remember these things. [13]I think it is right for me to help you remember these things while I am still living here on earth. [14]I know that I must soon leave this body. Our Lord Jesus Christ has shown me that. [15]I will try the best I can to help you remember these things always. I want you to be able to remember these things after I am gone.

We Saw Christ's Glory

[16]We told you about the power of our Lord Jesus Christ. We told you about his coming. Those things we told you were not smart stories that people invented. No! We saw the greatness of Jesus with our own eyes. [17]Jesus heard the voice of the Greatest Glory (*God*). That was when Jesus received honor and glory from God the Father. The voice said, "This is my Son and I love him. I am very pleased with him." [18]And we heard that voice. It came from heaven while we were with Jesus on the holy mountain.

[19]This makes us more sure about the things the prophets* said. And it is good for you to follow closely what the prophets said. The things they said are like a light shining in a dark place. That light shines until the day begins and the morning star rises in your hearts. [20]Most important, you must understand this: No prophecy* in the Scriptures* ever comes from a person's own interpretation. [21]No! No prophecy ever came from what a man wanted to say. But men were led by the Holy Spirit* and spoke things from God.

---

prophets   People who spoke for God. Their writings are part of the Old Testament.
prophecy   Teaching from God, given by a person who speaks for God.
Scriptures   Holy Writings—the Old Testament.
Holy Spirit   Also called the Spirit of God, the Spirit of Christ, and the Comforter. He is joined with God and Christ. He does the work of God among people in the world.

False Teachers

2 In the past, there were false prophets* among *God's* people. It is the same now. You will have some false teachers in your group. They will teach things that are wrong—teachings that will make people be lost. And those false teachers will teach in a way that will be hard for you to see that they are wrong. They will even refuse to accept the Master (*Jesus*) who bought their freedom. And so they will quickly destroy themselves. ²Many people will follow them in the evil (*bad*) things they do. And other people will say bad things about the Way of truth because of those people. ³Those false teachers only want your money. So they will use you by telling you things that are not true. But the judgment against those false teachers has been ready for a long time. And they will not escape the One (*God*) who will destroy them.

⁴When angels sinned, God did not let them go free without punishment. No! God sent them to hell. God put those angels in caves of darkness. They are being held there until the judgment. ⁵And God punished the *evil* people who lived long ago. God brought a flood to the world that was full of people who were against God. But God saved Noah and seven other people with Noah. Noah was a man who told people about being right *with God*. ⁶And God also punished the *evil* cities of Sodom and Gomorrah.* God burned those cities until there was nothing left but ashes. God made those cities be an example to show what will happen to people who are against God. ⁷But God saved Lot *from those cities*. Lot was a very good man. He was troubled because of the dirty lives of evil people. ⁸(Lot was a good man, but he lived with those evil people every day. Lot's good heart was hurt by the evil things that he saw and heard.) ⁹*Yes, God did all these things*. So the Lord *God* will always save the people who serve him. He will save them when troubles come. And the Lord will hold evil people and punish them, while waiting for the day of judgment. ¹⁰That punishment is mostly for those people who live by doing the bad things their sinful selves want, and for people who hate the Lord's authority (*power*).

false prophets People who say they speak for God but do not really speak God's truth.
Sodom and Gomorrah God destroyed these cities to punish the evil people who lived there.

These *false teachers* will do anything they want, and they boast about themselves. They are not afraid to say bad things against the glorious *angels*.* ¹¹The angels are much stronger and more powerful than these false teachers. But even the angels don't accuse the false teachers and say bad things about them to the Lord. ¹²But these false teachers speak evil against things they don't understand. These false teachers are like animals that do things without really thinking—like wild animals that are born to be caught and killed. And, like wild animals, these false teachers will be destroyed. ¹³These false teachers have made many people suffer. So they themselves will suffer. That is their pay for what they have done. These false teachers think it is fun to do evil things openly *where all people can see*. They enjoy the evil things that please them. So they are like dirty spots and stains among you—*they bring shame to you* in the meals that you eat together. ¹⁴Every time they look at a woman, they want her. These false teachers are always sinning this way. They lead weaker people into the trap *of sin*. They have taught their own hearts to be selfish. They are under a curse.* ¹⁵These false teachers left the right way and went the wrong way. They followed the same way that Balaam went. Balaam was the son of Beor. He loved being paid for doing wrong. ¹⁶But a donkey told Balaam that he was doing wrong. And the donkey is an animal that cannot talk. But that donkey spoke with a man's voice and stopped the prophet's (*Balaam's*) crazy thinking.

¹⁷Those false teachers are like rivers that have no water. They are like clouds that are blown by a storm. A place in the deepest darkness has been kept for them. ¹⁸Those false teachers boast with words that mean nothing. They lead people into the trap *of sin*. They lead away people who are just beginning to come away from other people who live wrong. Those false teachers do this by using the evil things people want to do in their sinful selves. ¹⁹These false teachers promise that those people will have freedom. But the false teachers themselves are not free. They are slaves of things that will be destroyed. A person is a slave to the thing that controls him. ²⁰Those people were made free from the

---

the glorious angels Literally, "the glories" or "the glorious ones."
under a curse Literally, "children of a curse," meaning that God will punish them.

evil things in the world. They were made free by knowing our Lord and Savior Jesus Christ. But if those people go back into those evil things, and those things control them, then it is worse for them than it was before. ²¹Yes, it would be better for those people to have never known the right way. That would be better than to know the right way and then to turn away from the holy teaching that was given to them. ²²What those people did is like this true saying: "When a dog vomits (*throws up*), he comes back to his vomit."* And, "After a pig is washed, the pig goes back and rolls in the mud again."

Jesus Will Come Again

3 My friends, this is the second letter I have written to you. I wrote both letters to you to help your honest minds remember something. ²I want you to remember the words that the holy prophets* spoke in the past. And remember the command that our Lord and Savior gave us. He gave us that command through your apostles.* ³It is important for you to understand what will happen in the last days. People will laugh *at you*. Those people will live following the evil things they want to do. ⁴Those people will say, "He (*Jesus*) promised to come again. Where is he? Our fathers have died. But the world continues the way it has been since it was made." ⁵But those people don't want to remember what happened long ago. The skies were there, and God made the earth from water and with water. All this happened by God's word. ⁶Then, that world was flooded and destroyed with water. ⁷And that same word *of God* is keeping the skies and the earth that we have now. The skies and the earth are being kept to be destroyed by fire. The skies and the earth are kept for the day of judgment and the destruction of all people who are against God.

⁸But don't forget this one thing, dear friends: To the Lord a day is like a thousand years. And a thousand years is like a day. ⁹The Lord is not being slow in doing what he promised—the way some people understand slowness. But God is being patient with

---

"When...vomit" Quotation from Proverbs 26:11.
prophets People who spoke for God. Their writings are part of the Old Testament.
apostles The men Jesus chose to be his special helpers for telling the Good News to the world.

you. God doesn't want any person to be lost. God wants every person to change his heart and stop sinning.

¹⁰But the Day when the Lord comes again will be like a thief. The sky will disappear with a loud noise. All the things in the sky will be destroyed with fire. And the earth and everything in it will be burned.* ¹¹In that way, everything will be destroyed like I told you. So what kind of people should you be? You should live holy* lives and do things to serve God. ¹²You should wait for the Day of God. You should want very much for that Day to come. When that Day comes, the sky will be destroyed with fire, and everything in the sky will melt with heat. ¹³But God made a promise to us. And we are waiting for what he promised—a new sky and a new earth. That will be the place where goodness lives.

¹⁴Dear friends, we are waiting for this to happen. So try as hard as you can to be without sin and without fault. Try to be at peace with God. ¹⁵Remember that we are saved because our Lord is patient. Our dear brother Paul told you that same thing when he wrote to you with the wisdom that God gave him. ¹⁶Paul writes like this about these things in all his letters. Sometimes there are things in Paul's letters that are hard to understand. Some people explain those things falsely. Those people are ignorant and weak in faith. Those same people also falsely explain the other Scriptures.* But they are destroying themselves by doing that.

¹⁷Dear friends, you already know about this. So be careful. Don't let those evil people lead you away by the wrong things they do. Be careful so that you will not fall from your strong *faith*. ¹⁸But grow in the grace (*kindness*) and knowledge of our Lord and Savior Jesus Christ. Glory be to him now and forever! Amen.

---

will be burned Many Greek copies say, "will be found." One copy says, "will disappear."
holy A holy person is pure, belongs only to God, and does only the things that God wants.
Scriptures Holy Writings—God's message to people through the writers of the Bible.

1 John

1 We tell you now about something that has existed (*lived*) since before the world began:

This we heard,
we saw with our own eyes,
we watched,
we touched with our hands.

We write to you about the Word (*Christ*) that gives life. ²That Life was shown to us. We saw it. We can give proof about it. Now we tell you about that Life. It is life that continues forever. This is the Life that was with God the Father. God showed this Life to us. ³Now we tell you the things that we have seen and heard. Why? Because we want you to have fellowship* together with us. The fellowship we share together is with God the Father and his Son, Jesus Christ. ⁴We write these things to you so that you can be full of joy with us.

God Forgives Our Sins

⁵We heard the true teaching from God. Now we tell it to you: God is light* (*goodness*). In God there is no darkness (*sin*). ⁶So if we say that we have fellowship* with God, but we continue living in darkness (*sin*), then we are liars—we don't follow the truth. ⁷God is in the light* (*goodness*). We should live in the light, too. If we live in the light, then we share fellowship with each other. And when we live in the light, the blood (*death*) of Jesus cleanses us from all sin. (Jesus is God's Son.)

⁸If we say that we have no sin, we are fooling ourselves. The truth is not in us. ⁹But if we confess (*admit*) our sins, then God

---

fellowship Associating with people and sharing things together with them. Christians share love, joy, sorrow, faith and other things with each other and with God.
light This word is used to show what God is like. It means goodness or truth.

will forgive our sins. We can trust God. God does what is right. God will make us clean from all the wrong things we have done. [10]If we say that we have not sinned, then we make God a liar—we don't accept God's true teaching

Jesus Is Our Helper

2 My dear children, I write this letter to you so that you will not sin. But if any person sins, we have Jesus Christ to help us. He is the righteous (*good*) One. Jesus defends us before God the Father. [2]Jesus is the way our sins are taken away. And Jesus is the way that all people can have their sins taken away, too.

[3]If we obey what God has told us to do, then we are sure that we truly know God. [4]A person says, "I know God!" But if that person does not obey God's commands, then that person is a liar. The truth is not in him. [5]But when a person obeys God's teaching, then God's love has truly arrived at its goal in that person. This is how we know that we are following God: [6]If a person says that God lives in him, then he must live like Jesus lived.

God Commanded Us to Love Other People

[7]My dear friends, I am not writing a new command to you. It is the same command you have had since the beginning. This command is the teaching you have already heard. [8]But also, I write this command to you as a new command. This command is true; you can see its truth in Jesus and in yourselves. The darkness (*sin*) is passing away and the true light is already shining.

[9]A person says, "I am in the light.*" But if that person hates his brother, then he is still in the darkness (*sin*). [10]The person that loves his brother lives in the light, and there is nothing in that person that will make him do wrong. [11]But the person who hates his brother is in darkness. He lives in darkness. That person does not know where he is going. Why? Because the darkness has made him blind.

---

light   This word is used to show what God is like. It means goodness and truth.

¹²I write to you, dear children,
    because your sins are forgiven through Christ.
¹³I write to you, fathers,
    because you know the One who existed (*lived*)
      from the beginning.
I write to you, young men,
    because you have defeated the Evil One (*the devil*).
¹⁴I write to you, children,
    because you know the Father.
I write to you, fathers,
    because you know the One who existed (*lived*)
      from the beginning.
I write to you, young men,
    because you are strong;
    the word of God lives in you,
    and you have defeated the Evil One (*the devil*).

¹⁵Don't love the world or the things in the world. If a person loves the world, the love of the Father (*God*) is not in that person. ¹⁶These are the *evil* things in the world:

Wanting things to please our sinful selves,
Wanting the sinful things that we see,
Being too proud of the things we have.

But none of those things come from the Father (*God*). All of those things come from the world. ¹⁷The world is passing away. And all the things that people want in the world are passing away. But if a person does what God wants, then that person lives forever.

Don't Follow the Enemies of Christ

¹⁸My dear children, the end is near! You have heard that the Enemy of Christ* is coming. And now many enemies of Christ are already here. So we know that the end is near. ¹⁹Those enemies of Christ were in our group. But they left us. They did not really belong with us. If they were really part of our group, then they would have stayed with us. But they left. This shows that none of them really belonged with us.

Christ The "anointed one" (the Messiah) or chosen one of God.

²⁰You have the gift* that the Holy One (*God or Christ*) gave you. So you all know *the truth*. ²¹Why do I write to you? Do I write because you don't know the truth? No! I write this letter because you do know the truth. And you know that no lie comes from the truth.

²²So who is the liar? It is the person that says that Jesus is not the Christ.* A person that says that Jesus is not the Christ is the enemy of Christ. That person does not believe in the Father (*God*) or in his Son (*Christ*). ²³If a person does not believe in the Son (*Christ*), then he does not have the Father. But the person who accepts the Son has the Father too.

²⁴Be sure that you continue to follow the teaching that you heard from the beginning. If you continue in that teaching, then you will stay in the Son (*Christ*) and in the Father (*God*). ²⁵And this is what God promised to us—life forever.

²⁶I am writing this letter about those people who are trying to lead you into the wrong way. ²⁷Christ (*or God*) gave you a special gift.* You still have this gift in you. So you don't need any person to teach you. The gift he gave you teaches you about everything. This gift is true. It is not false. So continue to live in Christ, like his gift taught you.

²⁸Yes, my dear children, live in him. If we do this, we can be without fear (*have confidence*) on the day when Christ comes back. We will not need to hide and be ashamed when he comes. ²⁹You know that Christ is righteous (*good*). So, you know that all people who do what is right (*good*) are God's children.

We Are God's Children

3 The Father (*God*) has loved us so much! This shows how much he loved us: We are called children of God. And we really are God's children. But the people in the world (*people who don't believe*) don't understand that we are God's children, because they have not known him (*God*). ²Dear friends, now we are children of God. We have not yet been shown what we will be in the future. But we know that when Christ comes again, we will

---

gift The word in the Greek text is "anointing." This might mean the Holy Spirit. Or it might mean teaching or truth like in verse 24.
Christ The "anointed one" (the Messiah) or chosen one of God.

be like him. We will see him like he really is. ³Christ is pure. And every person who has this hope in Christ keeps himself pure like Christ.

⁴When a person sins, he breaks *God's* law. Yes, sinning is the same as living against *God's* law. ⁵You know that Christ came to take away people's sins. There is no sin in Christ. ⁶So the person who lives in Christ does not continue to sin. If a person continues to sin, he has never really understood Christ, and has never known Christ.

⁷Dear children, don't let any person lead you into the wrong way. Christ is righteous (*good*). To be good like Christ, a person must do what is right (*good*). ⁸The devil has been sinning since the beginning. The person who continues to sin belongs to the devil. The Son of God (*Christ*) came for this: to destroy the devil's work.

⁹When God makes a person his child, that person does not continue to sin. Why? Because the new life* God gave that person stays in him. So that person is not able to continue sinning. Why? Because he has become a child of God. ¹⁰So we can see who God's children are. Also, we can know who the children of the devil are. The people who don't do what is right are not children of God. And the person who does not love his brother is not a child of God.

We Must Love One Another

¹¹This is the teaching you have heard from the beginning: We must love each other. ¹²Don't be like Cain.* Cain belonged to the Evil One (*the devil*). Cain killed his brother (*Abel*).* But why did Cain kill his brother? Because the things Cain did were evil, and the things his brother (*Abel*) did were good.

¹³Brothers *and sisters*, don't be surprised when the people of this world hate you. ¹⁴We know that we have left death (*sin*) and come into life. We know this because we love our brothers *and sisters in Christ*. The person who does not love is still in death. ¹⁵Every person who hates his brother is a murderer.* And you

new life   The Greek text says literally, "his seed."
Cain, Abel   Sons of Adam and Eve. Cain was jealous of Abel and killed him (Genesis 4:1-16).
Every...murderer   If a person hates his brother in Christ, then in his mind he has killed his brother. Jesus taught about this sin to his followers (Matthew 5:21-26).

know that no murderer has eternal life in him. ¹⁶This is how we know what real love is: Jesus gave his life for us. So we should give our lives for our brothers *and sisters in Christ*. ¹⁷Suppose a believer is rich enough to have all the things he needs. He sees his brother *in Christ* who is poor and does not have the things he needs. What if the believer who has things does not help the poor brother? Then the believer who has the things he needs does not have God's love in his heart. ¹⁸My children, our love should not be only words and talk. No! Our love must be true love. We should show our love by the things we do.

¹⁹⁻²⁰That is the way we know that we belong to the way of truth. And when our hearts make us feel guilty, we can still have peace before God. Why? Because God is greater than our heart (*conscience*). God knows everything.

²¹My dear friends, if we don't feel that we are doing wrong, then we can be without fear (*have confidence*) when we come to God. ²²And God gives us the things we ask for. We receive these things because we obey God's commands and we do the things that please God. ²³This is what God commands: that we believe in his Son Jesus Christ, and that we love each other. This is what he commanded. ²⁴The person who obeys God's commands lives in God. And God lives in that person. How do we know that God lives in us? We know because of the Spirit* that God gave us.

John Warns Against False Teachers

4 My dear friends, many false prophets* are in the world now. So don't believe every spirit. But test the spirits to see if they are from God. ²This is how you can know God's Spirit*: One spirit says, "I believe that Jesus is the Christ who came to earth and became a man." That spirit is from God. ³Another spirit refuses to say this about Jesus. That spirit is not from God. This is the spirit of the Enemy of Christ. You have heard that the Enemy of Christ is coming. And now the Enemy of Christ is already in the world.

Every...murderer If a person hates his brother in Christ, then in his mind he has killed his brother. Jesus taught about this sin to his followers (Matthew 5:21-28).
Spirit The Holy Spirit. Also called the Spirit of God, the Spirit of Christ, and the Comforter. He is joined with God and Christ. He does the work of God among people in the world.
false prophets People who say they speak for God but do not really speak God's truth.

⁴My dear children, you belong to God. So you have defeated them (*the false teachers*). Why? Because the One (*God*) who is in you is greater than the one (*the devil*) who is in *the people of* the world. ⁵And those people (*the false teachers*) belong to the world. So the things they say are from the world, too. And the world listens to what they say. ⁶But we are from God. So the people who know God listen to us. But the people who are not from God don't listen to us. That is how we know the Spirit* that is true and the spirit that is false.

Love Comes from God

⁷Dear friends, we should love each other because love comes from God. The person who loves has become God's child. And so the person who loves knows God. ⁸The person that does not love does not know God, because God is love. ⁹This is how God showed his love to us: God sent his only Son into the world to give us life through him. ¹⁰True love is God's love for us, not our love for God. God sent his Son to be the way that God takes away our sins.

¹¹That is how much God loved us, dear friends! So we also must love each other. ¹²No person has ever seen God. But if we love each other, then God lives in us. If we love each other, then God's love has reached its goal—it is made perfect in us.

¹³We know that we live in God and God lives in us. We know this because God gave us his Spirit.* ¹⁴We have seen that the Father sent his Son to be the Savior of the world. That is what we tell people now. ¹⁵If a person says, "I believe that Jesus is the Son of God," then God lives in that person. And that person lives in God. ¹⁶And so we know the love that God has for us. And we trust that love.

God is love. The person who lives in love lives in God. And God lives in that person. ¹⁷If God's love is made perfect in us, then we can be without fear on the day when God judges us. We will be without fear, because in this world we are like him (*Christ or God*). ¹⁸Where God's love is, there is no fear. Why? Because God's perfect love takes away fear. It is *God's* punishment that

---

Spirit The Holy Spirit. Also called the Spirit of God, the Spirit of Christ, and the Comforter. He is joined with God and Christ. He does the work of God among people in the world.

makes a person fear. So *God's* love is not made perfect in the person who has fear.

[19]We love because God first loved us. [20]If a person says, "I love God," but that person hates his brother *or sister in Christ*, then that person is a liar. That person can see his brother, but he hates him. So that person cannot love God, because he has never seen God! [21]And he (*God*) gave us this command: The person who loves God must also love his brother.

God's Children Win Against the World

5 The people who believe that Jesus is the Christ* are God's children. The person who loves the Father (*God*) also loves the Father's children. [2]How do we know that we love God's children? We know because we love God and we obey his commands. [3]Loving God means obeying his commands. And God's commands are not too hard for us. [4]Why? Because every person that is a child of God *has the power to* win against the world. [5]It is our faith that has won the victory against the world. So who is the person that wins against the world? Only the person who believes that Jesus is the Son of God.

God Told Us About His Son

[6]Jesus Christ is the One who came. Jesus came with water* and with blood.* Jesus did not come by water only. No, Jesus came by both water and blood. And the Spirit* tells us that this is true. The Spirit* is the truth. [7]So there are three witnesses that tell us *about Jesus*: [8]the Spirit,* the water,* and the blood.* These three witnesses agree. [9]We believe people when they say something is true. But what God says is more important. And this is what God told us: He told us the truth about his own Son. [10]The person who believes in the Son of God has the truth that God told us. The person who does not believe God makes God a liar. Why? Because that person does not believe what God told us about his

Christn The "anointed one" (the Messiah) or chosen one of God.
water This probably means the water of Jesus' baptism.
blood This probably means the blood of Jesus' death.
Spirit The Holy Spirit. Also called the Spirit of God, the Spirit of Christ, and the Comforter. He is joined with God and Christ. He does the work of God among people in the world.

Son. ¹¹This is what God told us: God has given us eternal life. And this eternal life is in his Son (*Jesus*). ¹²The person who has the Son has *true* life. But the person who does not have the Son of God does not have life.

We Have Eternal Life Now

¹³I write this letter to you people who believe in the Son of God. I write so that you will know that you have eternal life now. ¹⁴We can come to God with no doubts. This means that when we ask God for things (and those things agree with what God wants for us), then God cares about what we say. ¹⁵God listens to us every time we ask him. So we know that he gives us the things that we ask from him.

¹⁶Suppose a person sees his brother *or sister in Christ* sinning (sin that does not lead to *eternal* death). That person should pray for his brother *or sister* who is sinning. Then God will give the brother *or sister* life. I am talking about people whose sin does not lead to *eternal* death. There is sin that leads to death. I don't mean that a person should pray about that sin. ¹⁷Doing wrong is always sin. But there is sin that does not lead to *eternal* death.

¹⁸We know that any person who has been made God's child does not continue to sin. The Son* of God keeps God's child safe. The Evil One (*the devil*) cannot hurt that person. ¹⁹We know that we belong to God. But the Evil One (*the devil*) controls the whole world. ²⁰And we know that the Son of God has come. The Son of God has given us understanding. Now we can know God. God is the One who is true. And our lives are in that true God and in his Son, Jesus Christ. He is the true God, and he is eternal life. ²¹So, dear children, keep yourselves away from false gods.

Son The Greek says literally, "The one who was born from God keeps him (or himself) safe."

2 John

From the Elder.*

To the lady* chosen *by God*, and to her children:

I love all of you in the truth.* Also, all those people who know the truth love you. ²We love you because of the truth—the truth that lives in us. This truth will be with us forever.

³Grace (*kindness*), mercy, and peace will be with us from God the Father and from his Son, Jesus Christ. We receive these blessings through truth and love.

⁴I was very happy to learn about some of your children. I am happy that they are following the way of truth, like the Father (*God*) commanded us. ⁵And now, dear lady, I tell you: We should all love each other. This is not a new command. It is the same command we had from the beginning. ⁶And loving means living the way he commanded us to live. And God's command is this: that you live a life of love. You heard this command from the beginning.

⁷Many false teachers are in the world now. These false teachers refuse to say (*confess*) that Jesus Christ came *to earth* and became a man. A person who refuses to say (*confess*) this fact is a false teacher and an enemy of Christ. ⁸Be careful! Don't lose the reward that you have worked for. Be careful, so that you will receive all of your reward.

⁹A person must continue to follow only the teaching of Christ. If a person changes the teaching of Christ, then that person does not have God. But if a person continues following the teaching of Christ, then that person has both the Father (*God*) and the Son (*Christ*). ¹⁰If a person comes to you, but does not bring this

Elder This is probably John the apostle. "Elder" means an older man. It can also mean a special leader in the church (like in Titus 1:5).

lady This might mean a woman. Or, in this letter, it might mean a church. If it is a church, then "her children" would be the people of the church.

truth The truth or "Good News" about Jesus Christ that joins all believers together.

teaching, then don't accept him into your house. Don't welcome him. [11]If you accept him, then you are helping him with his evil work.

[12]I have much to say to you. But I don't want to use paper and ink. Instead, I hope to come visit you. Then we can be together and talk. That will make us very happy. [13]The children of your sister* who was chosen *by God* send you their love.

---

sister Sister of the "lady" in verse 1. This might be another woman or another church.

3 John

From the Elder.*
To my dear friend Gaius that I love in the truth*:

²My dear friend, I know that your soul is doing fine. So I pray that you are doing fine in every way. And I pray that you are feeling well. ³Some brothers *in Christ* came and told me about the truth* in your life. They told me that you continue to follow the way of truth. This made me very happy. ⁴It always gives me the greatest joy when I hear that my children are following the way of truth.

⁵My dear friend, it is good that you continue to help the brothers *in Christ*. You are helping brothers that you don't even know! ⁶These brothers told the church (*believers*) about the love you have. Please help them to continue their trip. Help them in a way that will please God. ⁷These brothers went on their trip to serve Christ. They did not accept any help from people who are not believers. ⁸So we should help these brothers. When we help them, we share with their work for the truth.*

⁹I wrote a letter to the church. But Diotrephes will not listen to what we say. He always wants to be their leader. ¹⁰When I come, I will talk about what Diotrephes is doing. He lies and says evil things about us. But that is not all he does! He refuses to help those brothers *who are working to serve Christ*. Diotrephes also stops those people who want to help the brothers. He makes those people leave the group of believers.

¹¹My dear friend, don't follow what is bad; follow what is good. The person who does what is good is from God. But the person who does evil has never known God.

Elder This is probably John the apostle. "Elder" means an older man. It can also mean a special leader in the church (like in Titus 1:5).
truth The truth or "Good News" about Jesus Christ that joins all believers together.

¹²All the people say good things about Demetrius. And the truth* agrees with what they say. Also, we say good about him. And you know that what we say is true.

¹³I have many things I want to tell you. But I don't want to use pen and ink. ¹⁴I hope to visit you soon. Then we can be together and talk. ¹⁵Peace to you. The friends (*believers*) here with me send their love. Please give our love to each one of the friends there.

---

truth The truth or "Good News" about Jesus Christ that joins all believers together.

Jude

From Jude, a servant of Jesus Christ and a brother of James.

To all those people who have been called by God. God the Father loves you, and you have been kept safe in Jesus Christ.

²All mercy, peace, and love be yours.

God Will Punish People Who Do Wrong

³Dear Friends, I wanted very much to write to you about the salvation we all share together. But I felt the need to write to you about something else: I want to encourage you to fight hard for the faith that God gave his holy* people. God gave this faith once, *but it is good for all time.* ⁴Some people have secretly entered your group. These people have already been judged guilty for the things they are doing. Long ago, *the prophets** wrote about these people. These people are against God. They have used the grace (*kindness*) of our God in the wrong way—to do sinful things. These people refuse to accept Jesus Christ, our only Master and Lord.

⁵I want to help you remember some things that you already know: Remember that the Lord saved his people by bringing them out of the land of Egypt. But later the Lord destroyed all those people who did not believe. ⁶And remember the angels who had power, but did not keep it. They left their own home. So the Lord has kept these angels in darkness. They are bound with everlasting chains. He has kept them to be judged on the great day. ⁷Also remember the cities of Sodom and Gomorrah* and the other towns around them. They are the same as those angels. Those towns were full of sexual sin and wrongdoing. They suffer

holy   God's people are called holy because they are pure and belong only to God.
prophets   People who spoke for God. Their writings are part of the Old Testament.
Sodom and Gomorrah   God destroyed these cities to punish the evil people who lived there.

the punishment of eternal fire. Their punishment is an example *for us to see.*

⁸It is the same way with these people *who have entered your group.* They are guided by dreams. They make themselves dirty with sin. They reject *God's* authority (*rule*), and say bad things against the glorious *angels.* ⁹Not even the archangel,* Michael, did this. Michael argued with the devil about who would have the body of Moses. But Michael did not dare to condemn the devil with criticizing words. But Michael said, "The Lord punish you." ¹⁰But these people criticize things they don't understand. They do understand some things. But they understand these things not by thinking, but by feeling, the way dumb animals understand things. And these are the things that destroy them. ¹¹It will be bad for them. These people have followed the way that Cain* went. To make money, they have given themselves to following the wrong way that Balaam went. These people have fought against *God* like Korah did. And like Korah, they will be destroyed. ¹²These people are like dirty spots in the special meals you share together. They eat with you and have no fear. They take care of only themselves. They are clouds without rain. The wind blows them around. They are trees that have no fruit when it is time, and are pulled out of the ground. So they are dead two times. ¹³They are like wild waves in the sea. The waves make foam. These people do shameful things like the waves make foam. These people are like stars that wander in the sky. *A place in* the blackest darkness has been kept for those people forever.

¹⁴Enoch, the seventh descendant* from Adam, said this about these people: "Look, the Lord is coming with thousands and thousands of his holy angels. ¹⁵The Lord will judge every person. The Lord is coming to judge all people and to punish all people who are against God. He will punish these people for all the evil things they have done against God. And God will punish these sinners who are against God. He will punish them for all the bad things they have said against God."

¹⁶These people always complain and find wrong *in other people.* They always do the *evil* things they want to do. They

archangel   The leader among God's angels or messengers.
Cain   The son of Adam and Eve who killed his brother Abel (Genesis 4:1-16).
descendant   Someone born into the family of a person after that person dies.

boast about themselves. The only reason they say good things about other people is to get what they want.

A Warning and Things to Do

[17] Dear friends, remember what the apostles* of our Lord Jesus Christ said before. [18] The apostles said to you, "In the last times there will be people who laugh *about God.*" These people do only the things they want to do—things that are against God. [19] These are the people who divide you. These people do only what their sinful selves want. They don't have the Spirit.*

[20] But dear friends, use your most holy faith to build yourselves up strong. Pray with the Holy Spirit.* [21] Keep yourselves in God's love. Wait for the Lord Jesus Christ with his mercy to give you life forever.

[22] Show mercy to those people who have doubts. [23] Save other people. Take those people out of the fire. Be careful when you show mercy to some people. Hate even their clothes that are dirty from sin.

Praise God

[24] He (*God*) is strong and can help you to not fall. He can bring you before his glory without any wrong in you and give you great joy. [25] He is the only God. He is the One who saves us. To him be glory, greatness, power, and authority through Jesus Christ our Lord for all time past, now, and forever. Amen.

---

apostles   The men Jesus chose to be his special helpers for telling the Good News to the world.
Spirit, Holy Spirit   Also called the Spirit of God, the Spirit of Christ, and the Comforter. He is joined with God and Christ. He does the work of God among people in the world.

Revelation

John Tells About This Book

1 This is the revelation* of Jesus Christ. God gave Jesus these things to show his servants what must happen soon. Christ sent his angel to show these things to his servant John. ²John has told everything that he saw. It is the truth that Jesus Christ told him; it is the message* from God. ³The person who reads the words of this message from God is blessed (*happy*). And the people who hear this message and do the things that are written in it are blessed. There is not much time left.

John Writes Christ's Message to the Churches

⁴From John,
To the seven churches in the province of Asia*:
Grace (*kindness*) and peace to you from the One (*God*) who is, who *always* was, and who is coming; and from the seven spirits before his throne; ⁵and from Jesus Christ. Jesus is the faithful witness. He was first among those to be raised from death. Jesus is the ruler of the kings of the earth.

Jesus is the One who loves us. And Jesus is the One who made us free from our sins with his blood (*death*). ⁶Jesus made us to be a kingdom. He made us to be priests who serve God his Father. To Jesus be glory and power forever and ever! Amen.

⁷Look, Jesus is coming with the clouds! Every person will see him, even the people who pierced* him. All people of the earth will cry loudly because of him. Yes, this will happen! Amen.

---

revelation   An opening, uncovering, or making known of truth that has been hidden.
message   The teaching and commands from God that were made known to John.
Asia   The western part of Asia Minor.
pierced   When Jesus was killed, he was stuck with a spear in the side (John 19:34).

[8]The Lord God says, "I am the Alpha and the Omega.* I am the One who is, who *always* was, and who is coming. I am the All-Powerful."

[9]I am John, and I am your brother *in Christ*. We are together in Jesus, and we share these things: suffering, the kingdom, and patient endurance. I was on the island of Patmos* because I was faithful to God's message* and to the truth of Jesus. [10]On the Lord's day the Spirit* took control of me. I heard a loud voice behind me. It sounded like a trumpet. [11]The voice said, "Write in a book all these things you see, and send it to the seven churches: to Ephesus, Smyrna, Pergamum, Thyatira, Sardis, Philadelphia, and Laodicea."

[12]I turned to see who was talking to me. When I turned I saw seven golden lampstands. [13]I saw someone among the lampstands who was "like a Son of Man."* He was dressed in a long robe. He had a golden sash (*belt*) tied around his chest. [14]His head and hair were white like wool—wool that is white as snow. His eyes were like flames of fire. [15]His feet were like brass that glows hot in a furnace. His voice was like the noise of flooding water. [16]He held seven stars in his right hand. A sharp two-edged sword came out of his mouth. He looked like the sun shining at its brightest time.

[17]When I saw him I fell down at his feet like a dead man. He put his right hand on me and said, "Don't be afraid! I am the First and the Last. [18]I am the One who lives. I was dead, but look: I am alive forever and ever! And I hold the keys of death and Hades.* [19]So write the things you see. Write the things that happen now, and the things that will happen later. [20]Here is the hidden meaning of the seven stars that you saw in my right hand, and the seven golden lampstands that you saw: The seven lampstands are the seven churches. The seven stars are the angels of the seven churches."

Alpha...Omega First and last letters in the Greek alphabet. Means beginning and end.
Patmos A small island in the Aegean Sea, near the coast of Asia Minor (modern Turkey).
message The teaching from God about the way he made through Christ for people to have their sins forgiven and live with God. God uses his people to tell the world about this truth.
Spirit The Holy Spirit. Also called the Spirit of God, the Spirit of Christ, and the Comforter. He is joined with God and Christ. He does the work of God among people in the world.
"like...Man" These words are from Daniel 7:13. "Son of Man" is a name Jesus called himself.
Hades Place where people go after death.

Christ's Message to the Church in Ephesus

2 "Write this to the angel of the church in Ephesus:

"The One who holds the seven stars in his right hand and walks among the seven golden lampstands is saying these things *to you*. ²I know what you do. You work hard and you never quit. I know that you don't accept evil people. You have tested those people who say that they are apostles* but are really not. You found that they are liars. ³You continue to try without quitting. You endured *troubles* for my name. And you have not become tired of doing this.

⁴"But I have this against you: You have left the love you had in the beginning. ⁵So remember where you were before you fell. Change your hearts, and do the things you did at first. If you don't change, I will come to you. I will take away your lampstand from its place. ⁶But there is something you do *that is right*: You hate the things that Nicolaitans* do. I also hate what they do.

⁷"Every person who hears these things should listen to what the Spirit* says to the churches. To the person who wins the victory, I will give the right to eat *the fruit* from the tree of life. This tree is in the garden of God."

Christ's Message to the Church in Smyrna

⁸"Write this to the angel of the church in Smyrna:

"The One who is the First and the Last is saying these things *to you*. He is the One who died and came to life again. ⁹I know your troubles, and I know that you are poor. But really you are rich! I know the bad things that some people say *about you*. Those people say they are Jews. But they are not true Jews. They are a synagogue (*group*) that belongs to Satan (*the devil*). ¹⁰Don't be afraid of the things that will happen to you. I tell you, the devil will put some of you in prison. He will do this to test you. You will suffer for ten days. But be faithful, even if you have to die. If you continue faithful, then I will give you the crown of life.

---

apostles   Men Jesus chose to be his special helpers for telling the Good News to the world.
Nicolaitans   This is the name of a religious group that followed false beliefs and ideas.
Spirit   The Holy Spirit. He brings God's message (truth) to God's people.

¹¹"Every person who hears these things should listen to what the Spirit* says to the churches. The person who wins the victory will not be hurt by the second death."

Christ's Message to the Church in Pergamum

¹²"Write this to the angel of the church in Pergamum:

"The One who has the sharp two-edged sword is saying these things *to you*. ¹³I know where you live. You live where Satan (*the devil*) has his throne. But you are true to me. You did not refuse to tell about your faith in me even during the time of Antipas. Antipas was my faithful witness* who was killed in your city. Your city is where Satan lives.

¹⁴"But I have a few things against you: You have people there *in your group* who follow the teaching of Balaam. Balaam taught Balak how to make the people of Israel* sin. Those people sinned by eating food offered to idols* and by doing sexual sins. ¹⁵It is the same *in your group*. You have people who follow the teaching of the Nicolaitans.* ¹⁶So change your hearts! If you don't change, I will come to you quickly and fight against those people with the sword that comes out of my mouth.

¹⁷"Every person who hears these things should listen to what the Spirit* says to the churches!

"I will give the hidden manna* to every person who wins the victory. I will also give that person a white rock. On this rock a new name is written. No person knows this new name. Only the person who gets the rock will know the new name."

Christ's Message to the Church in Thyatira

¹⁸"Write this to the angel of the church in Thyatira:

"The Son of God is saying these things. He is the One who has eyes that blaze like fire and feet like shining brass. This is what he says *to you*: ¹⁹I know the things you do. I know about your love,

---

Spirit The Holy Spirit. He brings God's message (truth) to God's people.
faithful witness A person who speaks God's message truthfully, even in a time of danger.
Israel The Jewish nation (people).
idols Statues made from wood, stone, or metal that people worship as gods.
Nicolaitans This is the name of a religious group that followed false beliefs and ideas.
manna Food from heaven that God gave his people in the desert (Exodus 16:4-36).

your faith, your service, and your patience. I know that you are doing more now than you did at first. ²⁰But I have this against you: You let that woman named Jezebel do what she wants. She says that she is a prophet.* But she is leading my people away with her teaching. Jezebel leads my people to do sexual sins and to eat food that is offered to idols.* ²¹I have given her time to change her heart and turn away from her sin. But she does not want to change. ²²And so I will throw her on a bed *of suffering*. And all the people who do the sin of adultery* with her will suffer greatly. I will do this now, if they don't turn away from the things she does. ²³I will also kill her followers. Then all the churches will know that I am the One who knows what people feel and think. And I will repay each of you for the things you have done.

²⁴"But you other people in Thyatira have not followed her teaching. You have not learned the things that they call Satan's (*the devil's*) deep secrets. This is what I say to you: I will not put any other burden on you. ²⁵Only continue the way you are until I come.

²⁶"I will give power to every person who wins the victory and continues until the end to do the things I want. I will give that person power over the nations:

> ²⁷'He will rule them with an iron rod.
> He will break them to pieces like clay pots.'   *Psalm 2:9*

²⁸This is the same power I received from my Father. I will also give that person the morning star. ²⁹Every person who hears these things should listen to what the Spirit* says to the churches."

Christ's Message to the Church in Sardis

3 "Write this to the angel of the church in Sardis:

"The One who has the seven spirits and the seven stars is saying these things *to you*. I know the things you do. People say that you are alive. But really you are dead. ²Wake up! Make yourselves stronger while you still have something left. Make yourself stronger before it dies completely. I find that the things

---

prophet Person who spoke for God. He often told things that would happen in the future.
idols Statues made from wood, stone, or metal that people worship as gods.
adultery Breaking a marriage promise by doing sexual sin.
Spirit The Holy Spirit. He brings God's message (truth) to God's people.

you do are not good enough for my God. ³So don't forget what
you have received and heard. Obey it. Change your hearts and
lives! You must wake up, or I will come to you *and surprise you*
like a robber. You will not know when I will come. ⁴But you have
a few people *in your group* there in Sardis who have kept
themselves clean. Those people will walk with me. They will wear
white clothes, because they are worthy. ⁵Every person who wins
the victory will be dressed in white clothes like these people. I will
not take away that person's name from the book of life. I will say
that he belongs to me. I will say this before my Father and before
his angels. ⁶Every person who hears these things should listen to
what the Spirit* says to the churches.''

Christ's Message to the Church in Philadelphia

⁷''Write this to the angel of the church in Philadelphia:

''The One who is holy and true is saying these words to you. He
holds the key of David. When he opens something, it cannot be
closed. And when he closes something, it cannot be opened. ⁸I
know the things you do. I have put an open door before you. No
person can close it. I know that you are weak. But you have
followed my teaching. You were not afraid to speak my name.
⁹Listen! There is a synagogue (*group*) that belongs to Satan (*the
devil*). Those people say they are Jews, but they are liars. Those
people are not *true* Jews. I will make those people come before
you and bow at your feet. They will know that you are the people
I have loved. ¹⁰You followed the teaching about my patient
endurance. So I will keep you from the time of trouble that will
come to the whole world. This trouble will test the people who
live on the earth.

¹¹''I am coming soon. Continue the way you are now. Then no
person will take away your crown (*reward*). ¹²The person who
wins the victory will be a pillar* in the temple* of my God. I will
do that for the person who wins the victory. That person will
never again have to leave God's temple. I will write the name of
my God on that person. And I will write the name of the city of

Spirit   The Holy Spirit. He brings God's message (truth) to God's people.
pillar   One of the tall, carved stones used to hold up the roof of a building.
temple   God's house—the place where God's people worship and serve him.

my God on that person. That city is the new Jerusalem.* That city is coming down out of heaven from my God. I will also write my new name on that person. ¹³Every person who hears these things should listen to what the Spirit* says to the churches.''

Christ's Message to the Church in Laodicea

¹⁴''Write this to the church in Laodicea:

''The Amen* is the One saying these things *to you*. He is the faithful and true witness. He is the ruler of all that God has made. This is what he says: ¹⁵I know what you do. You are not hot or cold. I wish that you were hot or cold! ¹⁶But you are only warm—not hot, not cold. So I am ready to spit you out of my mouth. ¹⁷You say you are rich. You think you have become wealthy and don't need a thing. But you don't know that you are really terrible, pitiful, poor, blind, and naked. ¹⁸I advise you to buy gold from me—gold made pure in fire. Then you can be truly rich. I tell you this: Buy clothes that are white. Then you can cover your shameful nakedness. I also tell you to buy medicine to put on your eyes. Then you can truly see.

¹⁹''I correct and punish those people that I love. So start trying hard! Change your hearts and lives! ²⁰Here I am! I stand at the door and knock. If a person hears my voice and opens the door, I will come in and eat with that person. And that person will eat with me.

²¹''I will let every person who wins the victory sit with me on my throne. It was the same with me. I won the victory and sat down with my Father on his throne. ²²Every person who hears these things should listen to what the Spirit* says to the churches.''

John Sees Heaven

4 Then I looked, and there before me was an open door in heaven. And I heard the same voice that spoke to me before. It was the voice that sounded like a trumpet. The voice said,

---

new Jerusalem   This name is used to mean the spiritual city God built for his people.
Spirit   The Holy Spirit. He brings God's message (truth) to God's people.
Amen   Used here as a name for Jesus, it means to agree strongly that something is true.

"Come up here, and I will show you what must happen after this." ²Then the Spirit* took control of me. There before me was a throne in heaven. Someone was sitting on the throne. ³The One who sat on the throne looked like precious stones, like jasper and carnelian. All around the throne was a rainbow the color of an emerald. ⁴Around the throne there were 24 other thrones. There were 24 elders* sitting on the 24 thrones. The elders were dressed in white, and had golden crowns on their heads. ⁵Lightning flashes and noises of thunder came from the throne. Before the throne there were seven lamps burning. These lamps are the seven spirits of God. ⁶Also before the throne there was something that looked like a sea of glass. It was clear like crystal.

Around the throne, on each side, there were four living things. These living things had eyes all over them, in front and in back. ⁷The first living thing was like a lion. The second was like a cow. The third had a face like a man. The fourth was like a flying eagle. ⁸Each of these four living things had six wings. These living things were covered all over with eyes, inside and out. Day and night these four living things never stop saying:

"Holy, holy, holy is the Lord God All-Powerful.
He was, he is, and he is coming."

⁹These living things give glory and honor and thanks to the One who sits on the throne. He is the One who lives forever and ever. And every time the living things do this, ¹⁰the 24 elders* bow down before the One who sits on the throne. The elders worship him who lives forever and ever. The elders put their crowns down before the throne and say:

¹¹"Our Lord and God! You are worthy
to receive glory and honor and power.
You made all things. Everything existed
and was made because you wanted it."

Spirit The Holy Spirit. He brings God's message (truth) to God's people.
24 elders Elder means "older." These are probably great leaders of God's people. They may be the leaders of the twelve Jewish family groups, plus the twelve apostles of Jesus.

5 Then I saw a scroll* in the right hand of the One sitting on the throne. The scroll had writing on both sides. The scroll was kept closed with seven seals. ²And I saw a powerful angel. The angel called in a loud voice, "Who is worthy to break the seals and open the scroll?" ³But there was no one in heaven or on earth or under the earth who could open the scroll or look inside it. ⁴I cried and cried because there was no one who was worthy to open the scroll or look inside. ⁵But one of the elders* said to me, "Don't cry! The Lion (*Christ*) from Judah's family group has won the victory. He is David's descendant. He is able to open the scroll and its seven seals."

⁶Then I saw a Lamb standing in the center of the throne with the four living things around it. The elders* were also around the Lamb. The Lamb looked like it had been killed. It had seven horns and seven eyes. These are the seven spirits of God that were sent into all the world. ⁷The Lamb came and took the scroll from the right hand of the One sitting on the throne. ⁸After the Lamb took the scroll, the four living things and the 24 elders bowed down before the Lamb. Each one of them had a harp.* Also they were holding golden bowls full of incense.* These bowls of incense are the prayers of the believers. ⁹And they all sang a new song *to the Lamb*:

> "You are worthy to take the scroll
> > and to open its seals,
> because you were killed;
> > and with your blood (*death*) you bought
> > > men for God
> > from every tribe, language, race of people,
> > > and nation.
> ¹⁰You made these people to be a kingdom,
> > and you made these people to be priests for our God.
> > And they will rule on the earth."

¹¹Then I looked, and I heard the voices of many angels. The angels were around the throne, the *four* living things, and the

---

scroll A long roll of paper or leather used for writing on.
elders Elder means "older." These are probably great leaders of God's people. They may be the leaders of the twelve Jewish family groups, plus the twelve apostles of Jesus.
harp A musical instrument with strings.
incense Special dried tree sap used for a sacrifice. It was burned to make a sweet-smelling smoke.

elders.* There were thousands and thousands of angels—there were 10,000 times 10,000. [12]The angels said with a loud voice:

"The Lamb who was killed is worthy
to receive power, wealth, wisdom, and strength,
honor, glory, and praise!"

[13]Then I heard every living thing that is in heaven and on earth and under the earth and in the sea. I heard every thing in all these places. I heard them all saying:

"All praise and honor and glory and power
forever and ever
to the One who sits on the throne
and to the Lamb!"

[14]The four living things said, "Amen!"* And the elders* bowed down and worshiped.

6 Then I watched while the Lamb opened the first of the seven seals. I heard one of the four living things speak with a voice like thunder. It said, "Come!" [2]I looked and there before me was a white horse. The rider on the horse held a bow. The rider was given a crown. And he rode out, defeating the enemy. He rode out to win the victory.

[3]The Lamb opened the second seal. Then I heard the second living thing say, "Come!" [4]Then another horse came out. This was a red horse. The rider on the horse was given power to take away peace from the earth. He was given power to make people kill each other. This rider was given a big sword.

[5]The Lamb opened the third seal. Then I heard the third living thing say, "Come!" I looked and there before me was a black horse. The rider on the horse held a pair of scales in his hand. [6]Then I heard something that sounded like a voice. The voice came from where the four living things were. The voice said, "A quart of wheat for a day's pay. And three quarts of barley for a day's pay. And don't hurt the oil and wine!"

[7]The Lamb opened the fourth seal. Then I heard the voice of the fourth living thing say, "Come!" [8]I looked and there before

---

elders Elder means "older." These are probably great leaders of God's people. They may be the leaders of the twelve Jewish family groups, plus the twelve apostles of Jesus.
"Amen!" When a person says, "Amen," it means that person agrees strongly with something.

me was a pale colored horse. The rider on the horse was death. Hades* was following close behind him. They were given power over a fourth of the earth. They were given power to kill people by using the sword, by starving, by disease, and with the wild animals of the earth.

⁹The Lamb opened the fifth seal. Then I saw some souls under the altar.* They were the souls of those people who had been killed because they were faithful to God's message* and to the truth they had received. ¹⁰These souls shouted in a loud voice, "Holy and true Lord, how long until you judge the people of the earth and punish them for killing us?" ¹¹Then each one of those souls was given a white robe. They were told to wait a short time longer. There were still some of their brothers in the service of Christ who must be killed like they were. Those souls were told to wait until all of this killing was finished.

¹²Then I watched while the Lamb opened the sixth seal. There was a great earthquake. The sun became dark like *black* cloth made from hair. The full moon became red like blood. ¹³The stars in the sky fell to the earth like a fig tree drops its figs when the wind blows. ¹⁴The sky was divided. It was rolled up like a scroll.* And every mountain and island was moved from its place.

¹⁵Then all the people hid in caves and behind the rocks on the mountains. There were the kings of the world, the rulers, the generals, the rich people, and the powerful people. Every person, slave and free, hid himself. ¹⁶The people said to the mountains and the rocks, "Fall on us. Hide us from the face of the One who sits on the throne. Hide us from the anger of the Lamb! ¹⁷The great day for their anger has come. No person can stand against it."

The 144,000 People of Israel

7 After this happened I saw four angels standing at the four corners of the earth. The angels were holding the four winds of the earth. They were stopping the wind from blowing on the

Hades Place people go after they die.
altar Place where sacrifices or gifts are offered to God.
message The news that God has made a way through Christ for people to have their sins forgiven and live with God. When people accept this truth, God accepts them.
scroll A long roll of paper or leather used for writing on.

land or on the sea or on any tree. ²Then I saw another angel coming from the east. This angel had the seal of the living God. The angel called out with a loud voice to the four angels. These were the four angels that God had given the power to hurt the earth and the sea. The angel said to the four angels, ³"Don't hurt the land or the sea or the trees before we put the sign on the people who serve our God. We must put the sign on their foreheads." ⁴Then I heard how many people were marked with the sign. There were 144,000. They were from every family group of the people of Israel.*

⁵ From the tribe of Judah 12,000 were marked with the sign,
    from the tribe of Reuben 12,000,
    from the tribe of Gad 12,000,
⁶ from the tribe of Asher 12,000,
    from the tribe of Naphtali 12,000,
    from the tribe of Manasseh 12,000,
⁷ from the tribe of Simeon 12,000,
    from the tribe of Levi 12,000,
    from the tribe of Issachar 12,000,
⁸ from the tribe of Zebulun 12,000,
    from the tribe of Joseph 12,000,
    from the tribe of Benjamin 12,000.

The Great Crowd

⁹Then I looked and there were many, many people. There were so many people that a person could not count them all. They were from every nation, tribe, race of people, and language of the earth. These people were standing before the throne and before the Lamb (*Jesus*). They all wore white robes, and had palm branches in their hands. ¹⁰They shouted with a loud voice, "Salvation belongs to our God, who sits on the throne, and to the Lamb." ¹¹The elders* and the four living things were there. All the angels were standing around them and the throne. The angels bowed down on their faces before the throne and worshiped God. ¹²They said, "Amen*! Praise, glory, wisdom, thanks, honor,

Israel   The Jewish nation (people).
elders   Elder means "older." These are probably great leaders of God's people. They may be the
    leaders of the twelve Jewish family groups, plus the twelve apostles of Jesus.
Amen   When a person says, "Amen," it means that person agrees strongly with something.

power, and strength belong to our God forever and ever. Amen!''

¹³Then one of the elders* asked me, "Who are these people in white robes? Where did they come from?''

¹⁴I answered, "You know who they are, sir.''

And the elder* said, "These are the people who have come out of the great suffering. They have washed their robes* with the blood of the Lamb. Now they are clean and white. ¹⁵So now these people are before the throne of God. They worship God day and night in his temple.* And the One (*God*) who sits on the throne will protect them. ¹⁶Those people will never be hungry again. They will never be thirsty again. The sun will not hurt them. No heat will burn them. ¹⁷The Lamb at the center of the throne will be their shepherd. He will lead them to springs of water that give life. And God will wipe away every tear from their eyes.''

The Seventh Seal

8 The Lamb opened the seventh seal. Then there was silence in heaven for about half an hour. ²And I saw the seven angels who stand before God. They were given seven trumpets.

³Another angel came and stood at the altar.* This angel had a golden holder for incense.* The angel was given much incense to offer with the prayers of all the saints.* The angel put this offering on the golden altar before the throne. ⁴The smoke from the incense went up from the angel's hand to God. The smoke went up with the prayers of the saints. ⁵Then the angel filled the incense holder with fire from the altar. The angel threw the incense holder on the earth. Then there were flashes of lightning, thunder and other noises, and an earthquake.

The Seven Angels Blow Their Trumpets

⁶Then the seven angels with the seven trumpets prepared to blow their trumpets.

---

elder(s) Elder means "older." These are probably great leaders of God's people. They may be the leaders of the twelve Jewish family groups, plus the twelve apostles of Jesus.
washed their robes Meaning they believed in Jesus so that their sins could be forgiven.
temple God's house—the place where God's people worship and serve him.
altar Place where sacrifices or gifts are offered to God.
incense Special dried tree sap used for a sacrifice. It was burned to make a sweet-smelling smoke.
saints God's people are also called saints, which means "holy people."

⁷The first angel blew his trumpet. Then hail and fire mixed with blood were poured down on the earth. And one third of the earth and all the green grass and one third of the trees were burned up.

⁸The second angel blew his trumpet. Then something that looked like a big mountain burning with fire was thrown into the sea. And one third of the sea became blood. ⁹And one third of the living things in the sea died, and one third of the ships were destroyed.

¹⁰The third angel blew his trumpet. Then a large star, burning like a torch, fell from the sky. The star fell on one third of the rivers and springs of water. ¹¹The name of the star is Wormwood.* And one third of all the water became bitter. Many people died from drinking the water that was bitter.

¹²The fourth angel blew his trumpet. Then one third of the sun and one third of the moon and one third of the stars were struck. So one third of them became dark. A third of the day and night was without light.

¹³While I watched I heard an eagle that was flying high in the air. The eagle said with a loud voice, "Trouble! Trouble! Trouble for the people that live on the earth! The trouble will begin after the sounds of the trumpets that the other three angels will blow."

9 The fifth angel blew his trumpet. Then I saw a star fall from the sky to the earth. The star was given the key to the deep hole that leads down to the bottomless pit. ²Then the star opened the hole leading to the bottomless pit. Smoke came up from the hole like smoke from a big furnace. The sun and sky became dark because of the smoke from the hole. ³Then locusts* came down to the earth out of the smoke. They were given the power *to sting* like scorpions.* ⁴The locusts were told not to hurt the grass on the earth or any plant or tree. They could hurt only the people who did not have the sign of God on their foreheads. ⁵These locusts were given the power to give pain to the people for five months. But the locusts were not given the power to kill the people. And the pain that the people felt was like the pain that a scorpion gives

---

Wormwood Name of a very bitter plant, used here to give the idea of bitter sorrow.
locusts Insects like grasshoppers. Sometimes many locusts came and ate all plants (Exodus 10).
scorpions A scorpion is an insect that stings with a bad poison.

when it stings a person. ⁶During those days people will look for a way to die, but they will not find it. They will want to die, but death will hide from them.

⁷The locusts* looked like horses prepared for battle. On their heads they wore things that looked like crowns of gold. Their faces looked like human faces. ⁸Their hair was like women's hair. Their teeth were like lions' teeth. ⁹Their chests looked like iron breastplates. The sound their wings made was like the noise of many horses and chariots hurrying into battle. ¹⁰The locusts had tails with stingers like scorpions.* The power they had to give people pain for five months was in their tails. ¹¹The locusts had a king. The king was the angel of the bottomless pit. His name in the Hebrew (*Jewish*) language is Abaddon. In the Greek language his name is Apollyon (*Destroyer*).

¹²The first great trouble is past. There are still two other great troubles that will come.

¹³The sixth angel blew his trumpet. Then I heard a voice coming from the horns on the golden altar* that is before God. ¹⁴The voice said to the sixth angel who had the trumpet, "Free the four angels who are tied at the great river Euphrates." ¹⁵These four angels have been kept ready for this hour and day and month and year. The angels were freed to kill one third of all the people on the earth. ¹⁶I heard how many troops on horses were in *their* army. There were 200,000,000.

¹⁷In my vision* I saw the horses and the riders on the horses. They looked like this: They had breastplates that were fiery red, dark blue, and yellow like sulfur. The heads of the horses looked like heads of lions. The horses had fire, smoke, and sulfur coming out of their mouths. ¹⁸One third of all the people on earth were killed by these three bad things coming out of the horses' mouths: the fire, the smoke, and the sulfur. ¹⁹The horses' power was in their mouths and also in their tails. Their tails were like snakes that have heads to bite and hurt people.

²⁰The other people *on the earth* were not killed by these bad things. But these people still did not change their hearts and lives and turn away from the things they had made with their own

locusts Insects like grasshoppers. Sometimes many locusts came and ate all plants (Exodus 10).
scorpions A scorpion is an insect that stings with a bad poison.
altar Place where sacrifices or gifts are offered to God.
vision A vision is something like a dream that God used to speak to people.

hands. They did not stop worshiping demons* and idols* made of gold, silver, bronze, stone, and wood—things that cannot see or hear or walk. ²¹These people did not change their hearts and lives and turn away from killing other people. They did not turn away from their evil magic, their sexual sins, and their stealing.

The Angel and the Little Scroll

10 Then I saw another powerful angel coming down from heaven. The angel was dressed in a cloud. He had a rainbow around his head. The angel's face was like the sun and his legs were like poles of fire. ²The angel was holding a small scroll. The scroll was open in his hand. The angel put his right foot on the sea and his left foot on the land. ³The angel shouted loudly like the roaring of a lion. After the angel shouted, the voices of seven thunders spoke. ⁴The seven thunders spoke, and I started to write. But then I heard a voice from heaven. The voice said, "Don't write what the seven thunders said. Keep those things secret."

⁵Then the angel I saw standing on the sea and on the land raised his right hand to heaven. ⁶The angel made a promise by *the power of* the One who lives for ever and ever. He (*God*) is the One who made the skies and all that is in them. He made the earth and all that is in it, and the sea and all that is in it. The angel said, "There will be no more waiting! ⁷In the days when the seventh angel is ready to blow his trumpet, God's secret plan will be finished. This plan is the Good News* God told to his servants, the prophets.*"

⁸Then I heard the same voice from heaven again. The voice said to me, "Go and take the open scroll that is in the angel's hand. This is the angel that is standing on the sea and on the land."

⁹So I went to the angel and asked him to give me the little scroll. The angel said to me, "Take the scroll and eat it. It will be sour in your stomach. But in your mouth it will be sweet like honey." ¹⁰So I took the little scroll from the angel's hand. I ate the scroll. In my mouth it tasted sweet like honey. But after I ate

demons Demons are evil spirits from the devil.
idols Statues made from wood, stone, or metal that people worship as gods.
Good News The news that God has made a way through Christ for people to have their sins forgiven and live with God. When people accept this truth, God accepts them.
prophets People who spoke for God. Their writings are part of the Old Testament.

it, it was sour in my stomach. ¹¹Then I was told, "You must prophesy* again about many races of people, many nations, languages, and kings."

The Two Witnesses

11 Then I was given a measuring stick like a rod. I was told, "Go and measure the temple* of God, the altar,* and the people worshiping there. ²But don't measure the yard outside the temple. Leave that alone. That has been given to the people who are not Jews. Those people will walk on the holy city for 42 months. ³And I will give power to my two witnesses. And they will prophesy* for 1,260 days. They will be dressed in sackcloth.*" ⁴These two witnesses are the two olive trees and the two lampstands that stand before the Lord of the earth. ⁵If a person tries to hurt the witnesses, fire comes from the mouths of the witnesses and kills their enemy. Any person who tries to hurt them will die like this. ⁶These witnesses have the power to stop the sky from raining during the time they are prophesying. These witnesses have power to make the water become blood. They have power to send every kind of trouble to the earth. They can do this as many times as they want.

⁷When the two witnesses have finished telling their message, the animal will fight against them. This is the animal that comes up from the bottomless pit. The animal will defeat them and kill them. ⁸The bodies of the two witnesses will lie in the street of the great city. This city is named Sodom* and Egypt. These names for the city have a special meaning. This is the city where the Lord was killed. ⁹People from every race of people, tribe, language, and nation will look at the bodies of the two witnesses for three and a half days. The people will refuse to bury them. ¹⁰People who live on the earth will be happy because these two are dead. They will have parties and send each other gifts. They will do these things because these two prophets (*witnesses*) brought much suffering to the people who live on the earth.

prophesy To prophesy means to speak or teach things from God.
temple God's house—the place where God's people worship and serve him. Here, John sees it pictured as the special building in Jerusalem where God commanded the Jews to worship him.
altar Place where sacrifices or gifts are offered to God.
sackcloth A rough cloth of animal hair. People sometimes wore it to show sadness.
Sodom A town where very bad people lived. God punished them by destroying their city.

¹¹But after three and a half days God let life enter the two prophets again. They stood on their feet. All the people who saw them were filled with fear. ¹²Then the two prophets heard a loud voice from heaven say, "Come up here!" And the two prophets went up into heaven in a cloud. Their enemies watched them go.

¹³At that same time there was a great earthquake. One tenth of the city was destroyed. And 7,000 people were killed in the earthquake. The people that did not die were very afraid. They gave glory to the God of heaven.

¹⁴The second great trouble is finished. The third great trouble is coming soon.

The Seventh Trumpet

¹⁵The seventh angel blew his trumpet. Then there were loud voices in heaven. The voices said:

"The kingdom of the world has now become
　　the kingdom of our Lord and of his Christ.*
　And he will rule forever and ever."

¹⁶Then the 24 elders* bowed down on their faces and worshiped God. These are the elders who sit on their thrones before God. ¹⁷The elders said:

"We give thanks to you, Lord God All-Powerful.
　You are the One who is and who *always* was.
　We thank you because you have used
　　your great power
　and have begun to rule!
¹⁸The people of the world were angry;
　but now is the time for your anger.
　Now is the time for the dead people to be judged.
　It is time to reward your servants, the prophets,*
　　and to reward your holy people,
　the people who respect you, great and small.
　It is time to destroy those people
　　who destroy the earth!"

Christ The "anointed one" (the Messiah) or chosen one of God.
24 elders Elder means "older." These are probably great leaders of God's people. They may be the leaders of the twelve Jewish family groups, plus the twelve apostles of Jesus.
prophets People who spoke for God.

¹⁹Then God's temple* in heaven was opened. The holy box that holds the agreement* *that God gave to his people* could be seen in his temple. Then there were flashes of lightning and noises, thunder, an earthquake, and a great hailstorm.

The Woman and the Giant Snake

12 And then a great wonder appeared in heaven: There was a woman who was clothed with the sun. The moon was under her feet. She had a crown of twelve stars on her head. ²The woman was pregnant. She cried out with pain because she was about to give birth. ³Then another wonder appeared in heaven: There was a giant red snake there. The giant snake had seven heads with seven crowns on each head. The snake also had ten horns. ⁴The snake's tail swept a third of the stars out of the sky and threw them down to the earth. The giant snake stood in front of the woman who was ready to give birth to the baby. The snake wanted to eat the woman's baby when it was born. ⁵The woman gave birth to a son, a male child. He will rule all the nations with an iron rod. And her child was taken up to God and to his throne. ⁶The woman ran away into the desert to a place that God prepared for her. In the desert the woman will be taken care of for 1,260 days.

⁷Then there was a war in heaven. Michael and his angels fought against the giant snake. The snake and his angels fought back. ⁸But the snake was not strong enough. The giant snake and his angels lost their place in heaven. ⁹The snake was thrown down out of heaven. (The giant snake is that old snake called the devil or Satan. He leads the whole world into the wrong way.) The snake with his angels were thrown to the earth.

¹⁰Then I heard a loud voice in heaven say: "The salvation and the power and the kingdom of our God and the authority (*power*) of his Christ* have now come. These things have come, because the accuser of our brothers has been thrown out. He is the one who accused our brothers day and night before our God. ¹¹Our brothers defeated him by the blood (*death*) of the Lamb and by

temple God's house—the place where God's people worship and serve him. John sees the heavenly temple pictured to be like the temple of God's people in the Old Testament.
holy box...agreement In the Most Holy Place of the Old Testament temple, there was a box that had in it the agreement God gave to his people (Exodus 25:10-22, 1 Kings 8:1-9, Hebrews 9:4).
Christ The "anointed one" (the Messiah) or chosen one of God.

the truth they preached. They did not love their lives too much. They were not afraid of death. [12]So be happy you heavens and all who live there! But it will be bad for the earth and the sea, because the devil has gone down to you! The devil is filled with anger. He knows that he does not have much time."

[13]The giant snake saw that he had been thrown down to the earth. So he chased the woman who had given birth to the boy child. [14]But the woman was given the two wings of a great eagle. Then she could fly to the place that was prepared for her in the desert. In that place she would be taken care of for three and one half years. There she would be away from the snake. [15]Then the snake poured water out of its mouth like a river. The snake poured the water toward the woman so that the flood would carry her away. [16]But the earth helped the woman. The earth opened its mouth and swallowed the river that came from the mouth of the giant snake. [17]Then the snake was very angry at the woman. The snake went away to make war against all her other children. Her children are those people who obey God's commandments and have the truth of Jesus.

[18]The giant snake stood on the seashore.

The Two Animals

13 Then I saw an animal coming up out of the sea. It had ten horns and seven heads. There was a crown on each of its horns. It had a bad name written on each head. [2]This animal looked like a leopard, with feet like a bear's feet. It had a mouth like a lion's mouth. The giant snake *on the seashore* gave the animal all of his power and his throne and great authority. [3]One of the heads of the animal looked like it had been wounded and killed. But this death wound had healed. All the people in the world were amazed, and they all followed the animal. [4]People worshiped the giant snake because he had given his power to the animal. And the people also worshiped the animal. They asked, "Who is as powerful as the animal? Who can make war against him?"

[5]The animal was allowed to say proud words and very evil things. The animal was allowed to use his power for 42 months. [6]The animal opened his mouth to say bad things against God. The

645

animal also said bad things against God's name, against the place where God lives, and against all those who live in heaven. ⁷The animal was given power to make war against God's holy people (*believers*) and to defeat them. The animal was given power over every tribe, race of people, language, and nation. ⁸All the people who live on earth will worship the animal. These are all the people since the beginning of the world whose names are not written in the Lamb's book of life. The Lamb is the One who was killed.

⁹If a person hears these things, then he should listen to this:

¹⁰If any person is to be a prisoner,
    then that person will be a prisoner.
If any person kills with a sword,
    then that person will be killed with a sword.

This means that God's holy people (*believers*) must have patience and faith.

¹¹Then I saw another animal coming up out of the earth. He had two horns like a lamb but he talked like a giant snake. ¹²This animal stands before the first animal and uses the same power that the first animal has. He uses this power to make all the people living on the earth worship the first animal. The first animal was the one that had the death wound that was healed. ¹³This second animal does great miracles.* He even makes fire come down from heaven to earth while people are watching. ¹⁴This second animal fools the people that live on the earth. He fools them by using the miracles that he has been given the power to do. He does these miracles to serve the first animal. The second animal ordered people to make an idol* to honor the first animal. This was the animal that was wounded by the sword but did not die. ¹⁵The second animal was given power to give life to the idol of the first animal. Then the idol could speak and order all the people who did not worship it to be killed. ¹⁶The second animal also forced all people, small and great, rich and poor, free and slave, to have a mark on their right hand or on their forehead. ¹⁷No person could buy or sell without this mark. This mark is the name of the animal, or the number of his name. ¹⁸A person who has understanding can find the meaning of the animal's number.

miracles False miracles—powerful acts done by the power of the devil.
idol A statue made from wood, stone, or metal that people worship as a god.

This requires wisdom. This number is the number of a man. His number is 666.

The Song of the Redeemed

14 Then I looked, and there before me was the Lamb. He was standing on Mount Zion.* There were 144,000 people with him. They all had his name and his Father's name written on their foreheads. ²And I heard a sound from heaven like the noise of flooding water and like the sound of loud thunder. The sound I heard was like people playing their harps.* ³The people sang a new song before the throne and before the four living things and the elders.* The only people that could learn the new song were the 144,000 who had been redeemed (*saved*) from the earth. No one else could learn the song. ⁴These 144,000 people are the ones who did not do wrong things with women. They kept themselves pure. They follow the Lamb every place he goes. These 144,000 were redeemed (*saved*) from among the people of the earth. They are the first people to be offered to God and the Lamb. ⁵These people were not guilty of telling lies. They are without fault.

The Three Angels

⁶Then I saw another angel flying high in the air. The angel had an eternal gospel* to preach to the people who live on the earth—to every nation, tribe, language, and race of people. ⁷The angel said in a loud voice, "Fear God and give him praise. The time has come for God to judge *all people*. Worship God. He made the heavens, the earth, the sea, and the springs of water."

⁸Then the second angel followed the first angel and said, "She is destroyed! The great city of Babylon is destroyed! She (*Babylon*) made all the nations drink the wine of her adultery* and of God's anger."

Mount Zion   Another name for Jerusalem, the spiritual city where God's people live with him.
harps   Musical instruments with strings.
elders   Elder means "older." These are probably great leaders of God's people. They may be the leaders of the twelve Jewish family groups, plus the twelve apostles of Jesus.
gospel   The Good News that God has made a way through Christ for people to have their sins forgiven and live with God. When people accept this truth, God accepts them.
adultery   Breaking a marriage promise by doing sexual sin.

⁹A third angel followed the first two angels. This third angel said in a loud voice: *"It will be bad for* the person who worships the animal and the animal's idol* and gets the animal's mark on his forehead or on his hand. ¹⁰That person will drink the wine of God's anger. This wine is prepared with all its strength in the cup of God's anger. That person will be tortured (*hurt*) with burning sulfur before the holy angels and the Lamb. ¹¹And the smoke from their burning pain will rise forever and ever. There will be no rest, day or night, for those people who worship the animal and his idol or who get the mark of his name." ¹²This means that God's holy people must be patient. They must obey God's commandments and keep their faith in Jesus.

¹³Then I heard a voice from heaven. The voice said, "Write this: From now on, the dead people who were in the Lord when they died are blessed (*happy*)."

The Spirit* says, "Yes, that is true. Those people will rest from their hard work. The things they have done will stay with them."

The Earth Is Harvested

¹⁴I looked and there before me was a white cloud. Sitting on the white cloud was One that looked like a Son of Man.* He had a gold crown on his head and a sharp sickle* in his hand. ¹⁵Then another angel came out of the temple.* This angel called to the One who was sitting on the cloud, "Take your sickle and gather *from the earth*. The time to harvest has come. The fruit of the earth is ripe." ¹⁶So the One that was sitting on the cloud swung his sickle over the earth. And the earth was harvested.

¹⁷Then another angel came out of the temple* in heaven. This angel also had a sharp sickle. ¹⁸And then another angel came from the altar.* This angel has power over the fire. This angel called to the angel with the sharp sickle. He said, "Take your sharp sickle and gather the bunches of grapes from the earth's

---

idol   A statue made from wood, stone, or metal that people worship as a god.
Spirit   The Holy Spirit. He brings God's message (truth) to God's people.
Son of Man   This name is from Daniel 7:13-14. Jesus used this name when talking about himself.
sickle   A farming tool with a curved blade. It was used to harvest grain.
temple   God's house—the place where God's people worship and serve him.
altar   Place where sacrifices or gifts are offered to God.

vine. The earth's grapes are ripe." ¹⁹The angel swung his sickle over the earth. The angel gathered the earth's grapes and threw them into the great winepress of God's anger. ²⁰The grapes were squeezed in the winepress outside the city. Blood flowed out of the winepress. It rose as high as the heads of the horses for a distance of 200 miles.

The Angels with the Last Plagues

15 Then I saw another wonder in heaven. It was great and amazing. There were seven angels bringing seven troubles. These are the last troubles, because after these troubles God's anger is finished.

²I saw what looked like a sea of glass mixed with fire. All the people who had won the victory over the animal and his idol* and over the number of his name were standing by the sea. These people had harps that God had given them. ³They sang the song of Moses, the servant of God, and the song of the Lamb:

"Great and wonderful are the things you do,
　Lord God All-Powerful.
Right and true are your ways,
　King of the nations.
⁴ All people will fear you, O Lord.
　All people will praise your name.
　Only you are holy.
All people will come and worship before you,
　because it is clear that you do the things
　　that are right."

⁵After this I saw the temple (the tabernacle of witness*) in heaven. The temple was opened. ⁶And the seven angels bringing the seven troubles came out of the temple. They were dressed in clean shining linen cloth. They wore golden bands tied around their chests. ⁷Then one of the four living things gave seven golden bowls to the seven angels. The bowls were filled with the anger of God, who lives forever and ever. ⁸The temple was filled with

---

idol A statue made from wood, stone, or metal that people worship as a god.
tabernacle of witness The tent God told his people to build after they left Egypt. It was a place for worship and a symbol of God's living with them. (Read Exodus 25-27, 35-38.)

smoke from the glory and the power of God. No one could enter the temple until the seven troubles of the seven angels were finished.

The Bowls of God's Wrath

16 Then I heard a loud voice from the temple.* The voice said to the seven angels, "Go and pour out the seven bowls of God's anger on the earth."

²The first angel left. He poured out his bowl on the land. Then all the people who had the mark of the animal and who worshiped his idol* got sores that were ugly and painful.

³The second angel poured out his bowl on the sea. Then the sea became blood like the blood of a dead man. Every living thing in the sea died.

⁴The third angel poured out his bowl on the rivers and the springs of water. The rivers and the springs of water became blood. ⁵Then I heard the angel of the waters say *to God*:

"You are the One who is and who *always* was.
> You are the Holy One.
You are right in these judgments you have made.
⁶ The people have spilled the blood of (*killed*)
> your holy ones and your prophets.*
Now you have given those people blood to drink.
> This is what they deserve."

⁷And I heard the altar* say:

"Yes, Lord God All-Powerful,
> your judgments are true and right."

⁸The fourth angel poured out his bowl on the sun. The sun was given power to burn the people with fire. ⁹The people were burned by the great heat. Those people cursed the name of God. God is the One who had control over these troubles. But the people refused to change their hearts and lives and give glory to God.

---

temple   God's house—the place where God's people worship and serve him.
idol   A statue made from wood, stone, or metal that people worship as a god.
prophets   People who spoke for God.
altar   Place where sacrifices or gifts are offered to God.

¹⁰The fifth angel poured out his bowl on the throne of the animal. And darkness covered the animal's kingdom. People bit their tongues because of the pain. ¹¹People cursed the God of heaven because of their pain and the sores they had. But the people refused to change their hearts and turn away from the *bad* things they did.

¹²The sixth angel poured out his bowl on the great river Euphrates. The water in the river was dried up. This prepared the way for the kings from the east to come. ¹³Then I saw three unclean (*evil*) spirits that looked like frogs. They came out of the mouth of the giant snake, out of the mouth of the animal, and out of the mouth of the false prophet.* ¹⁴These evil spirits are the spirits of demons.* They *have power to* do miracles.* These evil spirits go out to the kings of the whole world. They go out to gather the kings for battle on the great day of God the All-Powerful.

¹⁵"Listen! I will come like a thief comes! Happy is the person who stays awake and keeps his clothes with him. Then he will not have to go without clothes, and people will not see the things he is ashamed for them to see."

¹⁶Then the evil spirits gathered the kings together to the place that is called Armageddon in the Jewish language.*

¹⁷The seventh angel poured out his bowl into the air. Then a loud voice came out of the temple* from the throne. The voice said, "It is finished!" ¹⁸Then there were flashes of lightning, noises, thunder, and a big earthquake. This was the worst earthquake that has ever happened since people have been on earth. ¹⁹The great city split into three parts. The cities of the nations were destroyed. And God did not forget *to punish* Babylon the Great. He gave that city the cup filled with the wine of his terrible anger. ²⁰Every island disappeared and there were no more mountains. ²¹Giant hailstones fell on the people from out of the sky. These hailstones weighed about 100 pounds each. People

---

false prophet A person who says he speaks for God but does not really speak God's truth.
demons Demons are evil spirits from the devil.
miracles False miracles—powerful acts done by the power of the devil.
Jewish language Aramaic, the "Hebrew" language in the first century.
temple God's house—the place where God's people worship and serve him.

cursed God because of this trouble of the hail. This trouble was a terrible thing.

The Woman on the Animal

17 One of the seven angels came and spoke to me. This was one of the angels that had the seven bowls. The angel said, "Come, and I will show you the punishment that will be given to the famous prostitute.* She is the one sitting over many waters. ²The kings of the earth sinned sexually with her. The people of the earth became drunk from the wine of her sexual sin."

³Then the angel carried me away by the Spirit* to the desert. There I saw a woman sitting on a red animal. The animal was covered with bad names written on him. The animal had seven heads and ten horns. ⁴The woman was dressed in purple and red. She was shining with the gold, jewels, and pearls she was wearing. She had a golden cup in her hand. This cup was filled with terrible (*evil*) things and the uncleanness of her sexual sin. ⁵She had a title written on her forehead. This title has a hidden meaning. This is what was written:

THE GREAT BABYLON
MOTHER OF PROSTITUTES
AND THE EVIL THINGS OF THE EARTH.

⁶I saw that the woman was drunk. She was drunk with the blood of God's holy people. She was drunk with the blood of those people who told about *their faith in* Jesus.

When I saw the woman I was fully amazed. ⁷Then the angel said to me, "Why are you amazed? I will tell you the hidden meaning of this woman and the animal she rides—the animal with seven heads and ten horns. ⁸The animal that you saw was once *alive*. But that animal is not *alive* now. But that animal will *be alive and* come up out of the bottomless pit and go away to be destroyed. The people that live on the earth will be amazed when they see the animal. They will be amazed because he was once *alive*, and is not *alive* now, but will come again. These are the

---

prostitute   A woman who is paid by men who use her for sexual sin.
Spirit   The Holy Spirit. Also called the Spirit of God and the Spirit of Christ.

people whose names have never been written in the book of life since the beginning of the world.

⁹"You need a wise mind to understand this. The seven heads on the animal are the seven hills where the woman sits. They are also seven kings. ¹⁰Five of the kings have already died. One of the kings lives now. And the last king is coming. When he comes he will stay only a short time. ¹¹The animal that was once *alive* but is not alive now is an eighth king. This eighth king also belongs to the first seven kings. And he will go away to be destroyed.

¹²"The ten horns you saw are ten kings. These ten kings have not yet received their kingdom. But they will receive power to rule with the animal for one hour. ¹³All ten of these kings have the same purpose. And they will give their power and authority to the animal. ¹⁴They will make war against the Lamb. But the Lamb will defeat them, because he is Lord of lords and King of kings. He will defeat them with his chosen and faithful followers—the people that he has called."

¹⁵Then the angel said to me, "You saw the water where the prostitute* sits. These waters are the many peoples, the different races, nations, and languages *in the world*. ¹⁶The animal and the ten horns (*ten kings*) you saw will hate the prostitute. They will take everything she has and leave her naked. They will eat her body and burn her with fire. ¹⁷God made the ten horns want to do his purpose: They agreed to give the animal their power to rule. They will rule until the things God has said are completed. ¹⁸The woman you saw is the great city that rules over the kings of the earth."

Babylon Is Destroyed

18 Then I saw another angel coming down from heaven. This angel had much power. The angel's glory made the earth bright. ²The angel shouted with a powerful voice:

"She is destroyed!
The great city of Babylon is destroyed!

---

prostitute   A woman who is paid by men who use her for sexual sin.

>   She (*Babylon*) has become a home for demons.*
>   That city has become a place for every
>   unclean spirit to live.
>   That city has become a place for every
>   unclean and hated bird.
> ³ All the peoples of the earth have drunk
>   the wine of her sexual sin and of *God's* anger.
>   The kings of the earth sinned sexually with her,
>   and the businessmen of the world grew rich
>   from the great wealth of her luxury.''

⁴Then I heard another voice from heaven say:

>   ''Come out of that city, my people,
>   so that you will not share in her sins.
>   Then you will not get any of the bad things
>   that will happen to her.
> ⁵ That city's sins are stacked (*piled*) up
>   as far as heaven.
>   God has not forgotten the wrong things
>   she has done.
> ⁶ Give that city the same as she gave to others.
>   Pay her back twice as much as she did.
>   Prepare wine for her that is twice as strong
>   as the wine she prepared for others.
> ⁷ She (*Babylon*) gave herself much glory
>   and rich living.
>   Give her that much suffering and sadness.
>   She says to herself, 'I am a queen
>   sitting *on my throne*.
>   I am not a widow*; I will never be sad.'
> ⁸ So these bad things will come to her
>   in one day:
>   death, sadness, and crying, and great hunger.
>   She will be destroyed by fire,
>   because the Lord God who judges her is powerful.''

⁹The kings of the earth who sinned sexually with her (*Babylon*) and shared her wealth will see the smoke from her burning. Then

demons Demons are evil spirits from the devil.
widow A widow is a woman whose husband has died.

these kings will cry and be sad because of her *death*. [10]The kings will be afraid of her suffering and stand far away. The kings will say:

"Terrible! How terrible, O great city,
  O powerful city of Babylon!
Your punishment has come in one hour!"

[11]And the businessmen of the earth will cry and be sad for her (*Babylon*). They will be sad because now there is no one to buy the things they sell. [12]They sell gold, silver, jewels, pearls, fine linen cloths, purple cloth, silk, and scarlet cloth, all kinds of citron wood, and all kinds of things made from ivory, expensive wood, bronze, iron, and marble; [13]Those businessmen also sell cinnamon, spice, incense, myrrh, frankincense, wine, and olive oil, fine flour, wheat, cattle, sheep, horses, carriages, and the bodies and souls of men.

[14]"*O Babylon,* the good things you wanted
  are gone from you.
All your rich and fancy things have disappeared.
  You will never have those things again."

[15]The businessmen will be afraid of her suffering and stand far away from her (*Babylon*). These are the men who became rich from selling those things to her. The men will cry and be sad. [16]They will say:

"Terrible! How terrible for the great city!
  She was dressed in fine linen, purple,
    and scarlet cloth.
  She was shining with gold, jewels, and pearls!
[17]All these riches have been destroyed in one hour!"

Every sea captain, all the people who travel on ships, the sailors, and all the people who earn money from the sea stood far away from Babylon. [18]They saw the smoke from her burning. They said loudly, "There was never a city like this great city!" [19]They threw dust on their heads. They cried and were sad. They said loudly:

"Terrible! How terrible for the great city!
All the people who had ships on the sea
     became rich because of her wealth!
But she has been destroyed in one hour!
²⁰Be happy because of this, O heaven!
Be happy, God's holy people and apostles* and prophets*!
God has punished her because of the things she did to you.''

²¹Then a powerful angel picked up a large rock. This rock was as big as a large millstone.* The angel threw the rock into the sea and said:

"That is how the great city of Babylon will be thrown down.
That city will never be found again.
²²The music of people playing harps and other instruments,
     flutes and trumpets, will never be heard in you again.
No workman doing any job will ever be found in you again.
The sound of a millstone* will never be heard in you again.
²³The light of a lamp will never shine in you again.
The voice of a bridegroom* and bride
     will never be heard in you again.
Your businessmen were the world's great men.
All the nations were tricked by your magic.
²⁴She (*Babylon*) is guilty of the blood (*death*)
     of the prophets* and God's holy people,
          and of all the people who have been killed on earth.''

People in Heaven Praise God

19 After this I heard what sounded like many, many people in heaven. The people were saying:

"Hallelujah (*Praise God*)!
Salvation, glory, and power belong to our God.
²   His judgments are true and right.
Our God has punished the prostitute.*
     She is the one who made the earth evil
          with her sexual sin.

---

apostles Men that Jesus chose to be his special helpers for telling the Good News to the world.
prophets People who spoke for God.
millstone A large, round stone used for grinding grain.
bridegroom A man ready to be married.
prostitute A woman who is paid by men who use her for sexual sin.

God has punished the prostitute* to pay her
    for the blood (*death*) of his servants.''

³Those people in heaven also said:

"Hallelujah (*Praise God*)!
She is burning and her smoke will rise forever and ever.''

⁴Then the 24 elders* and the four living things bowed down.
They worshiped God, who sits on the throne. They said:

"Amen, Hallelujah (*Praise God*)!''

⁵Then a voice came from the throne. The voice said:

"Praise our God, all you people who serve him!
Praise our God, all you people small and great
    who honor him!''

⁶Then I heard what sounded like many, many people. It
sounded like the noise of flooding water and like loud thunder.
The people were saying:

"Hallelujah (*Praise God*)!
    Our Lord God rules. He is the All-Powerful.
⁷ Let us rejoice and be happy
    and give God glory!
Give God glory, because the wedding
    of the Lamb (*Jesus*) has come.
And the Lamb's bride (*the church*)
    has made herself ready.
⁸ Fine linen was given to the bride for her to wear.
    The linen was bright and clean.''

(The fine linen means the good things that God's holy people
did.)

⁹Then the angel said to me, "Write this: Those people who are
invited to the wedding meal of the Lamb are blessed (*happy*)!''
Then the angel said, "These are the true words of God.''

¹⁰Then I bowed down before the angel's feet to worship him.
But the angel said to me, "Don't *worship me*! I am a servant like

---

prostitute A woman who is paid by men who use her for sexual sin.
24 elders Elder means "older." These are probably great leaders of God's people. They may be
    the leaders of the twelve Jewish family groups, plus the twelve apostles of Jesus.

you and your brothers who have the truth of Jesus. So worship God! Because the truth of Jesus is the spirit of prophecy.*"

The Rider on the White Horse

¹¹Then I saw heaven open. There before me was a white horse. The rider on the horse is called Faithful and True. He is right in his judging and in making war. ¹²His eyes are like burning fire. He has many crowns on his head. He has a name written on him, but he is the only one who knows the name. No other person knows the name. ¹³He is dressed in a robe dipped in blood. His name is the Word of God. ¹⁴The armies of heaven were following him. They were riding white horses. They were dressed in fine linen, white and clean. ¹⁵A sharp sword comes out of the rider's mouth. He will use this sword to defeat the nations. He will rule the nations with a rod of iron. He will squeeze *the grapes* in the winepress of the terrible anger of God the All-Powerful. ¹⁶On his robe and on his leg was written this name:

KING OF KINGS AND LORD OF LORDS.

¹⁷Then I saw an angel standing in the sun. The angel said with a loud voice to all the birds flying in the sky, "Come together for the great supper of God. ¹⁸Come together so that you can eat the bodies of kings and generals and famous men. Come to eat the bodies of the horses and their riders, and the bodies of all people, free, slave, small, and great."

¹⁹Then I saw the animal and the kings of the earth. Their armies were gathered together to make war against the rider on the horse and his army. ²⁰But the animal was captured. Also the false prophet* was captured. This false prophet was the one who did the miracles* for the animal. The false prophet had used these miracles to trick the people who had the mark of the animal and worshiped his idol.* The false prophet and the animal were thrown alive into the lake of fire that burns with sulfur. ²¹Their armies were killed with the sword that came out of the mouth of

---

prophecy Teaching from God, given by a person who speaks for God.
false prophet A person who says he speaks for God but does not really speak God's truth.
miracles False miracles—powerful acts done by the power of the devil.
idol A statue made from wood, stone, or metal that people worship as a god.

the rider on the horse. All the birds ate these bodies until the birds were full.

The 1000 Years

20 I saw an angel coming down out of heaven. The angel had the key to the bottomless pit. The angel also held a large chain in his hand. ²The angel grabbed the giant snake (that old serpent). The giant snake is the devil (or Satan). The angel tied him *with the chain* for 1,000 years. ³The angel threw the snake into the bottomless pit and closed it. The angel locked it over the snake. The angel did this so that the snake could not trick the people of the earth until the 1,000 years were ended. After 1,000 years the snake must be made free for a short time.

⁴Then I saw some thrones and people sitting on them. These were the people who had been given the power to judge. And I saw the souls of those people who had been killed because *they were faithful to* the truth of Jesus and the message* from God. Those people did not worship the animal or his idol.* They did not receive the mark of the animal on their foreheads or on their hands. Those people became alive again and ruled with Christ for 1,000 years. ⁵(The other dead people did not live again until the 1,000 years were ended.) This is the first raising of the dead. ⁶Blessed (*happy*) and holy* are those people who share in this first raising of the dead. The second death has no power over those people. Those people will be priests for God and for Christ. They will rule with him for 1,000 years.

⁷When the 1,000 years are ended, Satan (*the devil*) will be made free from his prison *in the bottomless pit*. ⁸Satan will go out to trick the nations in all the earth—Gog and Magog. Satan will gather the people for battle. There will be so many people that they will be like sand on the seashore. ⁹Satan's army marched across the earth and gathered around the camp of God's people and the city that God loves. But fire came down from heaven and destroyed Satan's army. ¹⁰And Satan (the one who tricked those people) was thrown into the lake of burning sulfur with the

message   The news that God has made a way through Christ for people to have their sins forgiven and live with God. When people accept this truth, God accepts them.
idol   A statue made from wood, stone, or metal that people worship as a god.
holy   God's people are called holy because they are pure and belong only to God.

animal and the false prophet.* There they will be tortured (*punished*) day and night, forever and ever.

People of the World Are Judged

¹¹Then I saw a large white throne. I saw the One who was sitting on the throne. Earth and sky ran away from him and disappeared. ¹²And I saw the people that had died, great and small, standing before the throne. And the book of life was opened. There were also other books opened. These dead people were judged by the things they had done. These things are written in the books. ¹³The sea gave up the dead people that were in it. Death and Hades* gave up the dead people that were in them. Each person was judged by the things he had done. ¹⁴And death and Hades were thrown into the lake of fire. This lake of fire is the second death. ¹⁵And if a person's name was not found written in the book of life, then that person was thrown into the lake of fire.

The New Jerusalem

21 Then I saw a new heaven and a new earth. The first heaven and the first earth had disappeared. Now there was no sea. ²And I saw the holy city coming down out of heaven from God. This holy city is the new Jerusalem.* It was prepared like a bride dressed for her husband. ³I heard a loud voice from the throne. The voice said, "Now God's home is with people. He will live with them. They will be his people. God himself will be with them and will be their God. ⁴God will wipe away every tear from their eyes. There will be no more death, sadness, crying, or pain. All the old ways are gone."

⁵The One that was sitting on the throne said, "Look! I am making everything new!" Then he said, "Write this, because these words are true and can be trusted."

---

false prophet   A person who says he speaks for God but does not really speak God's truth.
Hades   Place where people go after they die.
new Jerusalem   The spiritual city where God's people live with him.

⁶The One on the throne said to me: "It is finished! I am the Alpha and the Omega,* the Beginning and the End. I will give free water from the spring of the water of life to any person who is thirsty. ⁷Any person who wins the victory will receive all this. And I will be his God and he will be my son. ⁸But the people who are cowards, people who refuse to believe, people who do terrible things, people who kill, people who sin sexually, people who do evil magic, people who worship idols,* and people who tell lies—all those people will have a place in the lake of burning sulfur. This is the second death."

⁹One of the seven angels came to me. This was one of the angels who had the seven bowls full of the seven last troubles. The angel said, "Come with me. I will show you the bride, the wife of the Lamb." ¹⁰The angel carried me away by the Spirit* to a very large and high mountain. The angel showed me the holy city, Jerusalem. The city was coming down out of heaven from God. ¹¹The city was shining with the glory of God. It was shining bright like a very expensive jewel, like a jasper. It was clear as crystal. ¹²The city had a large high wall with twelve gates. There were twelve angels at the gates. On each gate was written the name of one of the twelve tribes (*family groups*) of Israel.* ¹³There were three gates on the east, three gates on the north, three gates on the south, and three gates on the west. ¹⁴The walls of the city were built on twelve foundation stones.* On the stones were written the names of the twelve apostles* of the Lamb.

¹⁵The angel who talked with me had a measuring rod made of gold. The angel had this rod to measure the city, its gates, and its wall. ¹⁶The city was built in a square. Its length was equal to its width. The angel measured the city with the rod. The city was 12,000 stadia* long, 12,000 stadia wide, and 12,000 stadia high. ¹⁷The angel also measured the wall. It was 144 cubits* high, by

Alpha...Omega   First and last letters in the Greek alphabet. Means beginning and end.
idols   Statues made from wood, stone, or metal that people worship as gods.
Spirit   The Holy Spirit. Also called the Spirit of God and the Spirit of Christ.
Israel   The Jewish nation—God's chosen people in the Old Testament.
foundation stones   The large rocks that are used as the bottom or first part in building.
apostles   Men that Jesus chose to be his special helpers for telling the Good News to the world.
stadia   One stadion was a distance of about 200 yards. It was one-eighth of a Roman mile.
cubits   A cubit is about half a yard, the length from the elbow to the tip of the little finger.

people's measurement. That was the measurement the angel was using. [18]The wall was made of jasper. The city was made of pure gold, as pure as glass. [19]The foundation stones* of the city walls had every kind of expensive jewels in them. The first cornerstone was jasper, the second was sapphire, the third was chalcedony, the fourth was emerald, [20]the fifth was onyx, the sixth was carnelian, the seventh was yellow quartz, the eighth was beryl, the ninth was topaz, the tenth was chrysoprase, the eleventh was hyacinth, and the twelth was amethyst. [21]The twelve gates were twelve pearls. Each gate was made from one pearl. The street of the city was made of pure gold. The gold was clear like glass.

[22]I did not see a temple* in the city. The Lord God All-Powerful and the Lamb (*Jesus*) are the city's temple. [23]The city does not need the sun or the moon to shine on it. The glory of God gives the city light. The Lamb (*Jesus*) is the city's lamp. [24]The peoples of the world will walk by the light given by the Lamb. The kings of the earth will bring their glory into the city. [25]The city's gates will never close on any day, because there is no night there. [26]The greatness and the honor of the nations will be brought into the city. [27]Nothing unclean will ever enter the city. No person who does shameful things or tells lies will ever enter the city. Only the people whose names are written in the Lamb's book of life will enter the city.

22 Then the angel showed me the river of the water of life. The river was bright like crystal. The river flows from the throne of God and the Lamb. [2]It flows down the middle of the street of the city. The tree of life was on each side of the river. The tree of life makes fruit twelve times a year. It gives fruit every month. The leaves of the tree are for healing all the people. [3]Nothing that God judges guilty will be there in that city. The throne of God and the Lamb (*Jesus*) will be in the city. God's servants will worship him. [4]They will see his face. God's name will be written on their foreheads. [5]There will never be night again. People will not need the light of a lamp or the light of the sun. The Lord God will give them light. And they will rule like kings forever and ever.

foundation stones The large rocks that are used as the bottom or first part in building.
temple A building where people worship God.

⁶The angel said to me, "These words are true and can be trusted. The Lord is the God of the spirits of the prophets.* God sent his angel to show his servants the things that must happen soon."

⁷"Listen! I am coming soon! The person who obeys the words of prophecy* in this book will be blessed."

⁸I am John. I am the one who heard and saw these things. After I heard and saw these things I bowed down to worship before the feet of the angel who showed these things to me. ⁹But the angel said to me, "Don't *worship me*! I am a servant like you and your brothers the prophets.* I am a servant like all the people who obey the words in this book. You should worship God!"

¹⁰Then the angel told me, "Don't keep secret the words of prophecy* in this book. The time is near *for these things to happen*. ¹¹Let the person who is doing wrong continue to do wrong. Let the person who is unclean continue to be unclean. Let the person who is doing right continue to do right. Let the person who is holy continue to be holy."

¹²"Listen! I am coming soon! I will bring rewards with me. I will repay each person for the things he has done. ¹³I am the Alpha and the Omega,* the First and the Last, the Beginning and the End.

¹⁴"Those people who washed their robes* will be blessed. They will have the right to *eat the food from* the tree of life. They can go through the gates into the city. ¹⁵Outside the city are the dogs (*bad people*), people who do evil magic, people who sin sexually, people who murder, people who worship idols,* and people who love lies and tell lies.

¹⁶"I, Jesus, have sent my angel to tell you these things for the churches (*groups of believers*). I am the descendant from the family of David. I am the bright morning star."

¹⁷The Spirit* and the bride say, "Come!" Every person who hears this should also say, "Come!" If a person is thirsty, let him

prophets People who spoke for God.
prophecy Teaching from God, given by a person who speaks for God.
Alpha...Omega First and last letters in the Greek alphabet. Means beginning and end.
washed their robes Meaning they believed in Jesus so that their sins could be forgiven.
idols Statues made from wood, stone, or metal that people worship as gods.
Spirit The Holy Spirit. Also called the Spirit of God, the Spirit of Christ, and the Comforter. He is joined with God and Christ. He does the work of God among people in the world.

come; that person can have the water of life as a free gift if he wants it.

[18]I warn every person who hears the words of the prophecy* of this book: If a person adds anything to these words, then God will give that person the troubles written about in this book. [19]And if any person takes away from the words of this book of prophecy, then God will take away that person's share of the tree of life and of the holy city, which are written about in this book.

[20]*Jesus is* the One who says that these things are true. Now he says, "Yes, I am coming soon."

Amen. Come, Lord Jesus!

[21]The grace (*kindness*) of the Lord Jesus be with all people.

---

prophecy   A message or teaching from God, given by a person who speaks for God.